This is the fifth volume in the majo
being prepared under the General
published in 1985, Volume II in 1990; both were edited by Professor Kirk himself.
Like its predecessors, the present volume (the first to appear from the hand of one
of Professor Kirk's four collaborators) consists of four introductory essays (including
discussions of similes and other features of narrative style) followed by the
Commentary. The Greek text is not included. This project is the first large-scale
commentary on the *Iliad* for nearly one hundred years, and takes special account of
language, style, and thematic structure as well as of the complex social and cultural
background to the work.

The Commentary is an essential reference work for all students of Greek
literature, and archaeologists and historians will also find that it contains matters
of relevance to them.

The Iliad: a commentary

Volume v: books 17–20

THE ILIAD:
A COMMENTARY

GENERAL EDITOR G. S. KIRK

Volume v: books 17–20

MARK W. EDWARDS

PROFESSOR OF CLASSICS, STANFORD UNIVERSITY

CAMBRIDGE
UNIVERSITY PRESS

CAMBRIDGE UNIVERSITY PRESS
Cambridge, New York, Melbourne, Madrid, Cape Town, Singapore, São Paulo

Cambridge University Press
The Edinburgh Building, Cambridge CB2 2RU, UK

Published in the United States of America by Cambridge University Press, New York

www.cambridge.org
Information on this title: www.cambridge.org/9780521309592

First published 1991
Reprinted 1995, 2000

A catalogue record for this publication is available from the British Library

Library of Congress Cataloguing in Publication data
Kirk, G. S. (Geoffrey Stephen)
The Iliad, a commentary.

Includes index.
Contents: v. 1. Books 1–4   v. 5. Books 17–20
Mark W. Edwards.
1. Homer. Iliad.   I. Homer. Iliad.   II. Edwards, Mark W.
PA4037.K458   1985   883'.01   84–11330

ISBN-13 978-0-521-30959-2 hardback
ISBN-10 0-521-30959-X hardback

ISBN-13 978-0-521-31208-0 paperback
ISBN-10 0-521-31208-6 paperback

Transferred to digital printing 2005

D M

H. D. F. Kitto
T. B. L. Webster

CONTENTS

FIGURES

PREFACE

The General Editor's invitation to prepare a volume in this series reached me at the perfect time. After some years of work on formulae, type-scenes, and narrative patterns in Homer, I was in the final stages of putting together a general book on the *Iliad*, which originated largely from teaching the poem to undergraduates. In this I could not examine in fine detail the compositional techniques the poet was using. I felt the time was approaching when I should demonstrate more fully how these techniques could be analysed for the fullest possible appreciation of Homer's genius, but I had not yet begun to work out how to do so. Professor Kirk provided the ideal opportunity, for which I am very grateful.

The type of commentary described in his invitation, and now embodied in the first two volumes of the series, emphasizes stylistic analysis and explanation, as well as the necessary historical, linguistic, and literary comment. This is very much in line with my own interests and wishes. In what follows, I have constantly drawn attention to the structural patterns in the poem, the preparation of the audience for what is to come, the use, adaptation, or avoidance of formular expressions, the techniques for expanding or contracting typical scenes, and the positioning of words within the verse. Our understanding of such characteristics of Homeric style has advanced a great deal since Leaf's time, and familiarity with them is essential for proper appreciation of the poet's craft.

The preparation of this volume was aided by a Fellowship for Independent Study and Research from the National Endowment for the Humanities for 1986–7, and by leave granted by Stanford University for the same period. Dr David W. Packard kindly lent me a prototype Ibycus computer system and a CD-ROM holding the *Thesaurus Linguae Graecae* Greek corpus, which made possible rapid searches of the text.

I am also grateful to Professor Kirk and the editors of the other volumes in the series for making valuable comments on drafts of my commentary and for sending me advance copies of their own work; to my colleagues M. H. Jameson and A. E. Raubitschek, who gave me much help with the Shield of Achilles; and to Andrea Nightingale, Rush Rehm, and Larry Woodlock, who read parts of my MS and gave me useful comments. I must also thank many scholars for sending me advance copies of articles pertinent to my work. David Briney, Megan Harbison, and Donald Hersey assisted me in checking references, and at a late stage the careful eye and good sense of Susan P. Moore of the Cambridge University Press saved me from many errors.

I have made frequent reference to notes which will appear in forthcoming volumes in this series, working from drafts kindly supplied by my collaborators. In some cases subsequent changes in their text may mean that the material to which I refer when I write (for instance) 'see 12.34n.' may actually appear in the note to (say) 12.32–6. I hope the convenience of such cross-references will more than make up for any possible inaccuracies.

This volume is dedicated to the memory of my two teachers, whose enthusiasm and originality of thought developed my love for Greek literature, and whose encouragement and help enabled me to enter a profession which has made my life a happy one.

Stanford University   M. W. E.
July 1990

ABBREVIATIONS

Books

Ameis–Hentze   C. F. Ameis and C. Hentze, *Homers Ilias* (7th edn, revised by P. Cauer; Leipzig 1913)

Apthorp, *Manuscript Evidence*   M. J. Apthorp, *The Manuscript Evidence for Interpolation in Homer* (Heidelberg 1980)

Arch. Hom.   *Archaeologia Homerica: die Denkmäler und die frühgriechische Epos*, edd. F. Matz and H. G. Buchholz (Göttingen 1967–)

Arend, *Typischen Scenen*   W. Arend, *Die typischen Scenen bei Homer* (Berlin 1933)

Beazley, *ABV*   J. D. Beazley, *Attic Black-figure Vase-painters* (Oxford 1956)

Bernabé, *PEG*   A. Bernabé, *Poetae Epici Graeci: Testimonia et Fragmenta* (Leipzig 1988)

Bolling, *Athetized Lines*   G. M. Bolling, *The Athetized Lines of the Iliad* (Baltimore, 1944)

Bolling, *External Evidence*   G. M. Bolling, *The External Evidence for Interpolation in Homer* (Oxford 1925)

Bremer, *HBOP*   *Homer: Beyond Oral Poetry*, edd. J. M. Bremer, I. J. F. de Jong, and J. Kalff (Amsterdam 1987)

Chantraine, *Dict.*   P. Chantraine, *Dictionnaire étymologique de la langue grecque* (Paris 1968–80)

Chantraine, *GH*   P. Chantraine, *Grammaire homérique* i–ii (Paris 1958–63)

Cunliffe, *Lexicon*   R. J. Cunliffe, *A Lexicon of the Homeric Dialect* (London 1924)

Davies, *EGF*   M. Davies, *Epicorum Graecorum Fragmenta* (Göttingen 1988)

Denniston, *Particles*   J. D. Denniston, *The Greek Particles* (2nd edn, Oxford 1951)

Dihle, *Homer-Probleme*   A. Dihle, *Homer-Probleme* (Opladen 1970)

Edwards, *HPI*   M. W. Edwards, *Homer: Poet of the Iliad* (Baltimore 1987)

Erbse   H. Erbse, *Scholia Graeca in Homeri Iliadem* i–vii (Berlin 1969–88)

Fenik, *Odyssey*   B. C. Fenik, *Studies in the Odyssey* (*Hermes* Einzelschriften 30, Wiesbaden 1974)

Fenik, *Rhesus*   B. C. Fenik, *'Iliad X' and the 'Rhesus': the Myth* (Brussels 1964)

Fenik, *TBS*   B. C. Fenik, *Typical Battle Scenes in the Iliad* (*Hermes* Einzelschriften 21, Wiesbaden 1968)

Fernández-Galiano and Heubeck, *Odissea*   M. Fernández-Galiano and A. Heubeck, *Omero: Odissea*. vi, libri xxi–xxiv (Rome 1986)

Fittschen, *Sagendarstellung*   K. Fittschen, *Untersuchungen zum Beginn der Sagendarstellungen bei den Griechen* (Berlin 1969)

Fittschen, *Schild*   K. Fittschen, *Der Schild des Achilleus* (*Arch. Hom.* N, Göttingen 1973)

Fränkel, *Gleichnisse*   H. Fränkel, *Die homerischen Gleichnisse* (Göttingen 1921)

Friedrich, *Verwundung*   W.-H. Friedrich, *Verwundung und Tod in der Ilias* (Göttingen 1956)

Friis Johansen, *Iliad*   K. Friis Johansen, *The Iliad in Early Greek Art* (Copenhagen 1967)

Frisk   H. Frisk, *Griechisches Etymologisches Wörterbuch* (Heidelberg 1954–73)

Griffin, *HLD*   J. Griffin, *Homer on Life and Death* (Oxford 1980)

Hägg, *Greek Renaissance*   R. Hägg, *The Greek Renaissance of the Eighth Century B.C.* (Proceedings of the Second International Symposium at the Swedish Institute in Athens, Stockholm 1983)

Hainsworth, *Flexibility*   J. B. Hainsworth, *The Flexibility of the Homeric Formula* (Oxford 1968)

Hainsworth, *Odyssey*   A. Heubeck, S. West, and J. B. Hainsworth, *A Commentary on Homer's Odyssey* i (Oxford 1988)

Heitsch, *Aphroditehymnos*   E. Heitsch, *Aphroditehymnos, Aeneas und Homer* (Hypomnemata 15, Göttingen 1965)

Heubeck, *Odyssey*   A. Heubeck and A. Hoekstra, *A Commentary on Homer's Odyssey* ii (Oxford 1989)

Hoekstra, *Epic Verse*   A. Hoekstra, *Epic Verse before Homer* (Amsterdam 1981)

Hoekstra, *Modifications*   A. Hoekstra, *Homeric Modifications of Formulaic Prototypes* (Amsterdam 1965)

Hoekstra, *Odyssey*   A. Heubeck and A. Hoekstra, *A Commentary on Homer's Odyssey* ii (Oxford 1989)

Hoekstra, *Sub-epic Stage*   A. Hoekstra, *The Sub-epic Stage of the Formulaic Tradition* (Amsterdam 1969)

HyAp, HyAphr, HyDem, HyHerm   *Homeric Hymns* to Apollo, Aphrodite, Demeter, Hermes

Janko, *HHH*   R. Janko, *Homer, Hesiod and the Hymns* (Cambridge 1982)

Abbreviations

de Jong, *Narrators*   I. J. F. de Jong, *Narrators and Focalizers: the Presentation of the Story in the Iliad* (Amsterdam 1987)

Krischer, *Konventionen*   T. Krischer, *Formale Konventionen der homerischen Epik* (Zetemata 56, Munich 1971)

Kullmann, *Quellen*   W. Kullmann, *Die Quellen der Ilias* (*Hermes* Einzelschriften 14, Wiesbaden 1960)

Leaf   W. Leaf, *The Iliad* i–ii (2nd edn, London 1900–2)

Lee, *Similes*   D. J. N. Lee, *The Similes of the Iliad and the Odyssey Compared* (Melbourne 1964)

Lenz, *Aphroditehymnos*   L. H. Lenz, *Der homerische Aphroditehymnos und die Aristie des Aineias in der Ilias* (Bonn 1975)

Leumann, *HW*   M. Leumann, *Homerische Wörter* (Basel 1950)

LfgrE   *Lexicon des frühgriechischen Epos*, edd. B. Snell and H. Erbse (Göttingen 1955–)

LIMC   *Lexicon Iconographicum Mythologiae Classicae* (Zürich 1981–)

Linear B 1984   *Linear B: a 1984 Survey*, edd. A. M. Davies and Y. Duhoux (Proceedings of the Mycenaean Colloquium of the 8th Congress of the International Federation of the Societies of Classical Studies, Louvain-la-neuve 1985)

Lohmann, *Reden*   D. Lohmann, *Die Komposition der Reden in der Ilias* (Berlin 1970)

LSJ   H. Liddell, R. Scott, and H. S. Jones, *A Greek–English Lexicon* (9th edn, Oxford 1940)

Macleod, *Iliad XXIV*   C. W. Macleod, *Homer, Iliad Book XXIV* (Cambridge 1982)

Marg, *Dichtung*   W. Marg, *Homer über die Dichtung* (Münster 1957)

Markoe, *Bowls*   G. Markoe, *Phoenician Bronze and Silver Bowls from Cyprus and the Mediterranean* (Berkeley 1985)

Martin, *Language*   R. P. Martin, *The Language of Heroes* (Ithaca 1989)

Moulton, *Similes*   C. Moulton, *Similes in the Homeric Poems* (Hypomnemata 49, Göttingen 1977)

MW   R. Merkelbach and M. L. West, edd., *Fragmenta Hesiodea* (Oxford 1967)

Nagler, *Spontaneity*   M. N. Nagler, *Spontaneity and Tradition: a Study in the Oral Art of Homer* (Berkeley and Los Angeles 1974)

Page, *HHI*   D. L. Page, *History and the Homeric Iliad* (Berkeley and Los Angeles 1959)

Page, *Odyssey*   D. L. Page, *The Homeric Odyssey* (Oxford 1955)

Page, *PMG*   D. L. Page, *Poetae Melici Graeci* (Oxford 1962)

Parry, *MHV*   A. Parry, ed., *The Making of Homeric Verse*. The Collected Papers of Milman Parry (Oxford 1971)

Pasquali, *Storia*   G. Pasquali, *Storia della tradizione e critica del testo* (Florence 1962)

Plutarch, *Vit. Hom.*   Ps.-Plutarch, *De Vita et Poesi Homeri* II (*Moralia* vol. VII, ed. G. N. Bernardakis, Leipzig 1896)

Reinhardt, *IuD*   K. Reinhardt, *Die Ilias und ihr Dichter* (Göttingen 1961)

Risch, *Wortbildung*   E. Risch, *Wortbildung der homerischen Sprache* (2nd edn, Berlin 1974)

Ruijgh, *L'Elément achéen*   C. J. Ruijgh, *L'Elément achéen dans la langue épique* (Assen 1957)

Ruijgh, τε *épique*   C. J. Ruijgh, *Autour de 'τε épique'* (Amsterdam 1971)

Russo, *Odissea*   J. Russo, *Omero: Odissea* V (Rome 1985)

Schadewaldt, *VHWW*   W. Schadewaldt, *Von Homers Welt und Werk* (4th edn, Stuttgart 1965)

Scheibner, *Aufbau*   G. Scheibner, *Der Aufbau des 20. und 21. Buches der Ilias* (Leipzig 1939)

Scott, *Oral Nature*   W. C. Scott, *The Oral Nature of the Homeric Simile* (Leiden 1974)

Shipp, *Studies*   G. P. Shipp, *Studies in the Language of Homer* (2nd edn, Cambridge 1972)

Thalmann, *Conventions*   W. G. Thalmann, *Conventions of Form and Thought in Early Greek Epic Poetry* (Baltimore 1984)

van der Valk, *Researches*   M. H. A. L. H. van der Valk, *Researches on the Text and Scholia of the Iliad* I–II (Leiden 1963–4)

van Leeuwen   J. van Leeuwen, J. F., *Ilias* (2 vols., Leiden 1912, 1913)

Ventris and Chadwick, *Documents*   M. Ventris and J. Chadwick, *Documents in Mycenaean Greek*[2] (Cambridge 1973)

von Bredow, *Thrakischen Namen*   I. von Bredow, *Die Thrakischen Namen bei Homer* ('Terra Antiqua Balcanica': *Acta Centri Historiae* I, edd. A. Fol, V. Zhivkov and N. Nedjalkov, Turnovo 1986) 133–86

von Kamptz, *Personennamen*   H. von Kamptz, *Homerische Personennamen* (Göttingen 1982)

Wace and Stubbings, *Companion*   A. J. B. Wace and F. H. Stubbings, *A Companion to Homer* (London 1962)

Wackernagel, *Untersuchungen*   J. Wackernagel, *Sprachliche Untersuchungen zu Homer* (Göttingen 1916, repr. 1970)

West, *Theogony*   M. L. West, *Hesiod, Theogony* (Oxford 1966)

West, *Works and Days*   M. L. West, *Hesiod, Works and Days* (Oxford 1978)

S. West, *Odyssey*   A. Heubeck, S. West, and J. B. Hainsworth, *A Commentary on Homer's Odyssey* I (Oxford 1988)

Wilamowitz, *IuH*   U. von Wilamowitz-Moellendorf, *Die Ilias und Homer* (Berlin 1916)

Willcock   M. M. Willcock, *The Iliad of Homer* (books I–XII, London 1978; books XIII–XXIV, London 1984)

Abbreviations

Journals

AC	Acta Classica
AJA	American Journal of Archaeology
AJP	American Journal of Philology
BAGB	Bulletin de l'Association G. Budé
BICS	Bulletin of the Institute of Classical Studies, London
CA	Classical Antiquity
CJ	Classical Journal
CP	Classical Philology
CQ	Classical Quarterly
CSCA	California Studies in Classical Antiquity
CW	Classical World
DA	Dissertation Abstracts
G&R	Greece and Rome
GRBS	Greek, Roman and Byzantine Studies
HSCP	Harvard Studies in Classical Philology
IF	Indogermanische Forschungen
JDAI	Jahrbuch des Deutschen Archäologischen Instituts
JHS	Journal of Hellenic Studies
LCM	Liverpool Classical Monthly
MDAI(A)	Mitteilungen des Deutschen Archäologischen Instituts (Athen. Abt.)
QUCC	Quaderni Urbinati di Cultura Classica
RBPh	Revue Belge de Philologie et d'Histoire
REG	Revue des Études Grecques
RFIC	Rivista de Filologia e di Istruzione Classica
RhM	Rheinisches Museum
SMEA	Studi micenei ed egeo-anatolici
SO	Symbolae Osloenses
TAPA	Transactions of the American Philological Association
UCPCP	University of California Publications in Classical Philology
WS	Wiener Studien
YCS	Yale Classical Studies

NOTE

| is used to mark the beginning or the end of a verse. The abbreviation '(etc.)' means that other grammatical terminations are included in the reference or total; it is used in such cases only where the fact may have some significance.

On 'Arn/A' (etc.) references see vol. 1 pp. 41ff.

INTRODUCTION

1. The narrator and the audience

The only indubitable fact that Homer gives us about himself in the *Il.* is that he lived later than the events he narrates; this is obvious from his occasional references to his heroes as men of an earlier and grander generation (5.303–4, 12.381–3, 12.447–9, 20.286–7; he calls them ἡμιθέων γένος ἀνδρῶν, 12.23), and from his account of the destruction of the Greek wall by Poseidon, Apollo, and the local rivers after the fall of Troy (12.10–33, cf. 7.445–63). Despite the scholiasts᾽ ἀεὶ φιλέλλην ὁ ποιητής (bT on 10.14–16, and often; see N. J. Richardson, *CQ* 30, 1980, 273–4), he does not speak as a Greek, or refer to the Trojans as enemies.

His intended hearers are similarly undefined, except that these same passages identify them as his contemporaries, and they are clearly already familiar with stories of the siege of Troy and other Greek heroic legends. The poet often assumes that they have such a background and a good deal of emotional effect would have been lost if they had not known, for instance, the fates of Priam, Andromakhe, and Astuanax; when Here concedes the future destruction of Argos, Sparta, and Mycenae the poet may expect a recognition of the fate of the Mycenaean empire (4.51–3, see note *ad loc.*). They must also know something about the main characters, who are not introduced to us unless an important occasion calls for special emphasis (as in the case of Nestor, when he attempts to mediate between Akhilleus and Agamemnon, 1.247–52). The world of the similes is their own world (see ch. 3, iii), from which poet and audience together, united in an emotional bond, look back together upon the heroic past. Though this remoteness in time is not obtrusive, it renders easy the foreshadowing which the poet often uses for emotional effect.

Recent theoretical studies of the means by which an author communicates with his audience have led to new understanding of the refinements of Homer's technique as narrator, and the results are summarized in the next section.[1] A further section examines the ways in which the future is foreshadowed in the *Il.*

---

[1] The most important work for the *Il.* is de Jong, *Narrators*. This includes an account of ancient approaches to the subject and a full bibliography. A recent work by S. Richardson,

The narrator and the audience

(i) *Persona* and character: the narrator's technique

Through the Muse, to whom he occasionally utters a direct appeal at especially important moments (see below), the poet knows the histories of long-dead heroes; and it is also presumably from this source, though this is not specified, that he is able to tell us of the thoughts and actions of the gods. His omniscience enables him not only to move from Greek camp to Troy and to Olumpos, but also to share with us (for instance) the poignant remarks about the future grief of the now unwitting relatives of a hero who is killed, the information about the deaths of Helen's brothers which comes as a climax to the depiction of her guilt and loneliness (3.243–4), and the divine reaction to a character's prayer (e.g. 2.419 ≅ 3.302).

The closeness between narrator and audience is promoted from time to time, in certain standardized ways, when he emerges in his own *persona* and speaks directly to us or to others (his Muse, and his characters) in our hearing. To do this he employs three main techniques.

(1) A direct address to us, his audience. This takes several different forms. The narrator may address us in the second person, as directly as one of the characters addresses a listener: οὐδέ κε φαίης | is used both by the narrator (4.429, 17.366) and by a character (3.392), and so is | φαίης κε (3.220, 15.697; Longinus, 26.1, said the change of person 'seems to involve the hearer, often placing him in the midst of danger', quoting the second passage). So too οὐκ ἂν γνοίης is used both by the narrator (5.85) and by a character (14.58); οὐκ ἂν βρίζοντα ἴδοις Ἀγαμέμνονα (4.223) is similar.

Slightly less direct, but also addressed to the listener, are the third-person 'imaginary spectator' expressions, such as ἔνθα κεν οὐκέτι ἔργον ἀνὴρ ὀνόσαιτο μετελθών (4.539, cf. 4.421, 13.343–4, 16.638–9) and the more specific variant οὔτ' ἂν κεν Ἄρης ὀνόσαιτο μετελθών | οὔτε κ' Ἀθηναίη (13.127–8, rephrased at 17.398–9), which is also used in direct speech (20.358–9).

Occasionally a rhetorical question may be addressed to the audience. De Jong, *Narrators* 47–8, considers this to be the case with the 'inexpressibility *topos*', τῶν δ' ἄλλων τίς κεν ᾗσι φρεσὶν οὐνόματ' εἴποι; (17.260, see note *ad loc.*), though this might, like some other instances (see below), be addressed to the Muses.

The Homeric Narrator (Nashville 1990), which the author has kindly allowed me to see in MS, includes the *Odyssey*. A review of these, and of another recent work, J. Peradotto's *Man in the Middle Voice: Name and Narrative in the Odyssey* (Princeton 1990), by S. Schein will appear in *Poetics Today* 12 (1991; I thank him for showing me his MS). There are shorter accounts by S. P. Scully, *Arethusa* 19 (1986) 135–53 and by Edwards, *HPI* 29–41. J. Griffin has studied the poet's sympathy with his characters (*CQ* 26, 1976, 161–85) and the differences in vocabulary between the narrator and the characters (*JHS* 106, 1986, 36–50). An earlier but still useful view, with many perceptive remarks, can be found in S. E. Bassett's *The Poetry of Homer* (Berkeley 1938) chapters 4 and 5. See also vol. II, ch. 3.

2

(2) A direct address to the Muse. Several times the narrator utters a request or a question to the Muse, usually referring to himself in the first person. The result is a special claim upon the audience's attention, a special emphasis upon an important passage (1.1 8, the procm; 2.484–93, the Catalogue of Ships; 2.761–2, the list of the best men and horses; 11.218–20, the *aristeia* of Agamemnon; 14.508–10, the major Greek rally while Zeus is otherwise engaged; 16.112–13, the firing of the ships). There is also an oblique reference to the Muse in the narrator's despair at not being himself divine: ἀργαλέον δέ με ταῦτα θεὸν ὣς πάντ' ἀγορεῦσαι (12.176).

The trope ἔνθα τίνα πρῶτον, τίνα δ' ὕστατον ἐξενάριξεν (etc.; 5.703–4, 11.299–300, 16.692–3, with a shorter version at 8.273), as de Jong has pointed out (*Narrators* 49–50), is also a veiled form of such an appeal to the Muse; to whom else could it be directed? Other rhetorical questions may also be best thought of as addressed to the Muse, though a question to the audience is also possible. Certainly the audience is addressed in a particularly effective example during the flight of Hektor: πῶς δέ κεν Ἕκτωρ κῆρας ὑπεξέφυγεν θανάτοιο, | εἰ μή οἱ πύματόν τε καὶ ὕστατον ἤντετ' Ἀπόλλων | ...; (22.202–4).

(3) A direct address to a character (*apostrophe*). Twice the poet addresses Patroklos with great sympathy: ἔνθ' ἄρα τοι, Πάτροκλε, φάνη βιότοιο τελευτή (16.787), and ἔνθα τίνα πρῶτον, τίνα δ' ὕστατον ἐξενάριξας, | Πατρόκλεις, ὅτε δή σε θεοὶ θάνατόνδε κάλεσσαν; (16.692–3), where the doomed hero is addressed instead of the Muse (see note *ad loc.*). There are six other examples of this personal address to Patroklos, some almost as poignant as these, and there are similar instances in the cases of Menelaos (7 ×; see 7.104n., 17.679–80n.), Apollo (15.365, 20.152), Akhilleus (20.2), and Hektor's cousin Melanippos (15.582). For detailed discussion see the notes to the above passages, Edwards, *HPI* 37–41, and now N. Yamagata, *BICS* 36 (1989) 91–103 (with whose conclusions I am afraid I cannot agree).

The highly stylized usage of this direct address with the name of the swineherd Eumaios (Εὔμαιε συβῶτα |, 15 × *Od.* in speech-introductions; in address by another character, only *Od.* 15.381) suggests the technique may have arisen when the vocative of a name was metrically more convenient than the nominative. But the instances with the highly sympathetic character Patroklos, which appear with increasing frequency and emphasis as his death approaches, and to a lesser extent with the likeable Menelaos, make it clear that the technique has been extended to characters whose names present no metrical problem in order to bring them vividly face to face with the narrator, and hence with the audience too.

The narrator's closeness to us is also enhanced when he tells us, as if privately, the thoughts of a character, or sees something through the character's eyes, for a moment uniting character, narrator, and listener. The explicit instances need little comment: the narrator tells us the intent of a speaker before he begins to speak (e.g. 1.24–5), the indecision in a character's mind (e.g. 1.188–92), the purpose of a character's action (e.g. 19.39), the reasons for his emotional state (e.g. 17.603–4), the thoughts of both suppliant and supplicated in a scene without direct speech (20.463–8). In the case of Zeus, the thoughts often foreshadow what is to come (e.g. 15.610–14).

The implicit presentation of a character's viewpoint is less obvious, and de Jong's demonstration of it (*Narrators* 118–22) deepens our appreciation of the poet's skill. Often without conscious realization, the audience is brought into a closer sympathy with the character, and hence into closer emotional involvement with the tale. After the inconclusive duel between Aias and Hektor, the Greeks lead off their champion κεχαρηότα νίκῃ (7.312), and we note, with an understanding smile, that in Aias' opinion he was victor in the encounter. Akhilleus takes twelve Trojans captive ποινὴν Πατρόκλοιο (21.28), and for a moment we see into his vengeful mind. The description of Akhilleus' hands as Priam kisses them, δεινὰς ἀνδροφόνους, αἵ οἱ πολέας κτάνον υἷας (24.479), is moving enough, but becomes especially so if we reflect that it presents Priam's own thoughts at the time as well as the narrator's and ours. It has often been suggested that the struggles of Trojans and Greeks which Helen is depicting in her weaving, οὓς ἕθεν εἵνεκ' ἔπασχον (3.128), show us the guilt and remorse she is feeling (de Jong notes a close parallel at 10.27–8; see also 18.237–8n.). Judgemental words and superlatives, though rare in the narrative, sometimes appear there when they represent the thoughts of a character (see 19.310–13n., 20.408–10n., and de Jong, *JHS* 108, 1988, 188–9). Occasionally a simile expresses a character's viewpoint (see ch. 3, ii).

A special technique is the presentation of the view of a group of characters by means of the ὧδε δέ τις εἴπεσκεν convention, in which the remarks of a group of characters are paraphrased by the narrator as a single direct speech; there is an elaborate double example at 17.414–23 (see note *ad loc.*). The technique, which occurs 14 × *Il.* (see de Jong, *Eranos* 85, 1987, 69–84), is perhaps a development of the narrator's explanation of characters' feelings in his own voice, which is seen a little earlier at 17.395–7 and more elaborately at 15.699–702 (see 17.285–7n.). A special form of this appears in the especially innovative language of Akhilleus, who once uses a single unnamed character to represent the emotions of many (see 18.122–5n.). The convention is also developed into the famous thoughts about Helen uttered by the old men on the wall of Troy (3.146–60).

The narrator sometimes expresses his opinion of a character's actions, inviting us to join him in viewing the scene and suggesting what our emotional reaction should be.[2] Several techniques are employed. A very obvious one is the stylized comment | νήπιος, ὅς..., used in varying tones. Unlike σχέτλιος, which is used almost exclusively from one character to another (29 × ; the exception is *Od.* 21.28, which may represent Penelope's thoughts), νήπιος (-ίη) occurs mainly in the narrator's voice, but always in the third person, i.e. the comment is addressed to the audience, not the character (so J. Griffin, *JHS* 106, 1986, 40). It may convey deep compassion, as in the case of Andromakhe, preparing a bath for Hektor in ignorance of his death (22.445); criticism, for Patroklos' pursuit of the Trojans after his victory over Sarpedon (16.686); sympathy, for the hapless Tros as he vainly supplicates Akhilleus (20.466); futility in the face of destiny, as in the case of the over-eager Asios (12.113); amused scorn, as when Akhilleus does not realize Aineias' weapon cannot pierce his shield (20.264; see de Jong, *Narrators* 86–7). For Patroklos, the form is once expanded to allow even greater explicitness: ὣς φάτο λισσόμενος μέγα νήπιος· ἦ γὰρ ἔμελλεν | οἷ αὐτῷ θάνατόν τε κακὸν καὶ κῆρα λιτέσθαι (16.46–7; cf. *Od.* 9.44, Hesiod, *Erga* 131). Similar in sense is the comment on Pandaros' yielding to Athene, τῷ δὲ φρένας ἄφρονι πεῖθεν (4.104).

Probably the best-known instance of expression of the narrator's opinion is the comment on Glaukos' foolishness in exchanging golden armour for bronze (6.234–6). There are many difficulties in the passage (see note *ad loc.*, and most recently W. Donlan in *Phoenix* 43 (1989) 1–15), but it cannot be other than an unusually overt remark by the narrator, very possibly displaying humour at the expense either of Glaukos or of the heroic tradition of exchange of armour. A less direct, but nevertheless obvious, viewpoint appears when Hektor's head is dragged in the dust, πάρος χαρίεν· τότε δὲ Ζεὺς δυσμενέεσσι | δῶκεν ἀεικίσσασθαι ἑῇ ἐν πατρίδι γαίῃ (22.403–4); there was a similar reproach to Zeus when he allowed Akhilleus' helmet to be thrown down into the dust (16.796–800). As one of the techniques used to prolong the description of Hektor's flight before Akhilleus, the narrator compares the two heroes (22.158–61), a direct expression of opinion much more personal than a simple use of superlatives (which are avoided in the narrative; see J. Griffin, *JHS* 106, 1986, 49–50).

In the case of judgemental words, often there can be no doubt that we have the narrator's opinion. μῆνιν... | οὐλομένην (1.1–2), though not necessarily a criticism of Akhilleus, expresses the narrator's regret at the results of his anger (see de Jong, *Narrators* 143–4), especially since elsewhere

---

[2] The views of the 'implied' narrator need not be those of the poet himself, though in the case of the unknown Homer there is little point in trying to distinguish them. More important, they are not necessarily the same as those expressed by the characters, though this is occasionally overlooked by critics; see Edwards, *HPI* 319–20, and R. Renehan, *CP* 82 (1987) 107–8.

the word occurs only in direct speech (3 × *Il.*, 10 × *Od.*). After a debate, the Trojans Ἕκτορι μὲν γὰρ ἐπήνησαν κακὰ μητιόωντι, | Πουλυδάμαντι δ᾽ ἄρ᾽ οὔ τις, ὃς ἐσθλὴν φράζετο βουλήν (18.312–13). But sometimes it is not clear whether judgemental words represent the opinion of the narrator or that of a character. De Jong, *Narrators* 136–46, suggests that they should be taken as the opinion of a character where possible, since such words occur most often in direct speech. This should always be borne in mind as a possibility, though often the total number of occurrences of a particular word is so small that the judgement must be subjective.[3] Important instances of ambiguity are the ἀεικέα...ἔργα which Akhilleus perpetrates on Hektor's corpse (22.395 = 23.24), and the κακὰ...ἔργα of his killing the Trojan captives at Patroklos' pyre (23.176); both of these are likely to represent, as de Jong points out (*Narrators* 138), the viewpoint of Akhilleus and the Trojans respectively, rather than that of the narrator (see also 22.395n., 23.176n.). The reference to Thetis' ἐξαίσιον ἀρήν 'disproportionate demand' for the Greeks' defeat (15.598), sometimes taken to be the poet's criticism (see note *ad loc.*), may similarly be the view of Zeus, since the passage relates what is in his mind (so de Jong, *Narrators* 139).

In accordance with the usual reticence of the narrator about espousing an opinion, the narrative makes virtually no use of aphorisms, though they are common on the lips of characters. There is a short and simple example at 21.264, θεοὶ δέ τε φέρτεροι ἀνδρῶν, but the only major instance is the three-verse reflection on the overwhelming power of Zeus which is uttered by the narrator and repeated by Hektor (16.688–90 = 17.176–8, see notes *ad locc.*). In the narrative context the passage becomes essentially an expansion of the preceding νήπιος-comment, which may account for its presence.

Virgil's narrative style is often characterized as subjective, and by contrast the very different style of Homer is likely to be called objective. The vagueness of both terms makes generalization unwise without a detailed comparison.[4] But though opinions, emotions, and moral judgements in the *Il.* are usually expressed by the words and actions of the characters, and though Homer tells us virtually nothing of his own circumstances, the narrator of the poem often emerges to stand by our side and in person draw our attention in a particular direction, to criticize an action, to reveal a character's thoughts and motives, to foreshadow the future (see the next section), and to illustrate the heroic events he describes by comparison with those within our common range of experience (see ch. 3). Furthermore, the values of the narrator are not identical with those of the characters. The general world-view which seems to be presented will of

[3] See also J. Griffin, *JHS* 106 (1986) 36–50; de Jong, *JHS* 108 (1988) 188–9; and G. S. Kirk, Introduction to vol. II, ch. 3.
[4] Cf. especially B. Otis, *Virgil* (Oxford 1964) 41–96.

course be differently perceived by different readers; I have given my own ideas on this elsewhere (Edwards, *HPI* 317–23).

(ii) Foreshadowing

The omniscient poet can tell us anything he wishes about the outcome of his plot and the future fate of his characters. There is no random chance in Homer, but a human or divine cause (often both) determines every situation and event. But Homer the story-teller sets limits, and his large-scale foreshadowing is confined to a few major characters and themes, and appears with its greatest force as the action approaches its climax.[5] The effect is to unite narrator and audience in the sympathy of a shared knowledge which is denied to the characters, to allow the outcome of a character's action or decision to be foreseen immediately it takes place, and often to involve the listener's emotions through the irony of his knowing something which the characters do not.[6]

Akhilleus is unique as the only character who knows in advance that his death is imminent; and the pathetic effect of this is intensified not only by his superiority on the human scale but by the constant juxtaposition of his mortality with the immortality of his mother Thetis. All humankind are mortal; and the sadness of this is superbly focused in Akhilleus, greater than ordinary men and with a goddess for mother, yet doomed not only to die young but to do so with advance knowledge and by his own choice.

The theme is introduced gradually. Akhilleus speaks of himself to Thetis as μινυνθάδιόν περ ἐόντα (1.352), but so are all humanity compared with her; and her own complaint, ὠκύμορος καὶ ὀϊζυρὸς περὶ πάντων | ἔπλεο (1.417–18), might also mean no more than this. But when she supplicates Zeus on his behalf there is more precision: ὠκυμορώτατος ἄλλων | ἔπλετ' (1.505–6). Then at the time of Akhilleus' fateful choice, his account of his alternative destinies confirms that if he continues to fight at Troy he will die there (9.412–13); and after the death of Patroklos the rapid approach of his death, by his own choice, is constantly on his lips and those of Thetis (see 18.95–6n.).

The manner of his death also becomes more and more explicit: his horse tells him he will be killed by 'a god and a man' (19.417); as he struggles with the river he declares he knows the god is to be Apollo (21.277–8); and

[5] There is a collection of examples in G. E. Duckworth, *Foreshadowing and Suspense in the Epics of Homer, Apollonius, and Vergil* (New York 1966). Edwards, *HPI* 32–3, gives a brief account. Duckworth also collected the often perceptive remarks of the scholiasts on προαναφώνησις and πρόληψις, *AJP* 52 (1931) 320–38. A modern critical approach is provided by de Jong, *Narrators* 81–90. Plutarch, *Vit. Hom.* 115, gives only a very sketchy account of divine πρόνοια.

[6] I cannot deal in detail here with the common hypothetical condition in the narrator's voice, 'Then *X* would have happened, had not *Y*...', which of course involves a kind of foreknowledge. See 17.319–25n. and 20.288–91n.

the dying Hektor names the man as Paris (22.359–60). The reiterated theme, especially when spoken by the hero himself, is always moving; the most effective passage of all, and perhaps the most original, is that where he addresses the young Lukaon (21.99–113, see note *ad loc.* and 18.117–19n.). Other scenes which are designed to reinforce the theme are his meeting with the ghost of Patroklos, with its assurance that Akhilleus too will die at Troy (23.65–107), and his dedication of his hair to his dead friend, declaring that he will not return to fulfil his vow to the river of his homeland (23.144–51).

Akhilleus' doom is foreshadowed almost exclusively in his own words and those of others. Only on one occasion does the poet make use of an alternative means, and even then this is not by a direct narrative statement. Instead, he presents the visual tableau of Akhilleus lying prostrate in the dust like a corpse, his grieving mother taking his head in her hands, the two of them surrounded by the lamenting sea-nymphs (18.26ff., see 18.22–31n.). The scene is that of Akhilleus' own funeral rites, as described at *Od.* 24.43–94. In a similarly allusive way, the divinely made armour worn by Patroklos, Hektor, and Akhilleus himself also foreshadows his death, as we realize that its power will not protect him any more than it has the others (see introduction to book 18). Akhilleus' death does not take place in the *Il.*, but throughout the poem, with increasing intensity, we share his knowledge that it is imminent, and we admire his resolution in facing it.

In contrast to this, the death of the entirely human and realistic Hektor is not known to him, being foreshadowed almost exclusively by the words of the gods and by the poet himself. The only exception to this is the dying Patroklos' prediction that he will die at the hands of Akhilleus (16.851–4), and this Hektor totally ignores. Hektor can be pessimistic, as he is with Andromakhe (6.447–65), and in his final minutes he realizes at last that there is no hope for him (22.296–303). But usually, in very human fashion, he either knows that he is ignorant of the future (6.367–8, 6.487–9), or else displays a brave man's optimism about his chances of success (6.476–81, 6.526–9, 18.305–9, 22.129–30, 22.256–9, 22.279–88). Much of the attractiveness of Hektor's character arises from this very human veering of his hopes and fears, which is portrayed especially in his farewell scene with his wife and in its less tense, more cheerful sequel as he greets Paris and returns to battle by his side.

Human characters often fear or hope for Hektor's death, but without definite foreknowledge of it. Zeus, however, foresees it clearly, and twice his reflections bring it before our eyes (15.68, 17.201–8). Thetis too twice mentions it to Akhilleus (18.95–6, 132–3). Besides this, the poet's voice prepares us in many ways. Andromakhe's first words to him declare that his courage will destroy him (φθίσει σε τὸ σὸν μένος, 6.407), and the idea is repeated for the predator to which he is compared in a simile (ἀγηνορίη δέ μιν ἔκτα, 12.46). The unconscious irony in her tale of Akhilleus' respect for her father's corpse after he killed him (6.416–20) is followed by the mourning in Hektor's house after his departure (6.500–2). Zeus's prediction of Hektor's glory and consequent death (15.59–68) is repeated when the narrator describes the scene of his triumph (15.596–614), and again before his victory over Patroklos (16.799–800). The final death sentence is expanded to considerable length, first by Zeus's hesitation and Athene's insistence (22.167–87), then by the tableau of the deadly scales (22.208–13). Hektor realizes his death is imminent only a few minutes before it occurs, but we ourselves have anticipated it long ago, and our sympathy for him is the keener because of his unawareness. Partly through these different types of foreshadowing, the poet has contrived that our emotional involvement with Akhilleus and with Hektor is of an entirely different kind.

The deaths of a few other significant characters are also foreshadowed by the poet, in a variety of ways. Patroklos is memorably doomed as he answers Akhilleus' summons, which will give Nestor his opportunity to propose his plan: ἔκμολεν ἶσος Ἄρηϊ, κακοῦ δ' ἄρα οἱ πέλεν ἀρχή (11.604). In Zeus's major pronouncement of the future, it is revealed that he will die by the hand of Hektor (15.65–7). The poet's foreboding voice is heard again, in a νήπιος-comment (16.46–7), as Patroklos supplicates Akhilleus, and his doom is confirmed as he departs for the battle by Zeus's refusal to grant Akhilleus' prayer for his safe return (16.250–2). As usual, as his death approaches more forebodings appear, and for Patroklos alone these take the form of poignant apostrophes: the uniquely fashioned ἔνθα τίνα πρῶτον, τίνα δ' ὕστατον ἐξενάριξας, | Πατρόκλεις, ὅτε δή σε θεοὶ θάνατόνδε κάλεσσαν; (16.692–3, see note *ad loc.*), and the final warmth of ἔνθ' ἄρα τοι, Πάτροκλε, φάνη βιότοιο τελευτή (16.787). Patroklos himself never knows of his coming fate. Neither does Sarpedon, despite his famous discourse on honour and death (12.310–28), though its approach is dramatized for us by the indecisiveness of his father Zeus (16.431–61), and has been anticipated by the earlier hint when he was wounded by Tlepolemos (πατὴρ δ' ἔτι λοιγὸν ἄμυνεν, 5.662) and by the fear he expresses of lying unburied (5.684–8).

Besides these individual deaths, two main general events are fore-shadowed in the poem. Διὸς δ' ἐτελείετο βουλή (1.5) announces, in the vaguest terms, Zeus's plan for the defeat of the Greeks while Akhilleus is absent, which is majestically ratified by him at 1.524–30 and repeated more explicitly at 15.49–77 and 16.644–55. On the other hand, the eventual fall of Troy, after the poem ends, has been predicted by portents; Odysseus repeats Kalkhas' prophecy at Aulis that the city would fall in the tenth year (2.323–9), and Nestor reminds the Greeks of a favourable sign from Zeus (2.350–3). Both sides know that the gods are angry with the Trojans, as appears in the predictions of Agamemnon (4.163–8), Hektor (6.447–9), and Diomedes (7.401–2). Two similes even more vividly confirm this (21.522–5, 22.410–11), and at the end of the poem the scene of the sacking to come is described in detail by Andromakhe (24.725–39).

The granting or rejection of prayers, the obituaries after a man's death, and the prediction in the Catalogue of Ships of Akhilleus' eventual return (τάχα δ' ἀνστήσεσθαι ἔμελλεν, 2.694), exemplify other uses of the poet's foreknowledge. In addition, the small-scale anticipations of important actions (see ch. 2, iii) and the foreshadowing in similes (see ch. 3, ii) also prepare the listener's mind to react as the poet intends. Priam's appeal to Akhilleus' love for his old father, in their climactic scene, has been led up to by a long sequence of father–son relationships – Zeus's loss of his son Sarpedon, Akhilleus' mention of the possible deaths of his old father and his son in his lament for Patroklos (19.321–37), his killing of Priam's sons Lukaon and Polydoros, and Hektor's dying prediction of Akhilleus' death at the hands of Priam's son Paris. Priam's first words, μνῆσαι πατρὸς σοῖο, are the culmination of this theme, which is finally universalized by the myth of Niobe's suffering at the loss of her children and her eventual control over it. Both this kind of anticipation and the more explicit foreshadowing prepare the listener's frame of mind for the emotional effect the poet wishes to produce.

2. Composition by theme

The word 'theme' has been used to cover several different types of compositional patterns in Homer which are as fundamental for the structure of the poems as the verbal formulae are for the verse. The variation, adaptation, and elaboration of these themes, together with their occasional innovative use for a purpose for which they were probably not intended, display the poet's inventiveness and mastery of his craft; though usually we cannot tell if the genius is that of the composer of the *Il.* or something he has adopted from a predecessor or a contemporary. The way in which these standard structures are employed, like Virgil's use of his Homeric models, shows not plagiarism but the power of taking over something already familiar to one's audience and making it distinctively one's own.

In the second chapter of volume II G. S. Kirk has identified the typical elements in the battle at the beginning of *Il.* 5, analysed the speeches of Andromakhe and Hektor in *Il.* 6, and described the operation of typical structures in battle-poetry. Here I shall give further consideration to: (i) type-scenes; (ii) story patterns and neoanalysis; and (iii) anticipation, preparation, and adaptation.

(i) Type-scenes

In his highly original work *Typischen Scenen*, Walter Arend studied Homeric scenes depicting arrival (including visits, messages, and dreams), sacrifice and meal-preparation, journeys by sea and by land, donning armour and clothing, retiring to sleep, deliberation, assembly, oath-taking, and bathing.[7] He showed that such scenes are each built up of a sequence of elements which normally occur in the same order, some elaborated to a greater or lesser extent to suit the circumstances, others appearing in minimal form or even omitted. Arend carefully plotted these elements, and gave indications of how the particular instantiations are adapted to their context. Coincidentally, the same year G. M. Calhoun published a paper

---

[7] As he freely acknowledged, Milman Parry had predecessors in his work on Homeric formulae. But Arend had none, at least in Homeric studies. His conception of the type-scene had actually been anticipated in V. V. Radlov's work on Turkic oral poetry, published in 1885 (see J. M. Foley, *The Theory of Oral Composition*, Bloomington 1988, 10–13), but Arend seems to have been unaware of this.

(*UCPCP* 12, 1933, 1–26) discussing not only repeated lines but also a number of repeated scenes; his analysis was much briefer than Arend's, but he too observed the effects of different examples of the same type-scene. Some years later, A. B. Lord pointed out the association of these and other 'themes' (including story patterns) with traditions of oral poetry, and J. Armstrong published the first detailed literary analysis of the examples of a certain type-scene, that of the arming of a warrior.[8] Other studies have followed.[9]

Type-scenes must not be considered occasional occurrences in the flow of Homeric narrative; in the *whole* of both poems, parallels can be found to the unfolding description of each scene and to the larger patterns of the narrative (and also to the structures of the speeches). For example, the battles of book 17 are organized upon several repetitions of each of two structural patterns, one a rebuke to a leader followed by a charge led by him, and the other a call for help and the response to it (see the introduction to book 17). Book 18 is the most complex in this volume. It begins with the arrival of a messenger, but the usual element of what the recipient is doing (cf. 9.186–9) takes the form of Akhilleus' sudden foreboding (see 3–4n.), and the usual mention of his companions (cf. 9.190–1) is postponed until after the message has been delivered (28–31). A submarine mourning scene (35–64) is followed by a divine visit (65–147), the last element of which, the deity's departure, is given unusually detailed treatment (see 18.65–9n.). After a short battle-scene (148–64), a divine visit by Iris (165–202) leads to elaborated scenes in which Akhilleus receives supernatural inspiration (203–14, cf. 5.1–8), gives a great battle-cry (217–21; for parallels see note *ad loc.*), and routs the Trojans. The Trojans then hold an assembly (243–314), the Greeks mourn and wash Patroklos' corpse, and after a very short conference scene between Zeus and Here (356–67) comes the much-expanded visit-scene of Thetis to Kharis and Hephaistos (see 369–467n.). Hephaistos' armour-making can be regarded as an unusually massive ecphrasis (cf. Pandaros' bow, 4.105–11). The book ends with the first element of a divine visit.

The following books are simpler in form. Book 19, after winding up the visit of Thetis to Akhilleus, is composed of an elaborate assembly, which concludes with gift-giving and oath-taking scenes (40–281); two successive scenes of mourning, by Briseis and Akhilleus (282–339); a divine visit (340–56; on the unusual handling of the element of the companions of the person visited see 19.351–2n.); and an expansive arming-scene. Book 20

---

[8] Lord: *TAPA* 82 (1951) 71–80; *The Singer of Tales* (Cambridge, Mass. 1960) 141–97. Armstrong: *AJP* 79 (1958) 337–54.
[9] There is a general account in Edwards, *HPI* 71–7 and 241–4. A bibliographical survey of work on Homeric type-scenes is in preparation for publication in *Oral Tradition*.

likewise begins with an assembly-scene (4–31), continues with a march out
to battle (adapted to include the gods; 32–74), interrupts this for a divine
visit (79–111) and a conference (112–55), and concludes with the first
stages of the long *aristeia* of Akhilleus (see introduction to book 20),
including another divine visit (288–340).

Verbal repetitions sometimes occur in instances of the same type-scene,
but they are not extensive. One might have expected the recurrent ritual
of sacrifice, for instance, to be described in a block of identical verses, but
in fact no two such descriptions are exactly alike, and in the majority of
such scenes only a few verses recur in identical form. As in the case of
similes, Homer's consummate control of his medium allows him to use
different phraseology (within the formular tradition) to convey often-
repeated material.

The structure of a type-scene is often complex; the most detailed of all,
that of a sacrifice, was analysed by Arend into twenty-one successive
elements, and more might be added.[10] The attention given to each of these
component elements varies in each instantiation of a particular type-scene.
It is a basic principle of Homeric technique that amplification is used to
signify importance,[11] and the normal way to expand a scene is by
elaboration of the elements of which it is composed. The amount of detail
given commands the audience's attention for a greater or lesser period of
time; and the nature of the material used for expansion conveys additional
meaning and often greater emotional depth. This is exemplified in the four
major arming-scenes, those of Paris (see 3.330–8n.), Agamemnon (see
11.15–46n.), Patroklos (see 16.130–54n.), and Akhilleus (see 19.356–424n.).
Paris is characterized as an archer, unused to the hand-to-hand battle he
will face against Menelaos, by his need to borrow a corslet (3.333);
Agamemnon's breastplate is described in detail – the one item of Akhilleus'
panoply which is *not* elaborated (11.19–28); Patroklos dons Akhilleus'
armour, but his inadequacy is revealed in his inability to wield Akhilleus'
mighty spear (16.140–4); and Akhilleus' own arming is illuminated by a
wealth of brightness and colour. In a different way, Homer's originality is
shown in Hektor's arming-scene, which is expanded not by a description of
the armour (which is, after all, that of Akhilleus), but by the forebodings
uttered both by the narrator and by Zeus as Hektor puts it on (17.192–212;
see part iii below).

In this way, comparison of the various instantiations of the same type-
scene, identifying the extent and nature of the elaboration given to its

[10] Certain type-scenes have been shown to be identical in structure in *Il.* and *Od.* (by
D. M. Gunn, *HSCP* 75, 1971, 14–31); this agrees with Arend's researches, and so far no
significant differences of this kind between the two poems have been detected.
[11] There are many comments on this in the scholia; see N. J. Richardson, *CQ* 30 (1980) 276
n. 36.

successive elements in each case, can throw light on the artistic effects and the poet's apparent purpose in the particular context.[12] The variations possible in the amplification of a type-scene can be illustrated by comparing the priest Khruses' visit to the Greek camp to ransom his daughter (1.12–33), which is elaborated only by the highly significant description of his holy insignia (as well as by brief direct speeches), with that of Priam to Akhilleus' dwelling to ransom Hektor's body, which if the preparations are included fills most of book 24 (see 24.469–691n.). A duel may occupy a verse or two, or be expanded into the lengthy (and yet inconclusive) confrontations of Diomedes and Glaukos (6.119–236) or Akhilleus and Aineias (20.79–352). The formal meal of reconciliation between Akhilleus and Agamemnon is compressed to two verses, because more important scenes are on hand and the poet, like the attendants, is working ἐσσυμένως (23.55); whereas Akhilleus' entertainment of the envoys, where everyone present (as well as the audience) is waiting in anxious anticipation of the dialogue to come, spreads over 16 verses (9.206–21, see note *ad loc.*). A different kind of originality is sometimes apparent when a normally short element of a type-scene is expanded to become an independent episode, as when the routine attempt to capture the horses and chariot of a victim is turned into the memorable scene of Zeus pitying the immortal horses as they weep over Patroklos (see 17.426–58n., and part iii below).

Conventions are natural in descriptions of frequently repeated action, and familiarity with the standard pattern doubtless assisted both the composer and the audience. How far such conventional descriptions are the result of the artistic moulding of poets, and how far they correspond to the regular sequence of actions in actual life (e.g. in the ritual of a sacrifice, or the more prosaic procedures of launching a ship), remains uncertain; and we must be cautious in assuming that the practices described are an accurate reflection either of the practices of the heroic age or of those of Homer's own time.[13] Regular structures for less formal procedures, like those for the reception of a guest (see 18.369–467n. and 18.380–1n.), the visit of a divinity, the deliberation before a decision, the description of family and guests retiring for the night, make it clear that these at least are creations of the oral technique rather than precise imitations of the formalities of actual life. What is important, for full appreciation of the poet's intent and craftsmanship, is to recognize – as the poet's original

---

[12] I have done this in detail for the scenes of *Il.* 1 in *HSCP* 84 (1980) 1–28. The article includes a brief bibliography (p. 3 n. 6); see also *TAPA* 105 (1975) 52 n. 7.

[13] See G. S. Kirk on the sacrifice type-scene in *Entretiens Hardt* xxvii (edd. Olivier, Reverdin, and Bernard, Geneva 1980) 41–80, and my article on Homeric funerals in *Studies in Honour of T. B. L. Webster* i, edd. J. H. Betts, J. T. Hooker, and J. R. Green (Bristol 1986) 84–92.

audiences must have done – the conventional structure, so that we may observe attentively the special features of each instantiation of every type-scene.

(ii) Story patterns and neoanalysis

The *Od.* includes a reference to songs about the Argonauts and several to episodes of the Troy story lying outside its plot and that of the *Il.* Many of its stories are ultimately derived from a general corpus of Indo-European myth, as D. L. Page in particular has shown.[14] The plot of the *Il.* too has clear affinities with age-old story patterns, and it is also very likely that the handling of some episodes is related to similar episodes in other oral epics on the Trojan story.

This is not the place to attempt to summarize recent scholarly work on the interpretation of Greek myth.[15] But in a more limited field, it is easy to identify in the *Il.* the universal themes described in Joseph Campbell's famous *The Hero with a Thousand Faces* (New York 1949) and Mircea Eliade's *The Myth of the Eternal Return* (tr. W. Trask, New York 1954). Their use is summarized by A. B. Lord, *The Singer of Tales* (Cambridge, Mass. 1960) 186–97, as withdrawal, devastation, and return.[16] Characteristically, the hero is isolated in some way, goes on a journey to a land of mystery, is tested, undergoes a symbolic death, and finally returns to those he left behind him. Akhilleus is twice separated from his society, by his withdrawal in book 1 and his refusal to accept Agamemnon's terms in book 9. His 'journey' is his estrangement from his peers. His absence causes 'devastation' among the Greeks. His 'return' appears in several forms: he returns to battle in the form of his surrogate Patroklos in book 16 and in his own person in book 20; he rejoins the Greeks as their colleague at the games in book 23; and he rejoins humankind by his kindness to his enemy Priam and his reunion with Briseis in book 24. On his lonely 'journey', the hero Akhilleus is, as often, accompanied by a companion (Patroklos); his test (or race) with a monster appears in his struggle with Skamandros in book 21 (which may also derive from the archetypal Near Eastern tale of the Flood: Nagler, *Spontaneity* 147–50); and he dies symbolically in the form of Patroklos. Similarly, Priam's journey to Akhilleus in book 24 has many parallels with a hero's visit to the Underworld: the Trojans lament as he

---

[14] *The Homeric Odyssey* (Oxford 1955); *Folktales in Homer's Odyssey* (Cambridge, Mass. 1973).

[15] Recently several collections of articles have appeared: J. Bremer (ed.), *The Interpretation of Greek Mythology* (London 1987); A. Dundes (ed.), *Sacred Narrative: Readings in the Theory of Myth* (Berkeley 1984); L. Edmunds (ed.), *Approaches to Greek Myth* (Baltimore 1990); and R. L. Gordon (ed.), *Myth, Religion and Society* (Cambridge 1981). See also G. S. Kirk, *The Nature of Greek Myths* (Harmondsworth 1974) and *Myth: its Meaning and Functions* (Berkeley 1970).

[16] See especially Nagler, *Spontaneity* 131–66 and 174–98; W. R. Nethercut, *Ramus* 5 (1976) 1–17; and Edwards, *HPI* 7–10 and 61–70.

departs; like the dead suitors at *Od.* 24.1–10 he is guided by Hermes; he passes by a tomb (24.349) and a river (24.350–1); with Hermes' help he enters through the barrier around Akhilleus' dwelling, and on his return is again guided by Hermes, explicitly crosses a river again (24.692–3), and is first seen by the visionary Kassandre (so W. R. Nethercut, *Ramus* 5, 1976, 1–17).

In addition to the inheritance of stories which came down from Indo-European ancestry along with the Greek language, there is increasing evidence that Homer and his peers were influenced by the myth and literature of the Near East. In an important recent article, *JHS* 108 (1988) 151–72, M. L. West not only accepts that certain themes and expressions of heroic glorification which Greek epic shares with early Indo-Iranian texts have their roots in Indo-European poetry, but goes so far as to say that

> The first poet who described Achilles raging over Patroklos' body 'like a lion whose cubs have been stolen', and later embracing his friend's ghost, must surely have been acquainted with the *Epic of Gilgameš*... It also provides the model for the episode in *Iliad* v where Aphrodite complains to Zeus and Dione of her maltreatment by Diomedes. (171)

W. Burkert has shown that the 'fatal letter' motif in the Bellerophon story and the theogonic themes in the Beguiling of Zeus recall the *Atraḥasis* and *Enuma Eliš* respectively.[17]

Even more important for our appreciation of the *Il.* is its relationship to other contemporary epic stories. In Homer's time, and for many years before him, songs had been sung in hexameter verse and with the same oral compositional techniques of formula and type-scene which appear in his own poems (see vol. II, ch. 2). Many must have dealt with tales of Troy, such as are mentioned by Hesiod in his account of the Age of Heroes (*Erga* 164–5). Some *Il.* episodes must share story patterns with these tales: the abductions of Khruseis and Briseis, and the resulting disasters, match that of Helen herself; the quarrel between Akhilleus and Agamemnon resembles quarrels we know of between Agamemnon and Menelaos (*Od.* 4.134–50), Akhilleus and Odysseus (*Od.* 8.73–80), and Odysseus and Aias (*Od.* 11.543ff.); the angry withdrawal of Akhilleus is like that of Meleager (9.553–99), and perhaps those of Paris and Aineias (*Il.* 6.326, 13.459ff.); the seduction of Here in book 14 is based on a traditional theme (see 14.153–351n.).

In recent years a succession of scholars, known as neoanalysts (though most of them in fact take a unitarian view of the *Il.*), have argued that the *Il.* used as direct sources the particular poems later known as the Epic

---

[17] In Hägg, *Greek Renaissance* 51–6. On the *Il.* and *Gilgamesh* see also R. Mondi's article in Edmunds' collection (above, n. 15) 141–98, D. M. Halperin, *One Hundred Years of Homosexuality and Other Essays* (New York 1990) 75–87, and G. K. Gresseth, *CJ* 70 (1975) 1–18.

Cycle. The first important figure to support such views was J. T. Kakridis in his *Homeric Researches* (Lund 1949); the most prestigious was W. Schadewaldt, especially in his article on the *Memnonis*, which first appeared in 1951 (reprinted in Schadewaldt, *VHWW* 155–202), the greatest contributions to the theory have been made by W. Kullmann.[18]

Many of the views put forward by some neoanalysts in the past would now be considered extreme. Few accept Schadewaldt's detailed reconstruction of the *Memnonis*, or believe that the *Aithiopis* attributed to Arctinus existed in written form before the composition of the *Il.*; and few would hold that passages in the *Il.* were taken verbatim from other epics. Kullmann has recently expressed the view (*GRBS* 25, 1984, 316) that the wrath of Akhilleus is the invention of one poet, but the frame of the plot of the *Il.* is traditional, and includes 'the semi-rigid use of motifs taken from other identifiable epics or their oral predecessors... This use, however, is not based on any stock of motifs.' Many Homerists would object to Kullmann's 'taken from' and would deny the validity of his second assertion, preferring the alternative view of Fenik, *TBS* 239, that the similarities between the *Il.* and the *Aithiopis* 'must be viewed against the background of an epic tradition in which myths proliferated, repetitions were popular, and doublets freely constructed... most of their similarities could have been the result of common epic material which both shared with many other poems now lost'.

But neither the *Il.* nor its poet must be considered in isolation. Homer must have learned his craft from other poets, and almost certainly even in his maturity would hear the songs of his contemporaries at festivals and competitions.[19] And the *Il.* (and perhaps the *Od.*) were not the only songs he sang; he must have known stories of Troy which find no place in his own great poem, as well as theogonies, Titanomachies, and legends of Thebes, Herakles, the Argonauts, the Calydonian boar, and so on (see vol. II, ch. 2). It is inherently likely that he had sung of them himself – and in the bardic oral tradition, in which Homer almost certainly still worked, to sing a song meant (to some extent at least) to compose it anew each time it was

<hr/>

[18] See Kullmann's summary of his views in *GRBS* 25 (1984) 307–23, his account of his methodology in *WS* 15 (1981) 5–42, and his *Quellen*, especially 303–35. See also Fenik, *TBS* 231–40; A. Heubeck in B. Fenik, *Homer: Tradition and Invention* (Leiden 1978) 1–17; E. C. Kopff, *Skrifter Utgivna Av. Svenska Institutet i Athen* 4, xxx (1983) 57–62; Thalmann, *Conventions* 49–51; G. Nagy, *The Best of the Achaeans* (Baltimore 1979) 164–7 and 205–7. There is a good bibliographic survey of neoanalysis by M. E. Clark in *CW* 79 (1986) 379–94. On the Epic Cycle generally see M. Davies, *The Epic Cycle* (Bristol 1989) and G. L. Huxley, *Greek Epic Poetry* (London 1969); the fragments have recently been re-edited in Bernabé, *PEG*, and Davies, *EGF*.
[19] See further my article in *CA* 9.2 (1990) 311–25, and M. Griffith in *Cabinet of the Muses* (*Festschrift* T. G. Rosenmeyer) edd. M. Griffith and D. J. Mastronarde (Atlanta 1990) 185–207.

performed. In such circumstances correspondences between famous episodes in the tales are very likely, as the poet modified and improved upon similar episodes in other songs, as sung by himself or by others.

At some date the monumental *Il.* became fixed in more or less its present form, possibly earlier than its commitment to writing (on which see vol. IV, ch. 3). Traditionally a little later than this, other songs likewise took permanent shape in the canonical *Cypria*, *Aithiopis*, *Iliupersis*, and other epics. How the *Aithiopis* corresponded to earlier tales we cannot know, but it is of particular importance to us here, because after telling the story of Penthesileia it continued with the killing of Akhilleus' friend Antilokhos by Memnon, Akhilleus' revenge, and his own death and funeral. Parallels with the Iliadic story of Patroklos are obvious; besides the revenge-motif itself, one notices the part played by Apollo in Akhilleus' death, the laborious rescue of his body by Aias and Odysseus, the mourning of Thetis and the Nereids, and the funeral games given in his honour. In addition, the wounding of the Akhilleus-like Diomedes in the foot by Paris (11.373–400) resembles Paris' killing of Akhilleus by a similar shot in the *Aithiopis* (see 16.777–867n.). It has been held (by H. Mühlestein, *SMEA* 15, 1972, 79–90) that the name of Patroklos' killer Euphorbos associates him with Paris (see 16.808n., 17.9n.).

Scholars have argued that other passages in the *Il.* are modelled on episodes in the *Aithiopis*. Nestor is rescued by Diomedes (8.80–129), but was more appropriately, and more poignantly, saved in the *Aithiopis* by his son Antilokhos, who in so doing lost his life (see 16.470–5n.); Sarpedon's body is removed by Sleep and Death (16.450–7, 666–83), and Memnon's may have similarly been borne off by the same figures (or by his mother Eos; see 16.419–683n.); Thetis' lament as she holds the grief-stricken Akhilleus (18.35–64) may be copied from her lament at his death, and her warning to him that he must die soon if he kills Hektor (18.95–6) may be derived from a similar prophecy she may have made when he set off to kill Memnon (see note *ad loc.*); Zeus's weighing of the fates of Akhilleus and Hektor (22.208–13) may be modelled on a scene in which he had to decide between the appeals of Thetis and Eos on behalf of their respective sons; and Akhilleus' threat to attack Troy after killing Hektor (22.378–84) parallels the plot of the *Aithiopis*, in which it was in his attack on Troy, after his victory over Memnon, that he was himself killed.

Though we know nothing of the early Memnon-tales on which Arctinus' *Aithiopis* was based, it is hard not to think that other elements in Memnon's story, as sung by Homer himself or by his rivals, suggested or influenced motifs occurring in the *Il.* Akhilleus' horses may have mourned him instead of Patroklos, and their warning of his approaching death (19.408–17) may have been suggested by a similar warning given when he entered battle for

the last time; the preoccupation with genealogies which characterizes the
challenges between Aineias and Akhilleus, both sons of goddesses, may have
appeared in the latter's encounter with Memnon, also a goddess's son and
on the side of his father Tithonos sharing much of Aineias' Trojan ancestry
(see 20.215–40n.); the careful contrivance to ensure that both antagonists
in the fateful duel between Akhilleus and Hektor are wearing armour made
by Hephaistos, and the long amplification of the making of Akhilleus'
replacement armour, may also have been suggested by the story of
Memnon, whose Hephaistos-made panoply was long famous (Virgil has
Dido ask *quibus Aurorae venisset filius armis, Aen.* 1.751; see 18.84–5n.).

The constant foreshadowing in the *Il.* of Akhilleus' death proves that a
knowledge of the Memnon tale is expected of the audience (it is referred to
at *Od.* 4.187–8, 24.78–9), and probably most Homerists will agree that a
similar expectation underlies the prominence of Antilokhos and his close
association with Akhilleus in the later books of the *Il.*[20] How much further
one carries the interrelationship of the two tales is likely to remain
subjective. My own view is that in many episodes of books 17–20 Homer
was conscious of parallels which existed in contemporary oral versions of
the Memnon tale, as sung by himself or by his rivals. This I have noted in
the introductions to books 17 and 18 and occasionally in the commentary.
See also the introduction to book 16.

(iii) Anticipation, preparation, and adaptation

The appearance of longer and shorter versions of any type-scene is
characteristic of Homeric composition, as explained in (i) above. Often,
however, it may be noted that a short form of a type-scene (or other
structural pattern) precedes a fuller version, as if to familiarize the hearer
with the concept before its most significant occurrence. Fenik, *TBS* 213–14,
has referred to this as the use of an 'anticipatory doublet'.[21] For instance,
Agenor stands alone to face Akhilleus, soliloquizes about what he should
do, decides to stand his ground in desperate hope, and then is pursued by
Akhilleus (Apollo acting as his surrogate; 21.544–22.20); a little later, the
final encounter of Akhilleus and Hektor begins with exactly the same
structure. The duel between these two has also been anticipated by their
two abortive meetings (20.364–80, 20.419–54), and Hektor's flight before
the greater hero has been prepared for by that of Aineias, recounted by
both heroes in turn (20.89–93, 20.188–90).

This feature of Homeric style is distinct from what is below termed

[20] This is argued by Kullmann, *GRBS* 25 (1984) 312, and M. M. Willcock in *Mélanges E.
Delebecque* (Aix-en-Provence 1983) 477–85 and Bremer, *HBOP* 185–94.
[21] See also my article in Bremer, *HBOP* 47–60.

'preparation', from ring composition (see ch. 4, ii), in which matching elements form one or more frames around a central core, and from foreshadowing by prediction of future events (see ch. 1, ii). It is widespread, and though many instances are almost certainly intentional, others may result simply from the repeated use of common themes, on different scales, without any specific design on the poet's part. The scale of the repeated structure varies from a motif of a line or two up to important components of the plot.

On the major scale, Akhilleus' respect for Priam and his agreement to the honourable burial of Hektor at the end of the poem has been preceded in microcosm by the respect and burial he offered to Andromakhe's father Eëtion (6.416–20). Priam's loss of his son Hector is preceded by Zeus's loss of Sarpedon and Ares' of Askalaphos (not to mention the many other times the father of a dying hero is referred to); and all these prefigure the loss Peleus will suffer after the action of the poem ends. Akhilleus' despatch of Patroklos on an errand at 11.598–616 anticipates his later sending him into battle in his stead (16.64ff.). Hektor's vitally important stripping of Patroklos' armour is preceded by Menelaos' stripping of Euphorbos, in both cases with some lack of precision in detail (see 17.123–39n., 17.90–3n.). Sarpedon's brief words to Hektor about the wife and infant son he left at home (5.480 and 5.688) anticipate the immortal scene of Hektor's leave-taking of his own wife and son (6.394ff.). The young Trojan Tros implores Akhilleus' mercy, but is killed by the implacable hero (20.463–72); and the brief episode, told by the narrator, reappears a little later amplified with the superb speeches of the Lukaon–Akhilleus scene (21.34–135). The portentous weighing of the fates of Hector and Akhilleus (22.208–13) was anticipated when Hektor γνῶ...Διὸς ἱρὰ τάλαντα (16.658; cf. also 8.68–72 and 19.223–4). See also 17.274–7n., 19.76–84n.

On a smaller scale, Hektor and Aias struggle over a single ship first briefly (15.416–18) and then at length (15.704–46; cf. Willcock on 15.416). Antilokhos receives the news of Patroklos' death in silence (17.695–6); so does Akhilleus (18.22–7). The obscuring mist about which Aias complains so memorably to Zeus (17.643–7) is mentioned briefly by him beforehand (17.243). Shortly before Akhilleus utters his mighty war-cry, which routs the Trojans (18.217–29), Hektor stands by Patroklos' corpse μέγα ἰάχων (18.160). The poet's brief comparison of a falling man to a diver, ἀρνευτῆρι ἐοικώς | κάππεσε (16.742–3), is followed by Patroklos' mocking development of it (16.745–50). The long and beautiful simile comparing the stones hurled over the Greek wall to snowflakes (12.278–89) is preceded by a shorter simile with identical content (12.156–8; cf. 11.546 and 11.548–57). In the long passage of description in the middle of the struggle over Patroklos three of the expansion techniques occur first in a brief and then in a more developed form (see 17.360–425n.). If this technique is appreciated, we can more easily understand the scene where Agamemnon remains sitting to address the assembly (see 19.47–53n., 19.76–84n.).[22]

One also notices cases where a fully developed scene is clearly related to a much briefer version, though there is no regular anticipation of the longer by the shorter form. For instance, the *Il.* contains four short invocations to the Muse; and de Jong has pointed out, *Narrators* 49–50, that there is a short version of such an appeal in the line ἔνθα τίνα πρῶτον, τίνα δ' ὕστατον ἐξενάριξεν; (3 × *Il.*, cf. also 8.273, *Od.* 9.14). Zeus's gloomy reflections on Hektor's folly in donning Akhilleus' armour (17.201–8) are rather like an elaborate νήπιος-comment; his proposal to save his son Sarpedon against μοῖρα (16.433–8), and Poseidon's rescue of Aineias in order to preserve what is μόριμον (20.300–5), are reflected in the short expression ὑπὲρ μόρον (see 17.321n.). The moving scene in which Zeus comforts the immortal horses which are mourning Patroklos is developed from the common motif of the capture of a man's horses after his death (see 17.426–58n.).[23]

Different from the anticipation of plot-themes, and often close to foreshadowing, is the poet's habit of giving the audience a brief preparation for an important action before it takes place, by providing in advance information which will assist in understanding a later scene. This technique was noticed by ancient scholars; among their comments[24] are that Nestor's advice κρῖν' ἄνδρας κατὰ φῦλα, κατὰ φρήτρας, 'Αγάμεμνον (2.362) prepares for the Catalogue (bT), that Pandaros is said to be surrounded by the ranks of his men when Athene visits him (4.90–1) so that they will be available to screen him with their shields when he shoots (4.113–15; bT) and (less convincingly) that Patroklos does not take Akhilleus' spear to battle (16.140) because the poet is preparing for Hephaistos' replacement of the panoply, and wood for a spear would not be available to him in the sky (A, from Megaclides). Fenik, *Odyssey* 88, notes (among a number of examples from the *Od.*) that the River Skamandros' angry thoughts of intervention against Akhilleus (21.136–8) precede his direct attack (21.211–327).

There are actually a large number of examples of this preparation technique, which assists the audience's comprehension and may well be characteristic of oral composition.[25] There is a good example in the long

---

[22] For further examples see 11.163–4n., 11.181–210n., 19.42–5n., and 20.46n.

[23] For further examples see 11.104ff. n. and 17.545–6n.

[24] They use the term προοικονομεῖν, sometimes (pardonably) confusing the technique with foreshadowing; see G. E. Duckworth, *AJP* 52 (1931) 324, and Erbse's Index III s.v.

[25] Though it can also be seen, for example, in Aeschylus, who often foreshadows in metaphorical form something that will later appear on stage: in the *Agamemnon*, Peitho (385) becomes incarnate in Klutaimestra when she is tempting Agamemnon (905–57); the bloodshed within the house (732) spreads over the crimson tapestries on the stage (908–11); the warning against Hubris (763–71) signals the entry of the king, who will tread upon the crimson as he enters the palace; the hope that the victorious army has observed proper piety

description of Zeus's inattentiveness during the battle at the wall (13.1–9), preparing for his beguiling by Here in the next book. Very often a character's direct speech initiates the preparation. Antenor's praise of Odysseus' eloquence (3.221–4) prepares for the leading role assigned him in the embassy to Akhilleus. Aphrodite's tribute to Here, Ζηνὸς γὰρ τοῦ ἀρίστου ἐν ἀγκοίνῃσιν ἰαύεις (14.213), is ironically recalled when Here's plan has succeeded and Zeus ἔχε δ' ἀγκὰς ἄκοιτιν (14.353). With more serious irony, Hektor declares that if he meets Akhilleus he will not fly before him but will stand his ground (18.305–8), long before he fails to keep his promise in book 22. Sarpedon's prayer to Hektor, μὴ δή με ἕλωρ Δαναοῖσιν ἐάσῃς | κεῖσθαι (5.684–5), prepares us (if we are attentive) for the significance of Zeus's orders for his burial (16.666–75); and Sleep and Death are identified as brothers some time before they enter the action together to remove his body (14.231; 16.681–3). Menelaos praises Antilokhos' speed of foot (15.569–70), a little later the rapidity of his flight from Hektor is illustrated by a simile (15.586–90), and both passages prepare for his dispatch from the battlefield to summon Akhilleus, when speed is vital (17.652–5 and 691–3). Menelaos worries that Akhilleus cannot fight without armour (17.711), preparing for the latter's amplification of the theme (18.188–95), his rescue of Patroklos' body without armour, and its replacement by Hephaistos. Akhilleus says that the Trojans do not see his helmet blazing near them, or they would take flight and fill the stream-beds with corpses, preparing for his later massacre in the river (16.71–2; so bT). He says he loved Patroklos ἶσον ἐμῇ κεφαλῇ (18.82), and a few lines later proves it by deciding to kill Hektor at the cost of his own life (18.98–9, 18.114–16). He makes a brief mention of Briseis (19.59–60), a little before she utters her moving lament over the dead Patroklos (19.282–300). Apollo warns Hektor not to try to capture the horses of Akhilleus (17.75–8) some time before the scene in which he actually makes the attempt (17.483–542). He tells Aineias of the importance of his ancestry, and warns him not to be scared by Akhilleus's threats (20.105–7, 20.108–9); and both lineage and verbal attack appear in full development later, in chiastic order (20.203–9, 20.178–98). τλητὸν γὰρ Μοῖραι θυμὸν θέσαν ἀνθρώποισιν he declares (24.49), preparing for Akhilleus' later words to Priam. Though not in direct speech, Here's plan to beguile Zeus is revealed to us by her thoughts, told to us by the narrator (14.159–65) before she goes into action.[26]

Occasionally it appears that the poet has adapted a conventional scene

(338–42) is shown to be false by the appearance of the violated priestess Kassandre in the victor's chariot; and so on (see especially A. Lebeck, *The Oresteia*, Cambridge, Mass. 1971). Plato has Socrates admit he has aroused hostility by asking questions of those reputed wise (*Apology* 21e) before he presents him interrogating Meletos (24d–7e).

[26] For further examples see the introduction to Book 20 and notes to 105–7, 108–9, 133–43, and 182–3 in that book; and 16.97–100n.

to suit a purpose for which it was not primarily intended. In section (i) above it was suggested that Hektor's arming-scene (17.192–212) and his attempt to capture Akhilleus' immortal horses (17.426–58) convey an emotion which is different from (and greater than) that which the type-scene normally carries. There is a simple but powerful example of this at 23.135–51, where first the Myrmidons cut their hair in the regular sign of mourning and lay it upon Patroklos' corpse, and then Akhilleus himself does the same with a speech restating his knowledge that he will never return to his home, thus intensifying the pathos of his own short life. In similar fashion, the *topos* that death came even to Herakles, the mightiest of men, is stated in normal form by Akhilleus (18.117–19, see note *ad loc.*) some time before he adapts the paradigm, in his famous words to young Lukaon, to embrace the death of Patroklos and finally his own (21.107–13). Helen's account of the Greek leaders (3.172–244) tells us more about her own guilt, remorse, and loneliness than it does about them (cf. A. Parry, *YCS* 20, 1966, 197–200).[27] In books 17–20 there are two major examples: the uses the poet makes of Patroklos' disguise in Akhilleus' armour, which extend from book 16 to book 22 and go far beyond that of a mere deception of the Trojans (see the introductions to books 16 and 18); and the suggestion of Akhilleus' funeral which underlies the scene of his first grieving for Patroklos (see 18.22–31n., 18.52–64n.).

These habits of composition may well have developed as aids both to the oral poet and to the listening audience. But like so much else in Homer, in his work they are refined into artistic techniques for shaping the hearer's response and increasing his emotional involvement.

[27] For further examples see 24.552–95n., 24.633–76n., and my article in Bremer, *HBOP* 53–9.

3. Similes

Homer's versatility and his inventiveness within the epic convention appear clearly in his similes.[28] As the following sections will show, the similes appear in different forms; the connexion between simile and narrative varies; although certain themes recur frequently, the phrasing is almost always different;[29] and the diction of the similes is formular, but with evidence of non-traditional usages and vocabulary. These features suggest a high degree of original composition.

Rare in Hesiod and the *Hymns*,[30] long similes of the Homeric type may have been most fully developed in the *Il.* and *Od.* Near Eastern antecedents are possible (see P. Damon, *Modes of Analogy in Ancient and Medieval Verse*, Berkeley 1961, 264–70). Totals given for similes by modern commentators vary, depending on the definition adopted and the treatment of multiple occurrences. Lee, *Similes* 3–4, counts 197 long similes ('Full', i.e. with a verb) in the *Il.* and 153 short ('Internal', i.e. without a verb), compared with 45 and 87 respectively in the *Od.*; Scott's listing, *Similes* 191–205, gives a total (for both types) of 341 for the *Il.* and 134 for the *Od.* A. Bonnafé, *RPh* 67 (1983) 82, counts 1,128 verses of simile in the *Il.*, or 7.2 % of the total 15,693 verses.

[28] In the extensive bibliography, Fränkel, *Gleichnisse*, is still the fullest and best treatment. Lee, *Similes*, has useful lists, though most would find his theories unacceptable and his polemics against Fränkel displeasing. Scott, *Oral Nature*, studies the preferred context of similes of particular subject-matter, but does not exhaust his topic, which is more fully studied by J. C. Hogan, *The Oral Nature of the Homeric Simile* (diss. Cornell 1966; *DA* 27, 1966, 1352A). Moulton, *Similes*, finds connexions between the similes and the narrative structure of the poem. S. A. Nimis, *Narrative Semiotics in the Epic Tradition: the Simile* (Bloomington and Indianapolis 1987) 23–95 makes many perceptive observations from the viewpoint of semiotic theory. M. Mueller, *The Iliad* (London 1984), O. Tsagarakis, *Form and Content in Homer* (Wiesbaden 1982), and Edwards, *HPI* 102–10, devote sections to the topic.

[29] In the *Il.*, five long similes are repeated verbatim: 5.782–3 = 7.256–7; 5.860–1 = 14.148–9; 6.506–11 = 15.263–8; 9.14–15 = 16.3–4; and 13.389–93 = 16.482–6. In addition, 11.548–55 ≅ 17.657–64 (see note *ad loc.*; there is variation only in the first two verses). In the *Od.*, 4.335–40 = 17.126–31 (this is within a longer repeated speech) and 6.232–4 = 23.159–61. C. F. Beye, *Studies Presented to Sterling Dow* (ed. K. J. Rigsby, Durham, N.C. 1984) 7–13, suggests that in many cases the repetition is significant, recalling the circumstances of the first appearance; but it is hard to accept this entirely.

[30] Examples occur at *Theogony* 594–601, 702–4, 862–6; *Erga* 304–6; *HyDem* 174–7; *HyHerm* 43–6, 55–6, 66–7, 349. There are seven in the *Aspis* (42–5, 374–9, 386–92, 402–4, 405–12, 426–34, 437–42); they show one obvious point of comparison, and are very simple by Homeric standards.

Similes

(i) Form

Similes are introduced by a variety of different words, the commonest being ὡς, ὡς (δ᾽) ὅτε, ἠΰτε, ἐοικώς, ἴσος, and οἶος (there is a list in Lee, *Similes* 62–4). There are short forms (i.e. without a verb expressed), and several types of long form.

(a) The short simile

Many of these, such as δαίμονι ἴσος (9 × *Il.*), ἠΰτε νεβροί (-ούς) (3 × *Il.*), θηρὶ ἐοικώς (2 × *Il.*), ἠέλιος ὡς (1 × *Il.*, 2 × *Od.*), have much in common with formular epithets. Like the latter, they convey emphasis and some decorative value, and often they end the verse after the bucolic diaeresis. Occasionally they may have a strong significance (see 24.572–5n.). There is a good deal of variety; Scott, *Oral Nature* 128, lists 13 short similes of this metrical shape, of which only δαίμονι ἴσος occurs more than 3 ×. Short comparisons like these are common in oral epic in other cultures (see C. M. Bowra, *Heroic Poetry*, London 1952, 266–7).

Again like other end-of-verse formulae, such similes can be expanded to suit metrical convenience. νυκτὶ ἐοικώς can be preceded by ἐρεμνῇ (*Od.* 11.606, *Il.* 1.47), and the familiar λέων (λύκοι) ὡς can be replaced by θηρὶ κακὸν ῥέξαντι ἐοικώς (15.586). Automedon darts in ὡς τ᾽ αἰγυπιὸς μετὰ χῆνας (17.460), a longer form of αἰγυπιὸς ὡς | (13.531). ἴσος (-ον) Ἄρηϊ and λαίλαπι ἴσος also probably served to end a verse without further extension, though in Homer the former is always preceded by βροτολοιγῷ (4 × *Il.*, 1 × *Od.*) and the latter by κελαινῇ or ἐρεμνῇ (3 × *Il.*).

A similar metrical flexibility is apparent in conventional comparisons of other metrical shapes. The poet may or may not precede ἀτάλαντος (-ον, -οι) Ἄρηϊ (11 × *Il.*) by θοῷ, and may or may not follow δέμας πυρός (17.366) by αἰθομένοιο | (3 × *Il.*). Andromakhe dashes to the wall of Troy either | μαινομένη εἴκυῖα (6.389) or μαινάδι ἴση | (22.460). | λαμπέσθην ὡς εἴ τε πυρὸς σέλας (19.366) is a version of ὡς εἰ σέλας ἐξεφάανθεν | (19.17), and ἔρνεϊ ἴσος | (18.56 = 437, *Od.* 14.175) is virtually repeated in the next verse as φυτὸν ὡς γουνῷ ἀλωῆς |. The common idea 'like a flame' can appear as φλογὶ εἴκελος after the mid-verse caesura (3 × *Il.*), or the verse can be completed by Ἡφαίστοιο | (17.88); when the phrase occurs a foot later, the poet completes the verse with ἀλκήν | (13.330, 18.154). He uses another version of the phrase, φλογὶ ἴσοι, before the mid-verse caesura (13.39). κόμαι Χαρίτεσσιν ὁμοῖαι | (17.51) also appears in the longer form κόμας ὑακινθίνῳ ἄνθει ὁμοίας | (2 × *Od.*). Once the poet expands λέων ὡς into αἱματόεις ὡς τίς τε λέων κατὰ ταῦρον ἐδηδώς (17.542), which is like an abbreviation of the common long lion–bull simile (cf. 17.657–64 etc.). He illustrates the glare of Akhilleus' armour by a succession of short comparisons of different form:

Similes

σέλας... ἠΰτε μήνης | (19.374), ἀστὴρ ὣς ἀπέλαμπεν | (19.381; cf. the fuller version at 22.317–19), and παμφαίνων ὥς τ' ἠλέκτωρ Ὑπερίων | (19.398).

(b) The long simile

The characteristically Homeric long simile appears in three main forms.

(1) Extensions of the short simile

The poet may expand a short phrase of comparison by adding an enjambing clause, connected usually by a relative pronoun: ἠΰτε νεβροί (-ούς) |, standing alone at 21.29 and 22.1, continues αἵ τ'... | ἑστᾶσ' at 4.243–5. The relative clause is often preceded by a runover adjective: λέων ὥς |, which occurs in short form at 11.129, continues at 20.164ff. into | σίντης, ὅν τε..., developing a picture which extends for 9 verses. λύκοι ὥς, occurring 3 × Il. at the end of the line, once continues in similar detail ὠμοφάγοι, τοῖσίν τε..., | οἵ τ'... (16.156–66). Idomeneus at 4.253 is simply συῒ εἴκελος ἀλκήν |, but for Aias at 17.281 the poet continues | καπρίῳ, ὅς... for two further verses. ὄρνιθες (-ας) ὥς | is followed by amplification at 3.3–7, and at 2.765 by two descriptive epithets and a participial phrase (without relative clause); in the form ὄρνιθι ἐοικώς | it is extended by a relative clause at Od. 5.51–3 (it is interesting that Sleep's metamorphosis takes the slightly different form | ὄρνιθι λιγυρῇ ἐναλίγκιος, ἥν τ' ἐν ὄρεσσι |..., 14.290–1). A similar kind of extension follows ὥς τε γυναῖκας | at 20.252–5. At 17.133–6 a short simile expands first into a qualifying phrase and then into a clause: ἑστήκει ὥς τίς τε λέων περὶ οἷσι τέκεσσιν, | ᾧ... The comparisons | οἷμα λέοντος ἔχων, ὅς... (16.752–4) and the longer | αἰετοῦ οἵματ' ἔχων μέλανος, τοῦ θηρητῆρος, | ὅς... (21.252–4) do not occur without the extending relative clause but could clearly be used in shorter form.

The characteristically Homeric long simile may have originated in such extensions of a short simile, but in our poems they make up only a small proportion of the total number of long similes. For this reason I here avoid the possibly misleading term 'extended similes' for similes containing one or more verbs.

(2) Other postpositioned long similes

In the category just mentioned the simile, like a relative clause, follows the reference to the thing to which the comparison is made. In another type of long simile the statement in the narrative is followed by an adverbial clause, or a new sentence, usually beginning with ὥς τε, ὡς (δ') ὅτε, or οἷον (the Wiesatz). At the end of the simile the correlative to the introductory adverb marks (in ring form) the return to the narrative (the Sosatz). Euphorbos falls dead, his braided hair blood-bespattered; and the statement is then

26

illustrated by the picture of a cherished and beautiful olive sapling thrown to earth by a storm, beginning οἷον δὲ τρέφει ἔρνος ἀνὴρ ἐριθηλὲς ἐλαίης... and ending τοῖον... (17.53–60).

It is not easy to find a simple example even of this very common type of simile, for Homeric flexibility is such that the form is often varied slightly in one way or another and the connexion with the narrative may be more or less close (see ii below). For instance, consider 17.262–6:

> Τρῶες δὲ προύτυψαν ἀολλέες· ἦρχε δ' ἄρ' Ἕκτωρ.
> ὡς δ' ὅτ' ἐπὶ προχοῇσι διιπετέος ποταμοῖο
> βέβρυχεν μέγα κῦμα ποτὶ ῥόον, ἀμφὶ δέ τ' ἄκραι
> ἠϊόνες βοόωσιν ἐρευγομένης ἁλὸς ἔξω,
> τόσσῃ ἄρα Τρῶες ἰαχῇ ἴσαν.

The comparison begins with ὡς δ' ὅτε, as if to introduce a parallel to Hektor's leadership of the Trojan charge; but as the description of the swollen river and stormy sea progresses βέβρυχεν and βοόωσιν bring in the idea of sound; and this, instead of the forward rush, becomes the main point of comparison in the concluding τόσσῃ... ἰαχῇ. One must watch for this kind of additional colour in any simile that follows the illustrated item, however simple the comparison may seem at first sight.

(3) *Pre-positioned long similes*

The tendency for a new idea to appear in the simile and then carry over into the narrative, as shown in the last example, attains its most obvious form when a simile begins the sentence and introduces the point of comparison before the narrative has yet reached it. Usually such a simile begins with ὡς δ' ὅτ(ε), which occurs 34× *Il.* (ὡς ὅτ(ε) occurs 28× *Il.*). There is a straightforward example at 17.520–2. Aretos is wounded by a spear in the belly:

> ὡς δ' ὅτ' ἂν ὀξὺν ἔχων πέλεκυν αἰζήϊος ἀνὴρ,
> κόψας ἐξόπιθεν κεράων βοὸς ἀγραύλοιο,
> ἵνα τάμῃ διὰ πᾶσαν, ὁ δὲ προθορὼν ἐρίπῃσιν,

and Aretos, like the bull, springs forward and collapses:

> ὡς ἄρ' ὅ γε προθορὼν πέσεν ὕπτιος.

This repetition of the same word to indicate the point of comparison is common in similes. There is another instance at 19.356–60:

> ...τοὶ δ' ἀπάνευθε νεῶν ἐχέοντο θοάων.
> ὡς δ' ὅτε ταρφειαὶ νιφάδες Διὸς ἐκποτέονται...
> ὡς τότε ταρφειαὶ κόρυθες λαμπρὸν γανόωσαι
> νηῶν ἐκφορέοντο...

27

A longer phrase is repeated, no doubt for pathetic effect, in the moving simile at 23.222–4, as Akhilleus mourns his dead companion:

ὡς δὲ πατὴρ οὗ παιδὸς ὀδύρεται ὀστέα καίων,
νυμφίου, ὅς τε θανὼν δειλοὺς ἀκάχησε τοκῆας,
ὣς Ἀχιλεὺς ἑτάροιο ὀδύρεται ὀστέα καίων.

Several of the most notable similes in the *Il.* are of this pre-positioned type, including Akhilleus' likening himself to a bird suffering hardship to bring back food for its young (9.323–7), and the description of men stretching an oxhide (17.389–93), which is not closely connected with the preceding account of the sweating, weary warriors but introduces the following picture of the two sides tugging vainly at Patroklos' body. The agglomerated similes which introduce the Catalogue of Ships (2.455–83) and the double similes at 20.490–2 and 495–7 are also of this type.

Homer's most splendid exploitation of the long simile appears when the illustration is so powerfully integrated into the narrative, looking both forward and backward, that its removal would be impossible. In the lion-simile at 17.61–7, Menelaos has killed Euphorbos and is stripping off his armour: ὡς δ᾽ ὅτε a lion has seized the best cow of a herd, breaks its neck, and gulps down the blood and entrails, while the dogs and herdsmen make a great noise from a safe distance but fear to confront (ἀντίον ἐλθέμεναι) the beast; ὣς the Trojans fear to confront (ἀντίον ἐλθέμεναι) Menelaos. The first parallel is between the lion's kill and Menelaos', continuing into the lion's killing and eating of its victim and Menelaos' stripping of Euphorbos' corpse; then the focus shifts to the frightened dogs and herdsmen, and as we return to the narrative their reluctance is transferred to the Trojans. The simile is thus actually both postpositioned and pre-positioned (see also p. 32).

(4) *Unusual forms*

There are two major examples in the *Il.* of the use of a negative to produce an intensifying effect, turning the simile into a kind of priamel. At 17.20–3 this takes the form of a triple disjunction:

οὔτ᾽ οὖν παρδάλιος τόσσον μένος οὔτε λέοντος
οὔτε συὸς κάπρου ὀλοόφρονος, οὗ τε μέγιστος
θυμὸς ἐνὶ στήθεσσι περὶ σθένεϊ βλεμεαίνει,
ὅσσον Πάνθου υἷες ἐϋμμελίαι φρονέουσιν.

At 14.394–9 (see note *ad loc.*) we find a similar but even more formal triple example, where the disjunctions are amplified into separate couplets comparing the clash of the two armies successively to the roar of the sea, to that of a forest fire, and to that of a wind storming through oak trees. The three repeated | οὔτε's conclude ὅσση ἄρα Τρώων καὶ 'Αχαιῶν ἔπλετο φωνή. The form of these similes resembles the priamels where Hektor tells Andromakhe his concern is not so much for the Trojans, or for Priam and Hekabe, or for his dying brothers, as for her (6.450–5), and where Zeus recites the names of his conquests who moved him less than Here does at the present moment (14.315–28).[31]

Glaukos' famous simile of the leaves is complete in sense within a single line: οἵη περ φύλλων γενεή, τοίη δὲ καὶ ἀνδρῶν (6.146). Then the poet repeats the main word of the simile and expands the sense (φύλλα τὰ μὲν..., 147–8), and returns to the narrative, repeating here the item to which he has compared the leaves (ὣς ἀνδρῶν γενεή..., 149). He is expanding and artistically reworking the short comparison φύλλοισιν ἐοικότες (21.464). An even more sophisticated form of comparison appears in Odysseus' famous comparison of Nausikaa to a palm tree, which begins with no specification at all (*Od.* 6.160–1):

> οὐ γάρ πω τοιοῦτον ἐγὼ ἴδον ὀφθαλμοῖσιν,
> οὔτ' ἄνδρ' οὔτε γυναῖκα· σέβας μ' ἔχει εἰσορόωντα

then introduces paratactically the vehicle of the simile (6.162–3):

> Δήλῳ δή ποτε τοῖον 'Απόλλωνος παρὰ βωμῷ
> φοίνικος νέον ἔρνος ἀνερχόμενον ἐνόησα

and only later reaches the point of comparison, repeated in both simile and narrative (6.166–8):

> ὣς δ' αὕτως καὶ κεῖνο ἰδὼν ἐτεθήπεα θυμῷ
> δήν, ἐπεὶ οὔ πω τοῖον ἀνήλυθεν ἐκ δόρυ γαίης,
> ὣς σέ, γύναι, ἄγαμαί τε τέθηπά τε...

Twice the rare figure *anadiplosis* is used with a simile; once at 22.127–8:

> ἅ τε παρθένος ἠΐθεός τε,
> παρθένος ἠΐθεός τ' ὀαρίζετον ἀλλήλοιιν

and at 20.371–2, where a further comparison follows immediately:

> εἰ πυρὶ χεῖρας ἔοικεν,
> εἰ πυρὶ χεῖρας ἔοικε, μένος δ' αἴθωνι σιδήρῳ.

Occasionally it is not quite clear whether the poet intends a simile or a divine metamorphosis. There is a simple instance at 19.350–1, where

---

[31] See W. R. Race, *The Classical Priamel from Homer to Boethius* (Leiden 1982) 34–41. The only other negative simile in Homer is at *Od.* 13.86–7, οὐδέ κεν ἴρηξ | κίρκος ὁμαρτήσειεν, ἐλαφρότατος πετεηνῶν. On such similes see R. J. Schork, *AJP* 107 (1986) 263 n. 8 and *APA Abstracts* (1989) 20. He says that apart from these three Homeric examples, the figure is found in Greek lyric, elegiac, and iambic only occasionally in Theocritus, Moschus, and Callimachus, and is common only in Propertius and Horace.

Athene swoops down from heaven like a hawk (ἄρπῃ ἐϊκυῖα τανυπτέρυγι λιγυφώνῳ) to infuse nectar into Akhilleus. ἐϊκυῖα usually implies a metamorphosis, but her purpose and action suggest that the poet intends only to emphasize her speed.[32] This is very obviously the case with ἴρηξ ὣς at 18.616, where Thetis is burdened with Akhilleus' new armour.

(ii) Connexion of simile and narrative

Ancient scholars perceived that besides the primary point of comparison between narrative and simile other parallels might be developed in the course of the simile-description and add to the effect. For example, when Athene brushes Pandaros' arrow aside from Menelaos 'as when a mother brushes aside a fly from her infant, when it is lying in sweet sleep' (4.130–1), the scholia comment 'The mother ⟨corresponds to⟩ the good disposition ⟨of Athene to Menelaos⟩; the fly to the ease with which it is scared away and darts off to another place; the ⟨child's⟩ sleep to ⟨Menelaos'⟩ being off guard and to the weakness of the blow' (bT on 4.130–1; cf. K. Snipes, *AJP* 109, 1988, 220–1). They see many parallels in the famous simile which compares Aias, reluctantly withdrawing from the onslaught of the Trojan spears, to a stubborn donkey in a cornfield, long ignoring and then at last yielding to the sticks of children:

> The simile ⟨represents his⟩ scorn of the Trojans, in that he yields not to them, but to Zeus; the animal's greediness in cropping the plentiful pasture ⟨represents⟩ the hero's immovability. The grazing donkey is a much better parallel than a pack-animal, for it is hard to move a pasturing beast. And heightening ⟨the parallel⟩ he calls the donkey lazy and used to many blows (11.559); many men have broken sticks on his back before this, and now he says that not men are beating him, but children. (bT on 11.558–62; see N. J. Richardson, *CQ* 30, 1980, 279–81)

On the other hand, schol. T on 12.41–8 insist that the simile here comparing Hektor to a boar or lion at bay illustrates only his being surrounded by the Trojans, and that the death of the beast (ἀγηνορίη δέ μιν ἔκτα, 46) and the spears hurled at it (43–5) are only ποιητικὸς κόσμος. Certainly Hektor does not die here, as the beast does, but it is hard not to recall Andromakhe's first words to him, φθίσει σε τὸ σὸν μένος (6.407), and there can be little doubt that the similar idea in the lion-simile for Patroklos, ἑή τέ μιν ὤλεσεν ἀλκή (16.753), foreshadows that hero's death (bT *ad loc.* make this point). A few modern scholars have denied that there is ever more than one point of comparison (e.g. D. L. Page, *CR* 10, 1960, 108; G. Jachmann, *Der homerische Schiffskatalog und die Ilias*, Opladen 1958, 267–338), but most

---

[32] On other instances of this ambiguity see 4.78–84n., 7.59–60n., 13.62–5n., and 17.547–52n., and in general H. Erbse, *Hermes* 108 (1980) 259–74; H. Bannert, *WS* 12 (1978) 29–42; F. Dirlmeier, *Die Vogelgestalt homerischer Götter* (Heidelberg 1967); de Jong, *Narrators* 134–5; and M. Coffey, *AJP* 78 (1957) 120 n. 29.

follow Fränkel, *Gleichnisse* 1–16 and passim, in accepting that further ideas significant for the narrative occur in the course of the simile. As Fränkel says, *Gleichnisse* 5–6, it would be foolish to restrict the parallel in the famous simile applied to the Trojan watchfires (8.555–61) to the number of fires and the number of stars, when the pictures also have in common the glittering points of light, the stillness, and the joy in the hearts of the shepherd and the victorious Trojans. One often feels, especially with similes which begin ὡς (δ') ὅτε..., that the poet is drawing a general illustrative picture rather than making a direct comparison between one item and another. The familiarity of pre-positioned similes (above, i (b) 3) makes this view even more probable. For other examples of multiple points of comparison see 13.795–9n. and 20.164–75n.

Often a repetition of the same word links narrative and simile. Fränkel however correctly insists that such a word (the *Kupplung*) is not necessarily the main point of comparison. One of his prime examples (*Gleichnisse* 8–9) is 7.4–7, where, like weary oarsmen *longing for* (ἐελδομένοισιν, 4) a wind, the Trojans have been *longing for* (ἐελδομένοισι, 7) the return of Hektor and Paris; but the most striking point of comparison is not the realization of the men's hopes but the vividly described exhaustion of the oarsmen (5–6) and so too (by implication) of the Trojans (see also 18.318–22n.). Occasionally the linking word recurs in a slightly different sense; in 16.428–30 κλάζειν is used in the simile for the screeching of fighting birds, in the narrative for the battle-cries of Sarpedon and Patroklos.[33] In the vivid comparison of men dragging at Patroklos' body to workers stretching an oxhide (17.389–95), the simile's key-words τανύειν, τανύουσι, τάνυται (390, 391, 393) are picked up in the narrative by εἷλκεον (395), but recur a little later in τοῖον Ζεὺς... | ...ἐτάνυσσε κακὸν πόνον (401; see note *ad loc.*).

Sometimes the ideas introduced in the course of the simile, though not directly relevant to the immediate action, serve to foreshadow the future.[34] Two instances have been referred to above (12.41–8, 16.752–3; see also 13.471–5n.). A simile comparing Sarpedon to a marauding lion concludes with alternative endings, perhaps foreshadowing Zeus's later uncertainty whether to save his son (12.299–306; cf. 16.431–61). The full-fed wolves to which the poet compares the battle-starved Myrmidons before they set off for the battle (16.156–63) may look forward to their coming victory under Patroklos' leadership (see note *ad loc.*).[35] In the simile describing Akhilleus'

---

[33] The example is given by M. S. Silk, *Interaction in Poetic Imagery* (Cambridge 1974) 16; on the theoretical background of Silk's work see the review article by J. M. Mueller in *CP* 72 (1977) 146–59.

[34] This is often mentioned in the scholia; see K. Snipes, *AJP* 109 (1988) 213–14.

[35] S. A. Nimis however has made the attractive suggestion that the wolves' eating and drinking represent and replace the communal meal usually shared by an army before battle (*Narrative Semiotics in the Epic Tradition: the Simile*, Bloomington and Indianapolis 1987, 23–33).

anguish over his dead friend there is a prediction of his subsequent pursuit
of the Trojans (18.318–22, see note *ad loc.*), and two similes foreshadow the
burning of Troy (21.522–5; 22.410–1). Conversely, as Akhilleus advances
for his first duel in the *Il.* an effective simile includes a reminder of the way
the hero has withdrawn from the war up to this point (20.164–75, see note
ad loc.).

Sometimes the connexion between simile and narrative can best be
described as elliptical.[36] Thus at 16.364–7, just before Hektor's retreat:

ὡς δ᾽ ὅτ᾽ ἀπ᾽ Οὐλύμπου νέφος ἔρχεται οὐρανὸν εἴσω
αἰθέρος ἐκ δίης, ὅτε τε Ζεὺς λαίλαπα τείνῃ,
ὡς τῶν ἐκ νηῶν γένετο ἰαχή τε φόβος τε,
οὐδὲ κατὰ μοῖραν πέρασον πάλιν.

Here the parallel seems to be not between the movement of the cloud from
Olumpos and the retreat of the Trojans, which is not close, but between the
noise, fear and confusion aroused by the hurricane (which is not explicitly
mentioned) and that prevailing here amongst the Trojans as the result of
Patroklos' charge. Similarly, at 10.5–10 Agamemnon's agony of mind is
compared not exactly to the storm of rain, hail, or snow which the simile
describes, but rather to the deep concern caused to humans when Zeus sees
fit to display his awful powers, though the simile does not explicitly mention
this. See also 19.356–64n.

Especially interesting are the instances (mentioned above, p. 28) where
an idea introduced in the simile anticipates its appearance in the narrative,
so that the simile plays an essential part in the sense and cannot be
removed. Aias advances through the foremost fighting-men like a boar,
which turns at bay and easily scatters (ῥηϊδίως ἐκέδασσεν ἐλιξάμενος) the dogs
and hunters; so Aias charges and easily scatters (ῥεῖα μετεισάμενος... ἐκέδασσε)
the Trojan ranks (17.281–5), where the essential action is repeated by the
same word. The technique appears twice in close succession at 15.622–37,
where first the Greeks are standing firm against the Trojans (622); Hektor
falls upon them like a storm-driven wave which strikes fear of death into the
sailors; *so* the hearts of the Greeks are torn with fear (629). Then Hektor
advances like a fierce lion which springs upon a herd and eats an ox as the
rest dash away in fear (630–6); *so* the Greeks were put to flight by Hektor
and Zeus (637). Other examples appear at 15.381–3, 17.263–8, 17.725–34,
and 17.737–41 (see notes *ad locc.*, and also Fränkel, *Gleichnisse* 6–7 and
104–7, and Edwards, *HPI* 107–8).

---

[36] This term, and the following analyses, are those of D. Petegorsky, *Context and Evocation:
Studies in Early Greek and Sanskrit Poetry* (diss. Berkeley 1982; *DA* 44, 1983, 162A) 9–74.

Occasionally the description in a simile appears to take on a life of its own, and to continue in a direction which veers away from the narrative. Menelaos looks everywhere for Antilokhos, like a sharp-eyed eagle, which spots a hare cowering in the undergrowth, seizes it, and kills it (17.674–8); but Antilokhos is not hiding, and Menelaos' intentions are not hostile. The Trojans surround the wounded Odysseus as scavenging animals press upon a wounded stag, consuming it until a lion drives them off and eats the carcase itself (11.474–81); Aias, like the lion, arrives and drives off the Trojans (486), but Odysseus is of course not killed and eaten (for other examples see Fränkel, *Gleichnisse* 106; Edwards, *HPI* 106–7). A certain shock when the simile ends and the narrative restarts may be intentional, as when the long description of a quiet snowstorm that muffles even the sea-surf contrasts violently with the thundering din of flying stones (12.278–88; see P. Damon, *Modes of Analogy in Ancient and Medieval Verse*, Berkeley 1961, 261–71; Edwards, *HPI* 106).

Conversely, in a few cases a simile is shaped to suit the narrative context rather than the realism of the scene it depicts. Two lions unrealistically carry off a goat, 'holding it high above the ground in their jaws', because the Aiantes are lifting up a body to strip off the armour (13.198–202). Seirios the dog-star, which rises at dawn at harvest-time, hardly shines then πολλοῖσι μετ' ἀστράσι (22.28, see note *ad loc.*). There is an egregious example at *Od.* 4.335–40, where the doe has been much criticized for her bizarre behaviour in leaving her fawns in a lion's lair (cf. S. West, *Odyssey ad loc.*) by those who have not seen that the poor animal's unnatural action results from the poet's desire to make it correspond to that of the suitors, who κρατερόφρονος ἀνδρὸς ἐν εὐνῇ | ἤθελον εὐνηθῆναι ἀνάλκιδες αὐτοὶ ἐόντες (4.333–4; the poet is also punning on ξύλοχος, the lion's den, and συν- + λέχος, λόχος, cf. σύλλεκτρος, ἄλοχος).[37]

Similes are usually related from the narrator's viewpoint, which is sometimes quasi-Olympian; I. J. F. de Jong, *Mnemosyne* 38 (1985) 263, following Fränkel, notes that the similes at 8.555–9, 12.278–89, 16.633–7, and 19.357–8 are seen from the gods' perspective. Sometimes, however, the simile embodies the thoughts and emotions of a character; Priam's seeing the approaching Akhilleus as the sinister dog-star is a superb example (22.26–32).[38] More complex is the simile at 4.275–82, where the Greeks around the Aiantes are compared to a black cloud which frightens a shepherd (the Trojans' viewpoint), but delights the heart of Agamemnon (4.283: see de Jong, *Narrators* 272 n. 73). Even a formular short comparison may show this perspective, as when the Trojans see Akhilleus τεύχεσι

[37] Fränkel, *Gleichnisse* 105, lists other improbabilities in the behaviour of animals in similes.
[38] De Jong, *Narrators* 123–36, has a detailed study of this phenomenon; see also J. M. Bremer, *Papers of the Liverpool Latin Seminar* 5 (1985) 367–72.

λαμπόμενον, βροτολοιγῷ ἶσον Ἄρηϊ (20.46). A close identification between listener and character results, as the former looks at the scene through the latter's eyes.

The emotional impact of the scene a simile portrays can be transferred to the narrative passage, with powerful effect. The immortal horses standing over Patroklos' body are compared to a grave monument for stillness, but it is the funereal association which is significant (see 17.434–6n.). The many points of comparison between Euphorbos and the uprooted young tree include a reminiscence of the care showered upon him by his loving parents, whom he mentions in his last speech (see 17.53–60n.). The fire-similes so frequent for Akhilleus in the later books include sinister forebodings of doomed cities (see 18.207–14n., 219–21n., 22.410–11n.). Akhilleus' shield shines like a fire which gives hope to sailors borne on unwillingly by a storm and far from home – and the Greeks too feel hope when they see it, and are likewise unwillingly far from home (19.375–8). Here, and in many other similes, the poet suggests much more than a single, simple point of comparison, and thus enriches both the visual and the emotional impact upon his audience.

(iii) The subject-matter of the similes

Though very few extended similes are repeated verbatim (see above, n. 29), many share common subject-matter. But just as different examples of the same type-scene vary greatly in length and in elaborative detail, so too similes with common content vary greatly in phraseology, the details emphasized, and the application to the narrative context. Among the commonest subjects of similes in the *Il.* are (as listed by Lee, *Similes* 65–73): lions (40 similes, plus seven of an aggressive θήρ which is probably a lion; see 15.586–8n.); birds (22); fire (19); cattle (18); wind and wave (18); and boars (12). On the other hand, Lee lists 31 subjects of *Il.* similes which do not recur in either poem,[39] and these are usually the most evocative and memorable. Their uniqueness makes it likely that they were composed especially for their context, and many of them are unforgettable: Apollo, leading the Trojan attack, overturns the Greek rampart like a boy kicking over a sandcastle (15.362–4); the weeping Patroklos looks up imploringly at Akhilleus like a little girl tugging at her mother's skirt and begging to be picked up (16.7–10); Athena turns Pandaros' arrow aside from Menelaos as easily as a mother brushes away a fly from her sleeping child (4.130–1);

---

[39] The unique subjects, as listed by Lee, are: mules, asses, worm, rainbow, wheatfield, dew, beans, milk, lead, oil, ivory, top, trumpet, stake, threshing, reapers, child and sandcastle, mother and child, woodcutters, potter, trick-rider, boy swineherd, husbandry, land-dispute, fishing and tanning. There are also (among Lee's 'Miscellaneous') five different similes expressing 'as far as'.

Aias, defending the ships, leaps from one to another as a trick-rider jumps from horse to horse (15.679–84). Within books 17–20 we find the unique pictures of the workmen stretching a hide (17.389); the mourning horses standing like a grave monument (17.434–5); weary mules struggling to drag a tree-trunk down a hill (17.742–5); a potter spinning his wheel (18.600–1); a light shining for frightened sailors (19.375–8); women quarrelling in the street (20.252–5); and oxen threshing grain (20.495–7).

The purpose of a simile is to encourage the listener's imagination by likening something in the narrative of the heroic past to something which is directly within his own experience; and so the majority of Homeric similes are drawn from everyday life.[40] This means that they, like Akhilleus' shield, give us a view of the world lying beyond the war, the world that existed in the poet's own day and long after him. The subjects may be grouped as follows (the division is largely that of J. M. Redfield, *Nature and Culture in the Iliad*, Chicago 1975, 188–9):

(a) Weather and other natural phenomena, including storms at sea, flooding rivers, snowstorms, forest fires, thunderbolts, a dust storm (13.334), an earthquake (2.781), and lightning and thunderbolts. Most of these recur frequently; nature is thus most often presented as violent and hostile to humankind.

(b) Hunting and herding, usually involving aggression by wild animals against domestic animals (the largest group). Here again the natural world is usually dangerous and destructive and must be confronted by humans, often without success. There is also a small number of similes depicting wild animals (especially birds) without human involvement; usually they are killing each other.[41]

(c) Human technology, including carpentry, weaving, threshing grain, irrigating a garden, and similar activities, showing mankind working productively with nature. Most of these peaceful subjects appear only once.

Thus the majority of *Il.* similes contain recurrent subject-matter depicting mankind in a losing struggle with nature. Such subjects refute the old idea that similes are introduced to give the listener relief from the relentless violence of the battlefield, for most of them depict conflict and suffering. In most of the similes, the departure from the narrative brings not a change

[40] As Aristarchus noted: ὁ γὰρ Ὅμηρος ἀπὸ τῶν γινωσκομένων πᾶσι ποιεῖται τὰς ὁμοιώσεις (Arn/A on 16.364). See also K. Snipes, *AJP* 109 (1988) 214–15. Long ago Robert Wood observed that descriptions in the similes show that Homer must have lived on the west coast of Asia Minor, because at 9.4–7 and elsewhere the west wind blows ashore (*Essay on the Original Genius and Writings of Homer*, Dublin 1776, 16–24).

[41] On Homer's treatment of animal subjects see most recently A. Schnapp-Gourbeillon, *Lions, héros, masques: les représentations de l'animal chez Homère* (Paris 1981), and S. H. Lonsdale, *Creatures of Speech* (*Beiträge zur Altertumskunde* 5, 1990).

from violence to peacefulness, but a change from the Trojan plain to hill, lowland, farmer's sheepfold, forest or sea, from nobly-born chiefs to farmers and shepherds, and from conflict brought on by human folly to that arising from mankind's unending struggle to survive in an often hostile world. The predominance of harsh subjects is to some extent, of course, due to the mainly martial subject-matter of the *Il.*; but it is also reminiscent of the uncomfortable and uncooperative world of Hesiod, 'a fallen and fundamentally alien environment in which we can survive as humans only in the protective bubble of that which finally defines us as human: our own creation, justice'.[42] Since this kind of subject-matter is so abundant in Homer it is likely to be traditional.

A minority of similes depict the peaceful activities of the domestic life of men and women, and their subjects appear only once in the *Il.* and *Od.* This peaceful domestic world of harvest, vintage, fishing, irrigated gardens, and working women is the same as the world of the pictures on Akhilleus' shield, and thus these similes are likely to be the poet's innovation. One often feels that the poet is describing, within his heroic frame, a little vignette that recently caught his attention as he went about the ordinary business of life.

The restriction of the similes to ordinary experience – for attacks on domestic animals by a big feline predator must be considered a regular part of life, as can be deduced from the scene on Akhilleus's shield (18.579–86)[43] – is confirmed by the virtual absence of comparisons with the battles of divinities, the Titanomachies and Gigantomachies which appear in Hesiod and are reflected in *Il.* 20–21. In one exceptional case, the earth shakes

---

[42] R. Lamberton, *Hesiod* (New Haven and London 1988) 124–5. The hostility of nature in Homer is well brought out in A. Bonnafé, *Poésie, Nature et Sacré* (Lyon 1984), especially 86–8. The climax is Akhilleus' battle with Skamandros (21.233ff.), in which the hero compares himself to a boy swineherd swept away while trying to cross a river (21.282–3). V. Leinieks, *Classica et Mediaevalia* 37 (1986) 5–20, suggests that when the same subject-matter recurs in similes, an experienced audience would feel overtones (e.g. of destructiveness) even if they are not explicitly mentioned in a particular instance.

[43] There is evidence for lions in Greece at least down to the classical period; see P. Warren, *JHS* 99 (1979) 123, S. West, *Odyssey* on *Od.* 4.335–40, and 15.586–8n. Probably this was not like the African lion, but a short-maned or maneless species which did not roar; lions do not roar in Homer, unless στενάχων conveys this (18.318 and 324), but cf. βαρυφθόγγων τε λεόντων at *HyAphr* 159 (see 10.485n.). G. E. Markoe, *CA* 8 (1989) 86–115, demonstrates that the attack of a (maned) lion on its prey is very common in Near Eastern and archaic Greek art (as it is on Mycenaean daggers), and holds that in Homeric similes too the lion symbolizes 'divinely conceived heroic triumph' (p. 89); but it is safer to make a distinction between the maned lion presumably hunted by kings for sport (the type of visual art) and the lion of the similes, which usually attacks domestic animals and is pursued by villagers and dogs. In *Il.* lion-similes where the prey or circumstances are identified, 21× the lion is attacking a domestic animal or a herdsman (or the place is identified as a σταθμός), compared with 7× that the scene is one of huntsmen or of a wild victim. (The count is based on Markoe's list, *op. cit.* 115, with the addition of 17.109ff., 17.133ff., and 18.317ff. Instances of θήρ should probably be included, as Markoe does at 15.323ff., in which case add also 10.183ff., 15.586ff.; in all three cases the victim is domestic.)

Similes

beneath the feet of the marching Greeks as it does when Zeus angrily lashes the ground around the prostrate Tuphoeus (2.781–4, see note *ad loc.*, and cf. 20.54–66n.).[44] There are, of course, many instances where great men are glorified by comparison to Ares or Zeus, beautiful women to Artemis or Aphrodite; but such expressions evoke our personal imagination in the present, not the mythical world of the past.[45] There is a notable reversal of this principle in the description of the dancing-floor of the young folk on the shield of Akhilleus, which is dignified by a comparison to that built for Ariadne in the heroic past (18.590–2).

A number of similes make alternative comparisons. In the washing-pools before Troy there are two springs; one is hot, ἡ δ' ἑτέρη θέρεϊ προρέει εἰκυῖα χαλάζῃ, | ἢ χιόνι ψυχρῇ, ἢ ἐξ ὕδατος κρυστάλλῳ (22.151–2). Sarpedon falls ὡς ὅτε τις δρῦς ἤριπεν ἢ ἀχερωΐς, | ἠὲ πίτυς βλωθρή (16.482–3). A simpler alternation of lion(s) and boar(s) occurs at 5.782–3 ≅ 7.256–7, 8.338, 11.293, 12.42. In a little-known dissertation J. C. Hogan examines these 'disjunctions' or 'multiple-term' similes in detail (he finds 44 of them in *Il.* and *Od.* combined), and suggests that formular and metrical considerations are the essential cause.[46] This may well be correct in some instances; certainly the disjunction ἀνέρος ... ἠὲ γυναικός | in the simile at 17.435 is based on the formular ἠδὲ (οὐδὲ, ἤ τε) γυναῖκες | (etc.). In most cases, however, it seems more likely that the extra terms of comparison are added to strengthen the essential idea of the comparison – coldness, aggressive violence, headlong fall – by treating it as the common feature of any number of occurrences, rather than of just one particular scene.

(iv) Language and style

Similes speak of the world of familiar and recurrent events, and this is reflected in their syntax and vocabulary. The particle τε, generalizing the statement of a familiar action, is very common, often repeated several times (6× at 5.136–42; see 5.137–42n., and Chantraine, *GH* II 240–1). The time is always the present; verbs may be in the present (or occasionally perfect) indicative, the timeless aorist indicative, or the generalizing subjunctive, and a combination of these may appear in the same simile (e.g. 16.259–65, 18.318–22; at 17.58 two aorists after several present indicatives suggest the sudden violence of a windstorm).[47] In shorter similes the verb is frequently

[44] S. A. Nimis, *Narrative Semiotics in the Epic Tradition* (Bloomington 1987) 73–9, suggests a parallel is intended between Zeus and Akhilleus, each establishing his honour.
[45] The lists of similes with gods or goddesses as subject given in Lee, *Similes* 68, are badly incomplete; add (partly from M. Coffey, *AJP* 78, 1957, 122 n. 36) 3.158, 3.230, 8.305, 11.638, 24.699, *Od.* 3.468, 4.14, 4.310, 8.14, 23.163.
[46] *The Oral Nature of the Homeric Simile* (diss. Cornell 1966; *DA* 27, 1966, 1352A) 131–51.
[47] Cf. Chantraine, *GH* II 185–7, 245 and 253. On possible imperfect tenses in similes see 15.272n. and Chantraine, *GH* II 187.

omitted. Parataxis is especially common (e.g. 3.33–7 and note *ad loc.*, 18.207–14, 20.164–75, and 22.26–32; cf. Chantraine, *GH* II 355–6).

Short similes often have formular metrical variants (see above, section i (a)). In one instance forms were also developed for long similes; besides λέων (δ᾽) ὥς (4 × *Il.*), there are ὥς τε (ὡς δὲ) λέων (7 × *Il.*), ὡς (δ᾽ ὅτε) τίς τε λέων (ὀρεσίτροφος) (4 × *Il.*, 2 × *Od.*), and ὥς τε λὶς (ἠϋγένειος) (3 × *Il.*; see 17.133–6n.). J. C. Hogan's study (see above, n. 46) has shown that long similes employ the formulae of ordinary narrative when the sense allows, e.g. when actions such as fighting, throwing, and hunting are described. This results in a very close connexion between the narrative and the simile, for the actions of human warfare are illustrated by the behaviour of animals or natural phenomena, which are in turn described in the language of *human* action (see 14.16–19n, 15.323–5n., 20.164–75n.).[48] Because of the often mundane subject-matter, however, the vocabulary of the similes is rather closer to the *Od.* than to the *Il.* narrative, and almost certainly closer to that of everyday life. There is naturally a high proportion of *hapaxes*; N. J. Richardson, in Bremer, *HBOP* 172, finds that 32 of the 151 *hapaxes* in books 21 and 22 occur in similes, six of them in the simile describing the irrigation of a garden and five in that depicting the melting of lard in a cauldron (21.257–64 and 21.362–5, see notes *ad locc.*). Hogan, *op. cit.* 3, also notes five *hapaxes* in 13.588–90 (threshing beans and chick-peas). There are, however, a few archaisms (see Shipp, *Studies* 146–7). As with the subject-matter of the similes, the poet is making use of the traditional language and formulae in innovative ways, and adding to them new elements from his everyday experience.

(v) Function, distribution, and arrangement

The scholia consider the similes contribute αὔξησις (fullness), ἐνάργεια (vividness), σαφήνεια (clarity), ποικιλία (variety) and κόσμος (decoration).[49] Occasionally they remark that they give relief from the battle (διαναπαύουσι δὲ τὸν πόνον αἱ παραβολαί, T on 15.362–4). Among modern scholars, M. Coffey, *AJP* 78 (1957) 118, has categorized their functions as illustrating the movement of an individual, a group, or a thing; the appearance of a hero, group, or thing; noise; measurement of time, space, and numbers; a situation; and psychological characteristics, including decision-making. W. A. Camps, *An Introduction to Homer* (Oxford 1980) 56, sums up the uses: to suggest inward feelings and states of mind; to illustrate the distinctive

---

[48] W. B. Ingalls, *TAPA* 109 (1979) 87–109, using a very small sample, also finds little difference in formular density between similes and narrative in the *Il.* The very different results of M. W. M. Pope, *AC* 6 (1963) 14–18, are based on too limited a definition of formula.

[49] See K. Snipes, *AJP* 109 (1988) 208–9 (on Eustathius), 215–17, and N. J. Richardson, *CQ* 30 (1980) 279.

qualities of things, actions, or processes; and to render effects of multitude and mass. More specifically, M. Mueller, *The Iliad* (London 1984) 108–24, notes that a simile marks a passage as worthy of special attention, slowing down the narrative as expansions and digressions do. 'Similes occur predominantly in battle scenes. Here they articulate change and are found when a warrior joins or withdraws from battle, defeats his opponent or is defeated by him' (109, with good examples; see also Scott, *Oral Nature* 12–55). In sum, we can say that a simile produces a pause in the action, prolongs the tension, and draws the audience's attention to an important point. Like the expansion of a type-scene, it adds colour and a new dimension to whatever is the focus of attention. Besides this, because of its characteristically everyday content the Homeric simile for a moment unites narrator and audience in *their* world, not that of the heroes, as together they marvel at the mighty deeds of the past.

In practice, in the *Il.* similes often occur during descriptions of general battle movement, and when a hero enters or leaves battle, or has a success or a disaster. Three-quarters of the long similes in the *Il.* occur in battle-scenes (Moulton, *Similes* 382–3); the proportion relative to the total lines in each book varies from 0% in book 1 to 15.6% in book 17, other high proportions occurring in books 12 (14.4%), 16 (13.7%), 11 (12.1%), and 15 (11.3%). Books 3, 4, 13, 21, and 22 are also above the norm.[50]

Similes are much less common in direct speech, and so books consisting largely of direct speech have low ratios (especially books 1, 6, 9, 18, and 24). In common with the usual vividness of his diction, Akhilleus has more than anyone else (four long and four short), and his long similes are all strikingly original in content and highly effective (the mother bird feeding its young, 9.323–5; the crying child clinging to her mother's skirt, 16.7–10; the boy swineherd drowned crossing a river, 21.282–3; the wolf and the lamb *not* lying down together, 22.262–5).[51] Other fine similes occur in speeches by Agamemnon (3.243–5), Poseidon (13.101–4), Aineias (20.252–5), and Asios (12.167–70; see also 13.102–4n.).

Similes often occur in groups; C. Moulton, *Hermes* 102 (1974) 387 n. 38, says that about 70 of the roughly 330 similes he counts in the *Il.* are successive, i.e. 'similes occasioned by the same event in the narrative, without more than one or two lines of recapitulation between them'. We may distinguish the following.

(1) Balancing pairs of similes. Similes for each side illustrate the two armies marching to battle at 3.3–7 and 3.10–14, 4.422–8 and 4.433–6; two especially powerful examples contrast the optimism of the Trojans after

---

[50] The figures are taken from A. Bonnafé, *RPh* 67 (1983) 82–6.
[51] See J. Griffin, *JHS* 106 (1986) 53; Moulton, *Similes* 100–1; Scott, *Oral Nature* 50–1.

their first success and the despair of the Greeks (8.555–9 and 9.4–7; the pairing is now obscured by the book-division). The same balance occurs in similes for warriors preparing for a duel: Paris and Menelaos (3.23–6 and 3.33–5), Akhilleus and Hektor (22.26–32 and 22.93–6). See also 15.263–70 and 15.271–8, 16.352–6 and 16.364–6.

(2) Two similes coupled together, or occurring in close succession, to describe different aspects of the same thing. A magnificent pair describes Akhilleus' charge; he sweeps against the enemy like a forest fire, and the dead are crushed beneath his chariot like barley threshed by oxen (20.490–9). Even better known is the pair in which Aias is described first as a lion baulked of its prey and then as a donkey stubbornly ignoring the sticks of children (11.548–61). Sarpedon falls like a tree, and faces his death as furiously as a bull attacked by a lion (16.482–9). Polupoites and Leonteus are like firm-rooted oaks as they stand fast (12.131–4), and like boars when they begin to advance (12.146–51).[52]

(3) A series of consecutive similes. These are reserved for especially impressive effects. The most prominent of them heralds the mighty march of the Greeks to battle (the Catalogue of Ships; 2.455–83, see note *ad loc.*), where (with gradually narrowing focus) the gleam from their armour is compared to fire, their numbers to wildfowl, leaves, flowers, and insects, and their marshalling by the leaders to goats divided up by goatherds; finally their leader Agamemnon is singled out for comparison to the gods in physique and to the leading bull of the herd for prominence. At the end of the long struggle over the body of Patroklos five similes follow each other in a more flexible technique, in which the action of the similes is each time carried back to the narrative before the next simile follows (17.725–59; see note *ad loc.*); then this climactic flourish is summarized in a final short simile, ὣς οἱ μὲν μάρναντο δέμας πυρὸς αἰθομένοιο (18.1), before the scene abruptly shifts to Akhilleus and Antilokhos. Zeus's glorification of Hektor before the firing of the ships invokes a series of similes, as the hero is compared to Ares (15.605–6), the opposing Greeks to a sea-cliff (618–21), and Hektor again to a storm battering a ship and a lion attacking cattle (624–36).

Sometimes similes not directly juxtaposed may nevertheless produce a cumulative effect. In different ways, Akhilleus is repeatedly compared with fire (especially fire burning a city) as he prepares to rejoin the battle, beginning with his terrifying appearance to the Trojans (18.207–14) and continuing at 19.375–80, 21.522–4, 22.135, and 22.410–11 (see also

[52] See also Moulton, *Similes* 19–27, and T. K. Hubbard, *Grazer Beiträge* 10 (1981) 59–67.

22.317–21n.). As Akhilleus dons his armour, the poet compares (in short similes) the gleam from his shield to the moon, that from his helmet to a star, and Akhilleus himself, fully-armed, to the sun (19.374, 19.381, and 19.398). The struggle by the Greek heroes to protect the body of Patroklos is illustrated by similes likening them to animals guarding their young (17.4–5, 17.133–6, 17.757 (possibly; see note *ad loc.*), and 18.318–22). These can be associated with other similes in which Akhilleus compares himself to a parent (9.323–7, 16.7–10, 23.222–4 and note *ad loc.*; Moulton, *Similes* 27–49 and 101–6, is not always convincing). M. Baltes, *Antike und Abendland* 29 (1983) 36–48, finds interconnexion in the similes of book 16; R. Friedrich, *AJP* 102 (1981) 120–37, and W. T. McGrath, *CJ* 77 (1982) 205–12, find the same effect in the lion-similes of the *Od.* See also 2.394–7n., 4.422–8n.

The largest number of *similes* in the *Il.* are drawn from a relatively few subjects depicting the harshness of the natural world; but the greatest number of *subjects* are used once only, in unique similes based on the commonplace and peaceful events of everyday domestic life (see section iii above). It is natural to suppose that the former group are traditional in content (though just as in repeated type-scenes, the expression is almost always different), while the latter result from Homer's own observation and creativity, and show his own choice of subject-matter, his unlimited inventiveness, and (like Akhilleus' shield) his totally un-Hesiodic enjoyment of ordinary life. In all cases, the interaction of simile and narrative is complex and rewards the listener/reader's closest attention. The Homeric long simile is a masterpiece of poetic art, and brings us as close as we can hope to get to the perceptions and sensitivities of the genius who constructed the monumental poem.

4. Style

In chapter 2 of the Introduction to volume 1, pp. 17–37, G. S. Kirk gives an account of the structural elements of Homeric verse, the positioning of word-groups and formulae within the rhythmical cola, and the disposition of sentences over two or more verses. In this chapter I will discuss some further characteristic features of Homeric style: emphasis by word-position; ring composition; metaphor; *hapax legomena*; and rhetorical figures of speech.

(i) Emphasis by word-position

We do not know how hexameter verse was sung or declaimed in Homer's time. But the beginning and end of a verse must always have been obvious, if for no other reason than the indifference to hiatus between verses and to the quantity of the final syllable (including the impossibility of replacing it by two short syllables). Words placed at the beginning of the verse must have been immediately identifiable, and often they are particularly emphatic, especially if they are runover words (i.e. standing in enjambment with the preceding verse and immediately followed by a pause). This is apparent especially in the speeches of Akhilleus. In the embassy-scene, no one can fail to observe the contrast between the slowly spoken, hesitant beginning of his response to Odysseus, in which most of the lines (except for the simile) are heavily end-stopped (9.308–29), and the increasingly frequent emphatic runover words, marked off by a following pause, as his bitterness and vehemence mount (9.330–41; see also 9.325–45n.):

> τάων ἐκ πασέων κειμήλια πολλὰ καὶ ἐσθλὰ
> ἐξελόμην, καὶ πάντα φέρων Ἀγαμέμνονι δόσκον
> Ἀτρεΐδῃ· ὁ δ᾽ ὄπισθε μένων παρὰ νηυσὶ θοῇσι
> δεξάμενος διὰ παῦρα δασάσκετο, πολλὰ δ᾽ ἔχεσκεν.
> ἀλλὰ δ᾽ ἀριστήεσσι δίδου γέρα καὶ βασιλεῦσι,
> τοῖσι μὲν ἔμπεδα κεῖται, ἐμεῦ δ᾽ ἀπὸ μούνου Ἀχαιῶν
> εἵλετ᾽, ἔχει δ᾽ ἄλοχον θυμαρέα· τῇ παριαύων
> τερπέσθω· τί δὲ δεῖ πολεμιζέμεναι Τρώεσσιν
> Ἀργείους; τί δὲ λαὸν ἀνήγαγεν ἐνθάδ᾽ ἀγείρας
> Ἀτρεΐδης; ἦ οὐχ Ἑλένης ἕνεκ᾽ ἠϋκόμοιο;
> ἦ μοῦνοι φιλέουσ᾽ ἀλόχους μερόπων ἀνθρώπων
> Ἀτρεΐδαι;

A similar development from end-stopped verses to more emotional enjambed lines can be seen in the words of Patroklos' shade (23.69–92, see note *ad loc.*).[53] Conversely, Agamemnon's despairing speech to the army at 9.17–28 begins with frequent enjambed lines as he complains vigorously about Zeus's bad faith, then concludes with four slow, resigned end-stopped verses (9.25–8), followed by three more from the narrator.

There are many other examples of runover words like the above carrying heavy emphasis. The most obvious instances are in the sentence describing the drawing of lots for the duel against Hektor, ἐκ δ' ἔθορε κλῆρος κυνέης, ὃν ἄρ' ἤθελον αὐτοί, | Αἴαντος· (7.182–3), and the double one in Here's malicious announcement of her triumph over Zeus, ἤδη ἀνὴρ γέγον' ἐσθλός, ὃς 'Αργείοισιν ἀνάξει, | Εὐρυσθεύς, Σθενέλοιο πάϊς Περσηϊάδαο, | σὸν γένος (19.122–4). Among the most poignant is in the disguised Hermes' speech to Priam about the Trojans' fear: τοῖος γὰρ ἀνὴρ ὤριστος ὄλωλε | σὸς πάϊς (24.384–5). Three times after his death Hektor's name is used as a runover, for pathetic effect (22.426, 24.501, 24.742, in gen., accus., and voc. respectively); Akhilleus has used it in the same way to express his hatred (18.115). The heavily emphatic νήπιος and σχέτλιος are normally used as runovers.[54] Further emphasis is often given by a following amplifying epexegetical clause, in the cumulative technique (see vol. I, pp. 34–7).

But in the Greek hexameter, *any* word standing at the beginning or end of a syntactical or metrical unit, i.e. preceded or followed by a pause, may derive special prominence from that position. Thus in the above passage, it is clear that in addition to the runover words mentioned above, some verse-initial words which begin a clause or sentence are also highly significant (ἄλλα, τοῖσι, ἢ μοῦνοι). Besides this, the strongly stressed δεξάμενος is verse-initial but in the middle of its clause, and there are many parallels for this (e.g. νῦν δ' ὅρκια πιστὰ | ψευσάμενοι μαχόμεσθα, 7.351–2; μὴ δὴ οὕτως... | νήστιας ὄτρυνε προτὶ ῎Ιλιον υἷας 'Αχαιῶν, 19.155–6).[55]

Sometimes there is a series of end-stopped lines with stress on the initial word of the line (5.529–32 ≅ 15.561–4):

---

[53] On sequences of end-stopped verses see G. S. Kirk, *YCS* 20 (1966) 121–4.

[54] See also 18.20–1n., 18.74–5n., 18.77n., 18.89–90n., 19.155–72n., 19.216–20n., 20.119–24n., 20.191–4n., 20.470–2n. On the use of words in this runover position see my article in *TAPA* 97 (1966) 140–8, opposing the view of S. E. Bassett, *TAPA* 57 (1926) 116–48, and Hoekstra, *Odyssey* 158–9.

[55] T. D. Seymour, *HSCP* 3 (1892) 91–129, argued that pauses in sense occurred mainly at the end of the verse and at the mid-verse caesura, and F. L. Clark, *CJ* 9 (1913–14) 61–6, tried to show that stress falls on the word preceding that caesura. I think, however, that the examples collected by both scholars make it clear that it is the word *following* the verse-end, i.e. the first in the next line, which is likely to be emphatic, or at least more significant for the sense, than the word *at* the verse-end; to a lesser extent this is sometimes true of the word following the mid-verse caesura. J. A. Scott's attempted refutation of their views (*CP* 10, 1915, 438–42) is vitiated by his failure to understand the form of threefolders (see vol. I, p. 20).

ὦ φίλοι, ἀνέρες ἔστε καὶ ἄλκιμον ἦτορ ἔλεσθε,
ἀλλήλους τ' αἰδεῖσθε κατὰ κρατερὰς ὑσμίνας·
αἰδομένων ἀνδρῶν πλέονες σόοι ἠὲ πέφανται·
φευγόντων δ' οὔτ' ἂρ κλέος ὄρνυται οὔτέ τις ἀλκή·

Akhilleus again provides an even more powerful example (9.406–9):

ληϊστοὶ μὲν γάρ τε βόες καὶ ἴφια μῆλα,
κτητοὶ δὲ τρίποδές τε καὶ ἵππων ξανθὰ κάρηνα·
ἀνδρὸς δὲ ψυχὴ πάλιν ἐλθεῖν οὔτε λεϊστὴ
οὔθ' ἑλετή...

There may be anaphora (23.315–18; see also 19.23–4n.):

μήτι τοι δρυτόμος μέγ' ἀμείνων ἠὲ βίηφι·
μήτι δ' αὖτε κυβερνήτης ἐνὶ οἴνοπι πόντῳ
νῆα θοὴν ἰθύνει ἐρεχθομένην ἀνέμοισι·
μήτι δ' ἡνίοχος περιγίγνεται ἡνιόχοιο·

A new sentence or clause often begins at the bucolic diaeresis, even when a common formular expression is available to reach to the verse-end. Often the reason for beginning a new sentence or clause at this position seems to be the desire to dispose of the initial connecting words and particles here, in the less emphatic verse-position, so that the important word can be placed at the beginning of the next line. There are many examples of this in book 20: αὐτὰρ Ἀχιλλεὺς | Ἕκτορος ἄντα... (75–6); αὐτὰρ ἐμὲ Ζεὺς | εἰρύσαθ', ὅς... (92–3); αἴ κεν Ἀχιλλεὺς | τόνδε κατακτείνη (301–2, of Aineias); οὐδ' ἄρ' ἔτ' ἔτλη | δηρὸν ἑκὰς στρωφᾶσθ' (421–2); οὐδ' ἂν ἔτι δὴν | ἀλλήλους πτώσσοιμεν (426–7); καὶ τό γ' Ἀθήνη | πνοιῇ...ἔτραπε (438–9).[56] This interplay of emphatic positioning and variety of pause within the line is one of the most remarkable features of Homeric verse, though it is often neglected by translators.[57]

(ii) Ring composition

Of the small-scale structural devices which are used to order the presentation of material in Homer, ring composition is probably the least familiar to us and the hardest to appreciate without our giving it special attention. The straightforward linear style, in which a similar line or phrase

[56] See also (in bk 20) 23–4, 38–9, 42–3, 92–3, 100–1, 191–2, 283–4 (= 441–2), 358–9, 458–9. In bk 19, see 23–4, 217–19, 319–20, 345–6, and the speech of the horse Xanthos (408–17), in which most of the verse-initial words carry heavy emphasis.
[57] For examples of the variety of pause-positions see vol. i, 23–4 and 30–7, and notes on 6.152–211, 6.344–58, 12.457–65, 18.79–93, 18.231–8, 18.305–9, 18.333, 19.13–17, 19.147–50, 19.191–4, 19.319–21, 20.119–24, 20.455–89, 20.463–72, 22.136–8, 22.208–13, 22.344–54, 22.416–28. There is a general overview in Edwards, *HPI* 55–60.

introduces a number of successive passages (*Ritournelkomposition* or parallel composition) is usually obvious, as in the Catalogue of Ships and in Agamemnon's approach to his captains in turn (with 4.250–1 cf. the parallel idea at 4.272–3, 4.292–3, 4.326 7, and 4.364–5). But ring composition, though extremely common in the *Il.* (Gaisser found it structuring all but one of the twenty-four 'digressions' she studied), was not well appreciated even in antiquity and only recently has its importance been fully realized.[58]

Thalmann, *Conventions* 6ff., notes that there is a very small-scale example of ring form in the figure known as hysteron-proteron, quoting οἴσετε ἄρν', ἕτερον λευκόν, ἑτέρην δὲ μέλαιναν, | Γῆ τε καὶ Ἠελίῳ (3.103–4), where the order is ABBA.[59] As he says (p. 7),

hysteron-proteron actually maintains clarity. Because it makes possible a short preview of all the forthcoming topics, it allows the poet to get his ideas in order before he proceeds to detailed treatment of each, and it lets the audience know what is to come, so that they never lose sight of the overall plan.

A familiar example is the responding to questions or suggestions from one character to another in reverse order. Antikleia's answering of Odysseus' questions in this way is familiar (*Od.* 11.170–203). S. E. Bassett, *HSCP* 31 (1920) 46, shows that when Hektor returns to Troy Hekabe (A) asks Hektor why he has come, suggesting it is to pray to Zeus on the citadel (6.254–7), and tells him to wait until she brings wine, so that he may (B) first pour a libation to Zeus (258–9), (C) then refresh himself from his weariness (260–2); Hektor responds (C') that wine will weaken him

---

[58] The important modern studies are: J. H. Gaisser, *HSCP* 73 (1968) 1–43; Lohmann, *Reden* 12–30 and passim, and *Die Andromache-Szenen der Ilias* (Spudasmata 42, Hildesheim 1988); Thalmann, *Conventions* 1–32; all of these mention earlier bibliography. R. Gordesiani, *Kriterien der Schriftlichkeit und Mündlichkeit im homerischen Epos* (Frankfurt am Main 1986) 26–67, sees the structure of both *Il.* and *Od.* as based on ring form. R. L. Fowler, *The Nature of Early Greek Lyric* (Toronto 1987) 53–85, shows that ring composition is also pervasive in early lyric poetry, and feels, perhaps correctly, that it is 'perhaps one of the most obvious and psychologically natural ways of organizing material' (p. 62). On Eustathius' comments see Thalmann, *Conventions* 7 and S. E. Bassett, *HSCP* 31 (1920) 54–62, and *The Poetry of Homer* (Berkeley 1938) 125. On large-scale ring structure see vol. vi, ch. 1.

[59] The verbal figure chiasmus is in some ways similar; examples are: βασιλεύς τ' ἀγαθὸς κρατερός τ' αἰχμητής (3.179), χερσὶν ἑλὼν δολιχὸν δόρυ καὶ σάκος ὤμῳ (15.474), ἐσθλὸς ἔφευγε, δίωκε δέ μιν μέγ' ἀμείνων (22.158), εἰσορόων ὄψίν τ' ἀγαθὴν καὶ μῦθον ἀκούων (24.632). Hysteron-proteron refers to the sequence of *ideas*, and is illustrated in ὦρτο διὲκ προθύρου, λίπε δὲ θρόνον ἔνθα θάασσε (15.124, see note *ad loc.*), οἱ δ' ἀνεσάν τε πύλας καὶ ἀπῶσαν ὀχῆας (21.537). This latter figure is discussed by S. E. Bassett, *HSCP* 31 (1920) 39–62 and *The Poetry of Homer* (Berkeley 1938) 119–28. He deals mainly with the answering of questions in reverse order, as at 6.254ff. (see below) and many times in the *Od.*, and discusses the extent to which the figure was identified by the ancient critics and its importance for ensuring continuity of thought. Aristarchus occasionally commented upon instances of hysteron-proteron (e.g. Arn/A at 2.763) and a chiasmus is noted (as *antithesis*, T on 22.158; see N. J. Richardson, *CQ* 30, 1980, 282). However, neither chiasmus nor hysteron-proteron occurs in Plutarch's listing of figures in Homer (*Vit. Hom.*).

(264–5), (B′) that he will not pray to Zeus with unwashed hands (266–8), and (A′) that she herself should go to pray to Athene in her temple (269ff.). In larger-scale ring structures this laying-out of successive elements and return to each of them in reverse sequence also alerts the hearer to what is to come and at the end gives a satisfying sense of completion.

The simple form of ring composition occurs when a short passage inserted into the narrative is framed by matching elements which introduce it and then return again to the main narrative. The major example is of course the long similes, where the introductory ὡς (δ᾿) ὅτε is normally picked up at the conclusion by a ὡς ἄρα or the like. As J. B. Hainsworth pointed out, *G&R* 13 (1966) 159–60, by carrying poet and audience back to the point from which the sequence began (especially in the case of similes, during which there may be no progression in the story), the device facilitates an easy resumption of the thread of the main narrative. An anecdote about a hero may be framed in a similar way: Meges is saved by his corslet (πυκινὸς δέ οἱ ἤρκεσε θώρηξ), and we hear how his father acquired it, and handed it down to him, before ὅς οἱ καὶ τότε παιδὸς ἀπὸ χροὸς ἤρκεσ᾿ ὄλεθρον returns us to the next action (15.529, 15.534). On a larger scale, in speeches a statement may be followed by one or more arguments, after which the statement (now justified) is repeated; thus Akhilleus' exhortation to Priam begins οὐ γάρ τις πρῆξις πέλεται κρυεροῖο γόοιο and ends οὐ γάρ τι πρήξεις ἀκαχήμενος υἷος ἑῆος (24.524, 24.550).

The more developed forms also differ from simple hysteron-proteron in that they have a central core which is surrounded by more than one ring. There is a clear example in the catalogue of Nereid names. The core of names itself has a linear structure, with repeated ἔνθ᾿ ἄρ᾿ ἔην... (18.39, 18.47), but it is framed by θεαὶ δέ μιν ἀμφαγέροντο and τῶν δὲ καὶ ἀργύφεον πλῆτο σπέος (37, 50) and an inner ring πᾶσαι ὅσαι (ἄλλαι θ᾿ αἵ) κατὰ βένθος ἁλὸς Νηρηΐδες ἦσαν (38, 49). Paradigms are often structured in this way. J. H. Gaisser, *HSCP* 73 (1968) 9, demonstrates this in Akhilleus' tale of Niobe, where the outer ring 'You may take your son' (24.599–601; 24.619–20) contains the inner 'Now think of food' (601; 618–19), within which is a further ring 'Even Niobe took food' (602; 613) encircling her story (603–12; see 24.599–620n.). See also Diomedes' paradigm of Lukourgos (6.128–43n.; also 18.394–407n.).

At 15.596–603 (see note *ad loc.*) the actions and thoughts of Zeus are disposed in complex ring form:

A   He roused (ἔγειρε) the strength of the Trojans (594–5)
B   in order to give honour to Hektor (596)
C   so that he may hurl fire on the Greek ships (597–8)
D   and Zeus may fulfil Thetis' prayer (598–9).

C′   So Zeus waited to see the flare of a burning ship, after which he
would grant glory to the Greeks (599–602).

B′, A′ So thinking, he roused (ἔγειρε) Hektor (602–4).

The narrative itself is sometimes structured by large-scale ring composition,
as at 6.394–9 and 16.364–93 (see notes *ad loc.*). On the larger scale, the
whole of book 14 falls into two concentric rings around the Deception of
Zeus, which itself is composed of three ring systems (see the introduction to
book 14, and 14.292–351n.).

In 15.596–603, analysed above, the circumstances have changed slightly
at the end of the ring; attention has shifted from the Trojans to Hektor in
particular. A similar development during the course of an insertion into the
narrative is often seen in similes (see ch. 3, ii). It is found both in insertions
into the narrative and in speeches. Gaisser uses as an example of this
Nestor's description of the battle between the Pylians and the Epeans
(11.732–61):[60]

A   The battle is joined, with prayers to *Zeus and Athene* (732–6);

B   Nestor is the *first* victor, killing Moulios; *he* drives off his horses
(737–46).

C   *Nestor* pursues and captures fifty chariots, killing two men in each
(747–9).

D   Only the Aktorione/Molione escape, borne away by Poseidon
(750–2).

C′   The *Pylians* pursue and massacre the Epeans (753–8).

B′   Nestor kills his *last* victim; the *Pylians* drive back their horses
(759–60),

A′   giving glory to the gods and to *Nestor* among men (761).

At the close of the ring Nestor has joined the gods in the hearts of his people,
and in the inner elements his victories inspire a corresponding success in his
countrymen. In Athene's unkind comparison of Diomedes to his father
Tudeus, at first she says Tudeus' son is not like him, but at the end
concludes that from Diomedes' behaviour he cannot be Tudeus' son (5.800,
5.812–13; see 5.800–34n.). In instructing his son Antilokhos in chariot-
racing Nestor begins by pointing out that though he is a good driver his
horses are slow, but concludes the outer of several rings by declaring that
if he manages well around the turning-post no-one will catch up with him
(see 23.301–50n.). Menelaos' complaint against the outrageous pride of
Euphorbos is first directed to Zeus, but at the end of his speech the
corresponding rebuke is addressed to the offender himself (17.19–23,
17.29–32; so Lohmann, *Reden* 23–4).

Van Otterlo, whose work on this topic is fundamental, wrote that ring

[60] *HSCP* 73 (1968) 40.

composition is not so much repetition of the beginning of a passage at its end, as anticipation of the end at the beginning.[61] Actually both aspects are present and significant: first comes an anticipation of the outcome of a passage, a special case of the common Homeric habit of anticipation (see ch. 2, iii); then the idea presented at the beginning is repeated at the end, sometimes reinforced (as in the case of similes) by intervening material or otherwise developed, and poet and listener alike return, with ease and security, to the narrative at the point at which it was dropped. Though the technique is not restricted to oral poetry, it is likely to have arisen both because of its usefulness to the composer and the sense of recognition, satisfaction, and completion it gives to the hearer.[62]

(iii) Metaphor

Like a simile, a metaphor focuses attention upon one (or more) similar elements in two otherwise dissimilar things; but instead of making a comparison (with 'like' or 'as'), a metaphor stands out by its violation of the normal order of things, stating as a fact what is actually an impossibility. Aristotle twice insists that metaphor is the most important thing for a poet or speaker to master, and cannot be learnt from anyone else, for it depends upon a natural ability to perceive resemblances (*Poetics* 1459a6; *Rhetoric* 1405a8). As usual Homer provides his model; νηῦς δέ μοι ἥδ' ἕστηκεν (*Od.* 1.185 = 24.308) and ἦ δὴ μυρί' Ὀδυσσεὺς ἐσθλὰ ἔοργεν (*Il.* 2.272, μυρία for πολλά; *Poetics* 1457b9). These are not very impressive rhetorically, but elsewhere he quotes several examples of metaphorical animation of inanimate things, remarking that it is these on which Homer's reputation for vivid realism rests (τῷ ἐνέργειαν ποιεῖν εὐδοκιμεῖ); these are Sisyphus' λᾶας ἀναιδής (*Od.* 11.598) and four cases of the 'eager flight' of a weapon (*Rhetoric* 1411b31).

The ancients' interest in metaphors often appears in the exegetical scholia.[63] Sometimes their comments merely explain the source of the metaphor, correctly or fancifully: there is a good example at 4.274, where νέφος... πεζῶν is explained as 'the denseness and frightening aspect of the phalanx is likened to a black and threatening cloud' (AbT), and less successful ones at 18.3, 18.158, 18.322, and 19.323 (see notes *ad locc.*). Often, however, they very appropriately draw attention to the emphasis given by a metaphor, usually describing it as 'vivid' (ἐμφαντική), paying particular

---

[61] *Untersuchungen über Begriff, Anwendung, und Entstehung der griechischen Ringkomposition* (Amsterdam 1944) 43, quoted by Thalmann, *Conventions* 16.

[62] Ring composition occurs in oral South Slavic epic; see A. B. Lord in J. M. Foley, *Oral Tradition in Literature* (Columbia, Mo. 1986) 19–64.

[63] There are detailed treatments in Plutarch, *Vit. Hom.* 19–20, and Porphyry, *Quaest. Hom.* 1.6 and 1.17.

48

attention (as Aristotle did) to cases of the animation of an inanimate object: for instance, on πρίν με κατὰ πρηνὲς βαλέειν Πριάμοιο μέλαθρα (2.414) they comment ἔμφασιν ἔχει ἡ ἀπὸ τῶν ἐμψύχων μεταφορά (see also 4.521n.). Like Aristotle, they note the vividness given by the animation of weapons: on an arrow ἐπιπτέσθαι μενεαίνων, they say ἐμφαντικῶς δὲ τὴν τοῦ βαλόντος προθυμίαν εἰς τὸ βληθὲν μετήγαγεν (bT on 4.126), sometimes stating that an adjective is transferred from the wielder of a weapon to the weapon itself (e.g. at 15.463-4, 15.542, 21.169). On the striking χήρωσε δ᾽ ἀγυιάς (5.642) they comment αὕτη ἡ μεταφορὰ τὴν μετὰ λύπης ἐδήλωσεν ἐρημίαν (bT; they do not mention that the verb has its literal sense at 17.36). Another metaphor is said to be close to a comparison: ἔφριξεν δὲ μάχη φθισίμβροτος ἐγχείῃσι: ἐγγὺς παραβολῆς ἡ μεταφορά (13.339; see note *ad loc.*). At 17.737-9, where the battle is compared to a fire driven raging through a city by the wind, there is the perceptive note that the poet elsewhere uses the metaphor μάχη καύστειρα (4.342 = 12.316), here reworking it (ἐπεξεργασάμενος) into a simile.

In recent times, the three most substantial works on Homeric metaphor are those of Milman Parry, W. B. Stanford, and C. Moulton.[64] Parry felt that Aristotle was wrong about the importance of metaphor in Homer (*MHV* 365), and may have had later epic poets in mind. He is correct in pointing out (*MHV* 371) that many metaphors appear in conventional formular phrases (ἔπεα πτερόεντα, ὑγρὰ κέλευθα), though this does not necessarily mean that they have lost all meaning. But he overstates the case in declaring that other metaphors have also lost all real sense, and that 'because [the reader] soon ceases in reading Homer to seek for any active force in such single words, they too finally become for him simply epic words with no more meaning than the usual term would have' (*MHV* 373). Of the expressions Parry quotes here, most would find some metaphorical force in at least χόλον καταπέψη (1.81), ἀναιδείην ἐπιειμένε (1.149), δημοβόρος βασιλεύς (1.231), ἔχετ᾽ ἐμπεφυῖα (1.513).

Stanford's work on Homeric metaphor is disappointing. He postulated that '*because words lacked precise definition in Homer's time Homer could not, even if he had so wished, have used daring metaphors*' (p. 121, Stanford's italics), and unwisely dismisses the metaphorical value of 'words of such loose sensory application as γλυκύς, δριμύς, ὀξύς, βαρύς, ἀμβλύς, πικρός, τραχύς' (p. 54; on δριμύς see 15.696n.). His concluding classification of metaphors by degree of imaginative force (pp. 129-39) is unsuccessful, because it is entirely subjective; I would not myself, for instance, include λάϊνον ἔσσο χιτῶνα (3.57) among 'less imaginative types', or γήραος οὐδῷ with 'more imaginative'.

---

[64] M. Parry, MHV 365-75 = *CP* 28 (1933) 30-43; W. B. Stanford, *Greek Metaphor* (Oxford 1936) 118-43; C. Moulton, *CP* 74 (1979) 279-93.

Moulton, on the other hand, argues for the 'poetic vitality of Homeric metaphor' (*CP* 74, 1979, 281). He assumes that a word used metaphorically can be said to retain live metaphorical force if it is used literally elsewhere; this is, however, far from conclusive evidence (cf. the English 'trademark', '*crushed* by adversity'), but occasionally lends some support to his view. He gives a sympathetic discussion of some prominent examples of metaphor, associating them with parallel expressions: λάϊνον ἕσσο χιτῶνα (3.57) and other 'garments'; 'blazing' war (6.328 etc.); χάλκεον ὕπνον (11.241) and other figurative uses of 'bronze'; Zeus's 'push' behind Hektor (15.693–5, but see R. Janko's note *ad loc.*); the 'honey' and 'smoke' of anger (18.107–10, see note *ad loc.*); Odysseus' very complex analogy of warfare and harvest (19.221–4; see note *ad loc.*); and Patroklos' of a man falling from a chariot and an acrobat (16.745–50). He also groups together the recurrent metaphors of personified weapons (p. 288), the weaving of plots, the cloud of war or death, and the 'stretching' of battle (see 17.389–95n.).

Ancient scholars were not very clear about the distinction between comparison and metaphor, and their terminology was imprecise; the definition, identification, and qualities of metaphor nowadays are hardly easier to comprehend, despite much recent work.[65] One modern critic[66] has suggested that good metaphors should be: *active*, 'lending the energy of animated things to whatever is less energetic or more abstract'; *concise*; *appropriate* 'in their grandeur or triviality, to the task in hand'; *accommodated to the audience*; and 'Finally [a good] metaphor should build a proper *ethos* for the speaker, building or sustaining his character as someone to be trusted.' Most Homeric metaphors fare well by such criteria. So far as actual metaphorical impact is concerned, the vivid impression of a violation of the normal order, one can only say that in Homeric style, just as in all authors, metaphors vary between the strikingly new and effective and the completely dead (like English 'earmarked', 'full-fledged'), and that the force of a particular instance may depend largely on the sensitivity, the experience, and the attentiveness of the individual hearer or reader. It is hard to doubt that when the gods themselves go to war, ἀμφὶ δὲ σάλπιγξεν μέγας οὐρανός (21.388) has a powerful rhetorical effect (though ancient critics were divided about its appropriateness: see note *ad loc.*); there is a similarly splendid flourish in σιδήρειος δ᾽ ὀρυμαγδὸς | χάλκεον οὐρανὸν ἷκε (17.424–5); and the striking χάλκεον ὕπνον (11.241) for a warrior's death,

[65] See M. H. McCall, Jr., *Ancient Rhetorical Theories of Simile and Comparison* (Cambridge, Mass. 1969). G. E. R. Lloyd, *The Revolutions of Wisdom* (Berkeley 1987) 172–214, gives a full account of the attitudes of Plato and Aristotle towards metaphor and also a bibliography of modern theories (173–4). There is an exhaustive modern theoretical discussion in E. F. Kittay, *Metaphor* (Oxford 1987).

[66] Wayne C. Booth, in *On Metaphor*, ed. S. Sacks (Chicago 1978) 54–6. Demetrius, *On Style* 78–90, said much the same.

Style

with both components metaphorical (a 'sleep' which cannot be broken? one caused by a bronze weapon?), must be used intentionally to replace the formular νήδυμον ὕπνον (5 × *Il.*, 3 × *Od.*). There must be an individual creativeness, like that of the similes, in the taut oxhide μεθύουσαν ἀλοιφῇ, 'drunken with oil' (17.390, in a simile).

In many formular expressions it is likely that the precise metaphorical sense has more or less vanished, but a considerable weight and impressiveness has remained. ἐπ' εὐρέα νῶτα θαλάσσης | (3 × *Il.*, 7 × *Od.*) probably conveyed the broad expansiveness of the sea, without the sense of an animate 'back'; μητέρα (-ι) μήλων | (3 × *Il.*, 1 × *Od.*) may have evoked an imaginary picture of a wide hillside, dotted with sheep, without adding much feeling of fertility or nurture; ποιμένα (-ι) λαῶν (44 × *Il.*, 12 × *Od.*) means simply 'leader of men', without any suggestion that the hero is being particularly protective or his followers especially ovine (though these characteristics of shepherd and sheep appear in similes, e.g. 4.475–9, 13.492–3). ἔπεα πτερόεντα may or may not differ from those where the metaphor is missing, but certainly the expression confers weight; and there must still be some special force in ἄπτερος ἔπλετο μῦθος (4 × *Od.*).[67]

Similarly, it would be hard (*pace* Stanford, *Greek Metaphor* 138) to insist upon animism in the repeated νηλέϊ χαλκῷ (11 × *Il.*, 8 × *Od.*), though the epithet retains its full force in νηλέϊ θυμῷ (3 × *Od.*); but the expression probably means not just 'weapon' but something like 'dreadful weapon'. But often, as the ancients pointed out (see above), it seems that the eagerness of the wielder of the weapon is transferred to it, and the result is effective: ἐγχείη ... | ... ἱεμένη χροὸς ἄμεναι ἀνδρομέοιο (21.69–70 ≅ 20.279–80); (δοῦρα) ἐν γαίῃ ἵσταντο, λιλαιόμενα χροὸς ἆσαι (11.574 = 15.317 ≅ 21.168); αἰχμή ... μαιμώωσα | πρόσσω ἱεμένη (15.542–3, see note *ad loc.*); οὐ μὰν αὖτ' ὀΐω ... | ... ἅλιον πηδῆσαι ἄκοντα (14.454–5, see note *ad loc.*); ἆλτο δ' ὀϊστός (4.125); ὀϊστοὶ | θρῶσκον (15.313–14). Spears 'bite' like predators (5.858, 13.830–1), and twice Ares deanimates one by taking away its μένος (13.444 (see note *ad loc.*) = 16.613). There are also examples in direct speech: ἐμὸν δόρυ μαίνεται ἐν παλάμῃσιν (8.111 ≅ 16.74–5).[68] A proper evaluation of the significance of such usages would require a broad examination of the personification of emotions and other abstract concepts in Homer. One feels, for instance, that a reference to a mental wound as if inflicted by a weapon is metaphorical (πένθεϊ δ' ἀτλήτῳ βεβολήατο πάντες ἄριστοι, 9.3); but what of the βέλος of labour-pains which the Eileithuiai send upon a woman (προϊεῖσι; 11.269–70)?[69]

---

[67] See most recently Martin, *Language* 30–5, and for a sound earlier view, F. M. Combellack, *CJ* 46 (1950) 21–6. For a review of the extensive bibliography on these phrases see *Oral Tradition* 3 (1988) 32–4 and Russo, *Odissea* v, on *Od.* 17.57.

[68] On these and other examples of animism in Homer see M. M. Kokolakis, *Mus. Philologum Londiniense* 4 (1980) 89–113.   [69] See Kokolakis (*op. cit.* in n. 68) 112.

The poet's consciousness of the possibilities of metaphor for enlivening a statement and adding a rhetorical flourish can be seen in his manipulation of the traditional expressions involving bronze and iron. The bronze of weapons is conventionally transferred to Ares (5 × *Il.*), but retains enough force to be applied once each, probably by the poet's originality, to the death-sleep of a warrior (11.241), a defensive 'fence' of warriors (15.567, see note *ad loc.*; as in the previous instance, the noun is metaphorical as well as the adjective), a pitiless sky (17.425), Akhilleus' terrifying war-cry (18.222; his voice has just been compared to a (bronze) trumpet), and a weariless ἦτορ (2.490). On the complex double metonymy for both weapon and reaping-hook see 19.221–4n.

Homer uses iron too as a metaphor, as freely and familiarly as the heroic bronze, though its comparative lack of formular associations (only αἴθωνι (-α) σιδήρῳ (-ον) |, 3 × *Il.*, 1 × *Od.*) shows its late entry into the tradition. It conveys not only inflexibility (our 'cast-iron ⟨resolution⟩') but also relentlessness and harshness, for instance with θυμός (22.357), ἦτορ (24.205 ≅ 521) and κραδίη (*Od.* 4.293). σιδήρειος δ' ὀρυμαγδός intensifies the sense of unremitting turmoil of battle around Patroklos' corpse (17.424), and μένος... σιδήρεον the brutality of the sacrifice of the Trojan victims at Patroklos' funeral (23.177, see note *ad loc.*); it is also used in the *Od.* for the sky looming over the wicked suitors (*Od.* 15.329 and 17.565). Its use in similes too suggests that the metaphor is alive; a man's μένος is compared to it (20.372), and Odysseus' steadfastly dry eyes as he faces his weeping wife (*Od.* 19.211).

Three times in the *Od.* the poet takes the trouble to explain a metaphor: νηῶν... αἵ θ' ἁλὸς ἵπποι | ἀνδράσι γίγνονται (*Od.* 4.708–9), and εὗρε' ἐρετμά, τά τε πτερὰ νηυσὶ πέλονται (*Od.* 11.125 = 23.272). The nearest *Il.* parallel is Patroklos' mocking explanation of why he uses κυβιστᾷ of a victim who has somersaulted headlong from his chariot (16.745–50). There are also cases where a metaphor is immediately followed by a matching and explanatory simile (νέφος εἵπετο πεζῶν | ὡς δ' ὅτ' ἀπὸ σκοπιῆς εἶδεν νέφος αἰπόλος ἀνήρ..., 4.274ff.). Porphyry (*Quaest. Hom.* 1.6) was struck by the way in which the poet can begin with a metaphor, Τρῶες μὲν κλαγγῇ τ' ἐνοπῇ τ' ἴσαν; continue with a comparison (*homoiosis*), ὄρνιθες ὣς |; and conclude with a simile (*parabole*), ἠΰτε περ κλαγγὴ γεράνων πέλει οὐρανόθι πρό (3.2–3). Or a metaphorical use may be followed by a literal use of the same concept, as in ἀϋτή τε πτόλεμός τε | ἄστυ τόδ' ἀμφιδέδηε... ἀλλ' ἄνα, μὴ τάχα ἄστυ πυρὸς δηΐοιο θέρηται, 6.328ff.). These are rather like the instances where an adjective is explained, as νῆας ἐΐσας | ἀρχεκάκους, αἳ πᾶσι κακὸν Τρώεσσι γένοντο (5.62–3); ποταμῷ... | χειμάρρῳ, ὅς τ' ὦκα ῥέων ἐκέδασσε γεφύρας (5.87–8); ἵππους | πηγοὺς ἀθλοφόρους, οἳ ἄεθλια ποσσὶν ἄροντο (9.123–4).

As with other rhetorical figures, Homer is perfectly adept both at

Style

employing what seem to be traditional forms of metaphor in conventional fashion, and at creating original expressions for occasional special effect. Though of course we cannot be sure, many of the examples mentioned above may well have been as unique as so many Homeric similes.[70]

(iv) *Hapax legomena*

A word which appears only once in Homer occurs on the average every 9.4 verses of the *Il.* and every 11.8 verses of the *Od.*; and 303 words in the *Il.* and 191 in the *Od.* appear only once in Greek. These figures are from Kumpf,[71] who collects in separate indexes words which occur only once in Homer (listed alphabetically and in order of occurrence in the text), proper names which appear only once in Homer (655 in all), and Homeric *hapaxes* which do not appear elsewhere in Greek (sometimes termed 'singularities' or 'absolute *hapaxes*'). He includes tables which give the number and frequency of *hapaxes* in each Book, a comparison of totals and frequencies between *Il.* and *Od.*, and the passages of 100 or more verses which do not contain a *hapax* (only one in the *Il.* 8.362–478), and three in the *Od.*).

M. Pope, in a discussion of the *hapax* πανᾱώριος (24.540; *CQ* 35, 1985, 1–8), raises the fundamental question about *hapaxes*: whether such a word is old or new. He points out that Shakespeare's *hapaxes* fall into three classes: words which are in fact common, but by chance occur only once (e.g. 'brighten'); 'nonce-words' and compounds coined for an occasion (e.g. 'self-glorious'); and everyday words referring to things the poet has little occasion to talk about (e.g. 'gorse'). For the *Od.*, he suggests (p. 4) as examples of these three types ἀναμιμνήσκω, συλλέγω, τίμιος (commonplace words), πανάπαλος (a nonce-word), and συβόσιον (a specialized term).[72]

N. J. Richardson, in Bremer, *HBOP* 165–84, continued the examination, and gives further examples of Pope's categories of *hapaxes* from *Il.* 21–2 (pp. 168–9). He points out that *hapaxes* of specific reference are more likely to occur in similes and unusual themes (such as Akhilleus' battle with the river), in passages of unusual emotional tension (such as the outbursts of

---

[70] See also the notes on 15.618–21, 16.524–6, 17.756, 19.313, 19.362, and 24.129.

[71] M. M. Kumpf, *Four Indices of the Homeric Hapax Legomena* (Hildesheim 1984) 206. The figures include proper names.

[72] Pope reckons (p. 3) that *hapaxes* make up about 40–45% of Shakespeare's vocabulary. He declares (p. 4) that *hapaxes* make up 35% of the vocabulary of the *Il.* and 33% of that of the *Od.*, without giving the basis for his figures. Though he uses 'the label *hapax* to mean a word that occurs only once in an author' (p. 3), he seems to treat the *Il.* and the *Od.* as works by different authors. Following the old and rather unconvincing figures suggested by Kumpf (3–4 and notes), Homer (*Il.* + *Od.*) uses about 9,000 words, of which 1,382 are proper names. This leaves a vocabulary of 7,618 words, of which Kumpf's 2,037 *hapaxes* are 26.74%. Pope (pp. 3–4) quotes figures of about 20% and 15% for *hapaxes* in the vocabulary of Ovid and Virgil respectively.

grief at the death of Hektor), and in speeches (especially in Andromakhe's lament, 22.477–514). He examines in detail examples of such passages, concluding that 'the very high frequency of the author's *hapaxes* does not accord well with the theory of a composer tied to the apron-strings of his tradition; and what we have seen of his technique in the passages considered here suggests a greater awareness of the force of the individual word than some have suspected' (p. 183).

Any close investigation will confirm that statistics alone are a very blunt instrument with which to examine the occurrence of *hapaxes*, and only the type of close examination carried out by Richardson will produce useful conclusions. Technical *hapaxes* naturally cluster together in certain passages, being found predominantly in descriptions of artifacts (e.g. the shield of Akhilleus), in certain practical procedures such as the yoking of Priam's mules (24.265–74) and the preparation of Nestor's drink (11.637–9), and in the physical details of killings and woundings in battle. Commonplace, but rarely needed, *hapaxes* occur especially in similes, and are also frequent in other non-military passages such as paradigms and obituaries. Sometimes one may suspect that a vernacular word is being used for striking effect – Akhilleus' κλοτοπεύειν (19.149) leaps to mind – but this is impossible to prove.

It is unsurprising to note that in the *Il.* (leaving aside proper names) books 21, 18, and 14, all with unusual subject-matter, have the highest proportion of *hapaxes*, and the battle-books 7, 17, and 8 the lowest. For what the figures may be worth, I counted a total of 1,142 *hapaxes* in the 15,693 verses of the *Il.*, an average of 1 *hapax* every 13·7 verses.[73] Of these *hapaxes*, 528 (46.2%) occur in narrative (apart from similes), 454 (39.8%) in direct speech, and 164 (14.4%) in similes.[74] When similes are included, the narrative portions of the poem total 8,636 verses (55.0% of the whole), and contain 692 (60.6%) of the *hapaxes* (1 every 12.5 verses), whereas the

[73] For the sake of statistical comparisons, I correlated Kumpf's Index II, which lists Homeric *hapaxes* in the order of their occurrence (i.e. words occurring only once in *Il.* and *Od.* combined, whether or not found in later Greek), with the figures for the number of verses in the direct speech of *Il.* characters provided in A. Fingerle, *Typik der homerischen Reden* (diss. Munich 1939: I am grateful to Dr W. Beck for a copy of the data from this work). I omitted proper names, some variant readings, and a few cases of dubious word-boundary (such as παλινόρμενος, 11.326). Uncapitalized titles of gods were admitted, though some of these might well be considered proper names. The four cases where a *hapax* occurs in a simile in direct speech were counted in both categories but only once in the total figures (6.148 ἐπιγίγνομαι; 9.323 ἀπτήν; 13.102 φυζακινός; 21.465 ζαφλεγής).

Note that the total figure for direct-speech verses in *Il.* 24 on Fingerle's p. 37 should read 452, and the figure for *Il.* 7 on his p. 68 should read 243. It is most regrettable that Fingerle's excellent work is not available in print. The figures given here differ slightly from Griffin's (*JHS* 106, 1986, 37 and 52).

[74] The percentages given here and in the following sentence total more than 100 because of the four cases where similes occur in direct speech (see last note).

portions in direct speech (7,057 verses, or 45.0% of the poem) have 454 (39.8%) of the *hapaxes* (including those in direct-speech similes), or 1 every 15·5 verses.

Of the characters, Akhilleus has 80 *hapaxes* in 973 verses (1 every 12.2 verses); Agamemnon 33 in 551 verses (1 every 16.7 verses); Hektor 30 in 521 verses (1 every 17.4 verses); and Nestor 29 in 532 verses (1 every 18.3 verses). The proportion of *hapaxes* is, however, considerably higher among characters with fewer verses; Phoinix, in his single speech of 172 verses, has 24 of them (1 every 7.2 verses), and the highest level of all I have noticed is attained by Sleep, with 6 in 30 verses (1 every 5 verses; Dione ranks next, with 6 in 36 verses, followed by Skamandros with 6 in 40 verses). Moreover, 5 of Sleep's *hapaxes* occur in the mere 20 verses of his first speech, none of them strikingly odd (πινύσσω, 14.249, see note *ad loc.*; ῥιπτάζω, 257; ζητέω, 258; δμήτειρα, 259; ἀποθύμιος, 261; his sixth *hapax* is παραπαφίσκω, 360). Nothing suggests that his speech, or Dione's or the river's, is intended to be peculiar, or especially elaborate or colloquial.

If we look at the words which occur only once in Homer and never elsewhere ('singularities'), the total of 201 is divided into: narrative (without similes) 93, similes 21, and direct speech 88.[75] Akhilleus is responsible for most of those in direct speech (18), Priam for 7, Agamemnon for 6, Poseidon for 5, and Hektor and Nestor for 4 each. The Greek orators who spoke in Troy, Odysseus and Menelaos, have 2 and 1 respectively. This is not the place to discuss the nature of these 'singularities' in detail, but it is clear that many of them are *ad hoc* compounds like φιλοκτέανος, some may well be local colloquialisms (τέττα, φολκός?), and some are neologisms which never became popular (παυσωλή?). Hardly any are likely to be from the old poetic vocabulary, as such words would survive mainly in recurrent formulae; βλοσυρῶπις is the clearest example of such unique occurrences.

Pope (p. 8) declared, irrefutably, that 'Homer was as much concerned with the individual word as other poets and prepared to coin a new one if he felt it necessary.' It may be added that he was also completely at ease in employing in his verse words which are not only non-formular but which must be considered (on our limited evidence) foreign to the usual epic vocabulary.

(v) Rhetorical figures of speech

Plato pokes gentle fun at the manuals of Nestor and Odysseus on *The Art of Oratory*, composed in their spare time at Troy (τὰς Νέστορος καὶ Ὀδυσσέως τέχνας περὶ λόγων; *Phaedrus* 261b6), and there was long warfare between the

[75] This is taken from Kumpf's listing, again ignoring proper names. Kumpf relied upon *LSJ*, not the *TLG* database. The one example occurring in a simile in direct speech (φυζακινός, 13.102) has been counted once in the gross total but in the subtotals both for similes and for the speaker (Poseidon).

philosophers and the rhetoricians about whether the artistic skills of Homer disproved the contention of the latter that their profession was initiated by the famous rhetoricians of the fifth and fourth centuries B.C.[76] The efforts to trace formal rhetorical devices back to Homer produced results conveniently available in the work known as *De Vita et Poesi Homeri*, which has come down to us among Plutarch's *Moralia*.[77]

The author sets out to prove that essentially everything in the form and content of literature, as well as in philosophical thought, was anticipated by Homer: figures of speech, adaptations of regular grammatical usage, figures of thought, styles of rhetoric, types of speech, and much else. The treatise lists about thirty-eight figures of speech and thought (there is some overlap between the two), and provides Homeric examples of each. It is significant that with a few exceptions (falling in the areas of military strategy and other practical aspects of culture) the author achieves his purpose without undue strain; all the figures identified by later teachers of rhetoric *do* occur in Homer, and the study testifies to the richness of the decorative features of Homeric style. This richness need not, of course, be the product of a sophisticated and highly developed literary style, still less of a formal rhetorical teaching, and many of the figures are natural features of speech, found in the ordinary discourse of uneducated people. However, the frequency and variety of their occurrence within the conventional epic diction suggests that in this respect, as in all others, Homer is both making the fullest use of techniques developed by his predecessors and surpassing their achievement.

A good example of the employment of the classical rhetorical figures of speech for intentional decorative effect is Nestor's mediation speech to Agamemnon and Akhilleus (1.254–84); this may be considered a show-piece, since his eloquence is elaborately praised beforehand: Νέστωρ | ἡδυεπής... λιγὺς Πυλίων ἀγορητής, | τοῦ καὶ ἀπὸ γλώσσης μέλιτος γλυκίων ῥέεν αὐδή (1.247–9). E. Bethe[78] drew attention to the repetitions of word and sound, listing Πρίαμος Πριάμοιό τε παῖδες (255), κεχαροίατο... πυθοίατο (256–7), οἱ περὶ μὲν βουλὴν Δαναῶν, περὶ δ᾽ ἐστὲ μάχεσθαι (258), κάρτιστοι δὴ κεῖνοι... | κάρτιστοι μὲν ἔσαν καὶ καρτίστοις ἐμάχοντο (266–7), πείθοντό τε μύθῳ· | ἀλλὰ πίθεσθε καὶ ὔμμες, ἐπεὶ πείθεσθαι ἄμεινον (273–4),

[76] See G. A. Kennedy, *AJP* 78 (1957) 23–35.
[77] It is printed in vol. VII of the Teubner edition, ed. G. N. Bernardakis (Leipzig 1906; I have not seen the new edition, (*Plutarchus*): *De Homero*, by J. F. Kindstrand, Uppsala 1990). On the sources of the work see F. Wehrli, *Zur Geschichte der allegorischen Deutung Homers im Altertum* (Borna–Leipzig 1928), and H. Schrader, *De Plutarchi Chaeronensis* Ὁμηρικαῖς Μελέταις *et de eiusdem quae fertur Vita Homeri* (Gotha 1899), together with his articles in *Hermes* 37 (1902) 530–81 and 38 (1903) 145–6. For recent works on rhetorical figures in Homer see Macleod, *Iliad XXIV* 50; there is a good summary of the doctrine in D. A. Russell, *Criticism in Antiquity* (London 1981) 143–7. The philosophical background is discussed by R. Lamberton, *Homer the Theologian* (Berkeley 1986) 40–3. [78] *Homer* I (Leipzig 1914) 197 n. 18.

μήτε σύ... μήτε σύ (275, 277), εἰ δὲ σὺ καρτερός ἐσσι... | ἀλλ᾿ ὅ γε φέρτερός ἐστιν (280–1). (He might have added ἴδον... ἴδωμαι, 262.) In addition, within the first few lines there is *metonymy* ('Αχαιΐδα γαῖαν, 254), *antithesis* (255–7), and *litotes* (261).[79]

A few rhetorical figures have already been discussed,[80] and many instances are listed in the indexes to this Commentary. Here I will deal in some detail with only three groups of figures, based on (1) sound-effects, (2) word-play and etymology, and (3) repetition of words or phrases.

1. Dio Chrysostom, *Or.* 12.68,[81] praises Homer lavishly for his invention of words, with which (he says) he could imitate the sound of rivers, forests, winds, fire, and the sea, and also of bronze and stone and of every living creature and implement, κ- ------- τε καὶ βόμβους καὶ κτύπον καὶ δοῦπον καὶ ἄραβον πρῶτος ἐξευρὼν καὶ ὀνομάσας ποταμούς τε μορμύροντας καὶ βέλη κλάζοντα καὶ βοῶντα κύματα καὶ χαλεπαίνοντας ἀνέμους καὶ ἄλλα τοιαῦτα δεινὰ καὶ ἄτοπα τῷ ὄντι θαύματα.[82] *Onomatopoeia* is indeed used with great effect. Famous verses describe the hoofbeats of the mules setting out to collect timber for Patroklos' pyre (23.116, see note *ad loc.*, 11.756n., and 17.456–8n.), and the bouncing fall of Sisyphus' stone (*Od.* 11.598). τριχθά τε καὶ τετραχθά is superb for the tearing of Odysseus' sails (*Od.* 9.71), though less apposite for Menelaos' breaking sword (3.363, see note *ad loc.*), suggesting the phrase has become formular. The sea splashes noisily in κύματα παφλάζοντα

[79] Though the ancients do not comment on it, like most speeches in the *Il.* this is in ring form. After the introductory exclamation and hypothetical statement (1.254–8), appeals to the chiefs to listen (259, 274) surround an inner ring, 'I have kept company with better men than you, and they listened to me' (260–1, 269–73), and at the centre is a short catalogue of these older heroes (262–8). Then the appeal is repeated specifically, to Agamemnon (275–6), to Akhilleus (277–81), and again to Agamemnon (282–4; cf. Lohmann, *Reden* 224).

[80] Chiasmus and hysteron-proteron have been mentioned in (ii) above, metaphor in (iii) above, apostrophe in ch. 1, i, and similes in ch. 3. On *aporia* see 17.260–1n. Among the most important figures not dealt with in detail here is *prosopopoeia*, the impersonation by a speaker of another character, of which there are moving examples linked to Hektor in particular (16.839–41, 6.460–1, 6.479, 7.89–90, 22.107; there is a more oratorical one by Odysseus, 9.254–8).

[81] Translated in D. A. Russell, *Criticism in Antiquity* (London 1981) 182. A number of approving comments on sound-effects in the scholia are mentioned by N. J. Richardson, *CQ* 30 (1980) 283–7; see also D. W. Packard, *TAPA* 104 (1974) 239–60, and Edwards, *HPI* 117–19.

[82] καναχή: 16.105 and 16.794 of a clanging helmet; 19.365 of chattering teeth; the verb is used of timbers struck by missiles (12.36). βόμβος: actually only βομβέω occurs, when a helmet (13.530) and a spearhead (16.118) fall to the ground. κτύπος occurs often for the noise of feet, including those of horses. δοῦπος is often used of general uproar, ἄραβος only once, of chattering teeth (10.375); but of course Dio is thinking of the formula δούπησεν δὲ πεσών, ἀράβησε δὲ τεύχε᾿ ἐπ᾿ αὐτῷ (6× *Il.*, 1× *Od.*). In a memorable line, the River Skamandros attacks Akhilleus μορμύρων ἀφρῷ τε καὶ αἵματι καὶ νεκύεσσι (21.325), and ἀφρῷ μορμύροντα is used of a river (5.599) and of the sea (18.403, nom.). κλάζω appears mainly in the form κεκληγώς (-οντες (on which see 16.430n.); 10× *Il.*, 3× *Od.*). On ἠϊόνες βοόωσιν see 17.263–6n. χαλεπαίνω has ἄνεμος as subject at 14.398–9 and ὥρη χειμερίη at *Od.* 5.485.

πολυφλοίσβοιο θαλάσσης (13.798, in a simile; see 13.795–9n.), and more peacefully in ἀφρῷ μορμύρων (see 18.403n.). Insistent repetition of the roots βελ-, βαλλ- signifies a noisy battle (see 16.102–8n.). Other noisy lines simulate thunder (see 17.593–6n.); a smooth line with alternating vowel sounds describes a flowing river (πὰρ ποταμὸν κελάδοντα, παρὰ ῥοδανὸν δονακῆα, 18.576, see note *ad loc.*); and another was praised by the ancients for its elegant use of hiatus (see 22.152n.).

A considerable degree of alliteration and assonance is inevitable in Greek,[83] but often in Homer the effect is so striking that it must be considered deliberate; and of course the repetition of the same sound is often included in the sound-effects described in the previous paragraph. For instance, nine of the 21 Homeric verses containing six π's refer to horses, and may be said to suggest galloping hoofs (Packard 243). Another verse with nine labials, κοῦφα ποσὶ προβιβὰς καὶ ὑπασπίδια προποδίζων (13.158) signals Deïphobos' advance to a duel. The eleven α's, as well as the dactylic movement and the repeated word-break after a final trochee, contribute to the effect of the notorious πολλὰ δ' ἄναντα κάταντα πάραντά τε δόχμιά τ' ἦλθον (23.116, cf. *Od.* 11.598). Alternation of α and ο is apparent in 18.576 (quoted above). The highest concentration of λ and ρ appears in τῶν νῦν αἷμα κελαινὸν ἐΰρροον ἀμφὶ Σκάμανδρον, a verse about the river. βουβών is Aristotle's word for the groin, and its only appearance in epic diction, βεβλήκει βουβῶνα (4.492), seems clearly due to its sound (see note *ad loc.*). Verses with repeated gutturals, like ἄκρην κὰκ κόρυθα· πλάγχθη δ' ἀπὸ χαλκόφι χαλκός (11.351), convey harshness. Shewan notes, *CP* 20 (1925) 208, a tendency towards alliteration in formulae, in single words (e.g. χαλκοκορυστής, καλλίκομος, ποντοπόρος), in two-word groups (μητέρα μήλων, κάρη κομόωντες), in noun–epithet combinations (φίλε Φοῖβε, αἰπὺν Ὄλυμπον), and in verb formulae (ἔπεα πτερόεντα προσηύδα, πρότερος προσέειπε). This too suggests, if further proof is needed, that the poets of the oral tradition appreciated its effects.

2. Word-play (*paronomasia*) is frequent.[84] Plutarch, *Vit. Hom.* 38, quotes as examples δὴν ἦν (6.131; this may well be accidental) and Πρόθοος θοός (2.758). This latter type is especially common; there are examples with the names of Hektor (Ἕκτορ...ἐξέμεν, 5.473n., 24.728–30n.), Astuanax (6.402–3n., 22.506–7n.), Peleus (both with Mt Pelion and with πῆλαι; 16.33–5n., 141–4n., 19.387–91n.), Apollo ἑκάεργος (ἀποέργαθε, 21.599n.), Phthie (φθίσεσθαι, 19.329–30n.), Damasos (whom Polupoites δάμασσε,

[83] A point well made by A. Shewan in his article on the subject, *CP* 20 (1925) 193–209. A much better documented study of the repetitions of consonants and vowels has now been provided by D. W. Packard, *TAPA* 104 (1974) 239–60. Many of the examples quoted here are drawn from these works. See also Macleod, *Iliad XXIV* 51.

[84] See generally Macleod, *Iliad XXIV* 50–3, and Edwards, *HPI* 120–3.

12.182–6), Moulios (with οὖτα etc., 20.472–5n.), Tros (Τρώεσσιν ἄνακτα, 20.230), Ate (ἢ πάντας ἀᾶται, 19.91), Ekhepolos the horse-owner (see 23.293–300n.), and perhaps even in κούρην οὐ γαμέω 'Αγαμέμνονος (9.388, see Martin, *Language* 221).

Examples of *figura etymologica*, the syntactic connexion and often juxtaposition of words related in stem, are commoner still. The figure may have been attractive because it both repeats the sound and contrasts the sense or the grammar. In books 17–20 appear (among others) γηράς... ἐγήρα (17.197), μέγας μεγαλωστί (18.26n., 16.776), ἀγορὴν ἀγέροντο (18.245 ≅ 2.788), ἤλειψαν λίπ' ἐλαίω (18.350 ≅ 10.577), τέμενος τάμον (20.184), and ἐν πεδίω πεπόλιστο πόλις μερόπων ἀνθρώπων (20.217; note the alliteration of π).[85] There may be a strong contrast, as in 'Αχαιΐδες οὐκέτ' 'Αχαιοί (2 × *Il.*) and ἀκμῆτες κεκμηότας (2 × *Il.*), and complicated forms such as οὐ μὰν ἔτι δηρὸν ἀπείρητος πόνος ἔσται | οὐδ' ἔτ' ἀδήριτος (17.41–2).

A similar figure is *polyptoton*, the use of the same word in different forms, as in κακὸν ἐκ κακοῦ (see 19.289–90n.), παίδων παῖδες (20.308), cf. the verb-forms δαιόμενον... δαῖε (see 18.225–7n.) and ὀλλυντάς τ' ὀλλυμένους τε (11.83). The crowning achievement of this technique is of course ἀσπὶς ἄρ' ἀσπίδ' ἔρειδε, κόρυς κόρυν, ἀνέρα δ' ἀνήρ (13.131 = 16.215; cf. 2.363, 14.382, *Od.* 7.120–1).

Delight in the sound of words, and in their clever interweaving, is also apparent in artfully crafted phrases like ἤ κε φέρησι μέγα κράτος, ἤ κε φεροίμην (18.308), ἕλοιμί κεν ἤ κεν ἁλοίην (22.253), ἤ τ' ἔβλητ' ἤ τ' ἔβαλ' ἄλλον (11.410), καί τε κτανέοντα κατέκτα (18.309). Formation of new words sometimes shows the same almost ostentatious skill, as in δυσαριστοτόκεια (see 18.54n.).

3. Repetition of a word or phrase can take a number of other forms. *Anaphora* is found with different parts of speech, as in the triple repetition of πολλά at 17.430–1 (introducing cola of elegantly diminishing length), the triple repetition of ἐν within the same verse (ἐν μὲν γαῖαν ἔτευξ', ἐν δ' οὐρανόν, ἐν δὲ θάλασσαν, 18.483, and with cola of different lengths at 5.740, 14.216, and 18.535). There may be a purposeful variation, as in | βέβληται μὲν... | οὔτασται δὲ... | βέβληται δὲ... (11.660–2 = 16.25–7).[86] In the case of adjectives, there is often *polyptoton* too: τῷ κ' ἀγαθὸς μὲν ἔπεφν', ἀγαθὸν δέ κεν ἐξενάριξεν (21.280; see section 2 above). κάρτιστοι δὴ κεῖνοι ἐπιχθονίων τράφεν ἀνδρῶν· | κάρτιστοι μὲν ἔσαν καὶ καρτίστοις ἐμάχοντο (1.266–7) is a good example of climactic repetition with case-variation. τρὶς μὲν... τρὶς δὲ... is a common means of emphasis (see 18.155–6n.), and ἔνθα τίνα πρῶτον, τίνα δ'

---

[85] D. Fehling, *Die Wiederholungsfiguren und ihr Gebrauch bei den Griechen vor Gorgias* (Berlin 1969) 153–62, gives many other examples.

[86] Fehling (*op. cit.* in n. 85) 187–234 quotes an enormous number of instances, arranged by parts of speech.

59

ὕστατον ἐξενάριξεν is formular (3 × *Il.*). Sometimes a proper name is repeated at the beginning of the next verse together with a patronymic or epithet (e.g. 2.837–8, 6.153–4, 7.137–8; Fehling, *op. cit.* (in n. 85) 184), or in three well-known cases an entire hemistich (see 20.371–2n.).[87] The contrast implicit in most instances of anaphora is usually signalled by μέν ... δέ, but sometimes there is asyndeton, as in the triple repetitions of μήτι and of Νιρεύς at the beginning of successive verses (23.315–18, 2.671–3). There may be a complex contrast between two phrases: εἴτ᾽ ἐπὶ δεξί᾽ ἴωσι πρὸς ἠῶ τ᾽ ἠέλιόν τε, | εἴτ᾽ ἐπ᾽ ἀριστερὰ τοί γε ποτὶ ζόφον ἠερόεντα (12.239–40), cf. Hektor's οἶδ᾽ ἐπὶ δεξιά, οἶδ᾽ ἐπ᾽ ἀριστερὰ νωμῆσαι βῶν (7.238).

Nowadays interest in the classical rhetorical figures is often slight, and the majority of Homer's *readers* are more likely to note (in the speeches of Akhilleus, for example) the intense dramatic effects produced by enjambment, emphatic positioning of words, and variation in the length of the cola (see (i) above), and the almost invariable presence of ring composition in a speech of any length. To these features little attention was paid in antiquity. But the rhetorical figures which were so important to the ancients also appear in abundance in Homer's poetry, and for *listeners* in particular the sound-effects which many of them produce add a great deal to its power. In this, as in so much else, Homer was the teacher of the ancient world.

---

[87] This is termed *epanalepsis*, *epanastrophe*, or *anadiplosis*, grouped by Plutarch, *Vit. Hom.* 32, under the general heading *palillogia*.

COMMENTARY

BOOK SEVENTEEN

Between the death of Patroklos and the announcement of the news to Akhilleus there intervenes a long struggle for possession of the corpse. The episode is expanded to great length, both to emphasize Patroklos' importance and to prepare for the devastating impact of his death on Akhilleus; the rescue of his body will not be accomplished until 18.238. According to the poet's habitual practice (see Introduction, ch. 2, iii), two similar but much briefer struggles have preceded, over the bodies of Sarpedon (16.530–683) and Kebriones (16.751–82); the poem will conclude with a further mighty adaptation of the theme, the 'struggle' of Akhilleus and Priam for the body of Hektor.

Two motifs which often occur, in brief form, in the acount of a victory are here much enlarged, both for added grandeur and for purposes of the plot. The first of these is the seizure of the victim's armour, the continuation of the theme of Patroklos' disguise in Akhilleus' Hephaistos-made panoply which the poet makes use of in so many different ways (see introduction to book 18). In this Book it is anticipated by Menelaos' stripping of the corpse of Euphorbos, and provides a constant reminder of the absent Akhilleus, of his consent to Patroklos' entering the battle, and thus of his responsibility for his friend's death. It prepares the way for his inability to rescue the corpse immediately (see 711n.), and for the making of the replacement armour in book 18.

In addition, the poet uses Hektor's donning of the armour to demonstrate his growing over-confidence, to which our attention is drawn by Zeus himself (see 194–209n.). This same aspect of the portrayal of Hektor is brought out by the second motif, that of the pursuit of the victim's horses and chariot; in this case the horses are immortal, and the motif is enlarged (again by the introduction of Zeus) into a moving elegy on the sorrows of humankind (see 426–58n.). The theme will reach a climax in Hektor's headstrong and defiant refusal to retreat before the threat of Akhilleus' return (see 18.284–309n.).

The battle must be continued inconclusively, and without the loss of major figures on either side, until Akhilleus intervenes to save the corpse of his friend. This expansion is achieved by repeated use of two motifs which reinvigorate first one army, then the other. One of these is a rebuke to a leader, followed by a charge led by him, a pattern which recurs five times (beginning at 70, 140, 319, 543, and 582). The other is a call for help and the response to it, used first when Menelaos summons Aias (115ff.), again when at Aias' prompting he calls to a number of Greek chiefs (237ff.), and finally in a much enlarged version when Aias suggests to Menelaos that Akhilleus himself be appealed to (626ff.). The message is conveyed through Menelaos and Antilokhos, reaching him at the beginning of book 18. The structuring of these motifs has been analysed (in slightly different ways) by Fenik, *TBS* 159–89, and A. Thornton, *Homer's Iliad; its Composition and the Motif of Supplication* (Göttingen 1984) 86–92.

It is very likely that the story of the battle over Patroklos was associated with narratives of the even grander struggle over the body of Akhilleus himself (see 288–303n.). The *Od.* refers to this famous event (24.36–42), and it was described at length in the *Aithiopis*. What actual poetic form this later episode in the Troy tale had taken at the time of the composition of our book 17 cannot be known, but the prominence of Antilokhos at the end of this Book and in the funeral games of book 23 is probably due to the fame of his death at the hands of Memnon the Ethiopian and the revenge taken by Akhilleus (see 377–83n. and Introduction, ch. 2, ii). It has been plausibly suggested that the carrying-off of Patroklos' corpse may be adapted from Aias' famous retreat bearing the dead Akhilleus (see 720–1n.). The immortal horses which mourn for Patroklos may also have mourned for Akhilleus himself (see 426–58n., 19.404–24n.).

1–69 Menelaos stands over the corpse of Patroklos, is challenged by Euphorbos, and kills him

Menelaos is unusually prominent in this Book, partly perhaps because so many of the Greek leaders have been wounded (19.47–53), partly also because the poet attributes the same considerate and sensitive nature to him and to the dead Patroklos; ἄμφω γὰρ ἤπιοι (bT on 1–2; they also point out that Menelaos wanted to spare Adrastos (6.37ff.), sympathized with Agamemnon (2.408–9, 10.25ff.), led the rescue of Odysseus (11.463ff.), and waited to bury a comrade at Sounion despite his haste to be home (*Od.* 3.284–5)). He receives several remarkable similes, and is twice directly addressed by the poet (679, 702; see 679–80n., and Introduction, ch. 1, i, 3).

1–2 The same sentence construction with οὐδ' ἔλαθ' recurs at 626–7, where again new proponents are introduced in the accusative, obviously with some emphasis, and a previously mentioned character is referred to again in the nominative in the runover position, also with some emphasis – here pathos, there resentment. The present book-division obscures the diversion of our attention from Hektor, glorying in victory and pursuing his victim's horses (16.864–7), to the struggle for the body of Patroklos; see 9–42n.

3–6 Verse 3 is formular (7 × *Il.*). On the action of πρόμαχοι see 3.16n. and vol. II 21–2. With 4–6 cf. 5.299–301, where ἀμφὶ δ᾽ ἄρ᾽ αὐτῷ βαῖνε is followed by λέων ὣς ἀλκὶ πεποιθώς, and 5.300–1 = 17.7–8. Here a different and expanded simile is inserted. πρωτοτόκος is *hapax* in Homer but not rare later. The later form εἰδυῖα for ἰδυῖα is not surprising in a simile; see West on *Theogony* 264. κινυρός appears as an epithet of γόος (Ap. Rh. 4.605) and of πέτηλα (Nonnus, *D.* 38.95: the 'sighing leaves' of the trees into which the daughters of Helios have been changed), which suggests the meaning here was taken to be 'lowing pitifully'; see Frisk s.v. But Leumann (*HW* 242–3) argues, with much probability, that there is no implication that the calf is dead (despite dead Patroklos), and that other similes of animals protecting their young suggest the Homeric meaning was 'threatening'; cf. 133–7 (where Aias stands over Patroklos' body like a lion over its young), *Od.* 20.14–15 (a bitch growling over her puppies), and the wasps defending their offspring (12.170, 16.265).

The simile, like that at 133–7, conveys the tenderness for Patroklos often expressed in this Book. Menelaos' emotion is mentioned at 92 and 139 and rises to a climax at 670–2, and Zeus's regard for him is stressed at 204 and 270–3. Patroklos' gentle character was well appreciated by the scholiasts; see N. J. Richardson, *CQ* 30 (1980) 268–9.

7–8 = 5.300–1; see note *ad loc.* and Hoekstra, *Epic Verse* 16–17.

9–42 Hektor's *aristeia* will continue as usual with the battle over the corpse of his victim; but just as after Patroklos' victory over Sarpedon (16.508ff.), the focus first shifts away from the victor. So the first Trojan attack on the corpse takes the form of a challenge to Menelaos by Euphorbos. Such challenges before a duel are common; that of Diomedes to Glaukos (6.119–236) develops into the famous lecture about fighting with gods, that between Hektor and Akhilleus (22.248–72) becomes a vain attempt to bargain for the return of the loser's body, anticipating the end of the poem. The Paris–Menelaos challenge at the beginning of book 3 has no direct speech between the contestants. Cf. also 5.630–54, 7.224–43, 13.809–32, 20.176–258, and Fenik, *TBS* 66.

9 Πάνθου is for older Πανθόου or Πανθόο᾽(ο); see Chantraine, *GH* I 48. The full name–epithet phrase Πανθόο᾽ υἱὸν ἐϋμμελίην Εὔφορβον is used at 59. The epithet seems to be very old (see Page, *HHI* 240–2; Hoekstra, *Modifications* 37–8) and probably belongs to Priam (καὶ Πρίαμος καὶ λαὸς ἐϋμμελίω Πριάμοιο, 4 × *Il.*; an untraditional alternative appears at 16.738). It is probably applied to Euphorbos because there is no common alternative (ἀρηΐφιλος and βοὴν ἀγαθός require the name to begin with a consonant); the explanation that Euphorbos won it by wounding Patroklos with an ashwood spear is possible but unlikely (so R. S. Shannon, *The Arms of Achilles and Homeric Compositional Technique*, Leiden 1975, 64–6). H. Mühlestein proposed that Euphorbos, 'providing good pasture', is a shepherd, a doublet of Paris, and hence can be given Priam's epithet (*SMEA* 15, 1972, 83; see 16.777–867n., 16.808–11n.). Eustathius approved the parechesis εὐμμελίης ἀμέλησε.

Here and at 23 a verb stands at the end of the line in the place of the name ᾽Εὔφορβος, but the association of this epithet with the name seems to be already established. εὐμμελίης is also applied to Peisistratus (before the 3rd-foot caesura; *Od.* 3.400), to Kuknos at *Aspis* 368, and to four different heroes in Hesiod (frr. 58.8, 180.16, and 167 MW before the 3rd-foot caesura; 25.15 following it). It must be, like ἄναξ ἀνδρῶν, a 'special epithet raided to furnish vocabulary for generic use' (Hainsworth, *Homer: Tradition and Invention*, ed. B. Fenik, Leiden 1978, 48).

10 Cf. 379, where most MSS read θανόντος for πεσόντος; the same variation occurs at the end of the line at 8.476. In the *Il.* θανόντος is used only for Patroklos (9 × ; one of the expressions recurs for him at *Od.* 24.77), and perhaps has special pathos; it is followed again by the effective ἀμύμονος at 379. Here, however, the picture which πεσόντος invokes of the corpse lying in the dust between the two fighters makes it more effective than θανόντος would be; cf. ἐν κονίῃσι πεσόντος (428).

13 An effective tricolon, the cola increasing in length, but the mid-verse caesura is not bridged. There is another example at 33 (see Macleod, *Iliad XXIV* on 24.479). ἔα: 15.347 has ἐᾶν in the same phrase and meaning, probably because it follows another imperatival infinitive.

17 μελιηδέα (-ος) usually of wine or food, but metaphorically in this μ. θυμόν formula 3 × , and also at *Od.* 11.100 (for homecoming) and *Od.* 19.551 (for sleep).

18–32 Scornfully, Menelaos begins by apostrophizing Zeus and continues with an aphorism, a simile, and a paradigm illustrating the folly of such presumption (24–8) before he deigns to address his opponent directly (29–32); then he concludes with a second aphorism (32). The disgruntled Aias similarly begins by ignoring Akhilleus (9.624–36). Similes of this length in speeches are not common; Akhilleus has four, Hektor two (so Moulton, *Similes* 100). The ineffectiveness of threats is also asserted by Hektor in response to Aias' challenge (7.235–6) and by Aineias and Hektor in turn to Akhilleus (20.200–2 = 431–3).

The use of the powerfully expressive μέγ᾽ ὀχθήσας here has caused surprise (cf. S. Scully, *TAPA* 114, 1984, 20), but it is in accordance with Menelaos' grief and rage (cf. μεμαώς, 8). Menelaos' scorn emerges in no less than five examples of litotes (19, 20 (2 ×), 21, 27–8; see F. P. Donnelly, *CW* 23, 1930, 145).

20–3 Another triple 'negative' simile, more elaborate than this, occurs at 14.394–9 (see note *ad loc.*, and Introduction ch. 3, i (b) 4).

21–2 σῦς is often used for domestic hogs, so κάπρος is added to specify a wild boar, as at 281–2, 5.783 = 7.257, 11.293. Species similarly follows genus in apposition in βοῦς... | ταῦρος (2.480–1), ὄρνισιν... αἰγυπιοῖσι (7.59), ἴρηξ | κίρκος (*Od.* 13.86–7). The hiatus can be avoided by reading κάπροι' (o). Leaf leans towards the reading μάλιστα (found in some MSS of the *h* family and in Plutarch, *Vit. Hom* 133), together with the variant μέγα for περί in 22 (only in one MS of the family). μάλιστα is found 1 × *Il.*, 4 × *Od.* in the same construction (a pause at the diaeresis, a relative pronoun, τε), and once after οἶός τέ (*Od.* 19.160); μέγιστος is predicative, so its enjambment with its noun is not harsh (*TAPA* 97, 1966, 125–30), but it is paralleled in position and construction only at 15.37 = *Od.* 5.185. The predominance of μάλιστα in this phrasing, together with its use with μέγα at 14.399, gives considerable support to Leaf's view.

23 A papyrus and some of the good MSS read φορέουσιν, supported by van Leeuwen with a number of post-Homeric usages. But μέγα φρονέοντες and other verb-forms are common for 'confidently', 'proudly', and θεοῖσιν | ἶσα... φρονέειν is presumptuous for a mortal (5.440–1), so Allen's reading (and Leaf's) seems preferable. There may also be intentional word-play in ὀλοόφρονος... φρονέουσιν. 'Not even so great (τόσσον) [is] the strength of a leopard... as Panthoös' sons are proud (ὅσσον... φρονέουσιν).'

24–8 Menelaos killed a Huperenor, presumably this brother of Euphorbos, at 14.516–19, without mention of any taunts. This is the only instance where the attempt to avenge a brother (a common motif) is so far separated from the brother's death (Fenik, *TBS* 162), and the small inconsistency (*pace* Fenik) is hardly surprising in an oral poem. Willcock, *LCM* 3 (1978) 13–14, with much probability considers it an example of a remark created by the poet to suit the immediate context, not a character's recollection of the past. 'It is Homeric to leave something out and report it later' (bT, quoting 20.90, 9.353, and 5.832).

Menelaos' complaint about the pride of Panthoös' sons (the prominent Pouludamas is another, 13.756) recalls his diatribe against the Trojans' appetite for war at 13.620–39. The poet presents a consistent and believable portrait of a sensitive man, very conscious of how he has been wronged, of his responsibility for Patroklos' death (92), and of his inferiority to many fighters on his own side (7.94ff., 17.587–8).

24 οὐδὲ μὲν οὐδέ (6 × *Il.*, 1 × *Od.* at the beginning of sentence and verse) is very emphatic; cf. note on 13.269–71. Here the first οὐδέ picks up οὔτε in

20 and 21, the second stresses βίη. βίη in all its cases is often used with a genitive or adjective to provide an extended proper-name phrase; the most familiar is βίη Ἡρακληείη, on which see 2.658–60n., 11.690n. The example here is paralleled in form at 5.781.

25 ἧς ἥβης is emphasized by its initial position. ἀπόνητο: 'have joy of', as at 11.763; for the form, see Chantraine, *GH* I 382. ὤνατο is a unique form (from ὄνομαι, 'scorn') which may be imperfect or aorist, and may have resulted from the juxtaposition of its near-homonym; see Chantraine, *GH* I 295.

30–2 The shift from indirect to direct command in κελεύω | ... ἰέναι, μηδ'...ἵστασ' is natural; cf. 24.148. The lines are repeated in Akhilleus' response to Aineias' challenge (20.196–8). The aphorism appears also in Hesiod's παθὼν δέ τε νήπιος ἔγνω (*Erga* 218), and Plato (*Symp.* 222b8); the same idea, less epigrammatically, is found in γνώῃς ἀποτίνων (23.487). Aphorisms usually occur at the end of a speech (e.g. 12.412, 14.81), and almost always in a character's voice (see 176–8n.). The compositional use of such gnomes is studied by Lohmann, *Reden* 66 n. 112; there are collections in West, *Works and Days* 211, E. Ahrens, *Gnomen in griechische Dichtung* (Halle 1937), E. Pellizer, *QUCC* 13 (1972) 24–37, and J. Russo, *Journ. of Folklore Research* 20 (1983) 121–30.

33–42 The narrator's interjected τὸν δ' οὐ πεῖθεν is unusual (on the structure of the line cf. 14.270 and 14.267–70n.), and so is this third speech in a challenge; but Euphorbos, between the threats that frame his speech (34–5, 41–2), neatly turns Menelaos' warning paradigm into a motive for revenge, and includes a second reference to Huperenor's wife and parents (cf. 27–8). The famous Diomedes/Glaukos challenge also concludes with a third speech, that too unusual in content (6.215–31). The grief of the young wife and the parents of a warrior is often expressed, e.g. at 11.241–5, 5.152–8; most fully, of course, in the case of Hektor himself.

35–7 On the relative clause followed by paratactic clauses see Macleod, *Iliad XXIV*, on 24.292–3. νέοιο here must mean 'new', but it usually means 'young', and there may be that implication also. Lines 36–7 are inserted by a papyrus after 23.223 (see note *ad loc.*).

37 The line is repeated in Andromakhe's lament at 24.741, the second-person verb given a different sense and greater pathos there by the following runover vocative Ἕκτορ. MSS vary at both occurrences between ἀρητόν, 'prayed against', and ἄρρητον, 'unspeakable'. The sense of the former is hard to explain (Willcock's note *ad loc.* '"prayed for", "wished for", i.e. the death of their son put into the parents a longing to express their grief' is not very convincing), but the form is accepted here by Chantraine, *GH* I 160. ἄρρητον is much simpler, and is preferred by Leaf (who has a good discussion), Ameis–Hentze, and van Leeuwen.

38–40 κατάπαυμα shows a common type of noun-formation (see Risch, *Wortbildung* 49–51), but does not happen to recur until the Septuagint. The consolatory gesture Euphorbos proposes was achieved in some tales: 'They brought the head of Euru3thcu3 to Λlkmcnc, and that of Melaɴippu3 tu Tudeus' (T on line 40; Erbse lists the references). Hektor is said to intend to cut off the head of the dead Patroklos (126, 18.175–6), and Akhilleus that of Hektor (18.334–5), though of course the poet, with book 24 in view, cannot have him do so. See C. Segal, *The Theme of the Mutilation of the Corpse in the Iliad* (Leiden 1971), esp. 20–1. In 40 Πάνθῳ is for Πανθόῳ; see 9n.

41–2 The thought, the testing of the alternative outcomes of a fight, is familiar, cf. 227–8 and 11.410, 12.328, 18.308–9, but the wording is unusual. The first hemistich of 41 is like 5.895; the nearest parallel in form to the second is *Od.* 23.249... ἀλλ' ἔτ' ὄπισθεν ἀμέτρητος πόνος ἔσται; ἀδήριτος is *hapax* (though regular in form; Risch, *Wortbildung* 20–1); and it is unclear whether ἀλκῆς and φόβοιο should be taken with πόνος, 'struggle of courage and fear', or with the adjectives, 'untried and uncontested, [to prove] either our courage or our fear'. In 42, Ameis–Hentze and van Leeuwen read οὐδέ τ' for the more forceful οὐδ' ἔτ'. Aristarchus read ἠδέ... ἠδέ, which discards the alternatives usual in this context, and some MSS οὔτε... οὔτε, which can hardly make sense. Successive ideas are introduced at the cost of grammatical precision: 'No longer shall the contest be untried, no longer unfought, either for triumph or flight!' Macleod, *Iliad XXIV* 51, suggests the assonance δηρὸν ἀπείρητος... ἀδήριτος conveys grim sarcasm, listing other examples.

43–50 Fenik, *TBS* 162–3, finds close parallels to the action at 11.434ff. and 14.402ff. On 44–5 see 3.348–9n. All the verses except 47 occur elsewhere. After 3.350 (= 17.46), Menelaos' prayer to Zeus is amplified into direct speech; here it picks up his words in 19. νύξ' is common in this position before a pause, with powerful effect; cf. βάλλ' (1.52), λάμπ' (11.45), κόπτ' (*Od.* 9.290).

47 κατ' ὀφθαλμοῖο θέμεθλα (14.493) is the only parallel. The boastful Euphorbos is fittingly wounded through the throat.

51–2 The D scholia say that χάριτες is a Macedonian and Cypriot word for a closely twisted myrtle-wreath, an idea which appealed to Bowra (*JHS* 54, 1934, 72) but not to Leumann (*HW* 270–1). Other D scholia understand 'hair such as the Graces have', which must be right; it is a shorter alternative for κόμας ὑακινθίνῳ ἄνθει ὁμοίας (2 × *Od.*), cf. νύμφαι Χαρίτεσσιν ὁμοῖαι | (Hesiod fr. 291.1). Golden spirals apparently for binding the hair are common in sub-Mycenaean and Geometric graves (E. Bielefeld, *Arch. Hom.* c 47–8, 58); or perhaps the reference is to an Asiatic custom, taken over later by the Ionians (S. Marinatos, *Arch. Hom.* b 3). ἐσφήκωντο means 'were pinched in [like a wasp's waist]', cf. σφής, 'wasp', perhaps alluding to the colour of yellow bands on black hair as well as to the constriction; the verb occurs only here in Homer, but cognates are used later with the same metaphorical sense (see Frisk and LSJ).

The unusual description of Euphorbos' finery does not seem condemnatory in tone, as it undoubtedly is for Nastes of Miletos, who χρυσὸν ἔχων ('wearing') πόλεμόνδ' ἴεν ἠΰτε κούρη, 2.872), but it emphasizes the contrast between his pride and his fall. The defiling with blood and dust of a dead warrior's hair is repeated at the death of Hektor (22.401–4 and note), the soiling of a helmet-plume is amplified at 15.535–8 and 16.795–800, and the manes of Akhilleus' immortal horses trail in the dust in their sorrow (17.439–40).

53–60 In this pathetic and famous simile several familiar motifs form a unique and moving whole. Akhilleus, Telemakhos, and (implicitly) Nausikaa also grew like young trees (18.56 = 437, *Od.* 14.175, 6.162–3), and warriors often fall like them (see note on 4.482–7; also at 5.560, 13.178–80, 13.389–91 = 16.482–4, 14.414–17). Windstorms often cause turmoil, e.g. at 11.297–8, 13.334–6, 13.795–9, 19.377–8.

There are more points of comparison than usual between simile and narrative. The strength of the ἐριθηλές and free-standing (54) young tree is like the young (16.811) Euphorbos' exceptional athletic prowess (16.808–9); the devoted care of the olive-grower recalls the love of his parents (28, 37); the breezes which gave the sapling strength (cf. ἀνεμοτρεφὲς ἔγχος, 11.256) may mirror Euphorbos' successes in previous battles (16.810); its beauty and pale blossoms (55–6) remind us of his lovely hair and its adornment (51–2; κόμη is used for foliage at 677). Finally, both tree and Euphorbos meet abrupt and violent destruction and lie prostrate. See Fränkel, *Gleichnisse* 39–40; Macleod, *Iliad XXIV* 49–50.

54–5 On the formular system around χώρῳ ἐν οἰοπόλῳ (3 × *Il.*) see 13.471–5n. Allen's text, ‚ὅθ'(ι) ἅλις ἀναβέβροχεν ὕδωρ, 'where plenty of water moistens ⟨it⟩', is acceptable, but ὅ θ'...'⟨a tree⟩ which plenty of water has moistened' is preferred in *LfgrE*. Leaf prints ὅ θ' ἅλις ἀναβέβροχεν, but approves Bentley's ὅ (ϝ)άλις, which Chantraine, *GH* I 130, mentions without comment. ἀναβέβροχεν (Zenodotus' reading) is the expected form (from βρέχω, 'to make wet'), but ἀναβέβρυχεν (the reading of almost all MSS) may have been derived from *βρύξ, 'water' (cf. Frisk I 274) or (following van der Valk, *GRBS* 23, 1982, 294–5) from βρύω, 'burst forth' (see LSJ s.v.). καλόν (etc.) beginning the line is often followed by a choriamb-shaped adjective, usually δαιδάλεον (6 × *Il.*, 3 × *Od.*).

58 The aorists ἐξέστρεψε (only here in Homer) and ἐξετάνυσσε, after the present tenses, stress the suddenness of the uprooting. The scholia point out the effective pathos of the harshness of sound in this line, after the smoothness of the first part of the simile.

60 The position of ἐπεὶ κτάνε is paralleled at 16.762; ἐπεί is placed like this also at 125 below. ἐσύλα is an inceptive imperfect, as at 15.524.

61–9 The paragraph-division before 61 in Allen's text is misleading, as the simile elaborates on what precedes, introducing the fear motif (67) and then carrying it back to the narrative; see Introduction, ch. 3, i (b) 3. The simile is composed mainly of recurrent phrases, but is expanded more than is usual with lion-similes, probably because Menelaos' importance will continue. ὡς δ' ὅτε τίς τε also begins verse and simile at 3.33 and 8.338, and the rest of 61 recurs at *Od.* 6.130 (cf. also 12.299, and 17.133–6n.); phrases with ἄριστος (etc.) like that in 62 (e.g. ὅσσοι ἄριστοι) are very common in this position. Verses 63–4 are repeated at 11.175–6, and there the simile ends; but here the Trojans' fear is anticipated by the continuation (by means of the effective runover δηῶν) into a picture figured in more detail on Akhilleus' shield (18.579–86), where lions consume the blood and entrails of a captured bull while dogs and herdsmen stand by helplessly.

κύνες τ' ἄνδρες τε (65) recurs at 658 (accusative); ἀντίον ἐλθέμεναι is repeated in simile and narrative, as often happens (67, 69), and the second hemistich of 67 is formular (4× *Il.*, 6× *Od.*, cf. 18.322); 68 is rather like 10.232 ἐνὶ φρεσὶ θυμὸς ἐτόλμα.

The main point of comparison is of course between the reluctance of the dogs and herdsmen to approach the lion and that of the Trojans to face Menelaos, but Fränkel, *Gleichnisse* 63–4, well points out the additional correspondence between the lion tearing at its victim's entrails and the warrior stripping off his enemy's armour. The broken neck of the cow (63) recalls Euphorbos' wound in the throat (47–9). The two successive long similes (53–69) give the duel scale and colour, which under Homeric battle conventions cannot be given by repeated physical actions.

63–7 Note the sound of ἐξ αὐχέν' ἔαξε; Ameis–Hentze *ad loc.* splendidly render it 'das Knacken der Knochen'. ἰύζουσιν (66; again at *Od.* 15.162, cf. ἰυγμῷ, *Il.* 18.572) is also onomatopoeic (from the cry ἰοὺ ἰού), extended by zeugma to the dogs.

70–139 Apollo, disguised as Mentes, rebukes Hektor, who charges against Menelaos; Menelaos decides to retreat, and summons Aias to help. Hektor carries off Akhilleus' divinely made armour. Aias bestrides Patroklos' corpse

The confrontation between Menelaos and Hektor over the body of Euphorbos (still wearing his armour; the three names are inscribed) is beautifully depicted on a well-known East Greek plate of the late seventh century (London A749; Friis Johansen, *Iliad* 77–80, 279, and fig. 18; K. Schefold, *Frühgriechische Sagenbilder*, Munich 1964, 8–9, 84, and pl. 75; Wace and Stubbings, *Companion* pl. 28). The scene suggests an actual duel between them, which does not occur in the *Il.* Schefold points out that the position of Menelaos, facing to the right, and that of Euphorbos' corpse (supine behind Menelaos and also facing right, instead of lying as if he had died facing his enemy), indicates that Menelaos will succeed in capturing his victim's armour; but he is probably wrong in holding that this implies an older version than that of the *Il.* (see Friis Johansen, and 90–3n.).

The stress laid upon the possession of Euphorbos' armour (70–1, 85, probably 91, see note *ad loc.*) anticipates the significance of Hektor's seizing and donning of the armour worn by Patroklos; see the introduction to this Book.

70 φέροι is optative, where the aorist indicative (with κε) would be expected. Leaf (on 5.311), van Leeuwen (on 4.223), and Chantraine, *GH* II 220–1, link the use of the optative here with such phrases as φαίης κεν, οὐκ ἄν...ἴδοις; cf. 366, 398–9, and note on 4.223–5. Chantraine renders the phrase here 'on eût vu l'Atride emporter...' If correct, this implies a personal 'authorial voice' without use of the second person. See Introduction, ch. 1, i, 1, and de Jong, *Narrators* 68–81.

72–4 θοῷ ἀτάλαντος Ἄρηϊ is used generically for heroes (7 × *Il.* with θοῷ, 4 × *Il.* without it), but has emphatic force here. On ἀτάλαντος see 256–9n. At 2.846 the leader of the Kikones is named Euphemos; possibly there has been some confusion with *Od.* 1.105 Ταφίων ἡγήτορι Μέντῃ.

75–81 The first of the four rebukes which structure this Book; the others are at 142ff., 322ff., and 582ff. When last seen (16.864–7), Hektor was hurling a spear at Automedon as the latter was carried away by Akhilleus' horses – 'those immortal horses, which the gods gave as splendid gifts to Peleus'. Hektor's longing for these horses, like his donning of Akhilleus' armour (see 194–209n.), is developed as a sign of his presumption; later he expresses this longing to Aineias (485–90), shortly after Zeus has explicitly refused to let him gratify it (448–50). The poet is also preparing for the major scenes with these horses which are to come (17.426ff., 19.392ff.). News of a comrade's death is again used to rally Hektor at 16.541–3 and 17.589–90.

75–8 ἀκίχητα is accus. pl., 'the unattainable' (*LfgrE*). Verses 76–8 are repeated at 10.402–4. δαΐφρων may not have much meaning here; but τὸν ἀθανάτη τέκε μήτηρ contrasts powerfully with θνητοῖσι in the preceding verse and is highly significant – Akhilleus has a divine parent, Hektor has not. The phrase is akin to Apollo's own formula ὃν ἠΰκομος τέκε Λητώ (1.36, 19.413, *Od.* 11.318), cf. also τὸν Ἀλφειὸς τέκε παῖδα (*Od.* 3.189 = 15.187, cf. 10.139), and the verse-ending τέκε μήτηρ (5 × *Il.*, 5 × *Od.*).

The implied warning to Hektor to know himself mortal is an anticipation of Zeus's even clearer admonition when he dares to put on Akhilleus' armour (see 194–209n.). On the motif 'only X could handle...' see 19.387–91n.

79–81 τόφρα = 'meanwhile', as at 18.338, 19.24 etc. A rebuke often includes the news of the death of a companion, as at 589 90. The long phrase for Menelaos both adds emphasis and enables Patroklos' name to be placed in juxtaposition with it and prominently at the beginning of the next line. Euphorbos' name and patronymic are similarly emphasized. Though an exceptional athlete, the victor over twenty men in battle (16.808–11), and the brother of Hektor's counsellor Pouludamas, Euphorbos was not literally 'the best of the Trojans', but the term is used loosely; Patroklos is ὤριστος 'Αχαιῶν (689) and ἀνὴρ ὤριστος is applied to Agamemnon, Alkathoös, Sarpedon, Eumelos (in the chariot race), and Hektor (see also 18.8–11n.). θούριδος ἀλκῆς (21 × *Il.*, 1 × *Od.*) always stands at the end of the verse after a verb, and follows ἔπαυσε again at 15.250.

82 = 13.239 and 16.726. In all three cases the god has taken the form of a mortal and departs unrecognized, suggesting human poignancy in the contrast θεὸς ἂμ πόνον ἀνδρῶν. It may also be significant that Hektor does not recognize the god here or at 591, whereas Aineias, son of a goddess and fated to survive the war, does so at 333.

83 On black φρένες see note on 1.103; S. West, *Odyssey*, on *Od.* 4.661–2; F. M. Combellack, *Grazer Beiträge* 4 (1975) 81–7.

84–6 The phrasing is unusual and effective. | πάπτηνεν δέ occurs thus 4 × *Il.*, 2 × *Od.*, and αὐτίκα ἔγνω | 3 × *Il.*, 2 × *Od.*, always at times of sudden change in the action, but this is the only time they are found in the same verse. Anaphora of τὸν μὲν... τὸν δὲ... at the beginning of the verse and the bucolic diaeresis occurs only here; ἡ μὲν...ἡ δὲ... is so found at 23.868. κείμενον often occurs in this position, and is again followed by a pause at 536 and the heavily emotional 22.43. The last phrase of 86 = 14.518.

87–9 Again the composition is partly formular, partly very unusual. Verse 87 is found 7 × *Il.* ὀξέα κεκληγώς (88) is repeated at 2.222 and 12.125 (-οντες). φλογὶ εἴκελος (-ον) occurs 3 × *Il.* in this position followed by an essential part of the sentence, much like a generic epithet such as δουρικλυτός, and 2 × after the 4th-foot caesura followed by ἀλκήν. It is not elsewhere extended by 'Ηφαίστοιο, but διὰ φλογὸς 'Ηφ. occurs 2 ×.

For 89, a repeat of 1 would have served well enough. Instead, there comes the runover ἀσβέστῳ, which is never used again like this. It causes a synecphonesis (-ῳ and οὐδ- scanned as one heavy syllable; see S. West, *Odyssey* on *Od.* 1.226), which is made especially harsh by the pause in sense. Bentley's ἀσπέτῳ is very attractive, cf. *Od.* 5.101. βοήσας | occurs 3 × *Od.* in the formula ὅσ(σ)ον τε γέγωνε βοήσας (plus ὧδε β., 1 ×), but in the *Il.* only here and at 334 (εἶπε β.). υἱὸν... 'Ατρέος is also unparalleled. The innovative language both adds splendour to Hektor (ἀσβέστῳ) and alerts Menelaos (who is stripping Euphorbos) to his presence (ὀξὺ βοήσας, repeating the formular ὀξέα κεκληγώς of 88 (3 × *Il.*)).

90–105 There are similar monologues at 11.403–10 (Odysseus), 21.550–70 (Agenor), and 22.98–130 (Hektor); see B. Fenik, *Homer: Tradition and Invention* (Leiden 1978) 68–90 and *TBS* 96–8, 163–4; S. Scully, *TAPA* 114 (1984) 11–27; and notes *ad locc*. All four begin ὤ μοι ἐγώ (91) and the pondering ends and the decision is made with ἀλλὰ τίη μοι ταῦτα φίλος διελέξετο θυμός; (97). Menelaos is the only one who decides to withdraw; in fact his decision leads up to the call for help which is a part of the recurrent pattern of this Book. In his article on the *Heldentod* in Homer R. Renehan terms this 'a striking example of truly unheroic conduct' (*CP* 82, 1987, 111).

The speech is tightly constructed, partly in ring form (cf. Lohmann, *Reden* 39 n. 64):

A   1. If I abandon the armour and Patroklos,
     2. the Greeks will resent it (91–3).
B   1. If I fight Hektor and the Trojans alone,
     2. I may be cut off by Hektor (94–6).
C   [*Decision marker*] But why do I hesitate (97)?
B′   1. If I fight Hektor, a god's favourite,
     2. I shall quickly be killed (98–9).
A′   2. So the Greeks will not resent it
     1. if I yield to Hektor (100–1).
C′   [*New thought*] If I could summon Aias (102–5)!

90–3 On the derivation of ὀχθήσας see S. Scully, *TAPA* 114 (1984) 14 n. 8. Menelaos' feeling that he will incur blame if he retreats is like that of Hektor (22.99–107) and Odysseus (11.408–10). The arms referred to are probably not Patroklos' but Euphorbos', cf. 85. Homer never makes it clear whether Menelaos managed to retain them or not (see 70–139n.). Later, the Argives had irrefutable evidence that he did: 'They say that Pythagoras, seeing a bronze shield in the Argive Heraeum, declared that he had been killed by Menelaos while bearing it, when he was Euphorbos. When the Argives turned the shield over they saw the inscription: "Euphorbos' ⟨shield⟩"' (T on 17.29–30). It was still on display in Pausanias' time (Paus. 2.17.3).

92 The line shows Menelaos' consciousness of being the cause of Patroklos' death, also suggested at 139 and perhaps at 670ff. and 689–90. The nearest parallel expression is *Od.* 16.31 σέθεν δ' ἕνεκ' ἐνθάδ' ἱκάνω, but there ἐνθάδε has none of the poignancy it has here. Verse 94 is a 'rising threefolder' (see vol. I, 18–24).

95 ἕνα and πολλοί are not so contrasted elsewhere; the latter leads on to the natural exaggeration πάντας in the next verse.

98–101 Overt divine aid to the enemy is an acceptable reason for retreat; so Nestor advises it at 8.139–44, Diomedes at 5.601–6, Agamemnon at 9.17–28 and 14.74–81 (with the epigrammatic βέλτερον ὃς φεύγων προφύγῃ κακὸν ἠὲ ἁλώῃ), and Aineias at 20.97–8. Aias' reaction is different (629–47). πῆμα is subject of κυλίνδω again at 688, 11.347, and *Od.* 2.163; the metaphor is from a breaking wave (cf. 11.307). κυλίσθη is a generalizing gnomic aorist.

100–5 ἐκ θεόφιν (also at 23.347, at the same place in the verse) was created as a metrical variant for ἐκ θεοῦ (Chantraine, *GH* I 238); otherwise θεόφιν occurs only in the old formula θ. μήστωρ ἀτάλαντος (3 × *Il.*, 2 × *Od.*). βοὴν ἀγαθοῖο (102) is used in the genitive only here, clearly as an almost meaningless epithet between the prominent Αἴαντος and πυθοίμην; cf. 13.123. ἄμφω (103) contrasts with μοῦνος ἐών (94), and καὶ πρὸς δαίμονά περ (104) echoes 98 (of course they will not really go against a god; no one does except Diomedes, under Athene's orders, in book 5). ἐπιμνησαίμεθα χάρμης: the narrative phrase μνήσαντο (λήθοντο) δὲ χάρμης occurs 7 × *Il.*, and direct-speech subjunctive or optative versions like this appear again at 15.477, 19.148, and *Od.* 22.73. On the significance see Martin, *Language* 78–80.

The final sentence (105) sums up the decision reached in the monologue; in form it resembles ἐπεὶ πολὺ φέρτερός (-όν) ἐστιν (etc., many times), but it is quite different in meaning. The thought of summoning Aias is put into effect a few lines later.

106–9 This is a good illustration of verse construction. The first two verses recur at 11.411–12 after Odysseus' monologue, but here the significant ἦρχε δ' ἄρ' Ἕκτωρ is substituted for the ornamental ἀσπιστάων (found also in the same verse at 4.221); on such variations see *TAPA* 97 (1966) 172–4. Similarly, 108 is like 11.461, but the latter has a different concluding phrase (αὖε δ' ἑταίρους); the phrase here was used between the first and second caesurae of 13. ἐντροπαλιζόμενος (109) is used (with a different second hemistich) for Aias' retreat (11.547) and (memorably) as Andromakhe returns home after her farewell to Hektor (6.496; also 21.492); ὥς τε λῖς ἠϋγένειος introduces a very different simile at 18.318.

It is clear from 113 that the corpse referred to in 108 is Patroklos'. On the derivation of λῖς see 11.239n. On ἠϋγένειος, perhaps 'long-whiskered' rather than 'heavy-maned', see 15.271–6n.

110–14 ὅς (without τε) with the subjunctive is found only here and at 16.260 (see Ruijgh, τε *épique* 871). The simile contrasts with that comparing Menelaos to the victorious lion at 61ff. A longer form of this simile is used when Menelaos retreats again at 657ff. (see note *ad loc.*) and Aias at 11.544ff. The courage and reluctance of the lion correspond to those of

Menelaos, and the 'turning back' of both (109) is picked up by μεταστρεφθείς (114); this verse recurs after the retreats of Aias (11.595) and Antilokhos (15.591).

112 παχνοῦται 'is chilled' occurs only here in Homer, but cf. πάχνη 'hoar-frost' (*Od.* 14.476) and Hesiod's ἐπάχνωσεν φίλον ἦτορ (*Erga* 360). Perhaps this, like φρεσὶ σῆσιν ἰανθῆς (19.174), is not a metaphor but a physiological phenomenon. Leaf considers the τ' 'a mere stopgap to save the hiatus', but it is best taken as the generalizing τε common in similes (Ruijgh, τε *épique* 655; Denniston, *Particles* 521).

114 = 11.595, 15.591.

115–22 This is the first of several calls for help (see introduction to this Book). Aias was last seen fighting over the body of Sarpedon (16.555ff.), and has not yet heard of Patroklos' death (cf. 123). Verses 116–17 = 682–3. Apollo (118) departed at 82 ἂμ πόνον ἀνδρῶν; he is never far away in this Book.

116–17 On the left, as seen by the Greeks; see 13.675n.

120–2 On πέπον see 13.120–3n. The heavily emphatic γυμνόν (and the rest of 122) is repeated when Menelaos dispatches Antilokhos to Akhilleus with the message (693), and again when he delivers it (18.21). This kind of exegesis of a runover word in the following part of the verse is characteristically Homeric, common from 1.2 onwards; it is also characteristic of the flexibility of Homeric verse-construction that this line fits easily after three different preceding verses.

Akhilleus too speaks of his friend's death and the loss of his armour in close juxtaposition (18.80–5). The dishonour of failing to defend a comrade is greatly increased by the loss of both his body and his armour.

123–39 The poet swiftly alternates the actions of Aias (123–4, 128) and Hektor (125–7, 129–31); then the account of the defence of the body by Aias and Menelaos (132–9) is amplified by a simile and leads up to the second rebuke to Hektor.

Menelaos had to abandon Patroklos' body at 108, so it is now in Hektor's possession. Menelaos' words (122) have reminded us that it is without armour. Then to show that the pathetic corpse is completely at Hektor's mercy the poet uses the formular ἐπεὶ κλυτὰ τεύχε' ἀπηύρα (125; cf. 11.334, and κλ. τ. δῦσαι (etc.) 3 × *Il.*). Actually helmet, spear, shield, and corslet were stripped from the *living* hero by Apollo in superb lines (16.793–804), the description of his fall was altered to fit the fall of an *unarmed* man (16.822; the regular formula is at 4.504 and 7 × *Il.*), and the dying victim protests that the gods struck off his armour (16.846). Zeus is similarly misled by the commoner situation of a warrior stripping off his victim's armour (205–6). See Combellack, *TAPA* 96 (1965) 47–50. The inconsistency is caused by use of an inappropriate type-scene element and

74

formula; there is a parallel in the heavy groaning of the dead Hupsenor (13.419–23n.). On the old scansion Αἴαντῑ (< *Aiwántei*) see M. L. West, *JHS* 108 (1988) 159. On the meaning of δαΐφρων see 5.181n.

126–7 ἕλκε is an inceptive imperfect. On the proposed mutilation see note on 38–40. The scholia remark that Hektor's intended savagery prepares for that of Akhilleus to Hektor's own corpse. The insight the narrator gives into Hektor's thoughts is noteworthy; cf. 5.845.

128–30 On the 'tower'-shield see 7.219–23n. and 11.485n. De Jong, *Narrators* 211, notes that the narrator does not tell us the reason for Hektor's retreat, whereas Glaukos explicitly attributes it to his fear of facing Aias (166–8).

131–2 Later (186ff.) Hektor decides to put on the armour instead of sending it back to Troy. On characters who make plans which the poet knows will not be fulfilled see Fenik, *Odyssey* 106ff. In 131 μέγα of course qualifies κλέος (so 3 × *Il.*, 4 × *Od.*), not ἄστυ, despite the formular ἄστυ μέγα Πριάμοιο (9 × *Il.*, 1 × *Od.*). The same syntactic flexibility occurs in προτὶ ἄστυ μέγα φρονέων (22.21). καλύπτω means 'put over as a covering', also at 5.315, 21.321, 22.313. Aias' protecting the corpse with his shield is doubtless suggested by his regular association with the tower-shield, which has just been mentioned at 128 (= 7.219, 11.485).

133–6 The introductory phrasing for this and two other lion-similes in this book shows a formular structure (in threefolder verses):

ἑστήκει ⎫		⎧ περὶ οἷσι τέκεσσιν (133)
αἱματόεις ⎬	ὥς τίς τε λέων	⎨ κατὰ ταῦρον ἐδηδώς (542)
βῆ δ' ἰέναι ⎭		⎩ ἀπὸ μεσσαύλοιο (657)

cf. | ὡς δ' ὅτε τίς τε λέων, 61 (the structure is noted by S. H. Lonsdale in *Creatures of Speech, Beiträge zur Altertumskunde* 5, 1990).

The difference between the cow lowing for its calf (Menelaos, 4–6) and the lion protecting its cubs (Aias here) is significant for the temperament of the two heroes; there is also a powerful contrast between this lion and the lion whose cubs were lost in the beast's absence, which is pathetically apt for Akhilleus (18.318–22). Zenodotus omitted these lines (which were not in the Chian text; see Apthorp, *Manuscript Evidence* 102–4, n. 11) on the grounds that male lions do not lead their cubs about; familiarity with the habits of lions had led him to alter the text elsewhere (see 13.198–200n., and cf. Pasquali, *Storia* 229). Aristarchus (Did/A) correctly understood that λέων and λίς are always grammatically masculine and sex is not involved; see Fränkel, *Gleichnisse* 92–3, on the gender of female animals. λέαινα does not occur until Aeschylus and Herodotus. τέκνα is also used for the young of sparrows (2.311), deer (11.113), wasps (12.170), and horses (19.400).

135–6 σθένεϊ βλεμεαίνει (etc.) occurs 6 × *Il.*; the verb is never found elsewhere. ἐπισκύνιον is the skin above the eyes; the word is *hapax* in Homer, and perhaps from the same root as κυνέη (< *σκυνέη, Hoekstra, *Modifications* 99. n. 4). The exegetical scholia explain that more than a frown is meant: the lion covers its eyes so as not to be frightened by the missiles hurled at it and so desert its cubs. κάτω recurs in Homer only at *Od.* 23.91, where Odysseus sits facing Penelope κάτω ὁρόων. κάλυπτον (with ἐπισκύνιον), the reading of many good MSS, is supported by R. R. Dyer in his analysis of the uses of this verb in early Greek (*Glotta* 42, 1964, 35); -ων is preferred by Aristarchus (Did/A), Eustathius, and most editors.

138–9 ἑτέρωθεν perhaps means 'back to back'. Verse 139 is another reminder of Menelaos' feeling of responsibility for Patroklos' death; the phrasing is like *Od.* 11.195 μέγα δὲ φρεσὶ πένθος ἀέξει (of Laertes' grieving for Odysseus).

140–236 Glaukos rebukes Hektor, who puts on the armour he has captured from Patroklos and urges on the Trojan allies with the hope of recovering Patroklos' corpse

140–68 Glaukos is not one of the famous heroes of the *Il.*, but he takes part in many big scenes. Introduced as a comrade of Sarpedon, from faraway Lycia, in the Trojan Catalogue (2.876–7), he enjoyed a memorable encounter with Diomedes (6.119–236) and killed a Greek at the beginning of the next book as a kind of follow-up (7.13–16); in book 12 he led a charge together with Sarpedon (102), listened to the latter's well-known disquisition on the roots of honour (309–30), and was wounded with an arrow by Teukros (387–91); he was present nevertheless at the rescue of the wounded Hektor (14.426). The dying Sarpedon appealed to him to rescue his armour, and after being healed by Apollo he rallied the Trojans, rebuked Hektor, and killed a Greek (16.492–547, 593–9). After 17.216 he is not seen again in the *Il.* He will be killed by Aias in the struggle over the corpse of Akhilleus (see 288–303n.).

C. Moulton, *Hermes* 109 (1981) 1–8, has made a careful study of this speech. Usually a rebuke includes criticism of the addressee, an account of the present problem, and a call to action. Glaukos amplifies this, going from insults to Hektor to a threat to withdraw his troops, a reproach for the abandonment of Sarpedon's body, a further threat to go home, a general criticism of the fighting spirit of the Trojans, the suggestion of exchanging Patroklos' body for Sarpedon's, and the accusation that Hektor is afraid of Aias. Fenik well remarks 'The poet is clearly allowing Glaucos to develop his thoughts as they come to him, much as Achilles does in his reply to Odysseus in the embassy' (*TBS* 121).

142 εἶδος ἄριστε: Glaukos knows how to hurt Hektor – this is the insult Hektor himself has hurled twice at Paris (3.39 = 13.769). The phrase is used elsewhere in the *Il.* only in compliment to women. Good looks are also a reproach to warriors at 5.787 = 8.228 and 2.673–5, but cf. 279. 'Falling short in the fight' is elsewhere expressed only with a negative (13.310, 23.670, 24.385). In fact Homer contrives that although Hektor's prowess is often glorified, he does not even wound any of the major Greeks. On the irresolvable synizesis in ἐδεύεο see Chantraine, *GH* 1 59–60, and Shipp, *Studies* 165; there are several such examples in the *Od.*

143 Ameis–Hentze take αὔτως as 'undeservedly' (*unverdient*), an unparalleled sense; better 'like this', with the common contemptuous connotation (cf. 450, 633), looking forward to φύξηλιν. φύξηλις occurs only here and in imitators, but the formation is normal; adjectives are often formed with -ηλος, and occasionally feminine nouns from them (see Risch, *Wortbildung* 165). The feminine gender adds to the insult (cf. 2.235, 7.96), which is repeated at 151 (κάλλιπες) and 166–8.

144–8 The complaint that the allies of the Trojans, with no families or wives to protect, bear the brunt of the fighting has been very forcefully made by Sarpedon at 5.472–87, and briefly by Glaukos himself at 16.538–40 (the position is reversed at 10.420–2).

145 οἶος is used in the same emphatic runover position near the beginning of Sarpedon's complaint to Hektor (5.474), but is there followed by σὺν γαμβροῖσι κασιγνήτοισί τε σοῖσι. Some MSS read γαμβροῖσι for λαοῖσι here, which may be a 'concordance-variant'; τοὶ Ἰλίῳ ἐγγεγάασιν ends the verse (after πᾶσι) at 6.493. Perhaps Sarpedon, more equal in rank to Hektor than Glaukos, is allowed the more personal reproach to Hektor's relatives; certainly his speech is even more vivid and passionate than that of Glaukos.

147–8 After ἐπεί the couplet recurs in Akhilleus' complaint to Odysseus (9.316–17). Both Hektor and Agamemnon have problems keeping their army in the field.

149–53 A powerful reason for the Lycians to withdraw; as the scholia (bT) point out, if Hektor will not fight to preserve Sarpedon's body for burial, what hope is there of proper treatment for the rest of them if they are killed?

In 149 the meaning needed is 'rescue from the tumult', but μεθ' ὅμιλον means '⟨go, come⟩ amongst the crowd' (cf. 14.21, 20.47). Zenodotus may have read ὁμίλου, but this could hardly give the needed meaning (the text is uncertain; see Erbse *ad loc.*). Ameis–Hentze quote 2.143, 9.54, and *Od.* 16.419 for μετά and accusative meaning 'from amongst', but the parallels are not very close. On Sarpedon see 16.419–683n.

151–2 ἑταῖρος in its wider sense refers to a hero's band of followers (117), but it can also be used for a close friend, as close as a brother (*Od.* 8.584–6); a ξεῖνος has even stronger claims (6.215ff.). See Hainsworth, *Odyssey*, on *Od.*

8.585–6; J. Pinsent, *Mélanges E. Delebecque* (Aix-en-Provence 1983) 313–18; H. J. Kakridis, *La Notion de l'amitié et de l'hospitalité chez Homère* (Thessaloniki 1963) 51–77, 87–105.

For Ἀργείοισιν a few inferior MSS read οἰωνοῖσιν, as in the similar verse *Od.* 3.271 (where Ἀργείοισιν would be impossible; cf. also *Od.* 5.473). ἀνδράσι δυσμενέεσσιν with the same following hemistich at 5.488 supports the usual reading.

153 ζωὸς ἐών is used in this emphatic runover position with three other pathetic epexegetical clauses: for Patroklos (478 = 672 = 22.436), for Protesilaos (2.699), and (with a different intonation) for Odysseus in the underworld (*Od.* 11.156).

155 ἴμεν is 1st person plural, present tense (with future sense); Aristarchus (Did/T) took it as infinitive after ἐπιπείσεται, less probably. πεφήσεται is a unique future perfect of φαίνω; a homonym from θείνω, 'strike', appears at 15.140 (-εαι at 13.829, *Od.* 22.217; Chantraine, *GH* I 448).

157–8 Verse 157 is a weighty threefolder, a powerful runover adjective followed by an epexegetical clause which is itself explained by an enjambing relative clause. In 158 a papyrus and some good MSS read δῆριν ἔχουσιν as at *Od.* 24.515 (the only other occurrence in Homeric MSS; but δῆριν θήτην is likely at 16.756, see note *ad loc.*).

160–5 This sensible plan of Glaukos' is the only Homeric instance of a proposed exchange of the bodies and armour of dead heroes; the poet is making the most of the irony that Glaukos does not know of the privileged treatment Sarpedon's corpse has actually received. Hektor's promise of spoils for anyone who can capture Patroklos' body (229–32) may be meant to indicate approval of the exchange. The importance of recovery of the corpse is intensified in the case of Patroklos and further still in that of Hektor. Sarpedon's armour was stripped off and sent back to the Greek ships just before Apollo bore his corpse away from the battle for burial (16.663–83).

161 On the spelling τεθνηώς see vol. IV, ch. 3, vi. χάρμης often has the connotation 'joy of battle', but cf. 4.509 for 'battle' alone; MSS also read χάρμη, -ῃ, even -α, but this construction is repeated at 5.456 τόνδ' ἄνδρα μάχης ἐρύσαιο.

164–5 πέφατ'(αι), 'has been killed', is from θείνω; see Chantraine, *GH* I 342 and 433. ὅς... θεράποντες was said by Patroklos in rallying the Myrmidons (16.271–2). There the meaning might be '⟨so that we may honour Akhilleus⟩... we too, his... followers'. Here καὶ ἀγχέμαχοι θεράποντες might be taken (awkwardly) as 'and his followers ⟨are⟩ hand-to-hand fighters'. It is probably best, however, to assume a zeugma and take the sense in both instances to be '⟨Akhilleus⟩ who is by far the best of the Greeks, and ⟨so are⟩ his hand-to-hand fighters'.

78

Book Seventeen

Akhilleus, though off-stage, is mentioned no less than 24 × in this book, a constantly recurring reminder of the peril in which Hektor and the Trojans now stand.

166–8 Cf. 128–30; Hektor also fears Aias at 7.216–18 and 11.542. The lines show an unconventional handling of formular expressions, and 167 is an impressive rising threefolder. στήμεναι ἄντα appears in different forms at 21.266 and 22.253; κατ' ὄσσε ἰδών is a unique and vivid expansion of ἄντι (the simple ἄντα ἰδών occurs 7 × Il., extended to ἐσάντα ἰδών 1 × Il., 3 × Od.); δηΐων ἐν αὐτῇ is unique. In 168, ἰθύς is only here used with μαχέσασθαι (without some verb of movement), and the usual πολὺ φέρτερός ἐστιν is altered to a more personal σέο φέρτερος, recurring only at 16.722 (where it is complimentary).

169–82 Hektor does not answer the earlier rebukes of Sarpedon (5.493) or Glaukos (16.548). His assertion of his prowess here is rather like his response to Aias' challenge (7.237–41), and his reference to Zeus's overwhelming power reminds one of Menelaos' words a little earlier (98–9). There are other angry replies to the accusation of hanging back in the *epipolesis* (Odysseus, 4.350–5; Sthenelos, 4.404–10).

170–2 τί ἢ δέ is sometimes written τίη δέ; cf. 6.55. ὑπέροπλον occurs in Homer only here and in Poseidon's complaint about Zeus's high-handed orders (15.185; 4 × in Hesiod, and cf. ἧς ὑπεροπλίῃσι, 1.205). Zenodotus' ὦ πέπον in 171 (Did/AT; not in most of the older MSS) is accepted by Leaf, but perhaps weakens 179; πόποι does not always have to begin a speech (cf. 13.99–101n., 14.49, Od. 13.209). Both Chantraine, *GH* II 344–5, and Denniston, *Particles* 532, see difficulties in ἤ τε (171), but the sense must be 'and yet', as at 236 and 18.13. Verse 171 ≅ 13.631 (which begins Ζεῦ πάτερ), where the angry Menelaos questions Zeus's incomprehensible support of the Trojans.

173–4 Verse 173 = 14.95. In 174, τε after ὅς is irregular, since the statement is not generic, and is probably added for the metre or to match ἦ τ' ἐφάμην in 171 (so Ruijgh, τε *épique* 407). πελώριον in 174 and 360 is as usual much more than merely ornamental; there are other powerful examples of its force at 18.83, 21.527 and 22.92 (see *TAPA* 97, 1966, 166). 'The adjective seems to denote not objective measuring of size but rather the subjective impressions and emotions of someone who is scared by the enormity of what he perceives' (de Jong, *Narrators* 130).

176–8 The verses recur at 16.688–90 in the poet's own voice, amplifying a typical νήπιος-comment. Though effective in both places, they fit the context best in 16, where 691 applies the aphorism to Patroklos' battle-fury, and Ruijgh, τε *épique* 836–7, argues cogently on linguistic grounds that the verses here are adapted from 16. Probably the poet intended the ironic parallel, that these solemn verses, which introduce the battle-frenzy by

79

which the gods doom Patroklos (Πατρόκλεις, ὅτε δή σε θεοὶ θάνατόνδε κάλεσσαν, 16.693), are repeated by Hektor just before he arrogantly dons the armour of Akhilleus and calls up the gloomy prognostications of Zeus (201–8). The desire for the parallel may account for the very rare utterance of an aphorism (176) by the narrator himself (see 30–2n.).

MSS at 16.688, and many MSS here, substitute the much more effective ἠέ περ ἀνδρός (less frequently -ῶν) for αἰγιόχοιο, and a papyrus and some good MSS omit 16.689–90. Van der Valk, *Researches* II 27–8, thinks that Aristarchus made the change to αἰγιόχοιο here to clarify the reference of ὅς in 177. ἀφείλετο (177) is a gnomic aorist coupled with the present φοβεῖ, as at 4.161. The power of Zeus over men is celebrated more fully in Hesiod, *Erga* 3–8; see also 20.242–3n.

179 This verse, so appropriate here, is also used by the disguised Athene to Odysseus (*Od.* 22.233; cf. also *Il.* 11.314).

183–7 It is a normal pattern for a hero to deliver a short speech of encouragement (*parainesis*) before he leaves the fighting line; Hektor does so when he returns to Troy (6.110–15), and Agamemnon and Eurupulos when they are wounded (11.275–9, 585–90). Verse 184 occurs 6× *Il.*, but perhaps the inclusion of the Lycians has special point here. Verse 185 is also common (7× *Il.*).

Homer does not tell us Hektor's motive for donning Akhilleus' armour; it might sound implausible after his boasting at 179–82. The exegetical scholia suggest he wished to protect himself, to encourage the Trojans, and to frighten the Greeks. Reinhardt, *IuD* 336–8, thinks it is Hektor's answer to Glaukos' rebuke. The *poet's* motives become clear later; see 194–209n., and the introduction to book 18.

187 The line is significantly repeated (with ἐνάριξε) at 22.323, when Akhilleus is about to deliver the blow which kills Hektor despite his divinely made armour. Both τά and βίην are accus. after ἐνάριξα; on βίην see 24n.

192–212 This is Hektor's only arming-scene, very different from those of Paris, Agamemnon, Patroklos, and Akhilleus in content, tone, and position in his *aristeia*. It is expanded, to give the proper emphasis, not by description of his actions or of the armour itself, but by the narrator's reflections on the significance of the armour and Zeus's on Hektor's presumption in donning it. See Introduction, ch. 2, i.

192 Both πολυδακρύου and -δακρύτου appear in good MSS. The latter is metrically impossible, as elsewhere the scansion is πολυδακρῦτου (1× *Il.*, 3× *Od.*). -δακρύου is acceptable on the analogy of the thematic nom. sing. δάκρυον, back-formed from the pl. δάκρυα (cf. Chantraine, *GH* I 222; Risch, *Wortbildung* 13). The regular formation πολυδάκρυος (Bentley; cf. nom. -υς, 544) is preferred by Leaf and van Leeuwen.

194–209 The immense distinction of the armour is stressed by the poet as Hektor puts it on; then his presumption is further amplified by the words of Zeus which follow. Probably only sons of divinities like Akhilleus and Memnon, and perhaps marriage-connexions like Peleus (but see 18.84–5n.), may properly wear armour made by Hephaistos; cf. Apollo's stripping of the armour from Patroklos (16.793–804), and his warning to Hektor at 76–8. Hektor's lack of a divine parent was remarked upon by Agamemnon (10.50) and will later be stressed by Here (24.58), and the armour was not a gift of the gods to *him*. Cf. also 205–6n., and 10.439–41, where the golden armour of Rhesos 'is not fitting for mortal men to wear, but for gods'. Virgil noted the passage: *maestissimus Hector | ... quantum mutatus ab illo | Hectore, qui redit exuvias indutus Achilli* (*Aeneid* 2.270–5).

Griffin, *CQ* 26 (1976) 178, points out that Zeus's speech (201–8) 'combines the motifs of "short life", "pathetic ignorance", and "no return home"'. There is also an implied rebuke for Hektor's arrogance in symbolically proclaiming himself the equal of Akhilleus; διδάσκει Ὅμηρος καθ' αὑτὸν ἕκαστον φρονεῖν, say the A scholia (on 201). In his own voice, the poet ascribed similar ominous thoughts to Zeus when he supported Hektor's attack on the ships (15.610–14); the bT scholia say he puts them into Zeus's own mouth here to make them more convincing. Before Patroklos' death Zeus pondered in a similar fashion, and allowed him too further glory before his end came (16.644–56). Zeus's pity here, a consistent character trait, is like that which he feels earlier for Hektor (15.12ff.) and for Sarpedon (16.431ff.), and later for the grieving horses (17.441ff.), Aias (17.648ff.), the grieving Akhilleus (19.340ff.), and the fleeing Hektor (22.168ff.).

Gifts of the gods such as Peleus' horses (16.381 = 867) and Penelope's cosmetics (*Od.* 18.191) are ἄμβροτα; but 194 and 202 are the only places where the phrase ἄμβροτα τεύχεα occurs, and it seems possible that an ironic contrast is intended between the immortal gifts and their failure to save the lives of Patroklos, Hektor, and Akhilleus himself. See introduction to book 18.

When he called for fire to burn the Greek ships Hektor gloried in the knowledge of Zeus's support (15.719–25). In this Book and the next that support is gradually withdrawn, and Hektor appears increasingly over-confident; see 18.284–309n.

195–6 οἱ is ethic dative of the pronoun, the equivalent of 'his...father'; cf. 4.219. In 196 the scansion reflects ἄρα (σϝ)ῷ (Chantraine, *GH* 1 146).

197 Chantraine, *GH* 1 380, thinks γήρας is aorist (< *γηράσας), Leaf less probably takes it as present (< *γήρημι). Note the word-play with ἐγήρα at the end of the line; Macleod, *Iliad XXIV* 50–3, has other examples. Of course the reference is not to the loss of the armour to Hektor (it is explicitly recovered after Hektor's death, 22.376), but to the pathos of Akhilleus' short life, contrasted with that of his father (so the AT scholia; see also 404–11n., and Griffin, *CQ* 26, 1976, 176). On the origin of this panoply see 18.84–5n.

199–201 θείοιο is for original θεῖοιο; see Hainsworth, *Odyssey* on *Od.* 5.11. Only gods ponder κινήσας ῥα (δὲ) κάρη: Zeus here and 442, Poseidon at *Od.* 5.285 and 376. In 201, ἇ δείλ᾽ expresses strong sympathy, as at 443, 11.816, and 24.518; sometimes there is a sarcastic tone (11.441, 452, 16.837). The Odyssean usage is similar. The rest of this verse is repeated for Odysseus' misleading reassurance to the Trojan spy Dolon (10.383).

202–4 MSS of the *h* family read ὡς...εἶσι, Aristarchus ὅς...εἶσι (Did/A). The rather less effective ὅς...ἐστί is supported by the parallel at *Od.* 2.284 (where Nauck read ὡς for MSS ὅς). καὶ ἄλλοι (203) is emphatic, distinguishing Hektor from '⟨all⟩ others' (cf. 18.106, *Od.* 21.152), not 'others ⟨as well as you⟩'. Verse 204 is repeated to Akhilleus in Lukaon's vain plea for mercy (21.96); on ἐνήης for Patroklos see 670–3n.

205–6 On the inconsistency over who stripped the armour from Patroklos see 123–39n. οὐ κατὰ κόσμον (4× *Il.*, 4× *Od.*) occurs in diverse contexts with the basic meaning 'improperly'. Normally there is nothing wrong in stripping the armour from a dead enemy, though Akhilleus did not do so when he killed Andromakhe's father Eëtion (σεβάσσετο γὰρ τό γε θυμῷ, 6.417), but Zeus considers Hektor's donning of armour presented by the gods to be presumptuous, just as he later refuses to let him capture the immortal horses (448–50; see 194–209n.). Verse 203 also suggests Hektor is paying too little regard to the might of Akhilleus. Van Leeuwen takes οὐ with εἵλευ and thinks the impropriety lay in Hektor's not actually stripping the armour from the corpse himself, but this is an impossible violation of formular style; there is more merit to the objection in the A scholia, that Hektor carried off the armour though he did not kill Patroklos himself.

On the formular ἀπὸ κρατός τε καὶ ὤμων see 5.7n. Hoekstra, *Epic Verse* 22, found 205–6 'incompatible with oral verse-making' on grounds of complexity of expression and syntax.

207–8 τῶν ποινὴν ὅ means literally 'a compensation for these things, that...', cf. 8.362. μάχης ἐκ νοστήσαντι | occurs again in the context of Hektor's death at 22.444 and 24.705. On Andromakhe and Hektor see 22.437–515n. 'Even if a hearer were inclined to be angry with Hektor for putting on Akhilleus' armour, when he learnt it would not be for long, he might even have pitied him' (AbT).

209 = 1.528; see note *ad loc.* The bT scholia here say that Zeus's nod, ratifying mighty suffering, τραγῳδίαν ἔχει.

210–12 There is an even more vivid description of the inspiring effect of donning divinely made armour at 19.384–6 (by Akhilleus). On the purely human level, the vital importance of a good fit of heavy bronze armour is stressed by V. D. Hanson, *The Western Way of War* (New York 1989) 76–83. δύω in this sense also occurs at 9.239 with Lussa as subject. ἐπικούρους emphasizes it is the Trojan allies who are important here.

213–14 Another grim reminder of Akhilleus. ϝιϝάχων is preceded by a lengthened vowel, as often with its cognates (Chantraine, *GH* I 139–40). ἰνδάλλετο δέ σφισι πᾶσιν means 'he appeared before them all'. Aristarchus (Nic/A) read μεγαθύμῳ Πηλείωνι, '⟨he resembled⟩ Akhilleus', but this meaning of ἰνδάλλομαι is not found elsewhere in Homer and strains both word-order and sense. If the genitive is right, Πηληϊάδεω 'Αχιλῆος (6 × *Il.*, 2 × *Od.*) would be expected. Though μεγάθυμος is generic, its relative unfamiliarity in these circumstances may give it more weight here and in the other two occurrences of this phrase (18.226, 19.75). On the whole question of development in formular usages see J. B. Hainsworth in *Homer: Tradition and Invention*, ed. B. C. Fenik (Leiden 1978) 41–50. τεύχεσι λαμπόμενος is reserved by Homer for those in golden Hephaistos-made armour (also at 18.510, 20.46).

215–18 A catalogue of Trojan leaders also follows a rebuke to Hektor and precedes their charge at 13.790–4 (expanded by Hektor's previous failure to find them and his interview with Paris) and at 12.88–104 (expanded by personal details); see Fenik, *TBS* 154–5 and 167. Here the catalogue is more succinct, but a *parainesis* follows it immediately; this is lacking in the other instances. In his study of Homeric catalogues, *HSCP* 68 (1964) 363–4, C. R. Beye points out that four of the ten names, an unusually high proportion, occur in the Trojan Catalogue in book 2; this is of course because it is the allies who have come to help the Trojans who are of prime importance in this context.

Mesthles the Maeonian appears only in the Trojan Catalogue (2.864). *Hippothoös the Pelasgian* (2.840) and *Phorkus the Phrygian* (2.862) will be killed by Aias later in this Book (288–318). *Ennomos the Mysian* is a seer who failed to foresee his own death in the river (2.858–61), which is not actually mentioned in book 21; another Ennomos (presumably) was killed by Odysseus at 11.422. *Asteropaios the Paeonian* arrived at Troy only some ten days before this (21.155–6), too late perhaps to get into the Catalogue except in Euripides' recension (2.848a), but he is chosen by Sarpedon, along with *Glaukos the Lycian*, as the bravest after himself (12.101–4); he dies after managing to wound Akhilleus (see 21.139–204n.), and his corslet and sword become prizes at the funeral games (23.560, 23.808). *Khromios* (494, 534) must be the same as *Khromis the Mysian* (von Kamptz, *Personennamen* 113–14), associated with Ennomos (2.858); the name ('Thunderer') is common. *Thersilokhos the Paeonian* will be killed in the river (21.209). *Medon* and *Deisenor* are otherwise unknown.

219–32 The speech-introduction (219) is omitted by two papyri and many good MSS (see Apthorp, *Manuscript Evidence* 150), but elegantly picks up 215 after the name-list; if an addition, a good one. A *parainesis* before an attack is common enough (e.g. Hektor's at 8.173–83), but some have felt that Hektor's words to his allies are surprisingly rough in tone ('These are harsh words' (Fenik, *TBS* 171); '[eine] heftige Scheltrede' (Ameis–Hentze *ad loc.*); 'an extraordinary statement' (D. B. Claus, *TAPA* 105, 1975, 20–1)). The scholia compare the 'un-Greek character' (βάρβαρον ἦθος) of the speech very unfavourably with that of Menelaos at 248–55. Perhaps, as Fenik suggests, ill-feeling between the Trojans and their allies played a part in tales of the war which were not elaborated in the *Il.*; they may be hinted at in the complaints of Sarpedon (5.472–92) and Glaukos (16.538–47, 17.142–68). The diversity of nations on the Trojan side is twice stressed by mention of the different languages they speak (2.803–4n., 4.437–8n.) and by the cacophony of their voices, compared with the silence of the Greeks (3.2–7, 4.429–36). However, Hektor's words are a necessary response to Glaukos' threat to withdraw his men, and their harshness must not be overstated; they can be paraphrased 'I brought you here not as a great mob of nobodies, but as fighting men. I pay you and feed you well. Now go in and fight!' This is not insult or ingratitude, but the goading any officer or sports coach occasionally gives.

The speech is arranged in three sections, each four lines long and each containing balancing declarations: 'Not so that *x*, but so that *y*' (221–4); 'I do *x*, therefore you should do *y*' (225–8); 'If anyone shall do *x*, I will do *y*' (229–32). There is some innovative use of formular expressions. In 220, μυρία φῦλα is not found elsewhere, and περικτιόνων occurs only 1 × *Od.* (and 1 × *HyAp*) with ἀνθρώπων; occurrences of περικτιόνεσσιν are clustered at 18.212, 19.104, 19.109. Verse 221 is like οὔ τι γάμου τόσσον κεχρημένος οὐδὲ χατίζων (*Od.* 22.50); διζήμενος occurs 5 × *Il.*, 6 × *Od.* in this position, but not elsewhere with χατίζων. Τρώων ἀλόχους καὶ νήπια τέκνα (223) is otherwise clustered 3 × in the same verse in book 6 (after ἄστυ τε καί); νήπια τέκνα | is common (11 × *Il.*, 3 × *Od.*). φιλοπτολέμων ὑπ' Ἀχαιῶν (224) occurs only here; it may be the regular alternative after a final vowel for ἀρηϊφίλων ὑπ' Ἀχαιῶν (4 × *Il.*, also 3 × with metrically identical participles). Elsewhere the epithet is generic, used in the dat. pl. to follow Τρωσί at the beginning of the verse (3 × *Il.*) or a variety of nouns after the mid-verse caesura (6 × *Il.*). It retains some force here. There is a unique expression in 228 (see note), and a careful anaphora of ἥμισυ in 231.

221 γάρ looks forward to τῷ at 227. διζήμενος and χατίζων go closely together. C. Moulton, *Hermes* 109 (1981) 6 n. 12, suggests as a possible translation 'I have not gathered each of you because I *needed*, and went searching for, a crowd (of allies)' (his italics), but the frequency of virtual synonyms in formular expressions ending the verse makes it unlikely that any real difference was intended in the meaning of the two participles; see K. O'Nolan, *CQ* 28 (1978) 23–37.

223–6 We are often reminded that the Trojans are fighting for their wives and children, e.g. at 8.57, 15.497, 21.587; this is of course dramatized in Hektor's parting from his wife and son in book 6. The impoverishment of Troy owing to the war is described in more detail at 18.288–92 (cf. 9.401–3). λαούς, 'my own people' (226), is placed in emphatic juxtaposition to ὑμέτερου.

227–8 This is said in many different ways in the *Il.*, most eloquently by Sarpedon (12.310–28); the wording is close to 15.502–3. For the sexual metaphor in πολέμου ὀαριστύς, 'the embrace of war' (< ὄαρ, 'wife'; the phrase does not recur), see 13.290–1n., 22.127n. Oaristus is personified on Aphrodite's girdle with Philotes and Himeros (14.216).

229–32 The offer to share the spoils with whoever recovers Patroklos' body presumably results from Glaukos' suggestion that it be exchanged for Sarpedon's (160–3); it leads to increased Trojan eagerness (286–7, 291). Special rewards for exceptional achievement in the war are mentioned also in the offers for volunteer Greek and Trojan scouts (10.211–17, 302–12), to Teukros, for killing eight Trojans in three lines (8.286–91), and in Akhilleus' taunt to Aineias (20.184–6). Note the chiasmus in 230, and the balanced phrasing of 231–2. τῷ before ἐνάρων in 231 is due to Aristarchus (Did/A) and doubtless right. Some good MSS have τῶν, to avoid the hiatus. εἴξη is constructed as if ὅς δέ κε had been εἴ κέ τις.

236 The poet's comment both concludes these actions among the Trojans and returns us to Aias and Menelaos, still (since 137–9) fighting back-to-back over Patroklos' body (ἐπ' αὐτῷ). The scholia (bT) note the foreshadowing (προαναφώνησις) of Aias' victories, *sc.* at 278ff. πολέσσιν (3 × *Il.*) is an artificial form developed to increase the flexibility of formular expressions beginning with πολέεσσι(ν) (Hoekstra, *Modifications* 117–19). On ἤ τε see 170–2n.

237–318 At Aias' suggestion Menelaos again calls for help, and the Greeks rally. Zeus shrouds the scene in a mist. After a brief Trojan success Aias again overpowers them

This is the second of the three calls for help in this Book (see introductory note). Aias Oïliades, Idomeneus, Meriones, and others respond.

237–9 εἶπε occurs several times with accusative, usually in recurrent verses (237 = 651; 12.60 = 210 ≅ 13.725; 17.334, 20.375, *Od.* 23.91, and perhaps *Il.* 23.155, where most MSS have a dative). Perhaps the use with accus. is influenced by that of προσέειπε. The reiterated ὦ appears in the same phrase at 6.55, followed by a different enjambing sentence; here the generic epithet διοτρεφές fills the space before the emphatic οὐκέτι νῶϊ | ..., similarly used at 8.352. αὐτώ περ, '⟨not⟩ even we ourselves ⟨shall return⟩', i.e. even without Patroklos' body (so Ameis–Hentze, Willcock, and E. J. Bakker in his detailed study of περ, *Linguistics and Formulas in Homer*, Amsterdam 1988, 99); Leaf prefers to understand 'we alone ⟨without help⟩', which suits the context less well.

240–4 Aristarchus (Arn/A) wondered whether Πατρόκλοιο is dependent on νέκυος or in apposition to it; 24.108 Ἔκτορος ἀμφὶ νέκυι suggests the former, but the latter would be more in accordance with Homer's way of referring to a dead man by his name (e.g. at 255). περιδείδια has a genitive in 240 and 10.93, a dative in 242 and usually. Ameis–Hentze say the first is a causal genitive, the second *dat. commodi*, but there seems to be little if any difference; the meaning of τῷ ῥα περίδεισαν (11.508) seems indistinguishable from that of 240. περι- is intensive.

Verse 241 is similar to 8.379 and 13.831, which are both amplified by the following verse δημῷ καὶ σάρκεσσι πεσὼν ἐπὶ νηυσὶν Ἀχαιῶν. κορέει is the correct form of the future tense (Chantraine, *GH* 1 449); some inferior MSS have κορέσῃ (aorist subjunctive), which would better express the sense of the paraphrase given below. Despite the truce for burials (7.421–32), it is often asserted that those whose bodies are not recovered will be preyed upon by dogs and birds; cf. 1.4–5, and Macleod, *Iliad XXIV* 16 n. 4. κεφαλή frequently means 'life', 'person'; cf. 18.82, 18.114, and 16.74–7n.

Greeks are occasionally said to feel fear in the face of a Trojan charge (Sthenelos 5.241–50, Diomedes 11.345–8, Menestheus 12.331–50), but Aias' outspoken concern here is unparalleled. Probably the thought is not 'I do not fear the dishonouring of P.'s body as much as I fear the danger of losing my own life', as if he were balancing one calamity against the other; this seems unworthy of Aias. His words clearly amplify αὐτώ περ (239, see 237–9n.), and the sense is that he fears not just that the body will be lost, but that their lives will be lost into the bargain: 'It is not ⟨just⟩ that I fear so much (οὔ τι τόσον περιδείδια) for the body of Patroklos, that it may soon glut the dogs and birds of Troy, as that (ὅσσον) I fear ⟨in addition⟩ that you and I shall lose our lives.' Fenik, *TBS* 172, acutely points out that the phrasing of 240–4 is like that of Hector's words to Andromakhe at 6.450–5. Here too the meaning is not '*x* or *y*' but '*x* or (*x*+*y*)'; 'It is *not only* ⟨the sufferings of other Trojans⟩ that concern me,...but *much more* yours...'

243–4 Possibly the νέφος is an 'anticipatory echo' of the mist (ἠήρ) which is often mentioned later in this book (268–70, 366–9, 643–7). The 'cloud of war' only occurs here, but there is a 'cloud' of foot-soldiers at 4.274 and 23.133 (cf. also 17.755), which probably underlies the meaning here, as the T scholia suggest (ὅ ἐστι τὸ πλῆθος). C. Moulton, however, in his study of Homeric metaphor, links it with θανάτου...νέφος (16.350): 'The cloud of death is virtually interchangeable with the cloud of war' (*CP* 74, 1979, 290). A 'cloud' of grief is found at 591 = 18.22.

Leaf and van Leeuwen reject 244 as originating in a marginal gloss Ἕκτωρ plus a version of 11.174, but it was read by the scholiasts and should be kept. Ἕκτωρ is best taken in apposition to νέφος (cf. 11.347, and Pindar, *Nem.* 10.9 μάντιν Οἰκλείδαν, πολέμοιο νέφος; both quoted by Leaf), rather than as subject of καλύπτει with νέφος as object; see R. R. Dyer's study in *Glotta* 42 (1964) 29–38. Fränkel, *Gleichnisse* 24, and van der Valk, *Researches* II 429–30, retain the line, for different reasons.

247–51 The line introducing Menelaos' call for help (247) occurs 6 × *Il.* (including 2 × with Τρώεσσι) when a hero has a special need of assistance. Menelaos' use of his own name in 249 is natural, but of course the line is formular (4 × *Il.* in the dative, with various introductory words). The third person verbs in 250 after the vocative seem harsh, but there are parallels at 5.877–8, 6.159–60, and *Od.* 9.275–6.

Agamemnon pointedly reminds Odysseus and Menestheus that the Greek chiefs feast at public expense (4.343–6; cf. 9.70–3, and O. Murray in Hägg, *Greek Renaissance* 195–9). Here, however, the principal idea is to remind the leaders of their privileges and consequent obligations, as in Sarpedon's famous exhortation to Glaukos (12.310–28; see W. G. Thalmann, *TAPA* 118, 1988, 6). Menelaos' words correspond to Hektor's (220–6), but he is much more courteous.

252–5 At 12.337–41 the poet describes how Menestheus needs reinforcements but cannot make himself heard above the din. Teukros and Akhilleus use ἀργαλέον δέ... like this at the beginning of a line (12.410 = 20.356), and the poet himself uses it to express his despair at attempting to describe the battle at the gates of the Greek camp (12.176). Perhaps this association inspires the poet's apostrophe to his audience a few lines later (260–1). τις (254) is used as in Hektor's *parainesis* (227); αὐτός = 'without being named'. Verses 254b–5 are expanded at 18.178–80. μέλπηθρα, 'a thing to give joy and entertainment', is also found in a similar context at 13.233; on the form, Risch, *Wortbildung* 43.

256–9 The list of names as the battle is renewed is like that of the Trojans given at 215–18 above; all of these will appear later in this Book. Aias Oïliades was last seen being exhorted by Patroklos, together with his namesake (16.555); Idomeneus has come from killing a Trojan at 16.342–51, Meriones from an encounter with Aineias and a lecture from Patroklos at 16.603–31. ὀξὺ ἄκουσε occurs only here, but ὀξὺ νόησε is common. On ὀπάων see 7.165n. and P. A. L. Greenhalgh, *BICS* 29 (1982) 84–6. The old formula ἀτάλαντος Ἐνυαλίῳ ἀνδρείφοντῃ occurs only for Meriones (4 × *Il.*), always following 258 (3 ×) or its equivalent (2.650). Ruijgh, *Linear B 1984* 157–8, 162–3, carries the formula back to Mycenaean

Μηριόνᾱς ͱατάλαντος 'Ενῡαλίῳ ἀνγχʷόντᾳ (so too M. L. West, *JHS* 108, 1988, 158). ἀτάλαντος = 'of equal weight', from α copulative (< *sm̥) + *talanta*.

260–1 This is *aporia*, the 'inexpressibility topos', or 'emphasis upon inability to cope with the subject' (E. R. Curtius, *European Literature and the Latin Middle Ages*, tr. W. R. Trask, Princeton 1973, 159). Here the rhetorical question serves to break off the enumeration of the list of heroes; cf. *Od.* 3.113–14, and de Jong, *Narrators* 47–9. The idea recurs at 12.176; at 2.484–93 an expanded version explains that only the Muses' help makes the proposed feat possible. See Introduction, ch. 1, i.

Zenodotus (Arn/A) omitted the couplet, and Leaf approved because no extraordinarily large numbers are involved; Bolling agreed (*Athetized Lines* 156). But these verses, together with the following simile and the thoughts of Zeus, form part of the expansion the poet is giving to the conflict in preparation for the Trojan defeat and Apollo's rebuke to Hektor (319ff.). The paragraph division editors mark after 262 is erroneous.

Several vase-paintings (the earliest of about 540) showing groups of warriors fighting over a naked corpse are identified with this scene by name-inscriptions for Aias (sometimes distinguished by the archaic 'Boeotian' shield), Hektor, and Patroklos. See Friis Johansen, *Iliad* 191–200, and Fittschen, *Sagendarstellung* 173–4.

262–87 A longish passage of general description, such as this, often opens a new phase in the battle before individual duels begin (see Fenik, *TBS* 79). Here a short account of Trojan attack and the Greek defence (262–73) is followed by a temporary Trojan success (274–7), after which a longer Greek rally under the magnificent Aias prepares for the individual conflicts (288–318), the Trojan repulse, and the third rebuke (319ff.).

263–6 A simile famous in antiquity for its sound-effects: 'He has compared the noise not only to the flowing of a river or to the sea surf, but he has combined them both. And one can see the great surf of the sea hurled against the current of the river, and roaring as it is beaten back, and the beaches on either side of the river resounding, which he has imitated by the diectasis of βοόωσιν' (bT). The scholia also draw attention to the sound of βέβρυχεν, ἐρευγομένης, and ἔξω. This simile caused both Plato and Solon, they report, to burn their own poetry in despair. Aristotle remarked how different the effect would be with ἠϊόνες κράζουσιν (*Poetics* 1458b31). Robert Wood, *Essay on the Original Genius of Homer* (Dublin 1776) 100–1, reports that the scene described closely resembles his own terrifying experience approaching the mouth of the Nile from the sea.

The ostensible point of comparison is of course between the clash of the two armies and that of surf and river, but as often it is the noise, introduced in the course of the simile (βοόωσιν), which is carried back to the narrative (τόσση ... ἰαχῇ); see Introduction, ch. 3, ii. The simile also anticipates the

Greeks' resistance. The clashing of the two armies is compared to the meeting of two torrential rivers at 4.452–6 (on which the scholia also have good comments); there is a similar picture at 747–51 below. διπετέος = 'falling from Zeus', or possibly 'swift' (if from the same root as διερός), on the meaning and spelling see 16.173–5; J. T. Hooker, *IF* 84 (1979) 115–17; R. Renehan, *Glotta* 50 (1972) 44; and van der Valk, *Researches* 1 256–8.

264–5 The *h* family of MSS read βεβρύχει (Aristophanes -η (Did/AT)). On the unusual enjambment of the adjective and noun ἄκραι | ἠιόνες see *TAPA* 97 (1966) 128. Leaf, with a few late MSS and Eustathius, avoids it by reading ἠιόνος. Note the personification in βοόωσιν.

266–8 The united spirit of the Greeks is stressed at greater length at 354–65. On this close-order formation see 13.126–35n. The metaphor in φραχθέντες (268) is from building a fence (cf. *Od.* 5.256); the verb is also used like this at 12.263, 13.130, and 15.566.

268–73 Mist or darkness is often spread over the battlefield (5.506ff., 15.668ff., 16.567ff., 21.6ff.), especially following a Trojan charge in this 'rebuke' pattern (Fenik, *TBS* 52–3, 206), but only in this Book is a full account given of its appearance, its continuation (366–76), and its dispersal (643–50); see 5.127–30n., and J. T. Kakridis, *Homer Revisited* (Lund 1971) 89–103. Kakridis well points out that Zeus does not necessarily intend the mist to assist the Greeks – he does that by encouraging them as well (καί, 273) – but to show his grief and respect for the dead man in the same way that he did for Sarpedon (16.567–8); the scholia agree ('He clearly does this in honour of Patroklos' AbT). The idea of a 'mist' must have arisen from the clouds of dust stirred up during an actual battle; cf. V. D. Hanson, *The Western Way of War* (New York 1989) 147–8, quoting Herodotus 8.65 etc.

The gods are much concerned with proper burial, especially of their favourites: Sarpedon (16.666–83), Hektor (24.35–8), even Niobe's children (24.612). Zeus's affection for Patroklos was also shown at 204. The passage increases the pathos of Patroklos' death, and again brings in the name of the still unaware Akhilleus.

272–7 This is the only occurrence of μισέειν in Homer; the accus. + infin. construction follows that of στυγέειν. Verse 274 recurs at 16.569, at the same point in an identical pattern of action (Fenik, *TBS* 173). The Greeks must yield, to allow for the resurgence of Aias; but none of them are killed, because Greeks cannot be treated as nonentities and an account of their deaths would interrupt the general description of the action. ἐρύοντο (conative) foreshadows the fuller account of the attempt to drag off the body (288–303).

276–8 Τρῶες ὑπέρθυμοι is formular (6 × *Il.*), but the epithet is meaningful here ('proudly victorious', 'on fire'); so at 9.233, 11.564 (nominative), and

Book Seventeen

14.15 (accusative) when the Trojans have the upper hand, and at 6.111 and 20.366 (vocative) where Hektor is encouraging them when they are in trouble. καί (277) is best taken as '⟨the Greeks⟩ in their turn', though the position of τοῦ is awkward. δὲ καί here almost = δ' αὖ (cf. Denniston, *Particles* 305 §7.ii). Van Leeuwen suggests μίνυνθα δὲ καί = οὐδὲ δηρόν. ἐλέλιξεν (278) was probably originally ἐϝέλιξεν from ἐλίσσω; see Chantraine, *GH* 1 132. The verb is neatly repeated for the boar of the following simile (283).

279–80 The lines are poignantly repeated when Odysseus sees Aias' shade in the Underworld (*Od.* 11.550–1); the same idea is expressed at 2.768–9, 13.321–5, *Od.* 11.469–70 = 24.17–18. περὶ μὲν..., περὶ δὲ... are also used in antithesis at 1.258, 21.214, and *Od.* 1.66; for the sake of the balanced phrasing the digamma before the formular ἔργα τέτυκτο (elsewhere 2 × *Il.*, 1 × *Od.*) is ignored.

281–3 The first part of the verse leads into a different simile (ἴρηκι ἐοικώς) at 16.582; the second part is found without the enjambing expansion at 4.253. The picture recurs at 11.324–5. On συῖ... | καπρίῳ see 21–2n. Aias charges like the boar; then the boar's rout of dogs and men is carried back to the narrative as Aias routs the Trojans (ἐκέδασσε 283, 285). On a boar's habit of turning at bay (ἐλιξάμενος, 283) see 725–34n.

285–7 ῥεῖα goes with ἐκέδασσε, as in 283. μετεισάμενος, 'hastening towards', is an aorist from the root (ϝ)ίεμαι (Chantraine, *GH* 1 412). On the forms of (ϝ)ερύω see Fernández-Galiano and Heubeck, *Odissea*, on *Od.* 22.373. The narrator occasionally tells us the thoughts of the common man; cf. 395–7, 15.699–702, and de Jong, *Narrators* 113–14.

288–303 The attempt to drag off Patroklos' corpse was anticipated at 277, and prefigures Akhilleus' dragging of the dead Hektor (22.395–404, 24.14–18). These are the only cases in the *Il.* in which a strap is tied to the dead man's leg; cf. 126–7n. The action may also reflect a tale of the death of Akhilleus himself, since on a Chalcidian amphora Glaukos is shown trying to drag off Akhilleus' corpse with a strap (Schadewaldt, *VHWW* 161 and pl. 26); he too was killed by Aias (Apollodorus, *Epitome* 5.3). See Fenik, *TBS* 233.

Hippothoös led the Pelasgians in the Trojan catalogue (2.840–3) and came on the scene at 217. On the typical pattern of the action of 288–318 (A kills B; C aims a spear at A; he misses and hits D; A ignores C and kills E) see Fenik, *TBS* 174. The sentence structure and word-order of the passage are sensitively analysed by G. S. Kirk, *Homer and the Oral Tradition* (Cambridge 1976) 79–81.

290–2 Inferior MSS have τένοντε. Tendons are usually plural unless ἄμφω, ἀμφοτέρω suggest the dual. χαριζόμενος may have special reference to Hektor's offer, 229–32; but this and the following verse recur at the killing of Pouludamas' charioteer (15.449–51, see note *ad loc.*). In both passages

90

ἱεμένων περ is read by the better MSS; Aristarchus read it here (Did/T), but at 15.450 (which he athetized) he allowed ἱεμένῳ περ as an alternative. The easier ἱέμενος περ appears in a few inferior MSS. E. J. Bakker in his study of περ (*Linguistics and Formulas in Homer*, Amsterdam 1988, 190) finds the usage with -ων here very unusual.

293–8 Presumably Hippothoös was bending down over the corpse (ἕλκε in 289 is conative), so a head-wound is natural. The piercing of helmet and skull is described in three other passages, each concluding ἐγκέφαλος δὲ | ἔνδον ἅπας πεπάλακτο· δάμασσε δέ μιν μεμαῶτα (11.97–8 = 12.185–6 = 20.399–400). Here the effects of the blow on helmet and brain are explained more fully, as part of the general expansiveness of the passage (see Kirk's analysis, mentioned at 288–303n.), and the victim is awarded a 3-line obituary (301–3) to match the significance of Patroklos and the present action. Many phrases are formular, but the idea of 297–8 is unique.

293–4 Cf. τό ῥ' υἱὸς Τελαμῶνος ὑπ' οὔατος ἔγχεϊ μακρῷ | νύξ' (13.177–8). 293–4 ≅ 12.191–2, and the 2nd hemistich of 294 = that of 12.183.

295 ἤρικε, 'split apart', occurs in Homer only here (intransitive aorist) and at 13.441 (present participle passive).

296 ἔγχεῖ τε μεγάλῳ is unique. To use ἔ. χαλκείῳ (6 × *Il.*, always beginning the verse) after | πληγεῖσ' would cause a most unusual rhythm, for only 6.2% of dactylic words in the *Il.* occur in the second foot, and only 1.4% of molossus-shaped words in the position that χαλκείῳ would take (bridging the mid-verse caesura). The appositive τε serves to turn ἔγχεϊ into a choriamb, a shape common in this position. ἔ. τε μακρῷ, formular (without τε) at the end of the verse (5 × *Il.*, 2 × *Od.*), would have been equally uncommon metrically (only 6.8% of spondees occur in the position μακρῷ would take), but anapaest-shaped words like μεγάλῳ are more commonly placed like this than anywhere else except in the 2nd and 3rd feet (35.8% of such words; all figures are from J. T. McDonough, Jr, *The Structural Metrics of the Iliad*, University Microfilms, Ann Arbor, 1967). Normal metrical usage has taken precedence over formular associations.

297 παρ' αὐλόν = 'along the socket' of the spearhead into which the shaft fitted; javelins are called δολιχαύλους (*Od.* 9.156), and such spearheads are known from Mycenaean and Geometric times (O. Höckmann, *Arch. Hom.* ε 297, 299, 307; A. M. Snodgrass, *Arms and Armour of the Greeks*, Ithaca, N.Y. 1967, 16–17, 38–9 and pl. 3, 13). The obscure helmet epithet αὐλῶπις is probably unconnected with this; see 5.182–3n., J. Borchhardt, *Homerische Helme* (Mainz am Rhein 1972) 10–11, Page, *HHI* 289 n. 99, H. L. Lorimer, *Homer and the Monuments* (London 1950) 241–2.

298–300 Kirk (see 288–303n.) observes that the runover words αἱματόεις and κεῖσθαι are not essential to the meaning of the preceding lines and are not followed by exegesis, as such words often are, but by additions to the narrative: 'the cumulative runover technique … is being used as a subtle extension of the range of enjambment and a means of combining inessential although usually desirable decoration with the essential onward flow of events' (p. 81). αἱματόεις is used with similar force at an even greater peak of emotion at 22.369, where Akhilleus strips off his own armour from the dead Hektor. κεῖσθαι always occurs in this runover position (9 × *Il.*, 1 × *Od.*), usually with pathetic effect; e.g. in Priam's picture of a young man killed in battle (22.69–73) and Sarpedon's prescient appeal to Hektor (5.684–5).

301–3 From οὐδέ the verses are repeated at 4.477–9, *before* the death of Simoeisios. θρέπτρα occurs only in these passages (and in imitators), but Hesiod has οὐδὲ μὲν οἵ γε | γηράντεσσι τοκεῦσιν ἀπὸ θρεπτήρια δοῖεν (*Erga* 187–8). Griffin, *CQ* 26 (1976) 164–5, points out that the verses combine the 'far from home' motif with two others, 'short life' and 'bereaved parents', which 'dominate the architecture of the whole poem, from the Achilles and Chryses scenes in *Iliad* i to the encounter of Achilles and Priam in xxiv'. On the location of Larisa see 2.840–1n. In 303 ὑπό goes with δουρί.

304–11 Missing one's target and hitting someone else is a common motif (e.g. at 4.91, 13.402–12, 13.516–18, 15.430); but H. Bannert, *Formen des Wiederholens bei Homer* (Vienna 1988) 36–9, notes that Hektor's participation in the battle after he has donned Akhilleus' armour is limited to doing this three times (here, 525–9, and 608–19), and suggests this foreshadows his failure against Akhilleus. A Phocian leader named Skhedios, but the son of Perimedes, was killed by Hektor at 15.515–16; see 15.515–17n., 2.517n., 2.518n. Obviously the poet has made some minor error.

304–10 The phrasing from ἀκόντισε to τυτθόν recurs at 13.183–5. In 306, the original form would have been *μεγαθύμοο Ϝιφίτο᾽ υἱόν (Hoekstra, *Modifications* 150 n. 1). On πολέσσ᾽ (308) see 236n. The description of Skhedios postpones the verb longer than usual, so for clarity the object is recapitulated by τόν (309). On the enjambment ἄκρη | αἰχμή (309–10) see 264–5n.

312 Φόρκυνα is required here, Φόρκυν at 218 and 318; the variation is unsurprising in view of analogies such as ἔριν, ἔριδα. For others with the name Phainops see 5.152–8n.

314–18 The first four lines all recur elsewhere, and the mention of stripping the corpses is commonplace. Here (and at 13.507–8) the γύαλον, 'curved ⟨plate⟩', must cover the belly; see 5.99–100n., 15.530–4n, and H. W. Catling, *Arch. Hom.* E 76–8. On μέγα ἴαχον (317, = 4.506) see 213–14n. Pausanias (10.26.2) declares that Phorkus was fighting without a shield, relying entirely upon his γύαλα for protection, but this is hardly warranted by the text. The ancient commentators (bT) were surprised that the entrails would gush out through a bronze corslet.

319–359 Apollo rebukes Aineias, who rallies the terrified Trojans, while Aias holds the Greeks steady over Patroklos' body

The rebuke, the third to a Trojan in this book, leads not to a call for help from a Greek, as usual, but to a *parainesis* from Aineias to Hektor and a Trojan rally. The Greeks resist, and the long, indecisive conflict is then described at length (360–425).

319–25 This is an example of Fenik's 'extreme situations that are saved by divine intervention' (*TBS* 176); others occur when Zeus stops Diomedes with a thunderbolt (8.130ff.), Apollo stops Patroklos by physical repulse and a stern warning (16.698ff.), and Apollo stops Akhilleus' pursuit of the Trojans into Troy by rallying Agenor (21.544ff.). On two other occasions a Trojan panic is stopped by counsel to Hektor and his response (6.73ff., where 6.73–4 = 319–20 here; and 13.723ff.). De Jong, *Narrators* 68–81, finds 38 such 'if not' situations in the *Il.*; there are accounts by S. Flory in *TAPA* 118 (1988) 48–9 and M. Lang in *GRBS* 30 (1989) 5–26.

321 Expressions meaning 'beyond fate' are quite common: ὑπὲρ αἶσαν (6.487; 3.59 has a weaker sense); ὑπὲρ μοῖραν (20.336), ὑπὲρ μόρον (2 × *Il.*, 3 × *Od.*), ὑπέρμορα (2.155). Here Διός is probably inserted not merely for metrical reasons, but to refer both to Zeus's decision in book 1 to have the Greeks defeated during Akhilleus' absence and to his promise to Hektor at 206–8 above. The unique expression ὑπὲρ θεόν in 327 is rather different, for there Apollo is referring forward specifically to his representation of the will of Zeus in 331–2.

The expression is a means of emphasis, not a theological doctrine. With perhaps one exception (16.780, see 16.780–3n.), nothing ever actually happens in defiance of the will of fate, as a god always intervenes to prevent it; Poseidon explains this explicitly when he decides to save Aineias (20.300ff.). Zeus's deliberation on whether to save his son Sarpedon is a highly developed version of this (16.431–61; see Introduction, ch. 2, iii). See also 2.155n., and S. West, *Odyssey* on *Od.* 1.34–5.

322–6 ἀλλά replaces εἰ μή, as at 5.23–4. Apollo often disguises himself as someone known to the hero, who receives a verse or two of biography; cf. 16.715ff., 17.72ff., 17.582ff., 20.79ff. Περίφας: the IE root *bhā, seen here after the intensive περί, may mean 'appear' or 'speak' (as in φαίνω or φημί); here probably the latter (von Kamptz, *Personennamen* 83, 224), cf. Periphetes, named for the occupation of his father, the infamous herald Kopreus ('Dungman') who carries Eurystheus' orders to Heracles (15.638–9, see note *ad loc.*). Periphas' father Eputes is named from ἠπύω, 'call', cf. the probably formular ἠπύτα κῆρυξ (7.384). Heralds usually have significant names (von Kamptz, *Personennamen* 264–5): others are Hodios,

'Traveller' and Eurubates, 'Wide-stepper' (9.170), Thoötes, 'Swifty' or 'Driver' (12.342). See also 5.59–64n., 5.842–3n., 7.384n., 13.386n.

Herodian (bT) held that the υ of κῆρυκ(ι) (324) was shortened to preserve the metre, but despite the writing of final -ι in the MSS it should probably be elided and the long υ preserved; see Chantraine, *GH* 1 7 and 86, and Leaf *ad loc.* Verse 326 (= 16.720, 20.82) is omitted by two papyri, and is considered by Apthorp, *Manuscript Evidence* 152, to be a post-Aristarchean interpolation.

325 μήδεα εἰδώς (3 × *Il.*, 2 × *Od.*) is qualified only here by φίλα φρεσί; the closest parallel is καὶ εὖ φρεσὶ μ. οἶδεν (*Od.* 11.445, of Penelope). Heralds elsewhere are πεπνυμένα μ. εἰ. (1 × *Il.*, 1 × *Od.*), which would not scan here; the most common usage must have been Ζεὺς ἄφθιτα μ. εἰ. (24.88, and 5 × in Hesiod, 1 × in *HyAphr*).

327–30 On ὑπὲρ θεόν see 321n. κάρτεῖ τε σθένεῖ τε (329) recurs at 15.108; cf. 322. ἠνορέη is not found elsewhere in this position, but the same combination of words is found at 8.226 = 11.9. Instances of hyphaeresis like that in ὑπερδέα < -εέα are rare (Chantraine, *GH* 1 74), and the phrase here may be modelled on νηλέα θυμὸν ἔχοντας (19.229), itself perhaps a modernization of νηλεὲς ἦτορ ἔχειν (so A. J. Nussbaum, *APA Abstracts* 1987, 24). The sense 'inferior in number' (so bT, Apollonius' *Lexikon* and Hesychius) fits well with the rest of the sentence and the further reference to the current presence of the Trojan allies is appropriate in the context. Brooks' emendation ὑπὲρ Δία is unnecessary (despite its good fit with 321 and 327), and would leave δῆμον ἔχοντας to be taken as 'protecting their city', which is awkward (despite πόλιν ἐξέμεν 5.473, quoted by Leaf in support of the emendation). Eustathius' interpretation of ὑπερδέα as 'undaunted' gives a weak sense here, but one wonders if there existed a phrase ὑπερδέα θυμὸν ἔχοντες in which it had this sense, cf. θεουδέα θ. ἔ. (*Od.* 19.364), ἀπηνέα θ. ἔ. (*Od.* 23.97), ἀνάλκιδα θ. ἔ. (16.355), | νηλέα θ. ἔ. (19.229). πλήθεϊ = 'superior numbers', as at 23.639 (see note *ad loc.*).

333–4 εἶπε βοήσας is unique, but more effective than the common εἶπε παραστάς of some MSS. Despite Apollo's disguise, Aineias realizes he has been accosted by a god but does not know which one (338). The same thing happens to Aias, in an expanded form (13.43–72). On the various forms a divine intervention may take see 20.330–9n.

336–7 αἰδώς is used 5 × *Il.* as an exclamation, 'Shame [on you]!' (see 13.95–6n.). Here the sense is reinforced by making it the predicate to ἦδε γε and (as at *Od.* 3.24) expanding it by an exegetical infinitive clause. Aineias repeats the poet's own words (336–7 ≅ 319–20).

338–41 'γάρ gives the reason for ἴομεν (340) by anticipation, while ἀλλά puts the whole sentence in opposition to what precedes' (Leaf). The accusative expression for Zeus recurs at 8.22. ἐπιτάρροθος is used only of divine helpers (7 × *Il.*, 1 × *Od.*). In 341 the use of v-movable with νηυσί to make position shows that the verse is innovative; see Hoekstra, *Epic Verse* 47.

343–4 ἐλελίχθησαν: see 278n. Λειώκριτος is the name of one of Penelope's suitors (*Od.* 2.242, 22.294), so spelt by most MSS in all occurrences. Here a few good MSS have Λειό-, a compromise between the original Λᾱο- and the spoken Λεω-.

Fenik, *TBS* 177, considers the following exchanges (344–55) typical in detail, though the combination of them does not occur elsewhere. On the phalanx-like formation which stops Asteropaios (354–65) see 13.126–35n. Lukomedes is one of the lesser Greek leaders, twice mentioned in groups of Greek captains (9.84, 19.240) and once together with Aias Oïliades (12.366); at the fall of Troy he was wounded in the wrist, according to the *Little Iliad* (fr. xiii Allen, 11 Bernabé, 12 Davies).

348–51 The couplet 348–9 is a maid-of-all-work, ≅ 11.578–9 (with Φαυσιάδην for Ἱππασίδην) and 13.411–12 (with Ὑψήνορα for Ἀπισάονα). καὶ δέ (351; 10 × *Il.*, 10 × *Od.*) = 'and also', here with no special emphasis. On Asteropaios see 215–18n.

353 The verse is unformular; but the first two of its three parts may have been suggested by the sound of ἴθυσεν δὲ διὰ προμάχων (2 × *Il.*) and Δαναοῖσι μάχεσθαι matches Τρώεσσι μ. (7 × *Il.*). καὶ ὅ, 'he too', i.e. like Aineias in 342; this usage does not recur in Homer.

354 Hoekstra, *Odyssey* on *Od.* 14.73, suggests that the original phrase was σάκεσσι ϝεϝέρχατο (pluperfect of ἔργω), the reduplication being dropped possibly owing to the influence of ἕρκος. The digamma could be restored here by reading δέ for γάρ (Chantraine, *GH* I 136).

356–9 πολλὰ κελεύων introduces a *parainesis* (as at 5.528), which is here given in indirect speech (357–9), rounded off by a speech-conclusion (360). The long general description which follows provides the expansion instead of a direct speech. προμάχεσθαι (358) means to advance alone in front of the close formation; imprudent behaviour, emphasized by ἔξοχον ἄλλων (see 3.16n., and H. van Wees, *CQ* 38, 1988, 9, with vol. II 21–2). Nestor gives the same order (4.303–5). In 359 a papyrus, some inferior MSS, and Eustathius read τε for δέ.

360–425 The long struggle continues

Sixty-five lines of general description and the episode of the grieving immortal horses intervene between the account of Aias' leadership and the attack of Automedon, giving a virtuoso display of the poet's expansion techniques. As usual, the length emphasizes the importance of the battle, which will lead directly to the intervention of Akhilleus.

The descriptive passage is composed of a number of motifs, some of them repeated. Often they are separated by summarizing lines, 'So they fought on' and the like, which reminds us of the general picture. After a summary of Aias' orders (360) comes a descriptive passage, stressing the bloodiness of the slaughter and the greater mutual support of the Greeks compared with the Trojans (360–5); then after another summary (366), the poet, in a direct address to his audience, makes another comparison, contrasting the mist over this part of the battlefield with the sunlight elsewhere (366–75). After a summary of this (375–7), comes a brief 'But *X* did not know...' motif (377–83); this anticipates a longer and more significant example (401–11; on such anticipations see Introduction, ch. 2, iii). Next, after another summary (384–5), comes a further description, the significant detail this time being the sweat running down the fighters' bodies (385–8). Then a simile (389–93), and after its summary (394–5) a brief account of the thoughts of the men on both sides (395–7); this motif again anticipates a more developed repetition later, given in direct speech (414–23). Another summary (397–8) leads on to a second comment in the poet's own voice (398–401), which concludes with a reference to Zeus, perhaps anticipating the coming scene between him and the immortal horses; in fact, the horses are actually mentioned in an unformular phrase, though this may not be significant (see 400–1n.). After the repetition of the two motifs already used (401–11; 414–23), with a linking descriptive couplet between them (412–13), comes a final summary (424); then the section concludes with a last description of the noise of the tumult, employing a striking double metaphor (424–5).

Then the picture of the immortal horses (a standard motif, much elaborated; see 426–58n.) is expanded into the equivalent of an Olympian scene, which reveals the intentions of Zeus but is still closely focused both on the battlefield action and on the theme of human suffering. In scale and effectiveness only the description of the flight of Hektor before Akhilleus (which uses the same techniques) can compare with this splendid passage. In the *Contest of Homer and Hesiod* (190–204), however, other passages are put first (13.126–33, 13.339–44). See also 15.592–746n.

360–2 πελώριος (360) is meaningful, as usual; see 173–4n. The structure of αἵματι... | ...πορφυρέω is regular; πορφύρεον, 'seething', enjambs in the same metrical position and sentence structure after κῦμα at 1.482 = *Od.* 2.428, and πορφυρέους, 'red/purple', similarly enjambs after τάπητας at *Od.* 20.151. Here the sense is surely more significant than in the other examples (for significant adjectives in this position cf. ὀξεῖα (372) and *TAPA* 97, 1966, 151 n. 93), and only here in Homer is the adjective used of blood. LSJ take it to mean 'gushing', but S. West, *Odyssey* on *Od.* 2.428, more cautiously accepts either this or 'crimson'. The mention of blood again three lines later tends to support the more vivid connotation of colour. The formular phrase is ῥέε δ' αἵματι γαῖα [μέλαινα] (4 × *Il.*).

ἀγχιστῖνοι, 'tightly packed', is from ἄγχιστα (Risch, *Wortbildung* 101). The second half of the verse is repeated (without following enjambment) 3 × *Od.* ὑπερμενής, 'supreme in strength' (362), is elsewhere reserved for Zeus or βασιλήων (1 × *Il.*, 2 × *Od.*). In similar metrical circumstances ἀγακλειτῶν ἐπικούρων is used at 12.101; τηλεκλειτῶν τ' ἐ. might also have done, despite the overlengthening (cf. 5.491, and 4 × *Il.* in the nominative or vocative, and κλειτῶν τ' ἐ. 2 × *Il.*). The epithet must reinforce the importance of the Trojan allies in this and the preceding book. It would have been simpler (and less effective) to end the verse with 'Αχαιῶν χαλκοχιτώνων and go straight on to 366.

364–5 The couplet was athetized by Zenodotus (Arn/A), but as usual we do not know the reason. The bT scholia praise the sentiment, perhaps because of Zenodotus' disapproval; co-operation is also praised at 13.237 (see H. van Wees, *CQ* 38, 1988, 6). φόνον αἰπύν occurs 2 × *Od.* in the 2nd–3rd feet. Many good MSS read πόνον αἰπύν, which occurs at 11.601 in the 2nd–3rd feet and at 16.651 at the end of the verse. The reading φόνον is attributed to Aristarchus by van der Valk, *Researches* II 165 n. 359, who (probably rightly) prefers πόνον. Hoekstra, *Odyssey* on *Od.* 16.379, agreeing with Verdenius, *Mnemosyne* 6 (1953) 115, takes the meaning of αἰπύς here as 'irresistible', and thinks this is probably a late formula created on the model of αἰπὺς ὄλεθρος (etc.). West, *Theogony* 329, suggests that the meaning 'steep' was extended to that of 'hard to overcome'.

366 Usually this verse ends with αἰθομένοιο and marks a change of scene (11.596, 13.673, 18.1). Here the poet shifts to a direct address to his audience (see Introduction, ch. 1, i, 1, and de Jong, *Narrators* 54–7). On δέμας, 'like' (only used so in this formula), see 13.673n. οὐδέ κε φαίης occurs 3 × *Il.*, 1 × *Od.*

368–9 The text is dubious, and it is not clear if the meaning should be '⟨they were enclosed in mist⟩ over all the battlefield where the bravest stood...' or '⟨they were enclosed in mist⟩ in the battle, all the bravest who stood...' The latter sense (reading μάχης ἔπι, ὅσσοι) is preferable; it is supported by the matching (ring-form) passage which concludes the section (376–7), and is approved by Ruijgh, τε *épique* 841, who finds τε inexplicable here and thinks it was inserted to avoid the hiatus. The better MSS offer μάχης (-η) ἐπί (ἔπι) θ' ὅσσοι ἄριστοι; Zenodotus (Did/T) read μάχης ἐπὶ τόσσον (though this use of the demonstrative is not Homeric: Ruijgh, τε *épique* 841), Aristarchus perhaps μάχης ἔπι θ' ὅσσον (van der Valk, *Researches* II 133–4). Aristophanes (Did/T) conjectured μάχη ἔνι ὅσσοι ἄριστοι, which is simple and matches 376–7; this was accepted by Leaf, who refused to believe that μάχης ἐπί θ' ὅσσον (read by Allen and Ameis–Hentze) can = ἐφ' ὅσον τε μάχης. The impressive phrase Μενοιτιάδῃ κατατεθνηῶτι occurs only here; but cf. 267. On the mist, see 268–73n.

370–7 This amplification of the mist theme is unique; nowhere else is the darkness localized like this, and much of the language is innovative and vivid. The contrast is strongly drawn between the more desultory fighting elsewhere (370–5) and the intense, exhausting battle over Patroklos' corpse (375–6, 384–8, 412–13). εὔκηλος (371) is only here used in this emphatic position. αὐγή is not elsewhere given an epithet; ὀξεῖα (372) is not otherwise used of light, and must be given the bright metaphorical sense 'piercing', in sharp contrast to the mist (its position is like that of πορφυρέῳ in 361, see note *ad loc.*). The enjambment of πάσης | γαίης is harsh, but is found elsewhere with γαίης/γῆς (*Od.* 1.406–7, 11.166–7 = 481–2). μεταπαυόμενοι (373) is *hapax* (but cf. μεταπαυσωλή, 19.201), its sense elaborated in the following lines. βέλεα στονόεντα (374) recurs at line-end only at *Od.* 24.180 (and after the 3rd-foot caesura, 2 × *Il.* in identical verses). ἄλγε' ἔπασχον (375) and νηλέϊ χαλκῷ (376) are common formulae, but the other phrases in those lines do not recur.

375–7 ὅσσοι... ἔσαν further defines τοί; τείροντο... χαλκῷ is parenthetical, explaining πολέμῳ.

377–83 The 'But *X* did not know...' motif is repeated at greater length below (401–11). Other notable examples are found at 1.488–92 (Akhilleus taking no part in assemblies or battles), 13.521–5 (Ares ignorant of the death of his son), 13.673–8 (Hektor unconscious of the defeat of his other wing), and 22.437–46 (Andromakhe unaware of Hektor's death). See de Jong, *Narrators* 66–7, and Edwards, *HSCP* 84 (1980) 23–5. κυδάλιμος (378) is used elsewhere only at the end of the verse (κυδαλίμοιο (-οισι) | 13 × *Il.*, 14 × *Od.*) and in the formular κυδάλιμον κῆρ | (3 × *Il.*, 1 × *Od.*). On the pathetic phrase for Patroklos in 379 (and the variant πέσοντος) see 1on. ἐνὶ πρώτῳ ὁμάδῳ (380) does not recur, but cf. ἐνὶ Τρώων ὁ. 15.689, ἐν πολλῷ ὁ. 19.81.

Antilokhos is mentioned here in preparation for his importance later in this book; more specifically, to identify his position on the battlefield, far away from the struggle over Patroklos, before the dispatch of the message to him (651ff.). His increasing prominence after Patroklos' death prepares for his rôle in the death of Akhilleus. On the sympathetic characterization of Antilokhos see M. M. Willcock, *Mélanges E. Delebecque* (Aix-en-Provence 1983) 479–85. His brother Thrasumedes has been mentioned before several times; his name is brought in here in preparation for his taking Antilokhos' place at 705. The two have been fighting side by side since 16.317–24. Thrasumedes survived the war, and his tomb was shown near Pylos (Pausanias 4.36.2).

381–3 The bT scholia and most editors take Nestor's injunction to have been to protect the bodies of the slain (or, alternatively, to avoid casualties) and prevent panic. Van Leeuwen and Fenik, *TBS* 179, refer it to his dispatching them to a certain part of the battlefield remote from this, of course before Patroklos' death; this suits the context and is justified by the emphatic position of νόσφιν. Homer did not record these instructions. On decisions about where to enter the battle see 13.308–10n.

384–8 The poet returns to those struggling over Patroklos (τοῖς δέ) with a general description of the battle; before the simile usual in such passages the heavy runover ἀργαλέης is amplified by a vivid physical description of the heroes' sufferings (cf. the sweat chafing Diomedes, 5.796–8).

384–5 νεῖκος is not used again with ἔριδος, but cf. νεῖκος... πολέμοιο 13.271. In 385 it would improve the metre to read ἱδρόϊ, but καμάτῳ τε καὶ ἱδρῷ must stand at 745.

387–8 The singular number of παλάσσετο is strange, and the traditional explanation that the dual μαρναμένοιϊν refers to the two armies is not very convincing. Hoekstra, *Modifications* 92, points out that καμάτῳ (385) is also odd (παλάσσω, 'befoul', is elsewhere used concretely), and very plausibly suggests that the expression is formular and was originally used in duels of two heroes, perhaps with phrasing such as * τεύχεα καλὰ | αἵματι καὶ λύθρῳ ἐπαλάσσετο μαρναμένοιϊν (see also 16.370–1n.). Verse 388 reminds us again of the absent Akhilleus.

389–95 The action is like that described more directly in the case of Kebriones' corpse (16.762–4) and sometimes depicted on later vases (see Friis Johansen, *Iliad* 192). Fränkel, *Gleichnisse* 59, wondered uneasily if the processing of the hide suggested some corresponding (and grisly) effect on the dead body, but decided it is only the tugging to and fro in a small space that is the point of comparison. He links the repeated τανύειν, τανύουσι, τάνυται (390, 391, 393) with τέτατο (15.413), where the battle is pulled tight like a carpenter's measuring-line, and with ἐτάνυσσε in 401; but the metaphor there is common (see 400–1n.), and the association is unclear. See, however, C. Moulton, *CP* 74 (1979) 290–2.

Nothing much is known about the process described; W. Richter, *Arch. Hom.* H 50 can add little to the information given here. The scholia (bT) take ἀλοιφή (390, 392) as olive oil, a view supported by C. W. Shelmerdine (*APA Abstracts* 1987, 103). Usually, however, the word means 'fat', and (nowadays at least) the brains are sometimes used in the process.

389–90 βοὸς... βοείην. The phrase recurs at 18.582, *Od.* 22.364. Macleod, *Iliad XXIV* 144 (on προδόμῳ δόμου, 24.673), quotes as other parallels to the redundancy αἰπόλος αἰγῶν (*Od.* 17.247), ποδάνιπτρα ποδῶν (*Od.* 19.343). μεθύουσαν must mean 'drunken'; a powerful and surprising metaphor.

392–3 κυκλόσ'(ε) (also at 4.212) should be read in preference to Zenodotus' κύκλῳ and Aristarchus' κύκλος; see Leaf on 4.212. ἰκμάς is *hapax*

99

in early poetry. The hiatus before it (there is no initial ϝ) can be removed by replacing τε with ἐξ or inserting ἐπ' or ἀπ' after it (Leaf), but metrical irregularity is perhaps hardly surprising in such an untraditional passage. 'La valeur d'aspect de l'aoriste ἔβη parmi les présents est sensible' (Chantraine, *GH* II 186, with other examples from similes); the moisture has gone, the ἀλοιφή sinks in and remains. τάνυται is present tense, from an athematic form τάνυμι, found only here (τανύεται is impossible in hexameters).

395–7 The second part of 395 recurs at 234 and 495, without the Τρωσὶν μὲν... αὐτὰρ Ἀχαιοῖς division which follows here; this division is elaborated when the motif is repeated at 414–23. The phrase ἔλπετο θυμός | is 'clustered' in this book, occurring in this position (besides the above instances) at 404 and 603 (ἔ. θυμῷ); elsewhere only at *Od.* 3.275 and in the 4th–5th feet at 15.288 (B. Hainsworth, *Studies... Offered to L. R. Palmer,* Innsbruck 1976, 86). Hainsworth also suggests (p. 84) clustering of δουρὶ φαεινῷ here (4 ×, as well as in books 13 and 16). F. X. Strasser, *Zu den Iterata der frühgriechischen Epik* (Königstein/Ts. 1984) 43–5, lists as other clusters in this book κύνες τ' ἄνδρες τε (65, 658) and Ἕκτωρ Αἰνείας τ' (513, 534). There is also an unusually long run of Ἕκτορος ἀνδροφόνοιο vs. Ἕ. ἱπποδάμοιο (5 × between 16.840 and 18.149, including 3 × in 17; R. Janko, *Mnemosyne* 34, 1981, 254). On other passages where the narrator tells us the thoughts of the characters see 285–7n.

398–9 ἄγριος is used as runover to lead on to the following expansion of the thought, as at 737. Ares and Athene are introduced (as at 13.126–8, see note *ad loc.*) as a variant of the 'imaginary spectator', a motif used at 4.421, 4.539, 13.343–4; see de Jong, *Narrators* 58–60. The two deities sometimes represent the opposing sides (4.439, 20.48–53), sometimes warfare itself (18.516, 20.358); the former might best be emphasized here, in view of the preceding contrasts (395–7, and earlier 361–5). λαοσσόος is applied in the *Il.* only to Athene (13.128), Eris (20.48), Apollo (20.79), and here to Ares; see 20.38–40n., and for the etymology, 13.126–8n. The phrasing οὐδ' εἰ μάλα... is similarly used at 5.645 and 8.22; cf. also χόλος δέ μιν ἄγριος ᾕρει (2 × *Il.*). μιν (399) naturally refers to either Ares or Athena. χόλος, which occurs as subject of a wide range of verbs, is used again with ἵκοι at 9.525.

400–1 ἀνδρῶν τε καὶ ἵππων is unique in Homer, and no MS variants are recorded here. Probably ἵππων τε καὶ ἀνδρῶν is more useful because it can be followed by an epithet (ἀσπιστάων at 8.214, αἰχμητάων at 17.740; 2 × *Il.* without epithet). Can the reversed order here be connected with the prominence of Patroklos' horses at 426ff.? Unconventional construction is also revealed by the genitive nouns governed by πόνον in the following verse (cf. *TAPA* 97, 1966, 132). ἤματι τῷ is elsewhere always picked up by a ὅτε clause (de Jong, *Narrators* 234–6). With ἐτάνυσσε... πόνον cf. τέτατο... ὑσμίνη

543, πτόλεμος τέτατο 736, μάχην ἑ. 11.336, ἔριδα... τάνυσσαν 2 × *Il.*, τείνειεν... τέλος 20.101. The metaphor seems to be from stretching a rope over something (for an awning or tent?), but it is not clear exactly what is envisaged; see 13.358–60n.

401–11 The reference to Akhilleus' ignorance of Patroklos' death prepares for the appeal for his help in rescuing the body, which will begin with Aias' words at 640ff. For other examples of significant reference to a character who is unaware of the present action see 377–83n. οὐδ' ἄρα πώ τι (401) also introduces the parallel passage on Ares' ignorance of his son's death (at the beginning of the verse: 13.521); its only other occurrence is at 22.279.

403–4 For the phrasing, cf. ἀπάνευθε νεῶν ἐχέοντο θοάων (19.356). τό (404) is probably best taken as looking forward to τεθνάμεν (Ameis–Hentze) and expanding upon τεθνηότα (402). Leaf's '*wherefore*, i.e. because they were so far away from the ships Achilles had not yet grown anxious (on account of their long absence)' is over-complicated.

Patroklos had been hard against the wall of Troy when he was repulsed by Apollo (16.700–9); he then fell back πολλὸν ὀπίσσω (16.710), but charged forward again four times before his death (16.783–6). At 18.453 the battle is said to have been at the Scaean Gates. As Akhilleus' surrogate, and perhaps also because of the influence of tales of Akhilleus' death, Patroklos dies where Akhilleus himself will die (22.360).

404–25 These lines were athetized by Zenodotus. Bolling, *External Evidence* 174–5, and Leaf also reject them on aesthetic grounds, which are hardly valid.

404–11 Akhilleus had carefully instructed Patroklos not to attempt too much (16.83–96), and had not expected him to try to sack (ἐκπέρσειν is conative) the city alone. From Thetis he knows this much (τό γε, 408): it is not Zeus's will that they sack Troy together (οὐδὲ σὺν αὐτῷ, 407). But he thinks the reason is that *he* will die before the sack of the city, not Patroklos; this is brought out more fully at 19.328–33, cf. 18.333. This notion is consistent with Thetis' prophecy that he will be killed by Apollo (21.277–8), though that was probably invented for its immediate context. The shortness of Akhilleus' own life has long been known to him (1.415–18), and the choice he mentioned at 9.410–16 between a long or a short life was never a very real option. His death before Troy's fall is explicitly accepted by him at 18.96 and insistently reiterated thereafter (see 18.95–6n.). Apollo too has already announced that Troy will not fall to either Patroklos or Akhilleus (16.707–9).

'He often arouses sympathy like this, when the greatest sufferers are unaware of disaster and are borne up by loving hopes, like Andromakhe [22.437–46], Dolon [10.350], and now Akhilleus' (bT on 401–2). Homer brings pathos from both gloomy predictions and unfulfilled hopes. In the midst of all the complications that other people's follies and his own emotions had caused, Akhilleus wished that he and Patroklos could sack Troy together and alone (16.97–100; the idea recurs, with less impact, from the lips of Diomedes, 9.48–9). Later, he recalls how he told Patroklos' father that they would both come home again together (18.324–7), and how he hoped that after his own death Patroklos would take his son Neoptolemos back to Phthie to assume his inheritance (19.328–33). Thetis' prophecy that the best of the Myrmidons would die before him is not mentioned until he guesses Patroklos is dead (18.9–11). Realism could be preserved by asserting that Akhilleus did not associate this prophecy with Patroklos, but of course the poet introduces or ignores such predictions as he chooses.

407 αὐτῷ is reflexive, like (ϝ)έθεν; Chantraine, *GH* II 157, quotes other such uses. The final phrase carries great weight, and introduces the ominous following lines.

408–9 In the rest of the *Il.* we do not hear that Thetis is constantly reporting Zeus's ideas to her son. Macleod, *Iliad XXIV* 96 (on 24.72–3), lists this with other examples of 'rhetorical overstatement' in Homer. The idea prepares the way for the prophecy Akhilleus recalls when he sees Antilokhos approaching (18.8–11, see note *ad loc.*).

410–11 δὴ τότε contrasts with πολλάκι and the verbs of repeated time in 408–9. The T scholia on 410 remark defensively that that verse is not superfluous, quoting 5.51 and 53 (where the sense is complete without 52, or without 52–4); and the Geneva MS shows an obelus beside 411. The reference to the passage in book 5 must have been made because of the similarity of the contexts: 'But this time his mother did not tell him...' / 'But this time Artemis could not help him...' Bolling, *Athetized Lines* 157, held that the scholium is intended to defend 411 against athetesis by some unknown scholar; van der Valk, *Researches* II 471 n. 443, that Aristarchus may have athetized both 410–11 or 411 alone; but the reference to the passage of similar meaning in book 5 seems to imply that both verses had been under fire. The sense is complete enough without both lines or without the second, but they form a good ring-form balance with 401–2, which introduce the passage (οὐδ'... ἤδεε ≅ οὔ οἱ ἔειπε: Πάτροκλον τεθνηότα ≅ φίλτατος ὤλεθ' ἑταῖρος), and add something to the emotional force. However, the juxtaposition τόσσον ὅσσον (410) is found only here in Homer, and the disapproval of an ancient scholar might well have fallen upon 411 because of the pleonastic μήτηρ; this may have suggested that the verse was fashioned after the similar verse at 655, where the initial εἰπεῖν is essential.

412–23 After a descriptive couplet, antiphonal choruses of Greeks and Trojans describe the desperate resolve of both sides. In the poet's way (see Introduction, ch. 2, iii), the short example of a motif (395–7) is followed later by this expanded version; and what the poet described in his own voice is now given in those of the characters. Now the hopeful expectations of the earlier expression of their feelings has changed to 'better death than defeat'. Their intense concern reflects the importance of the absent Akhilleus; 'Both armies are intent on getting possession of the corpse, the one side ashamed of wronging Akhilleus a second time, the others longing to avenge themselves on Akhilleus for what they had previously suffered' (bT on 415–22).

This is a more powerful version of the technique of giving the thoughts of the onlookers in direct speech, as at 3.297–301, 3.319–23, 7.178–80, and 7.201–5. At 15.699–703 the contrasting emotions of the despondent Greeks and the victorious Trojans are given, but in the poet's voice. On these τις-speeches see 6.459–62n. and de Jong, *Eranos* 85 (1987) 69–84.

412–13 τοὶ δ' ἀλλήλους ἐνάριζον marks a change of scene at 11.337 and 14.24–5; here it marks the change from narrator's voice to direct speech.

415–17 The metrical lengthening which appears in ἀπονέεσθαι is convincingly explained by A. Hoekstra, *Mnemosyne* 31 (1978) 18ff., as originating from an old, perhaps pre-Ionic formula προτὶ Ἴλιον αἰπὺ νέεσθαι. 'Sooner may earth yawn open for (me)' is expressed in slightly different words at 4.182 (2nd hemistich) = 8.150 (2nd hemistich) and 6.281–2. Hektor's words at 6.464 make it likely that the idea is that of the tomb receiving the body rather than Hades receiving the soul. ἄφαρ (417) = 'forthwith', as often. A shorter form of the expression, τό κεν πολὺ κέρδιον εἴη, is found at 7.28. Verse 419 ≅ 287.

420–2 There is no ὣς φάτο to conclude the first speech because the two are thought of as simultaneous, not consecutive (F. M. Combellack, *Univ. of California Pub. in Class. Philol.* 12.4, 1939, 48–9). In other such cases the second speech is introduced by ἄλλος δ' αὖτ' εἴπεσκε (*Od.* 2.331 = 21.401), which would not do here. Neither would a repeated ὧδε δέ τις εἴπεσκεν followed by a qualifying formula in the genitive (414, 3.297 = 319, 7 × *Od.*) or a descriptive phrase (5 × *Il.*, 7 × *Od.*), because there is no ready formula for the Trojans in the genitive. So 420 is reshaped, including the substitution of αὐδήσασκεν (elsewhere only at 5.786, in a different position) and the modification of the first part of the verse into the unique ὣς δέ τις αὖ. Usually ὥς refers to what precedes, and Leaf very tentatively suggests it might mean 'in the same way', which is not far from the ἄλλος δ' αὖτ' of the parallel passages and seems the best explanation. αὖ, like αὖτε, 'signals continuation within a series consisting of two...members' (J. S. Klein, *Historische Sprachforschung* 101, 1988, 251, 286–7).

Aristarchus athetized 420 (Did/T), and Bolling, *Athetized Lines* 157–8, was prepared to consider it an interpolation within an interpolation (404–25), treating the two speeches as one. Van der Valk, *Researches* II 471, retains 420 on the grounds that if there is only one speech, 421–2 are tautologous after 415–19. The mention of both sides in the parallel 395–7 also strongly supports the retention of the line. The final clause of 422 is based on πολέμου δ' οὐ γίγνετ' ἐρωή (2 × *Il.*).

424–5 Instead of concluding δέμας πυρὸς αἰθομένοιο (3 × *Il.*), the summarizing phrase (see 366n.) is amplified into a striking descriptive couplet, an expansion of the formular [δι' αἰθέρος] οὐρανὸν ἷκε (3 × *Il.*). This forms a bridge to the episode of the immortal horses. The noise of a classical battlefield is well documented by V. D. Hanson, *The Western Way of War* (New York 1989) 152–4.

Iron is often used metaphorically for the μένος, θυμός, or ἦτορ of a warrior, for the menacing sky overhanging the wicked suitors (*Od.* 15.329 = 17.565), and for the fire which consumes the Trojans slain at Patroklos' pyre (23.177; see note *ad loc.*). Obviously the metaphor means 'pitiless', 'inflexible'. The sky is bronze when the Greeks are having difficulties in the battle (5.504), but also when Telemakhos arrives in peace to visit Nestor (*Od.* 3.2). There is little point in trying to decide if the main point of similarity is brightness, strength, a metal dome (like a bronze shield; cf. *caeli lorica*, Lucretius 6.954), the home of the gods (Διὸς προτὶ χαλκοβατὲς δῶ 4 × *Il.*, cf. *Od.* 8.321), or the source of metal-bearing meteorites (see 15.18–31n.). On other metaphorical uses of 'bronze' see 18.222n. ἀτρυγέτοιο is used only here in Homer of anything other than the sea, but δι' αἰθέρος ἀ. is clearly an under-represented formula (cf. Hesiod fr. 150.35; *HyDem* 67, 457; Stesichorus, *PMG* 209.4); it would fit the verse at 19.351. See 14.203–4n., and on possible derivations, S. West, *Odyssey* on *Od.* 1.71–3; *LfgrE* s.v.; and A. Leukart, *O–o–pe–ro–si: Festschrift für Ernst Risch* (Berlin 1985) 340–5 (from α-copulative + *τρυγετός, 'noise', 'surf'). On αἰθήρ see 14.286–8n.

426–58 The immortal horses of Akhilleus stand motionless, grieving for their dead charioteer. Zeus speaks words of pity for those bound to or associated with the mortal lot, and gives them fresh energy

Capture of a victim's horses and chariot is a common sequel to a victory, e.g. at 5.25–6, 5.165, 5.589, 13.400–1. At 5.260–73 and 5.319–27 the capture of the splendid horses of Aineias by Diomedes and Sthenelos expands the episode of the Trojan's wounding and rescue. Here the motif, foreshadowed at 16.864–7 and 17.75–8, is enlarged into a superbly effective scene. Possibly a similar scene figured in epics telling of the death of Akhilleus himself. Here it is more than just a relief from the battle (bT on 426–8), or a pathetic vignette; it reminds us again of the absent hero, continues to build up our expectation of his own grief when he hears the news, and introduces once more, in a new form, the ever-present contrast between mortals and immortals. Cavafy reproduced this in his poem 'Τὰ ἄλογα τοῦ ᾽Αχιλλέως' (published 1897).

Homeric heroes pay a good deal of attention to their horses. Patroklos' care for these is mentioned at 23.281–2, and Andromakhe's for those of Hektor at 8.186–9; and Hektor, Akhilleus, Antilokhos, and Menelaos all address their horses (8.185–97; 19.400–3; 23.403–16; 23.443–5) – not to mention Zeus himself here (443–55). C. M. Bowra, *Heroic Poetry* (London 1952) 157–70, gives many examples from heroic epic of the closeness of a hero and his horse, and of the grief of the latter at his master's death.

426–8 Αἰακίδαο always occurs at the end of line except after | ἵπποι (etc., 3 × *Il.*). Forms of κλαίω generally stand at the beginning of the verse, often in the emphatic runover construction used here. ἡνιόχοιο (427), instead of Patroklos' name, movingly suggests the thoughts of the horses (de Jong, *Narrators* 104). Verse 428 is like 6.453, ἐν κονίῃσι πέσοιεν ὑπ᾽ ἀνδράσι δυσμενέεσσιν. The horses were close at hand when Patroklos died (16.864). Their feelings appear later in direct speech (19.408ff.), and their grief keeps them out of the chariot-race (23.279–84).

429–31 Automedon was last seen driving off the horses after Patroklos' death (16.866). It was he who was ordered by Patroklos to harness them, and given a complimentary couplet (16.146–7).

The elegant triple anaphora of πολλά, with cola diminishing in length, is achieved by adaptation of formular phrases. In 430 (a threefolder) the unique combination μάστιγι θοῇ is reshaped from expressions like ῞Ηρη δὲ μάστιγι θοῶς ἐπεμαίετ᾽ ἄρ᾽ ἵππους (5.748 = 8.392); θοῶς occurs in this position 8 × *Il.*, 15 × *Od.*, but the adverb will not do here and the adjective is substituted. θείνων is another innovation, the form occurring only here. μειλιχίοισ(ι) is normally accompanied by a noun, either beginning the verse (2 × *Il.*, 8 × *Od.*) or ending it (3 × *Il.*, 7 × *Od.*), though 2 × the noun is dropped to accommodate a name as object (4.256 (see note *ad loc.*), *Od.* 20.165). Once the inclusion of an object-noun forces μειλιχίοισι into the 2nd–3rd-foot position (6.214), which it occupies both here and in another rhetorical construction at 12.267 (ἄλλον μειλιχίοις, ἄλλον στερεοῖς ἐπέεσσι). ἀρειῇ, 'threat', is used again in contrast with μειλιχίοις ἐπέεσσιν at 21.339, and in conjunction with λευγαλέοις ἐ. at 20.109; on its derivation see Frisk and *LfgrE*.

432 The only other occurrences of ἐπὶ πλατὺν (-εῖ) ῾Ελλήσποντον (-ῳ) are when Hektor speaks of the σῆμα to be built there for his potential victim in the duel (7.86), and when the shade of Agamemnon describes the τύμβος of Akhilleus which the Greeks erected there (*Od.* 24.82). The mound can be seen from afar over the 'level' sea, and the association of the phrase with tombs suits the context and looks forward to the grave-stone simile two lines later.

434–6 The point of comparison is the stillness of the horses (μένει ἔμπεδον... μένον ἀσφαλέως) and that of a grave-stone, but in the context the funereal association is the more important. Fränkel, *Gleichnisse* 56, speaks of the solemn immobility of death. There may also be an allusion to the representation of chariots on Geometric grave-marker amphorae (though these are Attic), possibly even a reminiscence of Mycenaean shaft-grave steles with such scenes (J. Wiesner, *Arch. Hom.* F 65–9 and 41–2; M. Andronikos, *Arch. Hom.* W 32–4, 114–21). See also 13.437 (where the short simile ὥς τε στήλην may also suggest a pictorial representation) and note *ad loc.*

ἑστήκῃ (for MSS -ει) is G. Hermann's restoration of the subjunctive of indefinite time, which is common in similes (Chantraine, *GH* II 253). Both ἀσφαλέως and ἔμπεδον convey steadiness, often steady motion (see 13.141n., and 23.325). περικαλλής is formular with δίφρος (5 × *Il.*, 1 × *Od.*). On the δίφρος see 5.727–8n.

437–40 οὔδει ἐνισκίμψαντε; the phrase is derived from οὔδει ἐνισκίμφθη, the description of a spear stuck into the ground (528 = 16.612). The formular δάκρυα θερμὰ χέων (etc.; 4 × *Il.*, 2 × *Od.*) is here expanded over two verses (437–8), and the common phrase θαλερὸν κατὰ δάκρυ χέοντες (etc.; 4 × *Il.*, 10 × *Od.*) may have suggested θαλερή as epithet for χαίτη in 439. μυρομένοισιν | occurs 2 × in an aphorism (*Od.* 10.202 = 568); -οιῖν (in a few late MSS) perhaps reflects μαρναμένοιῖν | (2 × *Il.*; see 387–8n.). χαίτη | ...ζυγόν is repeated at 19.405–6 when Xanthos bows his head to address his master. The ζεύγλη is understood to be a kind of pad between the yoke and the animal's neck, like the upper part of a collar (J. Wiesner, *Arch. Hom.* F 18–19).

The sorrowing horses allow their manes to be soiled with dust, much as Akhilleus and Laertes pour dust over their heads in grief (18.23–4 ≅ *Od.* 24.316–17). Patroklos used to wash and oil their manes (23.280–2).

441–2 Verse 441 ≅ 19.340, 442 ≅ 200; see 199–201n. Macleod, *Iliad XXIV* 14–15, remarks that Zeus's sympathy goes to the horses, who are immortal, rather than to mankind. This is not quite true; Zeus has shown a similar sympathetic concern for Sarpedon (16.431ff.), Patroklos (16.644ff.), and Hektor (17.198ff.); cf. also 20.20–30n.

443–55 There is a good deal of innovative phrasing, i.e. careful composition, in this speech; see the following notes.

443–5 The gift of the horses is also mentioned at 16.381 and 867; presumably they were a wedding present (see 16.140–4n.). At 23.277–8 (see note *ad loc.*) they are said to have been the gift of Poseidon in particular – though according to 16.150 he was not their father, as he was of Pegasos

and Areion (L. Malten, *JDAI* 29, 1914, 181–4). Of course their grief here
– and Zeus's concern – includes the foreknowledge of Akhilleus' death too
(19.408–17). We may compare the happy life of Poseidon's horses, whose
master is immortal (13.23 38).

The hiatus after θνητῷ perhaps adds to the heavy stress upon it. The
word is only here used in the runover position, and it is followed by a
contrasting statement instead of the normal exegesis; | πρῶτον· ἔπειτα δέ... is
used in the same way (for other examples see *TAPA* 97, 1966, 143). The
contrast θνητῷ/ἀθανάτω is noteworthy; ἀγήρω τ' ἀθανάτω τε is a modification
of the old formula ἀθάνατος καὶ ἀγήρως, found in all 20 × in extant epic (see
R. Janko, *Mnemosyne* 34, 1981, 382–5). ἦ ἵνα (445) also introduces Akhilleus'
ironic question to Athena (1.203), the sarcastic remarks of Apollo and
Odysseus to her (7.26–7, *Od.* 13.418–19), and Penelope's despairing
thought that her son too must die far from home (*Od.* 4.710). δυστήνοισι μετ'
ἀνδράσιν does not recur, but ἀνδράσι(ν) is often preceded by a preposition
here.

446–7 The contrast passes from that between mortals and immortals to
that between mankind and other earthly creatures; it is man's love of excess
(bT), or (in the context) his awareness of his mortality which makes him
more wretched than they. In the similar couplet at *Od.* 18.130–1 it is
mankind's blind hopes, especially of escaping retribution, that makes
nothing 'more feeble than man' (ἀκιδνότερον...ἀνθρώποιο). A similar
change in meaning when a *topos* is used by a mortal or a god can be seen
in the simile of the falling leaves (6.146–9, 21.464–6).

448–50 The usual phrase is ἅρμασι κολλητοῖσι | (3 × *Il.*), but this chariot
must be *distinguished* from all others and so δαιδαλέοισιν (formular in the
phrase σὺν ἔντεσι δ. |, 3 × *Il.*, 1 × *Od.*) is substituted. This is careful
composition, not just a breach of formular economy. The plural may be
formular or scornful. οὐ γὰρ ἐάσω (449) is said by Hektor to Pouludamas at
18.296. The scholia (Did/T) mention a variant ending οὐδέ τις ἄλλος, which
appears in a few late MSS; the phrase occurs 4 × *Il.*, 11 × *Od.* (enjambing
in all but one case), but is weaker than the usual reading. | ἦ οὐχ ἅλις, ὡς
(ὅττι) (450) is used to introduce similar angry rhetorical questions at 5.349,
23.670, *Od.* 2.312. In 450, αὔτως does not mean 'vainly', as Leaf takes it
('because his triumph is soon to come to naught'), but has its basic
significance of 'like this', as in εὔχεαι αὔτως | (11.388) and αὔτως εὐχετάασθαι
(20.348). See 143n. These parallels support ἐπεύχεται here against ἀγάλλεται,
read in a papyrus and Ap. *Lex.* 170.14, though the latter occurs in a similar
context at 473 and 18.132.

Horses and chariot must be returned for the use of Akhilleus himself, but
the poet takes the chance to reiterate Zeus's concern over Hektor's
arrogance; cf. 75–81n., 194–209n.

451–3 Verse 451 conflates the phrases seen in μένος δὲ οἱ ἔμβαλε θυμῷ | (16.529; ἐ. θ. | occurs 5 × *Il.*, 2 × *Od.*) and ἐν δὲ βίην ὤμοισι καὶ ἐν γούνεσσιν ἔθηκε (17.569). γούνεσσιν, with the usual Homeric alternative ending (Chantraine, *GH* I 204–7), occurs only here and at 569 and 9.488, in unformular phrases, whereas γούνασι(ν) usually appears in formulae (10 × *Il.*, 8 × *Od.*). The contracted future βαλῶ is unique (Chantraine, *GH* I 63), and though it is not surprising in these unconventional surroundings perhaps βάλω (aor. subjunc.) should be read (with Leaf and a few good MSS). In the first person there is virtually no difference in meaning (Chantraine, *GH* II 207, 209–10). καί (452) indicates Automedon as well as themselves. The reference prepares for Automedon's big scene at 459–542. σφισι (453): the sense makes it clear that σφισι here and τοῖσι (459) refer to the Trojans. κῦδος ὀρέξω (etc.) is formular (9 × *Il.*, 1 × *Od.*).

454–5 = 11.193–4, 208–9. The details are inappropriate here, as the Trojans never again advance beyond the ditch (18.198, 18.215) and retreat before sunset (18.222ff., 18.239ff.), but the lines repeat the guarantee of Zeus's support which is given there and at 206–9. Verse 455 is omitted by a papyrus and a few good MSS, and may have been taken from 11.194.

456–8 ἐνέπνευσεν μένος recurs in different adaptations at 15.262 and 24.442. μένος ἠΰ | appears 5 × *Il.*, 1 × *Od.* οὐδάσδε (457) recurs at *Od.* 10.440. Verse 458 = 11.533 (of Hektor's chariot); for Helios' chariot, *HyDem* 89 substitutes the ending τανύπτεροι ὥστ' οἰωνοί. The dactylic movement of the line suggests speed. The physical action of the horses' shaking off the dust mirrors the change in their feelings, as when Akhilleus resheathes his half-drawn sword (1.220).

Zenodotus (Did/T) read μένος πολυθαρσὲς ἐνῆκε (2 × *Il.*, 1 × *Od.*) for the latter part of 456, and added αὐτὸς δ᾽ Οὔλυμπον δὲ [*sic* Erbse] μετ᾽ ἀθανάτοισι βεβήκει (cf. 1.221–2). The extra line may have been intended to prepare for 545–6, where Zeus seems to be back home. Bolling, *External Evidence* 175, thought the text of Zenodotus of Mallos was meant; this is rejected by van der Valk, *Researches* II 20 n. 101.

459–542 Automedon hands over the chariot reins to Alkimedon and fights on foot. Hektor's attempt to capture the immortal horses is foiled by Automedon and the two Aiantes

Before the next rebuke pattern begins (at 543), a further scene concludes the theme of Hektor's desire for Akhilleus' horses (see 75–81n.). It glorifies Automedon, and is framed by mournful references to Patroklos (459; 538–9). Hektor is kept in view; Antilokhos is still waiting off-stage (377–83n.). For parallels to the structure (two heroes decide to make a joint attack; one of their opponents summons others to his aid, and a conflict ensues) see Fenik, *TBS* 181.

459–60 ἀχνύμενός (-οί) περ ἑταίρου, despite its pathos and apparent utility, seldom occurs; twice of Hektor after the loss of two successive charioteers in a repeated passage (8.122–5 = 314–17), once of the friends of Kopreus' son after his odd slaying (15.651). 460 is like | φασγάνῳ ἀΐσσων (8.88). αἰγυπιὸς ὥς | expresses the speed of Meriones on foot at 13.531 (see note *ad loc.*, and 7.59–60n.).

461–3 The same anaphora of | ῥέα μὲν ... | ῥεῖα δὲ ... occurs in Hesiod, *Erga* 5–6 (see West *ad loc.*). Both forms are common in Homer; original *ϝρᾶα > ῥῆα in Ionic (spelled ῥεῖα), which further developed to *ῥέα (iambic), scanned as a monosyllable by synizesis (Chantraine, *GH* 1 66, 71; Leumann, *HW* 18 n. 10). Ruijgh, *Linear B 1984* 184 n. 58, thinks the form may conceal Lesbian ϝρᾶ. ὑπὸ (ὑπὲκ) Τρώων ὀρυμαγδοῦ occurs 3 × *Il.* πολὺν καθ' ὅμιλον ὀπάζων: 'pressing hard through the crowd'; see 5.334n. Verse 463 is unformular. Forms and compounds of σεύομαι (< *kyew-) generally treat the initial σ as a double consonant, as here.

464–5 There is no parallel to Automedon's behaviour. The circumstances are exceptional because of the quality of the horses and their rôle in reminding us of the absent but looming Akhilleus; in the few other cases where a major hero has been killed, attention does not shift to his charioteer.

οὐ γάρ πως ἦν occurs only here (2 × *Il.* at the end of the verse, with ἄρα for γάρ). ἱερῷ ἐνὶ δίφρῳ is unique. The poet needs a phrase for 'in a chariot' which scans ∪∪–∪∪–– and begins with a vowel. ἅρμα and ὄχος provide nothing. ἐνὶ δίφρῳ is familiar enough, preceded regularly by εὐξέστῳ (16.402; ἐϋξέστου ἐπὶ δίφρου 2 × *Od.*) and less regularly by ἐϋπλέκτῳ (23.335; Hesiod, *Aspis* 306 has ἐϋπλεκέων δ' ἐπὶ δίφρων). To furnish ∪∪– before it, the poet turns to ἱερῷ, ignoring the hiatus; the word is familiar in formulae and may have been common in phrases like ἱεροῖς ἐπὶ βωμοῖς (etc.; 1 × *Il.*, 1 × *Od.*) and ἱερῇ ἐνὶ Θήβῃ (*HyAp* 226). J. T. Hooker, ΙΕΡΟΣ *in Early Greek* (Innsbruck 1980) points out that ἱερός is cognate with Sanskrit *iṣirá*, 'strong', and takes the sense to be 'active', 'life-giving', 'life-partaking', appropriate here because of the chariot's rapid motion. Most recently M. L. West, *JHS* 108 (1988) 155 and 157–8, suggests 'full of impetus'. See also 16.407–8n. Hooker's sense is appropriate enough here, but may have no special force; the word also solves the poet's problem with the watchmen before Akhilleus' dwelling (ἱεροὺς πυλαωρούς |, 24.681) and the elders in the lawcourt (ἱερῷ ἐνὶ κύκλῳ |, 18.504). However, this *is* a very special chariot; cf. 448–50n.

466–7 ἑταῖρος ἀνήρ recurs only at *Od.* 8.584, where it does not introduce a proper name like this. The combination of the two nouns serves to take the verse up to the formular ἴδεν ὀφθαλμοῖσιν (9 × *Il*., 11 × *Od*.). Alkimedon is also known by the short form Alkimos; see von Kamptz, *Personennamen* 11, and 16.197n. He led a contingent of the Myrmidons to battle (16.197), is in charge of Akhilleus' horses at 19.392, helps serve him a meal at 24.474, and unyokes Priam's horses at 24.574–6.

469–70 The alternative νημερτέα βουλήν occurs 2 × *Od.* (and 3 × *HyAp*.). Cf. ἔπος νημερτὲς ἔειπες (3.204), ἔ. νηκερδὲς ἔ. (*Od.* 14.509). With ἐξέλετο φρένας ἐσθλάς cf. φρένας ἐξέλετο Ζεύς (2 × *Il*., expanded at 9.377) and φρένας ἐσθλάς | (3 × *Od.*; φρένες ἐσθλῶν 2 × *Il*.).

471–4 οἷον = 'how', strengthened with δή at 587, 13.633, 21.57. πρώτῳ ἐν ὁμίλῳ is repeated at 20.173, but neither adjective nor noun is elsewhere used like this (ἀνδρῶν ἐν ὁ. 1 × *Od.*). μοῦνος occurs often in this emphatic runover position; 11.406 is another good example. ἀπέκτατο (472) is found again only in ἀ. πιστὸς ἑταῖρος | (15.437). τεύχεα δ' Ἕκτωρ | is followed by an even more effective line at 18.82–3, and 473 recurs at 18.132 with a different (enjambing) clausula. Διώρης is contracted from *Διϝο-ϝήρης (Hoekstra, *Epic Verse* 36).

475–6 On τίς γάρ τοι...ἄλλος 'Who else...?', looking forward to the hortative ἀλλὰ σύ in 479, see Denniston, *Particles* 70–1. ἄλλος is not found with ὁμοῖος elsewhere. ἀθανάτων replaces the formular ὠκυπόδων. δμῆσις (< δμᾶ-, seen in δάμνημι etc.) occurs only here; ψυχή τε μένος τε occurs 3 × *Il*., χεῖράς τε μένος τε 2 × *Il*. ἐχέμεν means 'hold ⟨the mastery⟩' and 'control ⟨the strength⟩'.

477–8 The complimentary formula is generic, used for Priam and Peirithoös in the *Il*. and Patroklos and Neleus in the *Od*.; but θεόφιν (see 100–5n.) may have special effect here after ἵππων ἀθανάτων in the previous line. On ἀτάλαντος see 256–9n. νῦν αὖ occasionally has adversative value, as here (J. S. Klein, *Historische Sprachforschung* 101, 1988, 261–2). Verse 478 = 672 = 22.436; see 153n. θάνατος καὶ μοῖρα κραταιή go together 6 × *Il*. In 478 ϝ'(ε) αὖ (van Leeuwen, after Brandreth at 672) is plausible, but MSS at the similar line 22.436 (Hekabe's address to the dead Hektor) do not have σ' αὖ.

479–80 = 5.226–7, where Aineias invites Pandaros to take over his chariot, with the stronger ἀλλὰ σὺ μέν...substituted here for ἀλλ' ἄγε νῦν...

481–2 βοηθόον: at 13.477 (the only other occurrence; see note *ad loc.*) it qualifies Aineias and means 'running to the rescue'. Possibly that significance is transferred from Alkimedon to the ἅρμα here, but the phrasing is unconventional (ἐπορούω is not used elsewhere with ἅρμα, and usually takes a dative; see 5.793n.), the normal epithets εὔξοον (1 × *Il*.) and εὔτροχον (2 × *Il*.) will not fit, and the poet may have felt that 'swift-rescuing' was appropriate enough to describe a chariot. Inferior MSS read βοῇ θόον, which Aristarchus (Did/T) disapproved of. 482 = 24.441.

483 νόησε δὲ… is formular in this position (3 × *Il.*, 4 × *Od*). On the motif of an attempt to capture an enemy's horses see 75–81n., 426–58n.

485–7 Verse 485 = 5.180. The epithet formula is generic, adapted for Sarpedon and Idomeneus as well as Aineias. Except in this formula, χαλκοχιτώνων is reserved for the Greeks. The first half of 487 ≅ 24.332. κακοῖσι here must mean 'incompetent', not equal to the class of the immortal horses; the wording is unparalleled and lays unusual weight on the epithet.

488–9 Cf. ὁππότε θυμῷ | σῷ ἐθέλῃς (*Od.* 23.257–8), and (without enjambment) | εἰ σύ γε σῷ θυμῷ ἐθέλοις (23.894). σῷ stands first in the line, with emphasis, again at 4.99, 6.126, 16.708, and *Od.* 2.186. Good MSS offer both ἐθέλεις and -οις here and at 23.894. The indicative is best here, as Hektor can have little doubt of Aineias' co-operation; the optative reading is probably due to ἐελποίμην. At 23.894 (see note *ad loc.*) the circumstances are very different and the optative is preferable. ἐφορμηθέντε and νῶϊ are accusatives; this gives better sense and a much easier construction than taking the participle as nominative, and τλάω governs an accusative (*pace* Leaf) at 5.395, 5.873, and 18.433.

Hektor ignores Apollo's warning (75–8) that the horses are not for him.

490 A threefolder. The phrasing is unusual, based on (ἐν)αντίβιον and μαχέσασθαι, which usually begin and end the line, each 3 × *Il.*; cf. also | στῆναι ἐναντίβιον (21.266), μεμαῶτες Ἄρηϊ | (1 × *Il.*, 1 × *Od.*).

491–3 ἐΰς πάϊς is used only in this formula (3 × *Il.*). The first hemistich of 492 recurs at 12.330; with the second cf. νεφέλη εἰ. ὤ. (5.186), σάκεσιν εἰ. ὤ. (*Od.* 14.479). 'Their shoulders wrapped in oxhides, dry and stiff, and much bronze had been hammered upon ⟨them⟩' is a picturesque way of describing their shields, dignifying their advance. There is a more elaborate parallel as Sarpedon charges at 12.294–7, and a briefer one as Hektor leads his men forward at 13.804 (repeating the second hemistich of 493, with πολλός). The scholia (AbT) point out that the poet must be speaking of shields in general, since Hektor is actually now bearing Akhilleus' *golden* shield.

494–6 On Khromios see 215–18n. Aretos, 'longed-for' (< ἀράομαι; the name is also used for a son of Nestor, *Od.* 3.414 etc.), has not been heard of before; he is introduced so that Automedon has someone to kill, since Hektor and Aineias must of course survive. 495 ≅ 395, 496 ≅ 5.236.

497–9 The poet's foreshadowing comment adds some pathos to the colourless Khromios and Aretos before the scene shifts back to the Greeks. ἀναιμωτί recurs at 363 and 2 × *Od.* The first phrase of 499 recurs at 212, the remainder at 573 (cf. 83n.). In other occurrences of εὐξάμενος (-οι) Διὶ πατρί (16.253, *Od.* 13.51, 24.518) the subject proceeds to some bold action; here this does not come until 516. For the divine inspiration cf. 13.59–61, 15.262–70.

501–2 It is the job of a hero's charioteer to hold the horses close behind him in case he needs to escape (5.230–4, 15.455–7, 17.610–15; see 13.383–401n., and Fenik, *TBS* 29). Horses also literally breathe down the neck (shoulders) of heroes at 13.385 and 23.380–1. οὐ γὰρ ἔγωγε occurs at the end of the line with enjambment 3 × *Il.*, 3 × *Od.*

504–5 Use of the dual number allows the formula καλλίτριχας ἵππους (etc., 11 × *Il.*, 4 × *Od.*) to be divided (only here) by βήμεναι; many examples of such insertion of a dactylic verb-form into a noun–epithet formula are collected by G. Nagy, *Comparative Studies in Greek and Indic Meter* (Cambridge, Mass. 1974) 68–71. χρυσάμπυκες ἵπποι, the formula for horses which draw the chariots of the gods, is so divided 3 × ; see 5.363n. ἵπποι for 'chariot' is common (see 3.265n.), and the poet probably did not notice the oddity of the regular epithet for horses in these modified circumstances; the alternative κρατερώνυχε would have been no better. See Hoekstra, *Modifications* 114–15. στίχας ἀνδρῶν elsewhere enjambs only with | ἡρώων (2 × *Il.*, 1 × *Od.*).

506 The sentence is complete after the subordinate clause πρὶν... βήμεναι... φοβῆσαί τε..., but then an alternative possibility is added co-ordinate with the main clause, ἤ κε... ἀλοίη, 'or he might be killed'.

507–8 Both here and at 668 the need to address the two Aiantes and a third hero requires a unique, though simple, form of speech-introduction. On the meaning of Αἴαντε see 2.406n., 13.46n., and for parallels E. Courtney, *Commentary on the Satires of Juvenal* (London 1980) 504 (on *Quirinos*). Aias Oïliades joined the battle over Patroklos at 256–7, but has not been mentioned since. Verse 508 is formular, ending χαλκοχιτώνων 2 × and Μηριόνη τε at 669.

509 τόν = 'the corpse there'. τοῖς must be understood as antecedent to οἵ; the omission is rare when it is in a different case from the relative, but cf. 1.230, 2.295, 8.401, 19.235, 19.265, *Od.* 4.196 (Leaf). The scholia (bT) remark that now that Hektor has withdrawn from the struggle over the corpse Aias might venture to leave its defence to the others.

512–13 The second hemistich of 512 does not recur, but cf. ἐς πόλεμον θωρήσσετο δακρυόεντα 2 × *Il.* The names of Hektor and Aineias (513) occur together only here and at 534, and for want of an epithet formula the common ὅς τις ἄριστος (οἵ περ ἄ.) is expanded (cf. *Od.* 2.51).

514 Here and when the line recurs at 20.435 (where Hektor faces Akhilleus) the tone is one of hope despite the admittedly greater prowess of the adversary; in the *Od.* usages (1.267, 1.400, 16.129) the alternatives are left quite open. The image is from spinning (in a sitting position) the thread of fate (ὡς γὰρ ἐπεκλώσαντο θεοὶ δειλοῖσι βροτοῖσι, 24.525), or less probably (*pace* Leaf) from laying offerings on the knees of seated statues; see 6.90–2n.

515 The second hemistich is similar to 23.724; there is a longer version at 5.430. On κε with the future indicative see Chantraine, *GH* II 225–6.

516–24 The killing of Aretos (516–19) is formular; see 5.537–40n. A dying warrior is also compared to a bull at 13.571–2, 16.487–9, and 20.403–5, but in each case the scene is different. The point of the comparison here lies not in the first link to the narrative, 'Automedon struck Aretos' shield, as when a powerful man...,' but in the developed picture of the bull springing forward, which is likened to Aretos' attack (προθορών 522, 523). When hit by the spear, Aretos falls on his back, which of course the bull does not. See Introduction, ch. 3, ii.

αἰζήϊος ἀνήρ (520) recurs at *Od.* 12.83; otherwise the form is αἰζηός (etc.), usually ending the verse (see 5.92n.). The sacrificial action is described more fully at *Od.* 3.442–50. The scholia (bT) remark that the tmesis in τάμη διά (522) imitates the cutting action, and that it is natural for bulls to fall forward when struck, all other animals backward. ἐρίπῃσιν (522) is the subjunctive of indefinite time common in similes (Chantraine, *GH* II 253). κραδαινόμενον (524) must have been taken over from a phrase such as 13.504–5 = 16.614–15, where a spear which has missed its mark sticks 'quivering' in the ground. See 13.442–4n. μάλ' ὀξύ is best taken with ἔγχος (as Willcock takes it); the adjective is found in formulae with most kinds of weapon (though not with ἔγχος), its postponement is common enough (see 360–2n.), and it picks up ὀξὺν...πέλεκυν of the narrative (520; cf. the repetition of προθορών). To take it adverbially with κραδαινόμενον gives a poor sense.

526–9 The lines are repeated at 16.610–13, and separate verses often occur elsewhere; see 13.442–4n., 13.502–5n., 22.274–6n.

530–3 The phrase (αὐτο)σχεδὸν ὡρμήθησαν (ὁρμηθῆναι) | introduces three successive new combats at 13.496, 13.526, and 13.559. Here it signals the arrival of the Aiantes. μεμαῶτε (etc.) ends a verse after a verb-form scanning ∪ – ⏖ – 8 × *Il.* With the second hemistich of 532 cf. ἑταίρου τεθνηῶτος 19.210. De Jong, *Narrators* 77, discusses this and five similar 'if not' situations. ὑποταρβέω (533) is *hapax*; ὑπο- = 'somewhat'.

535–6 Ἰδαῖον...λίπεν (24.470) is similar. δεδαϊγμένον (etc.) ὀξέϊ χαλκῷ | is formular (5 × *Il.*; 2 × an enjambing clause replaces ὀ. χ.), but δεδαϊγμένον ἦτορ recurs only at *Od.* 13.320, where the sense is metaphorical. On κείμενον (536), followed by a pause, see 84–6n. The generic compliment to Automedon (536; cf. 72–4n.) has some point, since he is about is celebrate his victory.

538–9 Automedon, whose first words were of Patroklos (475ff.), ends his big scene with a very human sentiment. In two other places a hero boasts that he has had the *better* of the exchange (13.446ff., 14.471ff.), but this inversion brings the speaker alive. Only Μενοιτιάδαο θανόντος is formular (2 × *Il.*, 1 × *Od.*); it may be genitive absolute or dependent on ἄχεος, in which case its position in the verse preceding that in which ἄχεος stands is unusual (see 400–1n.) but not surprising in such innovative lines. γε, only here after ὀλίγον, is particularly moving.

541–2 Cf. | ἂν δ᾽ ἄρ᾽ ἔβαιν᾽ αὐτός (3.311), of Priam stepping into the chariot after loading the sacrificial lambs. πόδας καὶ χεῖρας ὕπερθεν | is formular (6 × *Il.*, 3 × *Od.*), but the nearest parallel to the construction here (after αἱματόεις in the following line) is at 21.453, πόδας...ὕπερθεν | δήσειν. A hero's hands are spattered with blood and gore (λύθρῳ) at 6.268 and 11.169 ≅ 20.503, but the only real parallel to these lines is the description of Odysseus after he has slain the suitors (*Od.* 22.402–6), which includes a fuller version of the same simile (but does not connect αἱματόεις with πόδας...ὕπερθεν). The scholia (T) suggest, as at 522, that the tmesis κατὰ...ἐδηδώς imitates the torn-up bull.

Automedon receives the emphasis of blood and simile to round off his vengeful satisfaction before he disappears. We hear nothing more of him or the horses until he prepares them for Akhilleus' entry into the battle (19.392ff.). No one seems to have wondered that he did not, on his return, tell Akhilleus of Patroklos' death before Antilokhos arrived with his message.

543–81 Athene encourages and strengthens Menelaos. He kills Hektor's friend Podes

The final and most extended instance of the rebuke and call-for-help pattern upon which this Book is constructed (see introduction to book 17) has already begun with the Trojan attack on Automedon (483ff.), though that was in fact repelled by the Aiantes (530ff.). Now the second part of the pattern, the Greek defence, is led by Menelaos on the inspiration of the disguised Athene. The third part, the rebuke to a Trojan and his charge against the enemy, follows at 582. The final elements, the call for help by a Greek, the response (by Akhilleus himself), and the consequent Trojan retreat, begin at 626; they are greatly expanded, and conclude in book 18. Fenik's analysis of this part of book 17, *TBS* 182–9, gives an excellent account of the often atypical details, but somewhat obscures the regular overall pattern because he does not deal with its completion in book 18.

543–4 On the image in τέτατο see 400–1n. Of the 31 occurrences of κρατερὴ ὑσμίνη | (etc.) in the *Il.* this is the only instance of the nominative case; ἀργαλέος is common in this position, but πολύδακρυς occurs only in the formular πολύδακρυν Ἄρηα (3 × *Il.*), πόλεμον π. Ἀχαιῶν (2 × *Il.*), and at 192 (see note there). ἔγειρε δὲ νεῖκος Ἀθήνη is reminiscent of ὣς ἄγε νεῖκος Ἀθήνη

(11.721) and ἔ. δὲ φύλοπιν αἰνήν (3 × *Il.*), and is picked up by ἔ. δὲ φῶτα ἕκαστον at 552.

545–6 'Zenodotus athetized ⟨these verses⟩, and others omitted them' (Arn/T), because Zeus is still on Mt Ida (594) whilst Athene descends οὐρανόθεν. Bolling, *External Evidence* 175–6, thinks the athetesis was that of Aristarchus, and that Zenodotus and Aristophanes omitted the couplet (which is in all MSS). The language is not unusual. οὐρανόθεν καταβᾶσα (-βάς) occurs 2 × *Il.*, 2 × *Od.*; δὴ γάρ (more emphatic than γὰρ δή) is common (8 × *Il.*, 9 × *Od.*); the second hemistich of 546 is like ἦ καὶ νόος ἐτράπετ' αὐτῆς | at *Od.* 7.263, though there αὐτῆς is emphatic and here αὐτοῦ is otiose and rather unnatural.

A change of mind on Zeus's part is not very convincing here, since before and after this point he is supporting the Trojans (206–8, 453–5, 593–6). He has, however, just taken measures to prevent Hektor capturing Akhilleus' horses. Athene's visits to mortals in the *Il.* normally occur at the behest of Zeus (4.68ff., 19.340ff., 22.182ff.; also *Od.* 1.76ff., 24.477ff.), and Ζεὺς ἐξ οὐρανόθεν in the simile (548) fits well with this pattern. It can well be argued that 545–6 provide a condensed version of the conversation with Zeus which is the usual preliminary of Athene's missions to inspire a hero. The consistency of Zeus's purpose may well have been sacrificed for the sake of the usual type-scene of the despatch of Athene. The couplet also accounts for Athene's sudden appearance, for she has not been seen since she forcibly reminded Ares of Zeus's injunction to the gods to keep out of the battle (15.121–42), except for a momentary appearance to remove a mist which had not been heard of previously (15.668–70).

If the lines are interpolated, they skilfully imitate both the normal pattern of Athene's actions and the poet's habit of sometimes using a condensed version of a usually expanded type-scene. Perhaps they are an afterthought, to be grouped with the rather clumsy explanations of how Hektor can speak with a spear through his throat (22.328–9) and how Odysseus knows of a conversation between Zeus and Helios (*Od.* 12.389–90). Willcock retains the verses; Fenik, *TBS* 183, thinks it the easiest solution to drop them.

547–52 The formal point of comparison is the πορφυρέη ('dark-shimmering', 'lurid') rainbow and the πορφυρέη cloud which envelops Athene (547; 551), but as Fränkel remarks, *Gleichnisse* 29, the real parallel lies in the sufferings of the battle she stirs up (544) and the grim foreshadowings of the portent of Zeus (548–50). Far from being the sign of divine goodwill which it is in the Judaeo-Christian tradition (Genesis 9.13–17), for the Greeks the rainbow was associated with storm-clouds and trouble; Leaf compares πορφύρεος θάνατος (3 × *Il.*). In the other rainbow-simile (11.27–8) it is the colours and shape of the cobalt snakes on

Agamemnon's corslet which are compared to it, but the rainbow is again a τέρας μερόπων ἀνθρώπων (cf. 548). On the occasional merging of what is actually seen with that to which it is being compared see Introduction, ch. 3, i (b) 4. Willcock *ad loc.* and Fenik, *TBS* 182–3, hold that Athene actually assumes the appearance of a rainbow, but this is not necessary.

δυσθαλπής (549), 'hard to warm', is *hapax*, and ἀναπαύω (550) occurs only here in Homer; the genitive ἔργων before enjambment is also unusual. ἔθνος (552) is formular in ἔθνος ἑταίρων | (6 × *Il.*) and ἑτάρων εἰς ἔθνος (2 × *Il.*) but does not recur with a proper name. Such innovations are normal enough in a simile. ἕ (551) represents ἑ(έ) < ἑϝέ < *sewe* (Chantraine, *GH* i 264); the hiatus before it is due to the analogy of ʽ(ϝ)ε, where the digamma is almost always observed. Zenodotus' ἑωυτήν (Arn/A) is a later Ionicism.

553–5 The Aiantes went to assist Automedon (531–2), so Menelaos is again the main protector of Patroklos' corpse. The second hemistich of 554 is adapted with a negative for the memorable 22.295, where Hektor finds Athene/Deiphobos is *not* beside him to offer help. There are other variants at *Od.* 6.279 and 7.205. 555 ≅ 13.45, 22.227; there is a different version at *Od.* 2.268. On ἀτειρέα φωνήν see 13.45n.

Doubtless Athene chooses Phoinix to impersonate because with Antilokhos still waiting in the wings and Automedon and Alkimedon driving off in the chariot no other close associate of Akhilleus and Patroklos is available; the other leaders of the Myrmidons (Menesthios, Eudoros, and Peisandros) are never heard of after their appearance in the Myrmidon catalogue (16.173, 179, 193). Besides his rôle in book 9, Phoinix helps to comfort Akhilleus at 19.311 and serves as line-judge in the chariot-race (23.360).

556–9 κατηφείη καὶ ὄνειδος | recurs at 16.498. ἀγαυοῦ (< ἀγαυόο; 12 × *Il.*, 3 × *Od.*) is the alternative for ἀμύμονος (15 × *Il.*, 26 × *Od.*) before a consonant; cf. 186. Both words are fossilized in this position in the verse. The scholia (bT) remark on this further reminder of Akhilleus. τείχει ὕπο Τρώων (558) recurs at 404 and 23.81. Verse 559 = 16.501, the last words of the dying Sarpedon to Glaukos. λαὸν ἅπαντα | occurs elsewhere 1 × *Il.*, 2 × *Od.*, but otherwise the verse is (surprisingly) unformular.

561–2 It is impossible to guess what considerations led the poet to use διοτρεφές when Akhilleus uses this address to Phoinix (9.607) and παλαιγενές here. παλαιγενές recurs only in γρηῦ π., from Telemakhos to Eurukleia (*Od.* 22.395; in the dative at 3.386 and *HyDem* 101), whereas διοτρεφές is generic (and confined to this position; 20 × *Il.*, 17 × *Od.*). Some may even think it not entirely accidental that the combination Akhilleus uses, γεραιὲ διοτρεφές, recurs only at 11.648 and 11.653, where their mutual friend Patroklos uses it to address Nestor. Either epithet is slightly humorous when used to Athene – as is Menelaos' unwitting appeal to the goddess he is facing. ἄττα is otherwise used only to Eumaios by young Telemakhos (6 × *Od.*); on its origin see *LfgrE*. The second hemistich of 562 ≅ the second hemistich of 4.542.

563–4 παρεστάμεναι καὶ ἀμύνειν recurs at 15.255 (without the emphatic runover dative), and bridges the mid-verse caesura at 21.231. The runover name in 564 has pathos; Menelaos' love for Patroklos is also mentioned at 139 and 670ff. Akhilleus, seeing Hektor for the first time, says ἐγγὺς ἀνὴρ ὅς ἐμόν γε μάλιστ᾽ ἐσεμάσσετο θυμόν (20.425). εἰσμαίομαι, 'search deeply into', 'touch to the quick', occurs only in these two verses.

565–6 Menelaos has already complained of the divine help Hektor is getting at 98–101 (see note *ad loc.*) | χαλκῷ δηϊόων (etc.) is used 3 × *Il.* Ζεὺς κῦδος ὀπάζει is extended by a prefixed Κρονίδης at 8.141 and 21.570; κῦδος in this position is followed by a variety of ◡ – ◡ shaped verbs. Lohmann, *Reden* 64 n. 109, compares the antithesis Athene/Zeus here to the Zeus/Apollo antithesis in Akhilleus' warning to Patroklos (16.87–94).

567–8 The comparison editors make to the sentiment of *Od.* 3.52–3 means little, since there Athene is warmed by Peisistratos' courtesy to the old man she is pretending to be, a different thing from her appreciation here of Menelaos' choice of her godhead to turn to for help in his trouble. The scholia (bT) with more relevance quote Euripides: ἔνεστι γὰρ δὴ κἀν θεῶν γένει τόδε· | τιμώμενοι χαίρουσιν ἀνθρώπων ὕπο (*Hipp.* 7–8).

569 See 451n. The rhyming of 569 and 570 is doubtless unconscious.

570–3 Flies swarming over milk-pails are used as a comparison for the hordes of Greeks marching out to battle (2.469–73) and troops swarming over Sarpedon's body (16.641–3); and (as here) for the bold persistence of a fly which a mother brushes away from her child (4.130–1; see note *ad loc.*). Besides the θάρσος of both fly and Menelaos in the face of attack, the longing for blood is also a point of comparison.

Verse 570 ≅ 16.691. χροὸς ἀνδρομέοιο (571) is formular (3 × *Il.*). At 5.89, γέφυραι ἐεργμέναι ἰσχανόωσιν 'confining dikes hold back', the verb is a lengthened form of ἴσχω (ἔχω) (see note *ad loc.*). Here ἐργομένη is an incorrect form for the present tense ἐεργομένη (< ἐϝεργ-) and τε should be removed (Chantraine, *GH* I 136). Is ἰσχανάᾳ still the same verb, 'persists ⟨in biting⟩'? In that case χροὸς ἀνδρομέοιο is best taken with ἐργομένη, 'kept away from human flesh' (so Ameis–Hentze, and apparently Willcock). Or should we read (with Risch, *Wortbildung* 322) ἰχανάᾳ, 'desires', after the ἰχανόωσαν read in a papyrus and a few MSS at 23.300 (see note *ad loc.*), and put into the text (against the MSS) by von der Mühll at *Od.* 8.288? In that case χροὸς ἀνδρομέοιο can be construed after it. But the association of ἐεργμέναι and ἰσχανόωσιν at 5.89 is against reading the form ἰχανάᾳ here, and the sense 'desires' spoils the effect of λαρόν in the next clause. It is most natural to follow the MSS and understand '...which, though vigorously (μάλα) kept away from a man's flesh, persists in biting, for human blood is sweet to her'. E. J. Bakker, *Linguistics and Formulas in Homer* (Amsterdam 1988) 185–6, notes that the use of καί with μάλα περ is at variance with normal usage, and suggests it is an *ad hoc* solution to a versification problem. θάρσευς (573; disyllable) is a late Ionic contraction; at one time the pronunciation would have been θράσεος (trisyllable; Chantraine, *GH* I 58). On black φρένες see 83n.

575–7 | ἔσκε is used to begin a sentence like this again only 2 × *Od.* The longer equivalent | ἦν δέ τις is commoner (4 × *Il.*, 3 × *Od*), and Athenaeus (236c) and a few late MSS read it here (with ἐν for ἐνί). V. di Benedetto, *RFIC* 114 (1986) 276–7, identifies the *topos* of | ἦν (ἔσκε) δέ τις...introducing a minor figure, characterized by his wealth, who is destined to die immediately (5.9, 13.663, and here) or eventually (10.314, *Od.* 20.287). ἀφνειός τ᾽ ἀγαθός τε recurs only at 13.664. The wording of the second part of 576 is rather like τὸν μετ᾽ Ἀχιλλῆα ῥηξήνορα τῖε μάλιστα (16.146), but the runover δήμου ('community', as usual) is unique. On ἑταῖρος (577) see 151–2n. φίλος here conveys both affection and possession, as often (J. T. Hooker, *Glotta* 65, 1987, 44–65). εἰλαπιναστής, 'dining-companion', occurs only here in Homer, but cognate forms are common in both poems; the etymology is unknown.

The narrator takes care to give us the information that Podes is a close friend of Hektor, so that we may appreciate the effect of Apollo's words (589–90; cf. de Jong, *Narrators* 89–90). Athenaeus unsympathetically remarks (236d) that Podes is the first recorded 'parasite', and is fittingly wounded in the belly. As in the case of Euphorbos, Menelaos kills a man whose death causes Hektor special grief; cf. 80, 83. The mention of Hektor prepares for Apollo's second rebuke to him (586–90), and gives it additional effect. A man's wealth, or his father's, is often used to increase the pathos of a death; see 5.708–10n., 6.14–15n., 13.663–70n.

Presumably this Eëtion is not Andromakhe's father, king of Thebe, whose seven sons were killed by Akhilleus (6.421–4); there was also an Eëtion of Imbros who ransomed Priam's son Lukaon (21.42–3). The origin and meaning of the name are unknown (von Kamptz, *Personennamen* 372).

578–81 Verse 578 ≅ 5.615. A man is struck as he turns to flee at 5.45–6 and 16.307–9, in different circumstances. φόβονδε is found 4 × *Il.* in different positions and phrases. The second hemistich of 579 and the first of 580 are common formulae. The capture of the dead body is normal, e.g. 317–18, 4.506.

582–625 Apollo rebukes Hektor, who also receives a signal of Zeus's support. Idomeneus and other Greeks turn in flight

This is the last of the four rebukes in this book, and the Trojan attack which
follows leads on to the final call for help, which will reach Akhilleus in book
18. The episode has recently been examined by M. M. Willcock in Bremer,
HBOP 185–94.

582 A rising threefolder, giving emphasis to Hektor's name; he was last
seen in retreat (533–4), but his return has been prepared for by his
association with Podes (576–7). ἐγγύθεν ἰστάμενος (etc.) occurs 2 × *Il.* in this
position, and once begins the verse.

583 Another Phainops is mentioned at 312, and yet another at 5.152–8
(see note *ad loc.*). The scholia (bT) remark that Hektor will be shamed by
the rebuke from (apparently) a close friend. The enjambment ἁπάντων |
ξείνων is unusually harsh; see 6.498–9n.

585 = 326, 16.720, 20.82 (the variant Διὸς υἱός for ἑκάεργος is common in
the MSS). The verse is omitted in a papyrus and the better MSS, and
Apthorp, *Manuscript Evidence* 148, 150, is almost certainly right in
considering it a post-Aristarchean interpolation. Zenodotus' weird alternative for 582 (Arn/A) shows that 585 was unknown to him. Van der Valk
however, *Researches* II 504 n. 97, thinks Aristarchus omitted the verse
because of its repetition at 326.

586–8 Striking lines. ἄλλος Ἀχαιῶν, explained by Μενέλαον in the next
verse, is generally placed at the end of the verse (4 × *Il.*, 1 × *Od.*), but here
and at 20.339 that position is pre-empted by a long verb. οἷον δή also
introduces a reproach at 13.633 and 21.57, and without δή at 471 above.
πάρος γε, the reading of A and a few other MSS (against περ of the rest),
is definitely right. πάρος γε means 'though previously…, ⟨yet now…⟩',
contrasting the past with the present, and is here picked up by νῦν δέ (588);
cf. 18.386, 22.302–3, 24.641–2. πάρος περ (almost always after ὡς (ὅς etc.)
τό) means 'just as before, ⟨so now too⟩', as at 720–1.
On Menelaos' inadequacy as a fighter see 24–8n. μαλθακός (588) is found
only here in Homer; in Hesiod it is used once as an epithet of sleep (fr.
239.4). Plato remembered the phrase (*Sympos.* 174c1). Helenos and Hektor
speak of the unstoppable Diomedes as | ἄγριον αἰχμητήν (6.97, 6.278).

588–91 As at 79–81, the rebuke includes the report of a friend's death.
For exceptional emphasis the name of Podes is held back until after news
of the loss of a friend and the capture of his body (related hysteron-
proteron). ἐν(ὶ) προμάχοισ(ι)(ν) occurs 10 × *Il.* in various positions, and at
4.458 in this same phrase. Verse 591 = 18.22, *Od.* 24.315. On the metaphor
see 243–4n.

593–6 Two lines describe Zeus's impressive power; the third begins with
a noisy thunderclap (ἀστράψας), rumbles on over the mid-verse caesura
(μάλα μεγάλ'), and ends with two lesser crashes separated by a heavy bucolic
diaeresis (ἔκτυπε, τὴν δὲ τίναξε). Cf. Lucretius' reverberating *et rapidi fremitus*

et murmura magna minarum (5.1193). Then 596 carefully balances the different effects on Trojans and Greeks.

On the aegis see 2.446–51n., 15.18–31n., H. Borchhardt, *Arch. Hom.* ε 53–56, and most recently R. L. Fowler, *Phoenix* 42 (1988) 104–12. It has been suggested (see Fowler) that there is a connexion between the aegis, goatskins, and rain-magic, but only here is there a direct association between aegis and thunderstorms. αἰγίδα θυσανόεσσαν ends the verse 5 × *Il.*; the tassels are described at 2.448–9. μαρμαρέην = 'flashing'; the aegis is described as golden (24.20–1) and was made by Hephaistos (15.309–10). The epithet is also applied to the shield made by Hephaistos (18.480) and to the sea (14.273). μάλα μεγάλα (etc.) recurs in Homer only at 723, 10.172, and 15.695, all before the mid-verse caesura (which it here bridges). τήν (595) probably refers not to Mt Ida but to the aegis (so Ameis–Hentze and Willcock), for it is shaken to terrify the enemy at 4.167, 15.230, 15.320–1, and *Od.* 22.297. But at 20.56–60 Zeus's thunder and Poseidon's earthquake together shake 'all the feet' of Ida. τινάσσω is used often for brandishing weapons, but also with γαῖαν (20.57–8). Zenodotus dodged the problem by reading γῆν.

597 Peneleos was listed as one of the five leaders of the Boeotians (2.494), and fought victoriously in the attack inspired by Poseidon (14.486–505) and that led by Patroklos (16.335–41). On the name see von Kamptz, *Personennamen* 376; an original *Πηνέληος would not scan in hexameters, but Chantraine, *GH* I 197, points out that Πηνέλεος would always be metrically possible in our text. 'He is not a coward, as he yields to Zeus' (exegetical scholia).

598–600 The lines are unformular. Peneleos turned his left arm, bearing his shield, towards the enemy (πρόσω), and was wounded above the shield. ἐπιλίγδην, 'grazing', occurs only here, and λίγδην only at *Od.* 22.278; see Chantraine, *Dict.* 639, for cognate forms, and Risch, *Wortbildung* 365–6, for the termination. γράψεν is used in Homer only here and at 6.169 (for the 'writing' on Bellerophon's tablet), but ἐπέγραψεν has the same sense at *Od.* 22.280. ἄχρις (599) means 'up to'; see 4.522n. ῥ' in 600 conceals ϝ(ε).

The exegetical scholia comment on the variety given by the postponement of the attacker's name. Pouludamas was last mentioned with Glaukos at 16.535; he will have a big scene with Hektor in the next Book (18.249ff.). We are not told how Peneleos escapes; presumably by flight (597).

601–2 Leïtos was mentioned with Peneleos in the Catalogue of Ships (2.494) and when Poseidon exhorted the Greeks (13.91–2). He killed a Trojan at 6.35–6. Von Kamptz derives the name from ληΐς, 'booty', cf. Ἀθηναίη ληΐτιδι (10.460; *Personennamen* 249), but Hoekstra, *Modifications* 150 n. 1, points out that according to Herodotus (7.197) the Achaeans of

Southern Thessaly called their prytaneum λήϊτον, i.e. λάϝιτον < λαός. The name of his father Alektruon may be Mycenaean (Ventris and Chadwick, *Documents* 276–80). The phrase σχεδὸν... καρπῷ also describes the wounding of Aphrodite by Diomedes (5 458 = 883). χείρ includes the arm, so καρπός gives greater precision; similarly διὰ χειρὸς is preceded by τένοντες | ἀγκῶνος to specify the elbow at 20.478–9. In the latter episode the victim can only stand and await death at Akhilleus' hands. χάρμης (17× *Il.*, 1× *Od.*) always stands at the end of the verse, in a number of formular expressions; this one recurs at 12.389.

603–4 The first half of 603 recurs at 11.546. | ...ἔχων ἐν χειρί (χερσίν) is found 5× *Il.*, 1× *Od.*

605–6 Idomeneus was among those who responded to Menelaos' call for help (258). On his depiction generally see 13.210n. A verse including three proper names in different syntactical relationships to the same sentence must be rare; but the metrical shapes of all three make the cola very easy to handle, and the word-order lays the proper stress on Hektor. Verse 606 is an expanded example of the formular βάλ(λ)ε στῆθος παρὰ μαζόν | (4× *Il.*, 1× *Od.*); Chantraine, *GH* 1 200, notes other examples of the pluperfect of this verb, and renders the line 'Idoménée avait déjà frappe Hector comme il s'élançait...' Homer chooses not to mention that Hektor is now wearing the armour made by Hephaistos, which ought to be invulnerable; see 20.264–6n.

607–8 On the καυλός, 'tang' or 'socket', see 13.162n., where the verse is repeated with a different final enjambing phrase. τοὶ δὲ βόησαν | is used without enjambment at 23.847, but here would be ambiguous without | Τρῶες. This is Aristarchus' reading (Did/A) for τοὶ δ' ἐφόβηθεν (which occurs at 16.294), and seems to make better sense (*pace* van der Valk, *Researches* II 208). ἀκόντισε takes the genitive of the person aimed at, as at 8.118, 14.402. Usually it is followed by δουρὶ φαεινῷ (14× *Il*), with plural ἀκόντισαν ὀξέα δοῦρα (3× *Od.*; once the muddled form ἀκόντισεν ὀξέϊ δουρί occurs, *Il.* 4.490). But the final phrase is not essential to the sense, and sometimes (as here) a more important item is substituted (8.118, 13.502, 14.402, *Od.* 22.252, 22.255; see E. Visser, *Homerische Versifikationstechnik*, Frankfurt am Main 1987, 81–2).

609 The nearest parallel to the first hemistich is ἑστάοτ' ἐν δίφρῳ, of Priam returning with the body of Hektor (24.701). Heroes do not fight from their chariots, and the emphatically placed phrase indicates that Idomeneus has already climbed into Meriones' chariot (612–14) in order to retreat with the majority of the Greeks (595–6) after breaking his spear on Hektor's corslet (605–6). When a retreat occurs it is standard for men to be killed or wounded while standing in their chariots; cf. 5.38–41, 5.159–60, 20.460–2.

610 The second half of the verse looks formular, but occurs only here;

ὀπάων occurs only before or after ᾽Ιδομενῆος (4 × *Il.*), and ὀπάονα only here and for Phoinix (23.360). One would have expected the verse to end βάλ᾽ ἡνίοχον θεράποντα, as at 5.580 (this noun combination occurs 3 × *Il.* at the verse-end and 1 × *Il.* in the nominative before the mid-verse caesura). But βάλ᾽ does not appear until 617. Possibly the association of ὀπάων with Meriones led to the formation of the unusual phrase here, and left no room for the verb.

It is the job of a charioteer to stay close in order to rescue his superior if necessary; see 501–2n. Since Idomeneus walked to the battle (612–13), Meriones' driver looks out for him too, and observes his danger. I agree with P. A. L. Greenhalgh, *BICS* 29 (1982) 89 n. 72, that there is no need to substitute Idomeneus' name for that of Meriones, as Bentley and Düntzer did; for another view, see G. J. Stagakis, *Historia* 16 (1967) 414–21. No chariot is mentioned when the two talkative Cretans set out for battle (13.295–305), though the poet seems to have slipped into the assumption that they are driving at 13.326 (see 13.326–7n.). Fenik lists four other cases where a charioteer is killed by a weapon aimed at his leader (including the adaptation at 15.430–5; *TBS* 61). It is especially pathetic that Koiranos loses his life in saving that of Idomeneus.

611 On Luktos see 2.646–8n. αὐτῷ refers to Μηριόναο in 610 (*pace* Leaf); then πεζός clearly enough ignores both Meriones and Koiranos and carries the story-line back to Idomeneus. The lack of a verb in 610 produces a parenthesis, which explains in a kind of ring form why Idomeneus had need of Koiranos' help (612–13), between accounts of who he is (610–11) and what he is doing (614–15). Then 616 picks up 610, and the details follow.

613–15 The second half of 613 recurs at 206 and 11.753. ποδώκεας – ◡ ◡ ἵππους | appears only here and at 23.376 (nominative), but there is no metrical equivalent. At 15.352 κατωμαδόν takes the place of the epithet. φάος (615) and φόως are often used metaphorically (= 'help', 'victory'), as in the formular φόως Δαναοῖσι γένηαι (etc.) |. ἄμυνε δὲ (etc.) νηλεὲς ἦμαρ | is also formular.

617–19 The first verse, up to οὔατος, recurs at 13.671 (= 16.606) without the additional details given here. The only practical interpretation is that the victim's tongue was cut in half by the spear-point and his teeth were knocked out by the base (i.e. socket) of the spearhead or the forward end of the spear-shaft, which amounts to the same thing (cf. 16.348). LSJ render δόρυ πρυμνόν as '*the lowest part* of a spearhead (where it joins the shaft'). πρυμνόν as an adverb, 'by the roots', understood of the teeth (Leaf, van Leeuwen) is less likely. Possibly the wording was influenced by 5.292 τοῦδ᾽ ἀπὸ μὲν γλῶσσαν πρυμνὴν τάμε χαλκὸς ἀτειρής, though there the meaning is different. The first hemistich of 619 is a common formula; κατὰ (ἀπὸ) – ◡ ◡ χεῦεν ἔραζε | occurs 2 × *Il.*, 3 × *Od.*

620–3 Meriones was last seen challenging Aineias in the fight over the body of Sarpedon (16.619–25). On his background see 13.249–50n.; on his tendency to aim low, 13.567–9n. φίλῃσι seems to add a little emphasis, somewhere between 'his' and 'his own'; cf. 18.27, 23.99, *Od.* 5.462, 5.482. On ὅ τ(ε) (623) see Chantraine, *GH* II 288–9.

Meriones stoops to pick up the reins from the ground; from his hurried shout of μάστιε νῦν! to Idomeneus we assume that he hands them to him. The brevity of his speech and the omission of a mention of transferring the reins may be intended to convey the pressing emergency.

624–5 Usually it is χόλος which ἔμπεσε θυμῷ (4 × *Il.*). Idomeneus is going grey (13.361) and no longer quick on his feet (13.512–15). Meriones remains in the battle (668; Fenik, *TBS* 187, makes a rare slip here).

626–701 Aias complains of Zeus's help to the Trojans, and initiates the call for help to Akhilleus by sending Menelaos to find Antilokhos and send him as messenger. Antilokhos sets out, in tears

This final and much-expanded instance of the call-for-help pattern reaches its formal conclusion when Akhilleus routs the Trojans with his mighty war-cry (18.222–31).

626–55 Aias Telamonios is hardly renowned as an orator – Hektor rudely calls him ἁμαρτοεπές, 'word-bungler' (13.824) – but in fact his speeches in the *Il.* are composed with consummate care. His words to Akhilleus at the end of the embassy (9.624–42) begin with the rhetorically effective address to *Odysseus* (using words he might hesitate to speak to Akhilleus directly); only later does he turn to his host with the note of sincere comradely affection that makes him agree to remain at Troy. His challenge to Hektor includes the only reference by a character to the metaphorical whip of Zeus (13.812; in the poet's voice at 12.37), and a vivid picture of Hektor praying frantically to Zeus as he drives back to the city in terror (13.817–20). In his two powerful *paraineseis* during his defensive action at the end of book 15 he asks the Greeks if they expect to walk home if Hektor destroys their ships (15.504–5), declares that Hektor is not inviting them to dance, but to fight (15.508), demands in furious rhetorical questions if they think they have allies and a fortified city behind them (15.735–8), and concludes with the striking (and original?) aphorism τὼ ἐν χερσὶ φόως, οὐ μειλιχίη πολέμοιο (15.741). His claim to ἰδρείη (7.198) is well justified – and Hektor shows better judgement then, when he grants him πινυτή, 'good sense' (7.289).

Here Aias thinks aloud. Zeus is obviously favouring the Trojans (629–33); and Aias' reaction is nevertheless an attempt to figure out a way to rescue Patroklos' body, save their own lives, and rebuild the Greeks' spirit (634–9). The only way is to call for Akhilleus' help (640–2); but he cannot see anyone to carry the message, because of the mist (643–4). So his thoughts return defiantly to Zeus, and in famous words he asks him to let them see and challenges him to do his worst. The ring form is unobtrusive.

After Zeus has complied, Aias has meanwhile made up his mind whom to send, and despatches Menelaos to find Antilokhos (652–5). He does not pause to reflect on Menelaos' later concern (711) about how Akhilleus can fight without armour.

626–7 As at 1–2, the sentence construction switches to different characters (in the accusative), but maintains continuity by reference back to a linking subject (Zeus, mentioned previously at 593–6). ὅτε = 'that', not 'when', and might better be written ὅ τε (with Leaf; cf. Chantraine, *GH* II 289–90). ἑτεραλκέα νίκην is formular (4 × *Il.*, 1 × *Od*).

629–30 The same vigorous 'any fool can see that…' was used by Diomedes at 7.401–2.

631–3 βέλε' ἥπτετο occurs in this position in a verse repeated 4 × *Il.* For ἀφήῃ, MSS offer a wide choice of forms after both ἀφ- and ἐφ-, but the aorist subjunctive is clearly preferable to the optative; the weapons hurled are not a possibility, but a general fact. On the form, see Chantraine, *GH* I 459. ἔμπης is paraphrased ὁμοίως by the A scholia, ὅμως by the T scholia; the former meaning is surely better. αὔτως = 'like this'; see 143n., 448–50n. πίπτει (etc.) ἔραζε occurs 3 × *Il.*, 1 × *Od.*

634–6 The first two verses are repeated by Menelaos to Aias at 712–13 (after a different initial phrase); Menelaos however concludes with a formular verse (714), whereas Aias continues with an innovative verse (636) and goes on to recount the thoughts of his companions. αὐτοί περ = 'on our own' (as at 8.99 etc.), without Zeus's help. On the article with νεκρόν (635) see 509n. Leaf looked favourably on Bentley's νεκρόν τε, which preserves the digamma and avoids the article, but this will not serve at 509.

637–9 The enjambing phrase οὐδ' ἔτι φασὶν | occurs at the end of 9.234, after which 9.235 = 639 here (so too 12.106–7, 12.125–6). The additional verse 638 gives extra weight here, and should probably be taken as subject of the infinitives in 639. For a similar kind of amplification compare 18.444–5 with 16.56–9. Ἕκτορος ἀνδροφόνοιο begins the verse in only three of its 11 occurrences in the *Il.*, and here at least has special emphasis; see 6.498–9n. On χεῖρας ἀάπτους (638) see 13.317–18n.

637 ἀκηχέδαται, 'are troubled', is the perfect tense of ἀκαχίζω; the participle ἀκηχεμένη (-αι) is found at 5.364 and 18.29. See Risch, *Wortbildung* 342 and 343.

640–2 Cf. | νῦν δ' εἴη ὅς… (14.107), ἀλλά τις εἴη | εἰπεῖν… (*Od.* 14.496–7). λυγρῆς ἀγγελίης also begins the verse at 686 and 19.337 (accusative, of

Akhilleus' own death), and at 18.18–19 is split by enjambment. φίλος ὤλεθ' ἑταῖρος is expanded at 655, and is spoken by Akhilleus at 18.80 and by the poet at 17.411. Both phrases are used only of Patroklos and Akhilleus, which adds to the emotional effect.

643–4 On the mist see 268–73n.; it was also emphasized at 366–76, see note to 370–7.

645–7 Agamemnon similarly turns to address Zeus in mid-speech, after reproaching the Greeks (8.236); Menelaos, after denouncing the shamelessness and guilt of the Trojans (13.631); and Akhilleus, as he speaks to the assembly after the reconciliation (19.270). The technique is effective, especially here.

ἀλλὰ σύ with an imperative is common in Homer (5 × in *Il.* 17 alone), but is only otherwise used to Zeus by Thetis (1.508). The heavy spondees and balanced cola of 646 lend impressiveness to the prayer. καί (647) gives the intonation 'So long as it is in the light, *kill* us even, since that is what you want.' Editors quote approximate parallels at 5.685, 21.274, and *Od.* 7.224, but the effect here is uniquely powerful and moving. εὔαδε(ν) is aorist of ἀνδάνω, from root *σϝαδ- (with syllabic augment); the form is found only in the phrase ἐπεί (ὡς γάρ) νύ τοι εὖ. – – | (2 × *Il.*, 1 × *Od.*). J. T. Kakridis, *Homer Revisited* (Lund 1971) 98 n. 14, suggests that the audience would notice the oxymoron in ἐν δὲ φάει καὶ ὄλεσσον; on φάος = 'help', 'salvation' see 613–15n.

Aias' prayer was much admired in antiquity. 'Θαυμαστὸν τὸ ἦθος· he does not ask for protection, but that he may not be held back from brave deeds. So Zeus listens to him, although he is on the other side' (bT); 'Nobly (μεγαλοφρόνως) he asks not for protection, but for light to see by, so that they may accomplish something before they die' (A); 'Truly the feelings of an Aias, for he does not pray for life (this would be too base for a hero), but since in the baffling darkness he can put his heroism to no noble purpose he is angry that he can do nothing in the battle, and prays for light at once, so that at least he may find an end worthy of his courage, even with Zeus against him. Here Homer blows with a fair wind on the contest (οὔριος συνεμπνεῖ τοῖς ἀγῶσι)' (Longinus, 9.10).

648 The same line is used for Zeus's response to Agamemnon's despairing prayer at 8.245.

649–50 There seems to be no significant difference in meaning between ἀήρ and ὀμίχλη; the latter is once used of a dust-cloud (13.336), but also of the appearance of Thetis as a sea-mist (1.359). Note the chiasmus in 649. ἐπέλαμψε, 'shone out', is found only here in Homer. ἐπί with φαάνθη is also best taken of the sudden brightness, 'the whole battle lit up'.

652–5 The poet has taken care to tell us where Antilokhos is; see 377–83n. Aias' choice demonstrates his good sense; Antilokhos was known as the swiftest runner amongst the younger Greeks (23.756, cf. 15.570, *Od.* 3.112 ≅ 4.202), and was honoured by Akhilleus above all his companions except Patroklos (*Od.* 24.78–9).

αἵ κεν ἴδηαι | ζωὸν ἔτ᾽ is expanded in the simile which follows at 674–81. On 655 see 640–2n.

657–67 At 110–14 (see note *ad loc.*) Menelaos retreats reluctantly in the face of a Trojan charge led by Hektor, like a brave lion driven unwillingly away from a farm. In book 11 Aias is made fearful by Zeus and retreats slowly and unwillingly, and a simile follows which shares many verses with the one applied to Menelaos here (657 ≅ 11.548; 659–64 = 11.550–5; 666 = 11.557 as far as the bucolic caesura). In book 11 the simile is well integrated into both narrative and grammar, and besides the main point of comparison (reluctant retreat) τετιηότι of the simile is picked up by τετιημένος of the narrative (11.555, 11.556). Here, though the reluctance of Menelaos and the lion is the same, the motive for the retreat is different, and the relative clause introduced by ὅς (658) is never completed. But the description of the lion's withdrawal is needed to lead on to Menelaos' thoughts (666–7), which in turn climax in his characteristic appeal to the Greeks' love for Patroklos (669–72).

Only eight times is a simile repeated verbatim in Homer (see Introduction, ch. 3). C. R. Beye, *Studies presented to Sterling Dow* (ed. K. J. Rigsby; Durham, N.C. 1984) 7–13, has suggested with some plausibility that the present passage and the one in book 11 have in common the circumstances that Aias is dominant; a Greek is told to withdraw (Nestor and Machaon, 11.511ff.); and the withdrawal results in the bringing of information to Akhilleus (11.597ff.). The repetition of the simile thus rounds off, in a kind of ring form, the chain of events that began with Akhilleus' despatch of Patroklos (11.607ff.) and now is about to bring back to him the results of that action.

Leaf considers the simile pointless here, lines 669–72 'very weak', and the narrative 'at once late and poor'; but (characteristically) he shows a fine insight into the structure of the sentence: 'The Epic poet, always intolerant of long subordinate clauses, seems to use his two relatives at the beginning to indicate the general drift of his sentence and then does not attempt to follow out the details. Here ὅς is the necessary copula introducing the working out of the simile, and ἐπεί proclaims that the clause headed by it is preliminary and does not contain the real comparison.'

660 πάννυχον ἐγρήσσοντα is used at *Od.* 20.53. ἐρατίζων is found only in the phrase κρειῶν ἐ. |, here (= 11.551) and 2× in *HyHerm*. On its formation (< ἔραμαι, ἐρατός) see Risch, *Wortbildung* 298–300.

661–3 A spear 'rushing' from a hand is not a dead metaphor; see 5.657n., and Griffin, *HLD* 33–5. In 662 and 11.553 a papyrus and the older

MSS read ἀντίοι, cf. | ἀντίος ἀΐξας 15.694, *Od.* 22.90. Aristarchus read ἀντίον at 11.553 (Did/A *ad loc.*), whereas at 6.54 he read ἀντίος ἦλθε and Zenodotus ἀντίον (Did/b *ad loc.*). The vivid personification of the spears here makes the better-attested ἀντίοι preferable to Allen's text. θρασειάων ὑπὸ χειρῶν (662) is formular (6× *Il.*, 1× *Od.*). δετή (663), 'torch', occurs only here (= 11.553) and is next found in Aristophanes. The scholia (bT) explain 'torches of pieces of wood tied together'. The word probably comes from common speech (from δετός, 'tied ⟨in a bundle⟩').

664 τετιηότι θυμῷ | occurs only here (= 11.555) and 24.283; τετιημέναι (etc.) ἦτορ | is found 2× *Il.*, 6× *Od.*

666–7 περὶ γὰρ δίε is followed 2× by νηυσὶν Ἀχαιῶν |, 1× by ποιμένι λαῶν |, and 1× by an enjambing μή τις Ἀχαιῶν |. πρὸ φόβοιο seems to mean 'because of their rout', but the usage is almost unparalleled; Chantraine, *GH* ii 131, renders it 'en présence d'une panique, par suite d'une panique'. The scholia paraphrase ὑπὸ φόβου (Arn/A), the exegetical scholia (bT) comparing ἀθλεύων πρὸ ἄνακτος 'working for a master' (24.734).

668 Only here does ἐπιτέλλω directly introduce a speech. It is conventional for a hero to give a speech of encouragement before leaving the battle; see 183–7n.

669–73 On 669 see 507–8n. The two Aiantes were fighting side by side at 531–2. τις (670) refers to all the Greeks, not just the three leaders he addresses. ἐνηής is used of Patroklos by Zeus at 204 ≅ 21.96 and 23.252; otherwise only by Nestor of himself in proximity to a reference to Patroklos (23.648, cf. 646), and of Athene disguised as a friendly Phaeacian (*Od.* 8.200). The usages suggest that it may have been a conventional epithet for ἑταῖρος, in the *Il.* restricted to Patroklos for artistic reasons.

Similarly, the form δειλοῖο is used only in this formula for Patroklos (here and 3× in book 23), and he is the only person to whom μείλιχος is applied, here and when Briseis says that he was μείλιχος αἰεί (19.300; it is used with a negative for Hektor by Andromakhe, 24.739). Patroklos' gentleness is unique in the language of the poem, and seems to be recognized in the unusual number of direct addresses to him by the narrator (see Introduction, ch. 1, i, 3). Richardson, *CQ* 30 (1980) 268–9, discusses the sympathetic comments on Patroklos' character in the exegetical scholia.

'ἐπίστατο is used of disposition, not of intellect' (Leaf); so too at 14.92. εἰδέναι is similarly used (e.g. 325), and μανθάνειν (6.444). Verse 672 = 478, 22.436; see 153n., 477–8n.

674–8 Other eagle-similes compare the swiftness of the bird's swoop to a hero's charge (15.690–2, 21.252–3, 22.308–10, *Od.* 24.538). Here, however, the main emphasis is on its keen sight, already proverbial by the time of *HyHerm* 359–60, which corresponds to the urgent peering about of Menelaos; and the swiftness is transferred to the hare, to parallel that of

Antilokhos (see 652–5n.). The hare's epithet πόδας ταχύς (676) will be applied to Antilokhos when he approaches Akhilleus (18.2). Plutarch, *Vit. Hom.* 86, comments that the simile stresses both the eagle's keen sight (in its seeing from a great height) and its speed, by its seizing the swiftest animal. The exegetical scholia (bT) point out that its keen-sightedness is shown not only by its seeing from a height but by the camouflaged coat (τῇ χροιᾷ γεῶδες) and small size of its prey.

Fränkel, *Gleichnisse* 106, points out the incongruity between the action of the simile and that of the narrative; Menelaos does not kill Antilokhos when he finds him. Macleod notes a parallel in the description of Iris' mission to Thetis (24.78–82; *Iliad XXIV ad loc.*). At 22.308–11 Hektor charges as an eagle swoops to carry off a tender lamb or cowering hare; but his quarry Akhilleus charges furiously in return. Akhilleus' battle-starved followers are likened to *full-fed* wolves as they prepare to follow Patroklos into battle (16.156–63; but see Introduction, ch. 3, ii). It is even possible that κατακείμενος (of the hare, 677) carries the implication that Menelaos fears Antilokhos' absence may be due to his death, cf. εἰ…ἔτι ζώοντα ἴδοιτο (681), though the verb does not have any such special connotation. See also 676–8n. Denniston lists this as one of the passages with an accumulation of epic (generalizing) τε (5 × in 5 verses; *Particles* 521).

674 πάντοσε παπταίνων (etc.) is used of the frightened Harpalion as he retreats (13.649), of the dismayed suitors looking for fighting equipment (*Od.* 22.24), and of the rescued but still apprehensive Medon and Phemios (*Od.* 22.380). The connotation of nervousness is not unfitting for Menelaos after 666–7. The sense is repeated in ὄσσε φαεινώ | πάντοσε δινείσθην (679–80) as the narrative continues after the simile. φασί is used by the narrator only 2 × in the *Il.*, both times in a simile; here for a universally known fact, and at 2.783 for a statement which the narrator cannot himself confirm (de Jong, *Narrators* 237).

676–8 On πόδας ταχύς see 18.1–2n. πτώξ, 'hare', is of course connected with πτώσσω, ἔπτηξα, 'cower'; a fawn also tries to hide καταπτήξας ὑπὸ θάμνῳ at 22.191. ἀμφίκομος occurs only here and in a late imitation; κόμη is also used metaphorically of foliage at 14.398 and *Od.* 23.195, and cf. 53–6on. ἐξείλετο θυμόν | (678) recurs with accusative μιν at 15.460, and with genitives 2 × *Od.*

679–80 The poet directly addresses Menelaos seven times, always when the hero is evoking our sympathy or displaying some amiable emotion; twice when he is treacherously wounded by Pandaros (4.127, 4.146), once when he bravely accepts the challenge of the far stronger Hektor (7.104), once when he is about to make a remarkable speech (13.603; see 13.620–39n.), twice when he is desperately concerned to rescue the body of the gentle Patroklos (here and at 702), and finally when his anger is soothed by the handsome apology of his young friend Antilokhos (23.600). On this technique of the poet's see Introduction, ch. 1, i, 3. The vocative name falls in the second colon of the verse (except at 13.603), preceded by σοι, τοι, or σέθεν. Here and at 702 a generic epithet is added to fill the space before the formula which completes the verse. ὄσσε φαεινώ | is formular (6 × *Il.*).

Forms of δινεύω (680) have the meaning 'wander' with a person as subject at 4.541, 24.12, *Od.* 16.63 and *Od.* 19.67. Menelaos' journey to the left wing is not described, except by ἀπέβη in 673, and possibly the hero's bodily movements, as well as those of his eyes, are implied here.

681 It is most natural to read ἴδοιτο (with several of the older MSS) and understand Menelaos as subject, as Willcock does; the change from 2nd to 3rd person is not as difficult as Leaf maintains (cf. 705). Aristarchus (Did/A) took ὄσσε as subject, which is possible (it is followed by a singular verb, as if it were a neuter plural, at 12.466, 23.477, and *Od.* 6.131–2); he, or perhaps others, may have considered Menelaos an alternative subject (Arn/A). The plural ἴδοιντο mentioned in bT is an impossible Atticism (Chantraine, *GH* I 477; Wackernagel, *Untersuchungen* 95). ἴδοιο was preferred by οἱ ἀπὸ τῆς σχολῆς (T) and by van der Valk, *Researches* II 137–38, but this prolongation of the apostrophe would be unusual.

682–3 = 116–17 (see note), cf. 13.765–7. A few MSS continue with 683a = 118.

685–93 The same ring form (summons – description of the situation – summons) is used at 16.538–47 and 556–61 (Lohmann, *Reden* 125).

685–6 The first three cola of the tetracolon are repeated by Menelaos when he summons Antilokhos to answer the charge of cheating in the chariot-race (23.581). 686 ≅ 18.19; see 640–2n. The second hemistich ≅ that of 22.481b. Menelaos breaks the news more gently to Antilokhos than the latter does to Akhilleus.

687–9 οἴομαι εἰσορόωντα | γιγνώσκειν recurs at *Od.* 14.214–15. On πῆμα...κυλίνδει see 98–101n. On πέφαται (689) see 164–5n. Chantraine, *GH* I 85, writes ὤριστος. The usual phrase is ἀνὴρ ὤριστος (5 × *Il.*) or θεῶν ὤ. (2 × *Il.*); ἄριστος (-ον) Ἀχαιῶν (read here by several MSS of the *h* family and by Eustathius) occurs 7 × *Il.*, of Agamemnon, Diomedes, and Teukros as well as Akhilleus (see G. Nagy, *The Best of the Achaeans*, Baltimore 1979, 63); see also 18.10–11n.

690–3 Patroklos' name is often placed at the beginning of a line, but has special poignancy here; cf. 18.81, 22.387. The remainder of the verse ≅ 704, 11.471. αἴ κε...σαώσῃ is Menelaos' thought, not part of the message to Akhilleus; at 7.375 however a similar clause *is* intended to be the message, as the phrasing makes clear. Verse 693 = 122 (see 120–2n.).

695–6 = *Od.* 4.704–5; from τὼ δέ οἱ... also repeated at 23.396–7 and *Od.* 19.471–2. Thalmann, *Conventions* 8, notes the ring form (silence–tears–

silence). But silence is rare from epic personages, and in two of the above instances the dialogue soon continues (and in the third the character has been thrown from a racing chariot and a speech is hardly expected). Many of the older MSS read ἀφασίη. W. F. Wyatt, Jr, *Metrical Lengthening in Homer* (Rome 1969) 80–1, argues that the negative prefix appeared in Greek as ἀ- before a consonant and ἀν- only before a vowel, so the proper form would indeed be ἄφασίη; but since this is metrically intractable the first syllable was lengthened by inserting -μ- on the analogy of ἀμβροσίη. Since there is no reason to think this was not already done by Homer's time ἀμφασίη should stand in the text. ἔσχετο: 'was held back'; cf. 21.345; but see also S. West, *Odyssey*, on *Od.* 4.704–5.

Antilokhos' silence here prepares for that of Akhilleus himself when he hears the news (18.22ff.). 'The silence is more effective than any words' (bT).

698–9 Nowhere else does a hero take off his armour like this, but the situation is unparalleled. The scholia (bT) suggest Antilokhos does not take the chariot because he bears sad news, or in his grief does not think of it. Or one might think his swiftness of foot (see 652–5n.) will let him move faster through the mêlée than the chariot would. Actually Antilokhos' arrival and Akhilleus' horrified anticipation (18.2ff.) can be better handled without the presence of chariot and horses. This Laodokos is not heard of elsewhere; on his presence see 501–2n.

702–61 Menelaos returns to the continuing struggle over Patroklos' corpse. He and Meriones begin to bear it off the battlefield, while the two Aiantes hold off the Trojans. The desperate struggle is illustrated by a series of powerful similes

The attempt to carry off the body covers the time taken by Antilokhos to carry the call for help to Akhilleus, like the colloquy between Diomedes and Glaukos while Hektor returns to Troy (6.119–236), the struggle of Aias while Nestor carries the wounded Maçhaon back to his quarters (11.521–95), and the fighting at the ships while Patroklos makes his way back from tending the wounded Eurupulos (15.405–746; Fenik, *TBS* 185). Both poet and audience must often have thought of tales of the rescue of the body of Akhilleus himself (*Od.* 24.37–43; see 720–1n.).

702–5 On the direct address to Menelaos see 679–80n. 703 ≅ 18.129, which ends with the formular αἰπὺν ὄλεθρον; here an enjambing explanatory clause is substituted, itself explained by a clause (704) which must have been suggested by the memory of 690 just above. The three verses bring out Menelaos' concern for Patroklos, the poet's approval of him, and Antilokhos' prowess. Thrasumedes was mentioned at 378, perhaps to prepare for his service here.

708 κεῖνος (etc.) is often used in this position to refer to someone mentioned shortly before (e.g. 9.678, 14.48, 14.368, 19.344), but never so abruptly as this. Menelaos has no time or breath for names and titles.

709–10 If Virgil were the author, one would take πύθυς ιαχὺν here partly with κεῖνον, with which it fits so well; is it quite impossible to credit Homer with an oblique allusion like this? On the probable original form οὐδέ ϝ' ὀΐω (cf. 24.727) see Leaf's note. Whoever thought of the alternative ending κεχολωμένον Ἀτρείωνι for 710 (found on the inside margin of A) did not lack perception; the phrase occurs at 24.395.

711 Menelaos introduces the theme which will be developed in book 18. Thetis will announce the provision of replacement equipment (18.130–7), and Akhilleus will explain that he cannot wear anyone else's armour (18.188–95). This prepares both for the making of new armour and for Akhilleus' rescue of the corpse without it, enabling the poet to postpone his return to the battle.

712 ≅ 634, 713 = 635 (see note *ad loc.*); 714 reappears in the first hemistich of 16.782 and the second of *Od.* 12.157. φύγοιμεν (714) is well attested in the MSS, but the change from the preceding subjunctives would make no useful point.

Aias' first call for reliance on their own wits (634–6) led up to his plan of sending for Akhilleus. Menelaos has just explained it is unlikely that Akhilleus can help, so when he in turn says they have no recourse but themselves the supposedly dim-witted Aias (13.824) now comes up with another good idea.

716–19 ἀγακλεής is not common in early epic. The vocative occurs again at 21.379 (for Hephaistos), the genitive once for Priam (16.738) and once for Menelaos (23.529). Here it serves as initial-vowel alternative for διοτρεφές, which precedes ὦ Μενέλαε 1 × *Il.*, 2 × *Od.* ὑποδύντε (717) = 'getting under', 'shouldering', recurs at 8.332 = 13.421, where two companions carry off a wounded or dead hero. With 718 cf. 14.429 χερσὶν ἀείραντες φέρον ἐκ πόνου (of the wounded Hektor). The trochaic caesura in the fourth foot of 719 is irregular, violating 'Hermann's Bridge'. The difficulty of fitting in the metrically awkward μαχησόμεθα (which is not used elsewhere in Homer or Hesiod) forced the poet to accept the anomaly later in the verse.

720–1 ἶσον θυμὸν ἔχοντες recurs only at 13.704, of two yoked oxen straining to haul a plough together. They are compared to the two Aiantes as they struggle against Hektor's attack, and it seems probable that the use here is a conscious reminiscence of the earlier simile. ὁμώνυμοι does not recur in early epic. οἳ (ἢ) τὸ πάρος περ | is also used with a present tense at 12.346–7 = 12.359–60, 15.256–7, 20.123–4, 23.782–3. Macrobius, *Sat.* 5.15.13, quotes 720 with ἔχοντε (the hiatus would not be surprising at the caesura), and Aristophanes (Did/A) is said to have read μένοντε in 721. With 721 cf. μένει ὀξὺν Ἄρηα | (11.836). The second hemistich occurs 2 × *Il.*, 2 × *Od.* (dual and plural).

The two Aiantes fight side by side especially in book 13 (46ff., 197ff., 701ff.), and were together at 531–2 above. The emphasis on the presence of both of them here may be due to the desire to differentiate the episode from that of the rescue of the body of Akhilleus. The summary of the *Aithiopis* in Proclus says 'And in the mighty struggle over the fallen corpse Aias picks up the body and carries it off to the ships, while Odysseus fights off the Trojans' (p. 106 Allen). Odysseus' part on this occasion is confirmed by *Od.* 5.309–10, and the conjunction of the two heroes prepares for their rivalry for the armour of the dead man (*Od.* 11.543–6). There were, however, other early versions in which Odysseus carried the corpse; see G. L. Huxley, *Greek Epic Poetry from Eumelos to Panyassis* (London 1969) 150; Fenik, *Rhesus* 33 n. 2; and Bernabé, *PEG* 85–6. In representations in art Aias always bears the body (Bernabé, *PEG* 216; Friis Johansen, *Iliad* 73).

M. M. Willcock, in Bremer, *HBOP* 193, has suggested, with much plausibility, that this episode of Patroklos' body borne off by the second-class warriors Menelaos and Meriones while the two Aiantes protect it is secondary to the tale of the two mighty heroes, one carrying and the other defending Akhilleus' body; 'The imitator is likely to try to improve on his model.' Obviously the *Il.* poet cannot simply reproduce here the more famous rescue scene, and increasing the number of characters involved is a simple change to make; moreover, here the Trojans are led by both Hektor and Aineias (758), which of course could not have been the case at Akhilleus' death. If a little less grandeur results, that is only fitting for Patroklos.

The ancient commentators took a different view. 'This was altered by the later poets, who had Akhilleus carried off by Aias, while Odysseus protected him with his shield. If Homer had written of the death of Akhilleus, he would not have made the corpse be carried off by Aias, as the later poets did' (Arn/A on 719).

722–4 ἀγκάζομαι < ἀγκάς, 'in the arms', cf. πελάζω < πέλας (Risch, *Wortbildung* 297). It occurs only here and in late imitations. 'It would not be appropriate for the gentleness of Patroklos to drag him' (bT). On μάλα μεγάλως see 595n. ἴαχε(ν) always occurs in this position, and this phrase is repeated (without enjambment) at 13.834 (cf. 13.822). The same runover λαός... | Τρωϊκός (-ον) is seen at 16.368–9 and 21.295–6; here it contrasts with Ἀχαιούς and leads in to the following simile. αἴροντας is perhaps derived from *ϝαργω, a parallel formation to *ἀϝερϝω, which gives the usual ἀείροντας (Shipp, *Studies* 50).

725–61 The series of five similes which follows is paralleled only in the group which describes the Greek army arrayed before the Catalogue of Ships (2.455–83, see note *ad loc.*). There the similes follow each other in a formal uninterrupted sequence, introduced alternatively by ἠΰτε and τῶν (τοὺς) δ' ὥς, all describing the same army, its captains, and its leader with a gradually narrowing focus. Here the technique is more flexible. The first simile (725–34) compares the surging Trojans to dogs attacking a wounded boar; but the boar turns on them, they scatter in fear, and the action developed within the simile is carried back into the narrative as the two Aiantes repeatedly turn and terrify their attackers. After a short summary (735–6) the second simile describes a sudden blazing fire rushing over a city, and – again carrying the action of the picture back to the narrative – compares the roaring windstorm which accompanies it to the din of horses and spearmen (737–41). This general impression of the scene is followed immediately by a close-up of willing mules struggling to haul timber down a rough mountain trail; and the picture merges into that of the two heroes straining to carry off the corpse (742–6). After a quick summary (746; repeated from 735) we return to the Aiantes, now not retreating but unyielding as a wooded ridge holding back the streams of mighty rivers (746–753). Finally, after a couplet naming Aineias and Hektor as leaders of the attack, like screeching birds before a pursuing hawk the rest of the Greeks scatter before the two Trojans (753–9). The passage concludes with the poet's usual description of one item of the scene, the fallen armour lying around the trench, and a last line of summary (760–18.1).

Aineas and Hektor confront the two Aiantes while Menelaos and Meriones strain to carry the corpse; like a group of statuary, they are all frozen in position until the narrative returns to them at 18.148 and they spring to life again. The unusual agglomeration of similes is clearly intended to build this scene to a continuing climax while the narrative shifts to Akhilleus. This is different from the purpose of the series before the Catalogue.

The similes have in common the strains and struggles against opposition, not on the battlefield but in everyday life, which appear not only in human activities but in the conflict of natural forces and in the animal world. This unrelenting pressure, and the opposition to it, unify the different scenes described. For comparison, the long descriptive section at 360–425 (see note *ad loc.*) is composed of a number of separate motifs which present different aspects in turn by different techniques.

725–34 Boars are the fiercest of wild beasts (21–2), and like a boar easily scattering dogs and hunters Aias Telamonios easily broke the Trojan ranks at 281–5 (there are similar boar attacks at 11.324–5, 11.414–18, and 13.471–5). A dog pursuing a boar or lion expects it to turn on him

(8.338–40). 'The turning back [τὸ "ἐλίξεται", 728] is effective, for the boar alone of beasts turns at bay when it is pursued' (bT).

725–6 κύνεσσιν ἐοικότες, bridging the mid-verse caesura, is an example of a highly archaic formular system of comparisons (Hoekstra, *Epic Verse* 49–50). βλημένῳ, emphatic by position, shows it is not cowardice that causes the boar's retreat; similarly, the Aiantes retreat because of the need to get the corpse away (735). The wording is like 15.579–80, κύων ὥς, ὅς τ' ἐπὶ νεβρῷ | βλημένῳ ἀΐξῃ, where pathos replaces courage. The second hemistich of 726 does not recur.

727 ἕως has the same meaning as τέως, 'for a time', as at 730 and often in Homer. This is the only instance in the *Il.* of ἕως (or τέως) apparently scanned as a monosyllable; the *Od.* has five examples (and four of τέως; see Chantraine, *GH* I 11–12). Hoekstra, *Modifications* 34–5, notes that the traditional scansion as a trochee (*ἧος) could be restored here by omitting μέν, but μέν is required to set up the contrast with ἀλλ' ὅτε. The poet takes advantage, in the untraditional circumstances of a simile, of an option which synizesis has made available. διαρραῖσαι μεμαῶτες may be an untraditional formula; it is used again only in one of the similes leading up to the Catalogue of Ships (2.473) and in Nestor's tale of his exploits (11.713, 733).

728–9 ἐλίξεται (like ἀΐξωσι, 726) is aorist subjunctive of general or repeated time (Chantraine, *GH* I 245). ἀλκὶ πεποιθώς is another formula almost confined to similes (5 × *Il.*, 1 × *Od.*; also qualifying Hektor, 18.158). The first hemistich of 729 is repeated 1 × *Il.* (in a simile), the second occurs 3 × *Il.*, 1 × *Od.* (including modified forms).

730 ≅ 15.277, **731** = 15.278 and 3 × *Il.* elsewhere. In 730 εἵως (all MSS) would be preferable; see vol. IV, ch. 2, iv. On ἀμφιγύοισιν (probably of a spear-blade, 'curved on both sides') see 13.146–8n.

732–4 μεταστρεφθέντε repeats ἐλίξεται of the simile, again after ἀλλ' ὅτε δή. κατ' αὐτούς means 'among them' (Chantraine, *GH* II 114); cf. 13.556–7. σταίησαν (iterative; Chantraine, *GH* I 224–5) is the only example in Homer of this form of 3rd person plural aorist optative. L. R. Palmer (Wace and Stubbings, *Companion* 94; following Wackernagel, *Untersuchungen* 62) would read ἔστησαν, but the indicative does not give the sense of repeated action which is required here. Change of colour is the mark of fright at 3.35, 13.279, 13.284, *Od.* 21.412–13. The hiatus after the first foot of 734 may be due to the desire to place ἀΐξας in the normal position for this verb (Shipp, *Studies* 190). Forms of δηριάομαι with this scansion occur in this position 5 × *Il.*, 1 × *Od.*

735 ὥς...φέρον, the first part of the summary of the preceding action, is repeated after the close of the next simile (746). There the dual ἐμμεμαῶτε clearly refers to Menelaos and Meriones. Here, if the dual is to be pressed, it is hard not to take it with the two Aiantes. If the dual number can really refer to two *groups* (a view most recently championed by R. Gordesiani, *Philologus* 124, 1980, 163–74, and A. Thornton, *Glotta* 56, 1978, 1–4, neither referring to this example), it would well suit *both* pairs of heroes. Probably the poet is not so conscious of the duality of the form as modern scholars are. In 735, γ' ἐμμ- is to be preferred to the γε μεμ- of late MSS; see 13.775–87n.

736–41 The battle is as fierce as a fire sweeping over a city; then the roar of the fire and the windstorm is compared to the din of battle. This kind of anticipation of the narrative is common in similes; see Introduction, ch. 3, ii. Here there is no indication that the fire is other than accidental, doubtless a common occurrence. At 18.207–13 the fire in a city is an attempt to summon help, at 21.522–4 it is caused by the gods' anger, and at 22.410–11 it is that of Troy itself burning. It is hard not to think this sequence of similes rises to an intentional culmination. See also 21.522–5n. The scholia (bT) remark that the comparison is elsewhere compressed into a metaphor, μάχης καυστειρῆς (4.342 = 12.316).

736–8 On πτόλεμος τέτατο see 400–1n., 13.358–60n. The sudden blaze of fire is brought out in ἐπεσσύμενον, ὄρμενον, and φλεγέθει (cf. 18.211) as well as in ἐξαίφνης.

739 σέλαϊ appears only here, but γήραϊ λυγρῷ is formular and δέπαϊ is the normal form for δέπας. σέλᾳ is printed by Allen at 8.563, but the alpha should be short and σέλαι would be better (as von der Mühll prefers in his apparatus to *Od.* 21.246). See Chantraine, *GH* I 50, 209. τό refers back to πῦρ (737). ἐπιβρέμω, 'make roar', does not recur in ancient epic; ἐμβρέμω occurs at 15.627. ϝὶς ἀνέμοιο is an old formula designed to follow an imperfect or aorist verb-ending (3 × *Od.*; Hoekstra, *Odyssey* on *Od.* 13.276). Only here and perhaps at 21.356 (cf. Chantraine, *GH* I 143) is the digamma of ἴς neglected. A storm of wind accompanies forest fires at 11.156 and 20.492.

740–1 On the rare enjambment of a genitive noun–epithet formula dependent on a noun in the following verse see *TAPA* 97 (1966) 132. ἀζηχής (adj. and adv. 4 × *Il.*, 1 × *Od.*) is from *ἀ-δια-ἐχης, 'incessant' (Chantraine, *Dict.*). ὀρυμαγδός is not found elsewhere in this position in the verse. The four-word line is both harsh-sounding and impressive.

742–5 At 13.703–7 the Aiantes stand together like yoked oxen hauling a plough, and at 13.198–200 they bear off a victim's corpse like two lions carrying a captured goat high above the ground. But Patroklos is not the victim of his two bearers, and the comparison here lies in the difficult progress, the weight of the load borne, and the sweating effort exerted by the mules and the heroes. Subject, verb, and object, each with its qualifiers, fall neatly into the successive lines 742–4.

742–3 μένος ἀμφιβαλόντες: at 23.97–8 and *Od.* 17.344 the meaning of the active participle is 'throw ⟨one's arms⟩ around', and at *Od.* 23.192 Odysseus builds his bedroom 'throwing ⟨it⟩ around' the famous olive tree. Here the mules are 'throwing their mighty spirit around' the beam; as we should say, putting their backs into the work. Willcock renders it 'applying'. Cf. the description of the mules bringing in the timber for Patroklos' pyre (23.121–2). The beam is clearly dragged behind the mules, not slung between them, though this would better suit the comparison. ἀταρπός appears again at *Od.* 14.1, and ἀταρπιτός at 18.565.

745–6 See on 384–5. Verse 745 ends laboriously, with six heavy syllables. On 746 see 735n. The poet may be associating ἐμμεμαῶτε with the μένος of the simile (742).

747–51 River-similes all depict storm-swollen torrents; six are listed by Scott, *Oral Nature* 76, and 17.263–5 might be added. This is the only instance where the fury of the river is checked and rendered harmless.

747 Note the repetition of ἰσχανέτην, ἰσχάνει, and ἴσχει (750); all are forms of ἔχειν. There is a similar repetition (also in a simile) at 5.89–90. πρών, 'ridge', < *πρώϝων, cf. plural πρώονες (3 × *Il.*); the feminine form *πρώειρα > πρῷρα, 'prow' (Risch, *Wortbildung* 62).

748 Apart from this instance διαπρύσιον occurs in Homer only in the formula ἤυσεν δὲ δ. Δαναοῖσι (Τρώεσσι) γεγωνώς (6 × *Il*). The more flexible use here in the simile reflects that of *HyAphr* 19, 80 and *HyHerm* 336. In the Homeric formula and *HyAphr* it is used of voices, 'piercing', 'far-reaching'; here it must mean 'stretching right across ⟨the plain⟩'. What the author of *HyHerm* thought it meant we need not enquire. For the wording cf. *Od.* 10.87–8 πέτρη | ἠλίβατος τετύχηκε διαμπερὲς ἀμφοτέρωθεν. The correct Homeric form τετυχηώς (see Leaf, and Chantraine, *GH* I 428–9) has survived only in MS T and Eustathius 1700.40.

749 ἴφθιμος is elsewhere in Homer (27 × *Il.*, 18 × *Od.*) used only of humans or animals; its use here for rivers is in keeping with the innovative language of these similes. ἀλεγεινὰ ῥέεθρα occurs only here, but the adjective is found 1 × *Il.*, 3 × *Od.* with κύματα.

750–1 ἄφαρ ... πλάζων = 'and at once directs their (πᾶσι) flow over the plain, thrusting it ⟨back⟩'; see Chantraine, *Dict.* s.v. πλάζω. One wonders if the poet had a particular place in mind (cf. the descriptive ὑλήεις, 748). ἴσχει and πλάζων, similar in scansion, both followed by a pause, and both containing an *s* sound, are probably intended to suggest the floodwaters suddenly crashing against the barrier; cf. κῦμα δέ μιν προσπλάζον ἐρύκεται (12.285, again in a simile). σθένεϊ goes with ῥέοντες.

751 The better-attested reading is οὐδέ τέ μιν; τι is probably due to Aristarchus. See van der Valk, *Researches* II 126. ῥηγνῦσι < *ῥήγνυντι, since neither ῥηγνύουσι nor ῥηγνυᾶσι will scan in the hexameter; the circumflex is due to the analogy of Attic ἱστᾶσι etc. (Chantraine, *GH* I 189–90, 471).

754 Aineias and Hektor will play large rôles in books 20 and 22 respectively, so both are emphasized here and in 758; see 20.79–111n. The tricolon shape of the verse is common, cf. 1.7, 20.160.

755–9 Usually the hawk's speed in pursuit of prey is the point of comparison in a simile (e.g. 16.582–3; see Fränkel, *Gleichnisse* 80–1). Here the hawk represents Hektor and Aineias, but the main point of comparison is between the shrieking of the smaller birds at its appearance and the cries of the panic-stricken Greeks (οὖλον κεκλήγοντες 756, repeated at 759).

755 τῶν perhaps matches Τρώων (753), or looks forward to a noun understood from οὖλον κεκλήγοντες. There are similar changes of construction before and after a simile at 4.433–6, 15.271–5, and *Od.* 13.81–4. ψάρ = 'starling'; on the form see 16.582–3n. κολοιός = 'jackdaw'; both are pursued by a hawk at 16.582–3. With the 'cloud' cf. νέφος... πεζῶν 4.274, 23.133, Τρώων νέφος 16.66.

756 οὖλος = 'thick', 'curly', and describes wool, hair, twining plant stems, and smoke; it may be connected with εἰλέω (Chantraine, *Dict.*). It seems easy to transfer it, like πυκνός, to the idea of a large number of indistinguishable items, such as the continuous shrieking of a large flock of frightened birds (despite Leaf's '"a woolly cry"... is by no means in the Epic style'). W. B. Stanford, *Greek Metaphor* (Oxford 1936) 53, describes it as 'a cry which is thick and confused like wool'. Willcock, however, thinks it may be from ὀλοόν, 'dreadfully'. The word is not connected with οὖλος (Ἄρης) (< ὄλλυμι), but the poet may not have known this. The T scholia say τοῦ φόβου τὴν φωνὴν συστρέφοντος βοῶσιν ὀξὺ καὶ συνεστραμμένον. κεκλήγοντες shows an Aeolic use of the present ending on the perfect stem, and appears 4 × *Il.*, 1 × *Od.* beside the singular κεκληγώς; see Chantraine, *GH* 1 430–1.

757 κίρκος is used only here and 22.139; the more generic word ἴρηξ is commoner (6 × *Il.*, 1 × *Od.*). Once both words are used in apposition (*Od.* 13.86–7). Birds are also noisy, in different contexts, at 3.3–6 and 22.141. (σ)μικρός lengthens the preceding vowel here; in the other two Homeric occurrences this is not necessary and μικρός is written (5.801, *Od.* 3.296); see Chantraine, *GH* 1 176. On the word's meaning and usage see 5.800–1n.

Moulton, *Similes* 101, 105, considers σμικρῆσι... ὀρνίθεσσιν are the birds' nestlings, and links the simile with others of animals protecting their young. This view is supported by de Jong (see next note), and is of course possible. But if the poet thought the idea important, it is odd that he did not employ an explicit word such as νεοσσοῖσι (9.323) or τεκέ(ε)σσι(ν), used of the young of lions (133), birds (12.222), and bees (16.265).

758–9 I. J. F. de Jong, *Mnemosyne* 38 (1985) 276, points out that ὑπό presents the two Trojans from the viewpoint of the Greeks, as the hawk is seen by the flock of birds (756–7). With 759 cf. μνήσαντο δὲ (etc.) χάρμης 7 × *Il.*, 1 × *Od.*, οὐ λήθετο χάρμης 2 × *Il.* This is the only time warriors 'forget their war-spirit' in these words. Hoekstra, *Modifications* 151n., thinks these expressions are probably very old.

760 The scholia (bT) point out that the poet avoids saying directly that the Greeks throw their equipment away. ἀμφὶ δὲ τάφρον | is found 2 × *Il.*, but the ditch does not really enter into formulae. περί τ' ἀμφί τε recurs only at *HyDem* 276 (adverbially), but ἀμφὶ περί is found at 2.305, 21.10, 23.191, *Od.* 11.609.

761 Cf. πῖπτε κάρηνα | Τρώων φευγόντων (11.158–9; the only parallel). πολέμου...ἐρωή recurs at 16.302, where (as here) there is not a complete rout.

When the narrative returns to this scene at 18.148ff. the Greeks are still φεύγοντες. The exegetical scholia (bT on 755–7) carefully explain that the Greeks' cowardly behaviour is the result of Zeus's intervention, whereas when the same simile was used at 16.582–3 the Trojans fled because of the courage of a human hero, Patroklos.

BOOK EIGHTEEN

This book concludes the theme of Akhilleus' withdrawal from the battle and begins that of his revenge on the slayer of his best friend, preparing the way for his confrontation with Hektor. In an agony of grief at the loss of Patroklos, Akhilleus determines to seek revenge despite his mother's warning that it must quickly be followed by his own death. With Athene's assistance, he terrifies the Trojans (though he is now without armour), and the body of Patroklos is carried home. Before the first lament and the preparation of the corpse, the poet turns to Hektor, interweaving a scene which reinforces his over-confidence and his refusal to listen to good advice and withdraw from Akhilleus' fury. After the scene of mourning around Patroklos there is a short conversation between Zeus and Here, marking the end of Zeus's aid to the Trojans and foreshadowing their doom. Meanwhile, Thetis has journeyed to Hephaistos' home on Olumpos, and after affable greetings and a rehearsal of Thetis' sorrows the smith-god sets to work and makes a replacement set of armour, depicting on the great shield the mainly pleasant routines of everyday human life.

Just as the scenes with Akhilleus and Hektor alternate, so the two main themes of the Book interact with each other in a subtle irony. The short life of Akhilleus was lamented by Thetis when we first saw them together (1.414–18), and the renewed meeting between them at the beginning of this Book, in a tableau vividly invoking the image of Akhilleus' own funeral rites, reintroduces and reinforces the theme by the even more positive assertion that Akhilleus' death must quickly follow that of Hektor. This does not weaken his desire for vengeance on the slayer of Patroklos, and from this time on he will often refer to his swiftly-approaching fate.

These recurrent reminders of Akhilleus' mortality form an ironical counterpoint to the other theme of this book, that of the divinely made armour, which ought to confer invulnerability (an issue which Homer takes some care to avoid; see 20.264–7n.). Patroklos' disguise in the armour Akhilleus had received from his father Peleus was suggested by Nestor as a ruse to deceive the Trojans (11.798–801), but this aspect was ignored soon after it was put into effect (cf. 16.423–5, 543). The armour provided, however, a concrete symbol of Akhilleus' consent to Patroklos' leadership in the battle, and hence of his share in the responsibility for his death; this was heavily emphasized immediately before he died by the poet's reflections on the defilement of the splendid helmet (16.793–800). The following struggle for the corpse of Patroklos is combined with Hektor's seizing and donning of the armour, employed again as a symbol, this time of Hektor's hubris (see 17.194–209n.). The constant association of the death of Akhilleus' great friend and the dishonourable loss of the corpse and the armour too has already begun, and is continued into book 18 (e.g. 17.122, 17.472–3, 18.21, 18.82–5; see 165n., 180n.). Later, Akhilleus' armour on Hektor's shoulders will serve as a visible reminder of Patroklos' death when Akhilleus finally takes his revenge (22.323).

New armour must now be provided for Akhilleus, and the steps taken towards this are skilfully juxtaposed with the increasing clarity with which the hero's own death is predicted. The first Hephaistos-made panoply did not save Patroklos, and will not save Hektor; and with superb irony, Hephaistos himself, just as he sets about making the new imperishable equipment, declares that it cannot save Akhilleus (464–7). The craftsmanship of an immortal and the short life-span of the mortal are violently contrasted when Akhilleus finally dons the dazzling equipment and is at once given a further warning that it will not save his life (19.409–17).

Besides this symbolic value, the loss of the armour to Hektor also provides the poet with a realistic reason for Akhilleus not to enter the battle immediately to save his friend's body and kill Hektor, enabling the poet to bring about the reconciliation with Agamemnon and much else before the foes eventually meet. As it is, Akhilleus rescues the body without confronting Hektor. And of course the loss makes possible the brilliant description of the figures on the mighty shield.

It is probable that the loss and replacement of the divinely made armour was a theme peculiar to the monumental *Il.*, an invention of Homer (see 84–5n., and Ph. J. Kakridis, *Hermes* 89, 1961, 288–97.) When Akhilleus confronted Memnon after the latter had killed Antilokhos both heroes were wearing armour provided by the gods, and this tale may well have suggested the immensely more poignant background underlying the duel of Akhilleus and Hektor (see Introduction, ch. 2, ii). By introducing the disguise motif and the loss of Akhilleus' armour to Hektor, Homer produced (and magnificently exploited) the necessity of having Thetis provide new armour for him before he avenged Patroklos; and it may be that he transferred this motif here from its older place at Akhilleus' departure for the Trojan War, and to avoid duplication invented the tale that the Hephaistos-made armour Akhilleus took to Troy was given to Peleus at his wedding and handed on by him, in his old age, to his son (see 84–5n.). In so doing, Homer probably paralleled the gift of divinely made armour by Eos to Memnon when he left for Troy; but he incurred the embarrassment of Akhilleus' possessing, at the end of the *Il.*, *two* Hephaistos-made panoplies – so that in fact Aias and Odysseus could have had one each!

Several other scenes and themes in this Book may have been connected with the story of Akhilleus' vengeance on Memnon the Ethiopian for the death of Antilokhos, and his subsequent death at the hands of Paris and Apollo (see Introduction, ch. 2, ii). These episodes were narrated in the *Aithiopis*, attributed to Arktinos; of course we do not know what poetic forms the story may have taken at the time of composition of the monumental *Il.* In the *Aithiopis* both Memnon and Akhilleus were given immortality, a deflation of the *Il.*'s tragedy of heroic death which probably indicates the difference in tone between the two poems.

Excellent appreciations of this Book, which is perhaps the most striking in the poem for boldness, originality of artistic technique, and the brilliant composition of Akhilleus' speeches, can be found in Schadewaldt, *VHWW* 234–67, and Reinhardt, *IuD* 349–411.

1–147 Antilokhos brings the news of Patroklos' death to Akhilleus, who falls to the ground in an agony of grief. Thetis hears his cry in the depths of the ocean, and leads her nymphs in a lament for him; then they join him on the shore and she takes his head in her hands. Akhilleus declares his intention of killing Hektor in revenge, despite Thetis' warning that his own death must follow soon after Hektor's. Thetis forbids him to enter the battle until she returns with new armour made by Hephaistos

1–69 The scene is skilfully composed, directing all the attention towards Akhilleus; he has not appeared since he prayed in vain to Zeus for Patroklos' safe return (16.220–56), though a memorable account of him and his thoughts was given by the narrator during the recent battle (17.401–11). After a transitional verse (1) the setting is swiftly outlined (2–3), and Akhilleus' thoughts are given, first in the narrator's voice (4–5) and then in the hero's (6–14). Antilokhos' words (18–21) are brief, and do not turn our eyes away from Akhilleus, whose response is portrayed not in words (as is that of Priam and Hekabe to Hektor's death) but by his actions (22–35). Then, while Akhilleus lies prostrate and groaning, the lapse of time is covered by a shift in the narrative to Thetis, a lengthy catalogue of her nymphs, and her lament for Akhilleus himself. After this 35-verse expansion (35–69) we return to Akhilleus, still βαρὺ στενάχοντι (70).

1–2 Verse 1 is often used for a change of scene; see 17.366n. In 2, Ἀχιλῆϊ δαΐφρονι would have been more regular, as in 18 and 30 (cf. 3.121 Ἶρις δ' αὖθ' Ἑλένῃ λευκωλένῳ ἄγγελος ἦλθε, and *Od.* 12.374). πόδας ταχύς (-ύν) is conventional for Akhilleus (5 × *Il.*, including adaptations at 69 and 354 below), but its use is extended once each to Meriones (vocative; 13.249), Aineias (aptly; 13.482, see 13.481–4n.), and the hare to which Antilokhos is compared in a simile (17.676; see 17.674–8n.). Antilokhos' speed is important here (see 17.652–5n.), and the application of the phrase to him, in juxtaposition to Akhilleus' name, gives it special force. There is a similar separation of the units of a formula at 362. Antilokhos had been fighting at the left of the battle-line, whereas Akhilleus' ships are on the far right; see 17.377–83n.

3–4 The occupation of the person sought is a regular element in the type-scene of a messenger's arrival; here it takes the uniquely effective form of Akhilleus' sudden foreboding. Hektor has a similar monologue when he realizes the gods have doomed him (22.297–305; on such monologues see C. Hentze, *Philologus* 63, 1904, 12–30).

ὀρθοκραιράων is used of ships in the same phrase at 19.344, and of cattle 2 × *Il.*, 1 × *Od.* (and *HyHerm* 220). Risch, *Wortbildung* 139, traces it back to Linear B. The phrase is the plural equivalent of νεὸς κυανοπρῴροιο (1 × *Il.*, 8 × *Od.*), which is found 4 × *Od.* after προπάροιθε, μετόπισθε, and κατόπισθε and itself developed from the older unmetathesized νηὸς κ. (2 × *Il.*, 1 × *Od.*; Hoekstra, *Modifications* 124–6). If any particularized epithet existed to follow νηῶν or νεῶν it must have been lost before Homer's time. See also *AJP* 89 (1968) 261–2.

The first hemistich of 4 = 2.36, *Od.* 2.116; at 10.491 ἀνά is replaced by κατά, probably the preferred form when the metre allows (cf. the ubiquitous κατὰ φρένα καὶ κατὰ θυμόν). τετελεσμένος (-ον) ἐστί (ἔσται, εἴη) occurs 12 × *Il.*, 11 × *Od.*; this is the only example of the neuter plural and of the imperfect. The hiatus could have been avoided by using τελέεσθαι ἔμελλον, as at 2.36 and *Od.* 2.156, but ἦεν implies he is concerned about the past, 'what had happened' (cf. M. Finkelberg, *CP* 83, 1988, 207, 210). The scholia however seem to take it as looking towards the future (ἔστι δὲ τῶν ἐν ἀτυχίᾳ προληπτικὸς ὁ νοῦς, AbT).

6–14 This is the first of the four monologues Akhilleus utters in these later books (see 20.425–7n.). Lohmann, *Reden* 19–20, compares the structure of the speech to Agamemnon's at 14.42–51 (see note *ad loc.*), where he realizes Hektor's threat is coming true. It is in ring form:

A Why this panic-stricken flight to the ships (6–7)?
B May this not portend sorrow (8)
C as my mother once prophesied (9–11).
B′ Surely Patroklos must be dead (12)!
A′ though I ordered him to return to the ships (13–14).

7 Cf. ἀτυζομένω πεδίοιο | (6.38), ἀτυζόμενοι κλονέονται | (21.554).

8–11 Similarly in the *Od.* Poluphemos and Kirke recall forgotten predictions of Odysseus' coming after they have been outwitted (9.507ff., 10.330ff.), and Alkinoös remembers too late Poseidon's threat of retaliation for the Phaeacians' help to distressed sailors (13.172ff.). Here it is a very human touch for Akhilleus to guess the bad news before it is announced. The prophecy has been prepared for by 17.408–11, but must have been invented by the poet for its poignancy here. The 'best' fighter of a group is usually its leader, as Patroklos was when he was killed; cf. 17.79–81n., and H. van Wees, *CQ* 38 (1988) 21.

8 The *h* family of MSS read θυμοῦ, which Leaf thinks may be right, but the dative is preferable after μοι ('bring to pass sorrows for my heart'). At *Od.* 14.197 λέγων ἐμὰ κήδεα θυμοῦ the sense is different ('telling the sorrows of my heart').

10–11 With the second hemistich of 10 cf. the full-verse form ζώοντός γ' ἐμέθεν καὶ ἐπὶ χθονὶ δερκομένοιο at *Od.* 16.439. ὁρᾷ (etc.) φάος ἠελίοιο | is common (3 × *Il.*, 5 × *Od.*), but λείψειν φ. ἠ. recurs only at *Od.* 11.93 (with λιπών).

This couplet was omitted by Rhianus and Aristophanes, perhaps because Patroklos was said to be a Locrian from Opous (Did/AT); Aristarchus commented on and defended it (Arn/A, see Erbse *ad loc.* and Apthorp, *Manuscript Evidence* 82). Patroklos' father Menoitios brought him from Opous to Phthie (23.85–6), and was there again when the two young men joined the expedition to Troy (11.771–89); and Akhilleus promised to return Patroklos to Opous after the victory (18.324–7). However, Patroklos was to take Akhilleus' son back to his inheritance if the hero died at Troy (19.328–33).

12–14 Akhilleus realizes that the rout of the Greeks (6–7) and the remembered prophecy (7–11) must mean Patroklos is dead, despite his own attempt to prevent this (13–14). He is similarly quick to guess (and ostentatiously ignore) Athene's motives at 1.202–5 and Patroklos' at 16.7–19. Akhilleus' instructions to Patroklos were given at 16.87–96.

σχέτλιος is explained by the following sentence; see also 16.203–6n., 22.86n. Not 'my dear and wayward friend!' (Fitzgerald) but 'The fool! And yet I told him...' On ἦ τε see 17.170–2n.; the parallels weigh against Brandreth's ἦ F' here. ἂψ ἐπὶ νῆας ἴμεν is the reading of Aristarchus (Did/A), found in some late MSS and a papyrus; the older MSS and another papyrus read νῆας ἔπ' ἂψ ἰέναι. At 21.297 only Aristarchus' version appears (*h* have ἵναι), which supports that reading here; and ἂψ usually stands directly before the preposition.

16 The normal Νέστορος ἀγλαὸς υἱός (1 × *Il.*, 4 × *Od.*) is avoided here because it would produce a verse with no caesura in any foot but the first. The first hemistich = that of 381.

17 | δάκρυα θερμὰ χέων (etc.) is formular (4 × *Il.*, 2 × *Od.*), but perhaps we should recall its last occurrence, when Patroklos pleaded for permission to enter the battle (16.3). σὺν ἀγγελίη ἀλεγεινῆ | occurs at 2.787, but does not immediately introduce direct speech; here the lack of a normal speech-introduction is striking.

18–19 The normal vocative formula for Akhilleus is ὦ Ἀχιλεῦ, Πηλῆος υἱέ, μέγα φέρτατ' Ἀχαιῶν (16.21 = 19.216). Here the adaptation of the phrasing of 17.685–6, ὄφρα πύθηαι | λυγρῆς ἀγγελίης, causes a harsh enjambment between adjective and noun, which may be thought specially effective; see 17.640–2n. The scholia (AbT) comment that ὦ μοι shows Antilokhos' own suffering, as well as that of Patroklos and Akhilleus.

20–1 The asyndeton gives great emphasis, as in | κεῖται Σαρπηδών (16.541, cf. 22.386–7). Verse 21, with its emphatic runover and following exegesis, is repeated from 17.122 and 693; see 17.120–2n., 21.50n. Antilokhos blurts out all the terrible news at once, as the scholia (bT) remark – adding that the tragedians did not admire this but introduced long speeches for giving disastrous news to the unfortunate. Plutarch, *Vit. Hom.* 83, also praises the passage as forceful (εὔτονος). The capture of the armour adds disgrace and loss to grief, and Akhilleus himself will juxtapose it with Patroklos' death (80–5). See also 17.711n.

22–31 In his agony of grief Akhilleus defiles his head with dust, rolls on the ground, and tears his hair. The language of mourning is mingled with that of death, for defiling the head with dust is the sign not only of extreme grief but also of death on the battlefield. The presence of the lamenting women also suggests that Akhilleus is lying not in grief, but in death, and the way is prepared for the even stronger adumbration of this in Thetis' lament (see 52–64n., 65–9n.).

It is Patroklos' unique rôle in the *Il.* to be killed by Hektor – tradition forbade Antilokhos or any other major Greek figure to die thus and motivate Akhilleus' vengeance – and it is essential that we appreciate the depth of Akhilleus' grief for him so that we may understand, and perhaps sympathize with, his later barbaric behaviour towards Hektor's corpse. So Homer has already informed us of Akhilleus' great love for Patroklos from his prayer to Zeus for his friend's safe return (16.220–48), as well as from the foreboding passage at 17.401–11 and Aias' remark οἱ πολὺ φίλτατος ὤλεθ' ἑταῖρος (17.655), and here he portrays the hero in the extremity of grief (to Plato's dismay). See also 82n.

22–4 Verse 22 = 17.591; on the metaphor see 17.243–4n. These three verses are also used for the grief of old Laertes at the news of Odysseus' death, with χαρίεν...πρόσωπον replaced by πολιῆς ἀδινὰ στεναχίζων (*Od.* 24.315–17). The descriptions of Priam's grief go even further: κυλινδόμενος κατὰ κόπρον (22.414, cf. 24.163–5). αἰθαλόεσσαν (< αἴθω) literally = 'burnt', 'sooty' as at 2.415, *Od.* 22.239 (also of the thunderbolt, Hesiod, *Theogony* 72). The phrase looks forward to μέλαινα...τέφρη, 'ashes' (25). Modern commentators explain that ashes were available here from the altar which doubtless stood in front of the dwelling, but not how they came to be in Laertes' orchard (*Od.* 24.316).

There are significant echoes here of the defiling of Akhilleus' helmet in the dust when it fell from the head of Patroklos (especially ἀνδρὸς θείοιο κάρη χαρίεν τε μέτωπον | ῥύετ᾽ Ἀχιλλῆος, 16.798–9), and of the dragging of Hektor's head in the dust behind Akhilleus' chariot (κάρη δ᾽ ἅπαν ἐν κονίῃσι | κεῖτο πάρος χαρίεν, 22.402–3). See 22.401–4n. and references there (especially Griffin, *HLD* 134–48).

25 The contrast in 24 between the juxtaposed χαρίεν and ᾔσχυνε is followed by an even stronger one in 25, for νεκταρέῳ declares the divine associations of the tunic here marked with the signs of grief and death. νεκτάρεος qualifying clothing means 'perfumed with fragrant oil', as at its only other occurrence (for Helen's robe at 3.385; see 14.172n.), but the word, like ἀμβροσίη, is constantly associated with ambrosia and the immortals (see 19.37–8n.). It may also be thought relevant that Thetis had lovingly packed her son's clothes into his trunk when he left home, and the garment may have been a gift from her (16.222–4). Similarly, Hektor's hair is qualified by κυάνεος, normally reserved for the gods, when it is dragged in the dust (22.402; see note *ad loc.*). The compound ἀμφιζάνω is *hapax* in Greek literature.

26–7 αὐτός looks forward to δμῳαὶ δέ (28); cf. *Od.* 14.23. The couplet must be compared with | μαρναμένων ἀμφ᾽ αὐτόν· ὁ δ᾽ ἐν στροφάλιγγι κονίης | κεῖτο μέγας μεγαλωστὶ λελασμένος ἱπποσυνάων, used of Hektor's charioteer Kebriones at 16.775–6 and of Akhilleus himself at *Od.* 24.39–40 (changed to the second person). μεγαλωστί is normal in formation (Risch, *Wortbildung* 366), but occurs only in these passages in ancient epic; the same liking for parechesis appears in οἰόθεν οἶος (7.39) and αἰνόθεν αἰνῶς (7.97). With τανυσθείς | κεῖτο may be compared κεῖτο τανυσθείς | (3 × *Il.*) and | κεῖτο ταθείς (2 × *Il.*), both always used of a corpse (see also 17.298–300n.). The vivid ἐν στροφάλιγγι κονίης recurs (with μετά for ἐν) in a frivolous context at 21.503. | κεῖτο μέγας is used of a rock (12.381). ἱπποσύνη (etc.) is used 3 × *Il.* specifically for the driving skills of a charioteer (4.303, 23.289, 23.307), but also in the apparent formula | ἔγχεῖ θ᾽ ἱπποσύνῃ τε (11.503, 16.809), which has the wider sense of 'fighting with chariot and spear'. On tearing the hair as a sign of mourning see 22.77–8n.

In the present instance the couplet is appropriate and effective, not only describing the hero's grief but also suggesting his own death, which the conclusion of the scene will make both certain and imminent. One wonders if it recalled to some of the audience phrases they had heard in a contemporary poem about Akhilleus' slaying by Paris. In the parallel passage at 16.775–6, beautiful in itself (see note *ad loc.*, and Parry, *MHV* liii), μέγας μεγαλωστί is a little surprising for Kebriones, though he is the companion of Hektor and the final victim of Patroklos; and though this phrase befits Akhilleus, and might well describe his death-scene in another poem besides the *Od.*, λελασμένος ἱπποσυνάων is odd for him unless it can be given a wide general sense, which (as argued above) appears very possible. It is, however, rash to attempt to decide priority, as there is no way to determine if the more appropriate usage was followed by inferior imitations, or resulted from improvement upon less praiseworthy predecessors.

For other recent discussions see 16.775–6n., Heubeck, *Odissea* on *Od.* 24.39–40, and J. de Romilly, *Perspectives actuelles sur l'épopée homérique* (Paris 1983) 26–9; the major earlier treatments are Schadewaldt, *VHWW* 168, U. Hölscher, *Gnomon* 27 (1955) 395, and Kullmann, *Quellen* 38 and 330.

28–31 Cf. | καὶ δμώων οὕς μοι ληΐσσατο δῖος Ὀδυσσεύς (*Od.* 1.398). ληΐσσατο may be singular or plural (Chantraine, *GH* I 475). The clause alludes to the times Akhilleus and Patroklos fought side by side, as Akhilleus himself recalls at 341–2 and 24.7–8. On ἀκηχέμεναι (29) see 17.637n. The phrase enjambing from 30–1 is slightly modified for the Nereids at 50–1. The remainder of 31 = *Od.* 18.341; the formular system ((ὑπο)λύειν (etc.) ... γυῖα appears in a variety of different forms in both poems.

Technically, the maidservants may be regarded as the companions of the person visited, usually mentioned in the visit type-scene. Briseis too will grieve for the gentle Patroklos, who treated her well (19.287–300). φιλοπενθὴς γυνὴ βάρβαρος αἰχμάλωτος, say bT, perhaps from personal knowledge.

32–4 Simple changes produce μήτηρ δ᾽ αὖθ᾽ ἑτέρωθεν ὀδύρετο δάκρυ χέουσα at 22.79. The second hemistich of 33 ≅ 10.16. Verse 34 was rejected by Bentley, unjustifiably, though the changes of subject are admittedly harsh. The ancients saw only the question of whose throat was endangered – Akhilleus', Antilokhos', or even Patroklos', if Hektor thought to behead him! Antilokhos' fear that Akhilleus might harm himself is perfectly reasonable; so too the Trojans had to prevent Priam from rushing out of the gates of Troy as Hektor is being dragged in the dust (22.412–13), Odysseus in bitter disappointment thought of throwing himself overboard (*Od.* 10.49–51), and Aias' death by suicide seems to be understood at *Od.* 11.543–64 and appeared in the *Aithiopis* (fr. 5 Bernabé, 1 Davies). A hero, desperate with grief, turns to violent action (οἶδε γὰρ τοὺς μεγαλοψύχους ἐπὶ σφᾶς αὐτοὺς ἐν ταῖς συμφοραῖς ὁρμωμένους, T), whereas Andromakhe swoons (22.466). On ancient Greek attitudes to suicide see P. Walcott, *Studies in Honour of T. B. L. Webster* 1 (edd. J. H. Betts, J. T. Hooker, and J. R. Green, Bristol 1986) 231–7. Antilokhos now vanishes from the scene.

δείδιε is pluperfect, for *δεδϝ-; on the final -ε see Chantraine, *GH* I 438–9. ἀπαμήσειε is the reading of Aristarchus (Did/A; on the reading of T, ἀποτμήσειεν, see Erbse *ad loc.* and van der Valk, *Researches* II 118n.). The verb is found in tmesis with the sense 'cut off' at *Od.* 21.300–1, and uncompounded 2 × *Il.*, 1 × *Od.* with the meaning 'reap'. Zenodotus and all MSS, followed by Leaf, read ἀποτμήξειε, used with the meaning 'cut through' at 16.390 (and 3 × *Il.* for 'cut off' metaphorically). It is questionable whether Allen is correct in following the *lectio difficilior* against all the MSS. σίδηρος is used at 23.30 of a knife, and so presumably here, though μάχαιρα is commoner (and suitable metrically). It is used of an axe at 4.485, but of weapons only in the probably colloquial expression αὐτὸς γὰρ ἐφέλκεται ἄνδρα σίδηρος (2 × *Od.*).

35 Leaf (II p. 268) gives a very British point of view: 'It is needless to dwell on such obvious beauties as the profound truth of Achilles' grief – note how he first receives the cruel blow in silence, and only breaks out with groans (33) and wails (35) after the less-afflicted slave-women have been roused to shrieks at the first word.' σμερδαλέον is generally used with verbs meaning 'shout', but σμερδαλέον δὲ μέγ' ᾤμωξεν occurs at *Od.* 9.395.

36 = 1.358, after a similar preceding hemistich. Perhaps this is more than simple formular repetition, as the earlier meeting of Thetis and her son is recalled by her words a little later (74–7, see 73–7n.).

37–8 Thetis also contributes to the lament for Patroklos at 23.14 (μετὰ δέ σφι Θέτις γόου ἵμερον ὦρσε), and is found lamenting Akhilleus again at 24.84–6. The Nereids and Muses sing the lament at Akhilleus' funeral (*Od.* 24.47–62). ἀμφαγέροντο recurs only at *Od.* 17.33–4, in tmesis. Verse 38 ≅ 49; the repetition is not 'a "catchword"... a familiar sign of interpolation' (Leaf), but the normal ring form introducing and concluding a catalogue or a simile; cf. 14.315–28 (other examples are given by Lohmann, *Reden* 54). There is also an outer ring, for 37 is picked up by 50–1.

39–49 'The chorus of Nereids was previously athetized by Zenodotus too [*sc.* as well as Aristophanes], as being Hesiodic in character' (Did, Arn/A), implying that Aristarchus also athetized it (see Apthorp, *Manuscript Evidence* 118 n. 137). Kallistratos said the list was not in the Argolic text (A). The reason given for the athetesis is of no value, though it was approved by Leaf. Apthorp thinks (p. 116) the omission may have been due to the pronounced homoeoteleuton at 38 and 49, though this would involve a huge slip of the eye.

F. Krafft, *Vergleichende Untersuchungen zu Homer und Hesiod* (Göttingen 1963) 143–52 gives a review of scholarship on the list to that date; see also van der Valk, *Researches* II 437–9, and most recently J. Butterworth, *Studies in Honour of T. B. L. Webster* I (edd. J. H. Betts, J. T. Hooker, and J. R. Green, Bristol 1986) 39–45.

Most modern commentators have found the passage artistically satisfying. It is a kind of musical interlude, splendidly euphonious (see below), acting not perhaps as a relief from the scene of sorrow (as E. T.

Owen takes it: 'the mind finds rest and refreshment in sheer beauty that requires not the slightest effort to apprehend it', *The Story of the Iliad*, Toronto 1946, 157) but, like similes in the descriptions of battle, allowing the situation to be frozen into stillness to allow the time necessary for its proper appreciation. Alternatively, 'Perhaps the main function of such lists is to give a sense of reality to the narrative; the poet can put a name to Priam's sons or Thetis' companions, so they seem to be not merely "extras"' (Macleod, *Iliad XXIV* 110). On the aesthetic qualities of such lists see R. Lamberton, *Hesiod* (New Haven 1988) 82–4. In addition, these *dramatis personae* must not be forgotten, as they will be of significance visually in the coming scene (see 65–9n., 122–5n.). The names are translated in W. Arrowsmith's rendering of the passage (*Arion* 6.3, 1967, 347–8; reprinted in Edwards, *HPI* 271–2) and in the translation of the *Il.* by Robert Fagles (Viking Press, 1990).

Homer gives 33 names, of which 18 occur in the list of Nereus' daughters given in Hesiod's *Theogony* (243–62; this does not include Amatheia, a form of Hesiod's Psamathe, see 48n.). These are italicized in the notes below. It is significant that on the whole the names common to both lists occur in the same order. Glauke comes at or near the beginning (39: *Theogony* 244). Then verse 40 ≅ *Theogony* 245, with Nesaie (from *Theogony* 249) replacing Kumothoë and βοῶπις for ἐρόεσσα. Kumothoë (41) appears at *Theogony* 245, and Aktaie at *Theogony* 249 (from which Nesaie had been borrowed for the previous verse). Limnoreia may reflect Eulimene (*Theogony* 247). Melite and Agaue (42) also appear in the next *Theogony* verse (247). The next line (43) occurs as *Theogony* 248, after an additional verse (the uncertain sequence of 246 and 247 does not matter here). After the unmatched verse 44 (perhaps brought in for the Dunamene/Dexamene rhyme?), line 45 ≅ *Theogony* 250 (with the alliterating ἀγακλειτή for εὐειδής). Then Nemertes and Apseudes (46) are integral to the Hesiodic passage (Nemertes 235 and 262; Apseudes 233). Finally the Homeric passage adds two more verses (47–8), the *Theogony* a further twelve (251–62).

Of the 15 non-Hesiodic names in Homer, five have a clear or possible nautical connexion (Limnoreia, Amphithoë, Maira, Oreithuia, Amatheia), seven are suitable for high-ranking women (Iaira, Amphinome, Kallianeira, Kallianassa, Klumene, Ianeira, Ianassa), and two for goddesses (Thaleia, Dexamene; on the remaining name, Apseudes, see 46n.). The majority of the additions are thus likely to have been generic names for prominent females. (For the meaning of the names see notes *ad locc*.) Homer not only gives fewer names, but uses fewer epithets, and the passage may well have been abbreviated from a longer list. The presence of Nemertes and Apseudes would be hard to explain if we did not possess the Hesiodic passage (see 46n.).

The matching sequence proves that the Homeric and Hesiodic lists are connected. Butterworth, together with van der Valk and Krafft, holds that the Hesiodic list is modelled on the Homeric, but his reasons are not compelling. Lists like this were common; another obvious example of duplication is the list of Oceanids at *Theogony* 349–61, which has a good deal of overlap with the nymphs who play with Persephone at *HyDem* 418–24. There is no way of knowing if the two Nereid lists we have are interdependent or derived from a common source; and such a list is likely to have also featured in accounts of Akhilleus' funeral (cf. *Od.* 24.47–59), where it would add dignity and expansiveness and avoid the problem of recounting what words the Nereids actually sang. There may well have been a list in the *Aithiopis* too (Θέτις ἀφικομένη σὺν Μούσαις καὶ ταῖς ἀδελφαῖς θρηνεῖ τὸν παῖδα, Proclus: Bernabé, *PEG* p. 69; Davies, *EGF* p. 47). *Contaminatio* between lists is also very possible.

Butterworth draws attention to the links in sound: Thaleia (39) and θ' 'Αλίη (40); Kumodoke (39), Thoë (40), Kumothoë (41), and Amphithoë (42); Doto and Proto (43); Dunamene (43), Dexamene, and Amphinome (44). Kallianeira and Kallianassa are separated by one verse (44, 46), Ianeira and Ianassa juxtaposed (47). Schadewaldt's division into two four-line 'Stollen' and a two-line 'Abgesang' (*VHWW* 249) is unconvincing. On Nereids in general see West, *Theogony* 235–7.

39 *Glauke*: γλαυκή is an epithet of θάλασσα at 16.34; see West on *Theogony* 244. Thaleia (< θάλλω) is one of the Muses (*Theogony* 77) and one of the Graces (*Theogony* 909). *Kumodoke* is explained as ἢ κύματ'... πρηΰνει, 'calms' (*Theogony* 252–4).

40 ≅ *Theogony* 245. *Nesaie* < νῆσος; Neso also occurs (*Theogony* 261). *Speio* < σπεῖος. *Thoë* < θοός. *Halie* < ἅλς; Aristarchus (?Did/A) and (?) Herodian (A) supported this reading (Θόη θ' 'Αλίη), which is desirable after Thaleia in the previous line. West prefers to read θόη Θαλίη in Hesiod, to reduce the total of names to 50; see his note to *Theogony* 240–64 *and* 245.

41 *Kumothoë*: 'Wave-swift'. *Aktaie* < ἀκτή (see West on *Theogony* 249). Limnoreia < λίμνη + ὄρος (Risch, *Wortbildung* 136).

42 *Melite* < μέλι (also at *HyDem* 419). Iaira < *ϝιαρός, 'swift', cf. ἱαρὸς ὄρνις (Alcman fr. 26.4 Page; von Kamptz, *Personennamen* 121; Frisk s.v. ἱερός). Amphithoë < ἀμφί (intensive) + θοός. *Agaue* < ἀγαυός.

43 = *Theogony* 248. *Doto*: 'Giver', cf. Doris (45), Eudore (*Theogony* 244). *Proto* is perhaps connected with πεπρωμένον, cf. Proteus the prophet, or may be a short form of Protomedeia (*Theogony* 249; see West *ad loc.*). *Pherousa*: 'perhaps she who carries ships along, cf. *Od.* 3.300, 10.26, etc.' (West on *Theogony* 248). *Dunamene* < δύναμαι.

44 Dexamene is presumably one who accepts one's sacrifices and listens to one's prayers, though Willcock prefers 'she who protects', cf.

Θέτις... ὑποδέξατο κόλπῳ (398). The use of a participle as a name appears also in Odysseus' sister Ktimene (*Od.* 15.363, cf. ἐϋκτίμενος; so Risch, *Wortbildung* 54). Amphinome: fem. of Amphinomos, 'rich in pasture-land' (cf. Eurunome, -os). Kallianeira: fem. form of καλλι- + -ἀνήρ. Van der Valk, *Researches* II 439n., writes unconvincingly 'They bear a ship (Δεξαμένη), surround it ('Αμφινόμη) and lift it (Καλλιάειρα).'

45 ≅ *Theogony* 250. Doris: cf. 43n.; in Hesiod she is wife of Nereus and mother of the Nereids (*Theogony* 240–2). Panope: 'All-seeing', a common name in later poets. Galateia is perhaps from γάλα (Risch, *Wortbildung* 138), referring to the milk-white foam of the sea.

46 *Nemertes*, 'Infallible', and Apseudes, 'Truthful', must be connected with the attributes of Nereus, mentioned shortly before the Hesiodic list of Nereids begins (*Theogony* 233, 235; see West *ad loc.*). Their presence does not, however, prove that the present list is derived from the Hesiodic passage. Kallianassa: fem. form of καλλι- + -ἄναξ, 'Protector' (von Kamptz, *Personennamen* 85).

47 Klumene: 'Famous' < *κλεϝ-; Risch, *Wortbildung* 54, traces the masc. form back to Mycenaean. Ianeira (also at *HyDem* 421) and Ianassa are both from ϝίς, 'strength', + fem. forms of -ἀνήρ, -ἄναξ.

48 Maira, 'Sparkler', is derived from the root of μαρμαίρω (Risch, *Wortbildung* 137). Oreithuia: 'Mountain-rushing' (Risch, *Wortbildung* 136). G. S. Kirk suggests the wind that rushes down from the lee of a mountain on to the sea. Cf. Limnoreia (41). M. Finkelberg, *CP* 83 (1988) 208–9, suggests that καὶ εὐειδὴς 'Αμάθεια would have avoided the hiatus (cf. *Theogony* 250), but the Homeric scansion was most likely ἐϋ- (cf. *Il.* 3.48). Amatheia (most older MSS read -uia) < ἄμαθος, 'sand' (5.587); this is the same word as ἄμμος and ψάμμος, from which is derived Psamathe (*Theogony* 260; see Risch, *Wortbildung* 174).

49 J. T. Kakridis, *Homeric Researches* (Lund 1949) 75, thought that ἄλλαι (49) implies that the poet is omitting the rest of a list of fifty names which he had before him, but this does not seem probable. Cf. the similar expression at 2.649.

50–1 καί connects πλῆτο with ἀμφαγέροντο (37). ἀργύφεος (-υφος), 'shining white', is used for the robes of Kalypso and Kirke (*Od.* 5.230 = 10.543) and for sheep (24.621, *Od.* 10.85); here perhaps it contrasts the halls of the immortals with the ugly suffering on the shore. The first part is cognate with ἄργυρος; on the suffix see Risch, *Wortbildung* 171. The enjambing phrase ≅ 30–1; ἐξῆρχε γόοιο is formular (7 × *Il.*, including a shorter form at 24.723); see 316–17n.

52–64 Thetis must have lamented her son's death in the Memnon-story; in the *Aithiopis* she did so before bearing him from the pyre to the White Island (Proclus). It seems unlikely that her speech here could have owed

more than occasional phrases to other versions, for her account of Akhilleus'
life is framed in characteristic style by context-related couplets (52–3, 63–4;
see Lohmann, *Reden* 54), and concludes with a reference to his present
misery (61–2). Later on, she repeats seven verses to Hephaistos (56–62 =
437–43).

The insertion of the lament here is part of the building up towards
Akhilleus' decision to seek vengeance at the cost of his life (see 95–6n.).
Hektor too is lamented before his death by his wife and household
(6.497–502).

54 The first laments for Hektor begin in the same way: τέκνον, ἐγὼ δειλή
(Hekabe, 22.431), Ἕκτορ, ἐγὼ δύστηνος (Andromakhe, 22.477). The first
hemistich is also used by Odysseus as the storm arises (*Od.* 5.299). The three
final dirges for Hektor begin, perhaps more formally, with a vocative
without ἐγώ (24.725, 748, 762). The startling δυσαριστοτόκεια occurs only
here, though Euripides has a reminiscence of it (μ' ἄπαιδα γέννας ἔθηκεν
ἀριστοτόκοιο, *Rhe.* 909) and perhaps Stesichorus too (ἐγὼν [μελέ]α καὶ
ἀλασ[τοτόκος κ]αὶ ἄλ[ασ]τα παθοῖσα, fr. 13.2–3 Page, *Supplementum Lyricis
Graecis*). It is a more elaborate version of αἰνὰ τεκοῦσα, used by Thetis at
1.414 (cf. 1.418) and perhaps by Hekabe at 22.431 (see note *ad loc.*), formed
like δυσάμμορος (4 × *Il.*), Telemakhos' μῆτερ ἐμὴ δύσμητερ (*Od.* 23.97; also a
hapax) and Hektor's Δύσπαρι for Paris (3.39 = 13.769). There is a similar
oxymoron in αἰναρέτη (16.31, see note *ad loc.*). Eustathius records disapproval
of such triple compounds, on the grounds that they are seldom found in
serious authors and are particularly frequent in comedy (1130.24). But M.
Pope, *CQ* 35 (1985) 1–8, has shown that new coinages, as this probably is,
are not really rare in Homer; see also J. Griffin, *JHS* 106 (1986) 41–2.

55–60 Hekabe's laments for Hektor also tell of her pride in her splendid
son (22.432–6, 24.749–59).

55–7 The main clause to which ἐπεί ought to be subordinated never
appears. There is a similar anacoluthon at 436 and at 17.658, see
17.657–67n. ἀμύμονά τε κρατερόν τε | is formular (4 × *Il.*). Except for the
repetition at 437, ἔξοχος only here begins the verse, and ἔρνεϊ ἶσος recurs only
at *Od.* 14.175 (where Hoekstra, *Odyssey ad loc.*, comments that the phrase is
likely to be older than Homer, as loss of the digamma results in such a harsh
hiatus). The two comparisons are similar in sense; that in 57 is much
expanded at 17.53ff. γουνῷ ἀλωῆς is formular (3 × *Il.*, followed by
οἰνοπέδοιο | 2 × *Od.*).

58 The flexibility of the formular units can be seen by comparing νηυσὶν
ἐπιπροέηκα θοῇσιν | (17.708) and νήεσσι (νηυσὶ) κορωνίσιν Ἴλιον εἴσω | (*Od.*
19.182, 193). ἐπι- here must mean not 'to ⟨the ships⟩' but 'against ⟨the
enemy⟩'.

59–60 τὸν δέ refers to the same person as τὸν μέν (57) but with contrasting predication. Akhilleus repeats the enjambing phrase to his mother a little later (89–90); it is repeated at *Od.* 19.257–8, the verse completed there by the familiar φίλην ἐς πατρίδα γαῖαν.

The scholia (bT) sympathetically point out that Thetis suffers more than a mortal mother, since she can foresee her son's suffering and death. In the *Il.* it often appears that Thetis continued to live with Peleus after Akhilleus' birth, e.g. at 1.396–7, 16.222–3, 16.574, 18.332, and 19.422, but it is not necessary to assume (with Arn/A) that Homer did not know the tale that she deserted him.

61–2 ζώει(ν)...ἠελίοιο is formular (3 × *Il.*, 5 × *Od.*). On the contracted ὁρᾷ see Hoekstra, *Modifications* 133. With 62 cf. οὔ τις δύνατο χραισμῆσαι ὄλεθρον | (11.120). Here Thetis turns from the thought of Akhilleus' death to that of his present sufferings. The two themes were already linked in her response to him at 1.415–18. The pathetic frustration of 62 is intensely human, as well as (in view of her divine powers) ironical.

63–4 ἐπακούσω again calls to mind their earlier meeting; ἐξαύδα, μὴ κεῦθε νόῳ, ἵνα εἴδομεν ἄμφω (1.363). An unobtrusively innovative use of language can be seen in φίλον τέκος, found 12 × *Il.*, 4 × *Od.* but elsewhere always a vocative, as are Διὸς τέκος and ἐμὸν τέκος. In 64 it is ambiguous – and effectively so – whether ἀπὸ πτολέμοιο μένοντα means 'while' or 'although'. The phrase does not recur.

Thetis' ignorance (here and at 1.362) of Akhilleus' troubles, despite her prophetic powers (9–11, 17.408–9), is of course adopted so that Akhilleus may voice them to her himself. The A scholia sensibly remark τοῦτο ὡς ἐν ποιήσει ἀκουστέον.

65–9 Much is made here of the fact that all the Nereids accompany Thetis, and their dismissal at the end of the scene (139–45) is further stressed by her direct speech to them. Their presence should not be thought inimical to the intimate talk of mother and son; on the contrary, throughout the scene they add to the looming shadow of the funeral rites of Akhilleus, forming a chorus of mourning women around Thetis as she holds her son's head in her arms (see 71–2n.). They anticipate the lamenting women of Troy whom Akhilleus describes a little later (122–4). 'Schon hier herrscht die Gegenwart des Todes' (Schadewaldt, *VHWW* 250; see his analysis of the scene, *ibid.* 251–6).

Their arrival and departure also form a frame for the scene. Within this frame, in concentric rings, are the arrival and departure speeches of Thetis (73–7, 128–137), the two closely matched speeches of Akhilleus (79–93, 98–126), and, at the focal point, Thetis' two-line announcement of Akhilleus' doom (95–6; see Lohmann, *Reden* 142).

66–70 When Thetis leaves the sea at 24.96–7 the phrasing is λιάζετο κῦμα θαλάσσης. | ἀκτὴν δ' ἐξαναβᾶσαι... (*v.l.* εἰσ-), and at 1.496 ἀνεδύσετο κ. θ. |.

Perhaps greater speed, or the greater number of people, is suggested by ῥήγνυτο here. Thetis' first appearance is expanded with a simile (1.359). θαμειαί (68) = 'closely'. ἐπισχερώ (68) = 'in turn', perhaps from the root which appears in ἑξῆς, ἐφεξῆς. R. Janko has suggested that the original meaning may have been 'on the shore', from σχερός, 'shore' (*Glotta* 57, 1979, 20–3).

71–2 Taking Akhilleus' head in her hands is a gesture of mourning, as when Akhilleus holds Patroklos' head (23.136) and Andromakhe Hektor's (24.724; cf. also 24.712). She kneels or sits beside Akhilleus, who is still lying prostrate at 178. For other parallels and representations in art see 23.136n. and Macleod, *Iliad XXIV* 147. Here the gesture strengthens the foreshadowing of Akhilleus' approaching death; behind the picture of Akhilleus grieving for his dead friend the poet shades in a tableau of the mourning for Akhilleus' own death, which will come as a direct result of his grief and vengeance (96). In 72, Brandreth's ϝ' for ῥ' is probably right, for μ' occurs in this verse 5 × *Od.*

73–7 Verse 73 and the first half of 74 = 1.362–3, Thetis' first words when she came to Akhilleus on the earlier occasion. The repetition, like her next words, drives home the irony of the situation; Akhilleus has indeed been granted everything he asked Thetis for in book 1, and so he is himself responsible for the outcome, Patroklos' death. Thetis' apparent ignorance of what has happened (see 63–4n.) makes her appallingly tactless remark both plausible and pathetic – she hopes to be thanked for her success with Zeus! The two scenes between Thetis and Akhilleus are compared by Reinhardt, *IuD* 368–73.

74–5 Thetis' proud and happy τὰ μὲν δή τοι τετέλεσται | ἐκ Διός, with emphasis on Zeus (in the emphatic runover position), is repeated dully in Akhilleus' τὰ μὲν ἄρ μοι Ὀλύμπιος ἐξετέλεσσεν (79). χεῖρας ἀνασχών is formular after εὔχετο (etc.; 3 × *Il.*, 2 × *Od.*) and is used here although it is not consistent with 1.407–12.

77 Again the first words of the verse are heavily stressed. Homer probably considered the *hapax* ἀεκήλια (ἔργα) a contribution to the formular system that appears as ἔργον ἀεικές | (1 × *Il.*, 4 × *Od.*), ἀεικέα ἔργα | (*Od.* 4.694), ἀεικέα μήδετο ἔργα | (22.395 = 23.24), ἀεικέα ἔργ' ὁράασθαι | (*Od.* 16.107 = 20.317), ἔργα ἀεικέα ἐργάζοιο (24.733). The common and related ἀεικέλιος, and the analogy of ἀπειρέσιος–ἀπερείσιος, would have made this easy. The word probably originated, however (as Aristarchus saw: Arn/A, Herodian) as α-privative plus ἕκηλος, which would give the weaker sense 'unwished-for' (so *LfgrE* and Risch, *Wortbildung* 112–13).

79–93 Lohmann gives a fine analysis of this and the following speech by Akhilleus (*Reden* 142–5). They are similar in form. This speech (*a*) begins with his grief at the loss of his beloved friend and his armour at the hands of *Hektor* (79–84); then (*b*) the armour, the gods' gift to Peleus, leads to the thought of the marriage of Thetis and Peleus, and the *impossible wish* that it had never happened (84–7); for (*c*) <u>νῦν δέ</u> he is willing to go on living only if he can take vengeance on Hektor (88–93). The second speech again (*a*) begins with his grief at the deaths of Patroklos and other Greeks killed by *Hektor* (98–103); (*b*) goes on to the thought of his own failure to help them despite his prowess, his *impossible wish* that strife and anger might perish, and his resolution to overcome his anger against Agamemnon (104–13); for (*c*) <u>νῦν δέ</u> he is determined to be avenged on Hektor even at the cost of his own life (114–26). In both speeches, Akhilleus' grief leads to reflection and a frustrated wish for the impossible; then on to a sudden return to unpleasant reality, the inseparably linked death and need for vengeance. Patroklos' death and his own are insistently coupled together in his words, as they are in the mourning tableau against which he speaks.

The speech is also notable for the varied and flexible interplay of its sense-units and metrical cola. The first end-stopped line (79), ironically repeating Thetis' triumphant claim (74–5), is reminiscent of the memorable apophthegms Akhilleus spoke in answer to Odysseus' offer (9.318–20); this is followed by a short rhetorical question (ἀλλὰ τί μοι τῶν ἧδος; – reminiscent again of the furious string of questions at 9.337–41); and after the heavy mid-verse break in verse 80 begins an explanatory subordinate clause which is complete in sense at the verse-end but continues on into the pathetic runover name | Πάτροκλος. Here the heavy pause comes after these three syllables, but again the sense does not end here, but runs on into a relative clause which again is complete in sense at the verse-end (81) but continues into the long and emotional runover phrase | ἶσον ἐμῇ κεφαλῇ. After another heavy mid-verse break in 82 a new sentence starts, ending sharply two words later at the bucolic diaeresis, as if he is overpowered by emotion; τὸν ἀπώλεσα. Then the next sentence begins with the juxtaposition of heavily significant words, the weightiest of all placed in the most emphatic position (τεύχεα δ' Ἕκτωρ | δῃώσας ἀπέδυσε, 82–3). Then a conventional (but not meaningless) epithet and descriptive phrase for the armour conclude the verse (πελώρια, θαῦμα ἰδέσθαι |); but a further unexpected runover (καλά) carries on Akhilleus' thought to an enjambing relative clause coupling the armour with Thetis' marriage to his mortal father (84–5).

The next couplet expresses Akhilleus' regrets for the past, with balancing clauses for both his parents (σὺ μέν... | ...Πηλεὺς δέ, 86–7); he also voices an impossible wish like this at 16.97–100. Then he comes back to the actual situation with his characteristic νῦν δέ (88, see note *ad loc.*), and goes on to a long succession of subordinate clauses, which enjamb so as to place emphatic words at the beginning of each verse (89–93). This masterly exploitation of the resources of diction and metre is hard to match, even in other speeches of Akhilleus.

79 See 74–5n.

80 Cf. αὐτὰρ ἐμοὶ τί τόδ' ἦδος, ἐπεί… (*Od* 24.95). The second hemistich ≅ that of 17.642 (without enjambment).

82 κεφαλῇ = 'life' or 'self'; cf. 114 and | ὅσσον ἐμῇ κεφαλῇ περιδείδια (17.242); Akhilleus also uses it as a term of affection to Patroklos' ghost (23.94, see note *ad loc.*; cf. 8.281). τὸν ἀπώλεσα can mean 'I have lost him' (cf. 92, 460, 23.280 etc.) or 'I have destroyed him' (cf. 24.260 etc.; see Cunliffe's *Lexicon* s.v.). Van Leeuwen rendered the first meaning ('amicum… amisit'), Schadewaldt the second ('Ihn hab ich zugrunde gerichtet', *VHWW* 237). Griffin, *HLD* 163n., shows a mild preference for 'lost', and so apparently Ameis–Hentze ('Wiederaufnahme des Gedankens aus 80') and the scholia (περιπαθῶς πάνυ ὡς ἐπὶ κτήματος μεγάλου τοῦ φίλου bT). Leaf and Willcock do not comment. Probably ἀπώλεσα picks up ὤλεθ' ἑταῖρος from 80, and the immediate transition to the divine armour suggests the meaning should not be stronger than 'lost'. Akhilleus could, however, have held himself directly responsible for Patroklos' death on two grounds: that he sent him to battle in his own stead; and that he had asked Zeus (through Thetis) for the defeat of the Greeks. The ambiguity may of course be intentional.

In fact Akhilleus honours Patroklos *more* than his own life, as his next speech makes clear. Some ancients and a few moderns have thought that Akhilleus' great love for Patroklos was intended to imply a homosexual relationship; see 11.786n. and Stella G. Miller, *AJA* 90 (1986) 165–7. The idea is refuted by D. S. Barrett, *CB* 57 (1981) 87–93. The best account of their relationship is given by D. M. Halperin, *One Hundred Years of Homosexuality and Other Essays on Greek Love* (New York 1990) 75–87.

The loss of Patroklos and the loss of the armour are closely linked in Akhilleus' mind; see the introduction to this Book, and J. R. Wilson, *Phoenix* 28 (1974) 385–9. The shame felt at the failure to save a companion's armour is vividly stated by Sarpedon (16.498–500); cf. 6.417.

83–4 The second hemistich of 83 = that of 10.439 (of Rhesos' golden armour, not proper for men to wear, only gods; see 17.194–209n.). On πελώρια see 17.173–4n. The formula τεύχεα καλά is found 8 × *Il.*, 2 × *Od.* at the verse-end, 4 × *Il.* before the mid-verse caesura, and 2 × *Il.* at the beginning of the verse. It enjambs in the form τεύχεα δέξο | καλά (19.10–11) and τεύχεα.| καλά (22.322–3); the alternative ἔντεα καλά is also found in enjambment (10.471–2, 17.186–7). In this highly innovative passage the formular noun and epithet are split over *three* lines. In his illuminating study of formulae, P. Kiparsky remarks of this system 'The independence of formula from meter could hardly be better visualized than from these examples' (*Oral Literature and the Formula*, ed. B. A. Stolz and R. S. Shannon III, Michigan 1976, 87). The remainder of 84 ≅ 16.867, 24.534.

84–5 The armour Akhilleus lent to Patroklos is also said at 17.194–7 to be that given by the gods to Peleus at his wedding, and by him in his old age passed on to his son. But Friis Johansen, *Iliad* 92–127 and 257–60 (with figs. 23–41), has cogently argued that vase-paintings of the mid-sixth century showing Thetis handing over armour to her son depict not the scene which begins *Il.* 19, but an alternative version in which she presented him with Hephaistos-made armour in Phthie, before he left home for the war. A. Kossatz-Diessmann, *LIMC* I.1 71–2 and 122, agrees with him. The most cogent evidence from the monuments is a plate by Lydos (Athens, Nat. Mus. 507; *LIMC* I.1 Achilleus no. 187). which (like many others) includes an elderly man in the scene and (uniquely) names him Peleus; however, a representation by the Amasis Painter (Boston 01.8027; *LIMC* I.1 Achilleus no. 508) names this figure Phoinix. If the old man is intended to be Peleus, obviously the location is Phthie; and this is supported by the proposed identification of a young man in a Camtar Painter scene as Patroklos (Louvre, Campana 10521; *LIMC* I.1 Achilleus no. 201; D. von Bothmer, *Bull. of the Museum of Fine Arts, Boston* 47, 1949, 84ff.). Euripides twice seems to refer to a similar version: at *El.* 442–51, where the Nereids deliver the armour in Phthie, apparently to Akhilleus; and at *IA* 1068–75, where Akhilleus seems already to be wearing armour given him by Thetis when he lands at Troy.

Neither the vase-pictures nor the Euripidean references are conclusive (see my article in *CA* 9, 1990, 311–25), but the presumed non-Iliadic version parallels the gift of divinely made armour by Eos to Memnon, who in the *Aithiopis* left for Troy ἔχων ἡφαιστότευκτον πανοπλίαν (Proclus: Bernabé, *PEG* p. 68; Davies, *EGF* p. 47). It does not conflict with the *Cypria*, where the only wedding-gift specified is Cheiron's spear (fr. 3 Bernabé, 3 Davies), or with representations of the wedding of Peleus and Thetis, on which armour is not included among the gifts depicted. It avoids the embarrassment of Akhilleus' possessing, at the end of the *Il.*, *two* Hephaistos-made panoplies, which is awkward for the tale of the disastrous rivalry of Odysseus and Aias for Thetis' award (*Od.* 11.544–6; the tale is probably early, see M. L. West, *JHS* 108, 1988, 158–9). It is possible, perhaps likely, that Homer has altered the story of the gift of armour to Akhilleus in Phthie, attributing it to Peleus instead of to Thetis, in order to allow Thetis, without complaining of a repeat performance, to make a second (and identical) gift after the first panoply has been transferred to Hektor. The familiar tale of the gods' gifts at the wedding of Peleus and Thetis, and the obvious motif of a father handing on his armour to his son (cf. 7.148–9), would provide antecedents for the new version. See the introduction to this Book.

85 Cf. *HyAphr* 199, βροτοῦ ἀνέρος ἔμπεσον εὐνῇ, where again the bride was unwilling. But ἐμβάλλω is used when Aphrodite places her love-charm in Here's hands (14.218), and when the herald gives the speaker's staff to Telemakhos (*Od.* 2.37), so the verb itself does not imply violence. On the circumstances of Thetis' marriage see 429–35n.

86–7 αἴθ' is the reading of the older MSS and Apollonius Dyscolus for the vulgate ὡς. Akhilleus' first thought may be 'Would I had never been born!' (like Dionysius of Tarsus, who died μὴ γήμας· αἴθε δὲ μήδ' ὁ πατήρ, *Anth. Pal.* 7.309), but then he passes on (as 88–90 make clear) to the more sympathetic wish that Peleus had married a mortal wife because then she would not have to grieve for him forever, as Thetis will. The scholia approve the sympathy he shows for his mother's future suffering. To Asteropaios, grandson of a river-god, Akhilleus boasts of his divine descent on his father's side, from Peleus, son of Aiakos, son of Zeus (21.187–9). J. S. Clay, *The Politics of Olympus* (Princeton 1989) 165–70, puts forward the interesting idea that the end of the Age of Heroes was explained by Zeus's ending of the unions of deities and mortals by his disciplining of Aphrodite (*HyAphr* 45–52).

88 νῦν δέ (4× in these two speeches) is strikingly characteristic of the language of Akhilleus, used 26× by him compared with 7× by others in his presence (so P. Friedrich and J. Redfield, *Language* 54, 1978, 283). This (they say) 'is consistent with his combination of imagination and realism; his mind goes out into a world of possibility, and then abruptly returns to the situation before him'. See also Martin, *Language* 146–205, and S. E. Bassett, *TAPA* 64 (1933) 58–9. The ellipses of thought are 'But as it is ⟨you married Peleus⟩, ⟨so⟩ that for you too ⟨as well as for me⟩ there should be grief ⟨and for you it will be⟩ immeasurable...' Akhilleus' thought outstrips his language, as in the anacolutha at 101ff., 1.234ff.

89–90 The enjambing phrase occurred in Thetis' lament (59–60). The stress on the words which begin the verse is notable here, as throughout this speech. If logic is to be pressed, we must say that Akhilleus already knows he will not return home if he enters the battle and kills Hektor, because this will mean he has chosen the short, glorious life of which he spoke at 9.410–13; in which case, he says, ὤλετο μέν μοι νόστος, ἀτὰρ κλέος ἄφθιτον ἔσται (9.413). But it is likely that the poet is already anticipating Thetis' disclosure at 95–6, and allowing Akhilleus to speak in vague terms of a fate which becomes explicit only in her words.

90–3 οὐδέ (90) probably goes with ζώειν οὐδ'... μετέμμεναι, but οὐδ' ἐμέ 'not me either' (so Willcock; *sc.* 'any more than Patroklos') is a possible underlying thought. Verse 91 is an impressive expansion of the formular

Book Eighteen

ζωοῖσι μετέω (etc.; 2 × *Il.*, 2 × *Od.*). Verse 92 ≅ 11.433, 12.250, 16.861; a standard threat, fitted well to the context by | πρῶτος. ἕλωρ (cf. ἑλεῖν) and ἑλώρια (1.4) mean something preyed upon; ἕλωρα (only here) must be abstract, '⟨pay for⟩ his preying upon ⟨Patroklos⟩'. It would be preferable to read Μενοιτιάδα'(ο) with the better MSS.

95–9 The verses are quoted by Aeschines, *Tim.* 150, with an insignificant variant in 97 and a more important one in 99 (see 98–100n.).

95–6 ὠκύμορος is used only of Akhilleus in the *Il.*, and only by Thetis to him (1.417) and to Hephaistos (18.458). It occurs 3 × (in the same verse) of the suitors in the *Od.*, and once in each poem (in a different sense) for arrows. οἶ᾿ ἀγορεύεις | ('from what you say') is otherwise an Odyssean formula (6 × *Od.*), but ὡς ἀγ. | occurs 3 × *Il.*, 8 × *Od.* ἔπειτα = 'in that case', not simply 'afterwards'. ἑτοῖμος = 'ready', 'certain to be fulfilled', cf. 14.53–6n. Thetis' brevity is striking, and has plausibly been termed 'an oracular pronouncement' (by R. M. Frazer, *Hermes* 117, 1989, 385); but perhaps Akhilleus cuts her short (see 98–100n.).

Akhilleus' short life was lamented early in the poem, by the hero himself (1.352) and by Thetis (1.415–18; see Introduction, ch. 1, ii); at that point it was left effectively vague whether his life was short in comparison with other men's, or by contrast to her immortality (as M. Pope takes it, *CQ* 35, 1985, 8n.). Apollo has declared he will not live to sack Troy (16.709), and this is known to Akhilleus too (17.406–7, see 17.404–11n.). From now on the imminence of his death is insistently mentioned, by the hero himself (330–2, 19.328–30, 19.421–2, 21.110–13, 21.277–8, 23.150), by Hephaistos (464–5), by the horse Xanthos (19.416–17), by the dying Hektor (22.359–60), by the ghost of Patroklos (23.80–1), and by Thetis' continuing mourning (24.84–6, 24.91, 24.104–5, 24.131–2). The audience might have appreciated even more the difficulty she finds in accepting Akhilleus' mortality if they knew the tale of her fatal testing of her previous children, until Peleus stopped her, by throwing them into a cauldron of water (Hesiod, *Aigimios* fr. 300 MW).

In the *Aithiopis*, Θέτις τῷ παιδὶ τὰ κατὰ τὸν Μέμνονα προλέγει (Proclus), which can be taken to mean that she predicted his death must come soon after he killed Memnon (see Schadewaldt, *VHWW* 159 and 167, and Kullmann, *Quellen* 311 and *GRBS* 25, 1984, 310; G. L. Huxley, *Greek Epic Poetry*, London 1969, 145 translates 'Thetis tells her son about the coming fate of Memnon', which lacks point). But as U. Hölscher insists, *Gnomon* 27, 1955, 394–5, the motif is particularly effective here and need not have been imitated from the Memnon tale. The motif of a warrior first refusing to fight because of a prophecy that he will die in the battle, then fighting regardless of this, may have played a part in the story of Meleager, who in one account was killed in battle by Apollo (see 9.524–605n.; M. M. Willcock, *CQ* 14,

158

1964, 151–4; Edwards, *HPI* 227); this is suggested by Nestor's words at 11.794–5 ≅ 16.36–7. There was also a tale, perhaps in the *Cypria*, that Thetis warned her son, in vain, not to kill Tenes, or he would die at the hands of Apollo (Apollodorus, *Epitome* 26; see Kullmann, *Quellen* 213–14).

98–126 On the structure of this speech see 79–93n.

98–100 Every word counts heavily here. The repetition of αὐτίκα from 96 is striking; Macleod, *Iliad XXIV* 52, and Bassett, *HSCP* 31 (1920) 44, give examples of echoing of the words of a previous speaker (which Akhilleus has already done once, cf. 74–5n.), but none are so vivid as this. Lohmann, *Reden* 145, well suggests that Akhilleus *interrupts* Thetis with the repetition of the word she used – probably she had a good deal more to say; for her impetuous son's propensity for doing this cf. 1.292n., 19.76–84n. Moreover, he uses αὐτίκα in a different sense. Thetis has said '*Straightway after Hektor your fate is set*' (cf. Mimnermus fr. 2.9–10 West: αὐτὰρ ἐπὴν δὴ τοῦτο τέλος παραμείψεται ὥρης, | αὐτίκα δὴ τεθνάναι βέλτιον ἢ βίοτος), whereas Akhilleus means '*Right now* would I be dead, since...' (like Penelope's αὐτίκα νῦν, *Od.* 18.203, 20.63). Schadewaldt saw this ('Schnell bist du mir dann des Todes...' 'Wär' ich nur tot, gleich jetzt, da ich...', *VHWW* 238), and so did J. T. Sheppard ('Now, now at once, may I die', *The Pattern of the Iliad*, London 1922, 178). At this point Akhilleus' sense of guilt at not standing beside his friend is stronger than his desire for vengeance, which only returns at 114–15. His sense that he deserted his friend has been prepared for by Hektor's taunt to the dying Patroklos (16.837–8); Macleod, *Iliad XXIV* 25, remarks that Patroklos' life is the price Akhilleus pays for the harm he caused his comrades. His willingness to give up his own life for the sake of vengeance – as well as in atonement? – has been anticipated in 82 (see note *ad loc.*). On the ways in which Homer portrays heroes facing their own death see R. Renehan's perceptive article in *CP* 82 (1987) 99–116.

| κτεινομένῳ is emphatic by verse-position, and itself throws more weight on ἑταίρῳ ('I let my companion be killed') and ἐπαμῦναι ('when I could have saved him'). Then the formular but still pathetic τηλόθι πάτρης (5 × *Il.*, 1 × *Od.*; see J. Griffin, *CQ* 26, 1976, 164–7 and *JHS* 106, 1986, 55) leads on to the third successive powerful line-beginning ἔφθιτ', and the antithesis is repeated with the juxtaposed ἐμεῖο δέ.

The idiom οὐκ ἄρ' ἔμελλον '⟨It is now clear that⟩ I was not to...' recurs with similar pathos at 5.205 and 5.686 (ἄρα μέλλον would remove the forbidden trochaic cut in the 4th foot). Aeschines, *Tim.* 150, quotes 99 with the ending ὅ μοι πολὺ φίλτατος ἔσκεν (3 × *Il.*, 2 × *Od.*, with various forms of the verb) and omits 100. (He also gives a different speech-introduction at 97.) Van der Valk, *Researches* II 328–9, suggests that Aeschines altered the text deliberately, in order to make the relationship more like that of two lovers, but it may well be a slip of memory – the phrase begins the verse at 118. In 100 δῆσεν can hardly be right; the easiest correction is ἐμεῦ δὲ δέησεν (see Risch, *Wortbildung* 300). Elsewhere the aorist of δέω (< *δεϝ-), is ἐδεύησεν (*Od.* 9.483 = 540). On the old formula ἀρῆς ἀλκτῆρα, 'defender against harm', see 14.484–5n.

101–3 In the first three lines of the speech Akhilleus spoke of his death, and his failure to support his friend, in indefinite terms (τεθναίην, οὐκ ἄρ' ἔμελλον). The unspoken wish, 'If only I had ...,' ends as usual (see 88n.) in the νῦν δέ which brings him back to the unsatisfactory real world, and again juxtaposes his death with his lack of help to Patroklos and his other companions. The main verb is postponed until after the further νῦν δέ at 114; there are similar effective anacolutha at 6.242ff. and 22.111ff. Verse 101 = 23.150, where the main clause is completed in the following verse. On φάος (102) see 17.613–15n.

104 The heralds sent to abduct Briseis find Akhilleus ἥμενον by his ships at 1.330, cf. 1.416 and 1.421. He uses the word again (with similar distaste) of himself to Priam at 24.542 (see note *ad loc.*), where Macleod says 'It is a bitter paradox that Achilles is now far from idle at Troy, when he is killing Priam's sons ([ἧμαι ἐνὶ Τροίῃ] σέ τε κήδων ἠδὲ σὰ τέκνα)' (*Iliad XXIV ad loc.*). ἄχθος ἀρούρης is used in the same sense of 'encumbrance' at *Od.* 20.379. On Akhilleus' taste for vehement, colourful language see J. Griffin, *JHS* 106 (1986) 51–5. Plato paraphrases Akhilleus' words as μὴ ἐνθάδε μένω καταγέλαστος παρὰ νηυσὶ κορωνίσιν ἄχθος ἀρούρης (*Apology* 28d), but we need not conclude that his text was different.

105–6 Odysseus gently makes the same point at 19.216–20; this was why Patroklos has been told to counsel Akhilleus (11.788–9). Prowess in war and excellence in counsel are contrasted again in the figures of Hektor and Pouludamas (252) and often (e.g. 1.258, 6.78–9, and especially 9.438–43). See M. Schofield, *CQ* 36 (1986) 9–11, and G. Nagy, *The Best of the Achaeans* (Baltimore 1979) 45–9. Some editors rejected the couplet, but the self-praise is neither unheroic nor unjustified, and here Akhilleus is not boasting but reproaching himself. The b scholia appropriately remark ἔθος γὰρ τοῖς παλαιοῖς ἑαυτοὺς ἐγκωμιάζειν. διὰ δὲ τοῦ ἐγκωμίου ἑαυτοῦ κατηγορεῖ. Akhilleus' admission that he may not be the best in counsel leads on into the following curse on the emotions which confuse even a wise man's decisions. τοῖος ἐὼν οἷος (ἔσσι) is formular (1 × *Il.*, 2 × *Od.*). οἷος is also scanned as double-short (ὄγος) at 13.275 (see Chantraine, *GH* 1 168). Ruijgh, τε *épique* 656, points out that τε (106) suggests a general truth, i.e. καὶ ἄλλοι = not just 'other Greeks' but 'others than those who excel in battle'.

107–10 As at 86–7, Akhilleus goes on to voice a wish for the impossible. At 1.177 Agamemnon told him αἰεὶ γάρ τοι ἔρις τε φίλη πόλεμοί τε μάχαι τε (= 5.891, Zeus to Ares). On Eris in Homer see J. C. Hogan, *Grazer Beiträge* 10 (1981) 21–58; he finds the sense to be basically 'rivalry', not necessarily pejorative. At *Od.* 14.463–4 it is wine ὅς τ᾽ ἐφέηκε πολύφρονά περ μάλ᾽ ἀεῖσαι |. χόλος is much commoner in Homer than μῆνις (the poet's word for Akhilleus' anger), especially in direct speech (J. Griffin, *JHS* 106, 1986, 43, and P. Considine, *AC* 9, 1966, 22–3) Usually it is words of peace and reconciliation which are 'sweeter than honey' (e.g. 1.249, *Theogony* 83–4, 97), so the comparison has special point here. ἠΰτε καπνός (110) is also used of the departure of Patroklos' shade (23.100). Here the idea seems to be that of a swelling, *blinding* smoke (as Ate blinds her victims).

112–13 Akhilleus will repeat this couplet publicly at his reconciliation with Agamemnon (19.65–6). ἀλλὰ…ἐάσομεν appears also in his earlier words to Patroklos (16.60), followed there by a slightly different thought (οὐδ᾽ ἄρα πως ἦν | ἀσπερχὲς κεχολῶσθαι ἐνὶ φρεσίν). The enjambment of both lines 16.60–1 and 61–2 makes it likely that the phrasing there was modelled on this; see G. S. Kirk, *YCS* 20 (1966) 129. προτεύχω occurs only in these three verses and at Apollonius 4.84 (in tmesis: LSJ). ἐάσομεν and ἀχνύμενοί περ are both common in their respective positions, and occur together 4 × *Il.* (always spoken by or to Akhilleus) and 1 × *Od.* The scholia (bT) explain καίπερ ἠδικημένοι καὶ δικαίως ἂν ἐπ᾽ αὐτοῖς ἐπὶ πλεῖον μηνίσαντες. They also remark that this is the first example of reason overcoming anger.

Phoinix said δάμασον θυμὸν μέγαν to Akhilleus during the embassy (9.496). The only other use of the two words together is by Odysseus to Aias in the underworld, δάμασον δὲ μένος καὶ ἀγήνορα θυμόν (*Od.* 11.562; see J. Bremmer, *The Early Greek Concept of the Soul*, Princeton 1983, 54–6). ἀνάγκη: the necessity of avenging Patroklos.

114–26 On νῦν δέ see 88n. Akhilleus returns to the present action, as he tried to do at 101 before his thoughts reverted to his death, Patroklos', and his absence from his friends' struggle. In the concluding part of his first speech (88–93) Akhilleus declared he would only go on living if he could take vengeance on Hektor. The threat of his own death has not changed this, and he now restates his resolve in impressive ring form (see Lohmann, *Reden* 142–3):

A   I will go to kill Hektor (114–15)
B   and accept death when Zeus wills (115–16).
C   [*Paradigm*] For even Herakles died (117–19).
B′   So I shall die too (120–1),
A′   but now I shall win great glory (121–5).

Plato has Socrates justify his own life by reference to Akhilleus' choice of death over dishonour, quoting 96 and the first half of 98 and paraphrasing 104 (*Apology* 28c–d; the analogy is also suggested at *Crito* 44a–b). The exegetical scholia (AbT on 98) also approve ('a splendid example of friendship, when after not being persuaded by such magnificent gifts, he chooses even to die on behalf of his friend without them'), though their comments also contrast Akhilleus' words here with the regrets he expresses to Odysseus in the Underworld (*Od.* 11.489–91). On others in Greek myth who knowingly give their lives for what they think is right see Edwards, *HPI* 273.

114 On κεφαλή = 'life' see 82n. ὀλετήρ occurs only here in Homer. κιχείω suggests death, cf. the formulas θάνατος καὶ μοῖρα κιχάνει (3 × *Il.*, with a short form at 22.303) and μοῖρα κίχη (etc.) θανάτου (to end a pentameter; see R. L. Fowler, *The Nature of Early Greek Lyric*, Toronto 1987, 44). Some might see also an evocative poetic ambiguity in the whole phrase φίλης κεφαλῆς ὀλετῆρα κιχείω, which *could* mean 'meet *my own* life's destroyer'.

115–16 The couplet is repeated, obviously with special purpose, as Akhilleus stands over the dead Hektor (22.365–6), with τέθναθι replacing Ἕκτορα. Here the juxtaposition of Ἕκτορα, κῆρα, and ἐγώ is notable; κήρ = μοῖρα in the meaning 'death' (see 9.411n.) The T scholia say this was the source of Cleanthes' famous ἄγου δέ μ', ὦ Ζεῦ... (*SVF* 1 fr. 527), though 15.45–6 would be closer. Virgil gave the lines to the wicked Mezentius (*Aeneid* 10.743–4).

117–19 'Even Herakles died' is an example of a *topos* familiar in the *consolatio*; see E. R. Curtius, *European Literature and the Latin Middle Ages* (tr. W. R. Trask, Princeton 1973) 80–2. Here it is used, poignantly, to console the speaker as well as the listener. When Akhilleus 'consoles' young Lukaon he substitutes, with superb effect, first Patroklos, then himself, as paradigms (21.107–13). The *topos* appears in different forms at 15.139–40 and 24.551. On the strongly emphatic οὐδὲ γὰρ οὐδέ see 5.22n., on βίη Ἡρακλῆος 2.658–6on.

119–20 On Herakles' sufferings see 14.250–61n. Willcock (on 19.132–3) thinks that his death through 'Herē's baneful anger' may be Homer's invention; this does not, however, seem specially appropriate to the present context, through χόλος certainly recalls the χόλος which makes trouble at 108 and 111. (Is Homer anticipating Agamemnon's tale of Herakles, 19.95–125?) The phrasing is like Akhilleus' terrible line ἀλλὰ φόνος τε καὶ αἷμα καὶ ἀργαλέος στόνος ἀνδρῶν (19.214). ὁμοίη (120): i.e. the same as Herakles'; hardly 'mankind's common lot', as some have taken it.

121–5 νῦν δέ again returns from the indefinite to the matter in hand. With the final phrase of 121 cf. κλέος ἐσθλὸν ἄροιτο | (5.3, *Od.* 13.422), ἀροίμεθά κε κ. ἑ. | (5.273). The verse sums up the Homeric warriors' code, amplified and rationalized in Sarpedon's famous speech (12.310–28). The unusually long postponement of the main verb ἐφείην draws attention to the woman, weeping and tearing her cheeks, before the precise sense becomes clear. The brutal thought, indicative of the intensity of Akhilleus' feelings here, is expressed with much artistry, by the long and vivid description of a single lament; it is a highly developed form of the common ὧδε δέ τις εἴπεσκεν motif. Pindar similarly portrays a single Locrian maiden invoking Hiero in security (*Pythian* 2.18 20). Then the plural γνοῖεν (125) generalizes the significance of the picture drawn.

We must not forget that the stage (so to speak) is full of mourning women surrounding the still prostrate hero (see 65–9n.). With equal artistry (which again may indicate the poet's sympathy), Odysseus weeps at the tale of the sack of Troy like a widow led off into slavery after it (*Od.* 8.521–31), and Herakles 'widowed' the streets of Troy (5.642). Agamemnon, however, speaks of such a scene with characteristic brutality (4.238–9).

Τρωϊάδων καὶ Δαρδανίδων βαθυκόλπων (the terms are not synonymous: 20.215–40n.) recurs at 339 in a shorter nominative form, and cf. Τρώων καὶ Τρωϊάδων βαθυκόλπων (24.215). Otherwise the epithet is found only 2 × in ancient epic, applied to nymphs (*HyAphr* 257, *HyDem* 5); we do not know why Zenodotus read Μοῦσαι Ὀλυμπιάδες βαθύκολποι at 2.484. The epithet may have alluded to the deep folds of women's robes, but Aeschylus' θρῆνον... οἶμαί σφ' ἐρατῶν ἐκ βαθυκόλπων στηθέων ἥσειν (*Septem* 863–5) seems to refer to their cleavage. | ἀμφοτέρῃσι δὲ χερσί occurs at 23 and 1 × *Od.*, but without δέ (here and *Od.* 4.116) produces an unusual rhythm; van Leeuwen's χείρεσσ' ἀμφοτέρῃσι (cf. 12.382) is easier but without ancient authority. παρειάων ἁπαλάων occurs only here, but cf. παρειῶν | δάκρυ' ὀμορξάμενον (*Od.* 11.529–30). The first hemistich of 124 is formular (2 × *Od.*); with the second cf. ἀδινὰ στενάχοντα φέρεσθαι | (*Od.* 7.274); uncompounded στοναχέω occurs only here. ἐφείην and γνοῖεν make an emphatic chiasmus.

Actually this is only the third day of fighting that Akhilleus has missed, so far as we have been told; 3.1–7.380 described the first day, 8.53–488 the second, and the present interminable day, which began at 11.1, will not end until 18.242. But as Arn/A remark, μία ἡμέρα Ἀχιλλεῖ πολὺ ἦν ἀφεστῶτι. So too the Greeks will come to the assembly οὕνεκ' Ἀχιλλεὺς | ἐξεφάνη, δηρὸν δὲ μάχης ἐπέπαυτ' ἀλεγεινῆς (19.45–6).

126 The second hemistich is spoken by Hektor to Helen at 6.360; οὐδέ με πείσει(ς) | is common (7 × *Il.*, 1 × *Od.*). Lohmann unwisely wished to omit this verse, saying it disturbs the structure of the speech and is inconsistent with the rôle of Thetis. The latter point is not true (any son would consider 95–6, from a loving mother's lips, was intended as a deterrent), and even if the line does not fit within the ring form of 114–25 (which is arguable) it leads up well to Thetis' concession that his intent is the honourable one (128–9).

128–9 The scholia (Nic/A) already saw problems in punctuation here. The parallel ναὶ δὴ ταῦτά γε, τέκνον ἐμόν, κατὰ μοῖραν ἔειπες (*Od.* 22.486), and the Odyssean usages καί μοι τοῦτ' ἀγόρευον ἐτήτυμον, ὄφρ' ἐΰ εἰδῶ (7 × *Od.*), κείνου μέν τοι ὅδ' υἱὸς ἐτήτυμον, ὡς ἀγορεύεις (*Od.* 4.157) suggest that there should be a pause after ἐτήτυμον, which is predicative. 'This is surely true; it is not wrong...' τοῦτο of some late MSS is probably a simplifying emendation. The colon placed by Leaf after τέκνον violates both the normal run of the sentence and the formular usage. 129 ≅ 17.703, which has a different enjambing clausula.

Thetis realizes that opposition will be useless, and in motherly fashion seeks to help her son in his resolve, even though it will lead to his death. The scholia (?Porph/A) remark that she wishes his death to be noble. Akhilleus later implies that his entering the battle will avenge the deaths of others besides Patroklos (19.203–5); cf. 102–3 above.

130–7 The replacement of Akhilleus' armour is of course vitally important for more than practical reasons; it was prepared for at 17.711 as well as here. See Introduction, ch. 2, ii. The link between Hektor's donning of the armour and his death has already been made at 16.799–800 and 17.198–208.

130–1 ἔχονται is passive, with ἔντεα as subject; the plural is common after neuters meaning several concrete objects (Chantraine, *GH* II 17–18). ἔχονται (-το) is middle in Homer only where the meaning is strongly reflexive, 'hold ⟨in front of themselves⟩', 'hold ⟨on to each other⟩'. | χάλκεα μαρμαίροντα is formular for armour (3 × *Il.*), and the poet uses it unthinkingly for the armour Hephaistos will make from more precious metals; at 144 he is more careful (see note). | χρύσεα μ. occurs at 13.22 of Poseidon's house and could have been used here. The scholia (bT) note that a χαλκεύς gilds the horns of Nestor's sacrificial cow (*Od.* 3.432), and that the term is used of Hephaistos himself (15.309).

132–3 Verse 132 ≅ 17.473, where verse and sentence end with Αἰακίδαο. With the enjambing phrase cf. οὐδέ ἕ φημι | δηθ' ἀνσχήσεσθαι (5.103–4). ἐπαγλαϊεῖσθαι is otherwise found only in comedy and inscriptions, and ἀγλαϊεῖσθαι only at 10.331 (of Dolon) and never in tragedy, so there is probably a strongly colloquial and scornful tone here.

134–7 μή with the aorist imperative is found only here and in μή...ἔνθεο at 4.410 and *Od.* 24.248. Chantraine, *GH* II 230–1 and I 417, points out that καταδύσεο might be imperfect, but P. M. Smith, *HSCP* 83 (1979) 45–50, argues cogently that the forms arise from adaptations of the formular (κατ)ἐδύσατο τεύχεα καλά and ἔνθεο θυμῷ. μῶλον Ἄρηος is formular (3 × *Il.*), but occurs only here with καταδύσεο; this verb is regularly found with ὅμιλον (5 × *Il.*, 1 × *Od.*). Verse 135 is repeated at 190. πρίν with the subjunctive, instead of the usual infinitive, makes her promise more concrete and positive (Chantraine, *GH* II 264–5). The sense of 137 is also given by 617, but the latter verse shows off the conventional metrical mechanics by replacing καλά and ἄνακτος with μαρμαίροντα. The scholia (Arn/A) point out that Hephaistos has to work overnight.

138–41 Verse 130 occurs 4 × *Il.*, with different concluding phrases. On Thetis' dismissal of the Nereids see 65–9n. The sea formula recurs at *Od.* 4.435; a shorter form with ἁλός for θαλάσσης is found at 21.125. On the anonymous Old Man of the Sea see 1.358n. and S. West, *Odyssey* on *Od.* 4.349.

143–4 'To Akhilleus she stated definitely that she would without doubt bring armour from Hephaistos, but she speaks less certainly to her sisters; for it would be vulgar to speak too confidently to those of equal rank, as if she were going to give orders to Hephaistos' (bT). In 144 it would be better to read υἶι with Leaf (Chantraine, *GH* I 228). τεύχεα in this position is followed by ποικίλα χαλκῷ 6 × *Il.*, but the poet remembers that Hephaistos will provide something brighter than bronze. παμφανόωντα is formular with ἐνώπια (2 × *Il.*, 2 × *Od.*), but is also used with other objects.

145 Cf. ἀνεδύσατο κῦμα θαλάσσης (1.496). Thetis' departure in book 1 led on to Zeus's support for the Trojans and the whole tale of the result of Akhilleus' withdrawal from battle. Her departure here will lead to the gift of the armour, Akhilleus' return, and the concluding themes of revenge and consolation.

148–242 Meanwhile the struggle for Patroklos' corpse has continued, with Hektor fighting furiously against the two Aiantes. Herē sends Iris to rouse Akhilleus, who demurs because he has no armour; but she urges him to show himself to the Trojans, and with Athene's help his appearance and his mighty war-cry strike them with panic and allow the corpse to be borne back to the Greek camp

148–64 The picture is not quite consistent with that at the end of book 17, where the corpse was being carried by Menelaos and Meriones (17.717–18, 735–46) while the two Aiantes hold off the Trojans (746–53). Here the body is being dragged to and fro (155–6, 165, 176, 232), and there is no mention of the two bearers. Realism can be preserved if we hold that time has been passing during the previous scene and the struggle is now at a later (αὖτις, 153) and even more perilous stage.

148–50 Verse 148 ≅ 15.405. The scholia (bT) very properly comment on the unusual abruptness of the change of scene, not facilitated (as is usual) by the movement or observation of a character (though B. Hellwig seems to suggest that Akhilleus' concern for saving Patroklos' body provides a link (*Raum und Zeit im homerischen Epos*, Hildesheim 1964, 99)). The combination θεσπεσίῳ ἀλαλητῷ does not recur, but may be an under-represented formula; commoner phrases are | ἠχῇ θεσπεσίῃ (7 × *Il.*, 2 × *Od.*)

and μεγάλῳ ἀλαλητῷ (2 × *Il.*, 1 × *Od.*). Verse 150 ≅ 15.233, 23.2; ἵκοντο is conative.

151–2 The sense of οὐδέ κε...ἐρύσαντο is completed, after the intervening sentences, by εἰ μή...Ἶρις at 166. The variant οὐδ' ἄρα (mentioned by Did/T) does not improve the meaning. περ implies that the Greeks could have escaped to the ships themselves but could not get clear with the corpse. θεράποντ' Ἀχιλῆος is a unique and striking remodelling of the formular θεράποντες (-ας) Ἄρηος | (7 × *Il.*), clearly based on the similarity in sound. On the importance of sound in forming such analogies see Parry, *MHV* 73–4, and Nagler, *Spontaneity* 1–26.

153–4 Verse 153 is unformular. On the short simile in 154 see 17.87–9n. The need to insert τε prevents the use of Ἕκτωρ Πριαμίδης βροτολοιγῷ ἶσος Ἄρηϊ (11.295). The honour of the full-verse title for Hektor is balanced by that given to the Aiantes two verses later.

155–6 Zenodotus (Arn/A) altered the ending of 155 and continued with 176–7. Bolling, *External Evidence* 179–81, chose to eliminate 176–7 entirely, together with 156. One suspects that the repetition of ἑλκέμεναι μεμαώς (156) and ἑ. μέμονεν (176) had something to do with Zenodotus' alteration (though we know that he read 174, see note *ad loc.*); homoeoteleuton like this was suggested by Apthorp as a possible reason for the omission of 39–49 (see note *ad loc.*), and homoearchon for that between 17.133–9 (*Manuscript Evidence* 103–4). τρὶς μέν...τρὶς δέ is repeated at 228–9 and 4 × *Il.*, 2 × *Od.*; see 20.445–6n. Often there is a climactic 'but the fourth time...' (see 5.436–9n.). The trope often marks a decisive point in the action (see H. Bannert, *Formen des Wiederholens bei Homer*, Vienna 1988, 40–57). A corpse is also hauled by the foot at 16.762–3, cf. 17.389–95.

157–8 θοῦριν ἐπιειμένοι ἀλκήν is used only of the two Aiantes (3 × *Il.*, cf. *Od.* 9.214). The metaphor recurs in Akhilleus' forceful ἀναιδείην ἐπιειμένε to Agamemnon (1.149). ἀλκὶ πεποιθώς is otherwise confined to similes (5 × *Il.*, 1 × *Od.*).

159–60 ἄλλοτε...ἄλλοτε δ' αὖτε | recurs at 24.10. μέγα (or σμερδαλέα) ἰάχων often describes a victorious hero, but in view of Homer's habit of using a short form of a motif to anticipate an expanded form (see 17.360–425n.) he may be preparing the way here for Akhilleus' great cry at 217. On the scansion μέγᾰ ἰάχων (normal with this verb) see Chantraine, *GH* I 139–40, and Hoekstra, *Modifications* 53.

161–4 A typical lion-simile, unusually well fitted to the context. The two comparisons – lion/Hektor, herdsmen/Aiantes – are given equal weight, in chiastic order. Lions are also πεινάοντες in similes at 3.25 and 16.758, but there are no formular parallels. σῶμα is also used for a lion's prey at 3.23, but has much more point here since it is appropriate for both simile and narrative. δύω Αἴαντε κορυστά | recurs at 13.201; otherwise the epithet ('fully-armed') appears only in Τρώων ἕλεν ἄνδρα κορυστήν | (3 × *Il.*; see 4.457n.).

165 = 3.373, of Menelaos dragging Paris, in a similar construction. Note that though Hektor has already killed Patroklos and is wearing his armour, possession of the body too would mean additional honour for him and consequent dishonour for Akhilleus.

167 = 11.715, of Athene's help to Nestor's people. As often, θωρήσσεσθαι means 'prepare for battle', rather than literally 'arm oneself'; cf. 189, 2.526, 16.218. It is characteristic of the poet that Iris' purpose is announced in anticipation of her following words, and her secret dispatch by Here is signalled at 168 before she explains it herself (184–6).

168 κρύβδα occurs only here in Homer; κρύβδην is found 2 × *Od.* Here's dispatch of Athene (1.195) was described in the same words, extended by an epithet. Zeus has been portrayed as liking Patroklos (17.270–3), and he might well permit the rescue of his body, but Here's constant mistrust of her husband dominates her characterization as usual. Zeus was last seen on Mt Ida (17.594).

170 Verse 178 makes it clear that Akhilleus is thought of as still prostrate. ὄρσεο does not necessarily refer to this (it is used to the seated Priam at 3.250 and to others whose posture is not determined: 16.126, 21.331, *Od.* 6.255), but the phrase Iris applies to the hero is scornful; it was used by Agamemnon to Akhilleus (1.146), and will be used by the latter to the first of his victims (20.389).

171–2 Aristarchus' reading Πατρόκλου is mistaken; see Leaf's comment. ἀλλήλους ὀλέκουσι recurs at the beginning of the verse at 11.530.

174–5 προτὶ (ὑπὸ) Ἴλιον ἠνεμόεσσαν | occurs 7 × *Il.* Zenodotus' substitution of αἰπὺ θέλοντες (Arn/A) may have been due to the view that Ἴλιον should be neuter; see A. Hoekstra, *Mnemosyne* 31 (1978) 16–17. ἐπιθύουσι (elsewhere only at *Od.* 16.279) is from ἐπὶ + ἰθύω. A participle parallel to ἀμυνόμενοι would have been expected. μάλιστα δέ is strongly localized, always occurring in this position (9 × *Il.*, 4 × *Od.*) and often followed by a name or name–epithet formula.

176–7 With the phrasing cf. 13.202–3 κεφαλὴν δ' ἀπαλῆς ἀπὸ δειρῆς | κόψεν Ὀϊλιάδης. The walls of the city of the Phaeacians are σκολόπεσσιν ἀρηρότα (*Od.* 7.45). Aias Oïliades, not one of Homer's favourites, is the only hero who actually decapitates a corpse (13.202–3), though Euphorbos and Hektor think of it (17.38–40, 17.126) and Akhilleus promises to bring Hektor's head to Patroklos' pyre (334–5). Agamemnon and Peneleos behead enemies while fighting (11.146, 11.261, 14.496). On the unusual brutality of the threat see C. Segal, *The Theme of the Mutilation of the Corpse in the Iliad* (Leiden 1971) 22–4. The scholia (Arn/A on 154–6) claim that Iris is not telling the truth, as Hektor is actually following Glaukos' plan to exchange Patroklos' body for Sarpedon's (17.160–3). In similar fashion, Athene maliciously exaggerates Thetis' gesture of supplication to Zeus (8.371).

178–9 | ἀλλ' ἄνα, μή ... occurs 2 × *Il.*, 1 × *Od.* (plus 1 × *Il.* with εἰ). ἄνα = ἀνάστηθι. On the form κείσο see Chantraine, *GH* 1 474–5. σέβας, 'shame', occurs only here in the *Il.*, but cf. σεβάσσατο γάρ τό γε θυμῷ (2 × *Il.*). The *Od.* has σέβας μ' ἔχει εἰσορόωντα | 5 ×, with the sense 'wonder'. Verse 179 is repeated from 17.255 (where it depends on νεμεσιζέσθω); see note *ad loc.* The thought was in Hektor's mind at 17.127. As in 170, Iris' tone is calculated to rouse Akhilleus from grief-stricken immobility to vigorous action.

180 Later Akhilleus speaks of the λώβη of not having avenged Hektor's victims (19.208). τι ... ἠσχυμμένος refers to the barbarities of 174–9. αἵ κεν ... νέκυς ... ἔλθῃ can mean 'if the body is brought back' (Ameis–Hentze, Willcock), 'if the body goes ⟨away⟩' (Eustathius, τὸ ἔλθοι ἀντὶ τοῦ ἀπέλθοι), or 'if he goes to ⟨join⟩ the dead' (with νέκυς accusative plural, as at 7.420, *Od.* 24.417; Chantraine, *GH* 1 222). The last interpretation gives the best meaning (so Leaf), the second is the most natural.

182 Two papyri read ταρ, the older MSS τὰρ or τ' ἄρ. Allen's γάρ is almost certainly wrong; τίς γάρ belongs in a rhetorical question, as at 17.475, *Od.* 4.443, 10.383, 10.501, 17.382 (at *Od.* 14.115 Cobet's τάρ is preferable); see Denniston, *Particles* 70–1. Aristarchus' second edition (Did/A) read τάρ, which (as τ' ἄρ) is regular in surprised questions (188, 12.409, etc.; see Denniston, *Particles* 533) and is much to be preferred (so Leaf). Perhaps the τ' of τ' ἄρ is for τοι, cf. 17.469, rather than for 'connective' τε. Akhilleus' question is sensible enough after Thetis' injunction to him not to enter the battle (134–7, 189–91). He is similarly laconic at 1.216–18 and 24.139–40.

184–6 Here's name is put first for emphasis, and then Διὸς κυδρή παράκοιτις is the normal complimentary phrase to fill the space remaining, as at *Theogony* 328. It is also used for Leto at *Od.* 11.580. αἰδοίη replaces κυδρή to provide a longer form at 21.479. ὑψίζυγος is used only for Zeus and in this position (4 × *Il.*, 2 × Hesiod), and ἀγάννιφον only with Olumpos in this position (2 × *Il.*, 2 × Hesiod, 2 × *HyHerm*). On Zeus's ignorance see 168n.

188 Cf. 11.838 and *Od.* 3.22, both of which contain two half-verse questions. μετὰ μῶλον recalls μῶλον Ἄρηος in Thetis' command (134). κεῖνος also expresses dislike at 5.604 and 14.250.

189–90 J. C. Hogan has suggested (*CJ* 71, 1976, 305–10) that this use of double πρίν is especially associated with Akhilleus, but the evidence is not strong. On θωρήσσεσθαι see 167n. Verse 190 ≅ 135.

191–3 στεῦτο = 'promise', as at 5.832; on variations in meaning see Leaf. Leaf read παροισέμεν, against Aristarchus and the MSS, to provide a mid-verse caesura. This may well be right, though the compound verb does not elsewhere occur in Homer (except possibly at 4.97). ἄλλου... τευ is attracted into the case of τεῦ. Since the sentence can carry no sense until the relative clause is complete this does not seem harsh, though Leaf makes rather heavy weather of it. A similar attraction into the case of the relative occurs at 10.416–17, 14.75, 14.371. Wilamowitz, *IuH* 170–1, objected to ἄν (but cf. Chantraine, *GH* II 246) and read ἄλλου δ᾽ οὔ θην οἶδα ὅτευ κ. τ. δ. with some late MSS. Better than this is T. D. Seymour's suggestion that τεῦ... δύω; is parenthetical (*HSCP* 3, 1892, 123). With 193 cf. the formular Αἴας δ᾽ ἐγγύθεν ἦλθε φέρων σάκος ἠΰτε πύργον (3 × *Il.*). The shield is described at 7.219–23.

The scholia (AbT) provide a number of reasons why Akhilleus could not wear the armour of Patroklos, omitting the obvious ones that the poet wants to describe the new armour and to have both Hektor and Akhilleus arrayed by Hephaistos. Crates had the brilliant insight that Automedon had worn Patroklos' armour to impersonate him, as Patroklos impersonated Akhilleus, but (as Wolf acidly pointed out, *Prolegomena* I li) did not explain why in that case Akhilleus could not put on Automedon's equipment.

194–7 ἔλπομαι is only here in Homer used parenthetically. The first hemistich of 197 = those of 8.32, 8.463 (both are also spoken by goddesses). On ἔχονται see 130–1n.

198 A threefolder. αὔτως, 'just as you are', 'like this', as at 338, 1.520, 10.50 etc. Did/A thought that the reading αὐτός, preferred by Zenodotus and Aristophanes, was οὐκ ἄλογος, but it is not so effective in the context. Leaf preferred αὐτός as the *lectio difficilior*.

199–201 The lines are those used by Nestor to Patroklos (11.799–801, with σε τῷ εἴσκοντες for σ᾽ ὑποδείσαντες) and repeated by the latter to Akhilleus (16.41–3). τε (201) is generalizing (Ruijgh, τε *épique* 653). There is no reason to omit 200–1 here; Iris' speech would be unusually brief without them, and the omission in a papyrus and a few MSS may be due to homoeoteleuton. The repetition might well be thought significant, as Akhilleus is at last about to obey the injunction.

203–31 In this splendid passage the 'arming' of Akhilleus becomes a kind of epiphany, decorated with ornamental epithets and two vivid and apposite similes, and the resulting Trojan rout is described in almost impressionistic style. Griffin, *HLD* 38–9, quotes parallels from Near Eastern and Indo-European descriptions of warrior gods.

203–6 The impressively simple αὐτὰρ Ἀχιλλεὺς ὦρτο Διῒ φίλος signals the effective end of the hero's withdrawal, one of the turning-points of the poem; and in the same verse the goddess Athene appears to honour him, unheralded (any account of her journey would detract from the effect here). She arms him with the aegis, in place of corslet and shield, and the halo in place of a helmet. The language adapts formulae from arming-scenes. The function of conventional epithets is of course largely metrical, but here the ornamental and stately effect of Διὶ φίλος, δῖα θεάων, and χρύσεον is made more apparent by their separation from their nouns.

On the usage of Διὶ φίλος (17 × *Il.*, always in this position) see M. W. Edwards, *TAPA* 97 (1966) 163–4; on the form, 13.674–8n. The arming formula | ἀμφὶ δ᾽ ἄρ᾽ ὤμοισιν βάλετο ξίφος ἀργυρόηλον (βάλετ᾽ αἰγίδα θυσσανόεσσαν) (6 × *Il.*, once with substitution of an enjambing final phrase) is adapted to begin with Athene's name and to include the active form of the verb, leaving room for the preceding complimentary Διὶ φίλος and ἰφθίμοισι (otherwise used only with names of individuals and in the arming formula κρατὶ δ᾽ ἐπ᾽ ἰφθίμῳ κυνέην εὔτυκτον ἔθηκε, 3 × *Il.*, 1 × *Od.*). On the aegis see 2.446–51n., 15.18–31n., and 15.308–10n.

205–6 Cf. νεφέεσσι περιστέφει οὐρανὸν εὐρύν | Ζεύς (*Od.* 5.303–4). αὐτοῦ = the hero himself (though the exegetical scholia (AT) took it as τοῦ νέφους). φλόγα παμφανόωσαν | (also at 21.349) may recall the formular ἔντε᾽ ἐδύσατο παμφανόωντα | (2 × *Il.*). On golden clouds see 13.521–5n.

Athene similarly makes fire flash from the helmet and shield, head and shoulders of Diomedes as a surrogate arming-scene before his *aristeia* (5.4–7, see note *ad loc.*). C. H. Whitman declared 'The fire that shoots from Achilles' head denotes the *peripeteia* of the *Iliad*' (*Homer and the Heroic Tradition*, Cambridge, Mass. 1958, 137), and his exposition of the fire imagery is perceptive, though sometimes exaggerated (*ibid.* 128–53). Fire and light will be very prominent when Akhilleus finally arms himself for battle (19.369–98).

207–14 The simile is linked to the narrative at several points. The main comparison is between the fire flaming from Akhilleus' head and that from the walls of the besieged city; this city suggests Troy, whose fall is brought closer by Akhilleus' intervention in the battle. In addition, 'Achilles is identified with something suffering rather than something conquering... the elaborated description, taken as a whole, is suggestive of Achilles' psychological isolation' (D. M. Knight, *YCS* 14, 1955, 116). πανημέριοι στυγερῷ κρίνονται Ἄρηϊ (209) recalls the long day of fighting since book 11, and the setting sun (210) its swiftly approaching end (239–42). The islanders' hope of assistance (213) links the thought to the struggling Greeks, and the immediately reiterated flare from Akhilleus' head (214) appears like a light of hope for them.

On the sequence of similes describing burning cities as the doom of Troy becomes closer see 17.736–41n. Similes again look forward to future events at 16.752–3 (Patroklos' rash courage) and 18.318–22 (Akhilleus' pursuit of vengeance).

207 ≅ 21.522 (introducing another simile for Akhilleus and Troy).

Aristarchus, according to Dionysius Thrax, first accepted the reading in the text and then changed his mind and wrote ὡς δ' ὅτε πῦρ ἐπὶ πόντον ἀριπρεπὲς αἰθέρ' ἵκηται (Did/AT), which won the praise of Wolf (*Prolegomena* i xlviii n.36). This is now understood as what Aristarchus would have preferred (καὶ γὰρ ἄτοπόν φησι πῦρ εἰκάζεσθαι καπνῷ, T), not a correction in his text (Pasquali, *Storia* 238 n. 5 and references there). He did not see that the flame around Akhilleus' head is compared not narrowly with the smoke, but as usual with the whole picture given in the simile, in which after the daylong rising of the smoke the fires flash out far and wide as darkness falls. Eustathius (1138) found this passage more marvellous than Athene's glorification of Diomedes, and points out that in daylight smoke is seen better from a distance than fire, but at night the fire shines out.

208–14 MSS offer both indicative and subjunctive for ἀμφιμάχωνται and κρίνονται; Allen's reading is best (especially if οἱ δέ is accepted). Verse 209 ≅ 2.385. Heyne's conjecture οἱ δέ is tempting, as a change of subject from δήϊοι is needed; Leaf and Chantraine, *GH* ii 356, approve. The second hemistich of 210 is formular (3 × *Il.*, 1 × *Od.*). πυρσοί (211), 'beacon-fires', occurs only here in Homer but is common later. ἐπήτριμος occurs 3 × *Il.* and in a few late imitations; its meaning is uncertain, but the ancients took it to mean 'close together', from ἤτριον, 'warp'. See Risch, *Wortbildung* 105. On ἀρῆς ἀλκτῆρες (213) see 14.484–5n. Verse 214 ≅ 19.379 (concluding a simile for Akhilleus' shield). Eustathius (1138.57) points out that the mention of islanders is important, as signal-fires are more vital to them because no messenger can be sent on foot and the fire reaches both the mainland and other islands.

215–16 The ditch is thought of as being some distance beyond the wall; see 9.67n. μίσγεσθαι usually takes ἐν and the dative, but here ἐς and accusative indicates Akhilleus does not cross the ditch to join the Greeks.

217–18 ἀπάτερθε shows that Athene does not descend to stand beside Akhilleus, but her assistance makes the supernatural feat possible, as when she helps Herakles to support the sky on the famous metope at Olympia. The voice of the mortal Stentor was as great as those of fifty other men (5.786), and Poseidon's was like those of nine or ten thousand (14.147–52, see note *ad loc.*). Athene gives a war-cry to enhearten the Greeks at 11.10–12 and in the surrealistic scene at 20.48–50, and Apollo dismays them with one at 15.321. | ἔνθα στᾶσ' ἤϋσε is used for Here's encouragement to the Greeks (5.784) and for Athene's war-cry (11.10). On Παλλὰς 'Αθήνη see 5.1n. and 10.245n. In 218 Akhilleus is subject of the verb; the second hemistich ≅ 10.523.

219–21 A second comparison with the scene at a besieged city dignifies Akhilleus' symbolic war-cry announcing his return to the battle, his first public action since his withdrawal, and again suggests the doom of Troy.

The scholia (Arn/AT) rightly comment that Homer knows the trumpet but his heroes do not; in addition to this use in a simile it occurs in the splendid metaphor ἀμφὶ δὲ σάλπιγξεν μέγας οὐρανός (21.388, see note *ad loc.*). The earliest artistic representation is said to be on an amphora by the Amasis painter (Beazley, *ABV* 152/25; M. Wegner, *Arch. Hom.* υ 18–19). σάλπιγξ, like σῦριγξ and φόρμιγξ, is a loan-word (Risch, *Wortbildung* 175). ὡς ὅτε ... ὅτε τε is found again at 8.556–7. The first ὅτε introduces a general idea ('Akhilleus cries as when a clear voice ⟨is heard⟩'), the second specifies more particularly ('when a trumpet calls'); τε of course is normal in similes (see Introduction, ch. 3, iv).

220 περιπλομένων (etc.) is found elsewhere in archaic epic only with ἐνιαυτός (1 × *Il.*, 2 × *Od.*), but here it oddly controls the accusative ἄστυ. δηΐων ὕπο θυμοραϊστέων | (cf. θάνατος χύτο θυμοραϊστής |, 3 × *Il.*; see 16.588–92n.) recurs at 16.591 (also in a simile), where it amplifies ἐν πολέμῳ and means 'under the stress of murderous enemies'. Here ancient and modern scholars uneasily attach ἄστυ περιπλομένων to δηΐων, '⟨enemies⟩ surrounding a city'. But this involves a very harsh word-order, and it might be simpler to take ἄστυ περιπλομένων as dependent upon σάλπιγξ, 'the trumpet of those surrounding a city', and δηΐων ὕπο θυμοραϊστέων as an independent phrase (as at 16.591), amplifying the deadly nature of their attack. In either case, the expression is strikingly innovative even for a simile. With the usual interpretation, it is not clear if the trumpet is signalling the besiegers to attack or summoning the citizens to the defence; see Moulton, *Similes* 107 n. 51.

222 ἄϊον has ᾰ here and at 11.463, but ᾱ at 10.532 and 21.388. The usual feminine form χαλκείην will not fit, so the poet treats the adjective as if it were of two terminations. Zenodotus read χαλκέην with synizesis; χρυσέη (etc.) is often so scanned. Stentor was called χαλκεόφωνος at 5.785, and before the Catalogue of Ships the poet (perhaps in some confusion of mind) laments that he could not tell over all the heroes even if φωνὴ δ' ἄρρηκτος χάλκεον δέ μοι ἦτορ ἐνείη (2.490). 'Brazen' is also applied metaphorically to Ares, the hearts of fighting men, the sleep of a dead warrior (11.241; caused by a bronze weapon, or unbreakable? see note *ad loc.*), and the sky (17.425; see note *ad loc*). Here the metaphor recalls the preceding simile, and suggests that the σάλπιγξ was of bronze, not horn. There are other examples of a concrete item in a simile becoming metaphorical in the narrative: a 'cloud' of soldiers becomes a storm-cloud advancing over the sea (4.274–9, see note *ad loc.*); a wave 'raises its head' as Eris will do as she drives on the armies (4.424, 442, see notes *ad locc.*); as snow melts on the mountains, so Penelope's cheeks 'melt' into tears (*Od.* 19.204–8).

The poet has skilfully contrived that Akhilleus is essentially responsible for the rescue of Patroklos' body, without having him directly confront

Hektor or the other Trojans. His appearance and his war-cry perform the function of (and were suggested by?) the wind-storm which Zeus sent to end the struggle over Akhilleus' body (*Od.* 24.41–2).

223–4 πασιν ὀρίνθη θυμός is reserved for great occasions, when the Trojans are daunted by the attacks of Diomedes (5.29) and of the disguised Patroklos (16.280). With 224 cf. *Od.* 18.154 (ὁ) κακὸν ὄσσετο θυμῷ |, *Od.* 10.374 κακὰ δ᾽ ὄσσετο θυμός |.

225–7 Note the alliteration in ἴδον... | δεινόν... | δαιόμενον...δαῖε, especially the effect of the two verse-initial words. δεινόν can be taken as a runover epithet after πῦρ or adverbially with δαιόμενον; the latter is perhaps more effective, the former more natural in Homeric style. The repetition δαιόμενον...δαῖε...is matched by δαιομένη· δαίωσι δ᾽ (20.317, see 20.313–17n.), καιομένη· καίωσι δ᾽ (21.376), καιομένοιο...καίεται (19.376), and εἰλομένων· εἶλει δέ... (8.215; see note *ad loc.*). The generic epithet μεγαθύμου may carry more weight than the regular old Πηληϊάδεω ᾽Αχιλῆος; see 17.213–14n.

228–31 On τρὶς μὲν...τρὶς δέ see 155–6n. The account of the Trojan casualties, though terse, is a little fuller than that of Patroklos' last charge, τρὶς μὲν ἔπειτ᾽ ἐπόρουσε... | ...τρὶς δ᾽ ἐννέα φῶτας ἔπεφνεν (16.784–5). Groups of twelve nameless men are also killed at 10.488 and 15.746. καί (230) links ὄλοντο with κυκήθησαν. Scholars ancient and modern have found it hard to discover just what is meant by ἀμφὶ σφοῖς ὀχέεσσι καὶ ἔγχεσιν. The poet is not aiming at precision, and one should imagine only a sudden tumultuous flight, without pursuit, in which men die transfixed by the weapons of others (or even their own), trampled by horses and crushed under the wheels of chariots. ἀμφί has its common meaning of 'on and around'. Zenodotus (Arn/A) rewrote the couplet as ἔνθα δὲ κοῦροι ὄλοντο δυώδεκα πάντες ἄριστοι | οἷσιν ἐν⟨ὶ⟩ βελέεσσιν, a version rightly criticized by Aristarchus. See van der Valk, *Researches* II 58–60 (but his interpretation, 'if the Greeks had exploited their advantage, they would have killed 12 Trojans', is surely incorrect and inconsistent with his analysis).

Griffin, *HLD* 39, suggests that the motif of men dying from fear at the terrifying cry of a hero may underlie this unusual passage. At least we may say that the advance of a great hero into battle must be marked by enemy deaths, and here they cannot be provided by Akhilleus' prowess or that of other Greeks.

231–8 Notice the changing viewpoint and the variation of sense-pauses in these lines. After the change to the Greeks as subject in the final part of 231, a participial clause again enjambs and the sentence ends at the midpoint of 233; a short simple sentence turns from the Greeks in general to Patroklos' former companions, running over into the pathetic μυρόμενοι; then among them we see Akhilleus himself, and his emotions are described in two further enjambing verses (235–6), the first divided by syntax at the midpoint, the second falling into two balancing halves. The following couplet (237–8), again with enjambment, tells us his thoughts in the poet's voice.

234 The regular formulae are ποδάρκης δῖος Ἀχιλλεύς (21 × *Il.*), ποδώκεα (-ϊ) Πηλείωνα (-ι) (12 × *Il.*), and ποδώκεος Αἰακίδαο (8 × *Il.*, plus a variation at 20.89; 2 × *Od.*). Here, where a nominative is needed, ποδάρκης might have been expected. But ποδάρκης is fossilized in its one formula, whereas ποδώκης (in various cases) appears 6 × *Il.* in unformular usages, and is clearly the 'working' word which comes more readily to the poet's mind.

236 φέρτρον occurs only here in Homer, and (like φέρετρον) is very rare later. The root is that of φέρω, but the sense of both forms is restricted to 'bier' (cf. 'bier' itself from the root of the verb 'bear'; I owe the observation to N. J. Richardson). The second hemistich is formular (5 × *Il.*, clustered 3 × in book 19).

237–8 ἔπεμπε is meant literally, and conveys Akhilleus' sense of responsibility for Patroklos' death; the latter had no chariot or horses of his own. νοστήσαντα is also joined poignantly with οὐ... | δέξεται (-το) at 330–1 and 5.157–8. The poet leaves Akhilleus' grief speechless, as at 22ff., but in his own voice describes the self-reproachful thoughts in his mind, emphasizing our concern for him with ἦτοι, 'Verily, I tell you' (Denniston, *Particles* 553), 'ja nun allerdings' (Schadewaldt, *VHWW* 265). De Jong, *Narrators* 121–2, says that only 7.216–18 matches this as an approach to the 'stream of consciousness' technique.

239–42 It is Hektor's day of triumph, promised to him by Zeus at 11.191–4 and confirmed at 17.206, that Here brings to a premature end. The motif of hastening or delaying sunset or sunrise is found again at *Od.* 23.241–6 (Athene delays Dawn for the benefit of Odysseus and Penelope), and passes into the *topos* of erotic poetry. Here's intervention here also anticipates her bitterly anti-Trojan colloquy with Zeus at 356–67. The doom of Patroklos too is heralded by the setting of the sun (16.777–9). The passage may be compared with 8.487–8, Τρωσὶν μὲν ῥ' ἀέκουσιν ἔδυ φάος, αὐτὰρ Ἀχαιοῖς | ἀσπασίη τρίλλιστος ἐπήλυθε νὺξ ἐρεβεννή.

Ἤλιον δ' ἀκάμαντα is formular at the beginning of the verse (2 × *Il.*, 1 × Hesiod). Here the context gives the epithet special point. On Here's name–epithet formulae see 15.92n. ἀέκοντα: it is not yet time for Helios' departure, and his unwillingness to leave the scene perhaps increases the pathos of the passage; the word is common in this position. In 241 the wording is adapted to put Helios' name first, as in 239, and to include μέν; cf. | δύσετο (δύη) τ' Ἠέλιος (4 × *Il.*, 9 × *Od.*) and ὡς ἔφατ', Ἠέλιος δ' ἄρ' ἔδυ (2 × *Od.*). Then the second hemistich forms a chiasmus. | φυλόπιδος κρατερῆς

(242) recurs at *Od.* 16.268; see also 13.633–5n. On ὁμοίου πολέμοιο (< *ὁμοιῖοο πτολέμοιο) see 13.358n. and J. Russo, *Odissea* on *Od.* 18.264. The skill with which this short passage is composed is well brought out by J. I. Armstrong, *AJP* 79 (1958) 340. After the Trojan assembly we return to find the Greeks lamenting over Patroklos' body (314).

243–314 Dismayed by Akhilleus' reappearance, the Trojans immediately hold an assembly on the plain before Troy. Pouludamas prudently recommends that they withdraw within the city walls at once, and remain there the next day. But Hektor, not realizing he no longer has the support of Zeus, angrily rejects this good counsel and tells them to stay in their camp on the plain and join battle again when morning comes; he himself will not fear to face Akhilleus. The Trojans applaud and accept Hektor's advice

Greek and Trojan scenes alternate in this Book. The long presentation of Akhilleus' grief, his threat of vengeance, and his return to action is succeeded by this renewed depiction of Hektor's over-confidence, which has been mounting since he killed Patroklos (see 17.198–209n.). Next the account of Akhilleus' sorrow and anger will be renewed (314–55), and the withdrawal of divine assistance to the Trojans reaffirmed (356–67) before the Greek cause is taken up again on Olumpos.

Just as, in the previous scene, Thetis' warning to Akhilleus of the fated result if he killed Hektor brought out his own resolution and acceptance of his approaching death, so here Pouludamas' prudence throws into relief Hektor's arrogant over-confidence. See 284–309n.

243–83 The last Trojan assembly was held after they had driven the Greeks back within their ditch and wall (8.489–542); they approved, without a dissenting voice, Hektor's suggestion that they spend the night on the plain. On that occasion Hektor also utters threats, aimed then at Diomedes (8.532–41). Pouludamas was last seen fighting beside Hektor and wounding Peneleos the Boeotian (17.597–600).

243–5 The lines are composed of regular formulae. The genitive would be expected after ὑπό (244), but ἁρμάτων will not fit into a hexameter. The *schema etymologicum* ἀγορήν ἀγέροντο appears in a different form at 2.788 ἀγορὰς ἀγόρευον; see 2.785–9n. and 4.1n.

246–8 As often, the poet expresses a mental state by describing a physical action. Note the emphatic ἕζεσθαι and ἐξεφάνη placed at the beginning of each verse. ὀρθῶν ἑσταότων is used at *Od.* 9.442 for Poluphemos' uncomfortable unmilked ewes. οὕνεκ' Ἀχιλλεύς | ἐξεφάνη, δηρὸν δὲ μάχης ἐπέπαυτ' ἀλεγεινῆς here gives the thoughts of the Trojans, at 19.45–6 those of the Greeks before their assembly, and at 20.42–3 those of the gods before they join in the battle; the fact is of vital importance to all sides. Of δέ (248) bT say (as often) ὁ δέ ἀντὶ τοῦ γάρ, but it is hardly this; rather, it marks the new clause, with its shift to the viewpoint of the Trojans (so de Jong, *Narrators* 233).

249–53 Pouludamas is well enough known to us by now, but what he has to say here has unusual importance – this is the last chance for life for Hektor and many other Trojans – and so he is given this expanded introduction before his speech begins. On the technique see 15.281–5n. and Macleod, *Iliad XXIV* 123 and 137.

249–50 Pouludamas deserves better than most to be called πεπνυμένος, but this is the only time he receives the (probably) generic epithet; in the midst of battle, in similar metrical circumstances he is given Ares' ἐγχέσπαλος (14.449). The probably proverbial phrase ὅρα πρόσσω καὶ ὀπίσσω is repeated for Halitherses (*Od.* 24.452, again after οἶος) and adapted with different verbs and a following ὅπ(π)ως at 1.343–4 and 3.109–10. It always refers to the wisdom of experience, not prophetic powers. ὀπίσσω, 'backwards', otherwise means 'hereafter' of time (e.g. at 3.160), but here the expression refers metaphorically to someone who 'looks both before and behind him'.

251–2 Usually it is older men who are wiser (3.108–10, 19.218–19, 23.589–90), so Pouludamas' equality in age with Hektor emphasizes the surprising fact of his greater wisdom (so Solmsen, *TAPA* 85, 1954, 2); it also gives Hektor greater freedom to accept or reject his advice. On the antithesis in 252 see 105–6n. Pouludamas actually lectures Hektor on this topic at 13.726–35. ἔγχεϊ = 'warfare', by metonymy.

253–83 Pouludamas gives Hektor good advice at 12.61–79, 12.211–29, and 13.726–47; this is the only time we hear him speak publicly in assembly. At 13.744–7 he was wise enough to foresee the possibility of Akhilleus' return. 'He is adept at sizing up a military situation and its tactical possibilities, and then presenting a sensible assessment of their advantages and disadvantages (particularly the disadvantages) in support of his preferred solution' (M. Schofield, *CQ* 36, 1986, 19). He does not speak of honour and shame, as Hektor does. Hektor will remember his friend's words when he faces Akhilleus alone (22.100–2).

The speech, like the others by this speaker, falls into two parts; the first is in ring form, the second in parallel form (see Lohmann, *Reden* 30–3 and 178–82). In the second part, the parallelism is maintained by repetition of the italicized words:

I   A   *Go back to the city*; do not wait for morning (254–6).

    B 1. While Akhilleus was away, the fighting was easy, and I too was happy to pass the night by their ships (256–60).

2. But now I fear Akhilleus; we shall not fight on the plain, but for our city and our wives (261–5).

A′ Let us go back to the city! Listen to me (266)!

11 A Now, *night* has stopped Akhilleus (267).

   B If he finds us here *tomorrow* when he attacks, we shall know well what he is like (268–270).

   C [*Result*] We shall *be driven back to Troy*, and *dogs and vultures will eat many* (270–2).

   A′ If you do as I say, *tonight* we shall maintain our strength in the market-place, defended by the walls and gates (273–6).

   B′ *Tomorrow*, under arms, we will man the city towers; the worse for Akhilleus, if he attacks (277–9)!

   C′ [*Result*] He will *go back to his ships*; before he sacks our city, *dogs will eat him* (280–3)!

Hektor's speech in part repeats the structure (see 284–309n.).

254–5 κέλομαι γὰρ ἔγωγε | is found elsewhere 1 × *Il.*, 1 × *Od.* without enjambment. μίμνειν (etc.) 'Ηῶ δῖαν is formular (3 × *Il.*, 6 × *Od.*; < 'Ηόα, Chantraine, *GH* I 54).

257 Αἰακίδης (2 × *Il.*) would have fitted in place of οὗτος ἀνήρ, but the latter may well be pejorative; see 22.38n. Pouludamas also avoids using Akhilleus' name at 13.746–7.

259–60 χαίρεσκον recurs at *Od.* 12.380, where the meaning is more decidedly iterative than here. ἐπὶ νηυσὶν Ἰαύων | is almost a parody of the usual formula ἐ. ν. 'Αχαιῶν | (15 × *Il.*, with variants, 1 × *Od.*). The irregular lengthening of the final syllable of νῆας probably arises from adaptation of a formula; see Hoekstra, *Modifications* 125.

262 οἷος κείνου θυμὸς ὑπέρβιος is used at *Od.* 15.212 (by Menelaos of Nestor); in both instances the phrase gives the reason for the following clause. At 15.94 a similar verse ends ὑπερφίαλος καὶ ἀπηνής (by Here of Zeus), explaining what has preceded. The *Od.* passage shows that there is no need to read οὐδ' for οὐκ, as Leaf wished to do.

264–5 "Αρηος usually stands at the end of the verse, with ᾰ; in this position, with ᾱ, only at 2.767 and 3.128, where (as here) the phrasing is unique. Cf. 20.150–2n., 5.31n. Verse 265 ≅ *Od.* 11.403, 24.113.

266 Pouludamas reiterates his advice, rounding off the first part of his speech. ὧδε is taken by Lohmann, *Reden* 31, as a transition to what follows. But the run of the verse, with the two strong sense-pauses separating the sentences, suggests that the last phrase summarizes Pouludamas' description of the situation – 'That's the way it will be!' ὧδε can refer to what has preceded, as at 272.

267–83 He now presents the two alternatives: remain and face Akhilleus

Book Eighteen

in the morning (267–72); or follow his advice and return to the city (273–83).

267–8 | νύκτα δι' ἀμβροσίην occurs 4 × *Il.* (including an adapted form), 2 × *Od.*, and ἀμβροσίη νύξ | 3 × *Od.* Here ἀμβροσίη could not be fitted into the same verse as its companion νύξ, so it runs over into the next line, with no special emphasis. See Hainsworth, *Flexibility* 105–9. On the origin of ἄμβροτος and its cognates see 14.78n.

269–70 σὺν τεύχεσιν: *we* know of Thetis' mission to fetch armour, and we need not worry whether, and how, Pouludamas came to know it too. ἀσπασίως is used for the relief at escaping from a hypothetical undesirable activity at 7.118 and 19.72. Pouludamas' prediction comes true at 21.606–11.

271–2 Corpses to be eaten by dogs and vultures is a common motif, used for warnings, threats, taunts, etc.; see Griffin, *CQ* 26 (1976) 169–72. The second hemistich of 271 is repeated at 22.42, With 272 cf. 22.454 | αἳ γὰρ ἀπ' οὔατος εἴη ἐμεῦ ἔπος. The meaning is 'May I never hear of this!', perhaps based on a proverbial expression for *absit omen*.

274–6 Aristarchus (Arn/A) took the meaning of εἰν ἀγορῇ σθένος ἕξομεν to be τῇ βουλῇ κρατήσομεν, which is a sound paraphrase of the Greek but gives poor sense here; at this point Pouludamas is exhorting his listeners to seek the protection of the city, not to spend the night debating the best plan of action, and unless a strong local sense (with which Homer must surely have been familiar) is attributed to εἰν ἀγορῇ he seems not to be calling explicitly for a retreat within the walls. Other commentators (bT) took σθένος, like δύναμις in later authors, to refer to the army, so the sense would be 'tonight we will keep our army ⟨together⟩ in the marketplace', which makes good sense with what follows (so Ameis–Hentze and Willcock). Leaf will not accept this meaning of σθένος and renders 'we will keep (husband) our strength (by resting) in the agora', which is also possible. Fenik, in a thorough discussion of the passage (*Rhesus* 47–50), takes νύκτα as 'in the night' and accepts Aristarchus' rendering.

σανίδες are beams or boards (*Od.* 22.174), and the plural was used for the two door- or gate-leaves closing a large opening in a palace- or city-wall. These double gates were fastened by a 'supporter' crossbeam (ὀχεύς or ἐπιβλής) held by a pin (κληΐς). See 12.455–6 and notes; the account of city-gates by S. Iakovides, *Arch. Hom.* E 219, merely quotes this passage. ἐζευγμέναι (276), 'yoked together ⟨like two oxen⟩', is a fine metaphor for the barred double gates, and the spondaic verse-ending comes as culmination to the preceding heavy adjectives. εὐξέστῃς σανίδεσσι | is probably a formula (*Od.* 21.137 = 164); | μακρῷ εὐξέστῳ is used of an axe-handle at 13.613 (see note *ad loc.*). ἀραρυῖαι (275), 'smoothed', 'fitted', occurs 2 × *Il.*, 3 × *Od.* with σανίδες.

277–8 Though 277 occurs also at 8.530, it is not just its formular nature that makes Hektor repeat it at 303, with a very different ending to the sentence. He also picks up τῷ δ᾽ ἄλγιον at 306.

280–1 Our memory of Akhilleus' splendid immortal horses from 17.426–58 gives the jibe additional point. ἠλάσκω and -άζω always convey contempt of some kind, though Leaf's suggestion that the suffix -άζω may have this meaning is not borne out by Risch's fuller listing of such verbs (*Wortbildung* 297–8).

282–3 ἐάσει seems weak, as Leaf complains, if we translate 'His θυμός (anger? courage?) will not *allow* him to burst inside', but the sense is rather 'However great his anger, it will not permit him to…' With the second half of 283 cf. κύνες ἀργοὶ ἕποντο | (3 × *Od.*).

284–309 Hektor's speech skilfully refutes that of Pouludamas and impugns his motives (300–2). His arrogance has often been indicated before (see 12.231–50n., 13.54n., 13.825–9n., 17.194–209n., 17.448–50), and it rises to a climax here. This human fallibility will increase the pathos of his final duel with Akhilleus; pathetic too is the placing of his boastful challenge to Akhilleus (305–9) between the scenes of Akhilleus' meeting with his goddess mother and her procuring of divinely made armour for him. 'Der Dichter selbst sieht ihm zu mit einem Gefühl, in dem sich Bewunderung, Unmut und Mitleid seltsam mischen' (Schadewaldt, *VHWW* 258). See also J. M. Redfield, *Nature and Culture in the Iliad* (Chicago 1975) 128–53.

Lohmann, *Reden* 119–120 and 201–2, points out that Hektor's speech closely matches – almost parodies – Pouludamas' in construction and argument (see 253–83n.) and sometimes in language. Again the first part is in ring form:

I   A   I reject your advice to go back to the city (285–7).
      B   1. In the past, our city was wealthy (288–9).
           2. But now all these treasures have vanished because of Zeus' anger (290–2).
      A′ Now that Zeus has given me glory, do not utter such thoughts! No-one will listen to you (293–6)!

The second part does not of course offer the alternatives of Pouludamas' speech, but the recommended course of action again falls into three parts:

II   A Now, eat supper, post a watch, and do not concern yourselves too much with your possessions in the city (297–302).
      B Tomorrow, we will meet them in battle beside their ships (303–4).
      C [*Result*] If Akhilleus returns, I will fight him (305–9)!

On Hektor's preoccupation with honour and shame rather than the safety of his people see 22.100–10n. The formular content of the speech has been analysed by J. A. Russo in *Oral Literature and the Formula*, edd. B. A. Stolz and R. S. Shannon III (Ann Arbor 1976) 45–7, 51–3.

284–5 Hektor's rejection of Pouludamas' advice at 12.230-1 – another violent rejection of advice to retreat – begins with the same two verses.

286–7 | ὃς κέλεαι occurs in Hektor's previous argument with Pouludamas (12.235) and in Odysseus' with Agamemnon (14.96). ἀλήμεναι and ἐελμένοι are both from ἔλω, root ϝελ-. The word is common in this context, cf. 21.534n. Most of the expressions are formular, but κεκόρησθε and ἔνδοθι πύργων are not and give a frustrated vividness to 287.

288–9 There are two violations – or innovative uses – of normal formular conventions in this couplet. The old, incomprehensible formula μερόπων ἀνθρώπων | (7 × *Il.*, 2 × *Od.*, 6 × Hesiod, 1 × each in *HyDem* and *HyAp*; dative μερόπεσσι βροτοῖσι, 2.285) is used uniquely and unmetrically in the nominative. On its possible original meaning see 1.250n. and J. Russo, *Odissea* on *Od.* 20.49. The epithets πολύχρυσον πολύχαλκον |, occasionally used separately for ornament, are here combined and form the predicate of the sentence; they recur together only in the description of Dolon (10.315). Probably this is a regular combination of ornamental epithets (with neat anaphora) for a city, which happens not to be found in surviving archaic epic. Two weighty adjectives are also combined like this at 9.154, ἐν δ' ἄνδρες ναίουσι πολύρρηνες πολυβοῦται, and 11.390, κωφὸν γὰρ βέλος ἀνδρὸς ἀνάλκιδος οὐτιδανοῖο. M. L. West, *JHS* 108 (1988) 156, suggests this kind of pairing of adjectives with the same first element may go back to Indo-European poetry. The wealth of Troy before the war was legendary: cf. 9.401–3, and Akhilleus' more rhetorical statement at 24.543–6.

290–2 Hektor speaks of the Trojans' possessions again at 300–2, and he referred to the expenses of the war, especially those of supporting the allied contingents, at 17.225–6. The logistics of paying his allies, as well as hybris, are shaping Hektor's decision; he must counter the emotional attractions of a retreat to the Trojans' well-fortified and comfortable home, depicted at some length by Pouludamas (273–6), and he does it by portraying what the splendid city has already lost and will continue to lose in the future if Akhilleus is not stopped now. Verse 291 ≅ 3.401; on the Phruges and Meiones see 2.862–3n. and 864–6n. With 292 cf. Athene's question about Odysseus, τί νύ οἱ τόσον ὠδύσαο, Ζεῦ; (*Od.* 1.62).

293–5 After the ὅτε clause the main sentence should be 'you tell us to go back into the city!' But Hektor breaks off in vividly rhetorical disgust, and substitutes the more forceful 'You fool, don't speak such nonsense to the people!' νήπιε is also hurled mistakenly by Hektor at the dying Patroklos

(16.833), and Akhilleus will retaliate with it when Hektor in turn is dying (22.333). It will soon be picked up by the poet's own voice (311). The irony of Hektor's belief that Zeus will continue to support him will end with his realization of the truth at 22.301–3. But his self-confidence here is good for the troops' morale.

296 In the last line of the first part of his speech Hektor's οὐ... ἐπιπείσεται throws back at Pouludamas the πίθεσθέ μοι in the corresponding line at the end of his own appeal (266). The final abrupt οὐ γὰρ ἐάσω – note the repeated οὐ γάρ – is almost a mockery of Pouludamas' concluding ὧδε γάρ ἔσται; the phrase was used, perhaps not coincidentally, by Zeus when he refused to let Hektor capture Akhilleus' horses (17.449).

297 Having refuted Pouladamas' counsel. Hektor leads up to his own advice with a formular line (8 × *Il.*, 2 × *Od.*).

298–9 ≅ 7.370–1, spoken by Priam to the Trojans, and 298 ≅ 11.730, in Nestor's account of the Pylians' attack on their enemies (and ≅ 314 below, with an enjambing clausula). The expression is thus always used for those protecting a besieged city, not for the attackers.

300–2 See 290–2n. Verse 300 must be taken as a forensic imputation of an unworthy motive underlying Pouludamas' desire to return to the city, and 301–2 as an appeal to popular greed based upon it. Demagogy, in short. 'If you are so keen that the Greeks shall not have your property, share it out amongst us all and we will take good care of it!' 'He indicates that Pouludamas, being rich, is afraid to run risks' say the scholia (bT), and of the proposed share-out 'This is stimulating to the masses.' Only the order to eat is said to be executed (314).

Leaf sees 'an elaborate irony', which is true enough of Hektor's choice of words. κτεάτεσσιν ὑπερφιάλως ἀνιάζει is harsh in tone, 'is excessively distressed about his possessions'. καταδημοβορῆσαι is just the thing to bring laughter and cheers from the troops. Found only here, it is based on δημοβόρος βασιλεύς (1.231), which, like Hesiod's criticisms (*Erga* 260–4), was 'no doubt...something of a commonplace' (1.231–2n.); but here the sense of the compound is cunningly reversed – the δῆμος will devour the wealth instead of being themselves devoured by the princes.

303–4 Having discredited his opponent and won over his audience, Hektor repeats Pouludamas' words from 277, probably mockingly, as he does in 306 (though the verse is also used at 8.530). Then he completes the sentence with a standard incitement to battle (304 = 8.531; the second hemistich occurs an additional 3 × *Il.*).

305–9 Notice the variety of sense-pauses. The first verse (305) is filled by a single clause, the next has three strongly-marked sense-breaks and then enjambs into the emphatic | φεύξομαι (306–7); at the bucolic diaeresis a new sentence begins and enjambs into an equally emphatic and matching

| στήσομαι (307–8), which begins a 'threefolder'. Then a gnome fills up the final verse (309).

305–6 εἰ δ' ἐτεόν is very common (4 × *Il.*, 7 × *Od.* at the beginning of the verse, εἰ ἐτεόν γε (etc.) 4 × *Il.*, 2 × *Od.* at the end). Hektor pretends to leave room for doubt. ἄλγιον, αἴ κ' ἐθέλῃσι is repeated from Pouludamas' words at 278–9, and to make sense the rest of Pouludamas' sentence ἐλθών... ἄμμι μάχεσθαι must be understood. F. X. Strasser, *Zu den Iterata der frühgriechischen Epik* (Königstein/Ts. 1984) 51–2, gives examples of similar abbreviated repetitions.

306–7 Hektor has faced Akhilleus before (9.355). His brave words about standing his ground ironically anticipate his flight at 22.136–7. Verse 307 ≅ 11.590, where it is preceded by οὐδέ ἕ φημι | and followed by | ἵστασθαι.

308 Cf. 13.486 αἶψά κεν ἠὲ φέροιτο μέγα κράτος ἠὲ φεροίμην. In both cases there is an ellipse, here '⟨and we shall see⟩'. The use of the subjunctive for the first verb and the optative for the second also occurs in the longer alternative propositions at 16.648–51 and 22.245–6 (see note *ad loc.*), and at *Od.* 4.692. Chantraine, *GH* II 211–12, thinks that the optative in the second clause here shows 'une modestie vraie ou feinte', and S. West, *Odyssey* on *Od.* 4.692, agrees that this is the more remote possibility; but in this and the other examples quoted the second alternative is the one *preferred*, even if more remote, and the mood may convey this tone. Leaf's objection that this preferential implication is ruled out by the use of κε is not watertight, for the optative with κε sometimes has this meaning (Chantraine, *GH* II 218), and the analogy of κε with subjunctive in parallel alternative clauses might well lead to its retention. (A papyrus however reads φέροιτο, as at 13.486.) On the accentuation ἦ...ἦ see LSJ s.v. ἦ A II.

309 ξυνός is used with γαῖα at 15.193 and with κακόν at 16.262, with the sense 'shared ⟨by all⟩'. Here the context shows that the sense has become 'impartial'. No comma is needed after Ἐνυάλιος: 'The impartial Ares kills the would-be killer too.' ξυνὸς Ἐνυάλιος became (or already was) a maxim, cf. Aristotle, *Rhet.* II 21.11 and Archilochus fr. 110 West ἐτήτυμον γὰρ ξυνὸς ἀνθρώποις Ἄρης. Chantraine takes κτανέοντα as a future, with the sense of intention or will (the form, *GH* I 449; the sense, *GH* II 201); τε is generalizing.

Hektor's arrogant optimism (so different from Agamemnon's recurrent despair!) is good for the troops' morale. There is no hint that it is assumed. He showed the same confidence before his men, in similar circumstances, when Diomedes was the main danger (8.532–42), and even when facing Akhilleus alone he still maintains his hopes (22.130, 22.256–7) until the disappearance of 'Deiphobos'.

Homer likes the kind of word-play seen in these two lines; cf. ἦ τ' ἔβλητ' ἤ τ' ἔβαλ' ἄλλον (11.410), ἕλοιμί κεν ἤ κεν ἁλοίην (22.253; see Introduction, ch. 4, v, 2).

310 = 8.542. The scholia give a number of rather implausible reasons for the Trojans' approval, among them ἡ ἄνοια ἡ βαρβαρική (Λ), ἡ ἐλπὶς τοῦ δημοβορῆσαι (T), and the fact that if they had been persuaded by Pouludamas the rest of the *Il.* would have been irrelevant (ἐξαγώνιον: bT). Actually, the poet has portrayed Hektor as by far the more effective demagogue.

311 νήπιος-comments are a characteristic Homeric way of foreshadowing trouble for a character who is unaware of the outcome of an action, and emphasizing the pitiable futility of human designs. Often this is made explicit by a following οὐδὲ τὰ ἤδη or the like, as at 2.38 (see note *ad loc.*); here the following couplet explains the reason. Hektor's insulting νήπιε to the prudent Pouludamas shortly before (295) gives a special point here.

No special divine intervention is implied by ἐκ γάρ σφεων φρένας εἵλετο Παλλὰς 'Αθήνη; the expression is casually used for foolishness, usually in the mouths of characters (9.377, 12.234, 15.724, 17.470, 19.137) but again in one instance by the narrator (6.234).

313–14 Epaphroditus read the weaker οὔ τι, according to T. Verse 314 is formular up to the enjambing clausula (see 298–9n.).

314–55 Meanwhile, Akhilleus mourns over the body of Patroklos, speaking too of his own death and his promise of vengeance on Hektor. The corpse is washed, anointed, and clothed, and the Myrmidons lament through the night

Three different actions on three different stages take place during this night: the Trojans hold their assembly; the Myrmidons grieve for Patroklos; and Thetis makes her way to Olumpos and speaks with Hephaistos, who sets to work and fashions the new armour. The colloquy of Zeus and Here (356–67) may be added. Before the final day's battle the poet is carefully consolidating, in turn, the characterization of Hektor, the emotional state of Akhilleus, the preparation of the armour which makes the duel possible and enriches its meaning (see the introduction to this Book), and the divine savagery behind it all. The interweaving of the scenes has separated this lament from the recovery of Patroklos' body at 231–8.

314–15 The formular verse (see 298–9n.) is broken off to begin a new sentence and scene at the bucolic diaeresis, as often; see Edwards, *AJP* 89 (1968) 276–7. The scene is concluded at 354–5 by an amplified repetition of this description, beginning with | παννύχιοι and again ending with Πάτροκλον ἀνεστενάχοντο γοῶντες.

316–23 The two speech-introductions are separated by a descriptive line (317) and a simile, to recall Akhilleus' grief to our minds before his lament begins. Cf. the account of Pouludamas between his two speech-introductions (249–53).

316–17 This is the formular introduction for a formal lament, used again for Akhilleus (23.17), for the women who lead the dirges for Hektor (22.430, 24.723, 24.747, 24.761) and in shorter form for Thetis at 51 above. Apart from one occurrence for Ares and one for Lukourgos (at *Od.* 1.261 it is not formular), ἀνδροφόνος is reserved for Hektor and for the hands of the man who kills him (here, the repetition at 23.18, and the superb use at 24.478–9 where Priam kisses those hands). This is probably not accidental; cf. the poet's reserving of one death-formula for Patroklos and Hektor alone (16.856–7 = 22.362–3).

318–22 There are multiple connexions between simile and narrative. The formal point of comparison is between Akhilleus' groans and the lion's roar (στενάχων, 318 and 323), but the more significant emotional parallel is the loss and the consequent agonized grief of hero and lion (ἄχνυται, 320), followed by their anger (χόλος, 322; cf. χολωθείς of Akhilleus, 337). The circumstances are closely parallel too. Before its loss, the lion had left its cubs alone, and returned too late, as Akhilleus had failed to stand by Patroklos (98–9) and is now too late to save him; and the lion sets off in pursuit of the villain, thus foreshadowing Akhilleus' pursuit of Hektor. Similes often anticipate the narrative in this way, e.g. at 207–14, 16.751–3, 21.522–5 (see Introduction, ch. 3, ii). At 17.133–6 Aias protected the body of Patroklos like a lion protecting its young.

The parent–child theme is often used in similes to illustrate the Akhilleus–Patroklos relationship; see 23.222–5n. and Moulton, *Similes* 99–106. Gilgamesh mourns over Enkidu like a lioness deprived of her cubs (J. B. Pritchard, *Ancient Near Eastern Texts*[3], Princeton 1969, 88), and some have thought this may well be the origin of the simile here (M. L. West, *JHS* 108, 1988, 171; R. Mondi, in *Approaches to Greek Myth*, ed. Lowell Edmunds, Baltimore 1990, 150). But even without direct influence, the greatest hero of a tale is likely to be compared to the most dangerous predator, and when the context is one of grief a lion must be made to mourn its cubs, not its best friend; so a parallel creation is very probable.

318 ὥς τε λῖς ἠϋγένειος recurs at 17.109 (see note *ad loc.*). The exegetical scholia (AT) inform us that ἠϋγένειος is accurate, for the lioness has a magnificent (κάλλιστον) beard, the male lion (which does not care for the cubs) a mane; but see 15.271–6n. On λῖς see 17.133–6n.

319–22 σκύμνους and ἐλαφηβόλος occur only here in Homer, and ἄγκεα appears only in similes (3 × *Il.*, 2 × *Od.*). ὕστερος, 'too late' (320), may be picked up by σεῦ ὕστερος at 333, though the sense is different there. μετ' ...ἴχνι' ἐρευνῶν = 'following (after) the footprints', but ἴχνι' ἐρευνῶντες appears at *Od.* 19.436. δριμύς (322) qualifies χόλος only here; it does not appear in formulae, but cf. χλωρὸν δέος αἱρεῖ | (etc.) 4 × *Il.*, 6 × *Od.* Schol. bT say that the metaphor is from a bitter taste.

324–32 The first part of Akhilleus' lament balances the antithetical statements of the hoped-for return home (324–7) and the actual death and burial of both heroes at Troy (329–32), on either side of the gnomic 328. Lohmann, *Reden* 66 n. 112, quotes parallels. As before, Akhilleus immediately links Patroklos' death with his own.

324–7 ἤματι κείνῳ occurs 5 × *Il.*, elsewhere in the poet's voice. περικλυτός (etc.) is formular preceding ἀμφιγυήεις (6 × *Il.*, 3 × *Od.*), Ἡφαίστοιο (2 × *Od.*), and δῶρα (3 × *Il.*, including a separated form), and following ἀοιδὸς ἄειδε (4 × *Od.*) and ἄστυ (3 × *Od.*). Once it qualifies Antiphos, once ἔργα. It is always found in this position. Since its usage is otherwise so regular it is likely that in the exceptional phrase here it is not simply an ornamental line-filler but is predicative, 'I would bring his son home glorious' (the sense explained by 327), as the scholia (bT) and Ameis–Hentze took it. Cf. the comparable ambiguous significance of μεγαθύμου (335). The first hemistich of 327 is common; the second ≅ *Od.* 5.40 = 13.138.

Other accounts of the final conversations in Peleus' halls were given at 9.254–8 and 11.765–89. 'He not only laments for his death, but grieves for the loss of all that he had hoped for' (bT).

328 The thought is unexceptionable, but the nearest parallel to the wording is 10.104–5 οὔ θην Ἕκτορι πάντα νοήματα μητίετα Ζεὺς | ἐκτελέει.

329–32 The fuller expression at 11.394–5 ὁ δέ θ' αἵματι γαῖαν ἐρεύθων | πύθεται, οἰωνοὶ δὲ περὶ πλέες ἠὲ γυναῖκες clearly refers to an unburied corpse staining the soil. Here Akhilleus does not of course mean that their bodies will be unburied, but the words are more graphic and brutal than the usual κατὰ γαῖα κάλυψε or γαῖα καθέξει. ὁμοίην refers to their both dying at Troy, not to mankind's common fate (as van Leeuwen takes it). Aeschines, *Tim.* 144, quotes 329 with ἐρεύθειν. γέρων is formular before ἱππηλάτα in all but one (4.387) of the occurrences of the latter (9 × *Il.*, 2 × *Od.*), but may well be thought to carry pathos here.

333–42 In the second part of his lament Akhilleus returns to the real world (νῦν δέ, see 88n.) and promises to honour Patroklos' funeral rites with the armour and head of his killer, the sacrifice of twelve Trojans, and the unceasing lamentation of captive women. The expression is highly complex and poetic.

333 The line falls into no less than five parts, each semantically distinct: 'But *now*'; 'since then…'; the vocative 'Patroklos' (the pathos of which is commented upon in the scholia); the emphatic '*after* you'; and 'I myself shall die'. The nearest parallel to the last phrase is γαῖαν ὕπο στυγερὴν ἀφικοίμην (*Od.* 20.81). Akhilleus had expected to die before Patroklos; see 17.404–11n. Aeschines, *Tim.* 148, quotes φίλ' ἑταῖρε for Πάτροκλε; van der

Valk, *Researches* II 328–9, thinks the alteration deliberately suggests an erotic relationship, but it may well be a mere slip of memory (though the phrase does not occur in surviving epic).

334–5 κτεριῶ (better *κτερίω, Chantraine, *GH* I 451) is future of κτερίζω, an Ionic form created for metrical reasons from the original κτερεΐζω; see Ruijgh, *L'Elément achéen* 83, and Hoekstra, *Modifications* 142–3. Ἕκτορος is placed first in the clause for emphasis, though a genitive noun rarely appears in the verse preceding that in which its controlling noun stands; there may well be an intentional allusion to another striking instance, Hektor's taunt to the dying Patroklos that Akhilleus told him not to return πρὶν Ἕκτορος ἀνδροφόνοιο | αἱματόεντα χιτῶνα περὶ στήθεσσι δαΐξαι (16.840–1). In 335, μεγαθύμου Πριαμίδαο would have been possible (though the phrase does not actually occur), but instead Akhilleus says μεγαθύμου σεῖο φονῆος, and in a context with so many remarkable expressions it may be permissible to take the usually conventional epithet with σεῖο (genitive of σύ), as Leaf does (but Willcock does not), instead of with Ἕκτορος... φονῆος. This gives better sense, though giving the complimentary word to Hektor could also be taken as praise for the man he was great enough to kill. Allen regrettably reads σοῖο (< σός), with a few late MSS, which would require attributing the epithet to Hektor.

On beheading as a mark of vengeance see 176–7n. and 17.38–40n. The threat is not carried out in the *Il.*, doubtless because the poet has in mind the later restoration of the corpse to the Trojans; at 23.21 it is modified to dragging the body to the pyre and leaving it for the dogs. The fact that Hektor will die wearing Akhilleus' own armour is here ignored (did τεύχεα καὶ κεφαλήν occur in other such threats of vengeance?). Ph. J. Kakridis, *Hermes* 89 (1961) 288, thinks that in the Memnon-tale Akhilleus burnt the weapons and head of Memnon on the pyre of Antilokhos, but the evidence is very late; in the *Aithiopis* Eos carried her son off to immortality, and Akhilleus died before Antilokhos was buried.

336–7 These verses are repeated over the corpse at 23.22–3. ἀπο-δειροτομέω is used of cutting the throats of sheep at *Od.* 11.35, and without ἀπο- 3 × *Il.*, 1 × *Od.* It is a brutal word (see 21.98n.), clearly compounded from δειρή, 'neck'. Later the word was associated with δέρος, 'skin', and came to mean 'flay' (LSJ). χολωθείς picks up χόλος at 322 and 108; Akhilleus' anger at Agamemnon has now passed into anger at Hektor. The threat is again anticipated (in some detail) at 21.26–32 and carried out at 23.175–6 (see 23.166–76n.). The poet may be attributing to revenge an older practice of human sacrifice at a hero's burial; see Andronikos, *Arch. Hom.* w 27–9. On the frequency of strongly aggressive behaviour at funeral rites see W. Burkert, *Homo Necans* (tr. P. Bing, Berkeley 1983) 53, and on human sacrifice in Greek legend H. Lloyd-Jones, *JHS* 103 (1983) 88–9.

338–42 Though Patroklos died far from home, this is already the third time women wail for him (28–31; 50–64). The promise will be fulfilled at 19.282–302. In 338, τόφρα = 'meanwhile', as at 17.79, 19.24 etc.; αὔτως = 'as you are', i.e. unburied; cf. 198n. On the formula in 339 see 122–5n. Verse 340 ≅ 24.745, *Od.* 11.183. δουρί τε μακρῷ | (314) occurs 3 × *Il.*, but is not elsewhere preceded by βίηφι. Note the alliteration in 342. Verse 20.217, which shares the same second hemistich, outdoes this by beginning ἐν πεδίῳ πεπόλιστο.

Akhilleus thinks again at 24.6–8 of the fighting he had shared with Patroklos. The ghost of his gentle companion, significantly, speaks instead of the times they *talked* alone together (23.77–8).

343–55 The scene of grief is amplified by a detailed description of the washing, anointing, and clothing of the corpse. The type-scene has much in common with that of bathing a visitor; see Arend, *Typischen Scenen* 124–6.

344–5 Verse 344 ≅ 22.443, 23.40, *Od.* 8.434. ἀμφί is used because the tripod straddles the fire. Despite the conventionality of heating water for washing, in each of these instances the verse-ending ὠτώεντα which the diction provided (23.264, 23.513, *Erga* 657) is ignored and a new enjambing clause begun (different in each case; cf. 314–15n.). Verse 345 ≅ 14.7, 23.41, cf. 7.425; on βρότος, 'blood', see 14.3–7n. The double accusative Πάτροκλον... βρότον is not paralleled in the other instances, but cf. 16.667–8 αἶμα κάθηρον | ... Σαρπηδόνα. De Jong, *Narrators* 114, points out that it is not clear if these lines are part of Akhilleus' instructions or of his unspoken thoughts.

346–8 ≅ *Od.* 8.435–7. In 346 some MSS (including the *h* group) read the pluperfect ἔστασαν (or ἕ-) which is intransitive and must be wrong; see S. West, *Odyssey* on *Od.* 3.182. On the formula πυρὶ κηλέῳ see J. B. Hainsworth, *Odyssey* on *Od.* 8.435.

349–52 Verse 349 = *Od.* 10.360 (Odysseus' bath in Kirke's palace); on (ϝ)ῆνοψ, 'shining' (?), see 16.407–8n. The poet also stresses care for Patroklos' body at 19.23–39 and 23.184–91. The etymological play in ἤλειψαν λίπ' ἐλαίῳ recurs at 10.577. ἐννεώροιο apparently comes from ἐννέα + ὥρη, 'nine years old' (Risch, *Wortbildung* 189); a more complex suggestion is made by S. Marinatos in *Studies... D. M. Robinson* 1 (St Louis 1951) 131–2. Verse 352 ≅ 23.254; see note *ad loc.*

354–5 A shorter version of this couplet began the scene; see 314–15n.

356–68 Suddenly the scene changes to a conversation between Zeus and Here. He remarks that it must be she who has brought about the return of Akhilleus, adding teasingly that the Greeks must be her descendants. She replies that even humans seek to get their own way; all the more should she, highest of goddesses, bring misfortunes upon the nation she hates

A change of scene without some connexion through the narrative is highly unusual, but it happens both before and after this little conversation. Perhaps it is this oddity which led the poet to omit any indication of where it takes place. Ameis–Hentze, *Anhang* 118–19, and Leaf follow Zenodorus (bT) in considering the passage an interpolation, because of its abruptness, the number of lines which occur elsewhere, and the connexion with 168 and 181–6, which they find suspect on other grounds. On the other hand, such advance preparation for the scene is characteristically Homeric, and the short colloquy effectively marks the conclusion of Zeus's help to the Trojans and the beginning of Hektor's doom. This is similar to the careful matching of Zeus's giving support to Hektor and later withdrawing it (see 239–42n.).

Zeus's mocking tone towards his irritable consort, and perhaps a veiled concern for human suffering (cf. 20.20–30n.), match his words in the parallel scene before the general fighting begins (4.5–19, 4.31–49); and Here's savage disregard of any principle except her personal hatred for the Trojans is stated even more emphatically there (4.51–67). On the reasons for her hatred see 4.31–3n.; but as M. Davies says, 'This expression of enmity [4.51–67] would obviously be reduced and trivialised if the Judgement of Paris were explicitly mentioned by her or the poet as the ultimate inspiration of her hatred. Apparently motiveless malignity on the part of Hera or Athena creates an impression that is infinitely more formidable and sinister' (*JHS* 101, 1981, 56). In the *Il.* even Akhilleus' anger is not so implacable as that of the gods.

356 Single-verse speech-introductions including two names are uncommon, partly because the mention of two fresh characters is seldom needed; for other examples see *HSCP* 74 (1968) 15–16. The form of the verse gives equal weight to both characters, and the epithet phrase for Here anticipates the amplification at 364–6. Ἥρην δὲ προσέειπε πατὴρ ἀνδρῶν τε θεῶν τε would be more regular in phrasing (cf. 16.432) but lacks the emphasis necessary to introduce Zeus.

357–9 ἔπρηξας is emphatic by position. καὶ ἔπειτα with an aorist = 'then too', i.e. as well as on other occasions when she has succeeded in getting her own way (cf. *Od.* 8.520); with a future tense, the meaning becomes 'in the future too', as at 3.290 etc. Only Zeus uses this formal vocative title for Here (3 × *Il.*). Here a papyrus and some of the older MSS have βοῶπι, which may be right (*pace* Leaf; the -ῑ is original, see 14.49–55n., so βοῶπι should be written); this is the reading of older MSS at 8.471 and the *h* group at 15.49, where Did/AT record it as a variant and attribute the form with -ς to Aristophanes. Cf. the analogous vocative γλαυκῶπι, which ends the verse at *Od.* 13.389. The unusual enjambment σεῖο | ἐξ αὐτῆς ἐγένοντο (358–9) adds to the emphasis on the phrase, all the more irritating to the jealous Here because of course Zeus himself fathered the Trojan–Dardanian royal line by his affair with Electra (see 20.215–40n.).

361 This is Here's stock protest against her lord and master (6 × *Il.*); see 1.552n.

362–3 'Surely (δή) even (καί) any human is likely to achieve ⟨his purpose⟩ for ⟨another⟩ man.' βροτός is reinforced by θνητός in the next line. The expression is a variation of βροτὸν ἄνδρα τελέσσαι | (19.22), βροτὸν ἄνδρα παρεῖναι | (*Od.* 5.129), βροτοῦ ἀνέρος (85, *HyAphr* 199), βροτῷ ἀνδρί (5.604, *Od.* 4.397). The separation of the components of the formula is like that in verse 2. Verse 363 = *Od.* 20.46, where Athene contrasts a mortal's help with her own. The weight of MSS evidence in both occurrences is against τ', which may have been added for metrical reasons (but is accepted by Ruijgh, τε *épique* 446, as an unusual type of generalizing τε).

364–7 Completion of the sense of πῶς δὴ ἔγωγ' (by οὐκ ὄφελον, 367) is postponed longer than usual by the epexegetical relative clause ἥ... ἀρίστη and its amplification in 365–6 (= 4.60–1), but the sense is easy to follow. ῥάπτειν, 'sew together', is used metaphorically with κακά at *Od.* 3.118 and 16.423, with φόνον at *Od.* 16.379, and with θάνατόν τε μόρον τε at *Od.* 16.421–2. The noun κακορραφίη occurs 1 × *Il.*, 2 × *Od.*

369–467 Thetis reaches Hephaistos' home on Olumpos, finds him busy in his forge, and is greeted by his wife Kharis. The lame smith speaks warmly of Thetis' help to him in the past, and after hearing the tale of her unhappy son willingly agrees to fashion new armour for him

This pleasant scene comes as a relief after the sorrows which the human characters are now enduring and must endure to even greater degree in the future. It is related with much amplification, to suit the scale and importance of the following description of the shield: 'When we hear the exchanges between Thetis, Charis and Hephaistos – a total of five speeches repeating the themes of hospitality and past indebtedness and slowly advancing to the present need – we know that the arms must be extraordinary to require such ceremony and the need for them will be proportionately extraordinary' (N. Austin, *GRBS* 7, 1966, 309).

The structure follows the normal 'visit' type-scene, as described by Arend, *Typischen Scenen* 34–53; see also the analysis of the scene in *TAPA* 105 (1975) 62–3. The usual description of what the host is doing when the visitor arrives is expanded into the account of Hephaistos' tripod-making (372–81), and then his conventional surprise and welcome are further postponed by the intervention of Kharis, her presence gracefully circumventing the awkwardness of having the dignified matron Thetis received by a sweaty labourer in his workshop. The interruption in the regular succession of type-scene elements caused by the need to summon Hephaistos results in the omission of the usual meal shared by host and guest (see 387n.).

369–71 Homer often refers to the houses Hephaistos built for the Olympians; see 1.605–8n. This description is the most elaborate. The climate on Olumpos is described at *Od.* 6.42–6. ἀστερόεις is formular with οὐρανός (7 × *Il.*, 4 × *Od.* in the oblique cases), but is also used of the corslet of Akhilleus when Patroklos puts it on (16.134). The meaning thus may be simply 'shining', but one may also think of decorative ornaments or of the stars themselves. ἀθανάτοισι = ἀθανάτων δόμοις. The walls of Alkinoös' palace are also of bronze (*Od.* 7.86); probably the poet has in mind a bronze facing or ornament (see D. H. F. Gray, *JHS* 74, 1954, 3), but one may remember the striking χάλκεον οὐρανόν (17.425). κυλλοποδίων, 'little clubfoot', recurs at 20.270 and 21.331 (vocative). Hephaistos' lameness (its nature varies) is emphasized again at 397, 411 and 417–21, and his twisted feet or legs are often represented on vase-paintings of the Return of Hephaistos story; see F. Brommer, *Hephaistos* (Mainz am Rhein 1978) 11, 16.

372–9 Hephaistos' busy activity is conveyed by three participles in one clause (372–3). These wheeled tripods are not just easy to push but are self-propelled, like the 'automatic' gates of Olumpos (5.749 = 8.393) and Hephaistos' bellows (470–3). On the means of propulsion see 417–20n. Helen's silver work-basket, a gift from Egyptian Thebes, was fitted with wheels (*Od.* 4.131–2), and wheeled tripods and wheeled bronze stands from the ninth and eighth centuries are known (H. L. Lorimer, *Homer and the Monuments*, London 1950, 73). αὐτόματος (< αὐτός + the root that appears in μέ-μα-μεν, μένος) was a common word; it is also used of Menelaos' arrival unsummoned (2.408), and in Hesiod of the wanderings of diseases (*Erga* 103), of the earth's fruitfulness in the Golden Age (*Erga* 118), and in a proverbial expression (fr. 264 MW).

ἐϋσταθέος μεγάροιο | (374) occurs 6 × *Od.* ὑπό (375) goes with θῆκεν, but cf. τάλαρόν θ' ὑπόκυκλον (*Od.* 4.131). πυθμήν (375) here clearly = 'foot'; it is used for the supports of Nestor's cup (11.635) and for the base of a tree-trunk (2 × *Od.*). οἱ (376) is dative. The second hemistich of 376 also describes the Trojan women who 'will go before the divine assembly' to give thanks for Hektor's return (7.298; on ἀγών in this original meaning see 15.426–8n.). In place of this the scholia (Did/AT) report the reading θεῖον κατὰ δῶμα νέοιντο in 'inferior' texts (ἐν ταῖς εἰκαιοτέραις), with an Attic verb-form and poor sense (presumably omitting 377). Van der Valk, *Researches* II 614–15, thinks this is an alteration intended to reduce the miraculous element. The reading δύσονται (from 7.298) is recorded as a variant by Did/A and appears in a papyrus and many later MSS.

379 δεσμούς: 'fastenings', here the rivets which are to secure the handles to the body of the tripod. When Hephaistos plans the capture of Ares and Aphrodite the same wording must refer to chains (*Od.* 8.274–5). μείζων δὲ ἡ χάρις τοῦ καταλιπόντος ἡμιτελὲς τὸ ἔργον (bT). Usually in a visit-scene the host's attendants are mentioned, but because of the length of the description of his activity this element is here postponed to 417–21.

380–1 ἰδυίῃσι πραπίδεσσι is formular (4 × *Il.*, 1 × *Od.*), and used always of Hephaistos' craftsmanship. The πραπίδες seem to lie within the lower chest region and are a seat of thought and emotion, similar to but not identical with the φρένες (so S. D. Sullivan, *Glotta* 65, 1987, 182–93).

Verse 381 is omitted by a papyrus and many MSS (including two of the *h* family), and was added in the margin of A. It may have dropped out because of the homoiarchon (so Pasquali, *Storia* 219–20). Van der Valk, *Researches* II 515, decided it was unjustifiably removed by Aristarchus. Apthorp, however, in a long and judicious discussion (*Manuscript Evidence* 137–40), points out that the verse is supported by the close parallel in structure at 15–16 (ἧος... | τόφρα...), where again a visitor (messenger) arrives. On the other hand, he shows that 381 is not essential, arguing that ὄφρα may be picked up by δέ (382) and that τὴν for Thetis is acceptable (she was last mentioned at 372); and in fact Thetis does *not* 'come close to' Hephaistos here. He concludes that 381 is most likely to be a post-Aristarchean interpolation.

But Apthorp's remark (*ibid.* 138) that summarizing lines like 380–1 are not normal at this point in arrival type-scenes is not valid, because the scene itself is not normal. At this point in the regular sequence of an arrival-scene Thetis should stand beside Hephaistos and address him (Arend, *Typischen Scenen* 28; Teil IV). Instead, the poet switches over to the elaboration typical of a *visit*-scene, in which the visitor stands in the doorway and waits to be recognized by the host; and the host is now not Hephaistos, but Kharis (Arend, *ibid.* 35; Teil IV.1). Verse 381 thus takes the place of στῆ... ἐπὶ προθύροις (*Od.* 1.103, cf. *Il.* 11.777), returning our attention to Thetis so that we may observe her approach as Kharis does, and should not be removed. For more detail see *TAPA* 105 (1975) 62–3.

382 Aphrodite as Hephaistos' wife (as in *Od.* 8.269–70) would be an embarrassment here because of her pro-Trojan bias, so 'Grace' is substituted, a fitting consort for a craftsman; at *Od.* 6.234 = 23.161 Hephaistos χαρίεντα δὲ ἔργα τελείει. Verse 383 emphasizes the change from the more famous espousal. In Hesiod (*Theogony* 945) he is married to Aglaïe, the youngest of the Kharites (on whom see 14.267–70n.). The generic λιπαροκρήδεμνος occurs only here in Homer, but appears in two plus-verses (16.867a, *Od.* 12.133a), *Cypria* fr. 5.3 Bernabé (5.3 Davies), and 3 × in *HyDem* (see 16.867n.). On ἀμφιγυήεις see 1.607n.

385–6 Hephaistos repeats the greeting verbatim at 424–5, and Kalupso uses it (with necessary modification) to Hermes at *Od.* 5.87–8. The formular wording conveys readiness to attend to the visitor's wishes, affection, and the courteous implication that the visitor does not come often enough. τανύπεπλος is a generic epithet for women and goddesses. On πάρος γε see 17.586–8n. θαμίζεις is a 'timeless present' (J. Wackernagel, *Vorlesungen über Syntax* 1, Basel 1926, 158).

387 After the same verse at *Od.* 5.91 Kalupso produces a table loaded with ambrosia and nectar. Doubtless this element in the reception would have followed 390, but the summons to Hephaistos and his response breaks the sequence. Hephaistos himself bids his wife offer food to their guest (408), and presumably this is done off-stage; after his own greeting his guest launches immediately into her woeful tale (428ff.).

389–90 The formular wording is also used for the Hephaistos-made chair Here offers to Sleep (14.238–40).

392 ὧδε: 'this way'. Plato, burning his poems in despair (see 17.263–6n.), was supposed to have quoted this line with Πλάτων for Θέτις (A). Willcock comments on this 'charming bourgeois scene' of the wife calling her husband from his work-bench when an unexpected visitor arrives. In the *Il.* the more mundane aspects of life are shown through the gods rather than the humans.

394–409 Hephaistos begins with a paradeigma explaining why he is anxious to show his gratitude to Thetis. It is in complex ring form:

A   A goddess I respect is here (394),
B   who saved my life when my mother cast me out (395–7).
C   I would have suffered, if Eurunome and Thetis had not received me (397–8),
D   Eurunome, daughter of Okeanos (399).
E   For them I made many lovely things (400–1)
D′ as Okeanos' waters flowed around their cave (402–3).
C′ No one knew but Eurunome and Thetis (404–5),
B′ who saved me (405).
A′ Now Thetis is here, and I must reward her (406–9).

At 1.590–4 Hephaistos tells how Zeus (his father, *Od.* 8.312) hurled him from Olumpos when he tried to help Here, and the Sinties took care of him on Lemnos; in this version the fall must have caused his lameness. Zeus refers indirectly to this at 15.18–24. Here the unfortunate son describes a second fall, this time the result of his mother's disgust at his lameness; this is repeated in *HyAp* 316–21. The tales are doublets, both accounting for the natural association of lame men and smiths/craftsmen (see M. Detienne and J.-P. Vernant, *Cunning Intelligence in Greek Culture and Society*, tr. J. Lloyd,

Atlantic Highlands 1978, 269–75); at another level the lameness may also symbolize sexual impotence. There may even be a connexion with the visible fall of metal-bearing meteorites (cf. 15.18–31n.).

On the problematical circumstances of Hephaistos' birth see 14.295–6n. B. K. Braswell, *CQ* 21 (1971) 19–21, thinks (with good reason) that the tale of Hephaistos' second fall is a Homeric invention, to provide Thetis with a claim on his gratitude. The most recent detailed interpretation of the Hephaistos myth is that of R. Caldwell, *Helios* 6 (1978) 43–59; see also W. Burkert, *Greek Religion* (tr. J. Raffan, Cambridge, Mass. 1985) 167–8, and J. Griffin, *CQ* 28 (1978) 7 n. 18.

394 δεινή τε καὶ αἰδοίη: Macleod, *Iliad XXIV* 122 (on δείδοικα καὶ αἰδέομαι), gives many other Homeric examples of 'this mixture of considerations of reverence or honour with considerations of prudence'; cf. especially 3.172 (Helen to Priam) and 15.657–8. The warmer αἰδοίη τε φίλη τε is used by Kharis (386; because she too is female?) and Hephaistos himself when he greets Thetis (425).

395–6 Hephaistos' first fall is memorably described at 1.592–4, see note *ad loc.* κυνῶπις is used by Helen of herself (3.180, *Od.* 4.145), by Hephaistos of the faithless Aphrodite (*Od.* 8.319) and by Agamemnon of the villainous Klutaimestra (*Od.* 11.424). The masculine form is hurled by Akhilleus at Agamemnon (1.159). The characteristics of dogs include 'fawning gaze combined with unabashed sexual and excremental interests' (1.225n.). The scholia (?Did/T) record the polite variant βοώπιδος.

397–9 πάθον (etc.) ἄλγεα θυμῷ occurs 4 × *Il.*, 2 × *Od.*, with a lengthened form at *Od.* 1.4 and 13.90. The second hemistich of 398 is repeated when Thetis receives the terrified Dionysus (6.136; see also Fernández-Galiano, *Odissea* on *Od.* 22.470. The metre requires ὑπεδέξατο in the singular, rather harshly (1.255 is easier, as the verb precedes the nominatives). ἀψορρόου is one mora longer than Okeanos' usual βαθυρρόου, and is needed again at *Od.* 20.65 and *Theogony* 776.

Eurunome is mentioned by Hesiod among the daughters of Okeanos and Tethus (*Theogony* 358) and as mother (by Zeus) of the Kharites (*Theogony* 907–9); see West, *Theogony* 267. The amiable Hephaistos is courteously giving prominence to his mother-in-law, as the scholia (T) observe (but Braswell (see 394–409n.) did not). Her melodious verse (399) further adds to the charm and dignity of the passage.

400 χαλκεύω occurs only here in archaic epic; like χαλκεύς, it refers to metalworking generally. Word-end after a spondee is avoided in the 4th foot, and here 'Wernicke's Law' that the second syllable of a 4th-foot spondee should be long by nature is also violated (see A. M. Devine and L. D. Stephens, *Language and Metre*, Chico 1984, 12, 39–42; M. L. West, *Greek Metre*, Oxford 1982, 37; Leaf II 631–9). Perhaps the unusual rhythm imitates the craftsman's hammering. Presumably Hephaistos worked on Lemnos (cf. 1.592–4n., 14.229–30n., and Hainsworth, *Odyssey* on *Od.* 8.283). Part of the time he devoted to revenging himself on Here by fashioning a golden throne which imprisoned her when she sat on it (Pausanias 1.20.2); his consequent return to Olumpos to release her was often celebrated on vases, including the François Vase (see 369–71n.).

401 = *HyAphr* 163, where Ankhises lovingly undresses Aphrodite; doubtless a formular line for female adornment. There is slightly more detail when Ankhises first sees her (*HyAphr* 87–9):

> εἶχε δ' ἐπιγναμπτὰς ἕλικας κάλυκάς τε φαεινάς,
> ὅρμοι δ' ἀμφ' ἁπαλῇ δειρῇ περικαλλέες ἦσαν
> καλοὶ χρύσειοι παμποίκιλοι· ὡς δὲ σελήνη
> στήθεσιν ἀμφ' ἁπαλοῖσιν ἐλάμπετο, θαῦμα ἰδέσθαι.

πόρπαι are pins or brooches (the word is probably connected with the commoner περόνη). ἕλικαι γναμπταί are golden spirals, for the hair or as earrings. κάλυκες, 'buds', are presumably decorative rosettes. Homer mentions golden ὅρμοι, 'necklaces', 'pectorals', with amber beads (*Od.* 15.460, 18.295–6); the other words do not recur in the poems. See E. Bielefeld, *Arch. Hom.* c 5–8, 48–58 and illustrations, and S. Marinatos, *Arch. Hom.* A 36, B 3.

403 Notice the evocative sound of ἀφρῷ μορμύρων; the words recur in the accusative at 5.599 and in reverse order at 21.325. The construction is repeated at 24.697–9, οὐδέ τις ἄλλος | ἔγνω πρόσθ' ἀνδρῶν καλλιζώνων τε γυναικῶν | ἀλλ' ἄρα Κασσάνδρη.

406–7 Later MSS give the Atticism ἧκει for ἵκει; cf. C. J. Ruijgh, *Mnemosyne* 21 (1968) 121. The monosyllabic noun χρεώ, 'need', 'call', is common in both poems, and 'ne doit pas être corrigée mais constitue un trait ionien et relativement récent du dialecte épique' (Chantraine, *GH* I 70, II 40; see also Hoekstra, *Modifications* 37). It again takes the accusative + infinitive construction at 11.409–10. Θέτῑ here is the only occurrence of the dative case in Homer; on the declension see 15.598–9n. ζωάγρια (only here and from Nausikaa to Odysseus, *Od.* 8.462) = 'the price of one's life', 'ransom', from ζωγρέω, 'take a prisoner alive'.

408–9 On the offer of food see 387n. The subordinate clause replaces the expected co-ordinate clause after σὺ μέν.

410–11 The connotations of πελώριος are much like our 'monstrous'; the noun is used in Homer for the Cyclops (*Od.* 9.428) and Scylla (*Od.* 12.87). Here it clearly refers to Hephaistos' massive arms and torso, contrasting with his limping gait and shrunken legs (411). αἷητον may or may not be connected with the equally obscure ἄητον (21.395; see note *ad loc.*). L. R. Palmer, *The Interpretation of Mycenaean Greek Texts* (Oxford 1963) 339,

Book Eighteen

suggests a connexion with Mycenaean *a-ja-me-na*, a verb referring to some kind of craftsmanship. Risch (in *LfgrE*) supports a connexion with ἄημι, 'blow'. Willcock's 'heavily breathing, monstrous figure' conveys Homer's probable meaning. ἀραιαί, 'stunted' (?), was aspirated by Herodian (Λ) and in many MSS, but compounds and derivatives have ἀ-; initial ϝ- is evident, but the origin and meaning are unclear (Risch, *Wortbildung* 127). Verse 411 is repeated when Hephaistos advances with the other gods to battle (20.37); the a–b–a′ form (limping – nimble movement – stunted) is striking, and the 'bustling' idea is picked up again in 417.

412–16 Note the realistic detail. Verse 416 is an emphatic threefolder, the initial verbs in each colon stressing the god's urgent activity. A lesser poet might have used μέγα, as usual, to fill the place before the final phrase, but παχύ better draws attention to his need for support.

417–20 W. von Massow wondered if the two unidentified young women in the mule-cart in the company of Hephaistos on the chest of Cypselus might be these golden robots (*MDAI(A)* 41, 1916, 100; Pausanias 5.19.8–9). The gold and silver watchdogs which Hephaistos gave to Alkinoös may well have had their usefulness increased by movement and sense, and perhaps the torch-bearing *kouroi* too (*Od.* 7.91–4, 7.100–2). Their movement, as well as their intelligence and speech, is of course the result of magic, not machinery. Some say that the wooden horse was capable of moving its eyes, tail, and knees; the authority may have been Arctinus (*Iliupersis* fr. 2 Bernabé, 2 Davies). There are many other moving statues in Greek mythology, prominent among them those made by Daedalus which Plato mentions (*Meno* 97d–98a). On the whole topic see C. A. Farraone, *GRBS* 28 (1987) 257–80, and M. M. Kokolakis, *Museum Philologum Londiniense* 4 (1980) 103–7.

418 εἰοικυῖαι is unique for ἐϊκυῖαι (< *ϝεϝικ-), perhaps created for metrical convenience on the analogy of ἐοικώς and the metrical lengthening seen in the common form εἰλήλουθα (etc.); see Chantraine, *GH* I 129, 424. The normal form could be restored by reading νεήνισσιν, but this is unlikely to have been altered into the form in the text (which is in the older MSS).

420–2 With 420 cf. θεῶν ἄπο μήδεα εἰδώς (of Alkinoös, *Od.* 6.12), θεῶν ἄπο κάλλος ἔχουσα (of Nausikaa, *Od.* 8.457). The poet may have in mind the tale of the adornment of Pandore by all the gods after Hephaistos had created her (Hesiod, *Erga* 70–82), which may well be older than either this or the Hesiodic passage. The robot maidens scurry around (ἐποίπνυον); once the gods laughed to see their master himself bustling about (ποιπνύοντα, 1.600) to serve them wine. The stress on his lameness suggests that ὕπαιθα ἄνακτος means 'supporting him ⟨underneath his arms⟩' to match (in ring form) ὑπό... ῥώοντο ἄνακτι at 417, though otherwise it could mean 'keeping out of his way' (cf. 15.520, 21.255, 21.271) and 417 might = 'under his commands' (cf. 5.231). ἕρρων, 'stumbling', marks his lameness yet again, as the scholia (Arn/AT) point out. Verse 422 is a rising threefolder.

424–7 The first couplet repeats the words of Kharis (385–6), the second is a conventional greeting (used by Aphrodite to Here, 14.195–6, and Kalupso to Hermes, *Od.* 5.89–90). On τετελεσμένον and the neat word-play on τελέω see 14.194–7n. Verse 427 is omitted by two (perhaps three) papyri and a few late MSS, and Apthorp, *Manuscript Evidence* 140–1, makes the interesting argument that Hephaistos' offer of help is all the more generous without it: 'The addition of the cautious qualification of 427 would arguably sort ill with the spontaneity, emotion and abandoned generosity of his attitude' (*ibid.* 141). As Apthorp says, in the parallel passages both Aphrodite and Kalupso have good reason to exercise the caution which the line may convey. However, the homoiomeson of τελέσαι (also pointed out by Apthorp) is an adequate and safer explanation for the omission.

429–56 Thetis pours out all her troubles to her long-time and still grateful friend, whose soothing presence has already eased an embarrassing situation at 1.571ff. To him she can say things about her feelings for her husband which she could hardly mention to their son Akhilleus. 'He has portrayed the female character, as she does not answer his question but explains what she is upset about' remark bT sympathetically.

429–35 Cf. Penelope's πέρι γάρ μοι 'Ολύμπιος ἄλγε' ἔδωκεν | ἐκ πασέων, ὅσσαι... (*Od.* 4.722–3). ἀνδρὶ δάμασσεν: 'make subject to a ⟨mortal⟩ husband'; the noun is repeated in the next line to emphasize his mortality. The same use of ἀνήρ = 'mortal' is found at 20.97 and Pindar, *Py.* 2.29, 37, *Ol.* 11.20.

This may refer to the tale that Zeus married her to Peleus because of Themis' prophecy that she would bear a child greater than his father (Aeschylus, *Prom.* 907–27; Pindar, *Isth.* 8.26–48). However, a fragment of Philodemus reports that in the *Cypria* (fr. 2 Bernabé, 2 Davies) and the Hesiodic *Catalogue of Women* (fr. 210 MW) Thetis refused to marry Zeus in order to please Here, and in anger he swore to make her the wife of a mortal; this is likely to be the older version. At 24.60 Here says she brought up Thetis and ἀνδρὶ πόρον παράκοιτιν; this does not necessarily imply that the initiative was hers, and is not inconsistent with these other versions (though Thetis' rearing by Here may well be the poet's invention, as B. K. Braswell suggests, *CQ* 21, 1971, 23–4). In either case, Zeus's known interest in Thetis adds point to his concern at 1.518–21. Akhilleus, naturally with less precision, said 'the gods' brought about the marriage (85). For detailed discussions see A. Lesky, *Gesammelte Schriften* (Bern 1966) 401–9 = *Studi Italiani di Filologia Classica* 27/8 (1956) 216–26; J. R. March, *The Creative Poet* (*BICS* Supp. 49, London 1987) 4–10; L. M. Slatkin, *TAPA* 116 (1986) 1–24.

The strong aversion to her marriage which Thetis expresses here may be an allusion to the myth of her taking various shapes to avoid Peleus, which is well represented on vase-paintings (see F. Brommer, *Vasenlisten zur griechischen Heldensage*⁰, Marburg 1973, 321–9, and March, *op. cit.* 11–18). The intensely human characterization of this scene makes one wonder if she had really been so reluctant when Peleus was young and handsome instead of γήραϊ λυγρῷ | ... ἀρημένος. Poet and audience may well think here of a lament by Eos for her superannuated spouse in the Memnon-story. Thetis, however, according to the usual tale did not wait for Peleus to become old before she deserted him (but cf. 59–60n.).

With 434–5 cf. | γήρᾳ ὕπο λιπαρῷ ἀρημένον (*Od.* 11.136 = 23.283). ἀρημένος (only here in the *Il.*, 6 × *Od.*) is glossed by the scholia as βεβλαμμένος, 'hindered', and may be connected with the obscure ἀρή, 'harm', with ᾱ in place of reduplication; see 14.484–5n. and Chantraine, *GH* I 229. With ἄλλα δέ μοι νῦν we must understand Ζεὺς ἄλγε᾽ ἔδωκεν from 431.

436–56 Thetis goes on to her other sorrow, the sufferings of her splendid son, recapitulating the tale of his wrath and its result. Verses 437–43 are repeated from her lament when she heard his grief for Patroklos (56–62). On ἐπεί see 55n. γενέσθαι τε τραφέμεν τε | is formular (2 × *Il.*, 1 × *Od.*). Pasquali, *Storia* 244, gives parallels for this intransitive use of the aorist of τρέφω.

441 (= 60) was omitted in some ancient texts (Did/A) and in two (or perhaps three) papyri and one late MS. Apthorp, *Manuscript Evidence* 142–5, studies the evidence and spiritedly defends the case for considering it a post-Aristarchean interpolation. Retention of the line is supported not only by its occurrence at 60 but by two other instances of τὸν δ᾽ οὐχ ὑποδέξομαι (-δέξεαι) αὖτις | οἴκαδε νοστήσαντα (89–90, *Od.* 19.257–8, both quoted by Apthorp). On the other hand, abbreviation of a repeated passage is not unknown, and in fact is exemplified in this same speech (see 444–5n.); and the picture 441 suggests of Peleus and Thetis standing arm-in-arm at the gate of their home, waving excitedly as Akhilleus walks up the road from the harbour, might be thought to suit ill with the unusually strong distaste she has just expressed for her marriage. The usual sequence of verses could easily have given rise to concordance interpolation here. The heart of the question is: who is more likely, for aesthetic reasons, to have removed 441 from the passage as it occurs at 56–62; the superb poet Homer, or a literal-minded scholar-editor? My personal vote would be for the editor.

444–56 This passage was athetized by Aristarchus (Arn/AbT), on the grounds that there is no need for a summary here (similarly he athetized 1.366–92, see note *ad loc.*), and because it was not the prayers of Odysseus and Aias that persuaded Akhilleus to send Patroklos to battle but the latter's own request. But 448–52 do not necessarily imply anything other than the story of our *Il.*, and (as bT remark) it would be foolish for Thetis to complain about her marriage and say nothing about her reason for coming. Besides this, it is good to recapitulate the insult to Akhilleus and his withdrawal just as this part of the story is about to conclude; there is a similar summary at a similar point in the *Od.* (23.310–43). In addition, in a detailed examination of the passage, de Jong, *Narrators* 216–18, points out that Thetis does not (like most suppliants) remind Hephaistos of her previous favours to him (395–405), but appeals to his compassion for herself (with a mortal husband) and her son (with a mortal's short life); her tale explains both why he ἄχνυται (443) and why he needs new armour.

It is noteworthy that no scholia are recorded on the athetized verses (though they occur on the parallel 1.366–92). Presumably this is connected with the athetesis.

444–5 At 16.56–9 (see note *ad loc.*), Akhilleus amplifies 444 with δουρὶ δ' ἐμῷ κτεάτισσα πόλιν ἐϋτείχεα πέρσας, and 445 with Ἀτρεΐδης ὡς εἴ τιν' ἀτίμητον μετανάστην (= 9.648). Neither of the additional verses would come too well from Thetis' lips, and in this case I think the poet chose to omit (rather than adapt) them. But cf. 441n.

446–9 φρένας ἔφθιεν: the vivid image is repeated from 1.491, where Akhilleus φθινύθεσκε φίλον κῆρ. The latter phrase recurs at *Od.* 10.485. Chantraine, *GH* I 393, suggests that ἔφθιεν is a thematic aorist form understood as an imperfect. With 448–9 cf. τὸν δὲ λίσσοντο γέροντες | Αἰτωλῶν in the Meleager paradigm (9.574–5). ὀνομάζω is also used for the gifts which Agamemnon 'names' (9.515).

450–2 Both statements are true, but of course the events do not directly follow each other in the *Il.* Here Thetis is leaving out a good deal. αὐτός: de Jong, *Narrators* 217, points out that Thetis never uses Akhilleus' name in her speech, because she cannot think about anyone else.

453–6 Of course not all the day's fighting centred on the Scaean Gates, but Patroklos died near them (cf. 16.712) – and so will Akhilleus (22.360), who is so much on her mind. Verses 454–6 give an accurate summary of the end of book 16. The horse Xanthos repeats 456 to Akhilleus (19.414).

457–61 Verse 457 recurs 2 × *Od.* On ὠκυμόρῳ see 95–6n. Allen's reading υἱεῖ ἐμῷ ὠκυμόρῳ requires synecphonesis of -ῳ and ὠ-, which is possible enough (see S. West, *Odyssey* on *Od.* 1.226, and cf. 17.87–9n.), and perhaps intentionally conveys Thetis' emotional state. The scholia (Hrd/AbT) scan the line thus, commenting on the squeezing-out of the iota subscript. Leaf, Ameis–Hentze, and van Leeuwen (with a few late MSS) prefer to read υἷ' ἐμῷ with a harsh elision and correption of -ῳ, a solution again befitting distress of mind. Verse 459 is adapted from a formular arming-scene verse

(4× *Il.*); see 3.330–1n. In 460, for ὅ bT report that some preferred ἅ, doubtless understanding τεύχεα, which is in a few MSS; but after the mingled genders and numbers which precede it is natural and simple to attach the pronoun to θώρηκα alone. On the omission of the sword see 609–13n. In 461 she naturally describes Akhilleus as he was when she left him at 147; in the interim he has spoken with Iris and rescued his friend's body. The formular θυμὸν ἀχεύων (3 × *Il.*, 1 × *Od.*) returns to ἄχνυται (443) after the account of his troubles.

463–7 Verse 463 is formular (≅ 19.29, and 3 × *Od.*). The idiom of 464–6 is clearly explained by Leaf: 'This is the not uncommon formula where the certainty of one event is affirmed by contrasting it with the impossibility of another: "he shall have his armour as surely as I cannot save him from death", the latter clause taking the form of a wish.' J. T. Sheppard is more natural: 'I wish I could as surely hide your son away from lamentable death, as he shall surely have fine armour' (*The Pattern of the Iliad*, London 1922, 1). Cf. 4.178–9, 4.313–14, 8.538–41, 13.825–8, 16.722, and 22.346–8. F. M. Combellack, *AJP* 102 (1981) 116, is mistaken in implying that the speaker is not really expressing a desire for the impossible wish; here Hephaistos is sincerely wishing that Akhilleus need not die young. On the other hand, G. Nagy, *Studies Presented to Sterling Dow* (Durham, N.C. 1984) 237, is mistaken in insisting that the wish should always be considered possible, and that Hektor at 8.538–41 'can actually entertain the possibility of becoming a god himself'. As he sets about making the imperishable armour, Hephaistos knows that neither he nor it can save Akhilleus from an early death. The sentence superbly sums up the irony which the armour represents; see the introduction to this Book.

ὧδε (464), looking forward to ὥς (466), warns the hearer that this is not just a simple wish-clause. θανάτοιο ... νόσφιν ἀποκρύψαι is an unusual way to say 'save from death', and the poet may have in mind the tale of Akhilleus' being carried off by Thetis to the White Island, which appeared in the *Aithiopis* (Proclus, *Chrest.* 172; this was suggested to me by N. J. Richardson). ἱκάνοι (465), though referring to fact, is attracted into the optative by δυναίμην. But a papyrus, some MSS of the *h* group, and Eustathius read ἱκάνει, which may be right. In 466, Zenodotus and Aristophanes read παρέξομαι (Did/AT). τις ... | ἀνθρώπων πολέων = 'many a one of the many men there be' (Leaf). ὅς κεν ἴδηται | is formular (4 × *Il.*). Marg, *Dichtung* 36–7, sees the words of the poet himself behind those of the craftsman-god, as each creates his masterpiece.

Book Eighteen

Introduction to the Shield of Akhilleus

The making of the armour by Hephaistos can formally be considered a relocated expansion of Akhilleus' arming-scene, which will be resumed at 19.369 (after a short prelude). The huge scale of the expansion is proportional to the importance of Akhilleus' return to battle and, like the Catalogues of book 2, to the size of the *Il.* itself. But the poet boldly devotes almost the whole of the episode to a description of the pictures on the shield, which are introduced successively in the form of a catalogue. Like an immense simile, the description halts the action of the poem while the audience visualize the scene and feel its relationship to the ongoing story. The scale far exceeds the accounts of Agamemnon's corslet and shield, which perform a similar function in his arming-scene (11.20–40). Even more remarkable is the choice of decorative motif; the shield displays not monstrous horrors to terrify its bearer's opponents, as do the shield of Agamemnon and the baldric of Herakles (*Od.* 11.609–14), but scenes familiar to the poet's audience from their everyday life. He has other designs than to frighten us.

Literature

The fundamental general studies are:

> W. Marg, *Dichtung* 20–37.
> K. Reinhardt, *IuD* 401–411.
> W. Schadewaldt, *VHWW* 357–74.

Marg's is the most perceptive and sensitive of these. Schadewaldt summarizes the archaeological parallels and stresses the polarities in the choice of scenes and the comprehensiveness of the depiction of human life. Reinhardt stresses more – perhaps too much – the absence of the darker side of human circumstances and the emphasis on the aristocratic life. There is a good brief comparison of Homer's shield with Hesiod's *Aspis* in R. Lamberton, *Hesiod* (New Haven 1988) 141–4.

The archaeological evidence is best presented in:

> H. Borchhardt, *Arch. Hom.* E (Göttingen 1977) 1–5, 36–52.
> K. Fittschen, *Schild*
> H. G. Güterbock, 'Narration in Anatolian, Syrian, and Assyrian Art', *AJA* 61 (1957) 62–71.
> E. Kunze, *Kretische Bronzereliefs* (Stuttgart 1931).
> G. Markoe, *Phoenician Bronze and Silver Bowls from Cyprus and the Mediterranean* (Berkeley 1985).
> S. Marinatos and M. Hirmer, *Crete and Mycenae* (New York 1960).

Book Eighteen

A. Snodgrass, *Early Greek Armour and Weapons* (Edinburgh 1964) 37–68.
Wace and Stubbings, *Companion*.

Fittschen's work concentrates on Akhilleus' shield and that of Herakles in the *Aspis*, and has a good bibliography and useful illustrations. He also includes an interesting reconstruction of Akhilleus' shield by L. Weniger (Taf. vɪɪb). Borchhardt often gives more detail. Kunze and Markoe list, describe, study, and illustrate the Cretan shields and the Phoenician metal bowls respectively (see the following section); Markoe also gives useful accounts of the subject-matter of the scenes and of the techniques of presenting a narrative. Güterbock discusses the Phoenician bowls in the context of other narrative representations from Asia Minor. Marinatos and Hirmer illustrate and discuss the inlay technique of Mycenaean daggers. Snodgrass deals especially with the question of shield-bosses. Several of the chapters in Wace and Stubbings are still of use, but are seldom referred to in what follows as they have often been superseded by the relevant volumes of the *Archaeologia Homerica* series, which are up-to-date and have exhaustive bibliographies.

Construction and technique

The poet clearly visualizes a round shield, not the semi-cylindrical 'tower' shield or the various forms with cut-out sides which appear in Geometric art ('Dipylon', 'figure-of-eight', or 'Boeotian' shields, on which see most recently J. M. Hurwit, *CA* 4, 1985, 121–6). The usual Homeric round shield is made of a number of layers of oxhide, presumably stretched over a light wooden frame, with a bronze facing on the outside. Sarpedon's shield was made of closely-stitched oxhides on the inside, with a bronze layer beaten out (ἐξήλατον) on the outer surface (12.295–7), and Hektor's is ῥινοῖσιν πυκινήν, πολλὸς δ' ἐπελήλατο χαλκός (13.804; cf. 17.492–3). At 7.220–3 Aias' 'tower' shield (see 6.117–18n., 7.219–23n.) was made of seven oxhides and an eighth layer of bronze, and Hektor's spear penetrates the bronze and six layers (πτύχας) of hide, stopping in the seventh (7.247–8).

There are indications that the layers of hide were laid in concentric circles, diminishing in size towards the outer face of the shield. Akhilleus' spear hits Aineias' shield 'at the outer rim, where the bronze is thinnest, and thinnest is the oxhide laid' (20.275–6) and rips through, διὰ δ' ἀμφοτέρους ἕλε κύκλους; this seems to mean it tore apart the layer of bronze and the single layer of hide at the rim. A bronze plate beaten out over such layers of hide would itself take on a surface appearance of concentric circles, like a modern target, and this seems to be meant in the reference to Agamemnon's shield, ἣν πέρι μὲν κύκλοι δέκα χάλκεοι ἦσαν (11.33). Similarly,

Idomeneus' shield is ῥινοῖσι βοῶν καὶ νώροπι χαλκῷ | δινωτήν (13.406–7; see note *ad loc.*). Perhaps at one time the decoration followed these concentric bands, though on the shields from Crete the number of bands varies widely.

Adapting this mainly leather artifact to the metalworking of Hephaistos presents the poet with a problem. The god is said to make the shield of five layers (πτύχες, 18.481). At 20.259ff. Aineias' spear strikes this shield, but does not pierce it (20.268–72):

> χρυσὸς γὰρ ἐρύκακε, δῶρα θεοῖο·
> ἀλλὰ δύω μὲν ἔλασσε διὰ πτύχας, αἱ δ' ἄρ' ἔτι τρεῖς
> ἦσαν, ἐπεὶ πέντε πτύχας ἤλασε κυλλοποδίων,
> τὰς δύο χαλκείας, δύο δ' ἔνδοθι κασσιτέροιο,
> τὴν δὲ μίαν χρυσέην, τῇ ῥ' ἔσχετο μείλινον ἔγχος.

This would mean that the shield was constructed of two outer layers of bronze and two inner ones of tin, with a gold layer sandwiched between, which stopped Aineias' spear. Unfortunately, such construction makes little practical sense. Gold, though the divine metal *par excellence*, would not stop a bronze-headed spear; neither would tin; and in such an arrangement bronze alone would be visible on the outer face of the shield, the more decorative metals being hidden beneath it. It seems that in 268 (as at 21.165, the same verse) χρυσός means not 'the gold layer' but 'the golden ⟨shield⟩', and 269–72 are an uncomprehending addition to the text, as Aristarchus (Arn/A) perceived (see also 20.268–72n.).

How the poet thought the shield was actually built up thus remains uncertain. He can hardly have imagined Hephaistos laying oxhides over a frame in the manner of a human craftsman, and then superimposing the layers of metal. Fittschen, *Schild* 7, thinks of five layers of bronze. Probably Homer gave the matter little heed. 'All die Rekonstruktionen sind müssig, nichts als Verkennung der Dichtung. Jene Beziehungen sagen nichts mehr als dass die Phantasie des Iliasdichters im Raum des Realen bleibt' (Marg 26). The choice of five layers (481) may reflect the arrangement of scenes worked out by modern scholars (see below). It may, however, be a reference to the five components which form the surface and its decoration – bronze, tin, gold, silver (474–5), and κύανος, which forms οἶμοι ('stripes'?) on Agamemnon's corslet (11.24) and πτύχες on Hesiod's *Aspis* (143). Inlay-work can indeed be thought of as 'layers' of different materials, in a different sense from the superimposition of oxhides in a shield.

The decorative technique employed must be that of inlay of different-coloured metals. 'Gold gave the yellow colour, whiter if alloyed with silver and redder if alloyed with copper. Silver was white, and copper was occasionally used for red' (D. H. F. Gray, *JHS* 74, 1954, 3–4). Two other colours were used for Agamemnon's breastplate: ἐν δέ οἱ ὀμφαλοὶ ἦσαν ἐείκοσι κασσιτέροιο | λευκοί, ἐν δὲ μέσοισιν ἔην μέλανος κυάνοιο (11.34–5). Tin would give a duller white than silver. *Kuanos* is applied on the shield only to the ditch around the vineyard (564); it may be the blue glass-paste mentioned on Linear B tablets (see Fittschen, *Schild* 5 n. 22; F. Eckstein, *Arch. Hom.* L, Göttingen 1974, 40–1), or the usually black niello, of which Gray writes (4): 'Less obvious is the method of producing black, by mixing powdered sulphur with lead, copper, or silver to form the alloy known as niello; the black background of the Lily dagger from the fifth Shaft Grave is said to be a plate of iron and silver alloy. Depressions showing the patterns in blank outline were cut and hammered out of the cold bronze base. Thin plates of the inlaying metals were cut to the right shapes and hammered cold into the depressions. The niello was either applied in powder form and then fired, or first fired and cut out and then applied as a cold plate.' The technique can be seen on the well-known inlaid daggers from Mycenae, splendidly illustrated in colour in Marinatos and Hirmer, pl. xxxv–xxxviii; in a note to this last plate (p. 167) they remark 'At the moment of discovery the niello looked dark blue rather than black.' On a larger scale, the technique is used for the depiction of a frieze of six bulls' heads, in gold and niello on a silver background, on a fourteenth-century silver cup from Enkomi (*Companion* pl. 36c; the splendid polychrome effect is well brought out by the colour plate in H.-G. Buchholz and V. Karageorghis, *Prehistoric Greece and Cyprus*, tr. F. Garvie, London 1973, pl. 4). Gray suggests that Homer was familiar with artifacts of this type but not with the actual process of manufacture. The continuity of representations on the monuments from the Mycenaean to the Attic Geometric period has been demonstrated by J. L. Benson, *Horse, Bird and Man* (Amherst 1970) 109–23; he also lists a number of artifacts found in a context later than that of their manufacture.

No mention is made of a boss at the centre of the shield, despite the ubiquitous formula ἀσπίδες ὀμφαλόεσσαι (etc.; 11 × *Il.*, 1 × *Od.*). Bronze bosses are found on shields from the twelfth century on, one example also having a bronze rim (Snodgrass, *Arms and Armour of the Greeks*, Ithaca, N.Y. 1967, 32–3, 43–4; *Early Greek Armour and Weapons* 37–49); see 13.192–3n.

The nearest monumental parallels are bronze shields found in Crete, which may have come from Asia Minor or from Cyprus, and Phoenician silver and bronze bowls. The techniques used are repoussé, chasing, and engraving; inlay of different metals, like that described above, does not occur, though in a few cases gold foil has been applied to the figures alone on a silver bowl (see Markoe, *Bowls* 10). The Cretan shields have an omphalos, a lion's head, or a rosette in the centre, surrounded by concentric bands of decorative motifs and figured scenes, usually of the hunt; the best-preserved examples are Kunze no. 6 (Taf. 10–12 and Beilage 1 = Fittschen,

Figure 1. Bronze shield from the Idaean cave (Herakleion Museum, inv. no. 7).
From K. Fittschen, *Arch. Hom.* N Abb. 1.

Schild p. 8 Abb. 1; here fig. 1) and no. 10 (Taf. 26 = Schadewaldt, *VHWW*
Abb. 27). The Phoenician metal bowls or dishes, also of about Homer's
period (there are references to them at 23.741–4 and *Od.* 4.615–19 =
15.115–19), are catalogued, illustrated, and studied by Markoe. They too
show (usually on the interior surface) concentric rings of figure-scenes. Two
are particularly interesting. A silver dish from Amathus (Markoe no. cy4,
Fittschen, *Schild* Abb. 3, Schadewaldt, *VHWW* Abb. 28; here fig. 2), of
which about half is preserved, has a centre rosette, an inner band of
sphinxes, a figure-band of scenes from Egyptian religious myth, and an
outer band showing the siege of a city, with defenders on three towers
fighting off on each side attackers with scaling-ladders; beyond these, on
one side hoplites, archers, armed horsemen, and the horses of a (lost)

Figure 2. Phoenician silver dish from Amathus (British Museum, B.M. 123053). From K. Fittschen, *Arch. Hom.* N Abb. 3.

chariot approach; on the other, two armed horsemen ride up to two men felling trees in an orchard (ravaging the countryside?). The depiction is very close to Homer's City at War (18.509–50), especially as a second city may well have appeared symmetrically placed on the lost portion of the band. Another silver dish from Praeneste (Markoe no. E2; Fittschen, *Schild* Taf. viiib; here fig. 3) shows in the centre an unarmoured figure killing captives with a spear, then a frieze of horses, and an outer band depicting the 'Hunter's Day', a series of nine scenes presenting the narrative of a king who leaves a walled city, shoots, pursues, kills, and flays a stag, makes offerings to a deity, is attacked by an ape and rescued by the deity, kills the ape, and returns again to the same city-representation from which he left. The snake which encircles the whole scene may represent the ocean, which flows around Homer's shield too (see 607–8n.). A similar series appears on a silver bowl from Kourion (Markoe no. cy7), suggesting a well-known tale is being represented.

Figure 3. Silver dish from Praeneste (Villa Giulia, Rome, inv. no. 61565). From Markoe, *Bowls* 278.

Arrangement of scenes and descriptive style

Fittschen, *Schild* 4 n. 16, gives a lengthy list of scholars and artists who have been tempted to reconstruct the scenes on the shield. Homer introduces the five πτύχες of the shield and the decoration upon it in successive sentences (481–2), and the more recent reconstructions have followed this fivefold division. In the usual view, the heavenly bodies (introduced by ἔτευξε, 483) occupy the central position, surrounding the boss (if there is one), and the following scenes occupy successive bands moving outwards to the rim (607–8). However, the only evidence for this arrangement is the sequence of the poet's description, and it has been challenged by H. A. Gärtner, *Studien zum Antiken Epos* (edd. H. Görgemanns and E. A. Schmidt, Meisenheim am Glan 1976) 46–65.

Each scene is introduced by a new verb of action. The innermost band is divided between the City at Peace and the City at War (ποίησε, 490), and the next among the three scenes of the farmer's year (ploughing, reaping, and the vintage; ἐτίθει, 541, 550, 561). Then the next may contain either three scenes, the cattle (with the attacking lions) and the sheep (ποίησε, 573, 587) together with the dance (ποίκιλλε, 590; so Willcock *ad* 478–608); or the dance may be given a separate band, as in van Leeuwen's diagram (*ad* 483–608), which in view of contemporary artists' fondness for rows of similar figures is probably preferable. Ocean (ἐτίθει, 607) occupies the outermost band, just inside the decorated rim. The uncertainty whether the central and outermost scenes are included in the five bands makes it undesirable to attempt a more definite allocation.

There is no reason to suppose that Homer was describing an actual shield he had seen. In some scenes, however, it is possible he may have had some work of visual art in mind, and minor confusions in the details of his account may result from misinterpretation of a two-dimensional picture. Thus the δύω στρατοί depicted on either side of the city probably represent one army, depicted on either side of a city (see 509n.); the capture of the cattle and sheep is likely to be the work of attackers rather than the besieged inhabitants of the city (see 523–34n.); and the two talents in the lawsuit scene, though explicable as a reward for the best opinion, might well represent the compensation for a death in a different value system (see 507–8n.).

It is the normal Homeric technique for physical objects to be described by means of action and movement, as in the account of Pandaros' bow (4.105–11), Odysseus' brooch (*Od.* 19.228–31), and especially his boat (*Od.* 228–61; see Edwards, *HPI* 83–4). So here verbs repeatedly recall Hephaistos' ongoing action (478, 483, 490, 541, 550, 561, 573, 587, 590, 607), and there are occasional references to his technique, stressing colour and the appearance of light and dark (517–19, 548–9, 562–5, 574, 577); once the poet steps back and marvels at the artistic deception (548–9). Sometimes, however, he looks beyond the materials employed, and mentions the 'stone' seats of the elders (504) and the soft, finely spun clothing of the dancers (595–6).

Even more striking, however, is the constant emphasis on movement and progression of time; 'the predominant way of appropriating visual images is to translate them into stories' (so A. S. Becker in his theoretical study of ecphrasis, with special reference to the shield; *AJP* 111, 1990, 139–53). Just as in Homeric similes, there is life and action in every scene, including even that of the heavenly bodies (488; Marg, *Dichtung* 27–9). In the lawsuit scene, the antagonists appear two or three times; so do the inhabitants of the besieged city; the ploughmen turn and turn again at the headland; the cattle move from stall to river-bank; the dancers form now a circle, now straight lines (599–602). Even sound-effects are included: men and women are singing (493, 570–2), cattle are lowing, a stream babbling (575–6, 580). Homer does *not* stand back to reflect that the outcome of the lawsuit and the siege will never be known, as would Keats (*Ode on a Grecian Urn*) and the author of the *Aspis*, who says of his chariot-racers (310–11):

οἳ μὲν ἄρ' ἀΐδιον εἶχον πόνον, οὐδέ ποτέ σφιν
νίκη ἐπηνύσθη, ἀλλ' ἄκριτον εἶχον ἄεθλον.

For Homer does not intend to present a particular occurrence, but paradigms of ever-continuing human social activities.

Subject-matter of the scenes

In the first scene of this Book, Akhilleus made the decision between long life and everlasting glory which he had described in book 9; he chose to return to the battle and take vengeance on Hektor, then face the imminent death of which Thetis forewarns him. Now the poet portrays, on the shield which the hero will bear into the battle, the everyday human life which he has given up. All the scenes are full of ordinary people taking part in the activities of ordinary life. Akhilleus does not shoulder the burden of responsibility for these people, as Virgil's Aineias does for Rome's future (*attollens umero famamque et fata nepotum*, *Aeneid* 8.731). But the poet chooses to present this real and familiar life, just as he invariably presents it in the similes, instead of frightening us with terrifying forms such as the Fear, Strife, Panic, Slaughter (etc.) which begin the description of the *Aspis* (144–67) or the other mythological and heroic fictions which might have been expected here. Parallels have been drawn between his choice of scenes and those found on the miniature frescoes from Thera (see most recently S. P. Morris, *AJA* 93, 1989, 511–35). Marg, *Dichtung* 24–5, makes the good point that the scenes on Akhilleus' shield are described as the god fashions them on Olumpos, not (as are those on the shield of Aineias) when the hero receives and admires the armour on earth; the audience can appreciate them now, but Akhilleus could not properly do so until after his reconciliation with Priam, when he is more ready to appreciate life on ordinary human terms.

The poet constantly emphasizes, with a few vivid words, the pleasure the participants feel in their communal life. The women stand in their doorways admiring the wedding procession; the lawsuit will be decided by proper legal procedures without further bloodshed, and the fairest judge will win a reward; the βασιλεύς watches his workers with joy in his heart, and the ploughmen and reapers receive their refreshment; the busy vintagers sing along with the musician, the spectators enjoy the beauty of the dance. Except for the absence of the sea and ships, we might almost be in the wonderland of the Phaeacians. It is all far from the hardship, injustice, and gloom one finds in the dour Hesiod's pictures of human life. The same delight in the details of the daily round appears in those similes which have unique, non-traditional subject-matter (see Introduction, ch. 3, iii).

The scenes balance union and dissension, men and women, youth and age. It has also been held, rather implausibly, that they represent Dumézil's tripartite Indo-European society (see C. S. Littleton, *Arethusa* 13, 1980, 147 and references there). Connexions have been found between specific scenes on the shield and the plot of *Il.* itself (especially by Ø. Andersen, *SO* 51, 1976, 5–18), and between the general attitude and feeling of the descriptions and those expressed elsewhere in both poems (by O. Taplin, *G&R* 27, 1980, 1–21). Schadewaldt (tentatively; *VHWW* 367) and Marg (more firmly; *Dichtung* 36–7) adopt the suggestion that the poet represents himself in the ἀοιδός of 604. That verse may not belong in the text (see 604–6n.), but even without it, it is hard not to think Homer was aware of the parallel between the god's creation of human beings in essentially human circumstances and his own creation of the poem (as is argued by Marg, *Dichtung* 33–7). Certainly the irony of the doomed hero of the past who bears into battle the depiction of the continuing life of ordinary human folk is in harmony with the symbolic use made elsewhere of the divinely made armour (see the introduction to this Book), and with the famous simile of the leaves which fall to the ground but burgeon again in the spring; ὡς ἀνδρῶν γενεὴ ἡ μὲν φύει, ἡ δ' ἀπολήγει (6.149).

468–82 Hephaistos sets to work, and forges a mighty shield, decorated with many scenes

As usual in Homer a manufactured object is described by an account of the way in which it was made; cf. Pandaros' bow (4.106–11), the speaker's staff (1.234–7), and Odysseus' raft (*Od.* 5.228–61). The scholia (bT on 476–7) remark '⟨Homer⟩ himself has marvellously crafted the craftsman, as if wheeling him out (ἐκκυκλήσας) on the stage and showing us his workshop in the open.'

468–73 Hephaistos' bellows are 'automatic', like his tripods (375–9) and his robot attendants (417–20). Verse 468 ≅ 4.292 (= 4.364), *Od.* 17.254. χόανος (< χέω) recurs in Hesiod, *Theogony* 863, in the phrase ὑπό τ' εὐτρήτου χοάνοιο, and is usually taken to mean 'crucible', 'melting-pot' ('from which [metal] was run into the mould', LSJ) or 'furnace', the holes being those through which the draught was forced (so West *ad loc.*, Leaf). But

M. H. Jameson points out to me that the true meaning must be 'nozzle through which the blast is forced, tuyere'. This sense better fits the etymology and Hesiod's epithet (cf. Ar. *Thesm.* 18 δίκην δὲ χοάνης ὦτα διετετρήνατο (Reiske's emendation)), and the scholiast to Hesiod *ad loc.* understood the word thus (χωνευτῆρος· χόανον τὸ χωρήτικον ('container') τοῦ πνεύματος, τὰς φύσσας λέγει). It also matches the meaning of the later contracted form χώνη, 'funnel', 'cone'. εὔπρηστον (only here) < πρήθω, 'blow'. The bellows blow upon the fire and the work from all angles (παντοίην... ἀῦτμήν ἐξανιεῖσαι, cf. πνοιαὶ δονέουσι | παντοίων ἀνέμων, 17.55–6), on hand for the busy smith (σπεύδοντι παρέμμεναι) as he time and again requires their blast (ἄλλοτε μέν..., ἄλλοτε δ' αὖτε). ἄλλοτε δ' αὖτε means 'at another time again', not 'on the contrary', as Leaf and Willcock take it (i.e. ceasing to blow); when two clauses beginning with ἄλλοτε are contrasted, the contrast is signified not by αὖτε but by the verbs (e.g. ἄλλοτ' ἐπαΐξασκε..., ἄλλοτε δ' αὖτε | <u>στάσκε</u>, 159–60; cf. 24.10–11, *Od.* 4.102–3, 11.303–4, and on the meaning of αὖτε, J. S. Klein, *Historische Sprachforschung* 101, 1988, 286–7). ἄνοιτο: the ᾰ is unexplained, as *ἄνϝω becomes ἄνυω or ἄνω. Leaf reads ἄνυτο, but without good MS authority; see Chantraine, *GH* 1 51, for this form of the optative, and *GH* 1 161 for the vocalization of the digamma.

474–5 Cf. χαλκὸς ἀτειρής | (3 × *Il.*), ἀτειρέα χαλκόν | (1 × *Od.*), and χαλκὸν ἀτειρέα (bridging the mid-verse caesura, 2 × *Il.*). τιμῆντα is for τιμήεντα, cf. τεχνῆσσαι (*Od.* 7.110) and τιμῆς < τιμήεις (9.605, see note *ad loc.* and Chantraine, *GH* 1 32). χρυσὸν (-οῖο)... τιμῆεντα (-ος) | is found 2 × *Od.*

476–7 Cf. ἐν δ' ἔθετ' ἀκμοθέτῳ μέγαν ἄκμονα, κόπτε δὲ δεσμοὺς |... (*Od.* 8.274). ῥαιστήρ (< ῥαίω): lit. 'smasher'; πυράγρη (< πῦρ + ἄγρη): 'fire-pincers' (also at *Od.* 3.434; Risch, *Wortbildung* 207). He holds the hot metal in the pincers with one hand and hammers it with the other. D. H. F. Gray, *JHS* 74 (1954) 12–13, points out that the poet is visualizing iron-working rather than the handling of the softer metals listed.

Zenodotus (Did/AT) and some good MSS read κρατερόν; Eustathius supports the feminine form. Objects in -τηρ are otherwise masculine (Risch, *Wortbildung* 30, gives a list), and -ην is probably a change to improve the metre.

478–82 First the making of shield and shield-strap is mentioned in general terms, introduced by ποίει... πάντοσε δαιδάλλων (478–9; δαιδάλλων recurs in Homer only at *Od.* 23.200). Then the five layers are specified, and the ring form completed by the concluding ποίει δαίδαλα πολλά (482).

478–80 Verse 478 ≅ 609, the summarizing line at the end of the shield construction, in which τεῦξε replaces ποίει for metrical reasons. ἄντυξ, 'rim', is also used of the rail of a chariot. It is not clear what is meant by the 'triple' rim; it may be three decorative bands, like those on the bronze Cretan shields (see fig. 1, p. 204, and 607–8n.), or possibly a means of securing the layers of hide to the frame at the edges of a 'real' shield. Perhaps the poet is influenced by the formula | δίπλακα πορφυρέην, used 2 × *Il.* for an embroidered robe. On the τελαμών see 14.402–8n. and Borchhardt, *Arch. Hom.* F 1–5

483–9 The heavenly bodies

First the poet sums up the entire content of the decoration (483): the depictions of human life on the earth (in 490–606), the stream of Ocean which surrounds the whole (in 607–8), and the sky, which occupies the central position and is described in the following six verses (484–9). This seems preferable to envisaging an anthropomorphic Gaia, Ouranos, and Thalassa here (*contra*, O. Taplin, *G&R* 27, 1980, 19 n. 13.). The sun, moon, and constellations, besides being the eternal companions of human life, were watched closely because they indicate the passing of the day, the month, and seasons of the year respectively. Before a reliable calendar was developed a knowledge of the constellations was essential for farming, as Hesiod's *Erga* makes clear. Odysseus used the Pleiades, Boötes, and the Bear to sail by (*Od.* 5.272–3). How the poet envisages their depiction on the shield is unclear, and there are no good parallels from contemporary artifacts. On two gold signet-rings from Mycenae the sun is represented as a circle (once with spokes for rays) and the moon as a crescent (Marinatos and Hirmer, *Crete and Mycenae* 172–3 and pl. 207). A late Mycenaean amphora has figures which may be intended to represent the constellations (see J. Wiesner, *JDAI* 74, 1959, 45–6).

On Homeric and Hesiodic astronomy see D. R. Dicks, *Early Greek Astronomy to Aristotle* (London 1970) 27–38, esp. 36.

483 The central band of figures is introduced by ἔτευξε, the next band by ποίησε (490), the third by ἐτίθει (541, 550, 561), the fourth by ποίησε (573, 587), the last by ποίκιλλε (590), and the rim by ἐτίθει (607); cf. 478–80n. The same triple anaphora of ἐν recurs at 535, and also in similar descriptions at 5.740 and 14.216.

485 τείρεα is a form of τέρας, lengthened for metrical reasons (or to increase its impressiveness); on the ending see Risch, *Wortbildung* 87. τέρας, 'portent', usually means a meteor or comet (see 4.75–8n.), or a rainbow (17.548). The unchanging constellations may be so termed because of their significance for human life. τά τ' οὐρανὸς ἐστεφάνωται is rendered by Leaf '*has* set around it [sky or earth?] as a crown', by Willcock 'with which heaven is crowned', by Ameis–Hentze 'mit welchen der Himmel rings besetzt ist', and most recently by T. Worthen, *Glotta* 66 (1988) 1–19, 'stars which Ouranos encompasses like a diadem'. Parallel phrases with περὶ (ἀμφὶ)…ἐστεφάνωται (-το) mean '[Fear] has hung itself (has been hung) as a wreath around [the aegis]' (5.739; similarly at 15.153, *Od.* 10.195, *HyAphr* 120, *Aspis* 204), and even when there is no περί (ἀμφί), as here and at *Theogony* 382 (after ἄστρά τε λαμπετόωντα), it seems best to take the meaning as '[stars] which the sky (or Ouranos) has hung up as a wreath ⟨around the earth; or around his head⟩'. (I take the usage at 11.36 to be exceptional; but see note *ad loc.* Worthen, *op. cit.* 3, thinks it may well be the archetype of the others.) Did/A report that Zenodotus read οὐρανὸν ἐστήρικται and Aristarchus οὐρανὸν ἐστεφάνωκε. Zenodotus' phrase recurs in Hesiod, *Theogony* 779 (and cf. 4.443). Neither alternative appears in the MSS or has anything to recommend it, and the cause of their concern is not clear.

486 = Hesiod, *Erga* 615. The Pleiades mark the times for harvest and ploughing (Hesiod says Πληϊάδων 'Ατλαγενέων ἐπιτελλομενάων | ἄρχεσθ' ἀμήτου, ἀρότοιο δὲ δυσομενάων, *Erga* 383-4). For a detailed account see West, *Works and Days* 254-6. At *Erga* 619-20 Hesiod speaks of the Pleiades plunging into the sea to escape the σθένος ὄβριμον 'Ωρίωνος, as a sign that sailing-time is over. Both Pleiades and Hyades are close to Orion. J. H. Phillips, *LCM* 5.8 (1980) 179-80, points out that the risings and settings of these three constellations delimit the period May–November, during which the three main agricultural activities later described (541-72) take place.

The meaning of Πληϊάδες is obscure; possibly < *Πλεϊϊάδες < πλέω, because of their association with sailing. Hesiod (frr. 288, 289, 290 MW = Athenaeus 11.80) and later poets use the form Πελειάδες, 'doves'. Hesiod gives the names of the five Hyades (fr. 291 MW). The ancients said they were catasterized by Zeus after they died mourning their brother Hyas (Tzetzes on Hesiod, *Erga* 384), or because they reared Dionysus, who was called Ύης (schol. on Aratus 172). Their name may actually be derived from ὕω, 'rain', or from ὕς, 'pig', cf. their Latin name *suculae*, 'piglets'.

The older form 'Ωαρΐωνα, -ος is found in Pindar and later poets, but did not survive in our MSS of Homer and Hesiod; Pasquali, *Storia* 246, would (justifiably) restore it to the text here and at 488.

487-9 = *Od.* 5.273-5. Hainsworth, *Odyssey* on *Od.* 5.272-7, has a good discussion of the passage. The Great Bear is still known in England as Charles's Wain (wagon). Hainsworth refers to O. Szemerényi's demonstration (*Innsbrucker Beiträge zur Kulturwissenschaft*, Sonderheft 15, 1962, 190-1) that the Greek Ἄρκτος, 'Bear', is derived (through the form ἄρκος) from Akkadian *eriq(q)u*, 'wagon', and is thus a false etymology. See also A. Scherer, *Gestirnnamen bei den indogermanischen Völkern* (Heidelberg 1953) 134.

The idea that the Bear keeps a watchful eye on the great hunter Orion is an attractive touch, and brings out the all-pervasive sense of movement in the scenes depicted; West on *Erga* 620 gives parallels for the idea of constellations pursuing each other. Leaf points out that the Bear is close to the horizon, about to take his bath, when Orion rises and scares him away. Orion continues his hunting even in the Underworld (*Od.* 11.572–5). On his sexual randiness see most recently A. Griffiths, *JHS* 106 (1986) 66–70, on his catasterism J. Fontenrose, *Orion* (Berkeley 1981) 15 18. αὐτοῦ (488): i.e. without setting. οἴη: this is true of the constellations mentioned in Homer and Hesiod, and of others which do not set the Bear is the most obvious (as Aristotle noted, *Poetics* 1461a20–1); see Hainsworth, *Odyssey* on *Od.* 5.275.

490–508 The city at peace

The blessings of ordered communal life are represented by weddings, which unite different families and bring festivities for all, and the peaceful settlement of a dispute over a man's death by a city's judicial institutions. The Hesiodic *Aspis* also describes a wedding and other revels (272–85). The poet limits himself to two topics, which he (and the artist) can encompass in detail, rather than attempting to include religious ceremonies, funerals, games, and all the other public activities of a city.

491–6 καλάς: the single runover adjective is unexpected and effective, almost as if the sight called up an exclamation. In 492, Zenodotus read ἐς θαλάμους (Did/A), which is attractive (οὐκ ἀπίθανος, A) but not necessary; there is no MS support. δαΐδων ὕπο λαμπομενάων recurs 2 × *Od.*; ὑπό = 'accompanied by'. ἠγίνεον is trisyllabic. πολὺς δ' ὑμέναιος ὀρώρει | recurs at *Aspis* 274, in the more lengthy description of a wedding there; cf. πολὺς δ' ὀρυμαγδὸς ὀρώρει | (4 × *Il.*, 1 × *Od.*), πολὺς δ' ὑπὸ κόμπος ὀρώρειν | (*Od.* 8.380). ὀρχηστῆρες (494) recurs only in Hesiod fr. 123.3 MW and later imitations; the usual form is ὀρχηστής (2 × *Il.*). ἐδίνεον = 'turn', 'spin around'; see 606n. The women standing on their porches to watch (495–6) form a particularly attractive detail.

497–508 Organized communal life is further illustrated by the representation of the legal proceedings in the case of a man's killing. There is much dispute over what the legal issue is and what roles are played by the ἵστωρ, the elders, and the golden talents displayed. The most recent discussions of the problems are those by R. Westbrook (see 498–500n.), M. Gagarin, *Early Greek Law* (Berkeley 1986) 26–33, and Ø. Andersen, *SO* 51 (1976) 11–16; H. Hommel, *Politeia und Res Publica: Gedenkschrift R. Starks* (ed. P. Steinmetz, Wiesbaden 1969) 11–38 gives the fullest bibliographical listing and review of others' work; H. J. Wolff's article in *Traditio* 4 (1946) 31–87 (also [in German] in *Beiträge zur Rechtsgeschichte Altgriechenlands* 1961, 1–90) is of fundamental importance. A brief account is given by D. M. MacDowell, *The Law in Classical Athens* (Ithaca, N.Y. 1978), and the older literature is reviewed in R. J. Bonner and G. Smith, *The Administration of*

Justice from Homer to Aristotle I (Chicago 1930) 31–41, and Leaf II Appendix I §§ 23–31. The conclusion I reach here is much like that of J.-L. Perpillou, *Mélanges de linguistique et de philologie grecques offerts à Pierre Chantraine* (Paris 1972) 177–81.

497 λαοί = the citizens, distinguished from the women of the previous sentence. ἀγορή probably = 'meeting-place', as in similes at 16.387 and *Od.* 12.439 (cf. 274–6n.); elsewhere in Homer it has the earlier meaning 'assembly'.

498–500 Is the issue simply the practical one of whether the compensation for the man's death has or has not been handed over? This is the view of the scholiasts: ὁ μὲν διεβεβαιοῦτο λέγων δεδωκέναι τὸ ἀρκοῦν πρὸς ὅλον τὸ ἀδίκημα, ὁ δὲ ἠρνεῖτο (bT). Or – and this is a much more fundamental question – is it whether a monetary compensation for his death should, or must, be accepted? If it is not accepted, presumably either the killer must go into exile, or a blood-feud will begin (see 23.85–90n.).

Wolff (*op. cit.* 44–6), basing his interpretation on a wide comparative knowledge of the legal systems of early societies, points out that the 'defendant' (the one responsible for the death) speaks first, not the 'plaintiff'/'creditor' (the dead man's kinsman). He holds that the dead man's kinsman, acting under extra-judicial self-help, is about to seize or threatens violence against the person of the victim's killer, who now appeals for a legal trial before an arbitrator. This is consistent with either the failure to hand over an agreed compensation, or with refusal to accept such compensation. Wolff himself believes that the issue is whether compensation has actually been handed over, arguing that 'In all periods of Greek legal history ἀποδιδόναι [499] was technical for paying a debt already incurred' (p. 37); if the issue were whether the injured party might or might not refuse to accept compensation, he claims that ἀποτῖσαι would be required. However, he does not discuss the meanings of εὔχετο, ἀναίνετο, and ἐλέσθαι. Wolff's view here has been challenged with good general and specific arguments by A. Primmer, *WS* 4 (1970) 5–13.

Certainly ὁ μὲν εὔχετο πάντ᾽ ἀποδοῦναι can mean 'the one was claiming to have paid everything' (for this use of εὔχομαι with an aorist infinitive to refer to a past action cf. 8.254, 21.501, *Od.* 11.261). E. Benveniste, *Le Vocabulaire des institutions indo-européennes* (Paris 1969) II 233–43, and many earlier scholars have supported an alternative rendering 'the one promised to pay everything'. However, A. E. Raubitschek points out to me that in dedicatory epigrams εὐχόμενος means 'claiming', εὐξάμενος 'having promised'; εὔχετο will thus be the past form of the defendant's εὔχομαι, 'I am claiming', avoiding the semantic change in εὔξατο, 'he promised'. Furthermore, L. C. Muellner, in *The Meaning of Homeric* EYXOMAI *through its Formulas* (Innsbruck 1976) 100–6, holds (on the basis of other uses of the verb and an occurrence in Linear B) that only the significance 'asserts', 'says' is acceptable; though his own rendering, 'One man was saying he paid [the ποινή for murder] in full, the other [the victim's kinsman] was refusing to take anything' (105–6, Muellner's brackets), is rather illogical. The interpretation of J.-L. Perpillou, *REG* 83 (1970) 537 (also using the Mycenaean evidence), 'une des parties "proteste de son droit", ici à se libérer d'une dette de sang selon telle procédure', is preferable.

ἀναίνομαι with infinitive in Homer normally means 'refuse ⟨to do something⟩', as at 450. Only at 9.116 and *Od.* 14.149 can it be taken as 'refuse ⟨to admit the idea⟩', 'deny'. The obvious meaning of ὁ δ' ἀναίνετο μηδὲν ἑλέσθαι is thus not 'the other denied that he had received anything' but 'the other refused to take anything'. With this sense, μηδέν is correct (Chantraine, *GH* II 335, 'l'autre refusait de rien recevoir'), whereas if 'denied that he had received anything' were the meaning οὐδέν would be normal (though Wackernagel, *Vorlesungen* II 282, quotes Ar. *Eq.* 572 ἠρνοῦτο μὴ πεπτωκέναι to support his 'leugnete etwas erhalten zu haben'; E. Fraenkel, *Aeschylus Agamemnon*, Oxford 1950, III on *Ag.* 1653 follows him).

The straightforward interpretation of the two statements, closest to the normal meaning of the words, would thus be: 'The one man was claiming ⟨to be able, to have a right⟩ to pay everything (i.e. to be free of other penalties), the other refused to accept anything (i.e. any pecuniary recompense in place of the exile or death of the offender).' This is in accordance with Muellner's investigation of εὔχομαι (though it is not exactly his rendering of the passage), with Primmer's study of other word-usages, and with the parallels Andersen has drawn with the plot of the *Il.* (see below). There is no other example of this construction with εὔχομαι, but neither is there of its use in a legal context (except on the Linear B tablet discussed by Muellner and Perpillou). With this view, the problem of whether ἑλέσθαι can mean 'received' is also avoided. MacDowell's view (*op. cit.* 19–21) is similar to this. However, as W. Beck has suggested (*LfgrE* s.v. εὔχομαι), the clarity of the passage may have suffered from the effort to achieve structural parallelism between the two clauses.

After I had formulated the above views, R. Westbrook was kind enough to show me his article on the trial scene (forthcoming in *HSCP*), in which he compares this trial scene with what is known of legal procedures in cases of homicide in ancient Near Eastern and Mycenaean Greek societies. This evidence suggests that usually the dead man's kinsmen have the right to choose either to take revenge on the offender or to accept a ransom in lieu of it. In disputed cases, a court would decide: (*a*) whether revenge or ransom was appropriate, depending on the circumstances of the killing; and either (*b*) the appropriate limit of revenge (death of the culprit, death of his family too, whipping, humiliation, etc.); or (*c*) the appropriate amount of the ransom to be paid. Westbrook therefore holds that in this trial scene the killer is claiming the right to pay ransom (ποινή, 498) in full (πάντα, 499) on the grounds of mitigated homicide, the amount to be fixed by the court. The other party is claiming and choosing the right to take revenge, as in cases of aggravated homicide. The court must set the 'limit' (πεῖραρ, 501) of the penalty, i.e. whether it should be revenge or ransom, and also the appropriate 'limit' of either revenge or ransom. This view is identical with my own, and in accordance with the usual meaning of πεῖραρ (see next note).

If this interpretation is correct, the issue can be said (as Ø. Andersen has pointed out, *SO* 51, 1976, 14–16) to parallel the situation in the *Il.*, where Akhilleus has so far refused the recompense offered by Agamemnon, but will at last accept it in the following Book (19.238–75); and in fact he was rebuked by Aias with the words 'A man accepts (ἐδέξατο) compensation (ποινήν) even for the death of a brother or son, and ⟨the killer⟩ remains there among the people, after he has paid much' (9.632–4). Andersen also links the situation to Akhilleus' acceptance of compensation for the death of Patroklos: Thetis says to him ἀλλ' ἄγε δὴ λῦσον, νεκροῖο δὲ δέξαι ἄποινα (24.137).

Did/A report that ἀποκταμένου was read by Zenodotus καὶ ἐν ταῖς πλείσταις (i.e. the named or emended texts), but it does not appear in the MSS. Though this reading gives a stronger sense, it seems rash to print it in the text (with Leaf and others). δήμῳ πιφαύσκων: 'revealing' or 'declaring' it to the people. The verb is derived from the root seen in φά(ϝ)ος, 'light', but may have been confused with φημί. On the reduplication see Risch, *Wortbildung* 276. The man displays the recompense he is offering. De Jong, *Narrators* 118, draws attention to the vividness of the dramatization in these lines; only direct speech could go further, and that might be *too* remarkable on a work of visual art.

501 ἴστωρ is usually taken as < *ϝιδ-τωρ (Chantraine, *Dict.* s.v.), derived from the same root as οἶδα: 'one who sees and knows ⟨what is right⟩', or perhaps (Wolff, *op. cit.* 38) 'one familiar with the facts'. The meaning 'witness', which appears in the scholia and on a Boeotian inscription (LSJ), does not fit well here. However, E. D. Floyd, *Glotta* 68 (1990) 157–66, argues for a derivation from ἵζειν, 'seat', 'sit' and the meaning 'convener'. The word is used when Idomeneus proposes that Agamemnon arbitrate the dispute between him and Aias (23.486), and by Hesiod in the general sense 'wise' (*Erga* 792). Here it is not clear if the reference is to the elders as a body, to their presiding officer (if any), or to the eventual winner of the two talents (see 507–8n.). The last view is preferred by Wolff and MacDowell. The recourse to arbitration is like that suggested by Menelaos (23.573–8), not unlike the mediator's rôle played by Nestor and Hephaistos in turn in book 1. πεῖραρ is usually taken to mean 'judgement', an extension of the sense 'boundary between lands', since property is the object of adjudication (so A. L. T. Bergren, *The Etymology and Usage of* πεῖραρ *in Early Greek Poetry*, New York 1975, 43–5), but Westbrook's 'limit' (see previous note) is even closer to the normal meaning; see also 6.143n.

Presumably the dispute formed one scene on the shield, the hearing another, the litigants appearing in both (the 'episodic' form of narrative, Markoe 63).

502–3 ἐπήπυον: this compound of ἠπύω occurs only here, ἐπι- being amplified by ἀμφὶς ἀρωγοί. The Massaliotic text (Did/AT) read ἀμφοτέρωθεν (also favoured by Zenodotus and Aristophanes) and a variant (corrupted in the MSS) for ἐπήπυον. The animated and noisy scene can well be imagined. With 503 cf. | κήρυκες βοόωντες ἐρήτυον (2.97).

504–5 Thus the Phaeacian counsellors sit upon smooth stone seats in their assembly (*Od.* 8.6). The circle is sacred because Zeus presides over judicial matters (e.g. 9.98–9) and the public altars would be close to the assembly-place (cf. 11.807–8). Similarly threshing-floors are ἱεραί (5.499) because Demeter is at work there. J. T. Hooker, however, thinks the meaning may be 'massive'; see 17.464–5n. σκῆπτρα may be plural to match κηρύκων, the idea being that the elders are given the speaker's staff in turn by the heralds, when each wishes to speak (cf. 23.567–8 and note *ad loc.*); or possibly as holders of the judicial powers once belonging to a king, or as βασιλῆες (cf. 556–7n.), they each have a royal staff. ἠερόφωνος occurs only here; it may be connected with ἀήρ and mean 'whose voices resound through the air'; see Chantraine, *Dict.* s.v.

506 Ameis–Hentze, Leaf, Wolff, Hommel, and Willcock take this as '⟨The elders⟩ leapt to their feet with their staffs', but the abrupt action seems unlikely even in the heat of debate; elsewhere ἀΐσσω always conveys the idea of speed. It may be better to take the litigants as subject, 'To these elders then they dashed.' δίκαζον = '⟨the elders⟩ gave their judgements' (the same as δίκην... εἴποι, 507). δικάζω is used in the active for the decisions of Zeus and others (1.542, 8.431, 23.574, 23.579, *Od.* 11.547); if the meaning were that litigants presented their own cases the middle voice would be required (as at *Od.* 11.545, 12.440). Here the elders must be the subject, picking up τοῖσιν, with an abrupt but not un-Homeric change from the subject of ἤϊσσον. A. Primmer, *WS* 4 (1970) 5–13, points out that δίκαζον here must mean the elders are each giving their learned opinions, not handing down one majority decision. In its only other occurrences (*Od.* 18.310, *HyDem* 326) ἀμοιβηδίς also refers to a series of people acting in turn, not to two only.

507–8 δύω χρυσοῖο τάλαντα are the fourth prize in the chariot-race (23.269, 23.614), ranking after an unused cauldron and before a two-handled jar; see 23.269n. The talents are usually taken to be contributed (one each) by the parties in the suit, as an award for the one who 'speaks a judgement most straightly' (δίκη as at 16.542 and *Od.* 11.570, ἰθύς as at 23.580, *HyDem* 152, Hesiod, *Erga* 36). Wolff (43) and others compare *HyHerm* 324, though it is far from certain that the τάλαντα there are not simply the scales of Zeus. The equivalence in value to the chariot-race prize is reasonable enough – A. L. Macrakis considers that Homeric prices are consistent (*Studies Presented to Sterling Dow*, Durham, NC 1984, 211–15) – but of course by standards of the classical period this is an enormous weight of gold, even if it were the recompense which the defendant pointed to in 550. The matter has not yet been explained.

μετὰ τοῖσι: 'among the elders' (Wolff 39–40). Presumably the surrounding crowd decide which elder wins the award; Wolff (40–2) finds an analogy to this in early Germanic law. Verse 508 sounds much like an inscription on a prize, such as the Dipylon oinochoe: ὃς νῦν ὀρχηστῶν πάντων ἀταλώτατα παίζει (*IG* I Suppl. 492a; see most recently B. B. Powell, *Kadmos* 27, 1988, 65–86).

509–40 *The city at war*

The scene continues (there is no new 'he made') with the second city, this one under siege; a representation probably chosen by the poet not only because of the tale of Troy but because it was one of the recurrent circumstances of Greek city life. The picture includes an ambush and the capture of cattle. In similar fashion, the West House at Akrotiri contains miniature frescoes showing both pastoral and siege scenes (see most recently S. P. Morris, *AJA* 93, 1989, 511–35; P. M. Warren's article, *JHS* 99, 1979, 115–29, includes two colour plates).

509 Cf. στρατῷ εὐρέϊ λαῶν | (4.76). It has often been pointed out that the description seems to be based on a two-dimensional representation in which the besieged city appeared with the enemy forces on either side, as on the silver dish from Amathus (see fig. 2, p. 205, and Markoe 66–7). This also recalls the siege of a city by both sea and land on the north frieze from the West House at Akrotiri, and the well-known silver rhyton fragment from Mycenae (Fittschen, *Schild* 12, Taf. viiia; T. B. L. Webster, *From Mycenae to Homer*, London 1958, 58–9 and pl. 5), on which only the attack on one side of the city, by sea, survives. Nestor told of the siege of Thruoessa by the Epean army and its rescue by a force from Pulos (11.710–60), but that kind of episode does not seem to fit here. στρατός can have the meaning 'band', 'troop', e.g. at 8.472, so the meaning here may be simply 'two forces of ⟨armed⟩ men' or 'two camps', not necessarily two distinct armies. On the Hesiodic *Aspis* (237–70) one of the armies is that of the besieged city (cf.

9.529–30), but that would fit badly here with the ambush which follows. The scholia (AbT) offer divergent interpretations.

510–12 The divided opinion may well be, of course, within *one* attacking force. | τεύχεσι λαμπόμενοι (etc.) is reserved by Homer for Hephaistos-made armour, as at 17.214 when Hektor dons it, and at 20.46 when the Trojans shudder at Akhilleus' appearance in it. δίχα δέ σφισιν ἥνδανε βουλή | is formular (2 × *Od.*). In the same way Hektor, facing Akhilleus alone, wonders whether to offer that the Trojans give back Helen and divide with the Greeks the wealth of Troy (22.111–21), using in part the same words (511–12 ≅ 22.120–1; but 22.121 may be taken from here, see note *ad loc.*).

513 οἱ δέ: i.e. the townspeople. ὑπεθωρήσσοντο (only here in Greek): 'armed themselves secretly'. The ambush is called a δόλος in 526, and in general in the *Il.* is considered a cowardly stratagem (see A. T. Edwards, *Achilles in the Odyssey*, Königstein/Ts. 1985, 18–27).

514–15 The description evokes not only the Teikhoskopia (3.145–244), and Hektor's instructions for the defence of Troy while its army is camped on the plain (8.517–22), but the sufferings of women, children, and the old at the sack of innumerable cities; these are portrayed in Hektor's words to Andromakhe (6.450–65), in her lament over his corpse (24.731–8), and in the prediction of old Priam (22.66–76). Women are shown on the wall of the besieged city on the Mycenaean silver rhyton (see 509n.). Verse 514 ≅ 4.238.

516 οἱ δέ: i.e. the fighting-men of the city. Thus when the Trojans attack ἦρχε δ' ἄρα σφιν Ἄρης καὶ πότνι' Ἐννώ | (5.592). On the shield the presence of the gods must be pictured, not merely mentioned by the poet. The joint action of the deities, so often opposed to each other in the *Il.* (see 17.398–9n.), perhaps reinforces the generalized nature of the depiction.

517–19 The poet describes the artisan's technique, as at 548–9, 562–5, 574, and 577. On the well-known dinos by Sophilos in Athens the spectators are drawn much smaller than the contestants in the chariot-race. ἀμφὶς probably = 'apart', as at 15.709. ὑπολίζονες (519; Leaf's ὑπ' ὀλίζονες is preferable) is for ὑπό, 'beneath ⟨them⟩' and ὀλ(ε)ίζων < *ὀλειγγων, the old comparative form of ὀλίγος, found as a place-name at 2.717 and in inscriptions and later poetry (see LSJ).

520–2 Verse 520 ≅ 23.138. (ϝ)εῖκε is the imperfect of ἔοικα, 'it seemed fitting'. This tense is found only here in Homer. (Willcock, less plausibly, derives it from εἴκω, 'yield', as at 22.321). ἀρδμός (also at *Od.* 13.247) < ἄρδω, 'give water ⟨to cattle⟩'. βοτόν (cf. βόσκω) occurs only here in early epic, but is used in later poetry; this phrase must have been suggested by the frequency of βροτοῖσιν in this position, preceded by δειλοῖσι (3 × *Il.*, 3 × *Od.*) and other adjectives – once by πάντεσσι, as here (*Od.* 13.397). With 522 cf. κεκορυθμένος αἴθοπι χαλκῷ | (9 × *Il.*, 1 × *Od.*). The formular 'bright'

Book Eighteen

bronze is not very suitable for an ambush, and εἰλυμένοι is not used elsewhere in this position, so the poet may be creating a new phrase to describe the craftsman's technique rather than the men's armour.

523–34 The two scouts alert the men in ambush to the approach of the cattle; these are then seized and their herdsmen killed. Then the besieging army hears the bellowing of the cattle, comes to the rescue, and a pitched battle begins. It is possible that the poet has seen juxtaposed pictures of a siege and the capture of cattle, and has interpreted it as the seizing of the *besiegers'* cattle by the *townsmen*, though the reverse would seem a more likely event.

525–6 οἱ δέ: the cattle, though βοῦς (plural) is elsewhere feminine in Homer; by 527 they have become τά. τάχα: 'soon', not 'swiftly'. The second hemistich of 525 recurs at *Od.* 17.214. The happy, syrinx-playing herdsmen are straight out of later pastoral poetry – much unlike Hesiod's countrymen – and the swift pathos of their death is like that of the short 'anecdotes' which follow the death of so many minor characters in this poem. The syrinx is also mentioned at 10.13.

527–9 οἱ μέν: the men in ambush; οἱ δέ (530): the besiegers, owners of the cattle. προϊδόντες, 'seeing from a distance', as at 17.756. With 528–9 cf. βοῦς περιταμνομένους ἠδ᾽ οἰῶν πώεα καλά (2 × *Od.*). The poet has expanded the usual verse with βοῶν ἀγέλας (which occurs in various forms in both poems) and added, in enjambment, the colour-phrase | ἀργεννέων οἰῶν, modified from the older οἰῶν ἀργεννάων | (2 × *Il.*, once separated) and ἀργεννῆς ὀΐεσσιν | (1 × *Il.*, 1 × *Od.*). Zenodotus read πῶυ μέγ᾽ οἰῶν, which is formular (2 × *Il.*, 1 × *Od.*) but loses the importance of the colour here; it must mean he omitted 529. μηλοβοτῆρας occurs only here and *HyHerm* 286.

530–2 οἱ δέ: the besieging army, still debating the question presented at 510–12. εἰράων: apparently 'assemblies'; the word recurs only at Hesiod, *Theogony* 804. It may be connected with the root of εἴρω, 'speak' (Chantraine, *Dict.*) and is glossed by Arn/A as τὰς ἀγοράς. προπάροιθε suggests an audience sitting in a camp meeting-place listening to speakers who stood in front of them. ἵπποι ἀερσίποδες begins a verse 2 × *Il.*; on this kind of formular modification see J. B. Hainsworth, *Flexibility* 105–9, and M. W. Edwards, *TAPA* 97 (1966) 150–2. Of course chariots are meant.

533–4 ≅ *Od.* 9.54–5, which has παρὰ νηυσὶ θοῇσι in place of ποταμοῖο παρ᾽ ὄχθας (which recurs at 4.487). μάχην is best taken both as object with στησάμενοι (cf. φυλόπιδα στήσειν, *Od.* 11.314) and with ἐμάχοντο as cognate accusative. χαλκήρεσιν ἐγχείῃσιν | is formular (2 × *Il.*, 2 × *Od.*); the epithet here may or may not refer to the craftsman's material.

535–8 These verses also appear in the Hesiodic *Aspis* (156–9), with ἐθύνεον for ὁμίλεον in the first line. J. M. Lynn-George, *Hermes* 106 (1978) 396–405, has argued, with much probability, that the lines were composed for the *Aspis* and have been interpolated into the text of the *Il.* Lynn-George's main reasons (based on those of F. Solmsen, *Hermes* 93, 1965, 1–6) are: the lurid content of the lines, which much better suits the *Aspis* than Akhilleus' shield; the lack of parallels in the *Il.* to the activities of Eris, Kudoimos, and Ker, whereas at *Aspis* 248–57 the Keres behave in a similar way (Lynn-George (400) suggests *Aspis* 248–57 may have been the model for *Aspis* 156–9; other such doublets in the *Aspis* are discussed by R. Janko, *CQ* 36, 1986, 39–40); and the congruity of the sentence structure ἐν δ' Ἔρις... ὁμίλεον with the circumstances of the *Aspis*, where a completed shield is described, contrasted with the *Il.*'s depiction of the craftsman's actions in fashioning one (ἐν δ' ἐτίθει... etc.). ἐθύνεον of *Aspis* 156 was changed to ὁμίλεον to match ὡμίλευν (539) in ring form.

Lynn-George is also probably correct in maintaining (against Solmsen) that 539–40 follow smoothly after 534, with the same grammatical subject, and should be retained in the text; the sense (as he says) may be compared with 418, where Hephaistos' robots are ζωῇσι νεήνισιν εἰοικυῖαι. Both he and Solmsen (the latter uneasily) suggest that 608a–d (see 607–8n.) may have been interpolated in a similar way, but less successfully, at the same early period in the transmission.

535 On Eris see 107–10n., and on such personifications generally 4.440–1n. At 5.740–1 (the description of Athene's aegis) the anaphora is more shapely, in four cola of increasing length.

536–7 ἄουτος occurs only here and in the parallel *Aspis* passage, and the form (ἀ- for ἀν-) is unexplained; see Chantraine, *Dict.* s.v. οὐτάω. ἀνούτατος appears at 4.540, and νεούτατος at 13.539. Lynn-George (*op. cit.* 400) points out that this is rather a lot for a single Ker to handle, and that her grip on an unwounded man is strange. He suggests a 'somewhat jumbled reworking' of *Aspis* 248ff.

538–40 Elsewhere the form is always δαφοινός. The word-order | νεκρούς... τεθνηῶτας | recurs at 6.71. Ø. Andersen, *SO* 51 (1976) 11, following Marg, *Dichtung*, sees in the rescue of corpses an allusion to the struggle for Patroklos' body.

541–72 The farmer's year

The third band of decoration includes three scenes depicting the seasonal work of the farmer's year: ploughing, reaping, and the vintage. Each is introduced by ἐν δ' ἐτίθει (541, 550, 561). In all three scenes the pleasurable rewards of labour are emphasized – the refreshing cup of wine; the feast; the song and dance at the vintage. The pasture-land scene should perhaps be grouped here too (see 550n., 573–89n.).

541–9 'Lines 541–47 describe not a depiction of a field, but the plowing of a field, which includes movement and the desires of the depicted figures; the audience is thereby encouraged not to imagine the surface appearance of an image (the visual medium) but to imagine the world depicted therein... Lines 548–49 then call us back to the (visual *and* verbal) context of the scene' (A. S. Becker, *AJP* 111, 1990, 143).

541–2 πίειραν ἄρουραν is formular (1 × *Il.*, 2 × *Od.*); on the meaning and history of ἄρουρα see W. Richter, *Arch. Hom.* H 93–4 and Hoekstra, *Odyssey* on *Od.* 13.354. | νειῷ ἐνὶ τριπόλῳ is found at *Od.* 5.127 and Hesiod, *Theogony* 971. τρίπολον: 'thrice-ploughed' (cf. πολέω, 'plough', in Hesiod, *Erga* 462). Repeated ploughing not only kills weeds but by aerating the topsoil reduces the loss of moisture left by the winter rains; see H. Forbes, *Expedition* 19 (1976) 5–11, M. Jameson, *CJ* 73 (1977–8) 127, and P. Walcot, *Greek Peasants, Ancient and Modern* (Manchester 1970) 38–9. It is recommended in Hesiod (*Erga* 462–3), and is often referred to in later authors (see West's note *ad loc.*). There must be some association between τρίπολος and the name of the agricultural cult-hero Triptolemos, which appears as early as *HyDem* 153 and 474, and this suggests some possible ritual significance in three ploughings. E. A. Armstrong, *CR* 57 (1943) 3–5, suggested the translation 'triple-furrowed', an allusion to three ritual furrows ploughed by a king or priest, but there is no supporting evidence for this from Greece, though sacred ploughing rituals are known in Attica (Plutarch, *Mor.* 144a–b; see M. Jameson, *TAPA* 82, 1951, 49–61). For further discussion and references see W. Richter, *Arch. Hom.* H 101, and more recently West, *Works and Days* 274, *Theogony* 423, and Hainsworth, *Odyssey* on *Od.* 5.127.

543 ζεύγεα δινεύοντες: 'turning the yokes ⟨of oxen at the headland⟩'; the idea is elaborated in the next four verses. ἐλαστρέω is a form of ἐλαύνω, appearing in Theognis and occasionally later. The number of words describing motion, especially 'turning', in this passage is very noticeable. There is a similarly vivid description of ploughing at 13.703–7 (see note *ad loc.*).

544–7 τέλσον, 'turning-point', 'headland', comes from the root **qel*, 'turn', as does (τρί)πολον (542) too. (μελι)ηδέος οἴνου | occurs here, 2 × *Od.* and *HyDem* 206; it is declined (with digamma ignored) from μελιηδέα (ϝ)οῖνον |. τοὶ δέ (546): the refreshed ploughmen. ὄγμους here = 'furrows', as at *HyDem* 455. ὄγμος means a row or strip (perhaps from ἄγω or a postulated **ὄκμος*, 'furrow'; see Chantraine, *Dict.*), and is used of the swath cut by the reapers at 552 and 557 (and 11.68). See W. Richter, *Arch. Hom.* H 119–20.

The sudden insight into the labourers' minds (547) is noteworthy. Drinks would be frequent, but the wine would have been mixed with water, as usual (W. Richter, *Arch. Hom.* H 127).

548–9 The subject is ἡ ⟨νειός⟩ (from 541 and 547), but μελαίνετο refers both to the ploughed earth and to the representation of it on the shield; ὄπισθεν again refers to both the ploughing and the depiction of it. 'The physical similarity between depiction and depicted scenes serves to enhance the audience's respect for the ability of the visual image to reproduce significant aspects of the world. The result is an appreciation of Hephaestus' art' (A. S. Becker, *AJP* 111, 1990, 144). Then ἐῴκει returns us to the visual medium, and the narrator comments in his own voice: τὸ δὴ περὶ θαῦμα τέτυκτο (549). The poet must be thinking of the application of niello over a gold underlay, as at 562. περί is intensive, not local. θαῦμα: as Hephaistos promised at 466–7.

550–60 A similar reaping scene is described more briefly in a simile at 11.67–9, where again the rich (μάκαρ) holder of the arable land is mentioned.

550–1 Three post-Aristarchean papyri and some older MSS read βασιλήϊον, which is clearly correct (cf. 556); others βαθυλήϊον, perhaps under the influence of βαθὺ λήϊον in the similar description in Hesiod, *Aspis* 288 (and 11.560). Both readings were known to Did/AT. After 551 some texts added καρπὸν Ἐλευσινίης Δημήτερος ἀγλαοδώρου (T on 18.483), perhaps interpolated to give ἧμων an object. Agallis of Corcyra, a contemporary of Aristophanes of Byzantium, used the verse to support her view that the two cities on the shield were Eleusis and Attica.

On the τέμενος or royal estate, see 14.122–5n., Hainsworth, *Odyssey* on *Od.* 6.293, H. van Effenterre, *REG* 80 (1967) 17–26, J. Manessy-Guitton, *IF* 71 (1966) 14–38, and L. R. Palmer, *Mycenaeans and Minoans*[2] (London 1965) 100–4. The regular formular description appears at 6.194–5, καὶ μέν οἱ Λύκιοι τέμενος τάμον ἔξοχον ἄλλων | καλὸν φυταλιῆς καὶ ἀρούρης (≅ 20.184–5, cf. 12.313–14, which ends... πυροφόροιο). The *temenos* offered to Meleagros is half arable, half vineyard (9.578–80). At 14.122–4 grazing-land for cattle is added, and this is also implied at 12.319. These parallels suggest that the vineyard (561–72) and perhaps the pasture-land too (573–89) also belong to the βασιλεύς of 556.

The ἔριθος in Hesiod, *Erga* 602–3 (see West *ad loc.*), is a hired woman servant; Athene offers to be Nausikaa's συνέριθος with her laundry duties (*Od.* 6.32). The etymology is unknown. Later the meaning becomes 'wool-workers', perhaps from an assumed connexion with ἔριον. Here they are hired farm-hands; speaking of classical Attica, M. Jameson says 'The harvester is the typical hired man (Demosthenes 53.21, and woman, 57.45)' (*CJ* 73, 1977–8, 131). The distinction (if any) between them and θῆτες is not clear. See also W. Richter, *Arch. Hom.* H 17–19. On the form of the δρεπάνη see W. Schiering, *Arch. Hom.* H 154–8.

552–6 A δράγμα is literally a handful (< δράσσομαι); the cornstalks are grasped with the left hand and cut with the δρεπάνη in the right.

ἄλλα... ἄλλα: some of the handfuls are shown still lying μετ' ὄγμον, 'along the swath' (see 546–7n.), others are being gathered into sheaves. On ἐπήτριμα see 208–14n. ἐλλεδανοῖσι must mean 'sheaf-bindings', perhaps from *ἐλλέω (εἰλέω), 'turn' (Chantraine, *Dict.* s.v.) + the suffix -εδανός (Risch, *Wortbildung* 106). The 'handfuls' are gathered and bound into sheaves by the ἀμαλλοδετῆρες; then the children grab the sheaves (δραγμεύοντες), carry them off in their arms, and place them in stooks. πάρεχον: 'were at hand', as at 23.835.

556–7 The βασιλεύς must be the local landowner, the hereditary chief of the community, perhaps like the twelve noblemen who share power with Alkinoös of Phaeacia (*Od.* 8.390–1); in Linear B the *qa-si-re-we* seem to have been provincial officials (Ventris and Chadwick, *Documents* 121). See most recently P. Carlier, *La Royauté en Grèce avant Alexandre* (Strasbourg 1984) 136–230; I. M. Morris, *CA* 5 (1986) 98–9 and references there; and J. B. Hainsworth, *Odyssey* on *Od.* 7.49 and Introduction to *Od.* 8. On his staff see 2.109n. and R. Mondi, *Arethusa* 13 (1980) 206–12.

560 The second hemistich is a lengthened form of the formula ἐπὶ δ' ἄλφιτα λευκὰ πάλυνον | (1 × *Il.*, 3 × *Od.*). The wording has been interpreted to mean either that the barley is sprinkled over the meat – as over Eumaios' roast pork (*Od.* 14.77, 429) – for a general feast, or that the heralds are preparing the roast meat for the king and the women are making a kind of porridge for the workmen – though elsewhere the formula is used for *sprinkling* barley into wine, not boiling it in water (11.640, *Od.* 10.520 = 11.28). For this reason I find (with Leaf) the first interpretation more probable (taking ἀπάνευθεν as 'apart from the reaping', not 'apart from the women'); Willcock (*ad loc.*) and G. S. Kirk (*Homer and the Oral Tradition*, Cambridge 1976, 12) prefer the second. In either case, δεῖπνον must be in apposition to the sentence, 'as a meal'. ἐρίθοισιν: see 550–1n.

561–72 An ἀλωή is an orchard or vineyard, often marked off by a ἕρκος (564, 5.90); see W. Richter, *Arch. Hom.* H 97–8. Again the poet emphasizes the craftsman's skill and the happiness of the workers, and the song and dance anticipate the later dance-scene (590–605). The whole description is idyllic.

562–3 The visual impact of χρυσείην leads into the contrasting μέλανες δ'...; cf. 548–9. ἀλωή is understood as subject of ἑστήκει. Hesiod, *Aspis* 299, has ἀργυρέῃσι κάμαξι |, which may have been formular; κάμαξ is later used for any kind of pole or shaft. διαμπερές (< περάω, 'pass through'): 'through the whole vineyard-picture'; cf. 20.362, *Od.* 14.11.

564–6 The κάπετος (cf. Chantraine, *Dict.* s.v. σκάπτω) is a ditch, for irrigation (cf. 21.257–62; *Od.* 7.129–30), drainage, or both; see W. Richter, *Arch. Hom.* H 105–7. It is inside the ἕρκος, which protects it, marks the boundary, and keeps out wild and domestic animals. ἀταρπιτός: the form ἀταρπός appears at 17.743 and *Od.* 14.1. Both in Homer and later, τρυγάω, 'gather in', is used (like the English 'harvest') with an accusative of the crop (*Od.* 7.124) or of the place from which it is taken (as here, and Hesiod, *Aspis* 292).

567–8 Cf. ἠΐθεοι καὶ παρθένοι ἀλφεσίβοιαι | (593), παρθένος ἠΐθεός τε (22.127, 22.128), νύμφαι τ᾽ ἠΐθεοί τε (*Od.* 11.38). παρθενική appears as a longer alternative for παρθένος at *Od.* 11.39, Hesiod, *Erga* 699, and in later poetry. Uses such as παρθενικῇ ἐϊκυῖα νεήνιδι (*Od.* 7.20) perhaps made its adoption easy. ἀταλὰ φρονέοντες (etc). is formular (Hesiod, *Theogony* 989, *HyDem* 24); the shorter form ἀταλάφρονα occurs at 6.400. On the much-disputed derivation of ἀταλός (perhaps = 'tender') see C. Moussy, *Mélanges ... offerts à P. Chantraine* (Paris 1972) 157–68, who renders it here as 'qui ont la simplicité naïve de l'enfance'. Both halves of 568 recur 1 × *Od.*

569–70 On the φόρμιγξ see M. Wegner, *Arch. Hom.* U 2–18. λίνον: 'the Linos-song'. ὑπό: 'to the accompaniment of', as in *HyHerm* 502. καλόν is probably adverbial, like ἱμερόεν. The notion of Zenodotus (Arn/A) and others that λίνος here means the string of the cithara (subject of ἄειδε), though accepted by van der Valk, *Researches* I 153–4, seems on a par with Philochorus' tale (schol. T) that Linos was killed by Apollo because he substituted sheep-gut strings for λίνος, 'thread spun from flax' (or vice versa). Sheep-gut is said to be used for phorminx-strings at *Od.* 21.406–8. Aristarchus (AbT) correctly saw the parallel with παιάν, the song in honour of Apollo Paian.

On Linos see M. L. West, *The Orphic Poems* (Oxford 1983) 56–67 (with fragments and testimonia). Hesiod said that Linos was the son of Ouranie, ὃν δή, ὅσσοι βροτοί εἰσιν ἀοιδοὶ καὶ καθαρισταί, | πάντες μὲν θρηνεῦσιν ἐν εἰλαπίναις τε χοροῖς τε (fr. 305.2–3 MW). T quote an inscription in Thebes: ὦ Λίνε πᾶσι θεοῖσι τετιμένε, σοὶ γὰρ ἔδωκαν | ἀθάνατοι πρώτῳ μέλος ἀνθρώποισιν ἀεῖσαι | ἐν ποδὶ δεξιτερῷ. Μοῦσαι δέ σε θρήνεον αὐταὶ | μυρόμεναι μολπῇσιν, ἐπεὶ λίπες ἠλίου αὐγάς (= Page, *PMG* fr. 880, in drastically altered form). Pausanias (9.29.3, quoting 569–70) gives a fuller version, that Linos was murdered by Apollo for rivalling him in singing and is universally mourned, even by the Egyptians; Herodotus (2.79) repeats the Egyptian connexion, and gives a more likely one with the Phoenicians. The scholia and Eustathius (1163.53–1164.27) give further information.

Linos and the Linos-song probably developed from the cry αἴλινον; cf. Pindar fr. 128c.6 (Snell) Λίνον αἴλινον ὑμνεῖ; Aeschylus, *Ag.* 121 etc.; and Sophocles, *Ajax* 627. The cry is probably of oriental origin (Chantraine, *Dict.* s.v. λίνος); see E. Diehl, *RhM* 89 (1940) 81–114. The song is always referred to as a dirge, and it seems odd to sing it here on what is obviously a cheerful occasion. If Linos was actually a dying vegetation god, perhaps the song was proper to the autumn.

571–2 λεπταλέος (< λεπτός, 'thin', 'delicate') occurs rarely in later poetry. The meaning here is not obvious, but presumably complimentary; perhaps 'high'? ῥήσσοντες is not from ῥήγνυμι but from ῥήσσω (Attic ῥάττω), 'strike'; cf. *HyAp* 516 οἱ δὲ ῥήσσοντες ἕποντο and Ap. Rh. 1.539 πέδον ῥήσσωσι πόδεσσιν. ἁμαρτῆ: 'together' (< ἅμα), as at 5.656. On ἰυγμῷ see 17.63–7n. σκαίρω is used at *Od.* 10.412 of calves frisking around their mothers.

573–89 *Cattle and sheep herding*

The cattle and sheep are probably thought of as the property of the king (see 550–1n.), but reconstructions of the shield's design generally allot these two scenes a band of their own (van Leeuwen), or place them on a band together with the following dance-scene (Willcock). The change in the introductory verb (ποίησε, 573 and 587) suggests these two scenes should be separate from those which precede and follow. The season of the year is not emphasized (transhumance is not likely in the Mediterranean area at this period, according to P. Halstead, *JHS* 107, 1987, 79–81), though T (on 587–8) remark that sheep are driven to pasture only in the spring and O. Taplin, *G&R* 27 (1980) 7–9, holds that these scenes continue the farmer's year and portray winter. On depictions of cattle and sheep in early art see W. Richter, *Arch. Hom.* H 52–3, 59, and Markoe, *Bowls* 54–6.

573–6 On ὀρθοκραιράων see 3–4n. The scholia (bT) point out that the two metals provide different colours for the animals' hides; cattle in Homer are termed ἀργός (23.30), παμμέλας (*Od.* 3.6), οἶνοψ (13.703 ≅ *Od.* 13.32), and αἴθων (16.488, *Od.* 18.372). The onomatopoeic root μῦκ- appears in a number of forms in Homer and later Greek; cf. μεμυκώς (< μυκάομαι) at 580. μυκηθμός recurs at *Od.* 12.265. The use is extended to cover the groaning of gate-hinges (5.749 = 8.393, 12.460) and the clang of a shield struck by a spear (20.260). κόπρος can mean both 'dung' and 'stall', 'farmyard' as here and at *Od.* 10.411. The mention of the sound-effects accompanying the picture is remarkable, anticipating 580 and Keats' 'heifer lowing at the skies' (*Ode on a Grecian Urn*).

S. E. Bassett, *The Poetry of Homer* (Berkeley 1938) 156–7, claims 576 as the most beautiful verse in Homer, pointing to the way in which the second hemistich *almost* repeats the pattern of the first, the asyndeton stressing the parallels; different senses are appealed to by 'murmuring' stream and 'waving' reeds. W. B. Stanford, *The Odyssey of Homer* (London 1965) I xxii, also comments on the sound; besides its rippling dactyls the verse has nine short α's, alternating with short ο's, much alliteration (especially of -ον), anaphora at the mid-verse caesura, and a chiastic arrangement of noun–participle–adjective–noun, in which the first and third and second and fourth words match in metrical shape. On patterns of sounds in Homer see Introduction, ch. 4, v, 1.

The scholia, though often conscious of sound-effects (Richardson, *CQ* 30, 1980, 283–7), are here preoccupied with spelling. MSS give ῥοδανόν, which probably means 'waving' (cf. ῥοδάνη, 'spun thread', 'woof'), but Zenodotus read ῥαδαλόν (after διά) and Aristophanes and Aristarchus perhaps ῥαδανόν (Did/A; the text is corrupt); see Erbse and van der Valk, *Researches* II 44–6. The variation in root vowel is unexplained (Chantraine, *Dict.* s.v. ῥαδινός; the variation -ινός/-ανός is common enough). δονακεύς, 'reed-thicket', occurs only here and in Oppian, but words from the root are common.

578 The second hemistich is a lengthened form of κύνες ἀργοὶ ἕποντο | (3 × *Od.*, cf. 18.283).

579–86 The capture of the best cow in a pasturing herd by a lion, its consuming of the blood and entrails, and the powerless uproar of the herdsmen and dogs, are all described in a simile at 17.61–7. Besides the verbal parallels, which are natural in descriptions of a similar action, the shared content and sequence of ideas closely link simile and shield-scene. Cf. also 15.630–6, 18.161–2, and, on lions in Greece, Introduction, ch. 3, iii. Zenodotus' reading κυανέω δὲ λέοντε (Did/AT) reveals his imaginative critical methods; he obviously sought a colour-contrast with χρύσειοι (577), and one wonders if he could possibly have understood the dogs to be '*white-footed*'.

579–80 ἐν πρώτῃσι probably refers to position, the lions attacking one of the foremost animals, likely to be a prime bull. But βοῦν... ἥ τις ἀρίστη in the parallel description (17.62) suggests that the alternative 'among the best of the cattle' (cf. 15.643) should not be ruled out. ἐρύγμηλος occurs only here; it comes from the root of ἐρεύγομαι, 'bellow', cf. the Latin *rugio*. The sound of the word is important here, anticipating μεμυκώς.

581 Some late MSS have τώ for τόν; Zenodotus (Did/A) read τούς. Amid the rapidly changing subjects in these lines τόν is easiest for the audience to follow; τώ would give better sense, but τώ again in the next verse would then be weak.

582–6 There is a steady progression of time during these scenes, as in a simile. First the oxen leave the farmyard (575), then reach the riverside pastures (576); then the lions seize one of the foremost bulls (579–80), and now they are eating its carcase as the herdsmen try in vain to get the yapping dogs to attack. Bulls and lions are common on Phoenician bowls; see Markoe, *Bowls* 38–41.

583–4 Cf. αἷμα καὶ ἔγκατα πάντα λαφύσσει | (11.176 = 17.64). λαφύσσετον is imperfect; in historic tenses the ending should be -έτην, but -ετον is also found for metrical convenience at 10.361, 10.364 and perhaps 13.346 (see note *ad loc.*). αὔτως: 'in vain'. ἐνδίεσαν (only here) is imperfect active of δίεμαι, 'pursue', with prefixed ἐν-, 'towards', 'against', as in ἐντρέπω, ἐνορούω; i.e. they were sicking the dogs on.

585–6 ἀπετρωπῶντο is for an earlier -τροπάοντο; the alternatives -ο-, -ω- in the root occur in a number of -αω verbs, e.g. ποτῶνται (2.462), πωτῶντο (12.287); see Chantraine, *GH* 1 358. On 586 T comment γραφικῶς ἔδειξε τὸ πᾶν.

587–9 The description of the meadow for sheep-herding is much shorter than the other scenes and has no movement or human participants. Its presence is best defended by Marg, who draws attention to its peacefulness, intervening between the excitement of the lions' attack and the swift action of the dance; 'In der Knappheit so etwas wie ein Verlieren in der Landschaft, daher nichts Näheres mehr, kein Mensch zu erkennen, nur dies Andeuten der weissen Schäflein auf den Hängen (588). Ein Zwischenstück, eine Pause vor dem vollen Schluss' (*Dichtung* 27).

μέγας (-αν) is often used in this position to extend a preceding or following formula; the construction is paralleled by 6.194–5 (≅ 20.184–5) τέμενος... | καλὸν φυταλιῆς καὶ ἀρούρης. On σταθμούς see 5.140n.

590–606 *The dance*

The penultimate band depicts young men and women dancing amid spectators. Two kinds of dance movement are described, a round dance and one with rows of dancers facing each other. The dance is led by leaping solo dancers. The happy scene forms a fitting conclusion to the pleasant picture of human social life which the shield presents.

Representations of dances of men and women together, accompanied by a lyre-player, are discussed by M. Wegner, *Arch. Hom.* u 60–5 (with plates); see also Fittschen, *Schild* Taf. xa and b and Abb. 6.

590–2 χορός is best taken as 'a place for dancing', as at *Od.* 8.260, 8.264, 12.4, 12.318, rather than 'dance', as Schadewaldt, *VHWW* 484 n. 1, and others understand it. Marg, *Dichtung* 42 n. 50, gives good reasons for adopting the view taken here, including the parallel with νομόν at 587 and the use of ἔνθα at 593. The verb ποικίλλω occurs only here in ancient epic, but is common later. Possibly the word hints that this picture is more in the nature of a decorative frieze, like the rows of identical figures on Geometric vases, than a real-life episode like the others on the shield. εὐρείη (-αν, -ης) is used at the verse-end after ἐνὶ Τροίη (2 × *Il.*, 3 × *Od.*), ἐνὶ Σπάρτη (1 × *Od.*), ἐν Κρήτη (2 × *Od.*, including 1 × in the genitive), ἐν Λυκίη (1 × *Il.*), and ἀμφ' Ἑλίκην (1 × *Il.*). There may also be a formula Κρητάων... εὐρειάων | (*Od.* 14.199 ≅ 16.62). ἀσκέω is used of any kind of handiwork.

The simile compares the scene of daily life to the heroic past, an appealing reversal of the normal illustration of a heroic action by a familiar action of ordinary experience. The ancient scholars, however, argued much over whether it was ἀπρεπές to have Hephaistos imitating the work of a mortal (AbT). On Crete generally see 2.646–8n.; Cretans were famous dancers, and Aineias hurls a jibe at Meriones the Cretan about this (16.617, see note *ad loc.*). On Daidalos, a 'speaking name' from δαιδάλλω (< *δαλ-δαλ-*yω*, from the root *del- which appears in Latin *dolare*, 'hew'; von Kamptz, *Personennamen* 109), see most recently F. Frontisi-Ducroux, *Dédale* (Paris 1975). Ariadne's name is a divine title, 'most holy', from ἀρι-(intensive) + ἀδνός, Cretan for ἁγνός (but see *LfgrE*; Zenodotus [Did/AT] read Ἀριήδη, an unexplained form found also in Callimachus fr. 67.13; see Pfeiffer *ad loc.*). The conception of Daidalos' making a dancing-floor in Knossos for Ariadne, followed immediately by the description of a dance of young men and women, must be associated with the familiar tale of the Minotaur, the labyrinth, and the yearly tribute of young men and maidens (on which see H. Herter, *Gnomon* 16, 1940, 410–16; on the γέρανος-dance on Delos, A. Yoshida, *RBPh* 42, 1964, 9–10 and references there). Tablets from Knossos mention a Daidaleion and a Mistress of the Labyrinth (W. Burkert, *Greek Religion*, tr. J. Raffan, Cambridge, Mass. 1985, 23 and references there; on dancing and processions on Crete, 34), and three circular platforms dating from soon after 1400 have been identified as dancing-floors (P. Warren, *BSA* 79, 1984, 307–24). Theseus' abduction of Ariadne and her death on the island of Diē is related at *Od.* 11.321–5.

593–4 Dancers in Greece still hold each others' wrists, and a line of dancers is led by a person who does his own figures, in a semi-acrobatic way. ἀλφεσίβοιαι is derived from the root appearing in ἀλφάνω, 'yield', 'fetch' and -βοια < βοῦς (cf. Εὔβοια, Περίβοια, etc.; Risch, *Wortbildung* 138; W. J. Verdenius, *Hermeneus* 29, 1957, 4–7). The word occurs only here and in a similar phrase at *HyAphr* 119; it must be an old formula for 'maidens worth many cattle'. M. I. Finley, *Economy and Society in Ancient Greece* (Harmondsworth 1981) 293 n. 41, considers it the antonym of πολύδωρος; A. M. Snodgrass, *JHS* 94 (1974) 115 n. 116, lists 13 Homeric references to gifts given by the suitor to the bride's kin. On the vexed question of bridewealth and dowry in Homer see most recently I. M. Morris, *CA* 5 (1986) 105–15; Finley, *op. cit.* 233–45; Snodgrass, *op. cit.* 115–18. Verse 594 ≅ *HyAp* 196.

595–6 Helen leaves to go up to the wall ἀργεννῆσι καλυψαμένη ὀθόνῃσιν (3.141), presumably donning some kind of outer wrap or shawl. The χιτών is the normal wear of men. On the use of olive oil to give clothing a gloss (cf. the epithets σιγαλόεις, λιπαρός), a sweet scent, and perhaps softness see 14.172n. and S. Marinatos, *Arch. Hom.* A 4–6. Plutarch says that the use of olive oil gives long-lasting brightness to white cloth (*Alex.* 36). The grammatical structure of 595–6 and 597–8 matches almost word for word.

597–8 Both women holding garlands and men wearing daggers are common on Geometric vases; see Fittschen, *Schild* 16 and Taf. xa, b. This couplet was omitted by Aristophanes and athetized by Aristarchus (Arn/A) on the grounds that in Homer μάχαιρα cannot mean 'sword' (cf. 19.252–3, and 13.609–10n.) and that knives or daggers (its usual meaning) are not proper for a dance. Neither argument is compelling (*pace* Bolling, *External Evidence* 183). Apthorp, *Manuscript Evidence* 118 n. 139, suggests a copyist's omission before the time of Aristarchus, because of the similarity of 595 and 597 and the homoearchon in 596 and 598. Leaf adduces a reference in Lucian, *On Dancing* 12–13, to a chain-dance (ὅρμος) of young men and women, ὁ ἔφηβος τὰ νεανικὰ ὀρχούμενος καὶ ὅσοις ὕστερον ἐν πολέμῳ χρήσεται. There is evidence for certain dances as part of military training in Greece (see E. L. Wheeler, *GRBS* 23, 1982, 223–33), but here both men and women are dancing and nothing more than brilliance of costume need be intended. The gold and silver remind us again of the craftsman's technique.

599–602 ὁτὲ μέν... ἄλλοτε (δέ), 'at one time... at another time' is found again at 11.64–5 and 20.49–50. The shift in time, like that appearing in many of the other scenes, intensifies the ideas of movement and vividness. ἐπιστάμενος (etc.) elsewhere always qualifies a person, but the extension of usage is natural enough. On the spelling of ῥεῖα (ῥῆα in the Berlin papyrus) see 17.461–2n. ἄρμενον ἐν παλάμῃσιν | recurs at *Od.* 5.234. πειρήσεται is the generalizing aorist subjunctive common in similes (Chantraine, *GH* II 253).

The simile beautifully illustrates the speed and ease of the circling dancers. One wonders if the potter and his wheel came to the poet's mind because of the vases on which such friezes of dancers occur.

603 On the form πολλός see 13.802–5n.

604–6 Allen prints the text as it appears in the MSS and papyri. According to Athenaeus (180c–d), Aristarchus (or his school) added *Od.* 4.15–19 to the description of the wedding in Menelaos' palace, the last three verses running | τερπόμενος· μετὰ δέ σφιν ἐμέλπετο θεῖος ἀοιδός | φορμίζων· δοιὼ δέ... | ...κατὰ μέσσους. Later (181d) Athenaeus quotes 604–6 as they appear in our MSS, without μετὰ... φορμίζων, claiming that Aristarchus cut them from the *Il.* text. Wolf restored them (see his *Prolegomena* ch. XLIX n. 49). The verse τερπόμενος... ἀοιδός | recurs at *Od.* 13.27, enjambing with | Δημόδοκος in the next verse.

It is likely that the additional sentence was added to provide the dancers with music; there are traces of a similar effort at 606a (see below), which must have been added as an alternative. In an excellent recent discussion of the evidence and of previous opinions, Apthorp, *Manuscript Evidence* 160–5, opposes the view of van der Valk, *Researches* II 223–4, 527–30, and

Pasquali, *Storia* 232–3, that Aristarchus excised the sentence on the basis of internal evidence (i.e. the use of μέλπομαι to mean 'sing' instead of 'play') without MS support. The omission of an instrumental accompaniment to the dancing remains odd (*pace* Apthorp 164), especially since both the wedding and vintaging scenes concluded with phorminx-players (494–5, 569–70). Possibly the vulgate *Il.* and *Od.* versions represent shorter and longer variants of a standard dance-description, though elsewhere such variants differ by complete lines rather than by the four enjambing cola in question here. (Two of the obvious doublets in the Hesiodic *Aspis*, however, begin and end at the mid-verse caesura: 201–3, 209–11.) Schadewaldt, however, retains the sentence, suggesting that the singer may represent Homer himself (*VHWW* 367); Reinhardt, *IuD* 402, and Marg. *Dichtung* 30, take a similar view.

605–6 κυβιστητῆρε are leaping solo dancers, *Springtänzer*, like the two Phaeacians who show off their skill leaping to catch a ball and dance together with rapid exchanges of position (ταρφέ' ἀμειβομένω, *Od.* 8.370–80). Such dancers are figured on Geometric vases (M. Wegner, *Arch. Hom.* υ 65–8 and plates iiia, via, b, d). The word is also used of a diver plunging down for sea-squirts (16.745, 16.749, 16.750) and of fish jumping above the surface (21.354). κατ' αὐτούς: 'through them', 'among them', further defined in κατὰ μέσσους in the next verse; Athenaeus' (180e) κατὰ σφᾶς αὐτούς, i.e. 'by themselves', is incorrect.

606 The MSS ἐξάρχοντες (or -ε, with an unnecessary hiatus) is indubitably correct. It makes much better sense than Athenaeus' -ος (180d–e, 181d; with τοῦ ἀοιδοῦ understood), and a genitive absolute without the noun expressed is rare in Homer (only occurring at 11.458). See van der Valk, *Researches* ii 530. A proto-Attic amphora shows a row of women in long dresses led by an apparently naked male figure clapping his hands (M. Wegner, *Arch. Hom.* υ 52, no. 62; *BSA* 35, 1934–5, 176–7 and pl. 43). δινεύω (-έω) means 'turn', 'spin around', like the dancers in the marriage-procession (494); cf. also 543. There is no warrant for thinking they are somersaulting tumblers or acrobats (*pace* F. Chamoux, *L'Information Littéraire* 1, 1949, 69–71). See M. Wegner, *Arch. Hom.* υ 43.

After 606 the Berlin papyrus adds ἐν δ' ἔσ[σαν σύ]ριγγε[ς, ἔσα]ν κίθαρίς τ[ε] καὶ [αὐλοί]. The idea is like 494–5 and *Aspis* 278–80, but the phrasing does not recur.

607–8 The river of Ocean

Okeanos, ὅς περ γένεσις πάντεσσι τέτυκται (14.246), surrounds the pictures on the shield as he surrounds the flat disc of the earth on which men and women work out their lives.

607–8 It is not clear how this band is related to the 'triple rim' of 479–80; perhaps the poet thinks of it as sandwiched between two decorative bands. Okeanos is grouped with the rivers at 20.7, though he does *not* attend the extraordinary gods' assembly as they do; on his etymology and place in cosmogonies see 14.200–7n. It may be that Homer thinks of him represented here in the form of a snake encircling the shield, like the snake running round the edge of the silver dish from Praeneste (fig. 3, p. 206; see 14.244–8n., and R. B. Onians, *The Origins of European Thought*, Cambridge 1951, 315–17). In the *Aspis*, however, the depiction of Ocean included swimming swans and fish (314–17). The formula μέγα σθένος 'Ωκεανοῖο recurs at 21.195, preceded by the impressive βαθυρρείταο (see note *ad loc.*). With 608 cf. | ἄντυξ ἣ πυμάτη θέεν ἀσπίδος ὀμφαλοέσσης (6.118) and | ἄντυγ' ὑπὸ πρώτην (20.275).

After 608 the Berlin papyrus adds four extra verses, printed in Allen's apparatus and edited by S. West, *The Ptolemaic Papyri of Homer* (*Pap. Col.* III, Cologne 1967) 135–6. Verse 608a is adapted from *Aspis* 207–8; 608b runs together the first hemistich of *Aspis* 209 and the second of *Aspis* 211 (the text of the *Aspis* includes a doublet here); 608c = *Aspis* 212 (with a variant replacing a corrupt word in the *Aspis* MSS); 608d = *Aspis* 213 (with a minor error). Further additional verses continued in the next column. This is obviously another example of the interpolation of verses from the *Aspis* into the *Il.*, which was seen at 535–8 (see note *ad loc.*); it must have occurred before the doublet entered *Aspis* 209–11, i.e. early. One feels that the harbour-scene and fisherman of the *Aspis* would be out of place on the shield-rim, but the dolphins might be a fitting decoration for the stream of Ocean.

609–17 Hephaistos makes the rest of the armour and gives it to Thetis; she bears it down from Olumpos

609–13 The making of the corslet, helmet, and greaves is described as rapidly as possible, with little elaboration and simple repetitions of τεῦξε... The magnificence of the shield-description could only be diminished by further ornamentation here. The ancient scholars (T on 460) wondered why no sword is mentioned, and suggested that Nereus had received one from Hephaistos and passed it on through Thetis to Akhilleus. There was also a story that Hephaistos had made a sword for Peleus (Hesiod fr. 209.2–3 MW; see J. R. March, *The Creative Poet*, London 1987, 5–6). Patroklos had picked up a bronze sword, in the usual formular couplet (16.135–6, 3× *Il.*), as does Akhilleus himself when he goes to battle (19.372–3). Ph. J. Kakridis, *Hermes* 89 (1961) 297, thinks that Patroklos must have taken Akhilleus' sword, but that Homer overlooked this because of the formular verses employed in both arming-scenes. In Greek heroic tales a sword does not have the mystique it has in Teutonic and Celtic mythology, perhaps because of the importance of the spear, as in the case of Peleus (16.140–4) and ἐϋμμελίω Πριάμοιο (4 × *Il.*).

610 φαεινότερον πυρὸς αὐγῆς | is used of the goddess's robe at *HyAphr* 86. The comparison is amplified when Hektor gazes in terror at Akhilleus: ἀμφὶ δὲ χαλκὸς ἐλάμπετο εἴκελος αὐγῇ | ἢ πυρὸς αἰθομένου ἢ ἠελίου ἀνιόντος (22.134–5).

611–12 A shorter form of 611, without βριαρήν, appears at 13.188, and a variation at *Od.* 18.378. With the phrasing of 612 cf. (φόρμιγγι) | καλῇ δαιδαλέη, ἐπὶ δ᾽ ἀργύρεον ζυγὸν ἦεν | (9.187), (θρόνου) | καλοῦ δαιδαλέου· ὑπὸ δὲ θρῆνυς ποσὶν ἦεν | (18.390 and 3 × *Od.*) and 16.222, 19.380, and 22.314.

613 '[T]he choice of "soft tin" is proof that the poet did not conceive of effective bronze greaves' says D. H. F. Gray, *JHS* 74 (1954) 9; but the epithet is too obviously ornamental to carry such a weight. The greaves are of tin to differentiate them from the normal equipment, which must be understood to be of bronze (though only once said to be so: 7.41).

614–17 The scholia (A) perceptively point out that the poet very properly does not prattle about (καλῶς τὸ μὴ λαλεῖν) praise of Hephaistos, Thetis' thanks, or her gathering up of the armour; σπεύδει γὰρ πρὸς τὸν υἱόν. When vase-painters depict the scene they usually provide Nereids to help the goddess with her load (cf. my article in *CA* 9.2, 1990, 311–25), but the poet need not concern himself about how she can gracefully handle her burden. μητρὸς ᾽Αχιλλῆος (615) occurs only here; it is significant, not just a periphrasis.

ἴρης ὥς (616) is amplified at 13.62–5 (see note *ad loc.*); obviously speed, not disguise, is the point here. The gods always move quickly, and Thetis similarly hastens to join her beloved son at 24.121. ἴρηκι ἐοικώς | occurs 2 × *Il.*, once for Apollo and once for Patroklos. Verse 617 is a variant of 137. The type-scene of Thetis' journey continues at 19.3.

BOOK NINETEEN

At the beginning of the Book the new armour is delivered to Akhilleus; it is dawn, and the grieving and furious hero might naturally set off immediately to take vengeance on Hektor. But the plot of the poem and the purposes of the poet demand a fitting conclusion to the theme of anger, withdrawal, disaster, and return, before the vengeance-theme is in turn worked out. So Akhilleus calls an assembly – any oddness in his doing so at this juncture is mitigated by Thetis' instructions (34–6) – and much of the Book is occupied with the speeches of reconciliation and the handing over of Briseis and Agamemnon's gifts. Twice before this Akhilleus has rejoined the Greeks in a surrogate form: when he dispatched Patroklos in place of himself (book 16) and when he appeared before the Trojans and uttered his war-cry in order to drive them back from his friend's body (book 18). Now he actually charges into the battle at the head of his troops, but not until he has donned the new armour in a long and splendid arming-scene, at the close of which we are again reminded that his vengeance on Hektor brings his own death nearer. Such a vital turning-point in the action of the poem requires these long preliminaries.

The formal structure of the book has been analysed by J. B. Hainsworth (*G&R* 13, 1966, 158–66). The first item of the pattern of joining battle is the assembly (40–276). Then follow the meal, which is here adapted into Akhilleus' reluctance to eat or to allow others to do so (155–72, 205–37, 303–8) and his subsequent divine refreshment (347–54); the council of chiefs, here adapted into the mourning of the chiefs around Akhilleus (303–39); and the arming-scene which concludes the Book (357–20.2).

The dead Patroklos, still lying unburied, is kept before our eyes. In the first scene his body is preserved from decay, and the return of Briseis is dramatized by her lament for him, followed by a lament by Akhilleus himself and the Greek elders. Then immediately after his arming-scene Akhilleus reproaches his immortal horses with leaving Patroklos dead on the battlefield. Akhilleus' loneliness and grief are emphasized by his refusal to eat, which is amplified to considerable length (154–237) and leads up to divine intervention (340–56); the feast celebrating his reconciliation with Agamemnon, and the funeral feast for Patroklos, will not take place until book 23.

The Book displays fine insight into the psychology of guilt and of grief, and the characters' eloquent expression of their thoughts give it the highest proportion of direct speech in the poem (64.15%), except for book 9 (82.46%). Both Agamemnon and Akhilleus have to come to terms with the knowledge that their irresponsible actions, which they both attribute to Ate, have brought public and personal disaster. But their personalities are still totally incompatible, and even at their reconciliation Agamemnon tries to score off Akhilleus (see 76–84n.) and the latter's heedlessness about whether or not he receives Agamemnon's lavish compensation is humiliating to his superior (see 145–237n.). The fresh grief of Patroklos' death renews old sorrows for Briseis and the Greek leaders, and brings for her and for Akhilleus the agonizing loss of hopes which now can never be fulfilled (see 287–300n.). We hear more of Akhilleus' old father and his young son, preparing the way for the importance of that aspect of his life when he meets Priam in book 24; and his approaching death, brought out strongly in book 18, continues as a dark shadow in the background (see 18.95–6n.).

1–39 Thetis brings the new armour to Akhilleus, and finds him mourning Patroklos. In response to his concern about the corruption of his friend's body she protects it with ambrosia and nectar

1–3 The appearance of Dawn also hails the beginning of books 8 and 11, announcing the start of a new action. Here verses 1–2, like the book-division, interrupt the type-scene of Thetis' journey, and may well have been added when the book-division was made. ἡ in line 3 is unexplained except by reference to the previous Book.

On the other hand, Nagler has suggested (*Spontaneity* 141–3) that 'Thetis is symbolically identified with Eos, her attendance word φέρουσα being shared by close imagistic association between her own action and the generic light-bearing function of the dawn goddess, which is mentioned explicitly here (19.2 = 11.2, cf. 23.226f.); in fact, the ring-compositional anaphora of Thetis' approach before and after the description of Dawn suggests, by the traditional structure of such scenes, that Eos is the form taken by Thetis in order to appear to her son (18.61f. ≅ 19.3f.).' At all events, it is likely that Eos is in the poet's mind, as in the *Aithiopis* she similarly brought armour to her son Memnon, and the episode may well antedate Arctinus' poem (see Introduction, ch. 2, ii).

The various one-verse and two-verse formular expressions for 'Dawn came' are discussed at 2.48–9n. Here verse 2 is the same as 11.2 and *Od.* 5.2, but verse 1, instead of bringing Dawn from Tithonos' bed ('Ηὼς δ' ἐκ λεχέων παρ' ἀγαυοῦ Τιθωνοῖο | ..., 11.1 = *Od.* 5.1), puts together a unique combination of formulae to bring her from Ocean. It is tempting to see in this change additional support for Nagler's idea, since Thetis is associated with Ocean (18.402); a similar association, however, exists for Dawn (*Od.* 22.197). The poet may have preferred not to introduce the idea of a couple sleeping together in connexion with either Thetis or Akhilleus.

4–6 There are many examples in Homer of this contrast between the light-bringing dawn and the sorrows of humankind. Macleod, *Iliad XXIV* 47–8, gives a list, and comments on this passage 'The special favour from the god is set against the general blessing of light; but this favour is given to a sorrowing man, and is to bring sorrow to other men.' See also 23.109n. The direct mention of Patroklos' corpse drives home the specific contrasts between immortal goddess, god-made armour, and mortal men; see Introduction to book 18.

περικείμενον: 'embracing'; cf. ἀμφ' αὐτῷ χυμένη (284, of Briseis). Elsewhere (ϝ)ὸν φίλον υἱόν always follows προσεφώνεε(ν) and is in apposition to a preceding name (2 × *Il.*, 2 × *Od.*). Here an innovative (and effective) usage places Patroklos' name first and juxtaposes this phrase with it (without a proper name), ignoring the digamma. | κλαῖον (-ε)...λιγέως occurs 4 × *Od.* The second hemistich recurs at 2.417. There was a proverb ἀεὶ δ' ἀριδάκρυες ἀνέρες ἐσθλοί (AT, and bT on 1.349); Hoekstra, *Odyssey* on *Od.* 16.191, discusses the matter at length.

8–11 τοῦτον (as Ameis–Hentze and Leaf point out) is less sympathetic than τόνδε would have been. ἐάσομεν (aorist subjunctive) is common in this position, and is followed by ἀχνύμενοί περ 4 × *Il.*, 1 × *Od.* (including Akhilleus' own reference to his anger against Agamemnon, 18.112). On κεῖσθαι in this position see 17.298–300n. θεῶν ἰότητι occurs only here in the *Il.*, but 4 × *Od.* reproachfully, followed by μόγησα(ν), and 2 × *Od.* where the sense is positive (god-given wealth); so there is no rebuke inherent in the phrase, though Thetis' tone is no doubt unhappy as usual. The phrase is always found in direct speech, and always in this position. On τύνη see 12.237n. ἀνήρ (11) = 'mortal', as at 18.432, 18.433. The scholia (bT) remark that the praise is well-adapted to arouse the φιλότιμος Akhilleus.

12–13 Thetis' handing-over of her gift of arms to Akhilleus became a popular subject in art; see 18.84–5n., and for the later period Stella G. Miller, *AJA* 90 (1986) 159–70. Usually Nereids help Thetis carry the panoply, solving a practical problem which a poet can ignore.

13–17 βράχω is common for the clashing of armour; the compound recurs at *Od.* 21.48. With 14–15 cf. Ἕκτορα δ', ὡς ἐνόησεν, ἕλε τρόμος· οὐδ' ἄρ' ἔτ' ἔτλη | ... (22.136). οὐδέ τις ἔτλη | occurs 8 × *Il.*, 5 × *Od.* Presumably the Myrmidons do not see Thetis herself and are overawed by the glare of the armour alone, but the imprecision is effective. The description of their fear is dramatically expanded when the goddess comes with the Nereids to mourn her dead son (*Od.* 24.47–57). In 16–17, the first ὡς is temporal, the second demonstrative; 'When he saw them, then all the more...' See

Chantraine, *GH* II 255; there are close parallels at 14.294 (see note *ad loc.*) and 20.424, and different phrasing at 1.512–13. χόλος is used as subject with a wide range of verbs; it occurs again with ἔδυ at 9.553, and in an expanded phrasc at 22.94. Now of course Ἀkhilleus' anger is directed against Hektor, not Agamemnon. With the enjambing phrase in 16–17 cf. τὼ δέ οἱ ὄσσε | λαμπέσθην ὡς εἴ τε πυρὸς σέλας (365–6). Fire blazed from Akhilleus' head when he appeared to rescue Patroklos' body (18.206–14), and it is particularly associated with him from here on (the instances are collected by C. H. Whitman, *Homer and the Heroic Tradition*, Cambridge, Mass. 1958, 137–47).

Note the varied colometry (cf. vol. 1 18–24). Three successive strong breaks at the bucolic diaeresis lead up to a four-colon verse and a rising threefolder:

Μυρμιδόνας δ' ἄρα πάντας ἕλε τρόμος, οὐδέ τις ἔτλη
ἄντην εἰσιδέειν, ἀλλ' ἔτρεσαν. αὐτὰρ Ἀχιλλεὺς
ὡς εἶδ', ὥς μιν μᾶλλον ἔδυ χόλος, ἐν δέ οἱ ὄσσε
δεινὸν ὑπὸ βλεφάρων ὡς εἰ σέλας ἐξεφάανθεν·
τέρπετο δ' ἐν χείρεσσιν ἔχων θεοῦ ἀγλαὰ δῶρα.

18–20 The ancient variant ὀφθαλμοῖσιν ὁρῶν (T) is not without merit. The content of 19 is expressed in different phrasing at 24.633 and *Od.* 4.47. Martin, *Language* 30–7, suggests that the formula ἔπεα πτερόεντα is used to convey a directive, so that Akhilleus is giving his mother a strong hint to take measures to prevent the body's corruption; the idea is plausible enough here.

23–4 νῦν δέ is characteristic of Akhilleus; cf. 67, and see 18.88n. But just as in the middle of his triumphant speech over the dead body of Hektor his thoughts revert to the unburied Patroklos (22.385–90), so here too he immediately turns aside from donning this magnificent armour to worry about the care of his friend's corpse. The poet is thinking both of honouring the dead man by divine attention, as he honours the bodies of Sarpedon (16.666–83) and Hektor (23.184–91), and also perhaps that the body will not be burnt until book 23, after a great deal of dramatic time has passed. ἀλλὰ μάλ' αἰνῶς | is formular, and followed 3 × *Il.* by | δείδω μή... Notice how beginning the sentence at the bucolic diaeresis enables the important word to receive emphasis at the beginning of the verse; other important words begin each of the next three verses. As always, the poet takes the greatest care with Akhilleus' speeches. τόφρα: 'meanwhile', as at 17.79 etc.

25–7 χαλκότυπος in later Greek means a coppersmith; Xenophon (*Hell.* 3.4.17) distinguishes it from a χαλκεύς, 'blacksmith', and Plutarch, *Vit. Hom.* 16, uses it as an example of a common expression used for a different purpose. Here it must mean 'bronze-inflicted'. It may possibly be an under-represented formula, since there is no formular alternative (κατ᾽ οὐταμένην ὠτειλήν |, 2 × *Il.*, is a mora shorter), but the striking and unparalleled use suggests that it is an example of the exceptionally vivid and innovative language used by Akhilleus; cf. 149–50n., and J. Griffin, *JHS* 106 (1986) 50–7. The second hemistich of 26 recurs at 16.545. ἐκ δ᾽ αἰὼν πέφαται: 'the life has been struck out ⟨of him⟩'. The verb is from θείνω (the same root appears in φόνος; see Chantraine, *Dict.* s.v. θείνω), and is picked up by the second part of ἀρηϊφάτους in 31. αἰών usually has λείπω as verb (5.685, 16.453, *Od.* 7.224). The parenthesis is emotionally effective. With the second hemistich cf. οὐδέ τί οἱ χρὼς σήπεται (24.414). σήπω is also used of rotting ships' timbers (2.135). Leaf and Ameis–Hentze understand νεκρός as subject and χρόα as accusative of respect, which is possible but not necessary.

29–39 Hektor's corpse is similarly preserved by Aphrodite ῥοδόεντι… ἐλαίῳ | ἀμβροσίῳ (23.186–7), and Sarpedon's by Apollo, again with ambrosia (16.680). In both these passages it is rubbed on (χρίειν), just as humans anoint a corpse with olive oil (18.350, 24.587). Here ambrosia and nectar are dripped into the nostrils, which suggests a reminiscence of an embalming technique; cf. Herodotus 2.86.3 πρῶτα μὲν σκολιῷ σιδήρῳ διὰ τῶν μυξωτήρων ('nostrils') ἐξάγουσι τὸν ἐγκέφαλον, τὰ μὲν αὐτοῦ οὕτω ἐξάγοντες, τὰ δὲ ἐγχέοντες φάρμακα. This difference in the application of the substance is not discussed by G. G. E. Mylonas (in Wace and Stubbings, *Companion* 478–9) or M. Andronikos (*Arch. Hom.* w 4–7). On other uses of ambrosia see 5.775–7n., 14.170–1n. and S. West, *Odyssey* on *Od.* 4.429.

29–32 Verse 29 ≅ 18.463 and 3 × *Od.* φῦλα is common as a genre-term for mankind, gods, and women. The nearest parallels to this phrase are ἄγρια φῦλα Γιγάντων (*Od.* 7.206) and μελισσέων ἀγλαὰ φῦλα (Hesiod fr. 33(a) 16 MW). Verse 31 recurs at 24.415 with εὐλαὶ | ἔσθουσ᾽ replacing μυίας. ἀρηΐφατος occurs in these two verses and 1 × *Od.*, and occasionally in later Greek (in the form ἀρει-). On the form κεῖται (subjunctive, < *κείεται) see Chantraine, *GH* I 457. τελεσφόρον εἰς ἐνιαυτόν occurs only here in the *Il.*, but is formular (4 × *Od.*, 1 × in Hesiod, *Theogony*). ἀρείων (etc.) usually ends the verse, and follows ἢ καί like this at 16.557.

34–6 Thetis is made to propose the assembly and public renunciation of Akhilleus' μῆνις because the occasion must take place for purposes of the plot, and it would be implausible to have the idea enter the hero's mind in any other way; and to maintain the proper scale for the conclusion of the wrath-theme the episode must be considerably amplified. Page, *HHI* 313, does not see this, and prefers 'an earlier and better tale' which described Akhilleus' immediate return to battle.

The two participial clauses preceding the main clause are unusual, but since each verse is self-contained in sense the construction is not hard to follow. Verse 34 ≅ *Od.* 1.272 (Athene's advice to Telemakhos). With μῆνιν ἀποειπών cf. | μῆνιν ἀπειπόντος μεγαθύμου Πηλεΐωνος (75). The end of Akhilleus' anger against Agamemnon is driven home by repetition (in the same position) of the word which proclaimed it as subject of the epic in 1.1. ἀπō(ϝ)ειπών is found only here; ἀπō(ϝ)ειπεῖν (etc.) is normal, ἀπειπόντος at 75 is paralleled by ἀπειπέμεν at *Od.* 1.91; see Chantraine, *GH* i 135. With δύσεο δ' ἀλκήν | cf. εἰ μὴ σύ γε δύσεαι ἀλκήν | (9.231; also addressed to Akhilleus), and the formula (ἐπι)ειμένος ἀλκήν (4 × *Il.*, 2 × *Od.*), applied to Akhilleus when he begins his attack on the Trojans (20.381). The idea of armour giving strength to the wearer is made even more explicit at 17.210–12 and 19.386.

37–8 The second hemistich of 37 is formular (2 × *Il.*, 1 × *Od.*). Nectar constantly shares a verse with ambrosia (347, 353, *Od.* 5.93, 5.199, and 3 × in Hesiod). νέκταρ ἐρυθρόν | recurs at *Od.* 5.93 and *HyAphr* 206. Of course its colour comes from οἶνον ἐρυθρόν | (7 × *Od.*), not 'perhaps as supplying the place of blood' (Leaf). The word may be of Semitic origin; see Hainsworth, *Odyssey* on *Od.* 5.93.

The vulgate text omits the final element of the divine-visit type-scene, Thetis' departure. While she is still engaged, our attention shifts to Akhilleus. Some late MSS, however, add 39a, ἡ μὲν ἄρ' ὣς ἔρξασ' ἀπέβη Θέτις ἀργυρόπεζα (≅ 5.133), which seems to have been known to schol. T (Did?) and – apart from its lack of attestation – is acceptable enough.

40–144 Akhilleus summons a council of all the Greeks, and expresses before it his regret at the losses they have suffered in his absence from battle, and his willingness to end his anger and lead an attack on the Trojans. Agamemnon in turn declares that he must have acted under the influence of Ate, tells of her power over Zeus himself, and offers to hand over the promised gifts to Akhilleus

Lohmann, *Reden* 173–4, points out that this assembly presents the same themes as that in book 1, but reversed: regret for past actions, abandonment of anger, offer of gifts as reparation, and the return of Briseis. Both assemblies are called by Akhilleus, and in both he speaks first. The two scenes are also compared by Arend, *Typische Scenen* 117–18.

Page's treatment of this scene (*HHI* 311–15) illustrates the shortcomings of analysing it as if it were a historical event and disregarding the larger purposes of a creative poet. His long list of linguistic and metrical abnormalities (*HHI* 332–4) can be taken to show a flexible and innovative usage rather than ignorance of the tradition.

40–1 J. Griffin, *JHS* 106 (1986) 55–6, points out that the unhappy Akhilleus is often to be found alone on the sea-shore: 1.349–51, 23.61, and

24.11–12. παρὰ θῖνα θαλάσσης recurs in this position at *Od.* 4.432, 14.347; usually the longer παρὰ θῖνα πολυφλοίσβοιο θ. | is used. On σμερδαλέα (F)ι(F)άχων (7 × *Il.*, 1 × *Od.*) see 5.302–4n. and Hoekstra, *Modifications* 53.

42–5 The importance of this assembly is underlined by the presence of even the lowly non-combatant personnel, which is reiterated at 54. There is a precise parallel in the great assembly of the gods when Zeus turns them loose to enter the fighting (20.4–9), to which Themis summons even the rivers and nymphs. Both gatherings show that a climax is approaching. ἔσαν must be understood with κυβερνῆται; then the following phrase amplifies its meaning (cf. the expanded ἐπεὶ νηὸς γλαφυρῆς οἰήϊα νωμᾷς, *Od.* 12.218). The mention of the catering corps staff (44) perhaps anticipates the later emphasis on the need for the army to eat. νεῶν ἐν ἀγῶνι recurs at 15.428 = 16.500; Hoekstra, *Modifications* 127, suggests that it developed from νηῶν ἐν ἀ. (16.239). ἀγών here retains its original sense, 'gathering' (see *LfgrE*).

45–6 οὕνεκ' Ἀχιλλεὺς | ... ἀλεγεινῆς is a favourite clause of the poet's, repeated at 18.247–8 (see note *ad loc.*) and 20.42–3, and presumably (from its sense) created especially for the *Il.* Starting the subordinate clause at the bucolic diaeresis allows heavy emphasis on ἐξεφάνη at the beginning of the verse.

47–53 σκάζοντε, 'limping', is explained and amplified in 49, and the result of Diomedes' and Odysseus' wounds is that they go to the front row and *sit down* (50). Then the motif is repeated with more elaboration for Agamemnon, who arrives last of all (perhaps suggesting he is more seriously wounded). We are then reminded how he came by his wound (52–3), and later he remains sitting even when he addresses the assembly (see 76–84n.). This kind of repetition of a motif in shorter and longer forms is characteristic of Homer, and so is his care to give the audience information which will be of importance later on; see Introduction, ch. 2, iii.

47–52 Verse 47 is adapted from two old formulae, τὼ δὲ βάτην (5 × *Il.*, plus an expanded form at 1.327) and θεράποντες (-ας) Ἄρηος (7 × *Il.*). See Hoekstra, *Modifications* 134–5. The Atticism Ἄρεως appears in some (mainly late) MSS. μενεπτόλεμος (48) bridges the mid-verse caesura; cf. Ἀτρεΐδης τε ἄναξ ἀνδρῶν καὶ δῖος Ἀχιλλεύς (1.7). The wounded Diomedes, Odysseus, and Agamemnon are | ἔγχει ἐρειδόμενοι when they join Nestor to watch the battle (14.38). All were wounded in book 11 (373–8, 434–8, 251–3 respectively). The wounds are forgotten the next day, when all three take part in the funeral games. γάρ (49) is again lengthened in this position at 1.342. In verse 52 καί goes with τόν, 'him too'.

54 The verse is unformular. It is noteworthy that the formula for 'when they had gathered together', αὐτὰρ ἐπεί ῥ' ἤγερθεν ὁμηγερέες τ' ἐγένοντο (3 × *Od.*) is used to begin an assembly in the *Il.* only at 1.57 (and at 24.790 for the different purpose of collecting Hektor's bones). At 2.87–100 and

2.207–11 the descriptions of the gathering are much expanded, and in the depressed circumstances of 9.13 there is only | ἷζον δ᾽ εἰν ἀγορῇ τετιηότες. Here the innovative language makes room for πάντες, picking up the emphasis of 42–6.

56–73 Akhilleus' speech is low-keyed, heartfelt, and at the same time diplomatic; and as usual it is brilliantly composed. Addressing Agamemnon with a brief title ('Ατρεΐδη; see 146n.), he begins by linking them both closely together in shared responsibility for the quarrel, not with a blunt statement but in the delicacy of a rhetorical question. He minimizes the importance of Briseis, now just a κούρη he had captured, no longer the γέρας who had been given to him by the army, as we have been told so often (1.161–2, 1.356 = 507 = 2.240, 1.392, 9.367–8, 16.56, 18.444), and a woman whom he had come to love (9.336, 9.341–3). In doing this, he lays the blame on himself rather than Agamemnon, as well as implicitly reminding us of the force of his love for Patroklos. Finally, he expresses sorrow for the Greek deaths he has caused; and declaring the end of his anger, he calls for an immediate attack on the Trojans.

Lohmann, *Reden* 32–3, points out that like Hektor's response to Pouludamas (18.284–309, see note *ad loc.*) the first part of the speech is in ring form:

I   A   Was this quarrel the best thing for us (56–8)?
    B   Would that the woman had died first! Then Greeks would not have died (59–62).
    A′ This way was best for Hektor and the Trojans (63–4).

Then, as in Hektor's speech, the recommended course of action falls into three parts:

II A   But let us put this behind us. Now, I will end my anger (65–8).
    B   Quickly, let us attack the Trojans (68–71).
    C   [*Result*] Whoever escapes me will be glad to take rest (71–3)!

56–8 ἦ ἄρ τι is interrogative, as at 8.236 and 13.446. ἀμφοτέροισιν is reinforced by σοὶ καὶ ἐμοί and νῶϊ περ, as well as by the following dual participle and plural verb, to emphasize that the blame is shared between them. Did/AT tells us that for ἄρειον the Chian text read ὄνειαρ and the Massiliot ἄμεινον. ἔριδος πέρι θυμοβόροιο | is formular (3 × *Il.*); at 7.210 | θυμοβόρου (< οι'[ο]) ἔριδος begins the verse, for greater emphasis, and the dative is used here for the same reason, the hiatus being ignored. The epithet would seem to signify the destructive effects of *eris* on one's inner tranquillity, as θυμοδακής... μῦθος (*Od.* 8.185) is explained by δάκε δὲ φρένας

Ἕκτορι μῦθος (*Il.* 5.493); however, J. C. Hogan, *Grazer Beiträge* 10 (1981) 26–7, prefers to interpret θυμός as 'life' and the compound presumably as 'life-destroying', which better suits the usual context (3 × duels in battle, and the parody of this at 20.253) and is appropriate enough here. μενεαίνω has the sense of struggling eagerly and angrily; cf. 15.104, 15.617, and A. W. H. Adkins, *JHS* 89 (1969) 17–18.

59–60 Instead of Ἄρτεμις ἰῷ the formular Ἄ. ἁγνή (3 × *Od.*) might have been used. Women's deaths are commonly attributed to Artemis; cf. 6.205, 6.428, 21.483–4, etc. An account of the sacking of Lurnessos is given at 2.690–3.

61–2 This vivid phrase for 'biting the dust' occurs in several forms; like this at 24.738 and *Od.* 22.269; γαῖαν ὀδὰξ εἷλον (22.17); ὀδὰξ ἕλον οὖδας (11.749); and where an optative is needed, ὀδὰξ λαζοίατο γαῖαν (2.418). All the *Il.* examples are in direct speech. The second hemistich of 62 (with its reminder of μῆνιν, 1.1) recurs at 9.426, at the end of Akhilleus' angry response to Odysseus.

63–4 The advantage of the quarrel to the Trojans was Nestor's first thought when he tried to stop it (1.255–8). The long memories of the Greeks will be nourished not only by what they suffered but by songs like the *Il.* (cf. 6.357–8). Note the emphasis on | δηρόν.

65–8 Akhilleus spoke 65–6 to Thetis at 18.112–13 (see note *ad loc.*). Lohmann, *Reden* 32–3, follows Ameis–Hentze in rejecting the couplet here, without sufficient reason. In both places it is followed by the Akhillean νῦν δέ (see 18.88n.). Here Akhilleus' thought continues exactly as in his words to Patroklos at 16.60–1, ἀλλὰ τὰ μὲν προτετύχθαι ἐάσομεν· οὐδ' ἄρα πως ἦν | ἀσπερχὲς κεχολῶσθαι ἐνὶ φρεσίν, but uses the different phrasing οὐδέ τί με χρὴ | ἀσκελέως αἰεὶ μενεαινέμεν. Martin, *Language* 199, notes that elsewhere (except for *Od.* 19.118) the phrase is οὐδέ τί σε χρή | (12 × *Il.*, 9 × *Od.* with minor variants), so the formula has been adapted here for a different purpose. The meaning and etymology of ἀσκελέως are uncertain. The occurrences in the *Od.* (adverb 1.68, 4.543; adjective 10.463) suggest 'unrelenting'. On μενεαινέμεν see 56–8n.

69–73 Verse 69 ≅ 2.443; 70 ≅ 20.352 (Akhilleus speaking). The reference in 71–3 is to the Trojans' acceptance of Hektor's counsel, not Pouludamas' (18.310–13). The phrasing is slightly expanded (with added emphasis) from 7.118–19 φημί μιν ἀσπασίως γόνυ κάμψειν, αἴ κε φύγησι | δηΐου ἐκ πολέμοιο καὶ αἰνῆς δηϊοτῆτος (see note *ad loc.*). τιν' (71) is equivalent to 'many'; cf. 18.466.

75 On ἀπειπόντος see 34–6n., and on the use of the genitive absolute in Homer, Chantraine, *GH* ii 324. μεγαθύμου Πηλεΐωνος may have a more magnanimous connotation than the regular Πηληϊάδεω Ἀχιλῆος (see 17.213–14n.), but one would have liked the closer correspondence with 1.1.

76–84 A major problem about Agamemnon's speech is the position from which he delivers it. Clearly normal procedure (cf. 2.278–82n.) is not followed. Scholars have interpreted αὐτόθεν ἐξ ἕδρης οὐδ᾽ ἐν μέσσοισιν ἀναστάς (77) and ἑσταότος (79) to mean: (a) that he speaks without rising from his seat, because of the pain of his wound (so Arn/A); (b) that he speaks without rising, because of his humility before Akhilleus (or even his suppliant posture: so A. Thornton, *Homer's Iliad*, Göttingen 1984, 128–9), or so that his humble words shall not be heard (Epaphroditus/bT, dubiously approved by Arend, *Typischen Scenen* 118); or (c) that he stands up, but does not advance as usual into the middle of the assembly to speak. The last view is now commonly accepted, for example by Willcock, Erbse (*Glotta* 32, 1952, 243–7), van Leeuwen, Ameis–Hentze (though with 77 bracketed in the text) and 'as a last resource' by Leaf. (Other discussions are listed by Bolling, *External Evidence* 185.)

Allen's text is that read by Aristophanes (Did/AT). Alexander of Cotiaeium (Porph/A) declared that 77 was inserted by Aristarchus, because he misunderstood ἑσταότος (79) and thought Agamemnon remained sitting. Zenodotus (Arn/A) did not read 77, and for 76 read τοῖσι δ᾽ ἀνιστάμενος μετέφη κρείων Ἀγαμέμνων, which is irregular for someone who is not the first speaker (ἀνιστάμενος introduces the first speaker at 1.58 and 19.55; at 9.52 it is used for the third speaker, after applause, but the τοῖσι δὲ καὶ μετέειπε... form is mentioned there by Did/A and has been added in the margin of MS A). His use of ἀνιστάμενος presumably indicates he wished to make it clear that Agamemnon did stand up. The Massiliot and Chian texts (Did/AT) read the same line as Zenodotus and followed it with μῆνιν ἀναστενάχων καὶ ὑφ᾽ ἕλκεος ἄλγεα πάσχων, which has nothing to recommend it but shows awareness of the emphasis the poet has laid on the king's wound (51–3).

Clearly 76–7 can mean either 'he addressed them *from his seat*, not *standing up* in the middle', or 'he addressed them from his place, not standing up *in the midst of them*'. There is further ambiguity in 79–80. Is ἑσταότος (79) simply a synonym for 'speaker'? (Alexander of Cotiaeium paraphrases it as δημηγοροῦντος.) Or is Agamemnon distinguishing a 'standing' speaker from one in his own position, viz. sitting down (ὡς δηλονότι καθήμενος, Arn/A)? The emphasis thrown upon the word by its initial position in both phrase and verse suggests the latter interpretation; 'It is good to listen to *someone who is standing up.*'

Observation of Homeric technique supports this view. In the first place, it is common for the poet first to use a motif in a straightforward sense, and then to repeat it with more elaboration and often with a deeper meaning (see Introduction, ch. 2, iii). In this way, in the present passage first the wounded Diomedes and Odysseus arrive, limping and leaning on their spears, and sit in the front row (47–50). Then Agamemnon comes, last of all, and there is a longer account of his wound (51–53; much was made of this wound when he received it, 11.267–74). Together, the verses perform the function of giving us the information we shall need for the full understanding of a later passage; this is a second characteristic of Homeric composition (see Introduction, *loc. cit.*). Wounded men sit down; and αὐτόθεν ἐξ ἕδρης οὐδ᾽ ἐν μέσσοισιν ἀναστάς (77) stresses twice over the fact that Agamemnon not only sits down like the other two, but remains sitting during his speech.

With this understanding, ἑσταότος μὲν καλὸν ἀκούειν (79), with its prominently placed participle, means not 'It is good to *listen* to a standing ⟨speaker, so don't interrupt while I stand and address you⟩' but 'It is good to listen *to someone who is standing up* ⟨as Akhilleus was, whom you have just applauded; but I cannot stand, because of my wound⟩.' With this interpretation, the poet is using the 'wounded men sit down' motif to allow Agamemnon to taunt Akhilleus: Agamemnon suffered a particularly painful wound (11.267–72) while fighting valiantly, whereas Akhilleus has been conserving his energies, safe in his dwelling.

The same ungracious and jealous, not humble or apologetic, tone is apparent in the following clause, οὐδὲ ἔοικεν | ὑββάλλειν. The only other use of this compound in the sense of 'interrupt' was the *hapax* ὑποβλήδην at 1.292, where Akhilleus rudely interrupted Agamemnon in the final exchange of the quarrel. This was the last time they met. Agamemnon has not forgotten the insult, and alludes pointedly to it here. No one else is likely to interrupt him, even when he is sitting down; whereas Akhilleus' propensity for interruption reappeared not long ago, when he broke in on the words of his goddess mother (18.98–100, see note *ad loc.*); earlier still, he had not given even Athene a chance to utter a word before accosting her (1.202; see Edwards, *HPI* 180–1).

Akhilleus has just shown himself magnanimous enough to admit his mistake directly to the man who injured him. Agamemnon, characteristically, is not big enough to accept this without mean-spirited jibes at the man he hates. With similar gracelessness his next speech (185–97), though concerned with the handing-over of the gifts to Akhilleus, is pointedly addressed to Odysseus, not to the man he has injured. This is the same Agamemnon who, when obliged to send an offer of recompense, could risk destroying its effect by demanding that Akhilleus recognize him as βασιλεύτερος (9.160).

With this interpretation, it is still uneasiness and resentment towards Akhilleus, not humility or shame, that characterize Agamemnon, and he remains seated partly so that all may contrast his wounded condition with Akhilleus' unscathed physique. His publicly demonstrated physical incapacity allows him to save face when he tells his subordinate to lead the army into battle (139).

78–144 Agamemnon's speech falls into three parts: a short proem to the Greeks, asking them to hear him in silence (78–84); a long central portion, in which acknowledgements of his affliction by Ate (85–94, 134–8) enclose in ring form a paradigm demonstrating her power over Zeus himself (85–133); and a final address to Akhilleus, bidding him lead the Greeks into battle, first receiving the promised gifts if he so wishes (139–44). The speech is long, partly no doubt because of the importance of the occasion, partly perhaps (like those of Glaukos at 6.145–211 and Aineias at 20.200–58) because in an awkward situation it is best to keep talking.

78–84 Agamemnon begins with obvious awkwardness. He does not address Akhilleus directly, but tells the Greeks that he will 'make himself clear' to him, in a unique phrase (83); and he asks at some length for a quiet hearing. 'The disjointed character of all the exordium of Agamemnon's speech seems designedly to portray the embarrassment of his position, and indeed vividly expresses the peevish nervousness of a man who feels that he is in the wrong [better perhaps "has been put in the wrong"] and is under the disadvantage of following a speaker who by his frank admissions has won the sympathy of the audience' (Leaf on 85).

80–2 The participle ἐπιστάμενος is treated as an adjective, like ἐπιστήμων, and so is accompanied by ἐών. ἐπισταμένως is common. ἐν πολλῷ ὁμάδῳ: see 17.380n. βλάβεται is an ancient form of the present tense without the suffix seen in the usual βλάπτω (see Chantraine, *Dict.* s.v. βλάβη, and Hoekstra, *Odyssey* on *Od.* 13.34. λιγύς περ ἐὼν ἀγορητής | is used sarcastically by Odysseus to Thersites (2.246) and in the same tone by Antinoös to Telemakhos (acc. case, *Od.* 20.274). This may be another jibe at Akhilleus.

More men than usual are present (42–6), and they were delighted with Akhilleus' speech (74). Agamemnon alludes angrily to their applause for his enemy.

83 Πηλεΐδη...ἐνδείξομαι: 'I will make myself clear to Akhilleus', cf. Herodotus 8.141 ἐνδεικνύμενοι τοῖσι Λακεδαιμονίοισι τὴν ἑωυτῶν γνώμην. The verb is *hapax* in Homer. Instead of addressing him, Agamemnon uses the third person to refer to Akhilleus. With similar distaste, in his speeches in book 9 he never mentioned Akhilleus' name, but used τοῦτον (9.118) and the like. Lohmann points out, *Reden* 76–7, that Akhilleus once complained Agamemnon did not dare to meet him face to face (9.372–3), and that all Akhilleus' later speeches to Agamemnon go unanswered (146ff., 23.156ff., 890ff.). 'Selten...zeigt sich [Homers] sicheres Erfassen psychologischer Nuancen so deutlich wie hier' (Lohmann 77).

85–138 Agamemnon goes on to explain his past conduct as the result of his affliction by Ate. He proves her irresistible power by relating a long paradigm, the tale of her victory over Zeus himself at the time of Herakles' birth. Lohmann, *Reden* 77–80, points out that the narrative of the paradigm corresponds closely to Agamemnon's account of his own affliction, reinforcing the implied comparison between himself and Zeus. Agamemnon has been overcome by Zeus, Moira, and Erinus, as Zeus was by Here; it was when (ἤματι τῷ ὅτ', 89, 98) Agamemnon took away Akhilleus' prize, and when Alkmene was about to bear Herakles; Agamemnon insulted Akhilleus (the tale is not repeated, but replaced by 90, 'What else could I do? God accomplishes everything'), and Zeus swore a foolish oath (100–25); and Agamemnon's picture of Ate treading above men's heads and deluding them matches Zeus's hurling of his deceitful daughter out of Olumpos down to the land of mortals (126–31). Finally, Zeus's regret afterwards, when he saw Herakles disgracefully treated by Eurustheus (132–3), is paralleled by that felt by Agamemnon when he saw Hektor destroying the Greeks (134–6). Agamemnon does not draw attention to the lack of foresight and elementary caution which brought about both Zeus's error and his own. Nor, of course, does he seem to be aware of the ironic parallel that some modern critics have seen between the mighty Herakles' subordination to the inferior Eurustheus and that of Akhilleus to Agamemnon himself (so O. M. Davidson, *Arethusa* 13, 1980, 200).

Agamemnon has blamed Ate before, when he falsely said Ζεύς με μέγα Κρονίδης ἄτη ἐνέδησε βαρείη in tempting his troops to return home (2.111); and the poet ironically has him repeat the same line when in despair and utter sincerity he again proposes withdrawal after the Greek defeat (9.18). On that occasion too he repeatedly claims Ate is to blame (ἀασάμην, 9.116, 119). She is also blamed by Helen (*Od.* 4.261). Zeus's protestations (*Od.* 1.32–4) have been unable to stop this very human habit of attributing our follies to fate or the gods; as the scholia remark, 'Even now those who cannot defend themselves by the simple truth lay the whole blame on fate' (τῇ εἱμαρμένῃ; bT on 86–7).

Agamemnon does not explain the reasons why the three divinities dispatched Ate against him; probably we are to think he would agree with Akhilleus, that Zeus wanted death to come to many of the Greeks (273–4), and Zeus's reasons are often obscure. Here's reasons for deceiving Zeus are likewise unspecified, but are, clearly enough, her jealousy and irritation at his boasting about the greatness of his extra-marital offspring (101–5). In Phoinix's paradigm, Ate both φθάνει δέ τε πᾶσαν ἐπ' αἶαν | βλάπτουσ' ἀνθρώπους (9.506–7), without any reason given, and also (confusingly) may be sent by Zeus to punish a man who refuses to listen to supplication (9.511–12; in 24.480–2 the circumstances are again not clear).

Thus in putting forward Ate, Agamemnon is not suggesting that any wrongdoing on his part led to her attack. He is not humble or apologetic. However, as E. R. Dodds indicates in his famous discussion (*The Greeks and the Irrational*, Berkeley 1957, ch. 1), Agamemnon is not evading responsibility in the juridical sense, for he is willing to give compensation (137–8). It should be noted that it is the characters, not the poet, who attribute this 'temporary clouding or bewildering of the usual consciousness' to 'an external "daemonic" agency' (Dodds, p. 5); the poet himself would say νήπιος, ὅς... At the time of the quarrel Homer said nothing about Ate's presence, and there is obvious irony when Akhilleus, who wanted Zeus ἐπὶ Τρώεσσιν ἀρῆξαι, | τοὺς δὲ κατὰ πρύμνας τε καὶ ἀμφ' ἅλα ἔλσαι 'Αχαιοὺς | κτεινομένους (1.408–10), declares that *Zeus* wanted death to come to many of the Greeks (19.273–4).

Ate in Homer may thus be summed up as the heroes' personification of the impulse which led to a foolish and disastrous act, an act which with hindsight appears inexplicable and hence is attributed to an outside, i.e. superhuman, agency; Ate's intervention may be, but is not necessarily, a punishment for wrongdoing (cf. 9.505n.). Modern scholars take different (and often more specific) views. Besides Dodds' seminal work (mentioned above), there are recent articles by J. A. Arieti (*CJ* 84, 1988, 1–12); by W. F. Wyatt, Jr (with recent bibliography; *AJP* 103, 1982, 247–76), which concludes that ἄτη basically means 'remorse for an act' or 'a remorse causing act' (p. 273), a view which may not win general agreement; and by A. W. H. Adkins (*CP* 77, 1982, 324–6), concluding '*ate* is not used of what we should distinguish as moral error unless it fails, leads to unpleasant consequences'. See also 9.505n.; the *LfgrE* entries for ἀάτη (by H. J. Mette) and ἀάω (by H. J. Seiler); R. D. Dawe, *HSCP* 72 (1967) 95–101; and R. E. Doyle, *ATH: its Use and Meaning* (New York 1984). On ἄτη in Hesiod see most recently H. Roisman, *Hermes* 111 (1983) 491–6.

85–6 τοῦτον...μῦθον refers vaguely to the unfortunate occasion mentioned by Akhilleus (56–8); it is made more explicit partly by με νεικείεσκον in the next line, partly by 'Αχιλλῆος γέρας αὐτὸς ἀπηύρων (89). καί τε conveys a climax, as at 1.521; see Ruijgh, τε *épique* 774–5. νεικείεσκον here must mean 'kept finding fault with'; on the wide range of meanings of νεικείειν see A. W. H. Adkins, *JHS* 89 (1969) 7–21.

86–7 The sense is repeated in ring form at the end of this section of the speech (137). The same idea that the gods are αἴτιοι, not the humans, is expressed in similar words by the horse Xanthos to Akhilleus (409–10) and by Priam to Helen (3.164–5). It is Zeus who (men think) sends Ate amongst men, and who must have wanted trouble to befall the Greeks (273–4); Akhilleus himself said Zeus took away Agamemnon's wits (9.377). Moira sets the term of a man's life (24.209–10 etc.), and so is naturally involved with Ate's depredations. Erinus is somewhat surprising here, as her normal business in Homer is executing curses and punishing oath-breakers (cf. 257–6on.), but she employs Ate as her agent at *Od.* 15.233–4 and the association may be habitual. Possibly her guardianship of the proper order extends to seeing that Moira is not infringed upon (cf. 418 and note *ad loc.*, and Dodds 7–8). In any case, Agamemnon is exaggerating the forces arrayed against him. On ἠεροφοῖτις Ἐρινύς see 9.571n., 9.454n.

88 ἄτην should be capitalized here. This verse, 95, and *Od.* 11.61 are the only cases where ἄάτη, ἀάσατο (etc., < *ἄϝα-) cannot be restored; see Chantraine, *GH* 1 30 (he ignores the *v.l.* Ἀλεξάνδρου ἕνεκ᾽ ἄτης at 6.356 and 24.28). The trisyllabic form can also be restored in Hesiod, *Erga* 230 and *Theogony* 230. W. F. Wyatt, Jr, *AJP* 103 (1982) 268–73, discusses the various forms and suggests a connexion with ἄω (< *ἀάω), 'satiate'; E. D. Francis in C. A. Rubino and C. W. Shelmerdine, *Approaches to Homer* (Austin 1983) 87–103 connects it with the root of ἄημι, 'blow'.

89–90 On the implications of αὐτὸς ἀπηύρων see 1.185n. In an article in *CQ* 40 (1990) 16–20, A. Teffeteller argues that αὐτός in these cases is ambiguous, meaning either 'by (my) own hand' or 'by (my) own authority', and that ἰών at 1.138 need not necessarily imply motion. With the wording of 90 cf. ἀλλ᾽ οὐ Ζεὺς ἄνδρεσσι νοήματα πάντα τελευτᾷ (18.328).

91 πρέσβα = 'eldest', as at *Od.* 3.452; see 14.194–7n. Her seniority doubtless reflects not Agamemnon's taste for innovative genealogy (in Hesiod, *Theogony* 226–32, Ate is listed last but one of the unfathered offspring of Eris daughter of Night) but the exaggerated rank he attributes to the power that overcame him (as bT suggest); and perhaps also Homer's psychological insight. The *figura etymologica* becomes even sharper when Ἀάτη is restored (see 88n.). The word-play is repeated at 129 and 136.

92–4 This kind of graphic personification is of course seen at its best in the paradigm of Ate and the Prayers at 9.502–12. Here her feet are soft because she approaches undetected; her not touching the earth, but treading over (or among) the heads of men, reinforces the tenderness of her feet and strengthens the idea that she is unseen but may always be 'in the air'. Plato rather frivolously remarks that heads are not very soft (*Symp.* 195d–e).

The hiatus ἄρα ἥ γε (93) is strange; various emendations have been proposed. On the ancient form κράατα (with Aeolic ᾱ) see 14.175–7n. On βλάπτουσ᾽ ἀνθρώπους see 22.15n.; the phrase is also used for Ate's activities at 9.507. The metaphor in (κατα)πεδάω (94; shackling the feet) also occurs with Moira; see 22.5n. ἑτερόν γε might point to Akhilleus (who admits the charge, 270–4) or might be indefinite (as at 4.306, 21.437) with πέδησεν a gnomic aorist. Zeus's entrapment too is already in mind.

Verse 94 was athetized by Aristarchus (Arn/A) as superfluous – needlessly. As Page pointed out (*HHI* 333), δ᾽ οὖν is not found elsewhere in early epic, but the combination is common in Attic and in Herodotus and in the latter οὖν is often used (as here) between preposition and verb in tmesis (Denniston, *Particles* 460).

95–133 The paradigm is used to show how Ate can delude even Zeus, and so win sympathy and understanding for Agamemnon; it also explains how she was forced to quit Olumpos and came to practise her deceptions among mankind. For references to Herakles in the *Il.* see 8.362–9n. and W. Kullmann, *Das Wirken der Götter in der Ilias* (Berlin 1956) 25–35, and for Near Eastern parallels W. Burkert in J. Bremmer, *Interpretations of Greek Mythology* (London 1987) 14–19. The original purpose of the tale must have been to explain how Herakles came to be subjugated to the inferior Eurustheus. Here's craftiness must always have been responsible – even here she has a far bigger part than Ate in the story – and a personified Ate (at least in the sense of blind folly, not just disaster) need not necessarily have been involved as she is in Agamemnon's version. Diodorus' account (4.9.4) omits Ate, saying merely that Zeus predicted the birth, and Erbse, *Untersuchungen zur Funktion der Götter im homerischen Epos* (Berlin 1986) 11–17, thinks personified Ate is Homer's own creation.

95–9 In 95, Allen's reading Ζεύς is said (Did/AT) to have been in the better texts (ἐν ἁπάσαις, i.e. the emended ones; see vol. IV, ch. 3, iii) and was read by Aristarchus; it was considered ποιητικώτερον. Inferior texts (αἱ εἰκαιότεραι) read Ζῆν', which appears in all our MSS and is printed by Leaf, van Leeuwen, and Ameis–Hentze. The phrase Ἄτη ἣ πάντας ἀᾶται (91, 129) inclines one to supply Ἄτη as subject and read Ζῆν' (or Ζῆν; see Janko, *HHH* 62), but Ζεύς is more emphatic, and the passive sense is accepted (and preferred here) by H. Jankuhn, *Die passive Bedeutung medialer Formen untersucht an der Sprache Homers* (Göttingen 1969) 50. On the form ἄσατο see 88n.

With 95–6 cf. Menelaos' prayer Ζεῦ πάτερ, ἦ τέ σέ φασι περὶ φρένας ἔμμεναι ἄλλων, | ἀνδρῶν ἠδὲ θεῶν (13.631–2). Here the less said about Zeus's wisdom (φρένας) the better. θῆλυς ἐοῦσα is clearly derogatory; Agamemnon is as scornful of Zeus's wife as he was of his own (1.113–15). The juxtaposition of female gender and deceitfulness is doubtless not accidental. δολοφροσύνη (97) occurs only here and at 112; cf. δολοφρονέουσα (106), which is very much Here's word, also applied to her at 14.197, 14.300, and 14.329. ἀπάτησεν may be a pun on Ἄτη, though restoring this as Ἀάτη (cf. 88n.) would make it less likely. Hesiod keeps Ἄτη and Ἀπάτη apart (*Theogony* 224, 230), but R. D. Dawe, *HSCP* 72 (1968) 100–1, is convinced the Greeks would see an etymological connexion. On βίην Ἡρακληείην (98) see 2.658–60n. ἐϋστέφανος (etc.; 99) is elsewhere in Homer applied only to goddesses or women, but there is no metrically equivalent alternative and Hesiod has this phrase at *Theogony* 978 (and ἐϋστέφανον ποτὶ Θήβην occurs at *Aspis* 80). The allusion is to battlemented walls, as in Τροίης ἱερὰ κρήδεμνα (16.100).

101–2 Zeus uses the same impressive couplet at 8.5–6 (see note *ad loc.*) to begin his mighty proclamation to all the immortals, which reduces them to silence (8.28–9). Of course his boastful speech here makes his later foolishness all the more dramatic. According to Diodorus Siculus (4.9.2) he made his night with Alkmene three times as long as normal to give him time to beget an exceptionally strong child. The scholia (bT) ask how Agamemnon had heard of this conversation on Olumpos, and answer that the tale must have been common knowledge. There was a local angle for Agamemnon; Eurustheus' father Sthenelos had been king of Mycenae. Later MSS give κελεύει (as at 8.6) for ἀνώγει.

103 σήμερον, essential to the story, is put in the emphatic position. μογοστόκος Εἰλείθυια | is formular (3 × *Il.*, 2 × *HyAp*); on the etymology of both words see 11.270n. and Hoekstra, *Modifications* 132.

104–5 There was a formula περικτίονας ἀνθρώπους | (etc.; *Od.* 2.65, *HyAp* 274), modified at 17.220 to περικτιόνων ἐπικούρων |, on which the phrasing here is based. τῶν ἀνδρῶν is dependent on γενεῆς, which is a partitive genitive dependent on ἄνδρα (103; the structure of 111 is simpler). αἵματος ἐξ ἐμεῦ εἰσί is an easy combination of αἵματος ἐξ ἐμοῦ εἰσί (cf. 20.241) and ἐξ ἐμεῦ εἰσί (cf. 21.189). Zeus's pronouncement comes true because both Herakles and Eurustheus are of his lineage, though only the former is his son; Perseus, son of Zeus, fathered both Alkmene's father Elektruon and Sthenelos, father of Eurustheus.

107–9 ψευστέω, 'to be a liar', is found only here; the noun ψεύστης occurs at 24.261 in very bad company. Allen's text is Aristarchus' reading, and preferable as the *lectio difficilior*; the alternative word-division ψεύστης εἶς (mentioned by Hrd/T) is less likely. αὖτε: 'at a future time', as at 1.340. The second hemistich of 107 recurs at 20.369. Herē uses very strong language, doubtless knowing it will make her macho husband angry and even less wary than usual.

108–9 The demand for an oath (108) and the swearing of it (113), are told in very summary form. On the oath type-scene see Arend, *Typische Scenen* 122–3. Verse 109 ≅ 104.

110–11 πίπτω is often used as a middle or passive of βάλλω, e.g. when the Trojans 'hurl themselves' against the ships (9.235) and Odysseus' men 'were thrown out of' their vessel (*Od.* 12.417); so here πέσῃ = 'come to birth'. μετά: 'between'. A kneeling position for childbirth is indicated at *HyAp* 117–18 γοῦνα δ' ἔρεισε | λειμῶνι μαλακῷ.

The piled-up genitives in 111 are confusing, like those in 105, and the obscurity may well be intentional; Zeus intended to refer only to a son, while Here craftily widens the meaning to 'descendant'. The parallel at *Od.*

13.130, Φαίηκες, τοί πέρ τοι ἐμῆς ἔξ εἰσι γενέθλης, suggests that αἵματος is best taken as dependent on γενέθλης, though Leaf hesitantly prefers the reverse.

113–16 ἔπειτα is best taken to mean not 'afterwards' but 'therein', 'in that case' as at 1.547, 10.243. *Contra*, R. D. Dawe, *HSCP* 72 (1968) 98. Verse 114 = 14.225; see 14.225–30n. for descriptions of her locomotion. The formula Ἄργος Ἀχαιικόν is divided at 9.141 = 283; cf. also 3.75 = 258. The adjective distinguishes the Peloponnesian Argos from Pelasgic Argos in Thessaly; see 2.108n. In 116 note the 'new' irresolvable genitive Σθενέλου, compared with the old-style formula in 123.

117 ἣ δ' ἐκύει stands for κυέουσαν (after ἤδη), by the usual Homeric parataxis. Herē not only knew Sthenelos' wife, but knew she was pregnant with a son. μείς is the regular nominative form (< *mēns); Attic μήν developed by analogy from the oblique cases.

118–19 πρὸ φόωσδε is a birth formula, used after | ἐξάγαγε at 16.188 and after | ἐκ δ' ἔθορε at *HyAp* 119. ἠλιτόμηνον, 'missing the ⟨proper⟩ month', is very rare, but the first component (ἀλιτ-, ἀλιτ-, cf. ἀλιταίνω) is often found compounded with other words; cf. Chantraine, *Dict.* s.v. ἀλείτης, *LfrgE* s.v. ἀλιτεῖν.

Herē is not in ritual associated with motherhood and birth (W. Burkert, *Greek Religion*, tr. J. Raffan, Cambridge, Mass. 1985, 133), but exercises a similar control over Eileithuia in holding back the birth of Apollo (*HyAp* 97–101); at 11.270–1 and Hesiod, *Theogony* 922, the Eileithuiai are said to be her daughters. Homer uses the name in both singular and plural. Eileithuia was already worshipped in Mycenaean times; her name is derived from the root ἐλυθ-, 'come' (Burkert, 170–1; see *LfgrE* and 11.270n.).

120 The use of ἀγγελέουσα without a verb of motion is unparalleled in Homer, but here Here's return from Argos is unimportant; what matters is her malicious delight in personally making Zeus aware (αὐτὴ ἀγγελέουσα) of how she has tricked him.

121–4 ἀργικέραυνε also occurs in this position at 20.16 and 22.178; at 8.133 Zeus ἀφῆκ' ἀργῆτα κεραυνόν. The second hemistich recurs at *HyAp* 257 and is probably formular; cf. also 16.83. Here's revelation is crafted with immense skill: first comes the birth of a future king, then the surprise of his name (in the prominent position; cf. | Αἴαντος, 7.183) and his lineage, and finally the triumphant σὸν γένος, which again begins the verse. The litotes οὔ οἱ ἀεικές recurs at 9.70, 15.496, and 24.594.

125 The line is a more vivid version of the formular ἄχος κραδίην καὶ θυμὸν ἱκάνει (4 × *Il.*) and ἄχος πύκασε φρένας (3 × *Il.*). Neither τύπτων nor βαθύς is used elsewhere like this; perhaps a striking personification rather than a metaphor.

126–31 λιπαροπλόκαμος occurs only here and 1 × in Pindar. It is a variant of the formular λιπαροκρήδεμνος (18.382 and 3× *HyDem*) and καλλιπλοκάμοιο (1× *Il.*, 2× *Od.*). We cannot tell if it was formular or created for the special circumstances. Ameis–Hentze suggest the compliment marks Ate's seductiveness. Rather, it emphasizes Zeus's unusually violent action in grabbing her by the (glossy) hair to sling her out of Olumpos. Hephaistos was thrown out by the foot (1.591), but as the scholia (bT) very properly remark, it would be ἄτοπον γυναικὶ ῥίπτεσθαι ποδός. On 129 see 91n. περιστρέψας (131) is used of Odysseus hurling his discus in Phaeacia (*Od.* 8.189).

133 Athene repeats ὑπ' Εὐρυσθῆος ἀέθλων | when she tells how she was often sent by Zeus to relieve his son's sufferings (8.363, see note *ad loc.*).

135–6 ὀλέκεσκεν occurs only here, but the form is regular enough and the verb is common. There are several MSS variants. λελαθέσθαι is the ancient reduplicated aorist; see Chantraine, *GH* I 395–7. On the word-play in 136 see 91n.

137–8 The couplet is similar to 9.119–20, but significantly substitutes the exculpatory καί μευ φρένας ἐξέλετο Ζεύς for the more accurate φρεσὶ λευγαλέῃσι πιθήσας. After 137 (≅ 9.119) Athenaeus (11a) adds ἢ οἴνῳ μεθύων ἤ μ' ἔβλαψαν θεοὶ αὐτοί, claiming it is quoted by Dioscurides the pupil of Isocrates; the line does not appear in the MSS or scholia, but is mentioned by Eustathius 1176.11–14. W. F. Wyatt, Jr, *AJP* 103 (1982) 264, points to the association of ἀάω and wine in the cases of Elpenor (*Od.* 11.61) and the centaur Eurution (*Od.* 21.297).

139–44 In conclusion, Agamemnon urges Akhilleus to lead the Greeks into battle (139), and promises to hand over the gifts promised by Odysseus, if necessary before the battle begins (140–4). Akhilleus, as usual in Homer, will respond to the latter point first. Again Agamemnon does not address Akhilleus by name (see 78–84n., 83n.). His wound, made obvious to all by his sitting position (see 76–84n.), fortunately prevents his leading the army himself and saves him humiliation in handing over the leadership to Akhilleus.

139–41 Agamemnon used the first hemistich to Idomeneus in the Epipolesis (4.264), and Aias the second to Teukros (15.475). Verses 140–1 = 'I am here (ὅδε) to hand over all the gifts which ...'; the construction is like the infinitive after τοῖος (as at *Od.* 2.60) and in εἰσὶ καὶ οἵδε εἰπέμεν (9.688). χθιζός: actually the night before last.

142–4 Phoinix told how Meleager drove back the enemy but afterwards never received the promised gifts, and warned Akhilleus not to fall into the same trap (9.597–9, 9.604–5). Here the introduction of the idea allows Akhilleus to express his contempt for gifts from Agamemnon in the following lines. With 142 cf. 189 and ἐπειγόμενός περ ὁδοῖο | (3× *Od.*).

Martin, *Language* 115–16, points out Agamemnon's tendency to add a

gibe at the end of a speech, conspicuously at 9.158–61. Perhaps here
ὄφρα...δώσω has enough of the tone of Agamemnon's καί μοι ὑποστήτω,
ὅσσον βασιλεύτερός εἰμι | ἠδ' ὅσσον γενεῇ προγενέστερος εὔχομαι εἶναι (9.160–1)
to add even more point to Akhilleus' disdainful response (see next note).

*145–237 Akhilleus is not concerned with Agamemnon's gifts, but only with marching
out to battle immediately. Odysseus demurs, saying that the men need a meal before the
long day's fighting. The gifts, too, must be publicly displayed, and Agamemnon must
swear that he has not slept with Briseis. Agamemnon agrees, but Akhilleus still objects
to the delay. Odysseus will not yield; even after a personal loss one must eat in order
to continue the struggle*

Agamemnon's response to Akhilleus' acknowledgement of his mistake was
hardly gracious; and now Akhilleus in turn displays an offhandedness, or
even disdain (149–50), about receiving the gifts, and about their public
display, which humiliates the donor of so much property. See W. Donlan,
Phoenix 43 (1989) 5–6.

Leaf was perturbed by the long discussion of eating and drinking (see his
introduction to this Book), and Page has a good deal of fun with it ('More
than 180 lines have now passed since luncheon stole the limelight, and
nothing has been achieved', *HHI* 314). But as J. B. Hainsworth has shown,
G&R 13 (1966) 158–66, the meal is a regular part of the sequence of joining
battle at 2.399 and 8.53–4 (at 11.3ff. it is omitted, perhaps because the
immediately preceding scene was a meal (10.577–9), or because of the
spectacular intervention of Eris). The communal meal is also an important
element in social harmony, in which Akhilleus is still unwilling to
participate (see S. A. Nimis, *Narrative Semiotics in the Epic Tradition*,
Bloomington 1987, 23–42, and cf. 19.179–80 and the importance of
Akhilleus' attendance at Agamemnon's feast, 23.35–7). Here the element of
the meal is adapted to set Akhilleus apart from the rest of the Greeks (as in
books 1, 9, and 16) by dramatizing his reluctance to eat, or to allow others
to do so, before he has taken vengeance on Hektor. It may also prepare for
his later insistence that Priam eat despite his grief (see 199–214n.). The
theme is completed by his divine refreshment (347–54), which raises him
above the stature of other heroes.

146 Unlike Agamemnon, Akhilleus addresses his former adversary by
his proper titles, more formally than in 56. Is he embarrassed by
Agamemnon's awkwardness at 78–84?

147–50 Akhilleus' words are as individualistic as usual. He begins with
very short, chopped-up clauses, as though speaking slowly and with
difficulty (147–8a). Then, after his characteristic νῦν δέ (cf. 23, 67, and
18.88n.), comes an enjambing sentence ending at the next A caesura,

followed by an explanatory γάρ clause which enjambs over to the mid-verse caesura of the next line (149b–50a), itself followed by a further γάρ clause in the next hemistich (150b).

147–8 The construction is ambiguous. With Allen's accentuation, παρὰ σοί, the infinitives may be taken as imperatives, with αἴ κ᾽ ἐθέλησθα parenthetical ('Hand over the gifts, if you like, as is proper, or keep them with you'); or possibly after ἐθέλησθα, with an awkward ellipse of the main clause ('If you wish to hand them over, or to keep them, ⟨it's all right with me⟩'; cf. 6.150). Or πάρα σοί may be read (with Nicanor (bT), Ameis–Hentze, Leaf, and van Leeuwen), and taken as a separate clause (after a colon; so Ameis–Hentze) or as the main clause to which αἴ κ᾽ ἐθέλησθα is subordinate ('It is up to you, whether you wish to hand over the gifts, as is proper, or to keep them'), πάρα having its common meaning 'in one's power', 'at one's disposal'. This last rendering is the most effective, the first is the simplest. Akhilleus has not quite forgotten his words at 9.378 ἐχθρὰ δέ μοι τοῦ δῶρα· τίω δέ μιν ἐν καρὸς αἴσῃ.

There are only four examples of ἤ τε... ἤ τε, and a single ἤ τε is found only at *Od.* 16.216, in quite different circumstances. Ruijgh, τε *épique* 824–8, considers τε here irregular and artificial, and notes that all the examples could be replaced by the ancient form ἠέ. μνησώμεθα χάρμης: see 17.100–5n.

149–50 κλοτοπεύειν is obviously a vigorous way of saying 'waste time nattering', but has defied philologists (Risch, *Wortbildung* 333; Frisk lists some conjectures). It recurs only in Heliodorus (Hesychius glosses the noun -ευτής as ἀλαζών, 'boaster'). It may well be a colloquialism, as may his τρύζητε, 'coo', to the envoys (9.311) and μετατροπαλίζεο, 'turn back' (20.190). διατρίβω is only here used absolutely. ἄρεκτος (< ἀ-intensive + ῥέζω) is found in Greek only once again, in Simonides. On the uniqueness of Akhilleus' vocabulary see 25–7n., 201–2n., 20.188–90n., vol. II 34, and J. Griffin, *JHS* 106 (1986) 50–7.

151–3 These three lines, addressed to the Greeks in general, are more normal in structure and vocabulary. With Allen's punctuation ὡς κε is final, and ὧδε resumptive. With a comma after φάλαγγας (so Nicanor, Ameis–Hentze, Leaf, Willcock) they are correlatives, 'As each man sees...,so let him fight...' Akhilleus spoke of himself by his name at 1.240; Hektor does the same at 7.75 and Zeus at 8.22. Both hemistichs of 152 are formular. On ὑμείων see 20.119–20n.

154–83 Akhilleus' disregard for the meal schedule and the protocol of handing over compensation for an offence horrifies the practical-minded Odysseus, who as a good subordinate officer speaks up to see that the proper forms are observed after the two protagonists have reached agreement in principle. It was the outraged Odysseus who acted to punish Thersites' impropriety, and went on to address the assembly and brilliantly restore morale after Agamemnon's disastrous testing of the army (2.246–335); he led the attempt to mollify Akhilleus in book 9; and he spoke out vehemently against Agamemnon's weak-willed proposal to go home after the chiefs were wounded (14.83–102, see note *ad loc.*).

His exhortation falls into three parts: the army must eat (155–72); the gifts must be publicly displayed as they are handed over, and Agamemnon must swear that Briseis, Akhilleus' prize of honour, remains inviolate (172–80); and in future he must mend his ways (181–3).

155–72 Odysseus denounces Akhilleus' proposal to engage in battle without pausing for a meal; declares it will be a long time before they have another chance to eat; and urges that they eat and drink right now (155–61). After this brief ring-form synopsis he presents the alternatives at greater length: the utter weariness that engulfs the hungry fighter as the day draws on; the good spirit and energy of the one sustained by food and wine (162–70). He winds up by repeating that the meal must be taken now (171–2). See Lohmann, *Reden* 66–8.

Odysseus' vehemence is expressed by placing a high proportion of significant words at the beginning of the line (156, 158, 161, 163, 166, 169, 170, 173, 174, 175, 180). Though made from too 'historical' a viewpoint, the comment of bT on 154, 'Nestor is silent, for he is an object of suspicion (ὕποπτος) to Akhilleus because of Patroklos' death', shows the consistency of character which can be imposed upon the poem.

155 ἀγαθός περ ἐών was used with a negative command by Agamemnon to Akhilleus (1.131) and by Nestor to Agamemnon (1.275, see note *ad loc.*), and it will be used again by Apollo in an objection to Akhilleus' behaviour (24.53). The moral implications of the formula have been most recently discussed by M. Gagarin, *CP* 82 (1987) 303–6, and E. J. Bakker, *Linguistics and Formulas in Homer* (Amsterdam 1988) 192–3. 'It emerges from this passage, as from this book and the whole poem, that to be merely ἀγαθός is not enough' (Macleod, *Iliad XXIV* 93, on 24.53).

158–9 φύλοπις (-ιν) is formular in the fifth foot, followed by αἰνή (-ήν) (12 × *Il.*, 1 × *Od.*). The unusual usage in the runover position here adds to the emphasis. φάλαγγες (-ας, -ξι) at the end of the verse is preceded by forms of no less than 16 different verbs; this is the only instance of ὁμιλέω here. It is also the only time | ἀνδρῶν enjambs after φάλαγγες, though | Τρώων follows it 3 × *Il.*

161–2 Verse 161 = 9.706; 162 recurs (slightly adapted) 3 × *Il.*, 6 × *Od.* σίτου καὶ οἴνοιο corresponds to σίτου (163) and to οἴνοιο...καὶ ἐδωδῆς (167); on similar varied correspondences see Macleod, *Iliad XXIV* 124.

163 ἄκμηνος, 'fasting', occurs only in this book (4 ×, in non-formular expressions) and a few later imitations. Its origin is still unclear; the ancients derived it from τὴν ἀκμήν· οὕτω δὲ τὴν ἀσιτίαν Αἰολεῖς λέγουσι (AbT).

165–9 With 165 cf. ἵνα μή μιν λιμὸς ἵκηται | (348, expanded at 354). The second hemistich of 166 recurs at *Od.* 13.34. With 167 cf. σίτου καὶ οἴνοιο κορεσσάμενος κατὰ θυμόν (*Od.* 14.46). Both hemistichs of 168 are formular. Surprisingly, in view of its convenient metrical shape, 169 presents the only instance of θαρσαλέος etc. standing at the beginning of the verse (θαρσαλέως 2 × *Od.*, in a repeated verse). γυῖα is probably accusative of respect.

172–80 Odysseus now takes up the matter of the gifts, still firmly addressing Akhilleus. His proposal is in ring form (see Lohmann, *Reden* 66–8):

> A Agamemnon must hand over the gifts before all the Greeks (172–4);
> B *you*, Akhilleus, will be delighted with this (174).
> C He must swear that he has not slept with Briseis (175–7);
> B′ *you*, Akhilleus, will be mollified by this (178).
> A′ Then he must honour you with a formal banquet (179–80).

171–5 Verses 171–2 (to ὅπλεσθαι) ≅ 23.158–9. Akhilleus was insulted publicly, before the whole assembly; so the recompense should be handed over publicly too, and the oath sworn before all the Greeks. οἰσέτω (173) belongs to a common class of sigmatic aorists with thematic declension, developed for metrical convenience; see Chantraine, *GH* I 417–18. The formular system of which φρεσὶ σῇσιν ἰανθῇς (174) is a part is examined by Hoekstra, *Modifications* 122.

176–7 The couplet is taken from Agamemnon's earlier offer, repeated by Odysseus to Akhilleus (176 = 9.133, 9.275; 177 = 9.276 ≅ 134). Verse 177 is omitted in a papyrus and the MSS of the *h* family, as well as a number of others, and is not mentioned in the scholia. Here the couplet is clearly dependent on the occurrences in 9, as there τῆς refers to κούρη βρισῆος in the preceding line but here is without support except from understanding of the facts. Verse 177 may have been a concordance interpolation; on the other hand, it was as reasonable to borrow the whole couplet as the single verse 176, and 177 may have been omitted through prudishness. On the implications of ἢ θέμις ἐστίν see 2.73–5n. and 9.133–4n. (which quotes Genesis, 19.31, 'a man...to come in unto us after the manner of all the earth').

Verse 176 has six η's. D. W. Packard, *TAPA* 104 (1974) 247, lists other such verses and remarks 'One wonders whether it is coincidental that many of [them] deal with youth, beauty, and love-making.'

178 Sexual jealousy had formed a part of Akhilleus' fury at Agamemnon's abduction of Briseis; he had said angrily τῇ παριαύων | τερπέσθω (9.336–7), and admitted τὴν | ἐκ θυμοῦ φίλεον δουρικτητήν περ ἐοῦσαν

(9.342–3). So the oath will mollify him on the personal level, as well as the more formal one that the property seized must be restored undamaged.

179–80 This formal reconcilation banquet will not take place until 23.35–56, where Akhilleus at last yields himself to what he calls στυγερῆ...δαιτί (23.48). ἐπιδευές is a substantive, not an adverb; τι is adverbial.

180–3 Odysseus concludes with a short lecture addressed to Agamemnon. καὶ ἐπ᾿ ἄλλῳ (181) = 'to others as well ⟨as to Akhilleus⟩'. At 24.369, *Od.* 16.72, and *Od.* 21.133 the line ἄνδρ᾿ ἀπαμύνασθαι, ὅτε τις πρότερος χαλεπήνη is used to amplify νέος (νεώτερος): '(too) young to fight off someone who offers violence'. The adaptation in 183 is awkward, because to give acceptable sense τις must refer not to ἄνδρα but to βασιλῆα: 'it is not blameworthy for a king to appease a man fully, when one [i.e. a king] has begun the trouble'. τις now slightly softens the direct rebuke to Agamemnon. ἀπαρέσκομαι occurs only here in this sense; the prefix signifies completion (Chantraine, *GH* ii 93).

184–97 Agamemnon's assent and instructions are expressed directly to Odysseus (185–6, 192–5) and to the army (190–1); less directly to Akhilleus (188–9, cf. 194) and the herald Talthubios (196–7). His first three lines are end-stopped and slow, a little like the much longer sequence of end-stopped lines when Akhilleus began his answer to Odysseus (9.308ff.).

188–9 ἐπιορκέω occurs only here in Homer, but is later the usual word for 'forswear'. πρὸς δαίμονος: 'before God', as in σε πρὸς πατρὸς γουνάζομαι (*Od.* 13.324) = 'I implore you in your father's name'. Cf. also 1.239. τεῖος is for τῆος, scanned as a spondee before a consonant 3 × *Od.*; see Chantraine, *GH* i 11–12. It is explained by the ὄφρα...clause (190–1). MSS read τέως and follow it with περ or γε to repair the metre.

192–3 ἐπιτέλλομαι and κελεύω are again coupled at 10.61; on such doublets see K. O'Nolan, *CQ* 28 (1978) 23–37. κούρητες, 'young men', occurs only here and at 248 κούρητες Ἀχαιῶν. The formation is regular enough (see Risch, *Wortbildung* 18–19; Chantraine, *Dict.* s.v. κόρος), and the word is no doubt much older than Homer, but it appears otherwise only in the specialized senses of the nation (Κουρῆτες) and the legendary dancers (Κουρῆτές τε θεοὶ φιλοπαίγμονες ὀρχηστῆρες, Hesiod fr. 123.3 MW). Both here and at 248 it is not just a lengthened version of the formula κοῦροι Ἀχαιῶν | (7 × *Il.*, 2 × *Od.*), but retains the specific sense 'young men'. Cf. γυμνῆτες, 'light-armed soldiers', which is at least as old as Tyrtaeus (11.35) and may possibly have been known to the poet. Page's fulminations against 'this extraordinary aberration' (*HHI* 332–3) are unwarranted, as the meaning is of course *not* identical with (ϝ)ελίκωπες Ἀχαιοί and so there is no breach of formular economy. Elsewhere ἀριστῆες (-ας) Παναχαιῶν | (8 × *Il.*) is used as a substantive (at 2.404 γέροντας is in apposition). The slight change in grammar is like that at *Od.* 3.352, where Telemakhos' formula 'Οδυσσῆος φίλος υἱός | is incorporated into τοῦδ' ἀνδρὸς 'Ο. φ. υἱ. |; and cf. 395–7n.

If B. Sergent, *Homosexuality in Greek Myth* (tr. A. Goldhammer, Boston 1986) 310 n. 4, is right in saying that some hold the extraordinary opinion that these young men are intended for Akhilleus' homosexual gratification, the view must be corrected. They are of course needed to bring back the compensation.

194–5 The hiatus δῶρα ἐμῆς is perhaps permitted (as Leaf suggested) on the analogy of | χεῖρα ἑήν (9.420) < χεῖρα (ϝϝ)ήν (< *sw-); see Chantraine, *GH* I 146 and 272. Both ἐνείκεμεν and ἐνεγκέμεν appear in good MSS. The latter would be an Atticism, but is preferred by Wackernagel, *Untersuchungen* III–12; Chantraine considers the former correct, but an artificial form providing a dactylic equivalent for ἐνεῖκαι (18.334; *GH* I 395). γυναῖκας: Agamemnon's failure to distinguish Briseis from the other slave-women he will hand over is as graceless as his continued reference to Akhilleus as if he were not there. The poet *will* distinguish Briseis (245–6).

196–7 Talthubios was similarly sent to fetch the victims at 3.118–20. On that occasion lambs are sacrificed, not a boar. A boar was the victim when competitors took the oath to observe the regulations of the Olympic Games (Pausanias 5.24.9).

198–214 Akhilleus' riposte is in two parts, each in A: B: A' form (see Lohmann, *Reden* 86–7). Agamemnon should deal with these trivia at some other time; many Greeks lie slain by Hektor; yet Agamemnon bids the army eat (199–205)! Then turning more openly to his personal feelings, he declares he would lead them to battle now and dine later; he himself will not eat while his friend lies slain; he can think only of killing men (205–14). 'Saul had adjured the people, saying, "Cursed be the man that eateth any food until evening, that I may be avenged on mine enemies"' (1 Samuel 14.24).

Odysseus was similarly unsuccessful in persuading Akhilleus in book 9. Here, however, he will win his way after a further speech. In view of the amount of irony appearing in the *Il.* (see Edwards, *HPI*, Index s.v.) it is likely that the poet is conscious that at a later time Akhilleus himself will eloquently urge Priam to eat despite his overwhelming grief (24.601–19).

199 Again Akhilleus formally addresses Agamemnon, though ignored by him. ἄλλοτέ περ looks forward to the coming νῦν δέ (203), and καὶ μᾶλλον adds additional emphasis.

201–2 μεταπαυσωλή never occurs again in Greek, and may well be a neologism, suited to Akhilleus' highly individual diction. The nearest parallels are οὐ γὰρ παυσωλή γε μετέσσεται (2.386; spoken by Agamemnon) and μεταπαυόμενοι δὲ μάχοντο (17.373). Leaf and van Leeuwen write μετὰ παυσωλή, unnecessarily. ᾗσιν for ἔῃσιν may be an Atticism or an alternative ancient form; there are several such examples (see Chantraine, *GH* 1 286–7).

203–5 νῦν δ': see 18.88n. κέαται δεδαϊγμένοι, of the slain in general, is picked up by δεδαιγμένος... | κεῖται of Patroklos (211 12). 204 – 8.216, 11.300 (both in the narrator's voice). In 205, the dual number points to Agamemnon and Odysseus. βρωτύς (only again at *Od.* 18.407) seems to be simply a metrical alternative to βρῶσις (so G. P. Shipp, *Antichthon* 2, 1968, 25). ἦ τε always introduces a contrasting idea ('No, but *I* would...'), usually hypothetical (Ruijgh, τε *épique* 798).

207–8 νήστιας ἀκμήνους: in a defiant quotation, Akhilleus picks up two words Odysseus had used to begin verses in his protest against him (156, 163). In 208 a number of MSS, including a few early ones, read τεύξασθαι, which is printed by Leaf and others. The aorist infinitive is regular after a verb of command, but the future (unparalleled elsewhere) gives a more emphatic contrast with νῦν μὲν...πτολεμίζειν and is therefore preferable, especially from the vehement Akhilleus (so Willcock). The optative τισαίμεθα is attracted to the mood of ἀνώγοιμι; cf. 24.226–7. The reading μετά for μέγα appears in a few older MSS and is known to the scholia (bT), but has little to recommend it.

209–10 ἰείη should be ἴοι, as at 14.21, but has been formed on the analogy of ἰείη from ἵημι (Chantraine, *GH* 1 284–5). Confusion between forms of these verbs is only too easy. βρῶσίς (-ν) τε πόσις (-ν) τε | is formular (8 × *Od.*, including a variation at *Od.* 13.72). The formation of βρῶσις, βρωτύς and similar words is discussed by Chantraine, *Bulletin de la Société de Linguistique de Paris* 59 (1964) 11–23.

212–14 ἀνὰ πρόθυρον τετραμμένος: i.e. with the feet towards the door, the usual custom. ταῦτα (213): i.e. food and drink. The bloodthirsty line 214 has no parallel in form (except στόνον ἀνδρῶν |, 4.445), though similar accumulations of horrific terms sometimes occur ("Εκτορα δ' ἐκ βελέων ὕπαγε Ζεὺς ἔκ τε κονίης | ἔκ τ' ἀνδροκτασίης ἔκ θ' αἵματος ἔκ τε κυδοιμοῦ, 11.163–4; cf. 10.298). These, however, are in the narrator's voice; Akhilleus is the only character who speaks like this, and only in his present mood.

216–37 Odysseus is profoundly stirred by Akhilleus' last sentence, as well as by his continued insistence on an immediate attack. His response is grimly resigned to the realities of grief and fighting; this is the war-weary Odysseus who described himself and his fellows (14.85–7) as those

οἷσιν ἄρα Ζεὺς
ἐκ νεότητος ἔδωκε καὶ ἐς γῆρας τολυπεύειν
ἀργαλέους πολέμους ὄφρα φθιόμεσθα ἕκαστος.

On this side of his character see 14.83–102n. and B. Fenik in *Homer* (ed. B.

Fenik, Leiden 1978) 71–3. He uses no paradigm to prove his point (Akhilleus himself will use the Niobe tale when he makes the same argument to Priam, 24.602–13).

After an introductory self-justification (216–20), Odysseus declares he is glutted with battle (221–4). Then comes his argument, as usual in ring form:

A   Denying ourselves food is no way to mourn the slain (225);
B   far too many are killed for that (226–7)!
C   We must bury and weep for the dead for one day (228–9);
B′ then those who are so far spared by the battle (230)
A′ must think of food and drink, to take up the struggle again (231–3).

He concludes with a stern warning to anyone who ignores this summons to join the others against the Trojans (233–7). As a reflection on the reasons men go out to die in battle the speech bears comparison with the better-known thoughts of Sarpedon (12.310–28), but in Odysseus' way the argument is practical, not philosophical.

216–20 Probably Πηλέος υἱέ should be read, as in the better MSS; see 16.21n. Akhilleus himself more or less admitted that there were wiser men than he (ἀγορῇ δέ τ' ἀμείνονές εἰσι καὶ ἄλλοι, 18.106). Antilokhos presents the same argument from a younger man's viewpoint at 23.587–91, ending with the same apologetic phrase τώ τοι ἐπιπλήτω κραδίη; see also 18.251–2n. Notice the two emphatic runovers ἔγχει and πολλόν. πρότερος γενόμην (γεγόνει) καὶ πλείονα οἶδα (etc.) is formular (3 × *Il.*; the final phrase also 1 × *Od.*).

221–4 The precise meaning of this impressive metaphor and its application to the context were much debated in ancient times. The most recent discussions are those of F. M. Combellack, *AJP* 105 (1984) 247–57 (with a full account of the evidence and ancient views), and C. Moulton, *CP* 74 (1979) 285–6. The passage is imaginative and highly allusive, with several examples of words used with more than one concurrent significance.

The first line means basically 'men soon get tired of fighting'. This is related to the context both as a retort to the blood-lust expressed in Akhilleus' last words (214) and as an implicit renewal of Odysseus' claim that the men will tire the quicker if they are unfed. (Later he expresses the same idea in positive form: after they have taken food and drink, they will be able to fight νωλεμὲς αἰεί, 231–2.) Verse 222 continues 'of which ⟨fighting⟩ the bronze strews the stalks very thickly (πλείστην) on the ground'. χαλκός is a fascinating bivalent metonymy, meaning 'sickles' within the metaphor and 'weapons' in the narrative context. καλάμη must first be understood as the cornstalks cut by the sickle, the analogy between the falling stalks and the falling warriors being the same as that in the simile at 11.67–71 (see note *ad loc.*). πλείστην, which at first seems to give the reason for the fighters' κόρος, thus comes to mean primarily that there are many casualties. Combellack well quotes *Troilus and Cressida* v. 5.24–5:

> And there the strawy Greeks, ripe for his edge,
> Fall down before him like a mower's swath.

The next verse (223), however, begins ἄμητος δ' ὀλίγιστος, which is usually taken to mean 'the crop is smallest [very small]' (Combellack, *op. cit.* 247–50, presents the evidence). The antithesis with πλείστην... καλάμην indicates that the meaning of the latter has now shifted to 'straw ⟨after threshing⟩', as at *Od.* 14.214, which is its proper significance (so Eustathius 1181.49; LSJ incorrectly render 'stubble'). What 'crop' is meant? Some critics (including Eustathius 1181.31 and Moulton) take it as the men who survive, which seems quite inconsistent with the image. Others (including Combellack) think it represents the booty, i.e. the armour stripped from the dead.

An alternative rendering of 223 is 'the harvest-time is shortest', which is tentatively put forward by Combellack, though the evidence for this significance of ἄμητος is not strong (τὸν ἄμητον... μένει and μένεσκον τὸν ἄμητον in Herodotus 2.14.5 and 4.42.3 are ambiguous). The contrast with πλείστην then takes the form 'many men die, in a very short time'. Combellack explains this by arguing (from the following mention of Zeus's scales) that a sudden rout is meant. This seems, however, to draw too specific a picture from the very general language, and 'a very short time' works against Odysseus' purpose in using the metaphor.

The exegetical scholia (AbT) say that ἄμητος means 'harvest-time', relying on the feeble support of Hesiod's ἄρχεσθ' ἀμήτοιο (*Erga* 384), and ἀμητός means 'crop'. Both Porphyry (quoted by Erbse) and Eustathius (1181.39) provide different interpretations to fit each meaning.

It seems best to render the phrase 'but the harvest is very small', with the same general sense as the English carries, and take the meaning to be that the fighters profit little from hazarding their lives. The image of harvested grain, in this context, also suggests the meal which is so much in Odysseus' mind; the listening soldiers, about to risk their lives once again, have not even been fed!

The scales of Zeus (223–4) are familiar, symbolizing both the turning of battle and the fate of an individual (see 8.73–4n., 22.208–13n., and Combellack, *op. cit.* 251–2). But here the figure is coupled with what may have been a formula for Zeus, ὅς τ' ἀνθρώπων ταμίης πολέμοιο τέτυκται (= 4.84). Zeus thus holds his balance, not like Ares the gold-changer

(Aeschylus, *Ag.* 437–9), but like a steward weighing out supplies from the commissariat (cf. ταμίαι...σίτοιο δοτῆρες, 44). Again the idea of the meal is in the background. Homer has merged context and images in a highly poetic way.

Leaf's summary, 'Battle is a labour in which men must be kept up to the mark; for there is plenty of hard work and little reward – as with a farmer who should reap abundant haulm, and find but little grain to harvest... Soldiers require strengthening with food for such thankless work', is good, and closer to the sense than Moulton allows. Combellack properly stresses the importance of taking the context into consideration, but I think that the interpretation given above is preferable to his.

225 Cf. Odysseus' γαστέρα δ' οὔ πως ἔστιν ἀποκρύψαι μεμαυῖαν (*Od.* 17.286). In the *Od.* he is often preoccupied with the needs of the belly; see J. Russo, *Odissea* on *Od.* 18.44. Ruijgh, τε *épique* 837–8, points out that after the generalizing αἶψά τε (221) a co-ordinating καί would be expected here instead of δέ, but the intervening subordinate clauses – and the desire to begin the verse with the emphatic γαστέρι – lead to an anacoluthon.

226–7 This magnificent couplet brings in one by one the elements of the tragedy of warfare; 'to excess – many men – close together – day after day – they fall dead – shall we ever find rest from toil and suffering?' The ideas, in the Virgilian manner, are both general ('war is hell') and specific to the context ('too many are dying for us to mourn them properly'). On ἐπήτριμοι see 18.209–14n. ἀναπνεύσωσι πόνοιο | recurs at 15.235. Leaf is badly in error in limiting πόνοιο to 'toilsome *fasting*'.

229 νηλέϊ χαλκῷ (11 × *Il.*, 8 × *Od.*), νηλέϊ θυμῷ | (3 × *Od.*), and νηλεές ἦμαρ (7 × *Il.*, 2 × *Od.*) are formular, but this is the only occurrence of νηλέα (besides *HyHerm* 385). On the form see 17.327–30n. The epithet is also applied directly and reproachfully to Akhilleus at 9.632, 16.33, and 16.204, and there is some irony in Odysseus' counselling him to be obdurate here (the point is made by J. A. Arieti, *CJ* 82, 1986, 19–20). ἐπ' ἤματι means 'for one day', as at 10.48, *Od.* 2.284, etc.

230–2 There was a formula στυγεροῦ πολέμοιο | (2 × *Il.*). περὶ goes with λίπωνται, 'survive'. Leaf is mistaken in thinking this is 'a recommendation to eat when the battle is over'; Odysseus of course means those still alive must eat now. With 232 cf. μάρνασθαι δηΐοισιν ἐπ' ἀνδράσι νωλεμές αἰεί (9.317, 17.148).

233 Cf. τεύχεα ἑσσαμένω, ταμεσίχροα χαλκὸν ἑλόντε (23.803). χαλκὸν ἀτειρέα recurs in the same position at 20.108; cf. χαλκὸς ἀτειρής | (3 × *Il.*), ἀτειρέα χαλκόν | (only *Od.* 13.368, surprisingly). Perhaps ἀτειρής reinforces the thought of νωλεμές and νηλέα θυμὸν ἔχοντας (229), as well as looking forward to Odysseus' coming instructions to the army to return after the meal armed and ready for battle.

233–7 Odysseus, practical as ever, concludes with a warning to the troops to return after the meal to their ranks, ready to fight, without waiting for any further summons. This is the Odysseus who disciplined the troops as they ran for the ships in book 2. Shirking is far from unknown in the *Il.*, as H. van Wees illustrates (*CQ* 38, 1988, 13). λαῶν (234) is best taken with τις, though it could also be an objective genitive with ὀτρυντύν. In 235–6 it is best (with Leaf and others) to punctuate after ὀτρυντύς: 'Let no one of you all (λαῶν) hold back, awaiting some other summons ⟨to join ranks for battle⟩; *this* is the summons; there will be trouble (κακόν) for anyone left by the ships'; the summons to battle is described at length at 2.441–54, and the punishment for disobedience is made clear at 2.391–3. Cf. 351–2, where Athene finds the Greeks arming αὐτίκα when she comes to refresh Akhilleus. The scholia take it like this (αὐτοκέλευστος ἐξίτω, bT). As Allen prints it, the meaning must be '⟨If anyone waits for another summons to the ranks,⟩ this summons will be a bad ⟨one for him, i.e. to punishment⟩', which is too complicated. ὀτρυντύς occurs in Greek only here and in an imitation. The formation is regular (Risch, *Wortbildung* 40–1), and the name Otrunteus is found (20.384). On the omission of the antecedent to ὅς see 17.509n. Verse 237 = 4.352, cf. 318. ἐγείρομεν is subjunctive.

238–356 Odysseus' words are unanswerable, and the younger Greeks go off to bring the gifts from Agamemnon's quarters into the midst of the assembly. Agamemnon takes a formal oath, over a sacrificial boar, that he has not slept with Briseis. In a brief acknowledgement Akhilleus, like Agamemnon before him, blames their quarrel on Ate. The restored Briseis laments over the body of Patroklos. Akhilleus and the other Greek leaders lament too. In response to a suggestion from Zeus, Athene sustains Akhilleus with ambrosia and nectar

In structure the transfer of gifts is much like the restoration of Khruseis to her father (1.430–74). The donor produces the item(s) to be handed over; he makes a speech; the recipient makes an acknowledgement; and the gathering breaks up. In this case the prayer (oath) is made by the donor; in the Khruseis-scene it is made by the recipient. Akhilleus' graceful gift to Nestor during the funeral games is similarly accompanied by speeches from both parties (23.616–50).

The third element in J. B. Hainsworth's analysis of the structure of joining battle, after the army's meal, is the council of chiefs (*G&R* 13, 1966, 162–3). In this instance the usual refreshment is mentioned but rejected by Akhilleus (303–8), and the council meeting is adapted into a communal mourning over Patroklos, led by Akhilleus. The refreshment is supplied afterwards by the divine intervention (340–56).

238–40 'Nestor's sons' are Antilokhos and Thrasumedes, who are often found together (e.g. 17.377–83). Meges the Doulichian and Thoas the Aetolian are listed in the Catalogue of Ships (2.627, 638), and appear again with Meriones in an episode in Hektor's *aristeia* (15.281–304); Meges is grouped with major leaders at 10.110, and was wearing notable armour (15.530–4, see note *ad loc.*). Thoas is prominent enough for Poseidon to take his form to talk with Idomeneus (13.216–38). Lukomedes does little but avenge a friend at 17.344–51. Meges and Lukomedes were wounded in the *Iliupersis*, but Thoas returned home safely (Pausanias 10.25.2; 10.37.3). No Greek named Melanippos appears elsewhere in Homer; Trojans of that name (presumably different individuals) are killed three times, always at the end of a verse (8.276, 15.576, 16.695), so the name must be a regular line-filler.

242 'No sooner said than done' (Leaf). τετέλεστο δὲ ἔργον | recurs 1 × *Od.*, and is followed by Ἀχαιῶν | at 7.465. The proverbial phrase seems to have been ἅμα ἔπος τε καὶ ἔργον (*HyHerm* 46, Herodotus 3.135, cf. Ap. Rh. 4.103). Rather similar is οὔ πω πᾶν εἴρητο ἔπος ὅτ' ἄρ' ἤλυθον αὐτοί (10.540).

243–8 The list of gifts corresponds exactly to those Agamemnon offered to hand over immediately at 9.122–34. The further rewards he promised to give Akhilleus after the sack of Troy (the distinction is carefully made at 9.135, perhaps with the present scene in view) are ignored here; since Akhilleus, as well as the audience, knows that he will not live to see the fall of the city any mention of them here by Agamemnon, cold and awkward as he is, would be difficult to contrive effectively. See M. M. Willcock, *HSCP* 81 (1977) 48.

At 9.122 the tripods and the gold talents share a verse; here the tripods get one to themselves (243) and the talents are handled separately at the end, perhaps in order to bring in a reference to Odysseus, who is organizing all this (247–8). Cauldrons and racehorses appear in a repeated verse (244 = 9.123), but the latter are here shorn of the glorifying expansion Agamemnon gave them (9.124–7). The seven slave-women are as well-skilled as promised (245 ≅ 9.128), but their beauty and Lesbian origin (9.129–30) is passed over here. Briseis is summarily grouped with them, as her importance will be brought out later by her lament (see 282–302n.).

243–5 With οὓς οἱ ὑπέστη | cf. ἥν (ὥς) περ ὑπέστης | (2 × *Od.*) and τὰ πάροιθεν ὑπέστην | (2 × *Il.*). As usual MSS give ἔργ' εἰδυίας; see West, *Theogony* 241–2.

247–8 Verse 247 ≅ 24.232; στήσας again means 'having weighed out' at 22.350. ἦρχ': 'led the way ⟨back⟩'. On κούρητες Ἀχαιῶν see 192–3n.

249–68 The swearing of an oath may be simply narrated by the poet in a few lines, or it may be expanded by direct speech, a list of the powers in whose name the oath is sworn, and a sacrifice (see 14.271–9n. and Arend,

Typische Scenen 122–3). The only other instance of an oath-sacrifice is before the duel of Paris and Menelaos, when the truce is sworn to (3.268–313, see notes *ad locc.*) – a truce which must be heavily emphasized because it is to be broken. Here the expansion is necessary to dramatize the return of Akhilleus' prize of honour in pristine condition, but there are fewer details than in the earlier example.

249–51 Just as Akhilleus was insulted before all the Greeks, so must the restitution be displayed ἐν μέσσῃ ἀγορῇ, with the whole army sitting in silence and listening to the oath Agamemnon swears (255–6). The complimentary phrase for the herald is also applied to the bards Phemios and Demodokos (*Od.* 1.371, 9.4). At 3.268–70 there is the additional expansion of mixing wine and pouring water over the king's hands, prepared for at 3.246–8; see note *ad loc.*

252–5 The long postponement of the main verb, by three participles and a relative clause, is highly unusual in Homer. It throws emphasis on εὔχετο, brought out again by the repetition εὐξάμενος (257) after the description of the listening audience. The drawing of the knife is described in the same lines at 3.271–2. μάχαιρα, here distinguished from the sword, later takes on that meaning (see 13.609–10n.). The hairs are cut off as a first offering, and at a normal sacrifice are thrown in the fire (cf. εὔχετ᾽ ἀπαρχόμενος [here ἀπό … ἀρξάμενος] κεφαλῆς τρίχας ἐν πυρὶ βάλλων, *Od.* 3.446). Since there is no fire at an oath-sacrifice the hairs are distributed to the chiefs at 3.273–4 (see note *ad loc.*); in this shorter version that element is omitted. The enjambing clause in 254–5 is a version of the usual formula εὔχετο (etc.) χεῖρας ἀνασχών | (3 × *Il.*, 2 × *Od.*).

255–6 ἐπ᾽ αὐτόφιν must = ἐφ᾽ ἑαυτῶν, 'by themselves', cf. εὔχεσθε … | σιγῇ ἐφ᾽ ὑμείων (7.194–5); they watch not only apart from Agamemnon, but as individuals. On this occasional reflexive meaning of αὐτός see Chantraine, *GH* II 157–8. Every word here contributes to the intensity of the picture of Agamemnon, standing alone to take the solemn oath (249–50), watched by 'all the other Greeks, by themselves, sitting silently, in the proper way, listening to their king'.

257–60 Both hemistichs of 257 are formular. The aorist participle expresses an action contemporaneous with the main verb, as in ἐποτρύνας ἐκέλευσεν etc. (*Od.* 2.422); see Chantraine, *GH* II 187–8. Virtually identical powers are invoked at 3.276–80 (see note *ad loc.*); Zeus (in a different formula), Helios (with an added relative clause), then the rivers, Gaia, and the Erinues (not named, but with the same description; 260 ≅ 3.279). Zeus is supreme; Helios sees and hears everything (3.277); Earth is mother of all and in physical contact with all mankind; and the Erinues act against those who break an oath (cf. 264–5, and 3.278–9n., 9.454n.). ὑπὸ γαῖαν is the Erinues' home, and does not necessarily mean that they punish *dead* men there (*pace* C. Sourvinou-Inwood in Hägg, *Greek Renaissance* 36). A. Heubeck, *Glotta* 64 (1986) 147, holds that they punish the guilty man with death and so send him beneath the earth. Verse 258 = *Od.* 19.303. In 260 (≅ 3.279) the antecedent of ὅτις is omitted, as at 235 and 265.

261–3 The wording is more elaborate than that in Odysseus' proposal of the oath (176–7). The vulgate reading is ἐπενεῖκαι, but the indicative (which appears in some good MSS) is regular for a negative oath (cf. 10.330, 15.41–2) and the infinitive will not do after ἐγώ. πρόφασιν (adverbial accusative) occurs in Homer only here and at 302, in a similar construction; see G. P. Shipp, *Antichthon* 2 (1968) 22. It means the reason or purpose given for an action; 'neither seeking ⟨her⟩ for the purpose of the bed nor for any other'. On the complex significance of the word, especially in later authors, see L. Pearson, *TAPA* 83 (1952) 205–23 and *TAPA* 103 (1972) 381–94. οὔτε... οὔτε is used, despite the preceding μή, because the clauses are not a co-ordinate addition to what Agamemnon has sworn to in μή... χεῖρ' ἐπένεικα but only his exegesis of his meaning. ἀπροτίμαστος: 'unsought-out', a *hapax* formed from α-privative + προτί + μαίομαι.

264–5 Similarly at 3.297–301 the Greeks and Trojans invite the gods' punishment on themselves if they violate the oath they have just sworn. σφ'(ε) (265) is an Aeolic accusative plural, like ἄμμε, ὔμμε, but is elsewhere in Homer interpreted as a dual by analogy with the dual ending -ε. Chantraine, *GH* I 267, suggests that in some other places the Ionic σφεας (monosyllabic; cf. ἡμέας, ὑμέας) may have replaced an older σφε.

266–9 Verse 266 ≅ 3.292, which has ἀρνῶν for κάπρου. At 3.310 the lambs sacrificed at the oath-taking are carried off to Troy. The point seems to be that animals sacrificed at an oath-swearing are polluted and must not be eaten, and so here the boar's carcase is thrown into the purifying sea; see 3.310n., 1.313–14n. W. F. Wyatt, Jr, *AJP* 103 (1982) 258, says 'The boar here represents *ate* and Talthybius is acting as Zeus did when he cast *ate* out of heaven', which perhaps goes too far. The usual form of the sea formula (267) is μέγα λαῖτμα θαλάσσης | (3 × *Od.*). βόσις (cf. βόσκω) occurs only here and in later imitators, but the formation is common (cf. δόσις, λύσις etc.; Risch, *Wortbildung* 38–9), as is its use as an infinitive of purpose. Verse 269 does not recur, but ἀνστάς begins the verse 2 × *Od.* and φιλοπτολέμοισι(ν) in this position is applied generically to several nouns; cf. ἀλλ' ὅ γε οἷς ἑτάροισι φιλοπτολέμοισι μετηύδα (23.5).

270–5 It is necessary for Akhilleus to respond with a few words here, both as recipient of Agamemnon's gifts (cf. Khruses at 1.451–6, Nestor at 23.626–50) and as one involved in the matter of the oath (cf. Priam at 3.304–9). It is gracious in him to identify himself (in effect) with Agamemnon's remarks about the responsibility of Ate, thus implicitly accepting the king's explanation of his conduct; cf. his courtesy to

Agamemnon at 23.890–4. He also explicitly accepts that Odysseus has won in the matter of the meal (275). There is irony in his assertion that Zeus must have wanted death for so many Greeks, since it was Akhilleus himself who requested this (1.409–10). Ascription to Zeus of everything that happens is, however, normal; see for instance J. M. Redfield, *Nature and Culture in the Iliad* (Chicago 1975) 247–8. W. F. Wyatt, Jr, holds that '*Ate* has deprived Achilles of his friend Patroclus because he refused to accept Agamemnon's offer [in book 9]' (*AJP* 103, 1982, 256). I am not sure that this interpretation is correct, and I would not see this implication in Akhilleus' words here.

270 The plural of ἄτη also occurs at 9.115 and 10.391; here it = 'Ate-inspired actions'. διδοῖσθα (only here) is formed by adding the Homeric 2nd person perfect ending -θα (as in οἶσθα, ἦσθα) on to the Ionic form διδοῖς (accented as if from a contracted verb, as at 9.164). εἶσθα (10.450) and τίθησθα (2 × *Od.*) show the same ending. See Chantraine, *GH* 1 469–70, 298.

273–5 ἀμήχανος used of a person usually means 'unpersuadable', 'stubborn', and is applied to Hektor (13.726), Here (15.14), Akhilleus himself (by Patroklos; 16.29), and wryly by the sleepy Diomedes to Nestor (10.167). But at *Od.* 19.363 it clearly means 'helpless'. Ameis–Hentze accept the first meaning ('unbeugsam'), which makes good enough sense ('he would not have stubbornly insisted on taking the woman away against my will'). The ancients however (AbT; perhaps Nicanor and Didymus) recognize only the meaning 'helpless', saying it may be explained by what follows (*sc.* Zeus's wish that many Greeks die) or by what precedes (*sc.* the reference to Ate). The juxtaposition with ἀέκοντος favours the modern interpretation, but neither sense is easy to grasp. ἀλλά replaces εἰ μή.

Akhilleus addresses Zeus directly, as Agamemnon had just done, then goes on to speak of him in the third person. Aias reversed this (17.629–47). Verse 275 = 2.381.

276–7 Verse 276 = *Od.* 2.257; 277 = 23.3, ≅ *Od.* 2.258. Akhilleus dismisses the assembly, just as he summoned it (40ff.). αἰψηρήν need mean no more than 'quickly', though some ancients and moderns have taken it to refer to the urgent summoning of the assembly.

279–80 Ἀχιλλῆος θείοιο | occurs only here and at 297, but there is no alternative formula except the equally generic Ἀ. μεγαθύμου, used in the middle of the verse 1 × in each poem. On the original form (θεῖ- < *θεσιος) see Hainsworth, *Odyssey* on *Od.* 5.11. κάθισαν must mean something like 'settled in'.

282–302 Briseis' lament, in which the other slave-women join in formal antiphony (301–2; cf. 24.723–76), serves as the traditional mourning of women over the corpse of Patroklos; the motif has been anticipated three times (18.28–31, 18.50–64, 18.339–42; on the general arrangement of the funeral rites for Patroklos see M. W. Edwards, *Studies in Honour of T. B. L. Webster* 1, edd. J. H. Betts, J. T. Hooker, and J. R. Green, Bristol 1986, 86–8, and on formal laments 24.718–76n.). It also dramatizes the return to Akhilleus of his prize of honour without detracting attention from his grief for Patroklos; her own grief for him enlarges our comprehension of the loss he himself has suffered. Moreover, the picture of the mourning Briseis drives home the fact that she has been restored at the cost of Patroklos' life, and also, like Thetis' lament at the time of Akhilleus' first overwhelming grief, prefigures the mourning soon to come at Akhilleus' own death (see introduction to book 18). The scholia comment on the solemnity and emotional content of the lines (bT on 282–302).

282–5 The complimentary phrase is otherwise reserved for Kassandra (24.699) and Turo (Hesiod fr. 30.25 MW); Penelope twice receives the lengthened version Ἀρτέμιδι ἰκέλη ἠὲ χρυσέῃ Ἀφρ. (*Od.* 17.37, 19.54). Briseis laments ὡς ἴδε Πάτροκλον δεδαϊγμένον ὀξέϊ χαλκῷ (283), and a little later tells us that she saw her husband lying before his city δεδαϊγμένον ὀξέϊ χαλκῷ (292); 'the sight of Patroclus evokes memories of her own dead husband, and in the ensuing speech Briseis' grief for the husband she lost is integrated into her lament over Patroclus. In turn, Briseis' recollection of her dead husband activates the memory of the other women present (301–2)' (I. J. F. de Jong in Bremer, *HBOP* 113). The phrase ἀμφ' αὐτῷ χυμένη λίγ' ἐκώκυε is used for the woman mourning a husband killed in battle in the famous simile for the weeping Odysseus (*Od.* 8.527).

286 Only at 6.475 does εἶπε δέ again begin a verse. ἐϊκυῖα θεῇσι is formular, in all but one case (*Od.* 7.291) preceded by γυνή (2 × *Il.*, *HyAphr* 153) or δέμας (8.305).

287–300 Briseis' lament corresponds closely in structure and content to that of Akhilleus (315–37), as has been pointed out by D. Lohmann, *Die Andromache-Szenen der Ilias* (*Spudasmata* 42, Hildesheim 1988) 13–32 (cf. his *Reden* 102–5). The groups of mourners are almost equal in size (8 women (245–6) and 7 men (310–11); Lohmann notes (p. 22) the similarity with the facing groups on geometrical funeral amphorae, and remarks on the odd coincidence with the total of a Sophoclean chorus), and while Briseis' lament emphasizes one result of the assembly, her return to Akhilleus and the recompense paid, that of Akhilleus amplifies another, the communal meal before battle and his own absence from it. Both speakers begin, after a loving salutation to Patroklos, by contrasting their life when he was alive and the wretched present without him (287–90; 315–21). Then the speaker tells of other sufferings that (s)he has endured or might endure by the loss of other dear ones (290–4; 321–7). Finally, each ends (in ring form elaboration of the first theme) by describing a personal hope for the future which has now been destroyed (295–300, 328–37).

The speeches are moving because these are universal human sentiments. Both here and in the other laments in the *Il.* the poet acknowledges the intensely personal and lonely nature of grief. Mourners always speak of the loss that the death brings to their own lives (see Edwards, *HPI* 91 and 314), and this then calls to mind their other sorrows. This is made explicit in 302, where the other women weep Πάτροκλον πρόφασιν, σφῶν δ' αὐτῶν κήδε' ἑκάστη (see note *ad loc.*), and again at 339, where the elders mourn μνησάμενοι τὰ ἕκαστος ἐνὶ μεγάροισιν ἔλειπον.

In his Introduction to this Book Leaf said 'linguistic offences, which are freely scattered through the book, are [in Briseis' speech] heaped up in reckless profusion'. Each of the first two lines has a metrical anomaly, but there is little else to cause such concern and the sense and structure do not invite criticism.

287–8 The scansion Πᾰτρŏκλε appears only here; a vowel which remains short before mute + liquid is very rare unless the word cannot otherwise be used in a hexameter. Page, *Odyssey* 163, lists the exceptions; see also 20.383n., 16.554–5n., and Chantraine, *GH* 1 109. It is also the only Homeric example of an enclitic following a vocative, and attracted the attention of ancient critics (see Erbse); of course Πάτροκλ' ἐμοί is possible. (τῷ) ἐμῷ κεχαρισμένε θυμῷ | is used to Patroklos by Akhilleus (11.608), and also to Diomedes by Sthenelos, Athene, and Agamemnon, and to young Peisistratos by Telemakhos. It is clearly reserved for close friends. On the rare hiatus after the second trochee in 288 see 3.46n. Various emendations have been suggested, but the anomaly is best retained.

289–90 νῦν δέ is used by Akhilleus too (319). δέχεται is intransitive, 'follows upon', as at Hesiod, *Theogony* 800 ἄλλος δ' ἐξ ἄλλου δέχεται χαλεπώτερος ἆθλος. With κακὸν ἐκ κακοῦ cf. κακὸν κακῷ (16.111), κακὸς κακόν (*Od.* 17.217). But Akhilleus has not previously suffered as she has, and so he compares his grief with the future, not the past: οὐ μὲν γάρ τι κακώτερον ἄλλο πάθοιμι (321).

291–4 The capture of Briseis at the sack of Lurnessos was described in the passage explaining Akhilleus' absence from the Greek Catalogue (2.690–3; see notes there, and 9.343n., 16.56–9n.). The mention of the story here was prepared for by Akhilleus' brief reference at line 60. In the same raid Khruseis was captured at Thebe, the city of Andromakhe's father Eëtion, who was killed by Akhilleus (1.366–9; 6.414–16). Andromakhe also lost her brothers when Akhilleus caught them sheep-herding (6.421–4), and he nearly put an end to Aineias in similar circumstances (20.90–2). The story of this raid has been studied by Reinhardt, *IuD* 50–7. As usual, events preceding the beginning of the poem are narrated by a character, not the poet (see Krischer, *Konventionen* 93–4).

The scholia (bT on 296) assume that Munes, king of the city (296), was

Briseis' husband, but this is not explicit in Homer. That Briseis had been married adds to the pathos of her mourning a second time over a man δεδαϊγμένον ὀξέϊ χαλκῷ (283, 292); a third repetition of her sorrow will soon come when Akhilleus himself dies. The question whether Akhilleus could properly marry a widow will never arise except in the minds of commentators.

292–4 εἶδον < *ἔϝιδον, with loss of digamma and contracted vowels. There are two other examples of this 'flagrant breach of Epic law' (Page, *HHI* 334) at the beginning of the verse (11.112, *Od.* 10.194) and two at other positions (*Od.* 9.182, 11.162); see Chantraine, *GH* I 28. The second hemistich of 293 recurs at 3.238. κήδειος (294) appears as κήδεος at 23.160. From the general sense of κῆδος, 'care', come the specialized meanings 'honours to the dead' and 'relationship by marriage'; cf. κηδεμών, 'one who takes care for', 'patron' (Chantraine, *Dict.* s.v. κήδω). Here the sense must be simply 'beloved', perhaps with overtones of mourning. The rest of the verse is unformular, though ἦμαρ ὀλέθριον appears at 409; ὀλέθριον ἦμαρ at verse-end (parallel to δούλιον ἦμαρ |, νηλεὲς ἦμαρ | etc.) would cause the forbidden trochaic cut in the fourth foot.

295–7 οὐδὲ μὲν οὐδέ is very emphatic; see 17.24n. κλαίειν is postponed longer than usual, and emphasized by its position; cf. 252–5n. The iteratives ἔασκες, ἔφασκες are rather moving. On Ἀχιλλῆος θείοιο see 279–80n.; here (unusually) it is placed in the verse before that in which its controlling noun stands in order that κουριδίην ἄλοχον may be emphasized at the beginning of next verse.

298–9 Briseis left Akhilleus ἀέκουσα (1.348), he spoke of her as his ἄλοχον θυμαρέα (9.336), and he has expressed considerable affection for her (9.342–3). The relationship between them, though not romantic, shows the gentler side of Akhilleus and prepares for the effect of the final view of them together (24.676); but of course the passage here reflects the kindness of Patroklos rather than the passion of Akhilleus. There is also a sad irony, for Briseis does not know Akhilleus himself will not return to Phthie.

It is easiest (with Willcock) to consider Patroklos still the subject of ἄξειν and δαίσειν, rather than supposing a change to Akhilleus (with Ameis–Hentze, Leaf, and van Leeuwen, reading δ' for τ' in 298 with the inferior MSS). One supposes Thetis would have been responsible for giving the marriage-feast rather than Patroklos, just as Menelaos is found δαινύντα γάμον for his son and daughter at *Od.* 4.3–4, but the plan never approached reality. To give a funeral feast is δαινύναι τάφον (23.29 etc.).

300 The concluding verse recalls the beginning of her lament. Patroklos is the only person to whom μείλιχος is applied; see 17.670–3n. His kindness to an unhappy woman is like that of Hektor to Helen (24.767–72). ἄμοτον normally occurs with a form of μεμαώς (5 × *Il.*, 1 × *Od.*; with κεχολωμένος at

23.567 and τανύοντο at *Od.* 6.83), and probably derives from the same root with α-privative (so B. Forssman, *O-o-pe-ro-si: Festschrift für Ernst Risch*, Berlin 1986, 329–39).

301–2 Verse 301 = 22.515, 24 746; there are several adaptations. On πρόφασιν see 261–3n.; the women do not use the occasion as a 'pretext' to indulge their own grief, and still less need we think that γυναῖκες refers to the newly arrived women who did not know Patroklos (so schol. AT, Ameis–Hentze). Briseis' lament over the body of Patroklos is the 'reason' that they mourn their other personal sorrows, as suggested again at 339 and 24.167–8 (see 287–300n.). Briseis' own reference to her dead husband and brothers illustrates this (291–4). Πάτροκλον πρόφασιν became proverbial (e.g. Achilles Tatius 2.34).

303–39 Akhilleus' refusal to eat and the lament (together with the other leaders) which follows take the place of the meal and council of chiefs which usually follow an assembly (see 238–356n.). A formal meal will be required for the reconciliation, but will not take place until 23.35–56.

304–8 Verse 304 summarizes the leaders' entreaties that Akhilleus eat, his refusal, and his agony of mind (στεναχίζων), and also acts as introduction to the following direct speech. The absence of a normal speech-introduction is noteworthy, perhaps indicating Akhilleus' irritation at their insistence. Verse 305 ≅ 17.154. πρίν is not explained until 308, where πρὶν ἠέλιον δῦναι is altered to a more vivid expression.

310–13 The older and wiser chiefs remain to comfort Akhilleus. The others presumably go to eat. The mention of old Phoinix is noteworthy; he rarely appears outside book 9, but is brought in here when Akhilleus most needs his friends. τέρποντες, 'trying to comfort', is conative; for participles used like this cf. 1.159, 24.111 (quoted by Macleod, *Iliad XXIV* 100). πυκινῶς ἀκαχήμενος ἦτορ | and π. ἀκάχημαι (-ηται) | occur 1 × and 2 × *Od.* respectively. There are parallels to the powerful metaphor 'going down into the bloody jaws of war' in πτολέμοιο μέγα στόμα πευκεδανοῖο (10.8, see note *ad loc.*) and ὑσμίνης... στόμα (20.359); and the points of weapons are called κατὰ στόμα εἱμένα χαλκῷ (15.389). The comparison is clearly with the maw of a wild beast, and the variation in phrasing suggests it is not a dead metaphor. J. Griffin, *JHS* 106 (1986) 52, notes that Akhilleus alone uses αἱματόεις metaphorically, with πολέμοιο (9.650) and with ἤματα (9.326); and with a poet as careful as this it is not coincidental that the only other metaphorical use is here, when the narrator is expressing the thoughts in Akhilleus' mind. Similarly, the only occurrence of the common direct-speech word λίην (41 × in *Il.* and *Od.*) in narrative is when the narrator is describing Odysseus' thoughts (*Od.* 14.461; so Griffin, *loc. cit.*).

314–37 On the structure and content of Akhilleus' speech see 287–300n. Though the reference to the elders who mourn around him (338–9) suggests that this, like Briseis' preceding speech, is in a sense a formal lament, the thought with which it begins, Akhilleus' memories of when Patroklos used to serve his meals, arises directly out of the context.

314–18 μνησάμενος is repeated for the other mourning chiefs at 339, there taking an object. Here it provides a bridge from Akhilleus' refusal to eat to his lament for his dead friend. In the only other Homeric use of ἀναφέρω Herakles 'brought up' Kerberos from Hades (*Od.* 11.625). Here the middle voice must mean 'heaved a sigh', a sense which seems to reappear at Herodotus 1.86.3. The scholia, however, take it as bringing up ἐκ στέρνων τὴν φωνὴν ἀθρόαν (bT).

The heavily emphasized direct address to the dead man is noteworthy. In its three other occurrences δυσάμμορος is used by the mourners of themselves, not of the dead man. φίλταθ' ἑταίρων is applied by Idomeneus to his second-in-command Meriones (13.249; see 13.249–50n.) and (lengthened) by Athene/Mentor to old Laertes (*Od.* 24.517). Verse 316 seems to be an adaptation of λαρὸν τετυκοίμεθα δόρπον | (2 × *Od.*, once preceded as here by ἐν κλισίῃ). αἶψα and ὀτραλέως are linked together only here. Verse 318 = 8.516, cf. 19.237.

319–21 Up to this point in the speech the only significant pause in sense within the verse was that in 317, where the ὁπότε which followed prepared the way for Akhilleus' usual emphatic νῦν δέ (see 18.88n). Now the common ending ὀξέϊ χαλκῷ after δεδαϊγμένος (283, 292, etc.) is dropped in favour of a pause and the new beginning αὐτὰρ ἐμὸν κῆρ |, contrasting strongly with the preceding σὺ μὲν κεῖσαι and leading on to the emphatic runover ἄκμηνον; and the sentence ends with another runover, the unexpected and so doubly emphatic σῇ ποθῇ. On ἄκμηνον see 163n.

321 σῇ ποθῇ: σῇ is for the objective genitive σοῦ, like ἐμὴν... | ...ἀγγελίην at 336–7; cf. Antikleia's ἀλλά με σός τε πόθος... | ...θυμὸν ἀπηύρα to Odysseus (*Od.* 11.202–3) and 6.465. οὐ (instead of μή) shows that he speaks of a possibility, not a wish. Normally in this sense ἄν (κε) would be used with the optative, but cf. ἔπειτα δὲ καί τι πάθοιμι (21.274) etc. (Chantraine, *GH* II 213 and 216). Macleod, *Iliad XXIV* 106 (on 24.213–14) quotes 15.197 as a further example.

Like Briseis (290–4), Akhilleus compares this with other griefs. He associated Patroklos with Peleus and his home in Phthie at 16.13–16, and the association has often returned since his friend's death (18.88–90, 18.101, 18.330–2). The thought of fathers and sons will appear again, even more movingly, in his colloquy with Priam in book 24.

322–3 κεν τοῦ may be replacing an older κε οὗ < '(ϝϝ)οο, with the possessive pronoun serving as reflexive for all three persons, singular and plural, as in Vedic; 'my father'. The same may be the case (in the 2nd person plural) at 11.142 (see note *ad loc.*). See Chantraine, *GH* I 273–4 and (on the initial double digamma) 146–7, and Leaf 1 Appendix A. The second hemistich of 323 is formular.

324–5 With the first hemistich cf. 6.463 | χήτεϊ τοιοῦδ' ἀνδρός, and with the second | δήμῳ (γαίη) ἐν ἀλλοδαπῷ (-ῇ) (2 × *Od.*). The use of ὁ, followed later by the 1st-person verb, is very natural after the preceding τοιοῦδ' υἷος. Akhilleus is very conscious that he is fighting, and Patroklos died, far from home; see J. Griffin, *JHS* 106 (1986) 55. εἵνεκα often begins a verse, notably in Helen's own words | εἵνεκ' ἐμεῖο κυνός (6.356 ≅ 3.100). ῥιγεδανός (only here in Homer, and rarely later) is from the root seen in ῥιγέω, 'shudder', and the obscure suffix that appears in πευκεδανός, ἠπεδανός, ἐλλεδανός (see Risch, *Wortbildung* 106). Its sense is explained by Helen herself: πάντες δέ με πεφρίκασιν (24.775). The formular 'Αργείης 'Ε. would not scan here without adjustment, but that is not the only reason for use of the unique epithet.

326–7 τόν: *sc.* εἴ κεν ἀποφθιμένου πυθοίμην from 322. At 24.465–7 Hermes tells Priam to implore Akhilleus by his father, his mother, and his son (whom Priam actually does not mention), and in the Underworld Akhilleus' shade asks Odysseus about Neoptolemos and rejoices at the long account of his prowess in the last stages of the siege of Troy (*Od.* 11.492–540). Akhilleus' capture of Skuros is mentioned at 9.667–8.

As often in these later Books the poet has in mind episodes of the Trojan tale which occur after the end of the *Il.* (see Introduction, ch. 2, ii), but we do not know how these correspond to the versions given in the later Cyclic poems. According to Proclus' summary, in the *Cypria* Akhilleus landed at Skuros and married Lukomedes' daughter Deïdamia; their son was reared by Phoinix and named by him Neoptolemos, because his father was so young when he entered the war (fr. 21 Bernabé, 16 Davies). The story of the landing on Skuros, because of a storm, is told by the scholia here (T), but attributed to the *Little Iliad* (fr. 24 Bernabé, 4ᴬ Davies). The *Little Iliad* told how Neoptolemos was brought from Skuros by Odysseus after Akhilleus' death, given his father's armour, and visited by the shade of Akhilleus (Proclus; Apollodorus, *Epitome* 5.11). On the more detailed versions of the story and the problems they raise see Kullman, *Quellen* 190–1 and 266. Aristarchus and Aristophanes athetized 327 (Did/A) because Skuros is not far from Troy and Akhilleus would surely have heard if his son had died, and because they thought θεοειδής inappropriate. The epithet is of course generic, used in this position to follow many names in both poems, and the geographic factor can be ignored. Someone (Zenodotus?) went so far as to substitute Πυρῆς ἐμός, ὃν κατέλειπον.

328–33 Akhilleus has long known that he himself would never return home; see 17.404–11 n.

329–30 Macleod, *Iliad XXIV* 51–2, suggests there is a word-play on φθίσεσθαι and Φθίηνδε νέεσθαι: 'the echo here stresses the tragic irony – both

Achilles and Patroclus in fact die and fail to return to Phthia'. ἀπό = 'far from', as in the formular φίλης ἀπὸ πατρίδος αἴης etc. τε (330) has not been explained; Ruijgh, τε *épique* 699, finds it 'l'exemple le plus difficile de δέ τε', and is tempted to emend to δ' ἔτι.

331–3 τὸν παῖδα: τόν may be for ὅν, 'my'; cf. τοῦ πατρός (322 and note). δείξειας ἕκαστα: the digamma of (ϝ)έκαστος is normally observed; see Hoekstra, *Modifications* 50. Verse 333 = *Od.* 7.225 and 19.526; see 5.213n.

334–7 κατά goes with τεθνάμεν. In 336–7 the poet combines parts of the formulas ἐμὴν (σὴν) ποτιδέγμενος ὁρμήν | (1 × *Il.*, 1 × *Od.*), ποτιδέγμενος αἰεί | (3 × *Od.*), and | λυγρῆς ἀγγελίης (17.642, 17.686, cf. 18.18–19), and in doing so creates a very harsh enjambment between ἐμήν and its noun, throwing heavy emphasis on the pronoun; see 18.18–19n. (where there is another harsh enjambment in the speech of Akhilleus). On ἐμήν (= ἐμοῦ) see 321n. πύθηται is a fine example of formular adaptability, here transferred to a different construction from its use with λυγρῆς ἀγγελίης (17.685–6, 18.18–19).

Akhilleus pictures Peleus in a miserable old age, expecting only news of his son's death. A little later Priam, who already knows his own magnificent son is dead, with unconscious irony portrays Peleus still rejoicing in the hope of Akhilleus' return (24.490–2). In the Underworld, Akhilleus still has the same concern for his father (*Od.* 11.494–503). For tales of Peleus' miserable old age see 24.488–9n.

338–9 Cf. 301; the elders are portrayed as a chorus of mourners. On their grief for what they themselves have left behind see 287–300n. In 339 it would be safer to follow (with Leaf) the great majority of MSS and read ἔλειπε, though the plural would be more usual after στενάχοντο.

340–54 Having served as a mark of Akhilleus' grief, the motif of his fasting is now used to introduce a divine intervention, in which both Zeus and Athene honour him with their concern. The short episode is the equivalent of Athene's invigoration of Diomedes before his *aristeia* (5.1–3); the fire which she made blaze from Diomedes' shield and helmet (5.4–7) will appear again and again during Akhilleus' arming.

340 The same verse marks Zeus's pity for the immortal horses mourning over Patroklos (17.441). Change of scene by means of a reference to those watching is graceful and common.

342–3 ἑῆος was probably understood as a 2nd-person possessive pronoun, a metrical alternative for τεοῖο. Zenodotus here (Arn/A) and elsewhere read ἑοῖο, but there is no MS support. See 15.138n.; Chantraine, *GH* I 274; Willcock on 15.138; and Leaf I 562. οὐκέτι πάγχυ recurs at 13.747. μέμβλετ(αι) (< *με-μλ-εται) is perfect of μέλω (Chantraine, *GH* I 432). The teasing note in these two verses is characteristic of Zeus's dealings with the females of his family.

344–9 On ὀρθοκραιράων see 18.3–4n. ἄπαστος is elsewhere followed by ἐδητύος ἠδὲ ποτῆτος | (*Od.* 4.788 (where it is preceded by ἄσιτος), *HyDem* 200) with a variant at *Od.* 6.250. The coupling of adjectives with initial α-privative is a common figure, cf. ἀπτόλεμος καὶ ἄναλκις (3 × *Il.*), ἀκμῆτας καὶ ἀτειρέας (15.697), ἀσπουδί γε καὶ ἀκλειῶς (22.304). Verses 347–8 ≅ 353–4; 349 = 4.73 (see note *ad loc.*), 22.186, *Od.* 24.487.

350–1 The simile employs several rare words. The ἅρπη is a sea-bird, mentioned only here in poetry. τανύπτερυξ (2 × *Il.*), τανύπτερος (*HyDem* 89), τανυσίπτερος (2 × *Od.*) and later τανυπτέρυγος (Simonides, *PMG* 521.3) are useful metrical alternatives. λιγύφωνος does not recur in Homer, but ῾Εσπερίδες λιγύφωνοι | is formular in Hesiod (2 × *Theogony*) and is found in a non-formular usage in *HyHerm* 478. With 350 cf. Stesichorus, *PMG* 209 δι᾽ αἰθέρο[ς ἀτ]ρυγέτας κατέπαλτο (if the reading is correct, see Page *ad loc.*); ἐκκατέπαλτο (a *hapax*) may be from ἐκ + κατά + πάλλω, 'shake' (so Ameis–Henze: 'schwang sich herab') or ἐκ + κατά + ἐπί + ἄλλομαι, 'leap'; κατεπάλμενος at 11.94 supports the latter division, as does the meaning 'leapt out down towards'. ἐϊκυῖα suggests this is a metamorphosis, not simply a simile, but speed is the essential point and (as often) a decision is hard to make (see Introduction, ch. 3, i (b) 4).

351–2 The sudden switch to the other Greeks, donning their armour, seems abrupt (e.g. to Scheibner, *Aufbau* 60–1), but it can be explained as the next regular element of a visit type-scene, the description of what the companions of the person visited are doing. Thus when the envoys to Akhilleus arrive Patroklos is seen sitting across from him (9.190). See Arend, *Typische Scenen* 29, and *TAPA* 105 (1975) 61–7. The reference is picked up, in ring form, at 20.1–2. There is no comment in the scholia, but frr. of a second-century papyrus with a commentary on *Il.* 19, to appear in a future vol. of *The Oxyrhynchus Papyri*, refer to a text containing several plus-verses at this point, though they do not seem to ease the transition (I am grateful to Professor Michael Haslam for this information). αὐτίκα: i.e. immediately after their meal; cf. 235–6n.

352–4 We are not told if Odysseus and the other chiefs who remained with Akhilleus instead of joining in the army's meal (309–11) managed to grab a sandwich while Athene was at work. In 354 almost all MSS read ἵκηται, as in 348, and are followed by Ameis–Hentze and Leaf. Allen's ἵκοιτο is grammatically correct, but the emendation is hardly necessary, as both the proximity of 348 and the fact that Athene has Zeus's direct command in her mind make the more vivid subjunctive quite acceptable.

Ambrosia is used to preserve the corpses of both Patroklos and Hektor (see 29–39n.), and as a cleansing cream by goddesses (14.170–1, see note *ad loc.*; *Od.* 18.192–4). The word may mean 'containing life-force' (see S. West, *Odyssey* on *Od.* 4.429). In the Hesiodic *Catalogue* (fr. 23a MW), where the phrase [ἀμβροσ]ίην [ἐρ]ατε[ινὴν] | στάξε recurs (22–3), the ambrosia seems not only to restore Iphimede's body after her sacrifice by the Greeks but to make her immortal, an implication which may also be present at *HyDem* 237. There is irony in its application here to the hero whose mortality is so powerful a theme in the poem.

355–6 The last part of the formula παρὰ πατρὸς ἐρισθενέος Κρονίωνος | (*Od.* 8.289) is dropped in order to make room for πυκινὸν δῶ, attested only here, which is based on the formulae χαλκοβατὲς δῶ |, ὑψερεφὲς δῶ | etc. and πυκινὸν δόμον (2 × *Il.*, 3 × *Od.*). Mention of the return of the deity to Olumpos is the regular conclusion of a divine visit.

356–424 Akhilleus dons his armour, in the most elaborate of such descriptions in the poem. A simile sets the scene, illustrating the number of the armed men who come out to battle. The flashing of their armour fills the air, the earth resounds beneath their feet. Then Akhilleus' furious lust for combat is described, and the glare that blazes around as he takes up his armour and weapons. Finally, his immortal horses are yoked and he mounts the chariot behind them. He rebukes them for their failure to bring their driver Patroklos home from battle, and is answered by Xanthos with a reminder that Akhilleus' own death is near, though it will not come about through any fault of theirs. With a short rejoinder, in which he again accepts the inevitability of his death, Akhilleus leads the host into battle

On arming-scenes see 3.330–8n., 11.15–46n., and 16.130–54n. The importance of the image of shining fire in a warrior's arming, emphasized in Akhilleus' case by C. Whitman, *Homer and the Heroic Tradition* (Cambridge, Mass. 1958) 138–9, has been analysed in more detail by Krischer, *Konventionen* 23, 27, and 36–8.

356–64 The marching-out of an army to battle is a regular type-scene, much expanded at 2.441–83, very short at 11.49–50, and much adapted when the gods themselves join the mêlée (20.31–74). As often, a simile elaborates the description. Here the points stressed are the number and movement of the snowflakes, emphasized by the cold and wind of 358 (= 15.171, also in a simile; on snow-similes see E. M. Bradley, *TAPA* 98, 1967, 39). The sense of movement is picked up in ἐκφορέοντο (360), and the idea of brightness is added, to be amplified in 362 (though Fränkel's remark, *Gleichnisse* 31, that the comparison of the glitter of arms to the white glare of snow is the heart of the simile is overstated). 'The stream of armor from the ship is compared to the falling of snow because it is thick, and brilliant, and, above all, because it is irrepressible' (T. G. Rosenmeyer, *CSCA* 11, 1978, 215). When the army marches out at 2.455–8 the same gleaming of bronze is compared to a forest fire.

357–8 ταρφέες, 'thickly' (only the plural appears in Homer), is used of snowflakes at 12.158; θαμειαί takes its place at 12.278, and is repeated in the narrative (12.287) as ταρφειαί is here. On αἰθρηγενέος (358; 'born in the clear sky') and the North Wind see 15.170 n. Διός (genitive after the verb) is taken by some editors to mean 'sky', but this is not really necessary (any more than it would be to deny personification to Boreas in the next verse); 13.837 is quoted as a parallel, but see note *ad loc*. As often, the runover word ψυχραί is explained by the following phrase.

359–61 Cf. κόρυθες καὶ θώρηκες λαμπρὸν γανόωντες (13.265). γανάω, 'gleam', is from the same root as γαίω (which appears in the formula κύδεϊ γαίων; see 13.262–5n.). κραταιγύαλοι: perhaps 'with strong concave plates (γύαλα)'. The word occurs only here in Greek. It is not clear exactly what γύαλα are; see 17.314–18n. Several MSS of the *h* family place 361 before 360. Some late MSS read ἐκ νηῶν ἐχέοντο· βοὴ δ' ἄσβεστος ὀρώρει (= 16.267) after 361.

362–3 Cf. the longer version αἴγλη παμφανόωσα δι' αἰθέρος οὐρανὸν ἷκε (2.458), which also describes the gleaming of bronze as the army marches to battle. οὐρανὸν ἷκε is also used with noise as the subject (12.338, 17.425). Here the primary meaning of γέλασσε is 'shine'; Hesychius has γελεῖν· λάμπειν, ἀνθεῖν. See West on *Theogony* 40; Richardson on *HyDem* 14; Chantraine, *Dict.* s.v. γελάω. But the idea 'rejoices' may also be present, as it is in the Hesiod and *HyDem* passages. Similarly earth 'smiles' (μείδησε) at the birth of Apollo (*HyAp* 118). στεροπή, 'lightning', is used metaphorically for the flashing of bronze at 11.83 and 3 × *Od.*

As the Greeks go to battle with Akhilleus leading them, their armour flashes like lightning; the earth thunders beneath their marching feet. The same combination of light and sound, lightning and thunder is worked out more fully in two juxtaposed similes when the troops advance at the end of the Greek catalogue (2.780–5).

364–424 After the impressive simile the focus narrows down to Akhilleus, as it does upon Agamemnon after the similes introducing the Catalogue of Ships (2.477–9). For a detailed comparison of the four major arming-scenes see 3.330–8n. This is by far the most elaborate. The elements picked out for expansion are the unique proem (365–8); the shield, which receives an extended simile (373–80); the helmet, with a brief remark about Hephaistos' workmanship (380–3); the spear, given to Peleus by Kheiron (387–91); and the harnessing of the horses and mounting into the chariot, which includes the dialogue with the horse Xanthos (392–424). In addition, three verses describe the good fit and uplifting effect of the armour (384–6). The breastplate, which receives so much description in Agamemnon's arming-scene (11.19–28), is here given merely the usual formula (371).

364 This begins the proem to the arming-scene; cf. Αἴας (Πάτροκλος) δὲ κορύσσετο νώροπι χαλκῷ | (7.206, 16.130) and 3.328–9, 11–16. The structure may be altered here to avoid the mention of bronze, since Akhilleus' armour is of gold. The verb is picked up by κορυσσάμενος (397) at the conclusion of the arming.

365–8 The other arming-scenes offer no parallel to this personal description of the hero. The sentence τοῦ (τῶν)…πέλε occurs in Hesiod, *Aspis* 164, of the snakes on Herakles' shield; it may have been copied there from this place or have been a common formula. οὐχ ὡς Δόλων, remark schol. T (cf. 10.375). The other expressions in the passage are formular in Homer. Akhilleus is linked with fire (366), and fire in various forms will reappear often in this scene (374, 375, 381, 398; see Moulton, *Similes* 108). δύσετο (368) repeats κορύσσετο (364) in ring form; the same verb introduces the armings of Paris and Agamemnon (3.328, 11.16). 'Paris arms for shame, Agamemnon for security, Patroclus for loyalty and friendship, but Achilles arms in anger and grief for gentle Patroclus fallen' (J. I. Armstrong, *AJP* 79, 1958, 350).

Did/A report that according to Dionysius Sidonius, Aristarchus first athetized these four verses as grotesque (γελοῖον), but later removed the obeli, feeling the passage was poetic (ποιητικόν). They add that Aristarchus' pupil and successor Ammonius said nothing of this in his work on Aristarchus' successive editions (see R. Pfeiffer, *History of Classical Scholarship*, Oxford 1968, 216–17), and Did/T remark αὕτη τῇ προτέρᾳ ἐκδόσει συμφωνεῖ (if in fact the reference is to something in these verses; see Erbse *ad loc.*, and van der Valk, *Researches* I 424–5).

369–71 These three verses occur unchanged in all four of the major arming-scenes (= 3.330–2, 11.17–19, 16.131–3). In the other three examples the θώρηξ is commented upon, either attributed to its proper owner (Lukaon, Akhilleus) or described (Agamemnon's).

372–80 Verses 372–3 = 3.334–5, 16.135–6. Agamemnon's sword is further elaborated after the initial phrase, but Akhilleus' is never emphasized; see 18.609–13n. Here the usual shield-phrase, instead of concluding at the verse-end, is carried over by the enjambing εἵλετο, and the light from it compared to that of the moon. Then this light, which regularly precedes an *aristeia* (e.g. 5.4–8, 15.623; Krischer, *Konventionen* 38), is amplified by a remarkable simile. The blazing fire to which Akhilleus and his armour are often compared appears as the hearth-fire of a lonely shepherd in the mountains, seen from far off by wretched sailors on a stormy sea. One point of comparison is the light shining far through the darkness (so often seen in Aeschylus' *Oresteia*), but the illustration also brings out the longing with which the defeated Greeks, who like the sailors are οὐκ ἐθέλοντες and φίλων ἀπάνευθε (377–8), are looking towards this sign of safety. (*Contra*, Ameis–Hentze: 'Diese Zug ist aber für die Erzählung ohne alle Bedeutung.') The simile thus gives us a sudden insight into the minds of the Greeks who surround Akhilleus (see I. J. F. de Jong, *Mnemosyne* 38, 1985, 276) and, as so often, removes us from the horror of battle (cf. the view of Akhilleus' blood-lust at 365–8 above) to the hardship of ordinary life.

374 ἠΰτε μήνη(ς) | appears again in a simile only at 23.455, where the comparison is with a round, white mark on a horse's face. The image would, if necessary, support the view that a round shield is envisaged here. Later Akhilleus' helmet shines like a star, and the hero himself blazes like the sun (381, 398).

376–8 καιομένοιο... καίεται: this kind of repetition is not uncommon; cf. 18.227, 20.317 and notes *ad locc.*, and 8.215n. On the formular system around | χώρῳ ἐν οἰοπόλῳ (3 × *Il.*) see 13.471–5n.

379–83 Verse 379 recurs (with κεφαλῆς for σάκεος) when Athene makes fire flash around Akhilleus' head (18.214). The passage shares many expressions with the expanded version at 22.313–20, where Akhilleus makes his victorious charge against Hektor. σάκεος... | καλοῦ δαιδαλέου appears there in the nominative (22.313–14); the verses introducing the helmet are different, but they share the description περισσείοντο... | θαμειάς (22.315–16); and the short comparison ἀστὴρ ὥς (381) is expanded to a three-verse simile (22.317–19). As with the parallels in expression at the deaths of Patroklos and Hektor (16.855–7 = 22.361–3), there may be intentional allusion here as well as formular language. ἀστὴρ δ' ὥς ἀπέλαμπεν recurs at the beginning of the verse 1 × *Il.*, 1 × *Od.* ἵει (383) = 'set in place'; the aorist of the same verb was used when Hephaistos made the helmet (18.612).

384–6 This testing of the fit of the new armour naturally does not appear in the other arming-scenes, but there is a version of it when Hektor puts on the armour he has taken from Patroklos (17.210–2). In both cases the divinely made armour has a powerfully uplifting effect. δ' ἕο is for δὲ '(ϝ)ε'(ο) or δ' ἑ(ϝ)ε'(ο) (Chantraine, *GH* I 148). ἐντρέχω is very rare, but its meaning is obvious. εὖτε (386) has the sense of ἠΰτε, 'as', as at 3.10. Did/A report that Aristarchus at first accepted this (here and at 3.10), but later changed his mind and read αὖτε, somehow 'understanding' ὥς. This reading was found in some of the city editions (Did/A), but seems impossible (or at least much inferior). Aristophanes' ὥστε gives the sense but must be an emendation.

387–91 Paris picked up one spear, Patroklos two, in both cases with the formular close ὅ (τά) οἱ παλάμηφιν ἀρήρει (3.338, 16.139); Agamemnon seized two, which are given a few phrases of description (11.43–5). The Patroklos-scene continues with a verse explaining that he does not take up

Peleus' spear, and follows it with 388–91 (= 16.141–4, see note *ad loc.*). That passage prepares the way for this, drawing attention to the spear and explaining why it will still be available for Akhilleus. The amplification given by the descriptive verses is much in place here (as well as in book 16), because the spear is Akhilleus' best-known weapon and will be used to kill Hektor. Patroklos could not wield the mighty spear, but Akhilleus will do so to avenge him.

According to the *Cypria* (fr. 3 Bernabé, 3 Davies = schol. A on 16.140), Kheiron cut the ashwood shaft and presented it to Peleus, Athene polished it, and Hephaistos fitted it with a blade. Doubtless this reflects the concern that Hephaistos was not a wood-worker. Pausanias saw this famous spear in the temple of Athene at Phaselis (3.3.8). It had a bronze butt as well as a bronze blade.

σῦριγξ, occurring 2 × *Il.* for shepherds' pipes, is only here used for a spear-case, but the basic meaning 'pipe' gave rise to its use for various hollow objects in later Greek. δουροδόκη (*Od.* 1.128) is different, a rack for several spears. The chain of epithets (388) is used only for Peleus' spear, for the spear of Athene (5.746 = 8.390), and (perhaps with irony) for Patroklos' spear when Apollo shatters it (16.802); see H. Bannert, *WS* 18 (1984) 27–35. The laudatory motif 'only he could wield it' is also used for Akhilleus' horses (17.76–8 = 10.402–4), the gate-bar of his encampment (24.454–6), Nestor's cup (11.636–7; humorously?) and Odysseus' bow (much expanded; *Od.* 21.404–9); it is adapted for the cup Akhilleus kept for Zeus alone (16.225–7). It is similar to the motif 'two (three) men could not..., but the hero alone could...' at 5.303–4, 12.381–3, 12.447–9, and 20.286–7. Note the word-play πάλλειν... πῆλαι... Πηλιάδα... Πηλίου. Πηλιάδα μελίην recurs 3 × in Akhilleus' battles, in this position at 21.162, after | σείων at 22.133, and as Πηλιὰς ἤϊξεν μελίη at 20.277. The first two times it is used, against Aineias and Asteropaios, it misses its mark. The vulgate reading is τάμε, reflecting the version of the *Cypria*; πόρε survives in a papyrus and most of the *h* family MSS. Did/A mention both readings. See 16.141–4n.

392–424 The arming-scene concludes with the yoking of the horses to the chariot and Akhilleus' mounting behind them, with a final blaze from his armour (398). This part of the type-scene is expanded by his address to his horses, a prophetic response from one of them, and Akhilleus' reaction to it. At the conclusion of Patroklos' arming considerable expansion is given to the yoking of the horses to the chariot, including the symbolic attachment of the mortal trace-horse (16.145–54, see 16.152–4n.). The element is also included in the arming-scene of Here and Athene (8.374-83). After Agamemnon's arming a reference to the charioteers at large takes its place (11.47–8).

392–5 Alkimos is a shortened form of Alkimedon (see 17.466–7n.). He,

Automedon, and the horses took part in a scene together at 17.426–542. Surprisingly, there is no regular type-scene in Homer for harnessing horses, and the language is mainly unformular. The yoking of Here's horses to her chariot (5 729–33) and that of Priam's horses and mules (24.279 80; 24.266–74) are described quite differently from this passage. λέπαδνον is used in Homer only here and at 5.730, both times in the plural; the singular is occasionally found later, e.g. in the well-known ἀνάγκας ἔδυ λέπαδνον (Aeschylus, *Ag.* 218). The derivation is obscure. The yoke rested on the horse's neck, and the λέπαδνα were harness-straps, one passing in front of its chest below the neck and another behind its forelegs; see J. Wiesner, *Arch. Hom.* F 18, 54–5 and Abb. 13, and 107. The χαλινός is mentioned only here in Homer; see Wiesner 20. Three bronze bits are known from the Mycenaean period (Wiesner 56–7 and Abb. 14) and they are visible on frescoes from Mycenae and Tiryns (Wiesner 56–7, Abb. 14 and 15); an iron bit has been found in an early Geometric grave in the Athenian agora (Wiesner 71). γαμφηλαί appears elsewhere 2 × *Il.* of lions' jaws. The reins are sometimes shown running through guide-rings on the yoke, sometimes directly to the driver (Wiesner 108). κατὰ δ' ἡνία τεῖνεν ὀπίσσω is twice used in a slightly different sense when Priam picks up the reins to drive (3.261 and 311). κολλητός is used with δίφρος only here; it is an adaptation of the formular ἅρμασι κολλητοῖσι | (3 × *Il.*, 1 × *Od.*).

395–7 The action is common enough, but the form of the sentence is innovative. ὁ might refer to Akhilleus, or Automedon, or even Alkimos, until at last the name is reached. μάστιγα (-ι) φαεινήν (-ῇ) | (3 × *Il.*, 1 × *Od.*) is formular. | χειρὶ (χερσὶ) λαβών (etc.) occurs 4 × *Il.*, 1 × *Od.* (with adaptations at 3.385 and 21.286), usually beginning the verse, but here the addition of ἀραρυῖαν seems to require that χειρί be taken with it (as bT take it; cf. 3.338) instead of with λαβών. ἀραρυῖα (etc.) in its many other occurrences always ends the verse (20 × *Il.*, 14 × *Od.*), and is always amplified by a dative or an adverb, so it is hardly possible to take it absolutely as 'fitted ⟨with ornaments⟩'. (For a similar disruption of a normal formular association between adjacent words see 192–3n.). ἐφ' ἵπποιιν and ἀνόρουσεν do not occur together elsewhere (the last syllable of ἵπποιιν is again treated as long at 5.13, before the mid-verse caesura.) Finally, βῆ is never used elsewhere in metrical and grammatical circumstances like these. ἀνα- must be understood with it from ἀνόρουσεν.

398 Paris coming to meet Hektor τεύχεσι παμφαίνων ὥς τ' ἠλέκτωρ ἐβεβήκει (6.513). Here the proper name is added in apposition, as in *HyAp* 369. The connexion and etymology of ἠλέκτωρ, 'sun', and ἤλεκτρον (-ος), 'amber', 'electrum', remain obscure; see M. S. Ruipérez, *Mélanges... offerts à P. Chantraine* (Paris 1972) 231–41. The scholia (bT) aptly remark that the poet has compared Akhilleus' corslet with fire (18.610), his shield with the moon

(19.374), his helmet with a star (381), and now 'fittingly he likens the armed hero himself to the sun'. On Huperion see 8.480n.

399–403 Akhilleus gives no *parainesis* to the Greeks as he leads them into battle, as Patroklos does (16.269–74), perhaps because nothing is heard of them for so long after it commences. This short address to the horses may be thought of as taking its place, though it has none of the usual characteristics of a *parainesis* (see Fenik, *TBS* 48). In fact the formal structure is that of a rebuke, which (as often) brings a more or less indignant answer (e.g. 17.142–82). Hektor and Antilokhos also address their horses, though without eliciting a verbal response (8.185–97, 23.402–17).

The conversation allows Akhilleus to make a further allusion to his dead friend as he sets off to avenge him, and brings in a fresh reminder of his own imminent death (see 415–17n.). The immortal horses took part in a major scene during the battle over Patroklos' body (17.426–542), perhaps partly to build up their importance for Xanthos' coming speech. They play no part hereafter, except to increase the pathos by their continued grieving at 23.276–84.

ἐκέκλετο (399) always falls between the mid-verse caesura and the bucolic diaeresis, and the phrases occurring with it show an unusual regularity and fall neatly into the remaining three blocks of the verse (see Edwards, *HPI* 50–1). This is the only one of these verses where σμερδαλέον occupies the first place, and the concluding πατρὸς ἑοῖο has more impact than when used in the similar verse (23.402) by Antilokhos of Nestor's horses. On the gift of the horses to Peleus see 17.443–5n. τηλεκλυτός occurs only here and at *Od.* 1.30. The usual nominative epithets of this metrical shape (δουρικλυτός, πεπνυμένος, θεοείκελος) are unsuitable for horses (and not very appropriate for Orestes in the Odyssean verse), and the common τηλεκλειτός provided a model for this substitute. The names of the horses and those of their sire Zephuros and dam Podarge are given at 16.149–50 (see note *ad loc.*); two of Hektor's horses also bear the names Xanthos and Podargos (8.185). ἄλλως: i.e. better, as at 11.391, *Od.* 8.176, 20.211. ἡνιοχῆα: Akhilleus, as the parallel drawn with Patroklos in 403 makes clear; the latter too had Automedon as the actual driver (16.218–19). ἑῶμεν (< *ἥομεν) is subjunctive of ἄω, 'to have enough of', with Ionic η for ᾱ and quantitative metathesis (Chantraine, *GH* i 71); in other forms the Aeolic ᾱ is retained (as in ἄσασθαι, 307; Chantraine, *GH* i 21; T. Rüsing, *Glotta* 40, 1962, 162–4). The rough breathing (< *σα-) usually disappears but has survived in Attic ἅδην (cf. Latin *sa-tis*; in Homer the Ionic ἄδην is preferable, see Chantraine, *GH* i 185–6). C. Moulton, *CP* 74 (1979) 289, points out that metaphorical uses of ἄω are common in connexion with Akhilleus in the later books (though many of them are formular). μηδ' ὡς (403): the same type of abbreviated comparison occurs at *Od.* 21.427 and 24.199. The scholia (T) approve the naturalness of Akhilleus' words; 'for we are accustomed to blame those too who happened to be there'.

404–17 There was an association between the horse and death in Greek thought; see B. C. Dietrich, *AC* 7 (1964) 18, L. Malten, *JDAI* 29 (1914) 179–256, and for the wider picture J. Puhvel, *Comparative Mythology* (Baltimore 1987) 269–76. There was a formula Ἄϊδι κλυτοπώλῳ (3 × *Il.*). Wise or prophetic speaking animals are familiar from folktale and fable, and from epic in other cultures (see C. M. Bowra, *Heroic Poetry*, London 1952, 165–70). They occur in Greek poetry as early as Hesiod, *Erga* 203–12, but are unexpected in the severely unsupernatural *Il.* The horse's words, however, provide a further grim reminder of Akhilleus' mortality, and of his own awareness and acceptance of it, just as he sets out for his greatest battle, arrayed in his new divinely fashioned armour. The prediction is made the more powerful by the fresh detail that Akhilleus, like Patroklos, will be killed θεῷ τε καὶ ἀνέρι (417). The immortal horse is made to stress Apollo's part in both deaths with a clarity which could hardly be contrived in any other way; a fellow-god would hardly speak to a mortal like this in the *Il.*, and mere humans cannot perceive past and future divine actions so clearly.

This kind of warning would be more appropriate – if not necessarily more effective – if delivered to a hero setting out for the battle from which he would not return. Possibly Akhilleus (and perhaps other heroes) received a similar prophecy from this or another source in stories of his departure for his last battle. One wonders how bards delivered this speech; presumably its solemnity would discourage any equine intonation.

404–7 πόδας αἰόλος ἵππος is a unique noun–epithet combination perhaps with a connotation of shining hoofs as well as speed; cf. αἰολοθώρηξ 2 × *Il.*, αἰολομίτρης 1 × *Il.*, and the name Podarge, 'White-foot' (?). The word may have been suggested by the formula Φρύγας αἰολοπώλους (*HyAphr* 137, expanded at 3.185 (see note *ad loc.*)). The mane sweeping down to the ground is described as a mark of grief for Patroklos at 17.439–40 (see note *ad loc.*) and 23.283–4; here the motif shows the horse's additional sorrow for Akhilleus' own approaching death. Aristarchus (Arn/A) athetized 407 because of a supposed conflict with 418. But it is clear enough that normally Xanthos did not converse with his master, and Here is the natural person to be responsible for this sudden gift; cf. 1.55–6 and note *ad loc.*

408–17 The speech is in ring form:

A   We will save you now; but your death is near, at the hands of a god and destiny (408–10).
B   It was not because we were slow that Patroklos died (411–12),
C   but Apollo killed him (413–14).

B′ We are as swift as the wind (415–16);
A′ but it is your destiny to be killed by a god and a man (416–17).

408 καὶ λίην, 'certainly', always stands at the beginning of both verse and clause (3 × *Il.*, 8 × *Od.*). φαίδιμ' ᾿Αχιλλεῦ | is common (4 × *Il.*, 1 × *Od.*), and ὄβριμος is the usual formular alternative to φαίδιμος when an initial vowel is needed. But ὄβριμ'(ε) does not happen to occur elsewhere in Homer. This is one of the cases where one suspects that the sense of the word – something like 'heavy-handed' – may have induced the poet to shape the verse so as to include it, as Xanthos' comment upon Akhilleus' unfair rebuke. For other uses of formular epithets with a possibly significant sense see 20.497–8n. and *TAPA* 97 (1966) 153–4, 165–6, and 177.

409–11 ἦμαρ ὀλέθριον may be an under-represented formula; see 292–4n. Verse 410 is a significant variation on the usual (πορφύρεος) θάνατος καὶ μοῖρα κραταιή | 6 × *Il.*). βραδυτής and νωχελίη occur only here in Homer and are rare in Greek.

413–14 At 13.154 (the only other use) θεῶν ὥριστος refers to Zeus. Verse 414 = 18.456 (spoken by Thetis to Hephaistos). This is the first time Akhilleus has been told of Apollo's rôle in Patroklos' death. He had warned his friend against the god at 16.94.

415–17 Before this Akhilleus has known only that he would die soon after Hektor (18.95–6, see note *ad loc.*); the 'god and man' will be identified when the dying Hektor names Πάρις καὶ Φοῖβος ᾿Απόλλων (22.359). At 21.112–13 Akhilleus declares to Lukaon that someone will kill him with spear or arrow, and at 21.277–8 he reminds Zeus that according to Thetis he is to die by the shaft of Apollo. For further details see 21.113n. The same ironic contrast often drawn between Akhilleus' divinely made armour and his approaching death (see introduction to book 18) appears here between the unsurpassable speed of the horses and their powerlessness to prevent their master's fate.

Verse 415 is based on the formular ἅμα (μετὰ) πνοιῇς ἀνέμοιο | (2 × *Il.*, 3 × *Od.*) and | πνοιῇ ὕπο Ζεφύροιο (*Od.* 4.402, cf. *Od.* 10.25). Aristarchus' athetesis of 416–17 (Arn/A), on the grounds (*a*) that we already know that wind is the swiftest thing and (*b*) that it is incredible that a horse would say φασίν, 'like a well-read man', may be the least convincing of his contributions to criticism.

418 The narrator mentions the Erinues only here. They do not elsewhere in Homer clearly exert their later function as guardians of the natural order, and B. C. Dietrich has suggested (*AC* 7, 1964, 9–24) that they act here because of a connexion between them and the Harpuiai, one of whom was mother of these horses (16.149–50). In addition, Demeter Erinus bore the horse Areion to Poseidon (Paus. 8.25.4–10; see L. Malten, *JDAI* 29,

1914, 201–9). Much of Dietrich's argument is speculative, but some such association in the poet's mind may have played a part in his description here. It is more probable that Homer is thinking of their functions in punishing those who violated the rights of the gods (e.g. by breaking oaths; 259) and those of elder family members (9.454, 9.571, 15.204, 21.412, *Od.* 2.135, 11.280), and that these are extended here to cover maintaining the normal rules of behaviour, which bar horses from speech; just as at 87 they seem to be executors of Moira (see note *ad loc.*). It is also possible that the poet has in mind tales in which the Erinues are sent not to end the unnatural phenomenon of a talking horse, as here, but to prevent the disclosure of some secret or prophecy which must not be revealed to mortals; this may have been their rôle in the obscure Melampous story (*Od.* 11.291–3, 15.234); see A. Heubeck, *Glotta* 64 (1986) 154.

420–3 Akhilleus' assertion that he knows his death is near is perfectly placed as he drives out to the battle in which his killing of Hektor makes his own death imminent; see 18.95–6n. 'Achilles' acceptance of death transforms a cliché into a truly tragic insight, just as it is also that acceptance which ennobles and makes bearable his slaughter of Trojans in the last Books' (J. Griffin, *CQ* 28, 1978, 12).

421 οἶδα καὶ αὐτός otherwise occurs at the end of the verse (3 × *Il.*, 3 × *Od.*); here it is emphasized by εὖ at the beginning of the verse. The same idea is differently expressed at 8.32 and *Od.* 17.193.

422 The pathos of a death far from home is often brought out in Homer (see J. Griffin, *CQ* 26, 1976, 163–7) and so the motif is used here, though it is hardly appropriate in the case of Thetis. (ἀλλὰ) καὶ ἔμπης always ends the verse (2 × *Il.*, 1 × *Od.*); here it throws stress on οὐ λήξω at the beginning of the next verse.

423 Literally 'before driving the Trojans to satiety of war'; ἅδην is an accusative (ἄδην, with almost all MSS, would be preferable; see 400–3n.). Cf. οἵ μιν ἅδην ἐλόωσι καὶ ἐσσύμενον πολέμοιο (13.315) and 13.315–16n.

BOOK TWENTY

At the beginning of this Book the Greeks are arming in preparation for following Akhilleus into battle, and we expect his *aristeia* to begin. But the proper scale of events, and the tribute due to Akhilleus' greatness, demand that before he meets Hektor in the final duel not only must the furious hero cause devastation among the Trojans, but a good deal of time must elapse. In this Book two main episodes are used to expand the action: the preparatory scene for the Battle of the Gods, to be concluded in book 21, and a lengthy and inconclusive encounter with Aineias. Subsequent to this, Akhilleus has an abortive meeting with Hektor, which prepares the way for their final duel. The other Greeks receive a short exhortation from Akhilleus (353–63), but otherwise disappear from the action.

The formal structure of Akhilleus' *aristeia* is thus twice interrupted. Its first element, the arming, has been completed, but the scene then shifts to Olumpos for a divine council, after which the belligerent deities set off for war. The usual preliminaries of a new phase in the struggle are recounted: a catalogue of the forces; a description of the march out to battle; and perhaps an equivalent of the conventional duels (see 31–74n., 67–74n.). The main Battle of the Gods is then broken off until 21.385, though individually they are on hand in the interim to intervene in Akhilleus' conflicts with Aineias, Hektor, and Skamandros.

At this point a further interruption in the normal development of an *aristeia* takes place. Instead of a series of successful duels, there comes the long encounter between Akhilleus and Aineias, which is set up by Apollo and ended by Poseidon (79–352). Much of it is taken up with Aineias' account of his genealogy, which is both appropriate in its context and also significantly recapitulates the history of Troy and its close associations with the gods at the time when the city's doom is rapidly approaching. There may also be echoes of the Akhilleus/Memnon story (see 75–155n.). The tone and structure of this episode is much like that of other elaborated duels in the *Il.*, and rather incongruous with the furious anger against the Trojans earlier displayed by Akhilleus during his arming (19.365–8) and subsequently in his words to Lukaon (21.100–5). It has been plausibly suggested that a duel between Akhilleus and Aineias, the second-in-command on the Trojan side, was a standard part of the Troy-story which the poet wished to include in his poem, and that he failed to alter the normal polite conventions of such meetings (which appear, for instance, in the Diomedes/Glaukos encounter in book 6) to fit the ferocity of Akhilleus' mood at this point in his plot (see 75–155n.).

Poseidon's assertion that Aineias must survive the war so that his descendants may rule among the Trojans (307–8), and its virtual repetition at *HyAphr* 196–7, has led to speculation both in ancient and modern times that early epic poets knew of a family of kings in the Troad claiming such descent, and to recent comparisons of the language of this Aineias episode and that of the *Hymn*; see 75–155n.

The Book is unusually rich in examples of preparation for later episodes in the poem (see Introduction, ch. 2, iii). Besides the introduction to the Battle of the Gods, the way is prepared for the conflict of Skamandros and Hephaistos over Akhilleus (see 38–40n.), for the episode with Lukaon (see 79–82n. and 463–72n.), and for the final duel with Hektor (see 419–54n.), including the part played by Athene (see 452–3n.). Within the Book itself, there are advance preparations for the battle of pedigrees between Akhilleus and Aineias (105–7), for the threats they exchange (108–9), for Poseidon's concern and his rescue of Aineias (133–43, 195–8), and for the prediction of the later rule of his descendants at Troy (180–3).

There is an excellent account of this Book in Scheibner, *Aufbau*. The use made of the expansions (or retardations) has recently been examined by J. M. Bremer in Bremer, *HBOP* 31–46. There is an especially rich bibliography on the encounter between Akhilleus and Aineias (see 75–155n.).

1–74 Zeus summons a full assembly of the gods and invites them to take part in the battle before Troy, so that Akhilleus may not storm the city immediately. Accordingly they march out to war in two opposing groups, and sky, sea, earth, and the very Underworld are shaken by the fierce onslaught. The divine warriors pair off for duels

It has often been pointed out (e.g. by Reinhardt, *IuD* 446–50) that the introduction to the Battle of the Gods resembles that of a Titanomachy, though here the Olympians themselves are divided into two groups and only five duelling pairs are named; see 54–66n. The passage here prepares for the actual encounters between them (21.342–520), which of course descend into bathos.

1–3 This summarizing passage (standard in Homer; see 17.360–425n.) rounds off 19.352–3 in ring form and gives a long-range view of the Greeks, Akhilleus, and the Trojans, all armed and ready for battle on the plain, as the focus moves up to Olumpos. The human scene appears again at 41. On direct address to a character by the poet (2) see Introduction, ch. 1, i, 3, and Edwards, *HPI* 37–8. Here the device is undoubtedly intended to direct attention towards Akhilleus. There is a formula (δεινῆς) ἀκόρητος (-οι) αὐτῆς |

(13.621 and 3× in the Hesiodic *Aspis*), and probably μάχης ἀκόρητος is another (cf. Τρῶες δὲ μάχης ἀκόρητοι ἔασιν |, 13.639). Here Allen and most editors (supported by Scheibner, *Aufbau* 65 n. 1) print the better-attested reading ἀκόρητον, but ἀκόρητοι (printed by Leaf and supported by Willcock) much better suits formular style and gives a better sense – the Greeks are ready for anything now that Akhilleus has returned (and Odysseus has seen to it that they have been fed). Both readings were known in antiquity (Nic/AbT). Verse 3 = 11.56, ≅ 10.160. θωρήσσοντο must be supplied from 1.

4–12 At the divine council at 8.2ff. Zeus ordered the gods not to assist either Greeks or Trojans. Now he removes this prohibition. Because of the importance of the occasion this account of the council is much amplified, just as was the gathering of the Greeks for the reconciliation between Akhilleus and Agamemnon (19.40–53). Themis is ordered to assemble an expanded company, and Poseidon puts an introductory question (16–18). The gathering of the rivers, besides lending additional dignity to the assemblage, prepares for the part played by Skamandros in the coming Battle of the Gods (73–4; so T).

4–5 At 8.2 Zeus himself θεῶν ἀγορὴν ποιήσατο and addressed it immediately. But Themis ἀνδρῶν ἀγορὰς ἠμὲν λύει ἠδὲ καθίζει (*Od.* 2.69), cf. ἦ θέμις ἐστίν, ἄναξ, ἀγορῇ (1.33), and presides over the gods' feasts (15.95). On her rôle see 15.87–8n. and H. Vos, ΘΕΜΙΣ (Assen 1956) 6 and 42–7. The inflection with -στ- (again at 15.87 and *Od.* 2.68, and in θέμιστας (-ες -α) 7× *Il.*, 3× *Od.*) is probably a Thessalian aeolism; see Vos 36–8 and Hoekstra, *Sub-epic Stage* 19 n. 56. πολυπτύχου Οὐλύμποιο | occurs at 8.411, cf. Hesiod, *Theogony* 113 and the formula Ἴδης... πολυπτύχου (2× *Il.*).

7–9 Okeanos is θεῶν γένεσις (14.201, 246), closely identified with his element, and does not fit into the Olympian family; his presence here would be overwhelming. On Homeric theogony see 14.200–7n. Verse 8 ≅ *HyAphr* 97, verse 9 = *Od.* 6.124, *HyAphr* 99. Note the alliteration in 9, and the possible word-play νυμφάων... νέμονται. The nymphs are attendants upon the river-gods, as the Nereids are upon Thetis; on nymphs in Homer see J. B. Hainsworth, *Odyssey* on *Od.* 6.123–4.

11–12 Priam's palace was also equipped | ξεστῇς αἰθούσῃσι (6.243). Zenodotus' reading ἐφίζανον (Arn/A) arose from a misunderstanding of the meaning of αἴθουσα, 'a place for a fire', 'an outside passage-way', 'colonnade' (see *LfgrE* s.v. αἴθω ΙΙ). Verse 12 = 1.608.

13–18 Poseidon is given prominence because he is Zeus's brother, and claims to be his ὁμότιμος (15.186); because they are not on the best of terms (15.185–217) and he might have disobeyed the summons; and especially because he will play an important rôle in the coming Akhilleus/Aineias episode.

Book Twenty

With Διὸς ἔνδον cf. Ζεφύροιο...ἔνδον (23.200). νηκουστέω occurs only here in Greek; ἀνηκουστέω (with α-privative added to *n-, 'not') is the normal form (15.236 = 16.676 and in later authors; see 15.236–43n.). ἐξείρετο (15) introduces direct speech only here and in the same phrase at *Od.* 13.127; ἐξερέεινε does so 2 × *Il.* On its formular system see 15.592–5n. With 18 cf. ἀμφὶ μάχη ἐνοπή τε δεδήει | τεῖχος (12.35–6). The metaphorical use of this verb is very common.

20–30 Zeus's attitude here is often misinterpreted (and mistranslated). He does not lack sympathy for the human warriors, and it is the gods from whom he (justifiably) expects to get a good deal of amusement. Poseidon has just said 'The flame of battle is burning very close for Trojans and Greeks.' Zeus agrees (ἔγνως... ἐμὴν... βουλήν = 'You know what is in my mind' – βουλή usually means 'plans', but that would not make sense here). Then he goes on: μέλουσί μοι ὀλλύμενοί περ (21), 'I am concerned about them, dying as they are.' περ is intensive, as in ζωός περ ἐὼν φίλος ἦσθα θεοῖσιν (24.749; I thank E. J. Bakker for drawing my attention to this example) and *Od.* 1.315. (On the difficult question of intensive and concessive περ see Denniston, *Particles* 482, and E. J. Bakker, *Linguistics and Formulas in Homer*, Amsterdam 1988, passim.) ὀλλύμενοι refers back to Τρώων καὶ Ἀχαιῶν (17), *pace* Ameis–Hentze and Leaf; both sides are to be assisted by the gods – ἀμφοτέροισι δ' ἀρήγετε (25) – and Zeus cannot be partisan. In fact, he has often shown sympathy for each side (see 17.194–209n.).

Zeus himself, however (ἀλλ' ἤτοι μὲν ἐγώ, 22), will remain on Olumpos; and it is natural to understand ὁρόων φρένα τέρψομαι (23) as referring (at least primarily) to the enjoyment he anticipates (and receives at 21.388–90, see note *ad loc.*) from the preposterous divine conflict, not the human disasters. The rest of the gods (οἱ δὲ δὴ ἄλλοι, 23) may go to help whichever side they like. Now (26–30) his concern focuses explicitly on the Trojans, and what Akhilleus may achieve in his present frame of mind. Zeus here, as in book 17 and the early scenes of book 24, is not taking human affairs lightly or cold-bloodedly; but his very active sense of humour breaks through when he thinks about the antics some of his relatives will surely get up to now that he has turned them loose.

An excellent account of the gods as spectators of the human comedy, sometimes amused, sometimes pitying or grieving, is given by J. Griffin in *CQ* 28, 1978, 1–22. Of this passage he says '[Zeus] takes pleasure in watching [men] struggle' (p. 16), which I think is not quite accurate; though it might perhaps be said of other passages. L. Golden, *Mnemosyne* 42 (1989) 9–11, also denies Zeus any genuine concern for mankind here.

21–2 ὧν is neuter, amplifying the idea in the previous line. With 22 cf. κατὰ πτύχας Οὐλύμποιο (11.77).

26–7 οἶος: i.e. without divine help to the other side. μαχεῖται: the usual

Homeric future is μαχήσομαι (though μαχέονται appears at 2.366). Here the form (regular in Attic) is used by analogy with (ἐπὶ) (μετὰ) Τρώεσσι μάχεσθαι (-έσθω, -οιτο, -ωμαι, -οίμην) | (12 × *Il.*, 2 × *Od.*). Πηλεΐωνα: Macleod, *Iliad XXIV* 137 (on 24.585), lists other cases where a name in an oblique case refers back to the subject of the sentence, none so tautological as this; but here the formula gives added dignity.

28 καὶ δέ τέ μιν καὶ πρόσθεν: the first καί emphasizes the whole sentence, the second πρόσθεν in particular. Aristarchus (Did/AT) read τι, probably to reduce the number of conjunctions, and this appears in a few inferior MSS and (unfortunately) in Allen's text. Presumably it would have to be understood ironically. The vulgate τε is quite acceptable; the wording is like τόν τε τρομέουσι καὶ ἄλλοι (17.203). See Ruijgh, τε *épique* 697.

29–30 νῦν δέ is Akhilleus' own favourite expression (see 18.88n.). ἑταίρου: 'because of his companion'; cf. ἀχνύμενός περ ἑταίρου (8.125) and Chantraine, *GH* II 65. On ὑπέρμορον see 17.321n. and 21.516–17n.

The scholia (Did?/T) say that in place of 30 some texts read οὐ μέντοι μοῖρ' ἐστὶν ἔτι ζῳοῦ 'Αχιλῆος | 'Ιλίου ἐκπέρσαι εὖ ναιόμενον πτολίεθρον. | πέρσει δουράτεός ⟨θ'⟩ ἵππος καὶ μῆτις 'Επειοῦ. Verse 29 could not have stood together with these. The scholia go on to give the reason the lines were substituted, quite unnecessarily: πῶς γὰρ ὁ εἰδὼς 'μοῖράν τ' ἀμμορίην τε' [*Od.* 20.76] νῦν διστάζει; There is nothing wrong with the style of the verses (if ζῳοῖ' were read in the first line, as it should be also at *Od.* 17.115 and 19.272), and they may be quite early; Bolling, *External Evidence* 187, thinks they may go back to a cyclic epic.

31–74 The battle begins as usual with a catalogue of those marching out, which here lists the *deities* who are taking part (33–40). This is followed by a general description of the battle, including mention of both the human combatants (41–6) and the divine participants (47–53), in the one case balancing Greeks and Trojans, in the other Athene and Ares. A two-verse summary (54–5) leads into a brief cosmic-conflict passage, which takes the place of the simile which would be normal in such general descriptions (56–66, see 54–66n.). Then comes an odd section in which the pairs of 'duelling' gods are described (67–74, see note *ad loc.*). The same structure of catalogue–description–duels appears in the great catalogues of book 2 and the beginning of book 3, and again in book 4, where the Epipolesis (4.250–421) takes the place of a catalogue and the duels begin at 4.457. After the catalogue of Myrmidons (16.168–97) Akhilleus' *parainesis* and his prayer to Zeus are inserted into the sequence.

The gods are given no arming-scene, probably because this would be repetitive in the case of Athene (who has already armed herself twice: 5.733–47, 8.384–91) and too bizarre by the standards of the *Il.* in the case of some of the others. Instead of beginning duels, the gods merely square off

(67–74, if genuine; see note *ad loc.*), and at 75 the situation is summarized (ὡς οἱ μὲν θεοὶ ἄντα θεῶν ἴσαν) and a new action begins.

31–2 Cf. πόλεμος δ' ἀλίαστος ὄρωρε | (2.797), ὅμαδος δ' ἀ. ἐτύχθη | (2 × *Il.*). δίχα θυμὸν ἔχοντες: cf. ἕνα θ. ἑ. (4 × *Il.*, including a lengthened version at 13.487).

34–5 ἐριούνης | Ἑρμείας is again enjambed like this at *Od.* 8.322–3 (also following Ποσειδάων γαιήοχος). The technique is like that in which a name is picked up in the following verse by a patronymic and following relative clause, as Δηϊκόωντα | Περγασίδην, ὅν... (5.534–5); Hoekstra, *Modifications* 34, lists a number of examples (including many where the name occurs earlier in the first verse). ἐριούνης is derived from Arcado-Cypriot οὖνον, οὖνη with the intensive prefix ἐρι-, and seems to mean 'good runner'; see Chantraine, *Dict.* s.v., and K. Latte, *Glotta* 34 (1955) 190–202. In 35, ἐπὶ goes with κέκασται; cf. 24.535 and the name Epikaste (von Kamptz, *Personennamen* 57). κέκασται, which must be right, is Aristarchus' reading (Did/A) for -το of most MSS. φρεσὶ πευκαλίμῃσι occurs in this position at 15.81 and ends the verse 2 × *Il.* The epithet is probably always meaningful, as here (see F. M. Combellack, *Grazer Beiträge* 4, 1975, 84–5).

36–7 σθένεϊ βλεμεαίνων (-ει) | occurs 6 × *Il.*, twice of Hektor and three times of a wild boar or lion in similes. Verse 37 = 18.411.

Here, Athene, and Poseidon have of course always helped the Greeks. Hermes has so far played no part in the poem. He said nothing when the son of Phorbas the Trojan, his favourite shepherd, was killed in a particularly brutal manner (14.489–505), and his son Eudoros, the leader of one of the Myrmidon squadrons (16.179–86), plays no part in the battle. At 15.213–14 Poseidon groups Hermes and Hephaistos with Here, Athene, and himself as supporters of the Greeks, but that passage may be dependent on this. It seems likely that Hermes is brought in here to prepare for his prominence in book 24. Hephaistos is mentioned, as 73–4 makes explicit, so that he will be on hand to assist Akhilleus against the river-god (21.328–82).

38–40 κορυθαίολος is only here applied to anyone other than Hektor, and only here placed before a pause at the bucolic diaeresis. The normal epithet for gods in these metrical circumstances would be λαοσσόος, used for Ares at 17.398 as well as for Athene (13.128, *Od.* 22.210), Eris (20.48), and Apollo (20.79; for heroes only at *Od.* 15.244 and 2 × in the *Aspis*). χρυσήνιος, used for Ares (later in the verse) at *Od.* 8.285 and for Artemis at 6.205, would be another possibility, though it would cause an unpleasant over-lengthening. It seems likely that the choice of κορυθαίολος here, when less particularized alternatives were available, is due to its association with Hektor and the juxtaposition of Τρῶας. Φοῖβος ἀκερσεκόμης is an under-represented formula, found only here in Homer but occurring at *HyAp* 134 and 2 × in frr. of Hesiod. Some texts read Διὸς θυγάτηρ Ἀφροδίτη (Did?/T), thinking it more suitable to the context; this generic formula is gaining ground in Homer over the particularized φιλομμειδής 'A. (9 × against 6 × ; see J. B. Hainsworth in *Homer: Tradition and Invention*, ed. B. Fenik, Leiden 1978, 45).

Xanthos is here to prepare for his struggle with Akhilleus and Hephaistos (21.211–382), and Aphrodite has already been wounded in action (5.330–42). But Leto is an unlikely combatant; fortunately the amiable Hermes declines the bizarre duel with a lady and is cheerfully willing to let her claim the victory (21.497–501; see note *ad loc.*). Presumably the poet introduces her as the mother of the eager Trojan backers Apollo and Artemis; most of the appearances of her name are in the epithets which describe them. Her only other part in the poem was to help Artemis care for the wounded Aineias when Aphrodite was *hors de combat* (5.447–8). One expects her to comfort Artemis after she has been slapped by Here, as Aphrodite is by her mother Dione (5.370–417), but in fact that rôle is taken by Zeus (21.505–13) and Leto can only collect Artemis' abandoned weapons. She will feature later in Akhilleus' mighty Niobe paradigm (24.605–9), but it seems fanciful to invoke that as an additional reason for her presence here. Even more fanciful was the old explanation for her opposition to Hermes: ὅτι ὁ μὲν λόγος ἀεὶ ζητεῖ καὶ μέμνηται, ἡ δὲ λήθη τούτῳ ἐστὶν ἐναντίον (Plutarch, *Vit. Hom.* 102).

41–6 The matching descriptions of the feelings of Greeks and Trojans both serve to glorify Akhilleus, showing the contrasting ways he is seen through their eyes.

41–3 εἷος < *ἧος, τεῖος < *τῆος; both forms are here disyllabic. See Hoekstra, *Modifications* 34–5, and Chantraine, *GH* I 11–12. κυδάνω, an alternative for κυδαίνω, appears only here and at 14.73; see Risch, *Wortbildung* 271. Verse 43 = 18.248, 19.46 (also enjambing after οὕνεκ' 'Αχιλλεύς |); see 18.246–8n. Akhilleus said of lamenting Trojan widows γνοῖεν δ' ὡς δὴ δηρὸν ἐγὼ πολέμοιο πέπαυμαι (18.125). Verse 44 = 7.215.

46 The comparison is more than a formula; to the terrified Trojans Akhilleus looks like the war-god himself. τεύχεσι λαμπόμενος (etc.) is only used of those in Hephaistos-made armour: Hektor (17.214), and the two forces on the shield (18.510). βροτολοιγῷ ἶσος (-ον) "Αρηϊ | is used of Hektor 2 × *Il.*, of the Lapith Leonteus (12.130), and of the Phaeacian Eurualos (*Od.* 8.115). It is notable that the expression is used here just before Ares' actual battle-cry is described (51–3); similarly at 13.295 Meriones is said to be θοῷ ἀτάλαντος "Αρηϊ and a few lines later is given a full-scale comparison to Ares marching to battle (13.298–303; see note *ad loc.*). When Hektor stands facing Akhilleus, just before his fear overcomes him, the latter's fearful appearance is described by the unique verse ἶσος 'Ενναλίῳ κορυθάϊκι πτολεμιστῇ (22.132).

48–53 Eris, who is to some extent a personification, had never obeyed Zeus's confinement of the gods to Olumpos; see 11.73–5 and note *ad loc.* Athene and Ares also represent the opposing forces at 4.439, 17.397–8, and 20.358. There is a careful balance: Athene shouts standing at the ditch outside the Greek wall *and* on the beach beside the ships; Ares from the height of the citadel of Troy *and* running beside the Simoeis. This movement is the regular part of the motif of stirring up a battle; Hektor too is ὁτὲ μέν in the front ranks, ἄλλοτε δέ at the rear (11.64–5), and Ares is ἄλλοτε μὲν πρόσθ' Ἕκτορος, ἄλλοτ' ὄπισθε (5.595; so Fenik, *TBS* 80).

48–50 Aristarchus (Arn/A) took the Eris-clause with the preceding temporal clause and αὖε δ' Ἀθήνη as the main clause, which gives a good antithesis with αὖε δ' Ἄρης (51; αὔτει (50) carries on the same sound). Eris' presence is standard at the start of a big battle; it is heavily elaborated at 11.3–12 and less fully at 4.440–5. On λαοσσόος see 38–40n. Verse 49 ≅ 9.67. ὁτέ (49) is followed by ἄλλοτε at 11.64–5 and 18.599–602; there is a slight anacoluthon in pairing στᾶσ' with αὔτει. ἐρί(γ)δουπος (50) for the surf thundering on the sea-beaches is an innovative use. Besides its formular usages with Zeus and with αἰθούσης (-η), the epithet is applied once to horses' hoofs (11.152) and once to rivers (*Od.* 10.515). On the tremendous noise made by gods shouting see 14.147–52n., and for Near Eastern and other parallels Griffin, *HLD* 38–9.

51–3 ἐρεμνῇ λαίλαπι ἶσος is used of the Lycian leaders (12.375) and the metrical alternative κελαινῇ λ. ἴ. by Nestor of himself in his younger days (11.747). In 52, ὀξύ goes with κελεύων. θέων (53; not θεῶν) must be right, *pace* Aristarchus (Arn/A); 'running towards Pleasant Hill, ⟨which rises⟩ beside the Simoeis'. Kallikolone is mentioned again only when the pro-Trojan gods take a break there (151–2). Clearly his invention (?) stayed in the poet's mind.

54–66 After the summarizing couplet (54–5) the conflict rises to the cosmic level. In position and effect the passage takes the place of a simile, a parallel made more obvious by the concluding τόσσος ἄρα κτύπος ὦρτο θεῶν ἔριδι ξυνιόντων (66; a very similar verse actually ends a simile in Hesiod, *Theogony* 705). The involvement of sky, sea, earth, and the very Underworld in the strife, and the shaking of the mountains beneath the feet of the combatants, echo a standard theme common in descriptions of the Titanomachy (see R. Mondi, *TAPA* 116, 1986, 42–4). Hesiod gives three versions, one for the Titanomachy and two in Zeus's battle with Tuphoeus (the common elements are underlined); first, *Theogony* 678–83:

δεινὸν δὲ περίαχε πόντος ἀπείρων,
γῆ δὲ μέγ' ἐσμαράγησεν, ἐπέστενε δ' οὐρανὸς εὐρὺς
σειόμενος, πεδόθεν δὲ τινάσσετο μακρὸς Ὄλυμπος

ῥιπῇ ὕπ' ἀθανάτων, ἔνοσις δ' ἵκανε βαρεῖα
Τάρταρον ἠερόεντα <u>ποδῶν</u> αἰπεῖά τ' ἰωὴ
ἀσπέτου ἰωχμοῖο βολάων τε κρατεράων.

Next, *Theogony* 839–43:

[Zeus] σκληρὸν δ' ἐβρόντησε καὶ ὄβριμον, ἀμφὶ δὲ γαῖα
σμερδαλέον κονάβησε καὶ <u>οὐρανὸς εὐρὺς ὕπερθε</u>
πόντος τ' Ὠκεανοῦ τε ῥοαὶ καὶ τάρταρα γαίης.
<u>ποσσὶ</u> δ' ὕπ' ἀθανάτοισι μέγας πελεμίζετ' Ὄλυμπος
ὀρνυμένοιο ἄνακτος· ἐπεστονάχιζε δὲ γαῖα.

The same motif is adapted for the effects of Zeus's thunderbolt (*Theogony*
847–50):

ἔζεε δὲ χθὼν πᾶσα καὶ <u>οὐρανὸς ἠδὲ θάλασσα·</u>
θυῖε δ' ἄρ' ἀμφ' ἀκτὰς περί τ' ἀμφί τε <u>κύματα μακρὰ</u>
ῥιπῇ ὕπ' ἀθανάτων, ἔνοσις δ' ἄσβεστος ὀρώρει·
τρέε δ' Ἀίδης ἐνέροισι καταφθιμένοισι ἀνάσσων

(cf. 695–7). Homer, who very probably had himself sung Titanomachies in
verses similar to those above, adapts the conventional elements to the
present situation by: (*a*) having Zeus thunder not in threat, but ὑψόθεν, i.e.
from a safe distance, and leaving the shaking of the earth νέρθε to Poseidon,
whose presence makes it easy to drop the normal reference to the sea,
superfluous here; (*b*) elaborating the quaking of the earth by adding the
mountains (58; perhaps an alternative for Olumpos, *Theogony* 680), and
then linking this to the local topography by adding references to Mt Ida,
Troy, and the Greek camp (59–60); and (*c*) amplifying the motif of Hades'
fear (*Theogony* 850) into a vivid 5-verse description (61–5). To us, the
invocation here of these mighty cosmic conflicts verges on the mock-heroic,
especially when all the fireworks fizzle out a few lines later. Longinus,
however (9.6), found the passage awe-inspiring, though only if taken
allegorically.

A shorter evocation of a Zeus/Tuphoeus scene is used in a simile when
the Greek host marches out at 2.781–4 (see note *ad loc.*, and S. Nimis,
Narrative Semiotics in the Epic Tradition, Bloomington 1987, 73–84). West,
Theogony 20–31, gives an account of divine conflicts in Near Eastern myths;
the most recent studies of such tales in Homer and Hesiod are by R. Mondi
in *Approaches to Greek Myth* (ed. L. Edmunds, Baltimore 1990) 141–98 and
E. A. Havelock, *Oral Tradition* 2/1 (1987) 31–53.

55 ἔριδα ῥήγνυντο is an unparalleled phrase; G. S. Kirk, *The Songs of
Homer* (Cambridge 1962) 206, considers it 'an attempt at innovation and

improvement'. βαρύς is often used metaphorically, e.g. with ἄτη (2 × *Il.*, 1 × *Od.*).

56–8 Zeus, though a self-declared bystander, is involved in the activities because he features in the regular Titanomachy motif. Poseidon ἐτίναξε | γαῖαν in his rôles as γαιήοχος and ἐνοσίχθων. ἀπειρέσιος (58) is used with γαῖαν only here; the combination must be regarded as a metrical alternative for ἀπείρονα γαῖαν (2 × *Il.*, 5 × *Od.*). ὀρέων αἰπεινὰ κάρηνα | recurs at *Od.* 6.123, and Μυκάλης τ' αἰ. κ. | at 2.869.

59 With the 'foothills' of Ida cf. πόδα νείατον Ἴδης | (2.824). One wonders if the word was suggested here by the element in this type-scene of the earth trembling under the feet of the gods (*Theogony* 682, 842). For πολυπίδακος (preferred by Aristarchus, Did/A) the variant -ου is better attested by the MSS here, but -ος predominates at 218; both forms may go back to Homer (see 14.157–8n.).

61–5 Hades' fear is dwelt upon, perhaps to compensate for the fact that the subterranean Titan prisoners are not mentioned, as they are in the Hesiodic passages (*Theogony* 697, 851). J. Kroll, *Gott und Hölle* (Darmstadt 1963 (1932)) 367–8, draws parallels with Near Eastern tales of a descent into, or attack on, the Underworld by a god. The three brothers Zeus, Poseidon, and Hades are linked together with Gaia at 15.187–93; cf. Hesiod, *Theogony* 736–8 = 807–9 ἔνθα δὲ γῆς δνοφερῆς καὶ ταρτάρου ἠερόεντος | πόντου τ' ἀτρυγέτοιο καὶ οὐρανοῦ ἀστερόεντος | ἑξείης πάντων πηγαὶ καὶ πείρατ' ἔασιν.

61–3 ἔδεισεν... | δείσας; the repetition is emphatic – Hades is more accustomed to cause fear than to feel it. Cf. μείδησεν... | μειδήσασα (1.595–6 ≅ 14.222–3). ἄναξ ἐνέρων Ἀϊδωνεύς | recurs at *HyDem* 357, and the alternative expressions Ἀΐδης ἐνέροισι (καταφθιμένοισι) ἀνάσσων | at 15.188 and *Theogony* 850. Note the repetition ὑπένερθεν... ἐνέρων. ἐκ θρόνου ἆλτο: the usual phrase has ὦρτο (2 × *Il.*; ὑπό is substituted in the unusual circumstances of *Od.* 22.364). The substitution of ἆλτο here adds urgency. ἴαχε: there are many similar instances of this imperfect (?) form with ῑ and neglected digamma. It has been plausibly suggested that the form is an aorist, καὶ εὔαχε < *ἔϝϝαχε; see Chantraine, *GH* 1 140. The formular ἐνοσίχθων is especially pertinent here.

The T scholia remark ἐκπληκτικὸν τοῦτο, μὴ μόνον δεῖσαι, ἀλλὰ καὶ ἀναθορεῖν ⟨ἐκ⟩ τοῦ θρόνου. εἶτα καὶ τὸ ἴαχε κινητικὸν τῆς διανοίας τοῦ δείσαντος.

65–6 Verse 65 ≅ *Theogony* 739 and 810, with σμερδαλέ' replacing ἀργαλέ'. The workhorse σμερδαλέος, 'terrible' (always first in the line; 27 × *Il.*, 9 × *Od.*), is more suitable here than ἀργαλέος, 'grievous', since incarceration is not in question. εὐρώεις (etc.) is used in archaic epic only of the Underworld. Verse 66 ≅ *Theogony* 705 (in the Titanomachy), which begins τόσσος δοῦπος ἔγεντο; the second hemistich is repeated when Zeus enjoys the spectacle (21.390). Here it completes the ring form (with 54–5).

67–74 The gods pair off to fight, but the actual duelling is not described until 21.385ff., after the Skamandros–Hephaistos encounter. Poseidon and Apollo, as the powerful males who have been much involved before this, are an obvious match; so are Ares and Athene. Herē and Artemis are ill-matched, except in gender, and the outcome is humiliating in the extreme for the lesser goddess, despite her scornful rebuke to her brother (21.470–513). Leto and Hermes are an odder couple still; see 38–40n. Hephaistos and Xanthos are of course paired in preparation for their duel over Akhilleus (21.211–384). Aphrodite marched out with the others (40), but has no partner here. Later, however, her presence is recalled, and she will be manhandled by Athene while trying to assist the wounded Ares (21.416–26). The D scholia and Plutarch. *Vit. Hom.* 102, provide allegorical reasons for the various oppositions, deriving from Porphyry, who claims such explanations go back to Theagenes of Rhegium (see R. Lamberton, *Homer the Theologian*, Berkeley 1986, 31–2; K. Snipes, *AJP* 109, 1988, 203).

The passage performs no useful function, since the muster-roll of deities (in preparation for their combat in book 21) has already been called at 32–40, and it hardly serves either to diminish the bathetic failure to follow up immediately the resounding trumpetings of the divine march to battle or to add to the fun which the poet seems to be having with his gods. There is no parallel in Homeric battles to this listing of combatants as they line up to face each other; the nearest equivalent would be the lists of competitors in the games (23.288ff., 754ff., cf. 7.162–8), which are not however in pairs. Moreover, the opposing stances taken up by the various couples are broken up immediately, with unusual illogicality, as Apollo goes off to talk to Aineias (79–111) and Here calls her team into a huddle (112–43), after which both parties withdraw (144–55). There are also a number of oddities in language (see below). Though it never seems to have been seriously suspected in ancient or modern times, the passage conflicts with the norms of Homeric narrative structure and does not belong here; I think it has been added to the monumental poem at a later date, the pairings read back from the encounters in book 21. If it is removed, verse 75 (ὡς οἱ μὲν θεοὶ ἄντα θεῶν ἴσαν) following 66 provides a normal summary of the preceding general description before the action changes to Akhilleus.

In favour of retaining the passage it should be indicated that it might serve to represent the duels which normally occur at this stage in the structure of a battle (see 31–74n.); and (as Leaf observed in his introduction to this Book) this section may be held to prepare for the major divine battle in book 21 as the preparatory description of Zeus's inattentiveness (13.1–9) precedes the detailed account of his deception by Here in book 14. This is in fact a common Homeric narrative technique; see the introduction to this Book, and Introduction, ch. 2, iii. I do not, however, think these considerations justify the retention of the passage.

67–9 ἔναντα occurs only here in archaic epic, but appears in later poets. Ἀπόλλων Φοῖβος occurs in this position 4 × *Il.*, but includes the rare word-division after the second spondee; it is an unusual adaptation of the formular Φοῖβος Ἀπόλλων (36 × *Il.*). ἰὰ πτερόεντα is a neologism, showing analogies with the familiar ἔπεα πτερόεντα (which, however, never occurs at the end of the line) and the other unique occurrences πτερόεντες ὀϊστοί | (5.171) and | ἰοί τε πτερόεντες (16.773). Both the usual formulas for Apollo running from the feminine caesura repeat his name (ἄναξ ἑκάεργος [or Διὸς υἱὸς] Ἀπόλλων) and cannot be used here, so this phrase may have been invented for the occasion. The plural form ἰά occurs only here in Greek; E. Schwyzer and A. Debrunner, *Griechische Grammatik* ii (Munich 1950) 37, give other examples of words which have a masculine singular and neuter plural, and suggest they may be old collective forms. On Ares vs. Athene see 48–53n.

70–1 The formular Ἀρτέμιδος χρυσηλακάτου κελαδεινῆς | occurs at 16.183 (see note *ad loc.*), Hesiod fr. 23(a) 18 MW, and *HyAphr* 118, and also in the accusative at *HyAphr* 16 and the dative (without κελαδεινή) at *Od.* 4.122. This is the only place where the epithets are placed first. Ἄρτεμις ἰοχέαιρα appears first in the line only here. Such adaptations in the positioning of formulae are, of course, not surprising. Ἀπόλλωνος ἑκάτοιο | is also formular (2 × *Il.*, 1 × *HyAp*); κασιγνήτη ἑ. | may be so, but recurs only in a late Homeric Hymn.

72 The short form Ἑρμῆς (-ῆν, -ῇ) occurs only here in the *Il.* but 4 × *Od.*, only once at the end of the verse. Hoekstra, *Odyssey* on *Od.* 14.435, suggests very plausibly that it is the vernacular form familiar to the poet. ἐριούνιος (see 34–5n.) occurs in other combinations but only here before Ἑρμῆς. To complete the peculiarity, σῶκος, 'strong', as an adjective is virtually unknown in Greek except for this occurrence, though a Trojan of that name is killed by Odysseus (11.428–38); for possible etymologies see von Kamptz, *Personennamen* 142. Since ἐριούνιος has no digamma a metrical licence is involved in the lengthening of the last syllable of σῶκος. The use, and the combination, of ἐριούνιος and Ἑρμῆς are not surprising in an innovative passage like this, but the employment of the rare σῶκος (when the generic κρείων would have done) is very odd.

73–4 ποταμὸς βαθυδίνης | is found 5 × *Il.*, again lengthened by μέγας at 21.329. Ξάνθον...Σκάμανδρον: there are three other instances of alternative divine and human names in the *Il.*, and two in the *Od.* where a divine name is given without human equivalent; see 1.403–4n. West, *Theogony* 387, includes post-Homeric examples and a list of modern discussions. It is often said that the human name is that of everyday language, the divine that of the poetic tradition, but this is an over-simplification (see A. Heubeck, *Würzburger Jahrbücher für die Altertumswissenschaft* 4, 1949/50, 197–218). In the most recent discussion of the Xanthos/Skamandros pair, O. Szemerényi, *Tractata Mycenaea: Proceedings of the VIIIth International Colloquium on Mycenaean Studies* (Skopje 1987) 343–50, argues that Ξάνθος is derived from the name of the River Seha in western Asia Minor, through the form *S(e)hant-* and metathesis of the initial consonants, and Σκάμανδρος from the alternative form *S(e)ha-* with the suffix *-want-*, which gave the Greek -ανδρος (appearing also in Maiandros and other river-names), perhaps through association with Anatolian *ar(i)na*, *anra*, 'spring'. R. Lazzeroni, *Annali della Scuola Normale Superiore di Pisa* 26 (1957) 8, suggests that both divine and human names are mentioned here to show that the river-god is assuming a new status and character.

With the form of 74 cf. (ἥν) χαλκίδα κικλήσκουσι θεοί, ἄνδρες δὲ κύμινδιν (14.291). On the formular system used for Skamandros/Xanthos see 21.1–2n.; the short syllable before Σκάμανδρον is retained by a metrical licence, essential if the name is to be used in hexameters (see 12.21n.).

75–155 The divine conflict is now interrupted, and the scene is set for the duel of Akhilleus and Aineias. This is brought about by Apollo, who in the guise of Lukaon rebukes Aineias and inspires him to advance towards Akhilleus. On the other side, the worried Here summons Poseidon to discuss their strategy in support of the Greek hero. Poseidon counsels cautious monitoring of the situation, and all the gods withdraw, in two groups

The normal structure of an *aristeia* is interrupted by this encounter; see the introduction to this Book, and Krischer, *Konventionen* 27. It is, however, likely that a fight between the greatest Greek hero and the leader of the Dardanians, second-in-command on the Trojan side, was traditional, and since in much of the *Il.* Akhilleus is not engaged in battle this is the only place it can occur. The episode may also have been influenced – though we shall never know for sure – by tales of the encounter of Akhilleus with Memnon, who shared Aineias' Trojan ancestry on his father's side (see 215–40n.) and also had a goddess for mother. Aineias' prominence during Diomedes' *aristeia* in book 5 makes that episode in some ways a precursor of this. It has also been pointed out (especially by P. Smith, *HSCP* 85, 1981, 49–52) that the contrast between Aineias' salvation and Hektor's death, when each encounters Akhilleus, gives additional emotional depth to the later part of the poem. In a rather different way, Aineias and his account of the history of Troy contribute to the broader picture of the fall of the city, standing like a shadow behind the immediate tale of the revenge upon Hektor (see 200–58n.).

The structure of the encounter is regular enough: a rebuke, the response, and divine inspiration (79 111); a challenge, and the response, including a genealogy (176–288); a divine rescue, and the surprise of the remaining warrior (288–352). Diomedes' protracted battle with Aineias during his *aristeia* (5.166–488), and Paris' duel with Menelaos in book 3, afford many parallels. Lenz, *Aphroditehymnos* 160, finds a five-layered ring form, in which Aineias' despatch by Apollo (79–111) matches his rescue by Poseidon (318–40), the first conversation of Here and Poseidon (112–55) matches the second (292–317), and the advance of the two heroes (156–75) matches their combat (259–91). In the centre of the rings are the speeches (176–258), and the whole is framed by the initial description of Akhilleus' furious rage (75–8) and his concluding perplexed exhortation to himself (341–52).

But the expansive style of the narration, the relaxed tone of Akhilleus' speeches, and his willingness to listen to his opponent's lengthy discourse, are unexpected; Leaf (II 348) goes so far as to say 'Achilles is in a merciful and, indeed, bantering mood.' Certainly the emotional pressure is notably lower than it is in Akhilleus' next major encounter, that with Lukaon in the next Book. The general air is close to that of the Diomedes/Glaukos meeting (6.119–236), which is carried on with such careful regard for the proprieties and concludes so amiably; there are parallels in structure too (see 6.119n.). F. M. Combellack, *CP* 71 (1976) 49–53, has plausibly suggested that this episode presents the normal Akhilleus, not the furious avenger we see elsewhere after Patroklos' death, and that the encounter between them was a regular part of the Trojan story; 'the pull of his standard method of composition has in this instance ... caused the poet to retain features, and possibly even phrases, of this story of Achilles and Aeneas that do not fit the context into which he now places it' (p. 52).

As a reason for rescuing Aineias from Akhilleus, Poseidon says that the race of Dardanos must not die out; Zeus is now hostile to Priam's line, but that of Aineias will continue (307–8):

> νῦν δὲ δὴ Αἰνείαο βίη Τρώεσσιν ἀνάξει
> καὶ παίδων παῖδες, τοί κεν μετόπισθε γένωνται.

At *HyAphr* 196–7 Aphrodite expresses a similar sentiment to Ankhises:

> σοὶ δ' ἔσται φίλος υἱὸς ὃς ἐν Τρώεσσιν ἀνάξει
> καὶ παῖδες παίδεσσι διαμπερὲς ἐκγεγάονται.

In antiquity some thought the *Il.* passage meant that Homer knew of descendants of Aineias reigning in Phrygia; Dionysius of Halicarnassus writes ὑπολαβόντες οὖν τὸν Ὅμηρον ἐν Φρυγίᾳ δυναστεύοντας εἰδέναι τοὺς ἄνδρας (*Ant. Rom.* 1.53.5). Strabo (13.1.51–3) reports a version (among others) which located these Aineiadai at Skepsis in the Troad. The idea of a direct reference to a continuing royal line has been largely accepted by modern scholars since Robert Wood, and many have also thought that these latter-day Aineiadai were patrons of Homer whom he wished to please by such a reference (this view is championed by Reinhardt, *IuD* 450–3 and 507–21). The evidence has been given a full discussion in a recent article by P. M. Smith, *HSCP* 85 (1981) 17–58; cf. also his *Nursling of Mortality: a Study of the Homeric Hymn to Aphrodite* (Frankfurt am Main 1981). Lenz, *Aphroditehymnos*, is also important, and gives an account of earlier views (155–9).

Smith's conclusion is that the evidence does not support the existence of historical Aineiadai in the Troad, and that 'the two passages which inspired that hypothesis should be read ... as integral to their poetic contexts and not as composed to flatter "Aineiadai" in the poets' audiences. The future rule of Aineias which Poseidon predicts in the *Iliad* is the future rule which Hektor will not survive to enjoy. The future rule of Aineias which Aphrodite promises in the Hymn embodies the success with which Anchises will surpass the bounds of his inescapable mortality' (p. 52).

Aineias traditionally survived the war. Proclus, *Chrest.* 239, reports that in Arctinus' *Iliupersis* οἱ περὶ τὸν Αἰνείαν were so alarmed by the killing of Laokoön and one of his sons by two snakes that they withdrew to Mt Ida before the wooden horse disgorged the Greeks. In the *Iliupersis* of Stesichorus, Aineias and his family may have left for the west (Page, *PMG* pp. 110–1; see N. Horsfall, *JHS* 99, 1979, 39–43, who is very sceptical; G. K. Galinsky, *Aeneas, Sicily, and Rome*, Princeton 1969, 106–13; and L. Malten, *Archiv für Religionswissenschaft* 29, 1931, 42–8). Apollodorus has a different version, that during the sack of the city Aineias took up his father Ankhises and fled, and the Greeks let him go διὰ τὴν εὐσέβειαν (*Epitome* 5.21). There is no mention in the *Il.* of Ankhises (except in the formular παῖς Ἀγχίσαο etc.) or of Aineias' son, just as there is none of Memnon (see 236–8n.), but Aineias' wife Kreousa appeared among the women prisoners in Polygnotus' painting of the Fall of Troy (Pausanias 10.26.1). Representations of Aineias escaping from Troy with Ankhises on his back, and accompanied by a woman and one or two sons, suddenly become very common in the last quarter of the sixth century; K. Schauenberg lists 52 pictures on Attic black-figure vases and 5 in red-figure (*Gymnasium* 67, 1960, 176–91 and plates; cf. also *Gymnasium* 76, 1969, 42–53 and plates; F. Brommer, *Vasenlisten zur griechische Heldensage*[3], Marburg 1973, 386–89; Galinsky, *op. cit.* 122–5 and plates; and *LIMC* 1 386–8, nos. 59–91). Most of these vases of which the provenance is known come from Italy, especially

Etruria (*LIMC* 1 395); this sudden surge of interest is probably the result of attention to the Etruscan market rather than any new development in Greek epic, though Stesichorus' *Iliupersis may* have been a stimulus.

It is clear that hostility between Priam's line and Ankhises', both descended from Dardanos (see 215–40n.), was part of the conventional story; at 13.459–61 Aineias has withdrawn from battle because Priam does not honour him, and at 20.179–83 Akhilleus utters the taunt that Priam has sons whom he will reward before Aineias. There was a line of Dardanians in Thrace, and the tradition may reflect a Thracian occupation of Troy during or after the twelfth century (see 13.459–61n.; N. K. Sandars, *The Sea Peoples*, London 1978, 192–4; Scheibner, *Aufbau* 124–34).

The close connexion in wording between Poseidon's prophecy here and Aphrodite's in the *Hymn* suggests the possibility of common authorship. Reinhardt, *IuD* 507–21, suggests that the poet of the *Il.* also composed the *Hymn*; Heitsch, *Aphroditehymnos*, that the author of the *Hymn* inserted the Aineias-episode into the *Il.* However, the arguments from language and formular style have often been based on faulty assumptions, and Heitsch has been answered by H. Erbse, *RhM* 110 (1967) 1–25 (Heitsch responded in his further study *Epische Kunstsprache und homerische Chronologie*, Heidelberg 1968); Dihle, *Homer-Probleme* 65–83; A. Heubeck, *Glotta* 50 (1972) 129–43; and Lenz, *Aphroditehymnos* 218–55. The scholars who have most recently compared the language and formular style of this episode with that of *HyAphr* have concluded that the *Hymn* shows a later stage of development (Hoekstra, *Sub-epic Stage* 39–48; Janko, *HHH* 151–80), or at least a different author (N. Postlethwaite, *Phoenix* 33, 1979, 1–18).

Studies of language have not proved that the episode is alien to the author of the *Il.*, and (as the following commentary will indicate) the nature and handling of its component parts is fully consistent with the rest of the poem. It seems most likely that the monumental poet knew of a story that Aineias continued to rule somewhere in the Troad; this does not prove that a royal line of Aineiadai, perhaps originating in Thrace, survived (or claimed to) in the mid-eighth century, but it is a reasonable hypothesis. Virgil may have been alluding to, and contradicting, this version when he has his Aeneas tell Dido that if fate had allowed him his own choice, *recidiva manu posuissem Pergama victis* (*Aeneid* 4.344).

77–8 Πριαμίδεω occurs only here in a position where it is not resolvable into -ᾱ'(ο), but cf. Τυδεΐδεω Διομήδεος (16.74) and the many examples of the construction Τυδεΐδης, ὅς... quoted by Hoekstra, *Modifications* 34. The poet is availing himself of a new linguistic possibility to widen the use of an old sentence-structure. ἑ is Aristarchus' doubtless correct reading (Did/AT) for the γε of almost all MSS. Verse 78 = 5.289 and 22.267, which both follow πρίν γ' ἢ ἕτερόν γε πεσόντα |. On ταλαύρινον see 5.287–9n.

79–111 Apollo's motive in endangering Aineias is not made clear, though Erbse suggests he is keeping Akhilleus away as long as possible from his beloved Hektor (*RhM* 110, 1967, 18). The *poet's* motive is obvious enough – he wants the duel to take place (see 75–155n.), and employs conventional means to bring it about. There is a regular pattern of action in battle in which a god (in disguise) disapprovingly questions a hero who is for the moment not fighting; the hero responds; and the god persuades him to enter the battle, giving him fresh strength. Cf. Apollo's earlier approach to Hektor (15.243–70), Poseidon's approach to Idomeneus (13.206–45; the invigoration is omitted), Athene's to Menelaos (17.553–73; the goddess's second speech is omitted), and the spectacular version at 5.793–841, where Athene appears to Diomedes without disguise and to encourage him actually takes the place of his chariot-driver. See 13.206–45n.; Fenik categorizes this episode as an amalgamation of the 'rebuke' and 'consultation' patterns (*TBS* 27–9, 50–1, and 128–9).

This is Aineias' biggest scene, but he has always been second only to Hektor on the Trojan side. Earlier in the poem he had an important rôle in Diomedes' *aristeia* (5.166–446, 5.512–60), where he is likewise saved by divine intervention (that of Aphrodite and Apollo), and his prominence was reaffirmed (in preparation for this episode) as he charged beside Hektor in the attempt to capture Patroklos' body (17.753–9). He is linked with Hektor as the best of the Trojans both in fighting and counsel by Hektor's brother Helenos (6.77–9), and Idomeneus expresses a keen fear of him (13.481–4). The poet himself places him beside Akhilleus as ἀνέρες ἔξοχ' ἄριστοι (158). See Scheibner, *Aufbau* 10–18, and Reinhardt, *IuD* 128–37.

79–82 λαοσσόος: see 38–40n. and 13.126–8n. μένος ἠΰ is used after ἐνέπνευσε at 17.456. εἴσατο φωνήν | is an abbreviated form of the formular εἴκυῖα (etc.) δέμας καὶ ἀτειρέα φωνήν | (2 × *Il.*). Verse 82, and Aineias' response, show that the god also takes Lukaon's shape. Lukaon son of Priam has been mentioned only at 3.333, where Paris borrowed his breastplate. He is clearly referred to here in preparation for his memorable scene with Akhilleus later on (21.34ff.).

83–5 The accusation of boastful talk on social occasions is conventional, cf. σεο πατρὸς ἐνὶ μεγάροισιν ἄκουσα | εὐχομένης (1.396–7 ≅ 21.475–6; see M. M. Willcock, *HSCP* 81, 1977, 49–50). There is an expanded example at 8.229–34. Αἰνεία Τρώων βουληφόρε is formular (4 × *Il.*), followed 2 × by χαλκοχιτώνων. Similar expressions with βουληφόρε are used for Sarpedon and Idomeneus; the epithet 'is no idle compliment, but implies that [the hero] should live up to his responsibilities' (13.219–20n.).

86 ἀπαμειβόμενος προσέειπε: ἀπαμείβετο φώνησέν τε would be regular, as at 199, but overlapping speech-introduction formulae are not uncommon (see

M. W. Edwards, *CP* 64, 1969, 81–7, *HSCP* 74, 1968, 26). Yet another 'he answered' formula is used for Aineias at 5.217.

87–102 So too Pandaros, when reproached by Aineias, said that he had come to grips with the attacker previously without success and that some deity was standing beside him (5.184–91). Lohmann, *Reden* 161–9, analyses this and the later speeches, perhaps rather too rigorously. The first part of the speech, as is usual in telling a story, is in ring form:

A Why do you urge me to fight Akhilleus (87–8)?
B I fled from him before, when he sacked Lurnessos and Pedasos (89–92).
C Zeus saved me then (92–3),
B′ or he would have killed me, when he attacked the Leleges and Trojans (94–6).
A′ So no mortal can fight Akhilleus (97–102).

87–8 Verse 87 ≅ 332, 88 = 333. ὑπέρθυμος is used of Akhilleus only in these verses; it is used twice of Diomedes during his *aristeia*, but generally it is applied to the Trojans by angry Greeks. Clearly it is not purely formular but has a significant sense.

89–93 The same episode is used by Akhilleus at 187–94 as a paradigm showing why they should not fight. Capture for ransom of a Trojan caught in the countryside by Akhilleus is a motif appearing in the cases of Priam's sons Isos and Antiphos (11.104–6) and Lukaon (21.34–44), and Andromakhe's brothers were killed by him in similar circumstances (6.421–4). Aineias is the only one who escapes by flight; the incident was described in the *Cypria* (κἄπειτα ⟨'Αχιλλεύς⟩ ἀπελαύνει τὰς Αἰνείου βόας καὶ Λυρνησσὸν καὶ Πήδασον πορθεῖ, Proclus) and may be figured on a Cycladic relief pithos (M. E. Caskey, *AJA* 80, 1976, 35–6). The repeated account of the incident here anticipates the flight of Hektor before Akhilleus at 22.136ff. (which is thus not such a 'bold innovation' as was stated by Edwards, *HPI* 293).

89–90 ποδώκεος ἄντ' 'Αχιλῆος is paralleled (*pace* Dihle, *Homer-Probleme* 67) by πόδας ταχὺν ἀμφ' 'Αχιλῆα (18.354); cf. *Od.* 8.502. ἄλλοτε δουρὶ φόβησεν (-ῆσαι) is repeated by Akhilleus (187).

92–3 As often, beginning the sentence at the bucolic diaeresis allows the emphatic word εἰρύσαθ' to be placed in the runover position. ὅς μοι (οἱ) ἐπῶρσε μένος λαιψηρά τε γοῦνα is repeated for Zeus's aid to Hektor during his flight from Akhilleus (22.204), possibly to bring out the contrast between their eventual fates.

94–5 The protasis 'If Zeus had not saved me' is omitted; Macleod, *Iliad XXIV* on 24.439, quotes 3.53 and 5.885–7 as other parallels. As the scholia (bT) point out, Aineias saves face by stressing Athene's help to Akhilleus.

φάος (φόως) generally means 'salvation', as in the formular φόως Δαναοῖσι γένηαι (3 × *Il.*), but is here extended to mean 'protection'. Pedasos (92) was the chief town of the Leleges (21.86–7).

97–100 ἄνδρα = 'a mortal' (see 18.429–35n.). Verse 98 ≅ 5.603, where Diomedes complains that Ares is sheltering Hektor. The refusal to fight with an opponent whom a god is protecting is common, cf. 5.184–7, 17.98–9. See S. R. van der Mije, *Mnemosyne* 40 (1987) 241–67, who points out that here Aineias is reconciling his claim to be as good a fighter as Akhilleus and his reluctance to face him. καὶ ἄλλως (99) = 'even without this', as at 9.699, *Od.* 21.87. ἰθύ is adverbial. χροὸς ἀνδρομέοιο is normally an end-of-verse formula (17.571, cf. 21.70). περ (100) goes with εἰ, 'if only'. Lohmann, *Reden* 162, unwisely athetizes 99–102.

101–2 ἶσον τείνειεν πολέμου τέλος is made up from phrases like κατὰ ἶσα μάχην ἐτάνυσσε Κρονίων (11.336, cf. 12.436 = 15.413) and τέλος πολέμοιο κιχείω (3.291), ἐν γὰρ χερσὶ τέλος πολέμου (16.630). On the metaphor in τείνειεν see 17.400–1n., 13.358–60n., and A. Heubeck, *Glotta* 50 (1972) 135–43. οὔ κε... | νικήσει'(ε): both κε and με appear in good MSS, and ΝΙΚΗΣΕΙ has been taken as a vivid future indicative (reading με; κε is also grammatically possible, cf. Chantraine, *GH* II 225–6), as at 10.223–4, or as an optative (with κε), the final -ε elided as at *Od.* 11.585, 11.591, and perhaps *Il.* 2.4. The indicative (read by Willcock) would have greater force, but it is impossible to be certain how overtly confident Aineias is being here; the reservation expressed in 99 suggests the optative would better represent his degree of optimism. ῥέα recurs as a monosyllable at the verse-end at 12.381; Hoekstra, *Modifications* 37, suggests it may be a colloquialism. On the form see 17.461–2n. παγχάλκεος: there is a formular phrase κυνέη πάγχαλκος ἐπὶ κροτάφοις ἀραρυῖα | (2 × *Od.*), and παγχάλκεος is applied to a sword (*Od.* 8.403) and to Herakles' club (*Od.* 11.575), but this is the only metaphorical instance (though χάλκεος is so used, e.g. in the formular χάλκεος Ἄρης). Apollo once says to the Trojans, of the Greeks, οὔ σφι λίθος χρὼς οὐδὲ σίδηρος (4.510).

104 ἥρως is used as a vocative singular by Dolon to Odysseus (10.416) and by Patroklos to Eurupulos (in the apparently formular Εὐρύπυλ' ἥρως |; 11.819, 838); and in the *Od.* by Eidothea to Menelaos, Odysseus to Alkinoös, and Kirke to Odysseus. It seems to be a rather formal mode of address, suitable from the young Lukaon to the senior Trojan leader.

105–7 The comparison of the heroes' mothers prepares for Aineias' more detailed examination of their respective pedigrees at 203–9. Similarly Akhilleus boasts to Asteropaios that descendants of Zeus are stronger than sons of rivers (21.184–91): see Fenik, *TBS* 67. Perhaps there was something similar in a scene of Akhilleus' combat with Eos' son Memnon. Διὸς κούρης Ἀφροδίτης: this is the only instance of a genitive formula of this metrical shape for Aphrodite in Homer. In Hesiod and *HyAphr* πολυχρύσου Ἀφροδίτης is used, and in *HyDem* φιλοστεφάνου Ἀφρ. On the anonymous Old Man of the Sea see 1.358n. and S. West, *Odyssey* on *Od.* 4.349.

108–10 Verse 109 ≅ 21.339, which has μειλιχίοις for λευγαλέοις and also follows μηδέ σε πάμπαν | ... On ἀρειῇ, 'threat', see 17.429–31n.; here it prepares for Akhilleus' long challenge (178–98). Verse 110 = 15.262 (again Apollo inspiring Hektor).

112–55 A divine scene preceding a human encounter gives it added dignity; cf. the Zeus–Here conversation before Sarpedon's losing duel with Patroklos (16.431–61) and the debate on Olumpos before Hektor fights with Akhilleus (22.166–87). A second divine discussion, adding even more weight to Aineias' survival, will precede Aineias' actual rescue by Poseidon (291–339). Herē, like Apollo, seems no longer to be confronting an adversary as she was at 70–1; see 67–74n. οὐδ' ἔλαθ' is used to switch the narrative to new characters in the scene, with some emphasis; cf. 17.1–2, 626–7. 'It is a typical stylistic feature for the action on the battlefield to be interrupted for a scene among the gods, and then to be picked up again later at the same point where it was stopped' (Fenik, *TBS* 37). Herē's concern is not unjustified, in view of Apollo's actions against Patroklos (16.788ff.). Ἀγχίσαο πάϊς: cf. ἐὺς πάϊς Ἀγχίσαο | (3 × *Il.*).

113–14 On the formular ἀνὰ οὐλαμὸν ἀνδρῶν see 4.251n. For 114 Zenodotus read ἣ δ' ἄμυδις καλέσασα θεοὺς ῥεῖα ζώοντας, very properly corrected by Aristarchus (Arn/A; Did/AT). ἦ is used only after a speech, so here the article ἡ must be intended and the regular speech-introduction is required. Aristarchus (καὶ αἱ πλεῖσται, Did/AT) read στήσασα, but the MSS give καλέσασα, which it would be best to retain (with Leaf), particularly since it allows Here more initiative. The participle controls θεούς, as μετὰ μῦθον ἔειπε takes a dative.

115–17 This is an adapted version of ἡμεῖς δὲ φραζώμεθ' ὅπως ἔσται τάδε ἔργα (4.14 = 14.61); there is another single-line version at 14.3. Poseidon and Athene have both been involved in the battle previously and are the obvious people to turn to for help; Hermes and Hephaistos are ignored. Αἰνείας ὅδ' ἔβη: 'Here Aineias has moved out ⟨against⟩'; cf. 5.175–6n.

119–24 These lines are notable for their frequent strong sense-pauses and heavy emphasis. Four consecutive lines (120–3) begin with stressed runover words after enjambment; 121 is a threefolder with two strong breaks; 122 also has two strong breaks, but falling within and after the first hemistich; 123 repeats the shape of 121; then 124, with a weak mid-verse caesura, returns to the conventional form of 119. Herē is speaking with great forcefulness.

119–20 ἡμεῖς περ: contrasted with Apollo. The forms ἡμείων and ὑμείων occur 5 × *Il.* and 3 × *Od.*, and show a metrical lengthening perhaps based on the analogy of ἐμεῖο, σεῖο (Chantraine, *GH* I 271). The use here (after τις) may be suggested by the formular | οὐδέ (μηδέ, ὧδέ) τις ἡμείων (ὑμείων) (1 × *Il.*, 3 × *Od.*). αὐτόθεν...ἔπειτα: the temporal sense given by Leaf, 'at once...afterwards', does not allow a good alternative sense for ἤ. It is better to interpret αὐτόθεν as local, 'away from here', and ἔπειτα as 'alternatively' (cf. 13.743, 24.356, *Od.* 20.63).

121–4 παρσταίη, δοίη: When Here gave a command to everyone, herself included, she used the virtual imperative ἀποτρωπῶμεν (119); now that she addresses them all as individuals (τις) the optatives are more courteous. ἀνεμώλιος, 'empty', 'useless', is only here used of persons. For πάρος περ (123) one would have expected πάρος γε, since the gods defended Troy in the past but are now ἀνεμώλιοι (see 17.586–8n.). πόλεμον (-ου, -ῳ) καὶ δηϊοτῆτα (-ος, -ι) | occurs 10 × *Il.*, including split versions.

125–8 These lines were needlessly athetized by Aristarchus (Arn/A) on the grounds that Zeus had said otherwise at 26–7, and to protect Akhilleus' reputation for invincibility (on Aristarchus' view that Homer always represented Akhilleus in the best possible light see D. M. Schenkeveld, *Mnemosyne* 23, 1970, 165–70). One's day of death is determined at the day of birth (23.79). With the wording of 127–8 cf. τῷ δ' ὡς ποθι Μοῖρα κραταιὴ | γιγνομένῳ ἐπένησε λίνῳ, ὅτε μιν τέκον αὐτή (24.209–10; spoken by Hekabe of Hektor), and ἔνθα δ' ἔπειτα | πείσεται ἄσσα οἱ αἶσα κατὰ Κλῶθές τε βαρεῖαι | γεινομένῳ νήσαντο λίνῳ, ὅτε μιν τέκε μήτηρ (*Od.* 7.196–8). The metaphor is taken up in the name Κλωθώ (Hesiod, *Theogony* 218 = 905), Κλῶθες, 'Spinner(s)', and in the verb ἐπικλώθω (24.525 and 7 × *Od.*). See B. C. Dietrich, *Death, Fate and the Gods* (London 1965) 289–94, and Hainsworth, *Odyssey* on *Od.* 7.196–8. σήμερον· ὕστερον are contrasted again at the beginning of the verse at 7.30 ≅ 291 and 8.142. This is potentially the day of Akhilleus' greatest glory, and so of his greatest danger.

129–31 εἰ...οὐ...πεύσεται: in Homer, the negative is regularly οὐ when a protasis with indicative verb precedes the main clause (Chantraine, *GH* I 333; Leaf on 4.160). ὀμφῆς: cf. 2.41n. θεοὶ φαίνεσθαι (-ονται) ἐναργεῖς | recurs at *Od.* 7.201, 16.161, where, however, it is a sign of special favour.

133–43 Poseidon soothes the worried and angry Here, suggesting that the strife be left to mankind. Athene says much the same to Ares when she leads him from the battle during Diomedes' *aristeia* (5.31–4); she and Apollo also agree to suspend the fighting before the duel of Hektor and Aias (7.24–42). On Poseidon's attitude when he challenges Apollo to fight at 21.435–69 see note *ad loc*. The wisdom he shows here prepares for his later rôle in rescuing Aineias from premature death; see 292–320n.

133–5 παρ' ἐκ νόον, 'beyond reason' recurs at 10.391 and *HyAphr* 36. οὐδέ τί σε χρή | is formular (9 × *Il.*, 8 × *Od.*). With 134–5 cf. 8.210–11, where Poseidon tells Here οὐκ ἂν ἔγωγ' ἐθέλοιμι Διὶ Κρονίωνι μάχεσθαι and the second verse is the same (but with φέρτερός ἐστιν). There the sense is straightforward ('I would not wish that we others fight with Zeus'). Here the natural rendering would be 'I do not wish that we should set the other gods against each other', which gives an odd sense, or possibly '... that the gods should fight each other, we against the others', which violently changes the construction from that of 8.211. The latter meaning is approved by Scheibner, *Aufbau* 73 n. 2, and van der Valk, *Researches* II 509, but 135 is missing from most early MSS (though it appears in a sixth-century papyrus and the A scholia) and was probably copied from 8.211 at an early date. Leaf sensibly brackets it. θεοὺς ἔριδι ξυνελάσσαι | is paralleled at 21.394.

136–7 ἔπειτα: 'then', 'therefore', as at 9.444, 24.290. πόλεμος δ' ἄνδρεσσι μελήσει is also said by Hektor to Andromakhe, with a different connotation of ἄνδρεσσι (6.492). The phrase is formular, and is found with μῦθος (*Od.* 1.358), πόμπη (*Od.* 11.352, expanded at 332), and τόξον (*Od.* 21.352).

138–9 ἄρχωσι: this is the *schema Alcmanicum*, in which a dual or plural verb is placed following the first of two subjects, as at *Il.* 5.774, *Od.* 10.513–14. Here the subjects are coupled by the disjunctive ἤ instead of a conjunction, but the usage is still natural enough. Zenodotus (Arn/A) read ἄρχησι, unnecessarily (though Leaf gives some support). οὐκ stands in a protasis with subjunctive verb because it goes closely with εἰῶσι. 'Αχιλῆα is elided only here and at 174, but 'Οδυσῆα is elided 7 × *Od.* (5 × in this metrical position).

140 Almost all MSS read παρ' αὐτόφι, 'with [i.e. against] them', which is printed by Ameis-Hentze. The variant παρ' αὐτόθι, 'on the spot', is required at 13.42 and 23.147, but Chantraine, *GH* I 239–40, prefers αὐτόφι here, at 12.302, and at 23.640.

142–3 θεῶν μεθ' ὁμήγυριν ἄλλων | is an under-represented formula, found at *HyAp* 187 and *HyDem* 484. ἀναγκαίηφι δαμέντες is read by editors and a few MSS, but the vulgate ἀνάγκη ἶφι δαμέντας must be right; ἶφι δαμέντα (-ῆναι) | is formular, and follows the datives ἀνέρι (19.417), ἄορι (21.208), and ἔγχεϊ (*Od.* 18.156). Poseidon's prediction is fulfilled at 21.519, when the gods return to Olumpos οἱ μὲν χωόμενοι, οἱ δὲ μέγα κυδιόωντες.

145–8 On the background of the story see 21.441–57n. ἀμφίχυτος, 'of heaped-up ⟨earth⟩', occurs only here; a model might have been provided by the formular | νήσῳ ἐν ἀμφιρύτῃ (4 × *Od.*, including an adaptation). τὸ κῆτος: 'the sea-monster ⟨we all know about⟩'.

150–2 ἄρρηκτος, 'impenetrable', is only here used of a cloud. Besides the need for invisibility, conferred elsewhere by a merely 'dark' cloud (πορφυρέη νεφέλη, 17.551), is there perhaps danger from random missiles? On Kallikolone see 51–3n. ὀφρῦς is only here used metaphorically in early epic, but "Ιλιος ὀφρυόεσσα occurs at 22.411 and the very appropriate ὀφρυόεντα Κόρινθον | in Hesiod fr. 204.48. With 152 cf. | ὥς ῥα σύ, ἤϊε Φοῖβε

(15.365). In both places there is a slight emphasis on Apollo which might account for the apostrophe, but more likely the vocative is used because there is no metrical equivalent in the nominative or accusative. The expression occurs at the god's birth in *HyAp* 120. It must reflect the ritual cry ἰή (see 15.365–6n.). N. Yamagata, *BICS* 36 (1989) 97, points out that under similar metrical circumstances Zeus says ἔρχεο (εἰ δ' ἄγε) νῦν, φίλε Φοῖβε (15.221, 16.667), suggesting that the human veneration implied in the epithet is unsuitable from Zeus. πτολίπορθος (-ιος) is applied several times to Odysseus and Akhilleus and once each to Oïleus, Otrunteus, and the war-goddess Enuo (see 21.550n.). Its use with Ares may well be traditional, as there is no metrical equivalent with his name. The first syllable of Ἄρηα is scanned long again at 5.827 (in a different phrase); the varying quantity of the initial vowel (cf. 18.264–5n.) may be connected with a non-Greek origin of the word (see *LfgrE* s.v.).

154–5 δυσηλεγέος πολέμοιο | sounds like a formula, but the adjective ('ruthless', 'painful' < δυσ-+ἀλέγω) recurs only in the phrase θάνατόν γε δυσηλεγέα (*Od.* 22.325, *HyAp* 367) and in two unformular instances in Hesiod. With θάνατος it was probably dropped in favour of the equivalent τανηλεγέος θανάτοιο | (2 × *Il.*, 6 × *Od.*), but it may be the regular adjective with πολέμοιο, which does not appear with a metrical equivalent. ἥμενος ὕψι occurs only here, and reminds us that Zeus is still watching, πτυχὶ Οὐλύμποιο | ἥμενος (22–3). κέλευε is used absolutely, as at 11.65; the imperfect means 'it was Zeus who had bidden ⟨them⟩', recalling his injunction at 23–5. Herē and Poseidon converse again at 293ff., but the others will remain off-stage until 21.385.

156–258 As the two heroes confront each other, Akhilleus taunts Aineias with his lack of favour in Priam's eyes and with his flight when they previously met. In response, Aineias recounts his distinguished ancestry

156–60 The narrator briefly sums up the situation, as a bridge between the scene among the gods and the reintroduction of the two human heroes.

156–7 The same ideas appear in πλῆτο δὲ πᾶν πεδίον πεζῶν τε καὶ ἵππων | χαλκοῦ τε στεροπῆς (*Od.* 14.267–8; Odysseus' tale of his raid on Egypt). τῶν is explained by ἀνδρῶν ἠδ' ἵππων. καρκαίρω appears in Greek only here and in Hesychius, and is taken as the intensive reduplicated present of an onomatopoeic root; both ancient and modern scholars suggest the meanings 'shake' or 'resound'. Other examples of this kind of reduplicated present are given by Risch, *Wortbildung* 341.

158–60 A similar 3-line statement, beginning δύο δ' ἄνδρες ἀρήιοι ἔξοχον ἄλλων | ..., introduces Aineias' fight with Idomeneus (13.499–501). ἔξοχ' ἄριστοι | occurs 2 × *Il.*, 3 × *Od.* Verse 159 = 6.120 (Diomedes and Glaukos) and 23.814 (Aias and Diomedes), verse 160 ≅ 17.754 (Aineias and Hektor; a rising threefolder, like 1.7 etc.).

161–3 The motifs of the shield held before the chest, the nodding helmet-plume, and the brandished spear are regular, and appear in elaborated form when Akhilleus charges against Hektor (22.312–20). The language, however, is largely unformular. ἀπειλέω usually means to threaten with words; here apparently only by the actions described (so too at 13.582). νευστάζω appears 3 × *Od.*, but not in this martial context. The nearest parallel to | πρόσθεν ἔχε στέρνοιο is | τὸ πρόσθε στέρνοιο φέρων (7.224), and the nearest to τίνασσε δὲ χάλκεον ἔγχος is τινάσσων φάσγανον ὀξύ (22.311, cf. 12.298).

164–75 As usual the poet does not tell us when a hero leaves his chariot; cf. 15.352–4n. A warrior entering or re-entering the battle is often dignified by a simile, as is Diomedes at 5.87–94; see Fenik, *TBS* 10. Here the simile for Akhilleus balances Aineias' dialogue with Apollo. This is perhaps the most lifelike of the many lion-similes in the poem, although – perhaps because – it contains less action than most; it is also the longest. The beast is not hungrily seizing a domestic animal; he proudly ignores the hunters until struck by a weapon, whereupon he furiously attacks. The outcome is not revealed, as is fitting in this highly generalized description; it is the character of the animal that is important. The best appreciation of the simile is that of A. Schnapp-Gourbeillon, *Lions, Héros, Masques: les représentations de l'animal chez Homère* (Paris 1981) 86–7.

The main point of comparison is the kindled fury of the lion and of the hero, reinforced by the repetitions ἐποτρύνει (171) and φέρεται μένει (172) within the simile and ὄτρυνε μένος (174) in the narrative. There are other parallels too. The stress on the horde of men (πᾶς δῆμος, 166) seeking to kill a single animal may anticipate the isolated combat of Akhilleus against the Trojans until Hektor's death (cf. 356–9); the disregard of the animal for the hunters (ἀτίζων, 166) suggests Akhilleus' long withdrawal from the battle; the wound which provokes the lion's fury corresponds to the loss of Patroklos (rather than Fränkel's parallel with the threats of Aineias, *Gleichnisse* 63); the 'groan' the animal utters (169) suggests Akhilleus' lamentations; and ἐποτρύνει μαχέσασθαι and πρώτῳ ἐν ὁμίλῳ (173) suggest a battlefield rather than a hunt.

The formulae in 164–8 are identified by A. B. Lord, *HSCP* 72 (1967) 28. Modern editors print the whole simile (164–75) as a single sentence, and most of the lines enjamb without any pause at verse-end.

164 Though lion-similes are common, λέων ὥς at the end of the line occurs only here and at 11.129, in both cases preceded by ἐναντίον ὦρτο; in the latter instance the simile is not expanded in the following lines. On the ways of introducing lion-similes see Scott, *Oral Nature* 141.

165–7 σίντης (< σίνομαι, 'despoil') recurs only at 11.481 and 16.353, always in a simile and as a runover word qualifying a lion and wolves. It is found only in a few Homeric imitators. τε is the generalizing particle normal in similes; καί links σίντης and the following clause: the lion is destructive, and ⟨therefore⟩ the men seek to kill it. πᾶς δῆμος is probably formular in this position (1 × *Od.*, *HyDem* 271). For ὁ δὲ πρῶτον μὲν ἀτίζων some MSS of the *h* group have (or had before correction) ὁ δὲ κρειῶν ἐρατίζων, copied from the lion-simile at 11.551 (repeated in an identical passage at 17.660). The vulgate is much more effective here. ἀτίζω (= ἀτιμάζω) occurs only here in Homer, but appears in later poetry. ἀρηϊθόων αἰζηῶν and δουρὶ βάλη are formular (3 × *Il.*, 5 × *Il.* respectively), used elsewhere in martial contexts.

168–9 Verse 168 is a threefolder. ἐάλη < εἴλω, 'crouch', as at 278, 13.408 etc. The lion is not hiding but preparing to spring. στένει, like στενάχω (-ίζω), always seems to have a sense not only of oppression but of groaning aloud (cf. 23.230, 24.776). The word recalls Akhilleus' agony of grief (18.33, 18.78). The author of the *Aspis* however has μένεος... πίμπλαται ἦτορ in the parallel passage (*Aspis* 429). ἦτορ here must be taken as 'spirit' in a non-physical sense, as often, whilst κραδίη must mean 'heart' in the literal sense, as at (e.g.) 13.282 (so Erbse, *RhM* 110, 1967, 11). The various expressions underlying the present phrasing are discussed by E. Heitsch, *Epische Kunstsprache und homerische Chronologie* (Heidelberg 1968) 39–44.

170–1 'It has beneath its tail a black goad, like a little horn' (bT). The vividness of the description has convinced some scholars (including Fränkel, *Gleichnisse* 62n.) that the lion must still have existed in Asia Minor. Pliny, *NH* 8.49, says only that *terga ceu quodam incitamento flagellantur*. The *Aspis*, in a simile probably taken from this, has γλαυκιόων δ' ὄσσοις δεινὸν πλευράς τε καὶ ὤμους | οὐρῇ μαστιόων ποσσὶν γλάφει (430–1). ἑέ < *ἑϜέ < *sewe; see 17.547–52n. and Chantraine, *GH* 1 264. The hiatus before it is due to the analogy of ἑ(Ϝ)ε, where the digamma is almost always observed. With the second hemistich of 171 cf. αὐτὸς ἐποτρύνει μαχέσασθαι | (17.178 ≅ 16.690), used of a human fighter.

172–3 γλαυκιάω, 'glare fiercely', recurs in the *Aspis* simile (430), then only in late imitators; Catullus may have taken it to mean 'grey-eyed', 'blue-eyed' (*caesio...leoni*, 45.7; see R. J. Edgeworth, *Glotta* 65, 1987, 135). The use here may have been suggested by | μειδιόων (2 × *Il.*). With ἰθὺς φέρεται μένει cf. μένος χειρῶν ἰθὺς φέρον (5.506), μένος δ' ἰθὺς φέρον αὐτῶν (16.602). The sentiment 'kill or be killed' is commonly attributed to warriors; see 18.309n. πρώτῳ ἐν ὁμίλῳ recurs only at 17.471, where it means 'in the forefront of the battle'. Here it fits in with the military language of the simile.

174–7 Verse 174 shows an innovative adaptation of the formular ὡς εἰπὼν ὤτρυνε μένος καὶ θυμὸν ἑκάστου (10 × *Il.*, 1 × *Od.*) and θυμὸς ἀγήνωρ | (9 × *Il.*, 15 × *Od.*), switching the coupled nouns from object to subject. On ʼΑχιλῆ᾿(α) see 138–9n. The only instances of the combination μεγαλήτορος Αἰνείαο | occur in close proximity in this Book (again at 263, 293, 323), but there is no metrical equivalent and the clustering must be due to the formula, and the sentence-construction which requires it, remaining in the poet's mind. See J. B. Hainsworth, *Studies... Offered to L. R. Palmer* (edd. A. M. Davies and W. Meid, Innsbruck 1976) 83–6. Verses 176–7 = 21.148–9 (Akhilleus and Asteropaios).

178–98 A verbal exchange between warriors, in the form of a challenge of some kind and a response to it, is common before a heroic contest; there is a much briefer example at 429–37, and cf. more generally the taunting of Odysseus by Eurualos (*Od.* 8.158–85) and the 'flyting' between Beowulf and Unferth (*Beowulf* 499–606; see Martin, *Language* 68–75). The taunt levelled by Tlepolemos at Sarpedon (5.633–46) is very similar in tone to Akhilleus' words here; Diomedes' challenge to Glaukos (6.123–43) is closely linked to the mortals/immortals contrast which pervades his *aristeia*; Hektor's address to Akhilleus is modified into a request for a pact to hand back the body of the loser (22.250–9). As usual, the rest of the battle is forgotten while the conversation goes forward.

Lohmann's analysis of Akhilleus' speech, *Reden* 162–3, is less successful than usual, and involves the undesirable omission of 180–6. It is better to analyse the speech as a threatening question ('Why have you advanced to meet me?'), followed by two hypothetical answers, each of which is in turn rejected ('Is it so that you may rule the Trojans? But Priam would not allow that. Have you been promised a reward for killing me? But at our last encounter you fled and I was victorious'). Since neither hypothesis results in a desirable outcome for Aineias, the speech is rounded off with a recommendation that he withdraw (196–8).

Akhilleus' imaginative speculation about Aineias' motives for facing him has been linked with his vivid picture of Lukaon's fate (21.122–7) and the similes he uses as a poetic feature of his speech (by P. Friedrich and J. Redfield, *Language* 54, 1978, 273). The same aspect is demonstrated by J. Griffin, *JHS* 106 (1986) 53.

178–9 The usual phrasing is πολὺ προμάχων ἐξάλμενος ἔστη (17.342) or πολλὸν τῶν ἄλλων ἐξάλμενος (23.399). Here τόσσον ὁμίλου go together ('so far from the throng'), ἐπελθών replaces ἐξάλμενος, and πολλόν is retained. Dihle's explanation, *Homer-Probleme* 68, is less likely. Verse 179 ≅ 7.74.

180–6 Following his view that Akhilleus can do no wrong (see 125–8n.), Aristarchus (Arn/A) athetized these lines as 'mean in style and thought, and inappropriate for the character of Akhilleus'; the athetesis is supported by Lohmann, *Reden* 168–9. It would be easier to argue that the whole speech, especially its concluding warning to Aineias to retreat, is hard to reconcile with Akhilleus' fury against Hektor and all Trojans; see, however, 75–155n. Akhilleus' attempt to dissuade Aineias from fighting was foreseen by Apollo at 108–9.

180 Τρώεσσιν ἀνάξει(ν) is repeated in Poseidon's prediction (307). The dative is local ('among the Trojans'), and ἀνάξειν controls the genitive τιμῆς, which here means 'power', 'prerogative' as at 9.616, 15.189; cf. τιμῆς ἀπονήμενος ἧς περ ἄνασσες (*Od.* 24.30). With the use of the demonstrative in τιμῆς τῆς Πριάμου cf. υἱεῖς οἱ Δολίοιο (*Od.* 24.497).

182–3 ἐν χερὶ θήσει (etc.) also ends the line after πρεσβήϊον (8.289) and δέπας (24.101). ἔμπεδος, 'intact', normally qualifies μένος, φρένες, βίη, νόος, and the like, and is only here applied to a person; perhaps the proximity of ἀεσίφρων, with its suggestion of φρένες, made the usage easier. See Erbse, *RhM* 110 (1967) 10–11. ἀεσίφρων recurs in οὔ τι παρήορος οὐδ' ἀεσίφρων (23.603) and in the *figura etymologica* at *Od.* 21.301–2, ὁ δὲ φρεσὶν ᾗσιν ἀασθεὶς | ἤϊεν ἣν ἄτην ὀχέων ἀεσίφρονι θυμῷ (the line-end formula also occurs 3 × in Hesiod, *Erga*). The implied derivation from ἀάω, ἄτη is still accepted (see *LfgrE*), and ἀασίφρων might well be read.

The rivalry of the two Trojan royal houses has been mentioned before, perhaps in anticipation of this passage, when Aineias held back from battle because Priam did not sufficiently honour him (13.460–1, see note *ad loc.*; 13.361–454n.; and G. Nagy, *The Best of the Achaeans*, Baltimore 1979, 265–75). At 12.88–104 three groups of Trojans are led by Priam's sons Hektor (with Kebriones), Paris, and Helenos (with Deïphobos), Aineias leads the Dardanians, and Sarpedon the allies. The reference here looks forward both to Aineias' long account of his genealogy (208–41) and to Poseidon's prophecy of the future rule of his line at Troy (307–8).

184–6 Verses 184–5 ≅ 6.194–5, but the initial collocation ἦ νύ τί τοι does not recur in archaic epic and must be another peculiarity of Akhilleus' diction (see next note). Note the *figura etymologica* in τέμενος τάμον; on this, and on the meaning and origin of τέμενος, see 18.550–1n. Such inducements to fight are also offered at 10.303ff. and 17.229ff. χαλεπῶς δέ σ' ἔολπα: σε (ϝ)έ(ϝ)ολπα would give a better rhythm, providing a major word-break after the first syllable instead of after the trochee.

188–90 ἦ οὐ μέμνῃ ὅτε is formular (3 × *Il.*, 1 × *Od.*). In fact, the audience knows that Aineias remembers the occasion vividly (89–93). Eustathius (1203.8) points out that Homer skilfully varies the two accounts; Aineias merely says that he fled from Ida when Akhilleus arrived to seize the cattle and sack the towns, whereas Akhilleus tells the tale much more expansively.

Book Twenty

βοῶν ἄπο: Rhianus, Aristophanes, and the Chiot text (Did/AT) read βοῶν ἔπι, but ἐπί in this sense takes the dative (cf. 5.137, 6.424 etc.). μετατροπαλίζεο, 'turn back', is one of Akhilleus' nonce-words, never found again in Greek (see 19.149–50n.). Even the form without μετα- can be seen only in Hesychius. On such *hapax legomena* see Introduction, ch. 4, iv.

191–4 Notice the number of emphatic words which begin these lines, and the variety of position in the sense-pauses. On the story see 89–93n. and 19.291n. Among the captured women was Briseis (2.690–1). Verse 193 ≅ 16.831. ἐρρύσατο: A singular verb follows the first of two subjects, as at 2.858 etc. (cf. 138–9n.).

195–8 Aristarchus (Arn/A) athetized these lines, on the grounds that the last three are appropriate to Menelaos when he is struggling to save Patroklos' corpse and armour from his opponent (196 ≅ 17.30; 197–8 = 17.31–2), but not to the furious Akhilleus in his first encounter with a Trojan leader. This is a sound point; Lohmann, *Reden* 24 n. 31 and 164 n. 10, adds that the gnome at 17.32 (= 198) matches in ring form the gnome which begins Menelaos' speech (17.19). However, the warning to an adversary to retreat before he gets hurt is probably conventional (cf. 17.16–17 as well as 17.30–2), and though the sentiment is admittedly inappropriate to Akhilleus' rage against Hektor, it suits the leisurely and almost amiable tone of this whole episode. Moreover, the assertion in 195 that the gods will not save Aineias this time looks forward both to his account of his divine relatives and to his rescue by Poseidon. Verses 17.30–1 (≅ 196–7) fit well with 195, and the repetition not unnaturally carried along 17.32 as well, whether by the monumental poet's hand or some other. On 196–7 see 17.30–2n.

200–58 Much of Aineias' long discourse is taken up with the genealogy of the Trojan royal house; the rest is an eloquent diatribe against too much speechifying. Commentators have often indicated the irony of this, and it is true that there may be a semi-humorous characterization here (and also in the case of Glaukos in book 6) of a hero who knows he is the weaker and apprehensively keeps on talking. But expansion is natural here, because both heroes are of the greatest importance – Aineias because he is to be saved and to continue the royal Trojan line. It is common for Homeric warriors to recount their pedigrees with pride, because the glory of the fathers is reflected upon their sons. Glaukos is the prime example (6.145–211), but Idomeneus boasts of his own descent from Zeus as he challenges Deïphobos (13.448–54), and Akhilleus himself relates his ancestry in his vaunt over the dead Asteropaios (21.184–99). Recitation of genealogy is common in oral poetry in many cultures (see Martin, *Language* 85–6). It is also not unfitting that the splendid history of Troy's kings should be rehearsed just as the doom of the city is being prepared for by Akhilleus' pursuit of vengeance on its greatest warrior. The episode broadens the theme from revenge on Hektor to the fall of Troy. It has been well defended by A. W. H. Adkins, *CP* 70 (1975) 239–54.

The introduction of the genealogy is well motivated. The preparation is less obvious than in the case of Glaukos and Asteropaios, who are questioned about their pedigrees by Diomedes and Akhilleus respectively (6.123, 21.150), but Aineias' history of the two branches of his family, and the dealings between his forefathers and the gods, is clearly invited by Akhilleus' jibe at his relationship with Priam (179–83) and his assertion that the gods who saved him the first time they met will not save him now (195–6). And here, as in Glaukos' encounter, it is in fact the weaker man's distinguished ancestry which preserves his life from his mightier opponent, for Aineias reveals that he is not descended from Laomedon, who cheated the gods themselves (288ff.; 6.212ff.). He is a man in whose affairs the deities are bound to take a positive interest (as they did in book 5), and Poseidon will soon take appropriate measures to save him.

Aineias' verbose arguments against prolixity begin naturally enough (200–2), since Akhilleus has just tried to frighten him with words, as Apollo had warned he would do (108–9). After the comparison of their respective parents (203–10), the implicit contrast between fighting with words and with weapons is repeated at 211–12 to round off the first part of the speech in ring form, as usual (see Lohmann, *Reden* 91–3). This whole section takes the place of the usual introductory 'Why do you ask of my race?' (6.145 ≅ 21.153) – which carries the implication 'since it is so famous', here made explicit in 204. The theme of 'weapons, not words' is conventional, eloquently championed by Hektor (7.234–43) and epigrammatically expressed at 16.630–1; it reappears on Hektor's lips at 367–8 and 431–3.

Then comes the genealogy (213–41). This is related in linear form (see J. H. Gaisser, *HSCP* 73, 1968, 5–6), within a framing ring (213–14, 241). Many of the items in this are very much expanded, not only for their intrinsic interest but in order to give length and dignity to the whole (just as Nestor's speeches are long because of the importance of what he has to say; see Introduction, ch. 2, i). Ignoring this basic principle of Homeric style has led some scholars to complain of the improbability of such a genealogical disquisition at this time.

Then after a transitional gnome (242–3), the theme of 'weapons, not words' is taken up again (244–7, with repetition of νηπύτιοι ὥς from 200 and 211). It is expanded by several gnomes (248–50). Finally Aineias calls for the fight to begin (251–8), his challenge repeated in ring form after an amplifying simile (252–5). The expansion of these final sections of the speech may seem excessive to us, but it matches the expansion of the genealogy and is in keeping with Homeric style.

200–2 The rebuke is later repeated by Hektor to Akhilleus (431–3). On νηπύτιος see 13.292–4n. οἶδα (οἶσθα) καὶ αὐτός (-ή) | is formular (4 × *Il.*, 3 × *Od.*). Düntzer (approved by Leaf) proposed to read αἴσιμα, 'proper ⟨language⟩', for αἴσυλα, 'evil ⟨things⟩', to give a stronger contrast with κερτομίας, 'jeers', 'abuse', since ἠμὲν…ἠδέ imply an antithesis. But there may be contrast enough between a mocking taunt ('You've run from me already!') and a malicious false statement ('Priam won't honour you'), both summed up in ὀνείδεα μυθήσασθαι (246; so J. T. Hooker, *CQ* 36, 1986, 34). Neither adjective is found elsewhere with μυθήσασθαι | (except for ἐναίσιμα μ., *Od.* 2.159), and it is unwise to go against all the MSS.

203–4 The statement that they know each other's ancestry corresponds to the question τίη γενεὴν ἐρεείνεις; by which Glaukos and Asteropaios introduce their histories (6.145 ≅ 21.153). πρόκλυτος (only here in Greek) presumably means 'heard of old'. Leumann, *HW* 99 n. 59, preferred to read πρὸ κλύτ', taking the sense as 'indem wir zuvor ruhmreiche Worte hörten'. G. Nagy, with much plausibility, takes the passage to refer to epic poetry celebrating the exploits of the two heroes (*Oral Literature and the Formula*, edd. B. A. Stolz and R. S. Shannon III, Ann Arbor 1976, 248–50).

205–9 The verses were needlessly athetized by Aristarchus (Arn/AT) as superfluous.

205 The thought may seem odd; but it is linked to the preceding lines by the contrast ἀκούοντες… | ὄψει δ', and introduces in the following lines both the physical distance which separated their famous fathers Peleus and Ankhises and the mortal/immortal barrier which kept each from knowledge of the other's divine mother. The two heroes have much in common. One wonders if there is a reflection here of a conversation in another poem between Akhilleus and the other son of a goddess, Memnon.

207–9 ἀλοσύδνης recurs in the obscure phrase φῶκαι νέποδες καλῆς ἀλοσύδνης at *Od.* 4.404, which may refer to Amphitrite; see S. West, *Odyssey ad loc.* The first part is clearly connected with ἅλς, ἅλιος; the second may be from the root *ud-n-t-*, which appears in ὕδωρ, 'water' (Frisk, s.v. ὕδωρ). Verses 208–9 ≅ 5.247–8.

210–12 τῶν…ἕτεροι: one or other pair of parents. σήμερον is emphatic, both threatening and (together with the νηπυτίοισιν, repeated from 200) introducing the ring-form return to the 'actions, not words' theme (200–2). ἐξαπονέεσθαι: on the -ᾱ- see 17.415n.

213–14 = 6.150–1 (Glaukos to Diomedes); there is a shorter equivalent at 21.157. The ring form is completed by 241, just as 6.150–1 is by the same verse at 6.211.

215–40 The stemma is:

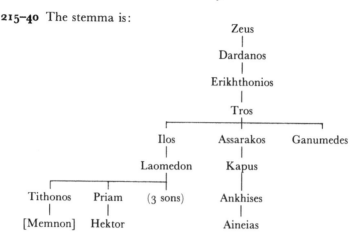

Zeus
|
Dardanos
|
Erikhthonios
|
Tros
|
Ilos   Assarakos   Ganumedes
| |
Laomedon   Kapus
| |
Tithonos   Priam   (3 sons)   Ankhises
| | |
[Memnon]   Hektor   Aineias

See 2.819–20n. The two lines of descent are kept separate in the Trojan Catalogue, where Hektor leads the Trojans, the largest contingent (2.816–18), and Aineias (with the two sons of Antenor) the Dardanians from the foothills of Mt Ida (2.819–23). Memnon is not mentioned, perhaps to avoid too obvious an allusion to his future rôle in Akhilleus' life, or to another epic – just as *Il.* and *Od.* do not refer to each other. Tithonos is first named as his father in Hesiod, *Theogony* 984–5.

215–18 Dardanos is the eponymous hero of the Dardanians, whose name lives on in the Dardanelles. It is usually taken to be Illyrian; see M. L. West, *JHS* 108 (1988) 164; von Kamptz, *Personennamen* 322–3; von Bredow, *Thrakischen Namen* 146–8, gives a full bibliography. The stories of early Trojan history are given in Dionysius of Halicarnassus, *Roman Antiquities* 1.61–2, and Strabo (13.1.48). Modern views are given in vol. II 36–50.

In 215 a few MSS, including some of the *h* family, read ἄρ for the vulgate αὖ, hesitantly followed by Leaf on the grounds that αὖ cannot introduce a narrative and may have slipped in from 219. This may well be right. However, αὖ occasionally marks the continuation or expansion of a previous thought, as at 2.618, 12.182, 16.603: 'If you want to hear what everyone knows, *well then*, Dardanos...' (cf. J. S. Klein, *Historische Sprachforschung* 101, 1988, 265–7). Δαρδανίη: the first line of the *Little Iliad* (fr. 28 Bernabé, 1 Davies) was Ἴλιον ἀείδω καὶ Δαρδανίην εὔπωλον. πεπόλιστο (217) suggests a walled city, as in [τεῖχος] πολίσσαμεν (7.453; see S. Scully, *Ramus* 10, 1981, 6). This verse has 6 π's, one of only 21 such verses in Homer, and a *figura etymologica* in πεπόλιστο πόλις. See D. W. Packard, *TAPA* 104 (1974) 243–4, who thinks 'It is at least possible that we can observe here a delight in sound for sound's sake.' The second hemistich is formular (3 × *Il.*, *HyAp* 42). ὑπωρείας, 'foothills', from ὑπό + ὄρος, occurs only here in ancient epic, but is common in Herodotus. On πολυπίδακος see 59n.

219 The presence of Erikhthonios in the Trojan royal line has not been satisfactorily explained. The name is Greek ('peculiarly of the earth', W. Burkert, *Homo Necans*, tr. P. Bing, Berkeley 1983, 156), and also appears in Attic myth and cult, associated or identified with Erekhtheus, ὅν ποτ' Ἀθήνη | θρέψε Διὸς θυγάτηρ, τέκε δὲ ζείδωρος ἄρουρα (2.547–8; see note *ad loc.*). According to a very fragmentary papyrus, Hesiod in the *Ehoiai* (fr. 177.13–15 MW) seems similarly to make Erikhthonios the son of Dardanos and to give him a brother Ilos, an addition which also appears in Apollodorus (*Library* 3.12.2; another Ilos is son of Tros, as at 232 below; see 230–2n.). In Dionysius, *Roman Antiquities* 1.62, the Arcadian Dardanos came to the Troad with his son Idaios, who gave his name to Mt Ida, received land from Teukros the king of the area, and had by Teukros' daughter a son Erikhthonios, who inherited the territory of both lines (cf. 220). Strabo (13.1.48) reports a version which identified the Erikhthonios of the Troad with the Athenian king. Many scholars have thought that the reference here, together with that to Boreas (223–5), is due to Athenian influence (see J. Griffin, *JHS* 97, 1977, 41; Heitsch, *Aphroditehymnos* 119–35; Dihle, *Homer-Probleme* 82–3); Lenz, *Aphroditehymnos* 299–301, thinks his name marks the territorial expansion from the foot of Ida across the plain, which is improbable. By his transparent name, and his description at 2.548, the Athenian Erikhthonios represented the indigenous inhabitants of the country (though the name is not securely attested in Athens until about 440–430; see R. Parker in *Interpretations of Greek Mythology*, ed. J. Bremmer, London 1987, 200–1). It is likely that for the bards who fashioned the genealogies before Homer and Hesiod, the Erikhthonios of the Troad also represented the indigenous inhabitants, and they connected him with Dardanos son of Zeus, the leader of the immigrant people, by making him his son. Alternatively, he may have represented the offspring of the union of the indigenous and the immigrant peoples, 'aboriginal' in the sense that they were the first 'Dardanians' born in the Troad; this is the version given by Dionysius. Verse 220 is adapted at 233, cf. *Od.* 1.219. On Erekhtheus/Poseidon see Burkert, *op. cit.* 149–56, and *Greek Religion* (tr. J. Raffan, Cambridge, Mass. 1985) 229.

220–9 In Dionysius (1.62) Erikhthonios is said to have been εὐδαιμονέστατος of all men because he inherited the property both of his father Dardanos and his maternal grandfather Teukros. In view of his name, it is interesting that horses were associated with the Underworld (see 19.404–17n.). At 5.265–7 and *HyAphr* 210–17 Zeus is said to have given superlative horses to Tros as a recompense for his abduction of Ganumedes, and it was for Laomedon's horses that Herakles sacked Troy (5.640).

Demokoön, a bastard son of Priam from Abydos, also has swift horses (4.500). The fame of the Trojans for horses is also reflected in the epithet ἱππόδαμος with their name and with Hektor's.

221–4 ἵπποι ... βουκολέοντο: For the 'mixed metaphor' Leaf compares οἰνοχόει ... νέκταρ (1.598). ἀταλῇσι: see 18.567–8n., and Lenz, *Aphroditehymnos* 226–35. καί (223) links the thought of ἀγαλλόμεναι to that of ἠράσσατο; they were lovely mares, *and so* he loved them. Presumably Boreas fell in love with and serviced only twelve of the mares (225). Cf. the siring of Akhilleus' horses by the West Wind (16.150–1). Aristarchus (Arn/A) was concerned about παρελέξατο used of a horse: ἵππος γὰρ οὐ παρακοιμᾶται, ἀλλ' ἐπιβαίνει. τινὲς δὲ γράφουσιν 'ἵππῳ δ' εἰσάμενος ἐμίγη φιλότητι καὶ εὐνῇ', which seems to be little improvement. The phrase παρελέξατο Κυανοχαίτης (of Poseidon) occurs at Hesiod, *Theogony* 278 and must have been formular; A Heubeck, *Glotta* 50 (1972) 133, thinks both this and the *Theogony* verse are adaptations of *τῇ δὲ Ποσειδάων παρελέξατο κυανοχαίτης. The epithet κυανοχαίτης is generally used of Poseidon, but occurs for Arion the horse at *Aspis* 120 and *Thebais* fr. 7 Bernabé, 6ᴬ Davies. The hiatus in 225 results from adapting the formular ἡ δ' ὑποκυσαμένη τέκετο (1 × *Il.*, 1 × *Od.*, 6 × Hesiod) to the plural.

226–7 σκιρτάω occurs only here (and 228) in Homer, but is common in later poetry. With 227 cf. Hesiod fr. 62.1 MW ἄκρον ἐπ' ἀνθερίκων καρπὸν θέεν οὐδὲ κατέκλα, of Iphiklos. ἀνθέριξ (probably 'corn-ear') is found in ancient epic only here and in the Hesiodic verse, but this illustration of swift-footedness may well have been a conventional motif.

229 ἄκρον ἐπὶ ῥηγμῖνος ἁλὸς πολιοῖο: this is the vulgate reading. The fossilized formula is ἐπὶ (παρὰ) ῥηγμῖνι θαλάσσης | (4 × *Il.*, 10 × *Od.*), the only other Homeric variant being ἁλὸς ῥηγμῖνα βαθεῖαν | (*Od.* 12.214). With the vulgate reading ἄκρον must be adverbial, for which there is no parallel; this is accepted by Erbse, *RhM* 110 (1967) 14–15. Leaf reads ἄκρον ἔπι ῥηγμῖνος, which is easier, but taking ἄκρον as a noun spoils the parallel with ἄκρον ... καρπόν in 227. Ahrens emended to ἐπὶ ῥηγμῖνα (adopted by Ameis–Hentze), which is better still, as the construction then parallels that of 227 (with ἄκρον as adjective); the change may have been made to avoid the hiatus after ῥηγμῖνα. Archilochus may have known ῥηγμῖνα (cf. his fr. 79a (Diehl), ἄκρον παρὰ ῥηγμῖνα); Apollonius of Rhodes, however, seems to have read ῥηγμῖνος, cf. *Arg.* 1.182. Heitsch, *Aphroditehymnos* 83–4, objected that ῥηγμίς must mean 'the edge of the sea', and that this is inconsistent with ἐπ' εὐρέα νῶτα θαλάσσης (228); and R. M. Frazer, *Glotta* 49 (1971) 24–7, supports ἄκρον ἐπὶ ῥηγμῖνος, taking the sense to be 'over the top of the water'. But K. Förstel, *Glotta* 48 (1969) 170–2, rightly points out that just as ἄκρον ἐπ' ἀνθερίκων καρπόν (227) is a specialized case of ἐπὶ ζείδωρον ἄρουραν in the previous verse, so here 'over the edge of the surf' (229), or better 'over the breaking wave-crests' (see R. Hiersche, *Studies...L. R. Palmer*, edd. A. M. Davies and W. Meid, Innsbruck 1976, 103–6) is a special instance of 228 'over the open sea'. This must be the proper sense, whether genitive or accusative is read. ἁλὸς πολιῆς (or in reverse order) is the normal form; here metrical need overcomes the usual grammatical gender.

230–2 Tros is of course the eponymous founder of the Trojan race, as the poet suggests by the *figura etymologica* in this line. Verse 231 ≅ 14.115. The tomb of Ilos was a well-known landmark (10.415, 11.166 (see note *ad loc.*), 11.371–2, 24.349). Twice Ilos is called Δαρδανίδαο, which may mean that the son of Dardanos is meant (see 219n.); or misunderstanding of the patronymic may have led to the invention of the earlier Ilos. He is of course the eponymous founder of Ilion; the tale is told in Apollodorus, *Library* 3.12.3. The name may be Phrygian (see von Kamptz, *Personennamen* 315–16; von Bredow, *Thrakischen Namen* 155–7). Assarakos appears in Homer only here and at 239, and is known only for fathering Kapus. The name may be Illyrian (von Kamptz, *Personennamen* 336; von Bredow, *Thrakischen Namen* 143). ἀντίθεος (232) is a generic epithet, occurring in this position with ten other names. The origin of the name Ganumedes is disputed (von Kamptz, *Personennamen* 64; von Bredow, *Thrakischen Namen* 144–5); it may be Greek (from γάνος, γάνυμαι and μήδεσθαι, μήδεα) or Thracian. In the *Little Iliad* (fr. 29 Bernabé, 6 Davies) Ganumedes was said to be the son of Laomedon, who received a golden vine in exchange for him. The version at *HyAphr* 202–17 (see P. Smith, *Nursling of Immortality*, Frankfurt am Main 1981, 71–7, and J. S. Clay, *The Politics of Olympus*, Princeton 1989, 186–7) agrees with that of the *Il.*, and in keeping with the mortal/immortal contrast in the context adds that he was made immortal and ageless.

233–5 It may seem to us that this version of the tale, that because of his beauty 'the gods' carried off Ganumedes to live among them and pour wine for Zeus, is bowdlerizing the pederastic element which is usually prominent in the myth (see 4.2–3n.). However, the researches of J. Bremmer, *Arethusa* 13 (1980) 286, suggest that the employment of noble youths as wine-pourers was an important part of their initiation into the world of men, so this aspect is not merely a polite disguise for Zeus's homoerotic ardour; cf. 1.470, 9.175, *Od.* 15.141, and Sappho fr. 203 Lobel–Page. Actually in Homer the divinities' cups are filled by Hebe (4.2–3) or, in humorous contrast to these beautiful attendants, by Hephaistos (1.597–600). Ganumedes' story is related here both to glorify his beauty and to explain why he had no descendants. In the longer version at *HyAphr* 202–17 it is Zeus who carries off the youth, and the erotic implication is more obvious.

καί (234), as at 223, links the two ideas; he was beautiful, *and so* they wanted him. ἀνηρείψαντο: the form occurs 4 × *Od.*, in three cases closing the verse after ἅρπυιαι; the verb is also used for Aphrodite's abduction of Phaëthon (Hesiod, *Theogony* 990). It may have been associated with ἅρπυια, ἁρπάζω, but is actually derived from ἀν(ά) + the root of ἐρέπτομαι, 'pluck', 'gather for oneself', and should be spelled -ηρειψ-; see *LfgrE*. For occurrences other than in Homer see West, *Theogony* 428. Verse 235 = *Od.* 15.251 (of Kleitos, carried off by Eos); cf. *HyAphr* 203. On οἰνοχοεύειν used of serving nectar see 1.598n.

236–8 Verse 236 ≅ 13.451, with similar repetition of the name: ἀμύμονα Δευκαλίωνα, | Δευκαλίων δ'... Laomedon had the walls of Troy built by Poseidon and Apollo; see 21.441–57 and note *ad loc.* Tithonos' abduction by Eos is alluded to at 11.1 = *Od.* 5.1, and described in detail in *HyAphr* 218–38 (see P. Smith, *Nursling of Immortality*, Frankfurt am Main 1981, 77–86). Their son Memnon is not mentioned here (see 215–40n.). Verse 238 = 3.147, where the three princes appear on the wall of Troy with Priam. All three names are Greek. Each of them loses a son during the battle at the ships (15.419–21; 525–43; 576–8).

239–41 Kapus is only a name – a Thracian name; see von Kamptz, *Personennamen* 375–6, and von Bredow, *Thrakischen Namen* 158–9. Verse 241 (= 6.211) also rounds off Glaukos' genealogy.

242–3 H. Fränkel suggested that in Pindar's view 'the will of the gods, or human limitations in general, often prevent the innate and hereditary qualities from taking effect; an idea which seems already to underlie a passage from the *Iliad*, 20.241–43' (*TAPA* 77, 1946, 136 = *Wege und Formen frühgriechischen Denkens*, Munich 1968, 29). This may be generalizing too much; the couplet can well be taken as a transition back to the 'weapons, not words' theme, referring to the explicit acknowledgement of Zeus's help by both parties when Aineias fled before Akhilleus, an occasion with which Akhilleus taunted his adversary at the end of his speech (192, 194; cf. 92–3). Lohmann, however, athetizes the lines (*Reden* 92n.). The same thought is expressed by other characters at 8.141–4, 15.490–3, and 17.176–8, and in the narrator's voice at 16.688–90.

244–58 This section of the speech has been heavily criticized for its repeated and time-consuming exhortations not to waste time talking. The two-part theme 'Let us not talk like children; we can both hurl insults' is first restated (244–7), matching 200–2 in ring form. This is followed by a two-line gnome (248–9) and a one-liner (250). Then Aineias rejects the strife and contention (*sc.* in words) between them (251–2), compares their behaviour to that of squabbling women (252–5), and rounds off with a call for the fight with their proper weapons to begin (256–8). The passage can thus be analysed as: the conclusion of the ring which began the speech;

three lines of gnomes; and a further ring-form structure surrounding a simile. It can also be argued that the expansion is not excessive, but matches that of the preceding genealogy (see 200–58n.).

However, Lohmann, *Reden* 66–7 and 92, excises 242–3, 247, and the simile (251–5), thus producing a series of gnomes surrounded by a ring, to which he lists many parallels (e.g. the gnomic passage at 19.162–70, ringed by 155–61 and 171–2). This is very drastic, and interpolations on such a scale are improbable.

244–5 Verse 244 = 13.292, where a new clause begins after the runover ἑσταότες (cf. also *Od.* 13.296). Here the poet has filled up the rest of the verse with an extension of the formular ἐν (αἰνῇ) δηϊοτῆτι | (9 × *Il.*, 3 × *Od.*) by means of a variation on | πρώτῃ ἐν ὑσμίνῃ (2 × *Il.*, cf. 11.297).

247 ἑκατόζυγος never occurs again. A ship with a hundred rowing-benches would be far larger than the ships of the Catalogue (see 2.509–10n.), and the number just means 'huge', as in ἑκατόμβη, ἑκατόμπυλος, etc. ἄχθος ἄροιτο: the meaning of the verb must be that of ἀείρομαι, 'bear', but the form is that of the aorist of ἄρνυμαι. Hoekstra, *Sub-epic Stage* 46 n. 2, correctly takes it as a formular conjugation of νέες ἄχθος ἄειραν | (*Od.* 3.312) on the analogy of κῦδος ἄροιτο |, κλέος ἐσθλὸν ἄροιτο |. Erbse, *RhM* 110 (1967) 15, thinks that ἄρνυμαι may bear the required sense.

248–50 The three verses are quoted as an example of antithesis by Plutarch, *Vit. Hom.* 173. πολὺς νομός: literally 'a wide field' for words to go this way and that; cf. Hesiod, ἀχρεῖος δ' ἔσται ἐπέων νομός (*Erga* 403), and *HyAp* 20. The metaphor appears to be the same as in English. The scholia however (T) gloss it as πολλὰ νεμηθῆναι, 'dispense'. With 250 cf. Hesiod, εἰ δὲ κακὸν εἴποις, τάχα κ' αὐτὸς μεῖζον ἀκούσαις (*Erga* 721).

251–5 Like Lohmann (see 244–58n.), Aristarchus (Arn/A) athetized these lines, on the grounds that they are out of place and a nuisance (ἄκαιροι καὶ ὀχληροί) after 244, the comparison is unworthy of the characters, and because παρὰ βαρβάροις δέ ἐστι τὸ τὰς γυναῖκας προερχομένας λοιδορεῖσθαι ὡς παρ' Αἰγυπτίοις (!). The simile is certainly unexpectedly vivid. The points of comparison are of course anger, *eris*, and abusiveness, with the added parallel that the antagonists meet μέσην ἐς ἄγυιαν ἰοῦσαι, cf. ἑσταότ' ἐν μέσσῃ ὑσμίνῃ (245).

253–5 The second hemistich of 253 is formular (3 × *Il.*); on its meaning see 19.56–8n. νεικεῦσ': the contraction is uncommon, but the uncontracted form could not be used in the verse; cf. οἰχνεῦσιν, εἰσοιχνεῦσαν (*Od.* 3.322, 6.157; Chantraine, *GH* I 62). In 255 Aristarchus (Arn/A) read πολλὰ τ' ἐόντα, probably to avoid lengthening the last syllable of ἐτεά, but the vulgate (followed by Allen) is clearly preferable. χόλος δέ τε καὶ τὰ κελεύει: τε may be the usual generalizing τε of similes, and καὶ τά ⟨οὐκ ἐτεά⟩ = 'anger makes them say also what is not true'. But Wackernagel's τά καὶ τά is tempting

(*Vorlesungen über Syntax* II, Basel 1928, 132; cf. Pindar, *Py.* 5.55, τὰ καὶ τὰ νέμων).

258 γεύομαι is used with the same sense elsewhere, but with a genitive of the weapon.

259–352 As the duel begins, each warrior hurls his spear and strikes the shield of the other. Akhilleus then charges with his sword, and Aineias seizes a huge stone. Poseidon however, concerned that Aineias may not live to fulfil his destiny, rescues him. Akhilleus unhappily realizes what has happened

A duel often begins with unsuccessful spear-casts. The stone picked up by Aineias recalls 5.302–10, where he is badly wounded by a stone hurled by Diomedes and is subsequently rescued by Aphrodite, as he is by Poseidon here. Fenik, *TBS* 33–5, compares the two scenes.

259–60 Aias' shield too is δεινός (7.245), but σμερδαλέος is unusual for armour and marks out the Hephaistos-made shield; cf. αἰγίδα... | σμερδαλέην (21.400–1). The common association of the word with noise (see 18.573–6n.) leads on well into the remainder of 260. δουρὸς ἀκωκῇ | is the reading of the older MSS, and the dative recurs at 17.295 and 23.821. The nominative is more common (3 × *Il.*, 1 × *Od.*), occurs in many MSS, and is possible here, though the sense is weaker.

261–3 The natural action of holding the shield away from the body to fend off the approaching weapon is repeated by Aineias (278) and Deïphobos (13.162–3). In each case the hero's fear is mentioned; here ταρβήσας is amplified in the following verses. ἀπὸ ἕο is for ἀπὸ ʽ(ϝϝ)έο < *sw- (Chantraine, *GH* I 146). φάτο: 'he thought', as often. ῥέα: see 17.461–2n.

264–7 The point is made again at 268 = 21.165 and at 21.594 θεοῦ δ' ἠρύκακε δῶρα. The invulnerability of god-given armour is carefully maintained by the poet when Patroklos' panoply is stripped from him by Apollo before his death (16.793ff.) and. Hektor is wounded above the neckline of the corslet (22.322ff.). Doubtless this was the reason for Akhilleus' own fatal wound in the heel (Apollodorus, *Epitome* 5.3, probably from the *Aithiopis*; the earliest evidence is a Chalcidian amphora of about 550–540, *LIMC* I Achilleus no. 850). There is irony in the contrast between the power of the armour and the deaths of all those who wear it; see the introduction to book 18. On the invulnerability of Hephaistos-made armour see O. Berthold, *Die Unverwundbarkeit in Sage und Aberglauben der Griechen* (Giessen 1911). Dihle, *Homer-Probleme* 71, objects that employing κατὰ φρένα καὶ κατὰ θυμόν with νοέω is contrary to Homeric usage, but it is clear that νήπιος, οὐδ' ἐνόησε go together (cf. 22.445, *HyAphr* 223) and the familiar formula fills up the verse. Verse 266 ≅ 10.403, 17.77. δαΐφρονος

(267) is generic, used in this position for many heroes (*pace* Dihle, *Homer-Probleme* 73).

268–72 Verse 268 recurs at 21.165, where χρυσός must mean 'the golden shield' or 'the ⟨top⟩ layer of gold'. δῶρα is also used of a gift consisting of more than one item at 14.238. The amplification which follows requires that the shield be fashioned of two outer layers of bronze and two inner layers of tin, with the layer of gold sandwiched between them. This makes no practical sense, either for the purpose or the appearance of the shield (see p. 201–2). Whoever composed the lines was combining Hephaistos' preparation of his materials (χαλκὸν δ᾽ ἐν πυρὶ βάλλεν ἀτειρέα κασσίτερόν τε | καὶ χρυσόν, 18.474–5) and his own familiarity with leather-layered shields, and (keeping the same sequence of metals) produced this improbable and impractical artifact. Whether the undesirable elaboration should be attributed to the monumental composer or some other remains a matter of taste.

The passage was much discussed by the ancients (see Erbse *ad loc.*). Aristotle knew the lines and found them perplexing (*Poetics* 1461a31); 269–72 were athetized by Aristarchus (Arn/A) and ἐνίοις τῶν σοφιστῶν (Did/T), and were omitted in some texts (Did/T); some were worried that the god's gift should be damaged, especially after what has just been said of it (265–6); others pointed to 17.607 and 21.164 as evidence to the contrary (T on 265). In modern times, 269–72 were bracketed by Ameis–Hentze, van Leeuwen, and Mazon, considered spurious by Leaf and Bolling (*External Evidence* 187–8), but supported by van der Valk (*Researches* II 423–4) on the unconvincing grounds that the duel is important and needs elaboration, and that Homer may not have been aware of gold's lack of strength. I am not convinced by A. Morard's defence of the lines (*Bulletin de l'Association G. Budé* 4.3, 1965, 348–59). If they are retained, note W. G. Thalmann's recent observation of the ring-form arrangement of metals here, bronze outside, then tin, then gold in the centre. 'This shows how naturally these poets thought in rounded, inversely symmetrical structures... The poet at this moment needs to name the metals of which the shield is composed and simply does so according to a scheme that is thoroughly habitual with him' (*Conventions* 190 n. 32).

271–2 ἔνδοθι: the context makes it clear that this means on the concave side of the shield. In 272 most of the better MSS have μείλινον, the rest χάλκεον, which is also the reading in Aristotle's quotation (*Poetics* 1461a33). χάλκεον is probably better, as it is possible the poet shows a preference for it when (as here) the bronze point of the spear, rather than its ashwood shaft, is particularly referred to; see R. Schmiel, *LCM* 9.3 (1984) 34–5. At 7.245–8 Hektor's spear penetrates the bronze and six oxhide layers of Aias' shield and is stopped (σχέτο) in the seventh oxhide.

273–7 The first two verses are formular. With 275–7 cf. ἄντυξ ἣ πυμάτη θέεν ἀσπίδος ὀμφαλοέσσης (6.118). ἐπέην can hardly mean that the oxhide was 'laid on top of' the bronze; this is the opposite of the description at 7.246 and makes no practical sense. Leaf says 'ἐπι- implies "to back it up"', presumably with the sense 'following in succession', like ἐπί at 13.799. Alternatively, the oxhide may be thought of as 'laid over' the bronze layer from the viewpoint of the warrior carrying the shield. Heyne emended to ὑπέην, which seems unnecessary. Πηλιὰς ἤϊξεν μελίη is an adaptation of Πηλιάδα μελίην (4 × *Il.*). λάκε is used again of bronze armour at 14.25. A spear again penetrates a shield, wholly or partially, at 5.281–2 and 7.251 = 11.435.

278–80 ἀπὸ ἔθεν: see on 261–3. ἐάλη is used again of a man ducking behind his shield at 13.408, cf. 168. With 279–80 cf. 21.69–70, where the same sentence continues... ἱεμένη χροὸς ἄμεναι ἀνδρομέοιο. However, ἱεμένη is used elsewhere of a weapon without further elaboration, as at 399, 15.543; on the animism implied see Introduction, ch. 4, iii. διά (280) goes with ἕλε; the two layers which the spear 'broke through' (less probably 'tore apart'; see 322–3n.) are those of bronze and oxhide mentioned at 275–6.

281–3 ἀσπίδος ἀμφιβρότης is formular (3 × *Il.*), and must have originally referred to a tower-shield. M. L. West, *JHS* 108 (1988) 157, notes that the short syllable before βρ is unusual and suggests an original * *amphimr̥tās*. The parenthetical clause in 282 is an innovative combination of the ideas seen in τὴν δ᾿ ἄχος ἀμφεχύθη (*Od.* 4.716), ἑ πένθος | ὀφθαλμοὺς ἐκάλυψε (11.249–50), and πένθος ... μυρίον (18.88); cf also 8.124, 17.591. Aineias feels ἄχος because his own shot was in vain, and fear because of his narrow escape.

283–7 From αὐτάρ to ἰάχων the verses ≅ 441–3. Then 285–7 ≅ 5.302–4, where Aineias is attacking Diomedes (Τυδεΐδης is substituted there for Αἰνείας). Verse 285 is also used when Hektor seizes a rock (= 8.321). The outcome is different in each case: here the rock is never thrown; in the Aineias/Diomedes encounter Aineias is seriously hurt and must be rescued; and Hektor's victim Teukros must be saved by his brother Aias. See 5.302–10n. and Fenik, *TBS* 33–5. The 'no two men now' motif also reappears at 12.447–9 (the last line = 287), cf. 12.381–3 and 19.387–91n. On σμερδαλέα ἰάχων see 5.302–4n. and 19.40–1n.; on χερμάδιον, 5.302–4n.; on μέγα ἔργον, 5.303n.

288–91 The lines are highly formular (see below) and the actions envisaged are conventional enough, but both Aineias' seizing of the rock and Akhilleus' charge with the sword are cast into the form of an unreal condition. The unreal condition itself is a normal technique, parallel to the many instances of 'Then the Greeks would have captured Troy, had not...' and the like, usually prevented by divine intervention (see 17.319–25n.);

they are described by Fenik as 'extreme situations' (*TBS* 175–6, 154). The double form here ('A would have ... and B would have') has been discussed at length by Dihle, *Homer-Probleme* 76–80; see also Erbse, *RhM* 110 (1967) 20; there are parallels at 17.319–22 and 8.130–2. De Jong, *Narrators* 70, accurately calls it 'a kind of compressed battle-scene'.

Verse 288 ≅ 16.411. In 289, ἤρκεσε λυγρὸν ὄλεθρον | is formular (3 × *Il.*, 1 × *Od.*, with a shorter form at 15.534); the relative clause is best taken as part of the unreal condition, with κε understood. In 289, notice the ἢ ... ἠέ alternative, showing that the 'truthful' poet can only speculate about events which never happen; see de Jong, *Narrators* 80. Verse 290 ≅ 16.828, 21.179. In 291, εἰ μὴ ἄρ' ὀξὺ νόησε occurs 6 × *Il.* with various name–epithet formulae.

292–320 As usual the human action stops dead during a scene among the gods, and begins again at 321; other examples are listed by Fenik (*TBS* 37; *Odyssey* 77–8). In much the same way Zeus wonders whether to rescue Sarpedon (16.431–61) and Hektor (22.166–87). The rescue of Aineias is similar to that at 5.311ff.; see 5.311–12n. The choice of the pro-Greek Poseidon as rescuer of Aineias, instead of Apollo (or even Aphrodite again, as she came on the scene at 40), has aroused comment, but (as Scheibner says, *Aufbau* 7) here Poseidon stands above the partisans of both sides to preserve the designs of destiny, and his motive is well suited to his senior status and serious demeanour. G. Nagy, *The Best of the Achaeans* (Baltimore 1979) 268–9, takes much the same view. Poseidon's intervention has been prepared for by his prominence at 132–50. Any assistance from Apollo, as Scheibner points out (*Aufbau* 6), has been carefully ruled out by Poseidon's threat to intervene himself if Apollo does (138–40) – and in any case Apollo is especially associated with saving Hektor (375ff., 443ff.). Finally, as bT remark, Aphrodite does not help her son, because of her fear of Athene.

295–6 Ἀπόλλωνος ἑκάτοιο (< (F)εκ-) is an old formula, found also at 7.83 and *HyAp* 1. It is competing with ἐκηβόλου Ἀπόλλωνος (2 × *Il.*, *Theogony* 94), which has the advantage of availability in the accusative and dative too. Verse 296 ≅ 2.873. It is not clear, and it would be a waste of time to speculate, how Poseidon knows that Apollo does not intend to help Aineias, or whether his words imply a threat to stop the junior god if he intervenes. The poet uses the idea to help justify Poseidon's own intervention.

297–9 ἀναίτιος and ἕνεκ' ἀλλοτρίων ἀχέων refer to Laomedon's outrageous behaviour towards Poseidon and Apollo (21.441–57); Aineias is not descended from Laomedon, as he made clear in the genealogy he has just recounted. The abduction of Helen by the Trojan prince Paris may also not be held against the Dardanians. Giving gifts to the gods is the recognized mark of piety, cf. 4.48–9, 22.170–2, *Od.* 1.66–7; there is an expanded version at 24.68–70. Presumably there was a line-end formula κεχαρισμένα δῶρα, of which the enjambing phrase is an adaptation, but it happens never to occur.

301–5 Verse 301 ≅ *Od.* 24.544, where the line ends εὐρύοπα Ζεύς. Here the enjambment allows emphasis on τόνδε at the beginning of the line. μή πως καί also begins the verse at 8.510, 10.101, and *Od.* 7.306, and always (as here) emphasizes the following word or phrase. The indicative κεχολώσεται after μή is unparalleled (except for the repetition at *Od.* 24.544); 10.330 (quoted by Chantraine, *GH* II 331) is different in sense. Perhaps, as Shipp suggests (*Studies* 144), the use was suggested by the frequent ambiguity (subjunctive or future) of forms like χολώσεαι, e.g. μή πώς μοι μετέπειτα χολώσεαι (14.310). μόριμος (302) is the regular formation from μόρος (like αἴσιμος etc.; Risch, *Wortbildung* 105), but occurs only here in ancient epic, and occasionally in later poetry. Its place is taken by μόρσιμος, of obscure etymology but greater metrical convenience (4 × *Il.*, 3 × *Od.*). ἄσπερμος is a strikingly innovative use, occurring only here in Greek in the sense 'without posterity'; it is used later for plants which do not produce seed. The form φίλατο (304; without augment) occurs only here, but the verse is based on expressions like ἔξοχα γάρ μιν ἐφίλατο Παλλὰς Ἀθήνη (5.61; cf. Hesiod fr. 141.21) and περὶ πάντων τῖον ἑταίρων (18.81). γυναικῶν τε θνητάων does not occur elsewhere. It was probably suggested by γυναικῶν θηλυτεράων | (2 × *Od.*, *Theogony* 590, 3 × *HyDem*).

306 At 4.44–9 Zeus professed great love for Troy, Priam, and his people. The poet is doubtless capable of changing the god's alignment according to the immediate need; but here we have only Poseidon's authority for Zeus's hostility to Troy, and Poseidon has been struggling against Zeus's support for the Greeks during much of the poem. There is, however, truth in bT's remark that Zeus is angry because of the Trojans' breaking of the oaths; cf. 4.157–68.

307–8 ≅ *HyAphr* 196–7. On the meaning of the couplet see 75–155n., and on the relationship of this and the *HyAphr* versions Janko, *HHH* 158, and Hoekstra, *Sub-epic Stage* 39–40. The poet's feeling for the continuity of the human race after the ending of the mighty Trojan saga appears also at 6.146–9 and 12.10–35. On the son Askanios later given to Aineias see 13.789–94n. Virgil renders the lines as *hic domus Aeneae cunctis dominabitur oris | et nati natorum et qui nascentur ab illis* (*Aeneid* 3.97–8); the first line translates Αἰνείω γενεὴ πάντεσσιν ἀνάξει, a Romanized version of 307 which is mentioned in the scholia (Arn/A) and quoted by Strabo (13.1.53, with Αἰνείαο γένος).

νῦν δὲ δή occurs only 3 × elsewhere (18.290, 21.92, 22.300), and can always (as here) have the meaning 'but as it is' rather than 'at the present time'. Αἰνείαο βίη is paralleled by Πριάμοιο βίην (3.105) and Πατρόκλοιο βίην

(2 × *Il.*) in this position, and in many cases the genitive of a name follows βίη (see 2.658–6on.).

312 ≅ 22.176, and is omitted by a papyrus and almost all the older MSS. It may well have been inserted here to supply an infinitive to follow ἐάσῃς, though this is not necessary; the sense 'abandon' is common, as at 456. For a similar probable interpolation see 24.556–8n., and for probably genuine infinitives after ἐάω, 15.472–5n.

313–17 πολέας...ὅρκους: not on many different occasions, but by the names of many different powers, as at 14.278–9, 15.36–40. Elsewhere Homer uses the plural ὅρκια. Verses 315–17 = 21.374–6, but here the vulgate reads δαιομένη δαίωσι, there και- και-. Certainty is impossible, but in view of δαιόμενον... δαῖε at 18.227 Allen was unwise not to follow the vulgate here. The repetition (cf. 18.225–7n.) splendidly conveys the vehemence of Here's hatred for Troy, and her happy anticipation of its eventual destruction.

319–20 Verse 319 = 5.167, but otherwise the phrasing (except for βῆ ῥ' ἴμεν) does not recur. ὁ κλυτὸς ἦεν 'Αχιλλεύς: cf. ὁ θρασὺς εἵπετ' 'Οδυσσεύς (*Od.* 10.436); the article is also used to extend a name–epithet expression at 10.231, 10.536, and *Od.* 23.306.

321–3 The second hemistich of 321 is formular (≅ 5.696, 16.344, 20.421, *Od.* 22.88). In three other cases a deity rescuing a hero hides him in a mist (ἐκάλυψε δ' ἄρ' ἠέρι πολλῇ, 3.381, 20.444, 21.597); the mist is not mentioned when first Aphrodite and then Apollo rescue Aineias from Diomedes (5.318, 5.445). Hephaistos rescues the son of his priest νυκτὶ καλύψας (5.23). εὔχαλκος is used elsewhere only of an axe (13.612), a helmet (7.12), and a cauldron (*Od.* 15.84). However, since no alternative epithet occurs after μελίη (etc.) in this position the expression may be formular. ἀσπίδος ἐξέρυσεν may be made consistent with ἐγχείη...ἐνὶ γαίη | ἔστη (279–80) if we suppose the spear pierced the shield and pinned it to the ground, which is realistic enough. Aristarchus (Arn/A) and others (bT) athetized 322–4 because of the apparent inconsistency (and perhaps also because of the god's menial service; cf. 3.424n.) but this weakens the effect of 345.

324–5 The return of his spear to a hero is a common motif. Athene does this again for Akhilleus during his duel with Hektor (22.276–7), and (with a different connotation) for Hektor himself (20.438–41); she does not disdain to return his horse-whip to Diomedes after Apollo has made him drop it (23.382–90). Once the poet takes care to have Akhilleus himself recover this very special spear (21.200). The second hemistich of 325 ≅ *Od.* 8.375.

326–9 Note the elegant anaphora in 326. The hiatus in 327 can be removed by reading θεοῖ'(ο). ἀπὸ χειρὸς ὀρούσας is used of launching a spear at 13.505 = 16.615. For τε (329) most MSS read δέ or κε. Editors read τε, but Ruijgh, τε *épique* 121–2 and 483, prefers δέ, considering the generalizing τε here possible but not probable. πόλεμον μέτα θωρήσσοντο: 'were armed for battle'. This does not necessarily imply that they were still putting on their armour; cf. 2.526 etc. Dolon says that the Kaukones are among those stationed next to the sea (10.428–9); Callisthenes, according to Strabo 12.542, found them a place in the Trojan Catalogue (see 2.853–5n.). A Greek race of the same name dwelt near Elis (*Od.* 3.366, Herodotus 1.147).

330–9 We are not told what form (if any) Poseidon took to speak to Aineias after the supernatural rescue. When they do not disguise themselves, deities occasionally appear to their favourites in their own form (1.197ff., probably 15.243ff. (ἄντην)), but more often they are just a disembodied voice (2.172ff, 20.375ff., 24.169ff.; see 11.199n.); χαλεποὶ δὲ θεοὶ φαίνεσθαι ἐναργεῖς (131). Aineias and Aias recognize a disguised god (17.333–9, 13.43–72; the latter hero makes the contrasting remark ἀρίγνωτοι δὲ θεοί περ, 13.72), but do not know which one. See 17.333–4n. Poseidon's words twice repeat the prediction that Aineias is fated to survive the war (336, 339), pay honour to the prowess of both heroes (334, 339), and once more predict the death of Akhilleus (337, cf. 127–8). A similar divine warning to a hero to avoid combat with a particular enemy is given at length at 11.181–209, and briefly at 375–8 below.

332–4 ἀτέοντα, 'crazed' (from the root of ἄτη), is trisyllabic, with initial ᾰ and synizesis of -εο-; see *LfgrE*, and on the synizesis Chantraine, *GH* I 58–60. The form recurs only in Herodotus 7.223.4 (the scholia quote ἀτέει from Callimachus), and is likely to be from contemporary speech. Verse 333 = 88; see 87–8n. Allen prints the reading of a few early MSS; the vulgate text is ἀντί᾽ Ἀχιλλῆος πολεμίζειν ἠδὲ μάχεσθαι, which is mentioned as an alternative in the scholia (Did?/A). Verse 334 is unformular.

335–6 συμβλήσεαι cannot be a sigmatic aorist subjunctive. Willcock takes it as future, quoting 9.167 as a parallel construction; but it is probably better to read Dindorf's συμβλήεαι, with Chantraine, *GH* I 455, and most editors. The variant συμβήσεαι, found in two MSS, may have influenced the form. ὑπὲρ μοῖραν: see 17.321n., 2.155n.

337–9 θάνατον καὶ πότμον ἐπίσπη | (etc.) is formular (3× *Il.*, 1× *Od.*); there is an alternative version θανεῖν (-έειν, -ον) κ. π. ἐ. | (1× *Il.*, 6× *Od.*). ἄλλος Ἀχαιῶν (339), usually placed at verse-end, has been forced out by the verb, which occurs there even more frequently; cf. 14.88–90n.

In fact the poet does not mention Aineias again in the *Il.*; Akhilleus too seems to allude to this at 349–50.

340–2 The parallel at 15.218, ὡς εἰπὼν λίπε λαὸν Ἀχαιϊκὸν ἐννοσίγαιος, supports Brandreth's ϝ᾽ ἔλιπ᾽ αὖθι. διεπέφραδε: 'revealed'; the same word is used of Thetis' prophecy to Akhilleus (18.9), and 2× *Od.* by superiors to inferiors (*Od.* 6.47, 17.590). μέγ᾽ ἔξιδεν ὀφθαλμοῖσιν clearly means 'stared';

Leaf quotes μέγα κρατέειν and κεφαλῆς ἐκδέρκεται ὄσσε (23.477) as the nearest parallels.

344–52 Akhilleus is given several monologues in these later Books (18.6–14, 20.425–7, and 21.54–63, as well as here), allowing us to see into his mind; see also 425–7n.

344–6 Verse 344 occurs 4 × *Il.* (with a variant at *Od.* 19.36); Akhilleus uses it again when he sees Lukaon (21.54). κατακτάμεναι μενεαίνων is formular in this position following a verb, usually ἐπόρουσε (as at 442); see Hoekstra, *Epic Verse* 16–17.

347–50 Akhilleus acknowledges a minor error, as he did a much bigger one at 19.56ff. φίλος ἀθανάτοισι θεοῖσιν is an unusual compliment, recurring only for Aiolos (*Od.* 10.2) and Peleus (Hesiod fr. 211.3 MW). αὔτως: 'like this'; see 17.448–50n. ἐρρέτω: 'The word is blunt and not at all elevated, as emerges from its use in Attic (e.g. Ar. *Lys.* 1240)' (Macleod, *Iliad XXIV* 109, on 24.239). It occurs (in various forms) 6 × *Il.*, 3 × *Od.*, always at the beginning of the line. The hiatus can be removed by reading ἐμεῖ'(ο). ὅς (350): a few late MSS have ὡς, which if better attested would be worthy of consideration, καὶ νῦν: 'now too', i.e. as he did on an earlier occasion (188–90).

351–2 The discomfited Akhilleus remembers the other Greeks, the thought introducing the following *parainesis*. Verse 352 ≅ 19.70.

353–418 Akhilleus exhorts the Greeks and Hektor the Trojans. But on Apollo's advice Hektor withdraws, and Akhilleus slaughters a number of Trojans, including Hektor's brother Poludoros

With these duels Akhilleus' *aristeia* returns to the normal structure, after the interruption of his encounter with Aineias (Krischer, *Konventionen* 27). The killings continue (Krischer counts fourteen in all) until 489.

353–72 The correspondences Lohmann finds between the two *paraineseis* (*Reden* 126–30) are perhaps taken too far; Reinhardt goes further still, thinking the second answers the first (*IuD* 429–30). There is certainly a parallel development: each hero first addresses his army (354–5, 366); then speaks of himself (356–7, 367–8); and finally describes his own proposed course of action (360–3, 371–2). Balancing *paraineseis* for each side are fairly common (e.g. 17.220ff. and 17.248ff.; 17.556ff. and 17.586ff.). Scheibner, *Aufbau* 83 n. 1, lists other examples; see also Edwards, *HPI* 92–3.

J. Latacz, *Kampfparänese, Kampfdarstellung und Kampfwirklichkeit in der Ilias, bei Kallinos und Tyrtaios* (Munich 1977) 171–4, refers to these *paraineseis* as an example of a means of transition from a duel of major heroes to a general battle. Akhilleus' initial exhortation to the Greeks to get closer to the enemy

(354–5) clearly expresses this. Actually, except for passing references such as those in 374, 21.32, and 22.3–4, nothing more is heard of the Greek army until after the death of Hektor, an almost surrealistic concentration of the audience's attention upon Akhilleus.

353–9 The second hemistich of 353, standing as the speech-introduction, closes a speech at 13.230. μηκέτι...ἑκὰς ἕστατε: cf. οὐ γὰρ ὀΐω | ...ἑκὰς ἱστάμενος πολεμίζειν (13.262–3). With 355 cf. μεμάτω Τρώεσσι μάχεσθαι | (4.304). Notice the innovative language in a couplet expressing an obvious idea. Similarly Sarpedon yells to his troops that he cannot break down the Greek wall single-handed (12.410–12; verse 356 here = 12.410). This is obviously a trope (cf. also 16.620–2), used here despite the absence from the action of the other Greeks.

358–9 θεὸς ἄμβροτος is formular in this position (3 × *Il.*, 1 × *Od.*). Ares and Athene represent the opposing armies; see 48–53n. καὶ πονέοιτο matches καὶ πᾶσι μάχεσθαι in 357, and has the sense of πονούμενος. The metaphor of the 'jaws of war' recurs at 10.8 and 19.313; the latter instance (see note *ad loc.*) again describes the thoughts of Akhilleus. The metaphor is probably from a wild beast; Leaf thinks that ἐφέπειν suggests driving a horse with bit and bridle, but this does not suit the other occurrences.

360–2 χερσίν τε ποσίν τε | (also at *Od.* 11.595) is a declension of χεῖράς τε πόδας τε | (4 × *Od.*). In 361 Allen prints the vulgate reading μ' ἔτι, Ameis–Hentze and Willcock μέ τί (the reading of a papyrus), Leaf οὐκέτι (with one MS of the *h* family) on the grounds that the pronoun is not usually expressed in such phrases. The absence of a preceding τι in the other instances of οὐδ' ἠβαιόν (-αί) | (6 × *Il.*, 3 × *Od.*) favours μ' ἔτι, and since this has point and is the best-attested reading it should be preferred. στιχός: sc. Τρώων. Elsewhere the plural is used (except for ἰῆς στιχὸς ἦρχε at 16.173), but στιχῶν is metrically intractable in hexameters. However, H. van Wees, *CQ* 36 (1986) 293, thinks that the singular is meaningful, 'all through a column'. On διαμπερές, 'right on through', see 18.562–3n.; it is followed by a genitive again at 12.429.

364–80 The encounter between Akhilleus and Hektor is here quickly aborted, thanks to Apollo's advice. At 419–54 it gets as far as a spear-cast and a charge in return before Apollo again intervenes and breaks it off. Hektor then drops out of sight until their final duel in book 22, allowing Akhilleus a long *aristeia* before it culminates in the slaying of Hektor. The short episode here anticipates the more important one at 419–54, and that in turn the ultimate contest. See Introduction, ch. 2, iii.

365 Both κέκλετο and ὁμοκλήσας are common in these positions, but they do not recur together. ἴμεναι: normally the initial vowel is short, and *Il.* MSS prefer the metrical equivalent ἰέναι; Allen's *Il.* text prints ἴμεναι only at 20.32, compared with ἰέναι 38 ×, and von der Mühls's *Od.* text gives ἴμεναι 16 × and ἰέναι 19 ×. The Aeolic ἴμεναι probably survived, in a losing competition with the Ionic ἰέναι, because of its similarity to the convenient metrical alternative ἴμεν; cf. Chantraine, *GH* I 486. Perhaps this unique form with ῑ- (or perhaps ἴμμ-, printed by Allen in his *OCT*) was someone's idea for a useful metrical alternative to ἰέναι, though it could be used only before a vowel. φάτο may mean 'intended' rather than simply 'declared'; but occasionally a direct speech is anticipated by a summary in indirect speech, as at 18.167, and that may be the case here (see de Jong, *Narrators* 117).

367–70 καὶ...ἐγών: 'I too', referring to Akhilleus' mention of the gods at 358–9. 'Fighting with words' is much talked about in this Book (211–12, 244–5, 431–2). The second hemistich of 369 ≅ 19.107. τελέει and κολούει (370) are presents, co-ordinate with the future ἐπιθήσει. Lohmann, *Reden* 129, is probably correct in taking this as a general statement; Akhilleus will not achieve all he speaks of, for ⟨even⟩ he accomplishes some things but is cut short of fulfilment in others. The expressions may be proverbial. Leaf, unnecessarily, reads κολούσει (with a few late MSS) and takes τελέει as future.

371–2 The epanalepsis (*epanastrophe, anadiplosis, palillogia*) of a hemistich recurs only at 22.127–8 and 23.641–2. It is probably an old oral technique, surviving also in more sophisticated forms like Ἠετίωνος, | Ἠετίων, ὅς... (6.395–6; cf. 2.849–50, 2.870–1, 6.153–4, 21.85–6). See 22.127–8n., and Hoekstra, *Modifications* 34. Here the figure seems intended to emphasize Akhilleus' association with fire, much stressed in his arming-scene; see 19.365–8n. It was much admired by the ancients (AbT; Plutarch, *Vit. Hom.* 32). χεῖρας ἔοικεν may once have been χεῖρε ϝέϝοικεν (Bentley).

Fire and iron are again linked at 23.177, ἐν δὲ πυρὸς μένος ἧκε σιδήρεον, when Akhilleus slays the Trojan captives on Patroklos' pyre. Macleod, *Iliad XXIV* 105, suggests that the metaphor of iron in these cases may be colloquial rather than a poetic tradition. See Introduction, ch. 4, iii.

373–4 The variant ἔσταν 'Αχαιῶν for ἔγχε' ἄειραν (mentioned by Did?/A) is doubtless taken from the formular ἐναντίοι ἔσταν 'Αχαιῶν (4 × *Il.*). ὦρτο δ' ἀϋτή | is formular (3 × *Il.*).

375–8 Apollo warns Hektor as Poseidon warned Aineias (332–9), allowing the hero to hold back without loss of face. Again we are not told if he took human form, or merely spoke (see 330–9n.).

375 The speech-introduction is unique in form. A formula like δὴ τότε Πουλύδαμος θρασὺν Ἕκτορα εἶπε παραστάς (4 × *Il.*, used also for Akhilleus and Agamemnon at 23.155) might have been expected, but there is no expression for Apollo of the required metrical shape, and the struggle for verse-end position between the metrically identical formulae Φοῖβος 'Απόλλων and (ϝ)εῖπε παραστάς was won by the name–epithet combination.

Speech-introductions including two names and a qualification (παραστάς) are very rare (see Edwards, *HSCP* 74, 1968, 15–16), because besides the possible metrical difficulties, the smoothness of scene-changes in Homer makes it unusual for two characters not already named to be introduced together. Here the mention of Hektor is hardly necessary, as the general description of the Trojan rally has lasted only two lines. On εἶπε with accusative see 17.237–9n.

376–80 σχεδὸν ἄορι τύψη (-ας) | is found again at 462, but otherwise 376–8 are unformular, though the wording is normal enough. On the formular οὐλαμὸν ἀνδρῶν (379) see 4.251n. A feminine form of θεοῦ (ϝ)όπα φωνήσαντος appears 2 × *Il.*, 1 × *Od.*

381–418 The first section of Akhilleus' massacre of the Trojans consists of his slaying of four named opponents; the last of these is Hektor's brother Poludoros, whose death brings Hektor back on stage. Following his rescue by Apollo, another series of killings (455–89) leads up to a general description of Akhilleus' attack (490–503). Reinhardt, *IuD* 430, draws attention to the pattern of three deaths followed by an especially significant fourth, cf. 445–8n.

381 εἰμένος ἀλκήν is an abbreviated form of ἐπιειμένοι (-ον) ἀλκήν, which occurs 3 × *Il.* (preceded by θοῦριν) and 2 × *Od.* (preceded by μεγάλην).

382–92 Several other heroes who die are given pathetic biographies which begin with their birth from Naiads; see Fenik, *TBS* 150–2. In a characteristic Homeric technique, the narrator gives us information about Iphition (383–5) which is necessary for us to appreciate Akhilleus' vaunt (389–92); see de Jong, *Narrators* 89, and Introduction, ch. 2, iii. The scholia (bT) remark that the elaboration of Iphition's fate is particularly apt, for after so many battles and killings the poet does well to use such decoration to avoid satiety, and to show that Akhilleus' first victim is not a nonentity.

382–7 Iphition is one of the Meïones, listed in the Trojan catalogue (2.864–6, see note *ad loc.*), whose leaders are (like him) associated with Mt Tmolos and the Gugaian Lake (390–1). Ὀτρυντεΐδην: the retention of ŏ before mute and liquid is rare, unless the word cannot otherwise be used in a hexameter; see Page, *Odyssey* 163, and Chantraine, *GH* I 108. The scansion is retained in 384 and 389. πολέων ἡγήτορα λαῶν | is probably an under-represented formula; it does not recur in Homer, but appears at *HyDem* 475 (without πολέων) and 3 × in Hesiod (frr. 25.36, 43(a).58, 136.18 (restored)). Strabo (13.4.6) could not find a Hude in Lydia, but says that some thought it was Sardis or its acropolis. He also reports, unsurprisingly, that some added line 385 after 2.866. In 386, E. Visser, *Homerische Versifikationstechnik* (Frankfurt am Main 1987) 301, argues well for reading τὸν ῥ' (resumptive) instead of τὸν δ' (connective). ἰθὺς μεμαῶτα

(-ος, -ε, -ι) (386) is formular in this position (5 × *Il.*). Verse 387 = 16.412, where Patroklos kills Erulaos with a stone.

389–92 Vaunts by a victorious warrior over his defeated enemy are common, and their tone and content vary widely; see Edwards, *HPI* 93–4, and Fenik, *TBS* 101. Here Akhilleus' words stress the bitterness of a death far from home, often brought out in the poet's own voice, e.g. at 17.300–3; see J. Griffin, *CQ* 26 (1976) 164–7. In this instance the poet's own pathetic note here appears at 394.

389 When Iris comes to rouse Akhilleus to save Patroklos' corpse she begins ὄρσεο Πηλεΐδη, πάντων ἐκπαγλότατ' ἀνδρῶν (18.170). Is it coincidence that in this vaunt over his first victim Akhilleus echoes her words? The disparaging phrase is elsewhere used only by Agamemnon to Akhilleus (1.146).

390–2 Some good MSS have the obviously wrong ἔνθα δέ. The juxtaposition of θάνατος and γενεή is noteworthy. γενεή again means 'birthplace' at *Od.* 1.407 etc. On τέμενος see 18.550–1n. Herodotus (1.80.1) describes a broad, bare plain in front of Sardis, watered by the Hullos and other tributary streams of the Hermos, which runs into the sea near the town of Phokaia. J. Griffin says that 392, 'with its massive epithets symmetrically spaced as the mind contemplates these serene and distant waters, is characteristic of Achilles' (*JHS* 106, 1986, 54); he compares Akhilleus' οὔρεά τε σκιόεντα θάλασσά τε ἠχήεσσα (1.157).

394–5 Leaf plausibly suggests ἐπισσώτροισι δατεῦντο, cf. ποσσὶ δατεῦντο (23.121). ἐπίσσωτρα are the metal tires on the rims of chariot-wheels; see 5.725n. and J. Wiesner, *Arch. Hom.* F 14, 43. The words anticipate 499–502, where the crushing of dead bodies under horses' hoofs and chariot-wheels is described at greater length. | πρώτη ἐν ὑσμίνῃ recurs at 15.340; here πρώτη is picked up by ἐπ' αὐτῷ, 'after him'.

395–6 Demoleon is not heard of elsewhere. ἀλεξητῆρα: the word is found only here in Homer and is rare, but occurs in Xenophon. ἐσθλόν at the beginning of the line is sometimes followed by a patronymic (3 × *Il.*, including 383 above), but Ἀντηνορίδην (7 × *Il.*, in various cases) will not scan after it, and perhaps for this reason the poet uses Ἀντήνορος υἱόν (5 × *Il.*) instead and apparently invents a new complimentary phrase to bridge the intervening space.

397–400 The lines (from κυνέης) ≅ 12.183–6, but ἱεμένη (399; see 278–80n.) replaces χαλκείη as an epithet for Akhilleus' spear, which was fashioned by Hephaistos (*Cypria* fr. 3 Bernabé, 3 Davies) and doubtless had a blade of gold; alternatively, χαλκείη in the previous line may have been copied in the one passage or the repetition avoided in the other. ἀλλὰ δι' αὐτῆς (398) replaces ἀλλὰ διαπρό. Similar expressions occur at 11.95–8, and there is a fuller description of such a head-wound at 17.293–8. πεπάλακτο:

the brain was spattered over the inside of the helmet. Friedrich, *Verwundung* 46–7, points out that this phenomenon could not be perceived from outside, but can well be imagined. He does not exclude the possibility that the verb-form here is thought of as derived from πάλλω, 'shake', but cf. 500–1n.

401 ≅ 11.423 (with Χερσιδάμαντα); Hippodamas is trying to escape, Khersidamas on the attack. Hippodamas appears only here; Reinhardt, *IuD* 431, plausibly suggested he is Demoleon's charioteer and owes his name to his profession. A hero's charioteer is again killed immediately after he himself has died at 484–9 and 11.122–47. Verse 402 = 5.56, which is expanded by ὤμων μεσσηγύς, διὰ δὲ στήθεσφιν ἔλασσεν. Here the following simile gives less precision but more colour.

403–6 The main point of comparison is of course the bellowing of the victim, both the warrior and the bull. A second parallel, the death of both, is brought in at the simile's conclusion. And like the bull, Hippodamas is in a sense the victim of Poseidon, who supports the Greeks. Homer ignores here the desirable assent of the animal to the sacrifice (see W. Burkert, *Greek Religion*, tr. J. Raffan, Cambridge, Mass. 1985, 56, and *Homo Necans*, tr. P. Bing, Berkeley 1983, 4 n.10). Dying warriors are often compared to bulls (see 17.516–24n.); at 17.520–4 a different aspect of a sacrifice is used.

404–5 Ἑλικώνιον: Helike was on the coast of Achaea, and had a famous temple of Poseidon (see 8.203 and n., and 2.570–5n.). Herodotus (1.148.1) says that the Panionion at Mukale was consecrated Ποσειδέωνι Ἑλικωνίῳ, and H. T. Wade-Gery, *The Poet of the Iliad* (Cambridge 1952), and others have assumed that this is what the poet has in mind. It is not yet clear, however, how early the cult there began; A. M. Snodgrass, *The Dark Age of Greece* (Edinburgh 1971) 419, thinks it may have been near the end of the eighth century, in which case a reference may have been intended; but L. H. Jeffery, *Archaic Greece* (New York 1976) 208–9, is quite uncertain.

With the second hemistich of 405 cf. γάνυται δ' ἄρα τε φρένα ποιμήν (13.493). τοῖς is taken by Ameis–Hentze to refer to the κοῦροι, and Fränkel, *Gleichnisse* 83, thinks Poseidon's delight in their strength parallels that of the poet's audience in the heroic prowess of Akhilleus; but this seems far-fetched, and in the context it is more likely that bulls are the antecedent, understood from ταῦρος.

406 λίπ' ὀστέα θυμὸς ἀγήνωρ | recurs at *Od.* 12.414; the shorter form λίπε δ' ὀστέα θυμός | occurs 2 × *Il.*, 1 × *Od.*, and another variant λίπη λευκ' ὀστέα θυμός | at *Od.* 11.221. The familiarity of the formula permits the addition of a second accusative τόν γ' ἐρυγόντα after λίπε.

407–18 The motif of the son whom his father would not allow to go to war, but who goes anyway, is used again at 11.717–21, where Nestor tells how his father went so far as to hide Nestor's horses without deterring him. The ugly death of Poludoros is used to motivate Hektor's return to face

Akhilleus. Together with his brother Lukaon (21.34–135), he is later mentioned by Priam as a possible victim of Akhilleus in his appeal to him not to add to the number of sons he has lost at his hands (22.46–55). The irony (for we know they have died, whereas Priam only fears it) much increases the pathos of his words. The pathetic Lukaon also mentions Poludoros' death (21.89–91). Scheibner, *Aufbau* 85 n. 2, points out that there is a special triumph in killing Priam's sons; Akhilleus kills three, Diomedes two (5.159–65), Agamemnon two (11.101–21).

408–10 Πριαμίδην...πατήρ: a good example of a runover word closely connected with the sense of what follows. γόνος is not elsewhere used in this collective sense, but it is a natural extension of its other meanings. νεώτατος (4 × *Il.*, 2 × *Od.*) is only here used by the poet himself, and φίλτατος too is rarely used in the narrative (3 × *Il.* against 20 × *Il.* in direct speech; so de Jong, *Narrators* 143). As J. Griffin, *JHS* 106 (1986) 49, points out, superlatives are commoner in speeches than in the narrative because of their greater evaluative and emotional content, and de Jong, *JHS* 108 (1988) 188, notes that the two superlatives are used here to present the feelings of Priam. ποσὶ πάντας ἐνίκα | occurs at 23.756 (of Antilokhos). The pride in his speed shown by this youngest of Priam's sons makes us sympathize with his adolescent folly in dashing through the battle-line, and understand Hektor's furious regret at his killing.

411–12 νηπιέη (3 × *Il.*, 2 × *Od.*) is formed by *diectasis* from *νηπιίη, *νηπίη, the abstract noun from νήπιος (Chantraine, *GH* I 83). Verse 412 = 11.342 (see note *ad loc.*). The first hemistich is also used at 5.250, where Sthenelos warns Diomedes against this fatal practice of running through the front line of fighters.

413–15 Literally 'He struck him (τόν) midway (μέσσον, with τόν) in the back (νῶτα, the part affected) of him dashing past (παραΐσσοντος).' Verses 414–15 = 4.132–3 (after ὅθι), where Menelaos is wounded from the *front*. The ζωστήρ, a belt made of, or decorated with, metal (παναίολος, 4.186 etc.; δαιδάλεος, 4.135) was put on above the θώρηξ and held it in place; the μίτρη was beneath (see H. Brandenberg, *Arch. Hom.* ε 119–43). Its ὀχῆες, 'fasteners', are mentioned only here (= 4.132). Since it presumably had some use as an additional defence against missiles it would not be surprising if the fastening, perhaps the weakest point, were at the back, where Poludoros was hit; but it is odd that the same wording is used as for Menelaos' belt, which fastened in front. Either (with Willcock) there is some carelessness in the use of formulae in one place or the other, or one of them has put on his armour back to front. In neither place is it clear what διπλόος ἤντετο θώρηξ means; a two-piece *metal* protection for the upper body would surely join under the arms, not in the middle of the chest (or back), so perhaps a kind of leather vest, overlapping where the flaps meet, is envisaged. See 4.132–3n., 4.137–8n., and Leaf 1 581. σύνεχον, 'come together', is intransitive, as at 478.

416–18 The first hemistich recurs at 5.100. παρ' (ἐπ') ὀμφαλόν occurs 4 × *Il.*; ἔγχεος αἰχμή, surprisingly, recurs only at 16.315 (in the dative) and 16.505 (separated); the equivalent δουρὸς ἀκωκή, with initial consonant, is commoner (7 × *Il.*, 1 × *Od.*). Verse 417 ≅ 5.68, where θάνατος replaces νεφέλη; the two ideas, together with that of κυανέη, are combined at 16.350, θανάτου δὲ μέλαν νέφος ἀμφεκάλυψεν |. κυάνεος is formular with νεφέλη (1 × *Il.*, 2 × *Od.*) and νέφος (2 × *Il.*). The nearest parallel to 418 is at 4.525–6 ≅ 21.180–1, οὖτα δὲ δουρὶ παρ' ὀμφαλόν· ἐκ δ' ἄρα πᾶσαι | χύντο χαμαὶ χολάδες; Xenophon describes a similar wound, *Anabasis* 2.5.33.

419–54 Hektor, enraged by his young brother's death, advances to face Akhilleus. They exchange challenges, but Athene intervenes on Akhilleus' behalf and Apollo then bears Hektor away to safety

This preliminary and inconclusive meeting of Hektor and Akhilleus, before their great duel in book 22, exemplifies a characteristic of Homeric style; a brief anticipation of a motif or type-scene before the major instance of it. Fenik, *TBS* 213–14, compares the two encounters of Hektor and Patroklos in book 16, and the short supplication of Tros to Akhilleus (463–72) preceding the expanded episode with Lukaon (21.34–135). See Introduction, ch. 2, iii.

419–21 Fenik, *TBS* 88, compares Hektor's distress at his brother's death with that of Koön at 11.248–50. The defence or avenging of brothers and other relatives is of course a standard motif; see H. van Wees, *CQ* 38 (1988) 6. The wording of 420 reflects that of 418. κατὰ δ' ὀφθαλμῶν κέχυτ' ἀχλύς also occurs 2 × *Il.*, 1 × *Od.* at the end of the line (on the ῠ of ἀχλύς see Chantraine, *GH* 1 222). In all cases but this the phrase signifies death. Here it is emotionally effective but not easy to explain – and commentators have not attempted to do so. It seems to be an impressionistic extension of the dark cloud of death which enveloped Poludoros so that it encompasses the grief-stricken Hektor too. Cf. 282, 17.591, and 5.127–30n.

423–4 The first hemistich recurs at 13.583; φλογὶ εἴκελος is formular in this position (6 × *Il.*). ὡς εἶδ', ὣς ἀνέπαλτο: the first ὡς is temporal, the second demonstrative; 'When he saw ⟨him⟩, then he bounded forward.' See 19.16–17n.

425–7 This short monologue is one of the four Akhilleus utters in these later books (the others are 18.6ff., 20.344ff., and 21.54ff.). Like the others, it shows us his thoughts, here reminding us of the reason for his savage anger against Hektor, as the armour Hektor wears again reminds us immediately before he is killed (22.322–3). The only other such 'perception'-monologues (as opposed to 'decision'-monologues) are those giving the soulful reflections of Zeus (17.201ff., 443ff.) and Hektor's final realization of his abandonment (22.297ff.). See Fenik, *TBS* 96–7.

ἐγγὺς ἀνήρ is used by Diomedes of *himself*, again beginning a speech (14.110). The difference in meaning in the two occurrences is noteworthy. τετιμένον is used as an adjective. οὐδ' ἄν is due to Aristarchus (Did/A), for οὐδ' ἄρ' of most MSS. The sense must be potential ('We will not...' or 'Let us not...'), and in Homer such an optative may or may not be accompanied by ἄν (κε) (cf. Chantraine, *GH* II 216–20), so it may be best (with Leaf) to retain the MSS reading. ἀλλήλους πτώσσοιμεν: 'cower away from each other'; the vivid verb (used of frightened animals) occurs only here with a personal object. On γεφύρας see 5.87–8n.

428–9 The speech-introduction marks off Akhilleus' monologue from his challenge to Hektor. On a challenge and the response to it before a duel see 178–98n. When upset, Akhilleus is often sparing with words (e.g. his gruff responses to Athene, 1.216–18, to his mother, 24.139–40, and 21.150–1) but he outdoes himself here (σύντομος ὁ λόγος τοῦ πρὸς τιμωρίαν σπεύδοντος. καίτοι πρὸς Αἰνείαν πλείους ἀποτέταται λόγους, bT). Diomedes, in more expansive mood, concluded his 21-line challenge to Glaukos with the same verse (6.143). Its second hemistich is a variant of ὀλέθρου πείρατ' ἐφῆπται | (2 × *Il.*, 2 × *Od.*). Macleod, *Iliad XXIV* 51, lists other examples of the kind of assonance seen in ἆσσον...θᾶσσον. On ὀλέθρου πείρατα see 6.143n.

431–7 Hektor admits Akhilleus' greater strength, but comforts himself with the thought that sometimes the weaker man wins; Agenor seeks the same vain solace at 21.568–70, and Hektor will do so again at 22.130.

431–3 = 200–2, where Aineias uses the lines in response to Akhilleus' 21-line challenge. After the terse 429 the effect may seem to verge on the comic, but actually the repetition fits well with the words/actions contrast so often made in this Book (see 200–58n.).

434–7 The scholia (bT), with unusual lack of understanding, say that 434 is intended ironically. Verse 435 is formular (2 × *Il.*, 3 × *Od.*); see 17.514n. πάροιθεν (437) is probably locative, 'before ⟨me⟩' (cf. 6.319 etc.) or possibly 'at the tip'. Diomedes similarly claims ὑπ' ἐμεῖο... | ὀξὺ βέλος πέλεται (11.391–2). Schol. T, however, take it as temporal, referring to Hektor's killing of Patroklos; but if such a meaning were intended one might expect it to be more clearly expressed.

438–40 The familiar formular verse ending προΐει δολιχόσκιον ἔγχος (7 × *Il.*, 2 × *Od.*) is broken off by the substitution of δόρυ and the start of a new sentence, which allows πνοιῇ to be placed emphatically at the beginning of the next line; its emphasis, and her divine strength, is then reinforced by ἧκα μάλα ψύξασα, 'breathing very gently'. 'Αχιλλῆος is ablatival genitive after ἔτραπε, as at 18.138. Athene acts more quickly and successfully here than when she moved to save Menelaos from Pandaros' arrow (4.127ff.). To save Diomedes from the spear of Ares she was obliged to take hold of it with her hand (5.853–4).

441–2 The expression, and the return of the spear, are like those at 324; see 324–5n. On 442 see 344–6n.

443–4 Hektor now vanishes, to reappear alone before the wall of Troy at 22.5–6. Verse 444 = 3.381 (Aphrodite rescuing Paris), ≅ 21.597 (Apollo rescuing Agenor); see 321–3n. Other examples of the ease with which deities perform such actions are listed by J. Griffin, *CQ* 28 (1978) 10.

445–8 As printed by Allen, the passage is a startling variation on 5.436–9, 16.702–6, and 16.784–7, where a hero (Diomedes, Patroklos) attacks three times and then the fourth time is repulsed by Apollo (cf. also 21.176–9, *Od.* 21.125–9). Reinhardt, *IuD* 434, thinks there is an intentional contrast with the earlier examples. The line which introduces Apollo's magisterial rebuff to Diomedes (5.439) and Patroklos (16.706) here introduces the words of Akhilleus (448). See 5.436–9n., 22.165n., and Fenik, *TBS* 46–8.

However, verse 447, 'But when the fourth time…', is omitted by most of the better MSS. Van der Valk, *Researches* II 517, holds that it was omitted by Aristarchus because it also occurred in the parallel passages (at 5.438 and 16.786). But (as Leaf points out) it is a very possible 'concordance interpolation', and the sense is much improved by its omission. Then the parallel is not (very awkwardly) with the passages where a god takes action the fourth time the hero charges, but with the simple τρὶς μὲν … τρὶς δέ motif, found 5 × *Il.*, 2 × *Od.* (see 18.155–6n.). It would be wiser to follow the MSS and omit 447, leaving 448 to follow naturally enough after 446.

449–54 Akhilleus' words are the same as those of Diomedes after Hektor has been struck and dazed by his spear (11.362–7). They do not fit the context so well there, as Apollo has not actually intervened; but Fenik, *TBS* 94–5, while pointing out other similarities, very properly refuses to think that this scene is the original of that in book 11. The reuse of an identical speech of this length – except in the case of a messenger – is however unparalleled in Homer. De Jong, *Narrators* 188, notes that both times the addressee is Hektor, and that both Diomedes and Akhilleus can properly display resentment that he has escaped, contempt for their opponent, and determination to kill him later. Macleod, *Iliad XXIV* 25 n. 1, groups this with other parallel passages where 'words which on their first appearance have no tragic consequences are later echoed with overtones of doom'.

449–51 αὖ νῦν = 'once again now', referring to Apollo's earlier removal of Hektor from the battle (375–80). It is not made clear there if Akhilleus realizes what has happened, but *we* know of it, and so his words make sense.

Book Twenty

On the use of κύον as a term of abuse see 22.345n. (where again Akhilleus hurls it at Hektor). δοῦπον ἀκόντων is also used at 16.361.

452–3 The thought looks forward to Athene's assistance to Akhilleus in the final duel (22.214ff.).

454 νῦν αὖ τοὺς ἄλλους: the vulgate reading is νῦν δ' ἄλλους Τρώων, which was printed by Leaf and is preferred by Scheibner, *Aufbau* 88 n. 1. Allen's reading appears in some late MSS, and is repeated at 11.367; Did?/A mention it here as a variant, but it is unwise to put it into the text. ἐπιείσομαι: from the root of ἵεμαι, but used as if it were from εἶμι; see Chantraine, *GH* I 412, and Fernández-Galiano and Heubeck, *Odissea* on *Od.* 22.89.

455–503 Akhilleus resumes his slaughter of the Trojans. This is followed by a general description of the enemy rout, which is concluded at the beginning of book 21

Most of Akhilleus' victims appear only to be killed. This was true of those in the first series (Iphition, Demoleon, Hippodamas, and Poludoros), though they are characters of some importance (except Hippodamas, who is probably Demoleon's charioteer, see 401n.). Of the current casualties, *Druops* and *Demoukhos* appear only here; *Dardanos* and *Tros* appear only here, but bear names famous in Trojan history (215, 230); *Laogonos* son of Bias appears only here (a man of the same name, son of Onetor, was killed by Meriones at 16.603–7); a *Moulios* was killed by Patroklos (16.696; another was one of Nestor's victims in his historic battle against the Epeans, 11.738–9); an *Ekheklos* was killed by Patroklos (16.694); *Deukalion* appears only here (another Deukalion was the father of Idomeneus, 13.452); *Rhigmos* appears only here; *Areïthoös* appears only here (another Areïthoös was a famous club-fighter, 7.8–10, 7.137–9). The 'Scheinrealismus' of the killings is examined by Friedrich, *Verwundung* 44–6.

455–89 The structure of the sentences and their arrangement within the line should be noted. One might expect a sequence of killings to fall into a catalogue of self-contained groups of a few lines each, set off from each other by end-stop. But the poet obviously takes great care to avoid such monotony, and to speed up the narrative by avoiding end-stop. The first victim is summarily despatched (455–6); the next is connected by a μέν... δέ link, starting at the 4th-foot caesura, and his name bears the emphasis of the verse-beginning (457). The double killing which follows (460–2) just fills 3 verses, but variety is provided by the matching τὸν μέν..., τὸν δέ of the last line. The name of Tros, the next victim, again begins the line, but the construction changes abruptly in mid-verse, and a long and beautifully crafted expansion follows (463–72; see note *ad loc.*). This ends in an

339

unexpected runover phrase (see 470–2n.), and so the fate of Moulios begins
at mid-verse, as does that of Ekheklos (474). Deukalion's name starts the
verse (478), but an inserted clause breaks the sense at mid-verse and the
sentence restarts after a runover word in the next line; in the six verses
devoted to Deukalion there is no end-stop. In the next killing (484–7)
Rhigmos' name is postponed to the beginning of the second verse, and his
actual death is omitted so that the description of his charioteer's wounding
can begin in mid-verse. The whole passage is turned from a monotonous
casualty list into a splendid display of restrained emotion and virtuoso
craftsmanship. On such techniques see Introduction, ch. 4, i, and vol. 1
18–24.

With his usual perspicacity, Scheibner, *Aufbau* 88, remarks that the
passage should be read aloud, and quotes the scholiast's comment (bT on
456) ἐπιτρέχει τὸν τῶν βαρβάρων θάνατον, ἐπὶ τῇ εὐχερείᾳ καὶ ὀξύτητι τοῦ
Ἀχιλλέως ταχύνας τὸν λόγον. There is similar variety in Patroklos' killings at
16.399–418, which however concludes with a remarkable name-only
catalogue.

455–62 As usual the details of the killings are different, but formular
expressions occur (αὐχένα μέσσον 4 × *Il.*, 1 × *Od.*; ἠΰν τε μέγαν τε (nom. and
acc.) 8 × *Il.*, 1 × *Od.*; ξίφεϊ μεγάλῳ also at 5.146; ἐξαίνυτο θυμόν 3 × *Il.*; 462
≅ 378). τὸν (τοὺς) μὲν ἔασ(ε) (456) is used in other lists of rapid-fire killings
(5.148, 11.148, 11.426, and expanded at 5.847).

458–60 κὰγ γόνυ: this is the only example of this type of apocope; see
Chantraine, *GH* 1 87–8. Pairs of brothers are often slain together; see Fenik,
TBS 11.

463–72 This short supplication scene anticipates the longer episode with
Lukaon at 21.34–135; on this Homeric technique see Fenik, *TBS* 213–14,
and Introduction, ch. 2, iii. Trojans often plead for their lives, always in
vain; sometimes the direct speech of suppliant and slayer are given as
expansion (6.46ff., 10.378ff., 11.131ff., 21.74ff., 22.338ff.).

The sentence-structure is unusual and effective. First the name of the
new victim is given in the accusative, repeating the accusatives used for the
previous casualties (460, 462; cf. the position and construction of |
Δευκαλίωνα, 478). This is picked up by a nominative pronoun introducing
a clause which describes his attempt to reach Akhilleus' knees, followed by
a couplet explaining what is in his mind (464–5; this replaces the usual
direct speech). Then instead of the response of Akhilleus (cf. his famous
words to Lukaon, 21.99–113), the poet himself describes the hero's mood
(466–8). A virtual repetition of the first clause (468) reiterates Tros'
reaching for Akhilleus' knees, explained by the summarizing ἱέμενος λίσσεθ'
(469); then comes Akhilleus' reaction, the sudden and violent ὃ δὲ φασγάνῳ
οὖτα καθ' ἧπαρ, at last providing a verb to govern the initial name and

patronymic of 463. Though Tros is not allowed to plead for mercy in direct speech, his final seconds are far from routine.

464 λαβών: the formulae (καὶ) λάβε γούνων | (4 × *Il.*, 4 × *Od.*) and λαβὼν ἐλλίσσετο γούνων | (1 × *Il.* with a variation at 21.71, 1 × *Od.* with a variation at 6.142) must have been in the poet's mind, but grammatically it seems impossible to take λαβών here with the subject of the main clause, though the rendering 'if he could grasp them [*sc.* Akhilleus' knees]' would make good sense. But the verbs of the clause make it clear that the proper sense is 'taking him ⟨prisoner⟩', which is preferred by Leaf and Willcock. There are examples of a similar break-up of the units of a formula at 18.2 and 18.362 (see notes *ad locc.*).

465–6 ὁμηλικίην ἐλεήσας: the implication is not that Tros is especially young, as Poludoros was, but that he and Akhilleus share the closeness that comes from being of the same age. This natural affinity within an age-group, perhaps arising from shared puberty-rites, is often stressed in Homer, e.g. at 3.175, 5.325–6, *Od.* 3.363–4, 6.23, 15.197, 22.209; on its importance in early Greece see most recently O. Murray in Hägg, *Greek Renaissance* 199. As in the case of Lukaon, Akhilleus' present mercilessness implies that he was not always like this (as the poet goes on to explain). Verse 466 = *Od.* 3.146.

467–8 γλυκύθυμος occurs only here in Homer and is very rare later. The same is true of ἀγανόφρων, but ἀγανοφροσύνη is attributed to Hektor by Helen (24.772, see note *ad loc.*) and to Odysseus by his mother (*Od.* 11.203). The litotes, common in Homer (see F. P. Donnelly, *CW* 23, 1930, 137–40, 145–6), is particularly effective here. ἥπτετο is probably conative.

470–2 αὐτοῦ: i.e. the liver. ἐνέπλησεν: Aristarchus (Did/A) unnecessarily read ἐνέπρησεν, 'inflate', which is used of the wind filling a sail at 1.481. Virgil translated the vulgate (*implevitque sinum sanguis*, *Aeneid* 10.819). τὸν δὲ σκότος ὄσσε κάλυψε | occurs 11 × *Il.* In only one other case is it followed by an enjambing word (| ἀσθμαίνονθ', 'gasping', 21.182), and it may not be coincidental that the enjambing phrase here, θυμοῦ δευόμενον, is also applied to gasping sacrificial lambs whose throats have been cut (3.293–4; see note *ad loc.*). As the dying victims gulp for breath the sentence drags itself past the end of the formula and into the next line.

472–5 One wonders if Moulios' name suggested his wound, or vice versa (Μούλιον οὖτα... | δουρὶ κατ' οὖς'... δι' οὔατος...). Ἀγήνορος υἱόν: probably not the Agenor, son of Antenor, who faces Akhilleus at 21.544ff. There he seems to be too young to have a son also fighting in the ranks, and his brother Akamas is said to be still a youth (11.59–60). The first hemistich of 475 recurs at 387 and 16.412. There was probably a formula φάσγανα κωπήεντα |, appearing in expanded form in φάσγανα καλά, μελάνδετα, κωπήεντα | (15.713); cf. also πλῆξας ξίφει αὐχένα κωπήεντι | (16.332).

341

476–7 = 16.333–4, ≅ 5.82–3 (see note *ad loc.*). The warming of the sword by the blood is admired by Plutarch, *Vit. Hom.* 26, as a means of emphasis.

478–80 Deukalion's name is placed first, and then picked up by τόν γε in the next line; a simpler version of the construction at 463ff. Alternative derivations of Deukalion's name have recently been proposed by R. Janko in *Glotta* 65 (1987) 69–72 (< *dl(e)uk-*, 'sweet') and by F. Bader in *O-o-pe-ro-si: Festschrift für Ernst Risch* (Berlin 1986) 463–88 (< *deu-k-*, 'shine', 'see'). ξυνέχουσι is intransitive, 'come together', as at 415. χειρός: 'arm', as often. In 480, a papyrus and many MSS of the *h* family read αἰχμὴ χαλκείη, which is very common in this position (10 × *Il.*) and is likely to be right. The formula does not otherwise occur in the dative. Possibly the nominative was altered in one line of the tradition to avoid repeating the beginning of 474.

480–1 There are a number of cases where a hero is first disabled and then killed (see Fenik, *TBS* 35), but none matches the sudden sharp pathos of πρόσθ' ὁρόων θάνατον. The nearest is 4.522–3, where the wounded man stretches out his hands to his companions; see note *ad loc.* R. Renehan, *CP* 82 (1987) 108, correctly emphasizes that the tone is one of pathetic helplessness; as he demonstrates, heroic defiance of death may be expressed by characters in Homer but is seldom portrayed by the poet.

482–3 τῆλ' αὐτῇ πήληκι κάρη βάλε: in the even more ghastly wounding at 14.493ff. the victor ἀπήρπαξεν δὲ χαμᾶζε | αὐτῇ σὺν πήληκι κάρη (14.497–8). αὐτῇ πήληκι: 'helmet and all'; on the development of this archaic use of αὐτός (cf. ἵπποι αὐτοῖσιν ὄχεσφιν, 2 × *Il.*) see A. M. Davies, *Linear B 1984* 88–9. σφόνδυλος (only here in Homer) is a vertebra, and later the drum of a column; the ending -ιος is doubtless adopted to avoid a cretic (cf. Risch, *Wortbildung* 122–3). ἐκπάλλω, 'spurt out', occurs only here in Greek. The phenomenon is anatomically impossible; see Friedrich, *Verwundung* 46, and on ancient ideas of the anatomy of the neck, 13.546–7n. κεῖτο τανυσθείς |: on the formula see 18.26–7n.

484–7 Rhigmos' father, the Thracian leader Peiroös (Peirōs), is listed at 2.844 and killed at 4.527–38. The generic epithet ἐριβώλακα (-ος, -ι) in this position follows a number of names in the *Il.*; it is again applied to Thrace at 11.222. The first hemistich of 486 is repeated at 413; the second ≅ 4.528, which in place of νηδύι has πνεύμονι, which is read here by a papyrus and some later MSS. The variant is mentioned in the scholia (Did?/A).

Normally the formular | ἤριπε δ' ἐξ ὀχέων (9 × *Il.*) is followed by a co-ordinate clause describing the man's death, the clatter of his armour, or the panic of his horses. Only here does it end the sentence and a new episode begin in mid-verse. It is unusual for a hero fighting on foot to kill an

Book Twenty

opponent in a chariot; Diomedes achieves it (5.159–65) and so does Agamemnon (11.101–21).

487–9 Areïthoös is Rhigmos' driver (cf. 401n.), but the name may be just an epithet; cf. ἀρηΐθόων αἰζηῶν (167), and see 15.319–17n. Charioteers are often killed as they expose themselves to attack while turning their horses; cf. 5.580–2, 8.256–7, 13.394–7. Both hemistichs of 488 are formular. οἱ (489) = '(ϝ)οι (dative). κυκήθησαν, 'were panic-stricken', is used elsewhere (2 × *Il.*) of warriors. The reference to the horses perhaps anticipates 498–502.

490–503 Akhilleus' *aristeia* continues in the usual pattern, with a description of his charge (see Krischer, *Konventionen* 27; Fenik, *TBS* 84–5). The resulting Trojan flight begins the next Book. There is a close parallel in Agamemnon's *aristeia* at 11.153ff., which again includes a fire-simile (11.155–7), a reference to a mêlée of horses and chariots, and the same description of the victorious hero (11.169 ≅ 20.503). There are shorter descriptions of charges by Diomedes and Hektor, each including a simile, at 5.85–94 and 11.304–9.

On paired similes see Introduction, ch. 3, v, 2. Here the contrast – or combination – of nature and culture is unusually clear.

490–4 Akhilleus was compared to fire at 371–2 (see note *ad loc.*), and will be again at 21.12–16. Here the fury and extent of the fire are compared with the hero's rage as he sweeps over the battlefield, and as the wind drives on the flames so he harries the dying Trojans. The intensity is driven home by the repetitions βαθέ'...βαθεῖα, πάντη...πάντη, θεσπιδαὲς πῦρ...δαίμονι ἶσος. At 11.155–9 the parallel drawn with Agamemnon's charge is slightly different. Burning woodlands appear in shorter similes at 2.455–6, 14.396–7, and 15.605–6.

490–2 ἀναμαιμάει: the compounded form occurs only here in Greek. βαθέ' ἄγκεα... | οὔρεος ἀζαλέοιο is an elaborated form of the formular | οὔρεος ἐν βήσσῃς (-ῃσιν) (5 × *Il.*). πάντη τε κλονέων ἄνεμος φλόγα εἰλυφάζει: cf. πάντη τ' εἰλυφόων ἄνεμος φέρει in the simile for Agamemnon (11.156), and νέφεα κλονέοντε πάροιθεν of Boreas and Zephuros at 23.213. εἰλυφάζω appears again in Greek only in Hesiod, *Aspis* 275, for the glare of torches (and cf. fr. 406, considered spurious by Merkelbach–West); εἰλυφόωντες (< -άω) is used of the thunderbolt at *Theogony* 692. The root is that of εἰλύω, 'wrap', but the -φ- is unexplained; see Frisk s.v. εἰλυφάω, and Chantraine, *GH* I 360. The metrically convenient suffix -άζω is a common alternative for -άω (cf. οὐτάω, οὐτάζω; Chantraine, *GH* I 337; Risch, *Wortbildung* 297).

494 κτεινομένους ἐφέπων: cf. ἔφεπε... | ...ἀποκτείνων (11.177–8). ῥέε δ' αἵματι γαῖα μέλαινα | is repeated at 15.715; a shorter form (without μέλαινα) occurs 2 × *Il.*; another variant ἐρυθαίνετο δ' αἵματι γαῖα (ὕδωρ) | occurs 2 ×

343

Il. Cf. also 11.394–5, 17.360–1. The picture of blood is amplified at 499–502.

495–502 In the second simile the comparison is between yoked oxen treading out grain on the threshing-floor and yoked chariot-horses trampling on the dead bodies lying on the ground. There may be an implication of the countless numbers of grain-ears and of the dead, and a suggested contrast between the life-giving harvests of domestic labour and the deadly destructiveness of warfare (as at 19.221–4, 21.254–62). The simile concludes with a gruesome but realistic parallel between the barley-ears forced out from the husks and the blood squeezed out of the corpses and splashing over the chariots. Other similes comparing the battle to a threshing-floor (5.499–505, 13.588–92, see notes *ad locc.*) stress different aspects.

The singular number of ἄξων and δίφρον, as well as the comparison with the disciplined oxen, suggest that it is Akhilleus' charging chariot that is envisaged, not those of the fleeing Trojans. Nothing has been said of Akhilleus' having mounted his chariot in order to pursue the Trojans, but omission of such details is normal; Hektor leaps out of his chariot at 8.320 but is wheeling his horses about at 8.348, leads the Trojans forward μακρά βιβάς at 15.306–7 and whips up his horses at 15.352. Here the return to the chariot both indicates that the Trojans are fleeing and allows the introduction of the grim and powerful simile.

495–6 βόας ἄρσενας εὐρυμετώπους: i.e. oxen; the metrical equivalent '(ϝ)έλικας βόας εὐρυμετώπους (*Od.* 11.289) refers to cattle generally. Cf. βοῦν ἄρσενα πενταέτηρον (*Od.* 19.420, split at *Il.* 7.314–15). ἐϋκτιμένη (-ην) ἐν (κατ') ἀλωῇ (-ήν) | is formular (2 × *Od.*). A papyrus and some late MSS read ἐϋτροχάλῳ ἐν ἀλωῇ, which appears at Hesiod, *Erga* 599 and 806. The variant ('well-rolled') is mentioned in the scholia (Did?/A), and has more point; Virgil rendered it *area...ingenti aequanda cylindro* (*Georgics* 1.178).

497–8 λέπτ(α) = 'shelled out from the husk', from λέπω, which is used of stripping a stake of leaves and bark at 1.236. Generally λεπτός is used as an adjective meaning 'small' or 'fine'. ὑπ' Ἀχιλλῆος μεγαθύμου: ὑπό may mean 'beneath' or (better) 'driven on by'. In the phrase μεγαθύμου Πηλείωνος, an alternative for the commoner Πηληϊάδεω Ἀχιλῆος, the generic epithet is sometimes thought to have some significant effect; see 17.213–14n., 18.225–7n., 19.75n., and 19.408n. A compliment might also be intended when Ἀχιλλῆος μεγαθύμου is repeated at *Od.* 3.189 (before φαίδιμος υἱός), but since there is no metrical alternative the epithet must be chosen (in both instances) to extend to the end-verse formula. It is unfortunate that the more appropriate Ἀχιλλῆος ῥηξήνορος (1 × *Od.*; 4 × *Il.* in accusative and dative) would not fit here.

499–502 ≅ 11.534–7 (Hektor's charge), which has στείβοντες for στεῖβον ὁμοῦ and δῦναι ὅμιλον for κῦδος ἀρέσθαι (502).

500–1 πεπάλακτο: here clearly from παλάσσω, 'splatter'; cf. 397–400n. On the ἄντυγες αἳ περὶ δίφρον ⟨ἦσαν⟩, the rails at the front and sides of a chariot, see J. Wiesner, *Arch. Hom.* F 15–16 and 104. ὁπλή, 'hoof', occurs only here in Homer (and the parallel 11.536), but is normal in later Greek; on the synizesis of -έων see Hoekstra, *Modifications* 36, and Ruijgh, *Linear B 1984* 165. With the final phrase cf. ἡνίοχον κονίης ῥαθάμιγγες ἔβαλλον | (23.502).

502–3 ἐπισσώτρων: see 394–5n. κῦδος ἀρέσθαι | is formular (9 × *Il.*, 1 × *Od.*). The savage line 503 ≅ 11.169, at the end of Agamemnon's charge, and cf. αἵματι καὶ λύθρῳ πεπαλαγμένον (6.268, *Od.* 22.402 = *Od.* 23.48); is there a suggestion that Akhilleus has become as brutal as Agamemnon? On χεῖρας ἀάπτους see 13.317–18n.

The sense and structure run on directly to the beginning of book 21, as is shown by the absence of any break in the parallel passage in Agamemnon's *aristeia* (11.169–70 ≅ 20.503–21.1).

INDEX

A fuller index of Greek words will be provided at the end of the whole Commentary.

347

Index

Index

heroic code, 162
Hippodamas, 334
Hippothoös, 83, 91
homosexuality, 155, 159, 185–6, 258, 319
horses of Akhilleus, 70, 96, 100, 105, 179;
  gift of Poseidon, 106–7; harnessing of,
  281; immortality of, 105; mourning of,
  18, 62, 104–5, 106, 283; names of, 282;
  speech of Xanthos, 282; association with
  death, 283; horses of Trojans, 317–18
Huperenor, 65, 66
Hyades, 212
hyphaeresis, 94
hysteron-proteron, 45–6, 119

Ianassa, 148, 149, 150
Ianeira, 148, 149, 150
Iaira, 148, 149
Ida, Mt, 120, 294–5
Idomeneus, 87, 121, 122, 123
ἱερός, 109
'if not' situations, 93, 113
Ilos (son of Tros), 316, 317, 319; (son of
  Dardanos) 317, 319
Iliupersis: of Arctinus, 18, 195, 264, 300; of
  Stesichorus, 300
'imaginary spectator', 2
ἵμεναι, 330–1
inlay, 202–3
Iphition, 332
Iris, 167, 168, 169
iron, 147; in metaphors, 52, 104, 304,
  331
irony, 139–40, 181, 182, 199, 246, 247, 258,
  262, 267, 270, 273, 276, 280, 284, 337

Kallianassa, 148, 149, 150
Kallianeira, 148, 149, 150
Kapus, 316, 319, 320
Kaukones, 328
Kebriones, 145–6
Ker(es), 221
Kharis, 189–91
Kheiron, 280
Khromios, Khromis, 83, 111
Klumene, 148, 150
Koiranos, 122
kuanos, 203
Kudoimos, 221
Kumodoke, 149
Kumothoë, 148, 149

lament, 150–1, 267–8, 271–2; *see also*
  mourning
Laodokos, 130
Laogonos, 339

Laomedon, 314, 316, 319, 325; horses of,
  317
lawsuit, on shield of Akhilleus, 213–18
Leiokritos, 95
Leïtos, 120
Leto, 292, 296
Linos, 225–6
lions, 33, 34, 41, 76, 126, 166, 184, 227–8,
  309–10; in Asia Minor, 310
Limnoreia, 148, 149
litotes, 57, 65, 251, 341
Little Iliad, 95, 273, 316, 319
Lukaon, 8, 10, 20, 118, 162, 302, 303, 335
Lukomedes, 95, 264
Luktos, 122
Lurnessos, sack of, 269

Maira, 148, 150
Medon, 83
Meges, 264
Melanippos, 264
Melite, 148, 149
Memnon, armour of, 19, 140, 156–7; death
  of, 62, 141, 158; duel of, with Akhilleus,
  18, 19, 298, 304, 315; given immortality,
  141, 186; goddess mother of, 18, 315;
  kills Antilokhos, 62, 140–1; not
  mentioned in Trojan royal stemma, 316
Memnonis, see Aithiopis
Menelaos, 116; carries off body of
  Patroklos, 132; considerate nature of, 62,
  65, 72, 87, 117, 130; depicted on East
  Greek plate, 69–70; directly addressed by
  poet, 3, 62, 128–9; gratifies Athene, 117;
  guilt and sorrow of, 62, 76; inferior as a
  fighter, 65, 119, 128
Meriones, 87, 122, 123, 264; carries off
  body of Patroklos, 132
Mesthles, 83
metamorphosis, *see* similes
metaphor, 48–53, 64, 73, 74, 85, 86–7, 89,
  99, 101, 112, 119, 126, 128, 135, 144,
  166, 172, 176, 178, 185, 189, 237–8, 248,
  251, 260–2, 271, 277, 282, 289, 294, 304,
  306, 307, 318, 321, 330; bronze and iron
  in, 52, 104, 260–1, 331
metonymy, 52, 57, 176, 260–1
mist, 86, 89, 96, 98, 125; for rescuing a
  hero, 327; of death, 336
Moira, *see* fate
monologues, 72, 142, 329, 336–7
motif, repeated, 23, 88, 96, 98, 107, 118,
  162, 163, 174, 280, 324
Moulios, 339, 341
mourning: of Akhilleus, 268–9; of Briseis,
  267–71; of Akhilleus' horses, 21, 104–5,

Index

Rhigmos, 339, 342
ring composition, 20, 44–8, 72, 122, 129–30, 142, 147, 152, 161, 163, 176–7, 179, 185, 210, 235, 241, 245, 247, 255, 256, 258, 260, 268, 275, 278, 283–4, 287, 295, 299, 303, 314, 315, 320, 323; in paradigms, 192
rivers, 35, 136
robots, of Hephaistos, 195
runover words, *see* sentence structure

sacrifice, 113, 264–5, 266, 334; human, 186
Sarpedon, 77, 93; armour of, 78; burial of, 18; foreshadowing of death of, 9, 10; son of, 20; speech to Glaukos, 87
Scaean Gates, 101
schema Alcmanicum, 307
schema etymologicum, see etymological play
sentence structure, 42–4, 71, 72, 73, 90, 185–6, 265, 340; interplay of sense units and metrical cola, 154–5, 173–4, 181–2, 237, 253–4, 257, 272, 305, 312, 339–40; runover words, 42–3, 63, 66, 74, 78, 91–2, 99, 105, 107, 110, 117, 129, 132, 144, 154, 173, 251, 255, 260, 272, 303, 305, 335, 340; *see also* emphasis
shield, 111; of Akhilleus, 69, 200–32, construction of, 201–5, 322–3, arrangement of scenes on, 206–8, movement depicted on, 207–8, subject-matter of scenes depicted, 208–9, relationship to similes, 200, 208–9, 227, and creativity of the poet, 199, 209, heavenly bodies on, 211–13, city at peace, 213–18, city at war, 218–21, the farmer's year, 221–6, cattle and sheep herding, 226–8, the dance, 228–31, the river of Ocean, 232; shield of Aineias, 323; 'tower' shield, 75, 201, 324
shield-strap, 210, 211
similes, 1, 24–41, 63, 68, 69, 73, 96, 99, 106, 114, 117, 126, 127–8, 151, 166, 172, 200, 227, 229, 230, 233, 275, 276, 277, 279, 314, 344; alternative comparisons in, 37; *anadiplosis* in, 29; connexion with narrative (point of comparison), 30–4, 69, 88, 106, 115, 128, 137, 170–1, 184, 278–9, 309–10, 321, 334, 344; cumulative effect of, 40–1; in direct speech, 39, 64; distribution of, 39; emotional impact of, 34; essential to the narrative, 28, 32; foreshadowing in, 10, 31–2, 88–9, 115, 170, 184, 293, 294; function of, 38–9; groups of, 39–41, 132–3, 135; *hapax legomena* in, 38, 54; in

Hesiod and *Homeric Hymns*, 24; language of, 37–8, 75, 172, 309–10; long similes, 26–8; and metamorphosis, 29–30, 115–16, 233, 275; and metaphors, 172; negative, 28–9, 65; repeated verbatim, 24, 126; snow similes, 20; sound effects in, 88–9; short similes, 25–6; subject-matter of, 34–7; unusual forms of, 28–30; viewpoint in, 33–4
Skamandros, 291, 292, 296; alternative divine and human names of, 297–8
Skhedios, 92
sound-effects, 57–8, 88–9, 109, 119–20, 135, 136, 147, 178, 193–4, 194, 198, 226–7, 256, 293, 308, 316, 341; *see also* word-play
spear, 233; of Akhilleus, 279–80, 333; return of, by a deity, 327, 337–8
Speio, 149
story patterns, 15–19, 303, 332; call for help, 62, 74, 85, 87, 114, 119, 123; joining battle, 234, 253, 263; rebuke pattern, 62, 74, 93, 114, 119, 298, 302; revenge of Akhilleus, 139, 234; withdrawal of Akhilleus, 139, 234; interweaving of, 139, 175, 179, 183
Strife, *see* Eris
suicide, 146
summarizing verses, 96, 133, 210, 287, 291, 293, 296, 308
sword, of Akhilleus, 232–3, 278
synizesis, 77, 172, 328, 345

τεῖος, *see* ἕως
temenos, 223, 312
Thaleia, 148, 149
themes, 11–23
Themis, 288
Thersilokhos, 83
Thetis: and Akhilleus' mortality, 7, 102, 145, 152; laments of, 147, 150, 158; parallels with Eos, 156–7, 235–6, 315; presents armour to Akhilleus, 156–7, 236; still living with Peleus, 152; prophetic powers of, 152; tactlessness of, 153; wedding of, 106, 156, 157, 196–7
Thoas, 264
Thoë, 149
θώρηξ, *see* corslet
Thrasumedes, 98, 130, 264
τις-speeches, 96, 102–3
Titanomachy, 287, 293–5
Tithonos, 316, 320
topos, see motif
tripods, of Hephaistos, 190
Triptolemos, 222

352

CORRIGENDA FOR VOLUMES I AND II

As promised in the preface to Volume II, details of corrections for Volumes I and II are listed here. All the corrections to Volume I, except for those in bold type, have already been incorporated in the second and later impressions of that book.

VOLUME I

p. 6, l. 27 — *for* 3.15 *read* 3.152
p. 26, l. 20 — *for* trochee *read* iamb
p. 46, l. 39 — *for* summon *read* elicit
p. 60, l. 42 — *read* may have useful divine echoes
p. 74, l. 33 — *read* determined, but see Leumann, *HW* 148ff. βοῶπις of Here suggests there
p. 80, l. 20 — *read* may be right in view of 262.
p. 85, ll. 2–4 — *for* do not make... known), but *read* proceed immediately to sacrifice hecatombs of bulls and goats to Apollo (315–17); and before that they
p. 91, l. 23 — *for* **366f.** *read* **366–9**
p. 91, l. 27 — *for* 416 *read* 425–8
p. 91, l. 28 — *for* Andromakhe *read* Andromakhe's mother
p. 92, l. 23 — *after* poem *add* ; see on 98
p. 95, l. 31 — *for* a form of *read* related to
p. 97, ll. 28–9 — *read* eleven days of divine concern over Akhilleus' treatment of Hektor's body, at 24.23–32.
p. 105, l. 27 — *for* not less than three *read* not one but two
p. 105, ll. 28–9 — *read* (31) (i.e. it lies for eleven nights in Akhilleus' hut (413)), and an
p. 105, l. 30 — *for* all *read* both
p. 105, l. 31 — *for* must *read* might
p. 105, l. 32 — *for* noted *read* discussed
p. 105, l. 34 — *for* three *read* pair of

p. 113, l. 3 — *read* Εὐμήλῳ
p. 113, l. 40 — *for* hobbling *read* bustling
p. 118, ll. 24–5 — *read* strictly 'sat upright', as apparently at 23.235; but the idea may be that he
p. 125, l. 36 — *for* whose exact... described *read* by Odysseus' ships according to 11.806f.
p. 127, ll. 32–4 — *read* διάκτορος could mean 'guide' (since the Homeric name Aktor is *nomen agentis* of ἄγω, and Hesychius glossed διάκτωρ as ἡγεμών).
p. 140, ll. 3–5 — *read* pot. ψεδνή means 'sparse', and ἐπενήνοθε is perhaps related to ἄνθος, 'flowered upon' (cf. 10.134), though cf. Chantraine, *Dict.* s.v. ἀνήνοθεν. The 'shambling
p. 155, l. 6 — *for* an unparalleled *read* a directly
p. 212, l. 13 — *for* Aigion *read* Aigai
p. 247, l. 17 — *for* the *read* any
p. 247, l. 24 — *before* second *read* third and
p. 247, l. 25 — *after* Troy VI *add*; Besik Tepe at the southern end of the Sigeion ridge is the best candidate, cf. Cook 173f., and a cemetery of Mycenaean date has recently been found there, see vol. II p. 49

Corrigenda for Volumes I and II

<table>
<tr><td>p. 252, l. 24</td><td>for μεμαότες read μεμαώς</td><td>p. 339, l. 30</td><td>for usual read not unusual</td></tr>
<tr><td>p. 262, l. 1</td><td>after value add ; but see on 5.181</td><td>p. 339, l. 31</td><td>after Iliad add ; see further on 5.168–9</td></tr>
<tr><td>p. 268, ll. 26 and 27</td><td>read δύω</td><td>p. 343, l. 30</td><td>for three read five</td></tr>
<tr><td>p. 277, l. 13</td><td>delete Leaf and</td><td>p. 343, l. 31</td><td>after 7.104 add , 13.603, 17.769</td></tr>
<tr><td>p. 277, l. 14</td><td>after prefer add with Leaf</td><td>p. 346, l. 7</td><td>for 36 read 35</td></tr>
<tr><td>p. 326, ll. 5–8</td><td>for , but contains... curiosity. read . The maidservants (as Professor R. M. Frazer reminds me) are the pair that accompanied Helen in 143, and not those awaiting her in the house; αἱ in 421 refers to Helen and them, rather than to Helen and Athene.</td><td>p. 347, l. 1</td><td>for shins read thighs</td></tr>
<tr><td></td><td></td><td>p. 355, ll. 2–3</td><td>delete (as well as... former)</td></tr>
<tr><td></td><td></td><td>p. 369, l. 3</td><td>after bridges. add See also on 5.87–8.</td></tr>
<tr><td></td><td></td><td>p. 369, l. 17</td><td>read ἱρή</td></tr>
<tr><td></td><td></td><td>p. 381, l. 20</td><td>for Kudoimos and Ker read Alke and Ioke</td></tr>
<tr><td></td><td></td><td>p. 386, l. 12</td><td>for Diores read Peiros</td></tr>
<tr><td></td><td></td><td>p. 386, l. 14</td><td>for Diores' read Peiros'</td></tr>
<tr><td>p. 336, l. 10</td><td>for 36f. read 35f.</td><td>p. 387, l. 24</td><td>for Boeotian read Euboean</td></tr>
<tr><td>p. 337, l. 20</td><td>after enjambment add ; see also the analysis on p. 36</td><td>pp. 402–3 (Index)</td><td>under Boeotian delete 387; under corslet delete 381f.; under Ganumedes read 113 for 114</td></tr>
<tr><td>p. 338, l. 16</td><td>after 1.44 add and see 7.19n</td><td></td><td></td></tr>
</table>

VOLUME II

<table>
<tr><td>p. 60, l. 4</td><td>read ἑκών, ἑκάς (twice)</td><td>p. 154, l. 13</td><td>for Odysseus read Telemakhos</td></tr>
<tr><td>p. 81, l. 26</td><td>for ἐς/ὅτε read ὅτ' ἐς</td><td>p. 229</td><td>restore missing ends of lines as (l. 1) 3.57), (l. 3) terminal, (l. 4) conclusion</td></tr>
<tr><td>p. 94, l. 29</td><td>before explained add seems to have, and delete at Paphos</td><td></td><td></td></tr>
<tr><td>p. 104, l. 27</td><td>for but blood itself read , something similar</td><td>p. 247, l. 38</td><td>read δεξιτερῆς</td></tr>
<tr><td></td><td></td><td>p. 279, l. 29</td><td>for or the like read , cf. 23.255</td></tr>
<tr><td>p. 118, l. 34</td><td>read κύμβαχος</td><td>p. 340, l. 35</td><td>delete f. after 557–8</td></tr>
<tr><td>p. 148, l. 42</td><td>for gates read doors</td><td></td><td></td></tr>
</table>

Lightning Source UK Ltd.
Milton Keynes UK
UKHW010027181022
410613UK00001B/160